faces of Anthropology

A Reader for the 21st Century

SECOND EDITION

EDITED BY

KEVIN RAFFERTY, PH.D.

DOROTHY CHINWE UKAEGBU, PH.D.

COMMUNITY COLLEGE OF SOUTHERN NEVADA

Pearson
Custom
Publishing

Cover Photo: "Java Market."

Printed in the United States of America

10 9 8 7 6 5 4 3 2

Please visit our web site at www.pearsoncustom.com

ISBN 0–536–02026-4

BA 990930

PEARSON CUSTOM PUBLISHING
160 Gould Street/Needham Heights, MA 02494
A Pearson Education Company

Copyright Acknowledgments

CONTENTS

SECTION ONE

Changing Faces of Anthropology:
The Subfields

THE SOUNDS OF SILENCE

Edward T. Hall and Mildred Reed Hall

Bob leaves his apartment at 8:15 A.M. and stops at the corner drugstore for breakfast. Before he can speak, the counterman says, "The usual?" Bob nods yes. While he savors his Danish, a fat man pushes onto the adjoining stool and overflows into his space. Bob scowls and the man pulls himself in as much as he can. Bob has sent two messages without speaking a syllable.

Henry has an appointment to meet Arthur at 11 o'clock; he arrives at 11:30. Their conversation is friendly, but Arthur retains a lingering hostility. Henry has unconsciously communicated that he doesn't think the appointment is very important or that Arthur is a person who needs to be treated with respect.

George is talking to Charley's wife at a party. Their conversation is entirely trivial, yet Charley glares at them suspiciously. Their physical proximity and the movements of their eyes reveal that they are powerfully attracted to each other.

José Ybarra and Sir Edmund Jones are at the same party and it is important for them to establish a cordial relationship for business reasons. Each is trying to be warm and friendly, yet they will part with mutual distrust and their business transaction will probably fall through. José, in Latin fashion, moved closer and closer to Sir Edmund as they spoke, and this movement was miscommunicated as pushiness to Sir Edmund, who kept backing away from this intimacy, and this was miscommunicated to José as coldness. The silent languages of Latin and English cultures are more difficult to learn than their spoken languages.

In each of these cases, we see the subtle power of nonverbal communication. The only language used throughout most of the history of humanity (in evolutionary terms, vocal communication is relatively recent), it is the first form of communication you learn. You use this preverbal language, consciously and unconsciously, every day to tell other people how you feel about yourself and them. This language includes your posture, gestures, facial expressions, costume, the way you walk, even your treatment of time and space and material things. All people communicate on several different levels at the same time but are usually aware of only the verbal dialog and don't realize that they respond to nonverbal messages. But

when a person says one thing and really believes something else, the discrepancy between the two can usually be sensed. Nonverbal-communication systems are much less subject to the conscious deception that often occurs in verbal systems. When we find ourselves thinking, "I don't know what it is about him, but he doesn't seem sincere," it's usually this lack of congruity between a person's words and his behavior that makes us anxious and uncomfortable.

Few of us realize how much we all depend on body movement in our conversation or are aware of the hidden rules that govern listening behavior. But we know instantly whether or not the person we're talking to is "tuned in" and we're very sensitive to any breach in listening etiquette. In white middle-class American culture, when someone wants to show he is listening to someone else, he looks either at the other person's face or, specifically, at his eyes, shifting his gaze from one eye to the other.

If you observe a person conversing, you'll notice that he indicates he's listening by nodding his head. He also makes little "Hmm" noises. If he agrees with what's being said, he may give a vigorous nod. To show pleasure or affirmation, he smiles; if he has some reservations, he looks skeptical by raising an eyebrow or pulling down the corners of his mouth. If a participant wants to terminate the conversation, he may start shifting his body position, stretching his legs, crossing or uncrossing them, bobbing his foot or diverting his gaze from the speaker. The more he fidgets, the more the speaker becomes aware that he has lost his audience. As a last measure, the listener may look at his watch to indicate the imminent end of the conversation.

Talking and listening are so intricately intertwined that a person cannot do one without the other. Even when one is alone and talking to oneself, there is part of the brain that speaks while another part listens. In all conversations, the listener is positively or negatively reinforcing the speaker all the time. He may even guide the conversation without knowing it, by laughing or frowning or dismissing the argument with a wave of his hand.

The language of the eyes—another age-old way of exchanging feelings—is both subtle and complex. Not only do men and women use their eyes differently but there are class, generation, regional, ethnic and national cultural differences. Americans often complain about the way foreigners stare at people or hold a glance too long. Most Americans look away from someone who is using his eyes in an unfamiliar way because it makes them self-conscious. If a man looks at another man's wife in a certain way, he's asking for trouble, as indicated earlier. But he might not be ill-mannered or seeking to challenge the husband. He might be a European in this country who hasn't learned our visual mores. Many American women visiting France or Italy are acutely embarrassed because, for the first time in their lives, men really look at them—their eyes, hair, nose, lips, breasts, hips, legs, thighs, knees, ankles, feet, clothes, hairdo, even their walk. These same women, once they have become used to being looked at, often return to the United States and are overcome with the feeling that "No one ever really looks at me anymore."

Analyzing the mass of data on the eyes, it is possible to sort out at least three ways in which the eyes are used to communicate: dominance vs. submission, involvement vs. detachment and positive vs. negative attitude. In addition, there are three levels of consciousness and control, which can be categorized as follows: (1) conscious use of the eye to communicate, such as the flirting blink and the intimate nose-wrinkling squint; (2) the very extensive category of unconscious but learned behavior governing where the eyes are directed and when (this unwritten set of rules dictates how and under what circumstances the sexes, as well as people of all status categories, look at each other); and (3) the response of the eye itself, which is completely outside both awareness and control—changes in the cast (the sparkle) of the eye and the pupillary reflex.

The eye is unlike any other organ of the body, for it is an extension of the brain. The unconscious pupillary reflex and the cast of the eye have been known by people of Middle Eastern origin for years—although most are unaware of their knowledge. Depending on the context, Arabs and others look either directly at the eye or deeply *into* the eyes of their interlocutor. We became aware of this in the Middle East several years ago while looking at jewelry. The merchant suddenly started to push a particular bracelet at a customer and said, "You buy this one." What interested us was that the bracelet was not the one that had been consciously selected by the purchaser. But the merchant, watching the pupils of the eyes, knew what the purchaser really wanted to buy. Whether he specifically knew *how* he knew is debatable.

A psychologist at the University of Chicago, Eckhard Hess, was the first to conduct systematic studies of the pupillary reflex. His wife remarked one evening, while watching him reading in bed, that he must be very interested in the text because his pupils were dilated. Following up on this, Hess slipped some pictures of nudes into a stack of photographs that he gave to his male assistant. Not looking at the photographs but watching his assistant's pupils, Hess was able to tell precisely when the assistant came to the nudes. In further experiments, Hess retouched the eyes in a photograph of a woman. In one print, he made the pupils small, in another, large; nothing else was changed. Subjects who were given the photographs found the woman with the dilated pupils much more attractive. Any man who has had the experience of seeing a woman look at him as her pupils widen with reflex speed knows that she's flashing him a message.

The eye-sparkle phenomenon frequently turns up in our interviews of couples in love. It's apparently one of the first reliable clues in the other person that love is genuine. To date, there is no scientific data to explain eye sparkle; no investigation of the pupil, the cornea or even the white sclera of the eye shows how the sparkle originates. Yet we all know it when we see it.

One common situation for most people involves the use of the eyes in the street and in public. Although eye behavior follows a definite set of rules, the rules vary according to the place, the needs and feelings of the people, and their ethnic background. For urban whites, once they're within definite recognition distance (16–32 feet for people with average eyesight), there is mutual avoidance of eye contact—unless they want something specific; a pickup, a handout or information of some kind. In the West and in small towns generally, however, people are much more likely to look at and greet one another, even if they're strangers.

It's permissible to look at people if they're beyond recognition distance; but once inside this sacred zone, you can only steal a glance at strangers. You *must* greet friends, however; to fail to do so is insulting. Yet, to stare too fixedly at them is considered rude and hostile. Of course, all of these rules are variable.

A great many blacks, for example, greet each other in public even if they don't know each other. To blacks, most eye behavior of whites has the effect of giving the impression that they aren't there, but this is due to white avoidance of eye contact with *anyone* in the street.

Another very basic difference between people of different ethnic backgrounds is their sense of territoriality and how they handle space. This is the silent communication, or miscommunication, that caused friction between Mr. Ybarra and Sir Edmund Jones in our earlier example. We know from research that everyone has around himself an invisible bubble of space that contracts and expands depending on several factors: his emotional state, the activity he's performing at the time and his cultural background. This bubble is a kind of mobile territory that he will defend against intrusion. If he is accustomed to close personal distance between himself and others, his bubble will be smaller than that of someone who's accustomed to greater personal distance. People of North European heritage—English, Scandinavian, Swiss and German—tend to avoid contact. Those whose heritage is Italian, French, Spanish, Russian, Latin American or Middle Eastern like close personal contact.

People are very sensitive to any intrusion into their spatial bubble. If someone stands too close to you, your first instinct is to back up. If that's not possible, you lean away and pull yourself in, tensing your muscles. If the intruder doesn't respond to these body signals, you may then try to protect yourself, using a briefcase, umbrella or raincoat. Women—especially when traveling alone—often plant their pocketbook in such a way that no one can get very close to them. As a last resort, you may move to another spot and position yourself behind a desk or a chair that provides screening. Everyone tries to adjust the space around himself in a way that's comfortable for him; most often, he does this unconsciously.

Emotions also have a direct effect on the size of a person's territory. When you're angry or under stress, your bubble expands and you require more space. New York psychiatrist Augustus Kinzel found a difference in what he calls Body-Buffer Zones between violent and nonviolent prison inmates. Dr. Kinzel conducted experiments in which each prisoner was placed in the center of a small room and then Dr. Kinzel slowly walked toward him. Nonviolent prisoners allowed him to come quite close, while prisoners with a history of violent behavior couldn't tolerate his proximity and reacted with some vehemence.

Apparently, people under stress experience other people as looming larger and closer than they actually are. Studies of schizophrenic patients have indicated that they sometimes have a distorted perception of space, and several psychiatrists have reported patients who experience their boundaries as filling up an entire room. For these patients, anyone who comes into the room is actually inside their body, and such an intrusion may trigger a violent outburst.

Unfortunately, there is little detailed information about normal people who live in highly congested urban areas. We do know, of course, that the noise, pollution, dirt, crowding and confusion of our cities induce feelings of stress in most of us, and stress leads to a need for greater space. The man who's packed into a subway, jostled in the street, crowded into an elevator and forced to work all day in a bull pen or in a small office without auditory or visual privacy is going to be very stressed at the end of his day. He needs places that provide relief from constant overstimulation of his nervous system. Stress from overcrowding is cumulative and people can tolerate more crowding early in the day than later; note the increased bad temper during the evening rush hour as compared with the morning melee. Certainly one factor in people's desire to commute by car is the need for privacy and relief from crowding (except, often, from other cars); it may be the only time of the day when nobody can intrude.

In crowded public places, we tense our muscles and hold ourselves stiff, and thereby communicate to others our desire not to intrude on their space and, above all, not to touch them. We also avoid eye contact, and the total effect is that of someone who has "tuned out." Walking along the street, our bubble expands slightly as we move in a stream of strangers, taking care not to bump into them. In the office, at meetings, in restaurants, our bubble keeps changing as it adjusts to the activity at hand.

Most white middle-class Americans use four main distances in their business and social relations: intimate, personal, social and public. Each of these distances has a near and a far phase and is accompanied by changes in the volume of the voice. Intimate distance varies from direct physical contact with another person to a distance of six to eighteen inches and is used for our most private activities—caressing another person or making love. At this distance, you are overwhelmed by sensory inputs from the other person—heat from the body, tactile stimulation from the skin, the fragrance of perfume, even the sound of breathing—all of which literally envelop you. Even at the far phase, you're still within easy touching distance. In general, the use of intimate distance in public between adults is frowned on. It's also much too close for strangers, except under conditions of extreme crowding.

In the second zone—personal distance—the close phase is one and a half to two and a half feet; it's at this distance that wives usually stand from their husbands in public. If another woman moves into this zone, the wife will most likely be disturbed. The far phase—two and a half to four feet—is the distance used to "keep someone at arm's length" and is the most common spacing used by people in conversation.

The third zone—social distance—is employed during business transactions or exchanges with a clerk or repairman. People who work together tend to use close social distance—four to seven feet. This is also the distance for conversation at social gatherings. To stand up at this distance from someone who is seated has a dominating effect (e.g., teacher to pupil, boss to secretary). The far phase of the third zone—seven to twelve feet—is where people stand when someone says, "Stand back so I can look at you." This distance lends a formal tone to business or social discourse. In an executive office, the desk serves to keep people at this distance.

The fourth zone—public distance—is used by teachers in classrooms or speakers at public gatherings. At its farthest phase—25 feet and beyond—it is used for important public figures. Violations of this distance can lead to serious complications. During his 1970 U.S. visit, the president of France, Georges Pompidou, was harassed by pickets in Chicago, who were permitted to get within touching distance. Since pickets in France are kept behind barricades a block or more away, the president was outraged by this insult to his person, and President Nixon was obliged to communicate his concern as well as offer his personal apologies.

It is interesting to note how American pitchmen and panhandlers exploit the unwritten, unspoken conventions of eye and distance. Both take advantage of the fact that once explicit eye contact is established, it is rude to look away, because to do so means to brusquely dismiss the other person and his needs. Once having caught the eye of his mark, the panhandler then locks on, not letting go until he moves through the public zone, the social zone, the personal zone and, finally, into the intimate sphere, where people are most vulnerable.

Touch also is an important part of the constant stream of communication that takes place between people. A light touch, a firm touch, a blow, a caress are all communications. In an effort to break down barriers among people, there's been a recent upsurge in group-encounter activities, in which strangers are encouraged to touch one another. In special situations such as these, the rules for not touching are broken with group approval and people gradually lose some of their inhibitions.

Although most people don't realize it, space is perceived and distances are set not by vision alone but with all the senses. Auditory space is perceived with the ears, thermal space with the skin, kinesthetic space with the muscles of the body and olfactory space with the nose. And, once again, it's one's culture that determines how his senses are programmed—which sensory information ranks highest and lowest. The important thing to remember is that culture is very persistent. In this country, we've noted the existence of culture patterns that determine distance between people in the third and fourth generations of some families, despite their prolonged contact with people of very different cultural heritages.

Whenever there is great cultural distance between two people, there are bound to be problems arising from differences in behavior and expectations. An example is the American couple who consulted a psychiatrist about their marital problems. The husband was from New England and had been brought up by reserved parents who taught him to control his emotions and to respect the need for privacy. His wife was from an Italian family and had been brought up in close contact with all the members of her large family, who were extremely warm, volatile and demonstrative.

When the husband came home after a hard day at the office, dragging his feet and longing for peace and quiet, his wife would rush to him and smother him. Clasping his hands, rubbing his brow, crooning over his weary head, she never left him alone. But when the wife was upset or anxious about her day, the husband's response was to withdraw completely and leave her alone. No comforting, no affectionate embrace, no attention—just solitude. The woman became convinced her husband didn't love her, and, in desperation, she consulted a psychiatrist. Their problem wasn't basically psychological but cultural.

Why has man developed all these different ways of communicating messages without words? One reason is that people don't like to spell out certain kinds of messages. We prefer to find other ways of showing our feelings. This is especially true in relationships as sensitive as courtship. Men don't like to be rejected and most women don't want to turn a man down bluntly. Instead, we work out subtle ways of encouraging or discouraging each other that save face and avoid confrontations.

How a person handles space in dating others is an obvious and very sensitive indicator of how he or she feels about the other person. On a first date, if a woman sits or stands so close to a man that he is acutely conscious of her physical presence—inside the intimate-distance zone—the man usually construes it to mean that she is encouraging him. However, before the man starts moving in on the woman, he should be sure what message she's really sending; otherwise, he risks bruising his ego. What is close to someone of North European background may be neutral or distant to someone of Italian heritage. Also, women sometimes use space as a way of misleading a man and there are few things that put men off more than women who communicate contradictory messages—such as women who cuddle up and then act insulted when a man takes the next step.

How does a woman communicate interest in a man? In addition to such familiar gambits as smiling at him, she may glance shyly at him, blush and then look away. Or she may give him a real come-on look and move in very close when he approaches. She may touch his arm and ask for a light. As she leans forward to light her cigarette, she may brush him lightly, enveloping him in her perfume. She'll probably continue to smile at him and she may use what ethologists call preening gestures—touching the back of her hair, thrusting her breasts forward, tilting her hips as she stands or crossing her legs if she's seated, perhaps even exposing one thigh or putting a hand on her thigh and stroking it. She may also stroke her wrists as she converses or show the palm of her hand as a way of gaining his attention. Her skin may be unusually flushed or quite pale, her eyes brighter, the pupils larger.

If a man sees a woman whom he wants to attract, he tries to present himself by his posture and stance as someone who is self-assured. He moves briskly and confidently. When he catches the eye of the woman, he may hold her glance a little longer than normal. If he gets an encouraging smile, he'll move in close and engage her in small talk. As they converse, his glance shifts over her face and body. He, too, may make preening gestures—straightening his tie, smoothing his hair or shooting his cuffs.

How do people learn body language? The same way they learn spoken language—by observing and imitating people around them as they're growing up. Little girls imitate their mothers or an older female. Little boys imitate their fathers or a respected uncle or a character on television. In this way, they learn the gender signals appropriate for their sex. Regional, class and ethnic patterns of body behavior are also learned in childhood and persist throughout life.

Such patterns of masculine and feminine body behavior vary widely from one culture to another. In America, for example, women stand with their thighs together. Many walk with their pelvis tipped slightly forward and their upper arms close to their body. When they sit, they cross their ankles. American men hold their arms away from their body, often swinging them as they walk. They stand with their legs apart (an extreme example is the cowboy, with legs apart and thumbs tucked into his belt). When they sit, they put their feet on the floor with legs apart and, in some parts of the country, they cross their legs by putting one ankle on the other knee.

Leg behavior indicates sex, status and personality. It also indicates whether or not one is at ease or is showing respect or disrespect for the other person. Young Latin-American males avoid crossing their legs. In their world of *machismo*, the preferred position for young males when with one another (if there is no older dominant male present to whom they must show respect) is to sit on the base of their spine with their leg muscles relaxed and their feet wide apart. Their respect position is like our military equivalent; spine straight, heels and ankles together—almost identical to that displayed by properly brought up young women in New England in the early part of this century.

American women who sit with their legs spread apart in the presence of males are *not* normally signaling a come-on—they are simply (and often unconsciously) sitting like men. Middle-class women in the presence of other women to whom they are very close may on occasion throw themselves down on a soft chair or sofa and let themselves go. This is a signal that nothing serious will be taken up. Males, on the other hand, lean back and prop their legs up on the nearest object.

The way we walk, similarly, indicates status, respect, mood and ethnic or cultural affiliation. The many variants of the female walk are too well known to go into here, except to say that a man would have to be blind not to be turned on by the way some women walk—a fact that made Mae West rich before scientists ever studied these matters. To white Americans, some French middle-class males walk in a way that is both humorous and suspect. There is a bounce and looseness to the French walk, as though the parts of the body were somehow unrelated. Jacques Tati, the French movie actor, walks this way; so does the great mime, Marcel Marceau.

Blacks and whites in America—with the exception of middle- and upper-middle-class professionals of both groups—move and walk very differently from each other. To the blacks, whites often seem incredibly stiff, almost mechanical in their movements. Black males, on the other hand, have a looseness and coordination that frequently makes whites a little uneasy; it's too different, too integrated, too alive, too male. Norman Mailer has said that squares walk from the shoulders, like bears, but blacks and hippies walk from the hips, like cats.

All over the world, people walk not only in their own characteristic way but have walks that communicate the nature of their involvement with whatever it is they're doing. The purposeful walk of North Europeans is an important component of proper behavior on the job. Any male who has been in the military knows how essential it is to walk properly (which makes for a continuing source of tension between blacks and whites in the Service). The quick shuffle of servants in the Far East in the old days was a show of respect. On the island of Truk, when we last visited, the inhabitants even had a name for the respectful walk that one used when in the presence of a chief or when walking past a chief's house. The term was *sufan*, which meant to be humble and respectful.

The notion that people communicate volumes by their gestures, facial expressions, posture and walk is not new; actors, dancers, writers and psychiatrists have long been aware of it. Only in recent years, however, have scientists begun to make systematic observations of body motions. Ray L. Birdwhistell of the University of Pennsylvania is one of the pioneers in body-motion research and coined the term kinesics to describe this field. He developed an elaborate notation system to record both facial and body movements, using an approach similar to that of the linguist, who studies the basic elements of speech. Birdwhistell and other kinesicists such as Albert Sheflen, Adam Kendon and William Condon take movies of people interacting. They run the film over and over again, often at reduced speed for frame-by-frame analysis, so that they can observe even the slightest body movements not perceptible at normal interaction speeds. These movements are then recorded in notebooks for later analysis.

To appreciate the importance of nonverbal-communication systems, consider the unskilled inner-city black looking for a job. His handling of time and space alone is sufficiently different from the white middle-class pattern to create great misunderstandings on both sides. The black is told to appear for a job interview at a certain time. He arrives late. The white interviewer concludes from his tardy arrival that the black is irresponsible and not really interested in the job. What the interviewer doesn't know is that the black time system (often referred to by blacks as C.P.T.—colored people's time) isn't the same as that of whites. In the words of the black student who had been told to make an appointment to see his professor: "Man, you *must* be putting me on. I never had an appointment in my life."

The black job applicant, having arrived late for his interview, may further antagonize the white interviewer by his posture and his eye behavior. Perhaps he slouches and avoids looking at the interviewer; to him this is playing it cool. To the interviewer, however, he may well look shifty and sound uninterested. The interviewer has failed to notice the actual signs of interest and eagerness in the black's behavior, such as the subtle shift in the quality of the voice—a gentle and tentative excitement—an almost imperceptible change in the cast of the eyes and a relaxing of the jaw muscles.

Moreover, correct reading of black-white behavior is continually complicated by the fact that both groups are comprised of individuals—some of whom try to accommodate and some of whom make it a point of pride *not* to accommodate. At present, this means that many Americans, when thrown into contact with one another, are in the precarious position of not knowing which pattern applies. Once identified and analyzed, nonverbal-communications systems can be taught, like a foreign language. Without this training, we respond to nonverbal communications in terms of our own culture; we read everyone's behavior as if it were our own, and thus we often misunderstand it.

Several years ago in New York City, there was a program for sending children from predominantly black and Puerto Rican low-income neighborhoods to summer school in a white upper-class neighborhood on the East Side. One morning, a group of young black and Puerto Rican boys raced down the street, shouting and screaming and overturning garbage cans on their way to school. A doorman from an apartment building nearby chased them and cornered one of them inside a building. The boy drew a knife and attacked the doorman. This tragedy would not have occurred if the doorman had been familiar with the behavior of boys from low-income neighborhoods, where such antics are routine and socially acceptable and where pursuit would be expected to invite a violent response.

The language of behavior is extremely complex. Most of us are lucky to have under control one subcultural system—the one that reflects our sex, class, generation and geographic region within the United States. Because of its complexity, efforts to isolate bits of nonverbal communication and generalize from them are in vain; you don't become an instant expert on people's behavior by watching them at cocktail parties. Body language isn't something that's independent of the person, something that can be donned and doffed like a suit of clothes.

Our research and that of our colleagues has shown that, far from being a superficial form of communication that can be consciously manipulated, nonverbal-communication systems are interwoven into the fabric of the personality and, as sociologist Erving Goffman has demonstrated, into society itself. They are the warp and woof of daily interactions with others and they influence how one expresses oneself, how one experiences oneself as a man or a woman.

Nonverbal communications signal to members of your own group what kind of person you are, how you feel about others, how you'll fit into the work in a group, whether you're assured or anxious, the degree to which you feel comfortable with the standards of your own culture, as well as deeply significant feelings about the self, including the state of your own psyche. For most of us, it's difficult to accept the reality of another's behavioral system. And, of course, none of us will ever become fully knowledgeable of the importance of every nonverbal signal. But as long as each of us realizes the power of these signals, this society's diversity can be a source of great strength rather than a further—and subtly powerful—source of division.

"THE SOUNDS OF SILENCE"

Edward T. Hall and Mildred Reed Hall

1) Language is more than the spoken word. What different modes of communication do Hall and Hall define in this article?

2) How are eyes used to communicate? Is all eye use conscious or are some eye gestures physiologically controlled?

3) How do urban blacks and whites use the language of the eyes differently?

4) Hall and Hall define four zones of distance used by white middle-class Americans. Define and discuss them.

5) Think of a time recently that you had trouble communicating with someone. In retrospect, was there some form of unspoken message that you may have been transmitting that interfered with your verbal message?

as a proxy for "stages" of sociocultural evolution that have succeeded one another over thousands of years.[4] The comparative method has been productive in anthropological inquiry, especially so in recent decades, owing to methodological improvements,[5] but it will always suffer from an inability to directly study sociocultural evolution where it actually took place. Ideally, comparative inquiry should complement direct archaeological investigation, but it was not until after World War II that the potential synergism of comparative and archaeological approaches could be fully realized. Anthropological archaeology advanced in its analytical concepts and field research methods, including the development of carbon-14 dating and other chronometric techniques.[6] These developments, coupled with a greater availability of research funding for substantial multidisciplinary, long-term field projects (especially from the United States' National Science Foundation), made it possible to acquire an unprecedented quantity and quality of new information about the human past.

We can add to these developments in archaeological method and funding levels the fact that, beginning around 1950, a "cultural ecological" theoretical orientation began to influence archaeological field research, contributing greatly to its ability to address broad evolutionary issues. Archaeologists were urged to use their data to address questions relating sociocultural change to ecological processes in a way that engaged the interests of a wide spectrum of natural and social scientists. Putting all of these elements together, it was evident that anthropology was on the verge of realizing a greatly expanded understanding of sociocultural evolution, a new synthesis that would be built on the combined efforts of researchers representing its various subdisciplines, including archaeology, as well as researchers from other disciplines.

The Rise of Cultural Ecology

Anthropologists, including Leslie White, Julian Steward, Elman Service, Karl Wittfogel, and Marvin Harris, and the economist Ester Boserup, among others,[7] proposed theories that connected various aspects of the material conditions of existence—environment, technology, exchange, production, population growth, and competition for resources—to sociocultural evolutionary change. An admirable feature of this materialist theoretical orientation was that its ideas could be evaluated through anthropological field investigations, including archaeological research. Past environmental conditions can be inferred from archaeological plant and animal remains (by ethnobotanists and ethnozoologists), including remains of pollen (palynology), and through the study of ancient landforms (geomorphology), among other sources of information. Population change could be measured through detailed archaeological surveys of large regions. Ancient production technologies could be reconstructed from the archaeological excavation of activity areas. Testing ecological theories through archaeological field studies is never easy. Problems abound, ranging from difficult working conditions to poor preservation of archaeological sites in some environments. Modern agriculture and construction destroy remains of past societies. And, the new theories placed stringent new demands on the quality and quantity of information that have to be collected by anthropological archaeologists and their colleagues. In spite of these challenges, much progress toward understanding the past can be and has been made within the framework of the long-term, multidisciplinary projects carried out in a cultural ecological theoretical framework.[8]

Most archaeological field research that drew from the cultural ecological theoretical orientation focused on "behavioral regions." Behavioral regions are naturally or culturally bounded territories, such as river floodplains, mountain valleys, or islands. Presumably, within such a region a human population adapted over an extended period to local environmental circumstances. A region-focused approach asks questions like: How have humans adjusted to the environmental features of a region, over time, through technological, social, and cultural changes? What local environmental factors were most important in determining aspects of change in social organization and culture? Has the environment (for example, climate) remained stable over time, or has it changed, and what have been the social consequences of environmental change? What has been the long-term history of population growth in the region? Has population stayed below carrying capacity (the number of people that could be sustained, as calculated from the availability of resources like cultivable soil and water), or has population exceeded carrying capacity? If population levels exceeded capacity, what were the social and environmental consequences?

One of the most stimulating suggestions was made by Julian Steward (Karl Wittfogel had a similar idea). He suggested that irrigation agriculture in major river floodplains in arid or semi-arid environments would entail the development of centralized social controls, bringing in their wake the evolution of complex society. Ideas like his spurred research efforts in important riverine regions, including the Nile Valley and Mesopotamia, and influenced the aims of archaeological research in the semi-arid highlands of Mesoamerica.[9]

Research Projects in the Valleys of Mexico and Oaxaca, Mexico

One of the most important region-centered cultural ecological projects ever carried out by anthropologists was already underway by the time I started my graduate studies at the University of Michigan. Eric Wolf, William Sanders, Angel Palerm, and René Millon, among others, proposed and initiated a long-term study of an important Mesoamerican region, the Valley of Mexico.[10] There, a succession of powerful states had developed, including one centered at the famous archaeological site of Teotihuacan, and later the Aztec empire, conquered by the Spanish in 1521. These states had been among the most influential social formations in prehispanic Mesoamerican civilization, making the valley an obvious choice for a major long-term research project. Many specialists contributed to the project, but the main research focus was a systematic archaeological settlement pattern survey of the entire region. In semi-arid environments like the Valley of Mexico, remains of ancient habitation sites and other ancient features (defensive walls, irrigation canals, agricultural terraces, public buildings, etc.) are usually visible on the ground surface except where obliterated by subsequent natural geological processes and human activity (especially, in this case, the massive growth of modern Mexico City). Numerous archaeological sites were located and recorded using surface survey methods. The sites ranged from the earliest small farming villages after about 1500 B.C. to the great prehispanic cities of the Classic period and the later Aztec empire. Ancient human communities show up as scatters of pot sherds, building stone, stone tools, plaster wall fragments, and sometimes more massive features such as pyramid platforms. In the best-preserved situations, even house foundations can be mapped. By analyzing settlement patterns (the spatial distribution of habitation sites), information from stratigraphic excavations, and environmental data, archaeologists can make inferences about many aspects of past social change through three thousand years of settled agriculture life prior to the Spanish conquest, as well as for periods subsequent to the conquest.[11] I spent three valuable, and enjoyable field seasons on the Valley of Mexico archaeological survey, which provided material for my Ph.D. dissertation and helped prepare me for my future research.

The regional study methods developed in the course of the Valley of Mexico project proved gratifyingly productive, and potentially applicable to similar regions elsewhere. Although much work remained to be done in the Valley of Mexico, I decided after three field seasons to apply a similar approach in another important Mesoamerican highland region, the Valley of Oaxaca in the southern highlands of Mexico. This region saw the growth of the Zapotec state, one of the most influential societies of ancient Mesoamerican civilization. There, another long-term, multidisciplinary regional project, Kent Flannery's Oaxaca Human Ecology Project, was in full swing, and clearly would stand to benefit from a systematic archaeological survey like the one I had helped to complete in the Valley of Mexico. Over a period of ten years and six field seasons, my colleagues and I were able to carry out the regional archaeological survey of the core region of Zapotec society, and extensions of the core-zone surveys continue to this day. To date we have located, described, and analyzed the data from more than six thousand archaeological sites in a 2,500 square kilometer area.[12]

Ecological Theory Challenged

The Valley of Mexico Project and the Oaxaca Human Ecology Project have proven to be among the most successful large-scale regional archaeological studies anywhere, providing an unparalleled record of past human occupation of two of Mesoamerica's most socioculturally significant regions. The results of decades of work are important to anthropological archaeology in many respects, but most importantly, from my point of view, in illustrating the complex causal interactions that obtain between political and economic structure, on the one hand, and patterns of population growth and agricultural intensification, on the other. For example, the massive social system of Teotihuacan (roughly 100 B.C. to A.D. 700) concentrated political, economic, and ritual functions of the entire Valley of Mexico, and beyond, primarily in one large capital center. This strongly centered regional structure—called a "primate" system—resulted in the growth of a massive city of more than 150,000 people, but a comparatively underpopulated and disadvantaged rural hinterland. Once this system was established, there was little further overall population growth or agricultural intensification over many centuries. By nearly the end of the prehispanic sequence, however (roughly A.D. 1200 to A.D. 1521), a new arrangement emerged, that we call "Aztec" society, characterized by the growth of a complex system of numerous cities and towns, each providing a variable mix of commercial, political, cultural, and ritual functions.[13] This complex social formation saw a rapid growth in population, to the highest levels of the prehispanic sequence (over one million in the valley alone), and the development of many new agricultural strategies, including sophisticated water-control facilities for large-scale irrigation projects.

How could systems so unlike one another evolve in the same region? I infer from discoveries like these that in our earlier cultural ecological theorizing, we had paid too much attention to how humans cope with the environment of their local region, thinking that the process of environmental adaptation alone would lead us to a better understanding of the nature of sociocultural change. While it is evident that environmental factors provide important constraints and opportunities for human actors, we still need to be attentive to the fact that contrastive social arrangements, such as Teotihuacan and Aztec, themselves generate distinct modes of population distribution, natural resource utilization, and technological development. Further, it is evident from these data that population growth was not a steady, constant factor in human affairs, driving the development of new productive technologies, or bringing about competition for resources, as cultural ecological theory had led us to expect. Differing social structures resulted in differing demographic patterns; some structural arrangements encouraged growth, while others retarded it.

What would explain the evolution of such distinct social systems? One of the most important aspects of society and culture largely ignored by the environmental adaptation theories was the role played by the population of a region in a larger system of interconnected regional populations. Mesoamerican civilization, a social system that extended all the way from what is now Central America to northern Mexico, was as much a part of the environment of an important city like Teotihuacan as was its local agricultural hinterland. While cultural ecological research had produced a vast quantity of useful information, by the late 1970s it was becoming clear to me and other researchers that a fuller explication of sociocultural change would develop out of a more complete and encompassing theory. A new approach would incorporate the most useful insights and findings of cultural ecology, but go beyond its adaptational and region-centered biases. A more robust theory would have to have the ability to explain how processes of change at the local level (including those found in households, and villages, and regions), influence, and are influenced by, processes of change taking place at larger spatial scales, including intersocietal interactions over long distances at the scale of whole civilizations (e.g., Mesoamerican, Central Andean, Greater Mesopotamian, Chinese). This more ambitious research agenda implies a need for a more broadly conceived method and theory, not to mention new kinds of field research.[14]

New Directions for Research

Anthropology has tended to see its subject matter as local culturally-defined groups that are relatively isolated, bounded, static, and adapted to their local environmental circumstances. But closer investigation shows that people migrate; groups coalesce or split up; local leaders manipulate concepts of ethnic identity to firm up control of a faction and outside powers create named cultural groups where none existed previously to manage a chaotic periphery.[15] To understand processes of change in a dynamic world, one must know more about the behavior of social actors as they respond to changing circumstances both locally and at larger spatial scales. One of the weak points of the cultural ecological approach, and of anthropological inquiry in general, is the failure to account fully for household behavior.[16] And yet, many fundamental processes of social, cultural, and environmental change in the evolution of early complex societies, as well as in the modern world, are outcomes of household choices concerning such things as migration, fertility, production intensity, passing on of wealth between generations, education, market participation, and consumption, among many others.

In our research in the Valley of Oaxaca, my colleagues and I noted what appeared to be substantial changes over time in household behavior related to fertility, craft production, food (including production, processing, and consumption), housing (and other aspects of consumer behavior), market participation, and migration. For example, at about the same time as the development of the region's first urban center (about 500 B.C.), households, even in rural communities, intensified agricultural production, built more substantial houses, engaged in more commercial transactions, and even invented the tortilla, indicating a change in everyday habits of food processing and consumption. We thought that changing household activity in this and other periods had important consequences for change in the larger social systems of the valley, and for those beyond its boundaries, and it seemed natural to pursue this line of investigation as a next step to learning more about Zapotec civilization and its transformations. An excavation program concentrating on houses would allow me to investigate change over time in household behavior, but I realized that little in the way of methodological or comparative data were available to aid me in the analysis and interpretation of this class of data. Given this, I decided to make a temporary career detour in order to make use of the possibilities of a comparative and cross-cultural approach.

My goal was to gain a broader perspective on household issues before pursuing further research in Oaxaca. While I realized a change in research approach would ultimately benefit my archaeological investigations, I made the change with some reluctance, because I find archaeological fieldwork to be one of the most enjoyable kinds of research. It combines intellectual stimulation with physical challenge, while at the same time allowing me to enjoy the beauty and pleasure of living in Mexico.

Effective interpretation of archaeological remains is dependent on a well-developed understanding of the relationships between human social behavior and material culture. In the case of households, this issue revolves in part around the house itself. What social factors influence household decisions regarding, for example, house size, building materials, and space use? The aim of my comparative project is to relate the formal properties of houses described in published ethnographic reports to household form and function, including household composition (nuclear family, extended household, etc.) and economic strategies of household members. Formal properties of the house include the use of space (such as gender-specific areas and activity specialization by room), size of the house, spatial arrangements of rooms, costliness and durability of building materials, decorative elaboration of the facade, and internal symbolic aspects of the house (to what degree is the house a cosmological metaphor?). To get at variation, I coded ethnographically and architecturally described rural houses from several localities where peasant houses and households are described in ethnographic works of high quality, including Japan, Java, Thailand, China, Nepal, India, Iran, Iraq, Syria, Turkey, Lebanon, Egypt, Yemen, Mexico, and Guatemala.[17]

There were definitely times when, sitting in my office in West Lafayette, coding data from published reports, I wished I could be back in Oaxaca doing archaeology. Still, I have been very gratified with what came out of this comparative work, and I am even planning to do more in the future. It accomplished exactly what I was hoping for, in that it provided me with a large and varied sample that I can use to better contextualize prehispanic Zapotec households and their changes. I was able to propose hypotheses to explain some aspects of the observed variation in households and their houses by placing the ethnographically-described cases within the contexts of community type and regional market structure.

For example, I found that in certain economic situations, senior generation members of households control the labor and marriages of their children in order to attain desired levels of social status in the community. In these cases, house forms reflect cosmological themes, with potent cultural symbols manifested in shrines and other features in the domestic built environment. Raising children in a house that is a cosmological metaphor evidently conditions them to more readily accept hierarchical social relations, by linking the activities of everyday home life to powerful symbols legitimizing inequality. Now I want to know (among many other questions): To what degree were ancient Zapotec houses cosmological metaphors, and how did this change over time? Although my comparative household research is a small step toward the larger goal of comprehending the evolution of a civilization, this foray into a new methodology has aided me in a pursuit of knowledge about sociocultural evolution, the origins of which can be traced back to Leslie White's courses.

Earlier, I alluded to anthropology's potential to develop a new synthesis that would combine the power of sociocultural and ecological theory with sophisticated archaeological methods. Has this come about? Not yet. But, by and large, we have moved in a direction that allows us to realize that potential. The most important outcome of the synthesis to date, besides an abundance of useful new data, is that we are able to see clearly the shortcomings of the excessively reductionist cultural materialist and population determinist ecological theories. Our data have opened our eyes to the need for more sophisticated approaches that better account for economic, political, and ideational factors in the growth of complex societies.

Notes

1. For example, Paul R. Ehrlich, *The Population Bomb* (New York: Ballantine, 1968); Garrett Hardin, *Population, Evolution, and Birth Control* (San Francisco: Freeman, 1964); Donella and Dennis Meadows, *The Limits to Growth* (New York: Universe Books, 1972); Taghi Farvar and John Milton, eds., *The Careless Technology: Ecology and International Development* (New York: Natural History Press, 1972).

2. Richard W. Franke, "Miracle Seeds and Shattered Dreams," *Natural History* 83 (1974); Mahmood Mamdani, *The Myth of Population Control: Family, Caste, and Class in an Indian Village* (New York: Monthly Review Press, 1973).

3. My training and interests have enabled me to participate in a Purdue University undergraduate program, funded by the Kellogg Foundation, designed to introduce social and humanistic perspectives to agronomic education, so that students develop an awareness of the social, moral, and environmental consequences of industrialized food systems.

4. Kent V. Flannery, "The Cultural Evolution of Civilizations," *Annual Review of Ecology and Systematics* 3 (1972): 399–426; Elman R. Service, *Origins of the State and Civilization: The Process of Cultural Evolution* (New York: W. W. Norton, 1975).

5. For example, the special issue titled "Cross-Cultural and Comparative Research: Theory and Method," *Behavior Science Research* 25 (1991).

6. Described, for example, in Colin Renfrew and Paul Bahn, *Archaeology: Theories, Methods, and Practice* (New York: Thames and Hudson, 1991).

7. Leslie A. White, *The Evolution of Culture* (New York: McGraw-Hill, 1959); Julian H. Steward, *Theory of Culture Change: The Methodology of Multilinear Evolution* (Urbana, IL: University of Illinois Press, 1955); Karl A. Wittfogel, *Oriental Despotism* (New Haven, CT: Yale University Press, 1957); Marvin Harris, *Cultural Materialism: The Struggle for a Science of Culture* (New York: Vintage Books, 1979); Ester Boserup, *The Conditions of Agricultural Growth* (Chicago: Aldine Atherton, 1965).

8. For example, Frank Hole, Kent V. Flannery, and James A. Neely, *Prehistory and Human Ecology of the Deh Luran Plain: An Early Village Sequence from Khuzistan, Iran* (Ann Arbor: University of Michigan Museum of Anthropology Memoirs 1, 1969); Douglas Byers, ed., *The Prehistory of the Tehuacan Valley, Volume One: Environment and Subsistence* (Austin: University of Texas Press, 1967), and subsequent volumes of the Tehuacan project reports.

9. Karl W. Butzer, *Early Hydraulic Civilization in Egypt: A Study in Cultural Ecology* (Chicago: University of Chicago Press, 1976); Robert McAdams, *Heartland of Cities: Surveys of Ancient Settlement and Land Use on the Central Floodplain of the Euphrates* (Chicago: University of Chicago Press, 1981); Angel Palerm and Eric R. Wolf, "Ecological Potential and Cultural Development in Mesoamerica," *Pan American Union Social Science Monograph* 3: 1–37; William T. Sanders, Jeffrey R. Parsons, and Robert S. Santley, *The Basin of Mexico: Ecological Processes in the Evolution of a Civilization* (New York: Academic Press, 1979).

10. Eric R. Wolf, "Introduction," in Eric R. Wolf, ed., *The Valley of Mexico: Studies in Pre-Hispanic Ecology and Society* (Albuquerque: University of New Mexico Press, 1976).

11. Wolf, "Introduction"; Sanders, Parsons, and Santley, *The Basin of Mexico*; René Millon, *Urbanization at Teotihuacan, Mexico, Volume One: The Teotihuacan Map, Part One: Text* (Austin: University of Texas Press, 1973). Sites of the "archaic" period previous to about 1500 B.C. have been found and studied but present difficult methodological problems for reconstruction of human social systems.

12. Richard E. Blanton, *Monte Albán: Settlement Patterns at the Ancient Zapotec Capital* (New York: Academic Press, 1978); Richard Blanton, Stephen A. Kowalewski, Gary M. Feinman, and Jill Appel, *Monte Albán's Hinterland, Part I: The Prehispanic Settlement Patterns of the Central and Southern Parts of the Valley of Oaxaca, Mexico* (Ann Arbor: University of Michigan Museum of Anthropology, Memoirs 15, 1982); Stephen A. Kowalewski, Gary M. Feinman, Laura Finsten, Richard E. Blanton, and Linda Nicholas, *Monte Albán's Hinterland, Part II: Prehispanic Settlement Patterns in Tlacolula, Etla, and Ocotlán, The Valley of Oaxaca, Mexico* (Ann Arbor: University of Michigan, Museum of Anthropology Memoirs 23, 1989).

13. Richard E. Blanton, Stephen A. Kowalewski, Gary M. Feinman, and Laura M. Finsten, *Ancient Mesoamerica: A Comparison of Change in Three Regions*, 2nd rev. ed. (Cambridge: Cambridge University Press, 1993), chapter 4; Frances F. Berdan, Richard E. Blanton, Elizabeth Boone, Mary Hodge, Michael E. Smith, and Emily Umberger, *Aztec Imperial Strategies* (Washington, DC: Dumbarton Oaks, in press).

14. The degree to which new theory is needed is currently an issue of contention, as some researchers are unwilling to accept the critiques of cultural ecology; this is discussed in Richard E. Blanton, "Theory and Practice in Mesoamerican Archaeology: A Comparison of Two Modes of Scientific Inquiry," in Joyce Marcus, ed., *Debating Oaxaca Archaeology* (Ann Arbor: University of Michigan, Museum of Anthropology, Anthropological Papers 84, 1990); cf. Blanton et al., *Ancient Mesoamerica*, chapter 1. In a study combining the Valley of Mexico archaeological data with early colonial Spanish descriptions of the region, I was able to show that the distribution of cities of the last two prehispanic periods is strongly predicted by market location theory, not environmental factors or carrying capacity. See Richard E. Blanton, "The Basin of Mexico Market System and the Growth of Empire," in Frances F. Berdan et al., *Aztec Imperial Strategies*.

15. Eric R. Wolf, *Europe and the People without History* (Berkeley: University of California Press, 1982).

16. Robert M. Netting, Richard R. Wilk, and Eric J. Arnould, "Introduction," in Robert M. Netting, Richard R. Wilk, and Eric J. Arnould, eds., *Households: Comparative and Historical Studies of the Domestic Group* (Berkeley: University of California Press, 1984).

17. Richard E. Blanton, *Households and Houses: A Comparative Perspective* (New York: Plenum, 1994).

Suggested Readings

Blanton, Richard E., Stephen A. Kowalewski, Gary M. Feinman, and Laura Finsten. *Ancient Mesoamerica: A Comparison of Change in Three Regions*, 2nd ed. Cambridge: Cambridge University Press, 1993. Compares the evolution of prehispanic Mesoamerican societies in three major regions, the Valleys of Mexico and Oaxaca, and the lowland Maya.

Harris, Marvin. *Our Kind: Who We Are, Where We Came From, Where We Are Going*. New York: Harper and Row, 1989. Broad-ranging overview of human social evolution from a cultural ecological perspective.

Netting, Robert M., Richard R. Wilk, and Eric J. Arnould, eds. *Households: Comparative and Historical Studies of the Domestic Group.* Berkeley: University of California Press, 1984. A large collection of papers indicating the range of household studies in anthropology.

Renfrew, Colin, and Paul Bahn. *Archaeology: Theories, Methods, and Practice.* New York: Thames and Hudson, 1991. Recent review of developments in archaeological method and theory.

Wenke, Robert J. *Patterns in Prehistory: Humankind's First Three Million Years,* 3rd ed. Oxford: Oxford University Press, 1990. Summarizes archaeological sequences for all major world areas.

"ARCHAEOLOGIST AT WORK"

Richard Blanton

1) What was Blanton's original research interests?

2) What is cultural ecology and why is it well suited to a regional approach to archaeology? What sorts of questions can you ask using this approach?

3) How did experiences from Blanton's own research in Mexico challenge the explanatory utility of cultural ecological theory?

4) In explaining cultural change, why does Blanton consider it important to begin with the level of household decision making?

5) In doing his cross-cultural comparative ethnological research, what social factors did Blanton identify that affected household decision making?

WORKING THE DEVIL'S MINES

Marguerite Holloway

Mornings on Cerro Rico, Bolivia's "Rich Hill," have been very much the same for centuries. At the Candelaria mine, the new shift gathers at about eight o'clock, and the miners sit chewing the coca leaves that will enable them to work for more than twelve hours without eating, drinking, or resting. At about ten o'clock, the men go inside the shacks near the mine entrance. They reappear in clothes covered with white dust, carrying picks, dynamite, and carbon lamps. By eleven the ghostly procession has been swallowed up by the *boca mina*, the "opening to the mine."

Just inside Candelaria, the light is still bright and the air cool. But soon the air becomes heavy and hot, and the mud in the narrow tunnel sucks at the miners' boots. Some 900 feet into the mountain, thirty-three-year-old Bernabé Mamani, who has been mining since he was fifteen and looks as if he were fifty, sits in front of the new life-size statue of the Devil, or El Tío, that he has just completed.

Each mine has its main Tío (Spanish for "uncle")—sculpted in red clay and featuring a large, erect penis—and each group of miners within a mine usually has its own small figure next to its work site. Since Cerro Rico may have 2,000 to 5,000 mine openings, there may be as many as 15,000 devil figures in this mountain. Every Tuesday and Friday the miners make libations, or *ch'alla*, when they visit their Tío, chatting with him and offering alcohol, coca leaves, and cigarettes. If there have been recent accidents, *ch'alla* becomes a desperate attempt to appease El Tío: they give him gifts so he stops desiring miners' flesh.

"The miners die because El Tío is angry with them," explains Vanancio Mercado Hurtado, a retired miner. "El Tío is the owner of the riches in the mountain. He gives to whom he wants to, and if he doesn't, you work in vain."

The miners are descendants of the Aymara-speaking people, who once ruled the region around Lake Titicaca, to the northwest of Cerro Rico, and of the Quechua-speaking Incas, who came to dominate what is now Bolivia a mere seventy-five years before the Spaniards arrived. Following the conquest, the Andean natives outwardly adopted Catholicism, but they maintained many of their own spiritual beliefs, particularly inside the mines, where they could es-

cape the Spaniards' scrutiny. El Tío is not precisely a counterpart to the Christian Devil—the Andeans did not have a concept of one supreme evil being. Some say he is a manifestation of Supay, a god of the underworld, or of Huari, one of many earth demons. All Andean figures "combine good and possibly destructive consequences, but not evil," explains June Nash, an anthropologist at the City University of New York who has documented the lives and beliefs of miners in Oruru, to the north of Cerro Rico.

Deep in Candelaria, Mamani greets his Tío with his customary salute, an insult: he calls him a drug addict and a *malcriado*, "one badly brought up." "This gentleman is totally of these depths," explains Mamani. The miners endeavor to treat El Tío as a comrade but are careful to avoid carrying pickaxes in front of him because he might take offense at the sign of the cross. When Mamani inadvertently utters the word *God*, he expresses his anguish by piling coca leaves on the figure and offering him more cigarettes.

Near where Mamani both insults and gently murmurs to his Tío, miners struggle up a ninety-foot incline with huge sacks of rocks on their backs. They dump their loads and, sweating and thirsty, race back down for more, their lamps bouncing at their waists.

Some 10,000 men work in or around the mountain, tapping the rich rivulets of metal laid down at least twenty million years ago by hot water escaping from magma. Cerro Rico has minerals from old magmas that have been recycled and reprocessed, as well as from younger, less refined magmas. Metals frequently form in clusters, but even by Andean standards, the mountain is exceptionally rich, yielding tin, tungsten, lead, zinc, copper, and silver.

According to one legend, the mountain's riches were discovered in early colonial times by an Inca who camped there while pursuing an escaped llama. At night, by the light of his fire, he saw a vein of silver. Another myth, reported by Uruguayan historian Eduardo Galeano, holds that the Incas had learned long before that the mountain contained precious metals, but that when they attempted to excavate them, a great voice proclaimed that the riches were reserved for "those who come from afar." The mountain was thereafter named Potojsi, which means "to thunder or to burst." Whether they were the intended people from afar or not, the Spanish conquistadors found Cerro Rico in 1545 and eagerly set to mining it, exploiting the labor of the native Andeans.

Rising some 2,800 feet above the surrounding 13,000-foot-high terrain, Cerro Rico yielded more silver than any other mountain or region in the Spanish empire—an average of sixty-seven tons (worth $12 million in today's market) per year between 1545 and 1825, according to Peter Bakewell of Emory University. Much of it was shipped out of Spain to Holland, Germany, and England, providing capital that financed the Industrial Revolution and Europe's burgeoning trade with Asia. Meanwhile, near the base of the mountain grew the city of Potosí, one of the most famous and important centers in colonial Latin America. By 1573 Potosí was bigger than Seville, Madrid, Rome, or Paris. A shield bestowed upon it by the Holy Roman Emperor Charles V read: "I am rich Potosí, treasure of the world, king of the mountains, envy of kings." Histories of the time chronicled the wild excesses of the young city—from the weeks of drunken revelry to the building of silver-laden churches.

"All that stuff praising the Cerro Rico is only Creole poetry," counters Roberto Carnaghi, an Italian educator who works with miners' children in Potosí. "For the Indian, the mountain is only death." By the 1570s, the silver lodes near the surface had been depleted, and mine owners were forced to excavate deeper and deeper inside the mountain. This intensive work would have been prohibitively expensive but for the *mita*, the Inca system of community labor that the Spaniards expanded and institutionalized as state servitude. Each year some 13,500 men were rounded up from their villages on the Andean plateau and forced to walk as much as 600 miles to Potosí.

Once in Potosí, the *mitayos* labored in the mines, where accidents were routine, or in the refining plants, where contact with the mercury used to extract silver from the rocks led to dementia and infirmity. In the late 1500s, historian Luis Capoche reported that "it is common to bring them out dead or with broken heads and legs, and in the mills they are injured every day." Many who survived their year of servitude remained in the fledgling city and risked the danger of continued employment in the refineries and the mines. By 1825, the mountain had meted out a wealth of corpses in addition to silver: untold thousands of Andean Indians had died in the mines.

In effect, Potosí maintains a modern-day *mita*, for the city of 112,000 provides jobs that cannot be found in the surrounding countryside, which is poorly suited for agriculture. And the human cost is still high. According to Balbina Martinez, a pediatrician at the main hospital in Potosí, the infant mortality rate is by far the highest in Bolivia: 250 deaths per 1,000, between birth and five years of age. At 13,189

feet above sea level, the city is not a place one easily adapts to, and many suffer from chronic mountain sickness.

The miners, some as young as fifteen, breathe in the fine particles that will incapacitate most of them before the age of forty. Julia Valdivia, a pulmonary specialist in Potosí, says that 90 percent of the active miners have silicosis and 90 percent of those, in turn, contract tuberculosis. The ones that have health insurance visit her ward, lying fully clothed for weeks at a time, their faces dark against the pink sheets. Valdivia holds up their X-rays, showing scarred lungs and enlarged hearts, which struggle to get oxygen. Later she reveals that the ten miners currently under her care have perhaps a year to live. "It is very difficult to see patients who are already done with. You can't help them." She pauses, then continues, "It makes one desperate to see them die, asking for air."

The mines have been unsafe for centuries. Rickety shafts collapse, tunnels flood, and explosions blow up or bury miners alive. Last year, for instance, a worker in one mine lit dynamite; moments later, his lamp ran out of fuel (after burning for eighteen hours), and he could not see where to run for safety. Two miners who went in to get his body a few days later were rendered unconscious by the fumes from the explosion, and although they were ultimately rescued, their lungs were damaged. Such accidents—the product of overly long shifts and poor equipment—are a regular occurrence.

Although they make up only 2 percent of the work force, the miners of Potosí and elsewhere in Bolivia have shaped their country's modern history more powerfully than any other segment of the population. Exploited first by the Spaniards and later by the "tin barons"—the Patiños, the Aramayos, and the Hochschilds—the miners led their country to revolution in 1952. "It cost the miners blood and grieving," recalls Dulfredo Durán, a leader of the Association of Retired Miners of COMIBOL (the Mining Corporation of Bolivia) who has marched on La Paz in protest many times. "That is why not only in Bolivia but also in other parts of the world the Bolivian miners are recognized."

The state bought out the biggest private owners and created COMIBOL to run the nationalized mines. Although seemingly the beneficiaries of the revolution, the miners instead found themselves operating depleted mines with little equipment and caught in a wildly fluctuating world market. The Bolivian government also proved unstable, and successive administrations sought to break the political power of the miners, shedding more blood.

By the early 1980s, COMIBOL was in financial turmoil as the price of tin plummeted. When the market crashed in 1985, 23,000 miners lost their jobs.

COMIBOL now produces virtually nothing. Most miners currently work in private mines or in cooperatives that lease the *bocas minas* from the state. Members of the cooperatives receive health insurance and earn between $12 and $40 a week. The cooperatives are themselves guilty of exploiting workers whom they hire for short periods, then fire to avoid paying health coverage.

Sitting in his dark, one-room apartment on the second floor of a dilapidated building, breathing heavily because half his lungs are destroyed, Durán becomes animated as he remembers his eighteen years with COMIBOL. "Work in the mine is very sacrificing, but it is beautiful, it is a marvel," he says, conveying a joy about the hard work that many of the miners in Potosí express. "I felt happiest with my comrades, because we lived there." Now fifty-one, Durán went to work at age sixteen after the death of his father. To support his brothers and his mother, he first worked in a cooperative mine that allowed underage miners.

Durán's mother, who is seventy-four, can be found every day in the Plaza Bolivian, just around the corner from Durán's house, where she has been selling cake, vegetables, and cinnamon drinks since she was fourteen. Standing in front of the wooden boards that she has piled high with greens and pomegranates, she tells of how proud she is of her son's activism.

There are few options for the wives or widows of miners: they can sell coca leaves, dry goods and supplies, or homemade food in the market or out of their houses. Women are generally not permitted inside the mines, and to earn money through metal, they pick over the rocks that the miners have rejected as too low in ore content. These gleaners are known as *palliris*, Aymara for "ones who choose." They spend their days hunched over, their backs exposed to the cold wind and the damp, lifting stones and carrying them in their shawls, then sorting them into piles.

While the miners look to El Tío for spiritual protection, the *palliris'* principal connection is to Pachamama, the spirit of the earth and the harvest. Every Monday, widows gather in the cemetery, pour alcohol for Pachamama, and offer her coca. According to historian Sabine MacCormack, Andean peoples "thought their ancestors had sprung from the land itself, from mountain or rock, lake or spring." They believed the living must talk to the dead, thus honoring the land and insuring a livelihood.

The cooperatives process the rocks collected by the *palliris*, paying them their share of the eventual proceeds. There used to be hundreds of *palliris* because a widow had the right to collect around her husband's mine. But now there are only 110, including the 50 *guardas* who protect the *bocas minas* from nighttime intruders. A big threat to the *palliris* is not just the low price of tin but the private interests that have set their sights on the tailings.

Several years ago, COMCO—a refining subsidiary of the mining corporation COMSUR, one of whose major shareholders is the current president of Bolivia—purchased the mountain's uppermost tailings. These rocks, originally unearthed by the Spaniards, yield high grades of silver in COMCO's hands. The cooperatives were willing to make the sale, because they could extract little of value from the rocks using their antiquated equipment. At worker-run refineries, bits of rock fly by the faces of the miners who shovel the shards into the grinders. Some of the men limp, others have hands that hang useless by their sides. Nearby, men sort the fine minerals, running their hands through corrosive water.

The miners' frustrations and lack of resources take another kind of toll on the women, according to Ruth Ortega Calderón, a lawyer at the National Organization for Children, Women, and the Family, who started a legal clinic in July 1995. Every Monday she finds, lined up outside her office, eight or nine women who have been raped or beaten by their husbands, victims of the libations that begin deep in the mine on Friday and continue all weekend. Every month or two, Calderón also hears of a family being blown up by dynamite set in the house or of someone who "opens up the gas and asphyxiates the entire family."

About eighty children live on the mountain, and few of them have access to schools. "It is a terrible world up there. At times it feels as though it eats you inside," says Carnaghi, who came to Potosí with his family five years ago from Italy with the intention of aiding children. Carnaghi converted an empty room at one of the mines into a school. "The solitude is incredible," he says. "Sometimes you are walking and walking in the sun and you hear nothing except wind. Then you hear a little sound of hammering. And in the cold shadows is a woman, alone, breaking rocks."

To many in Potosí the future seems as bleak as Cerro Rico itself. There has been strong pressure in Bolivia to continue to privatize all sectors of the economy. Every now and then rumor sweeps Potosí: the Japanese are going to buy the mountain, reduce it to rubble, and extract the remaining silver. Many migrate from Potosí to La Paz or to the Chapare to grow coca.

After centuries of mining, Cerro Rico is denuded of vegetation and wormholed with mines and collapsed shafts. But the mountain has long provided a living, and the miners can only believe it will continue to do so. Just when it seems that the minerals are depleted, another vein opens—as one did this year—and a surge of people migrate to Potosí from the countryside.

"WORKING THE DEVIL'S MINES"

Marguerite Holloway

1) Who is Tio and why is he important in the everyday lives of the miners?

2) What dangers and stresses do the miners face daily?

3) How do the miner's problems impact on their families?

4) What religious figure do the women in the mining towns revere? What themes or ideological concepts does she represent?

5) The article discusses the religious beliefs of Bolivian miners as combinations of two different religious systems, a *syncretism* of these beliefs. What belief systems have been syncretized, and what different elements of each system can be identified from the article?

Epistemology:
How You Know What You Know

Kenneth L. Feder

Knowing Things

The word *epistemology* means the study of knowledge—how you know what you know. Think about it. How does anybody know anything to be actual, truthful, or real? How do we differentiate the reasonable from the unreasonable, the meaningful from the meaningless—in archaeology or in any other field of knowledge? Everybody knows things, but how do we really know these things?

I know that there is a mountain in a place called Tibet. I know that the mountain is called Everest, and I know that it is the tallest land mountain in the world (there are some a bit taller under the ocean). I even know that it is precisely 29,028 feet high. But I have never measured it; I've never even been to Tibet. Beyond this, I have not measured all of the other mountains in the world to compare them to Everest. Yet I am quite confident that Everest is the world's tallest peak. But how do I know that?

On the subject of mountains, there is a run-down stone monument on the top of Bear Mountain in the northwestern corner of Connecticut. The monument was built toward the end of the nineteenth century and marks the "highest ground" in Connecticut. When the monument was built to memorialize this most lofty and auspicious of peaks—the mountain is all of 2,316 feet high—people knew that it was the highest point in the state and wanted to recognize this fact with the monument.

There is only one problem. In recent times, with more accurate, sophisticated measuring equipment, it has been determined that Bear Mountain is not the highest point in Connecticut. The slope of Frissell Mountain, which actually peaks in Massachusetts, reaches a height of 2,380 feet on the Connecticut side of the border, eclipsing Bear Mountain by about 64 feet.

So, people in the late 1800s and early 1900s "knew" that Bear Mountain was the highest point in Connecticut. Today we *know* that they really did not "know" that, because it really was not true—even though they thought it was and built a monument saying so.

Now, suppose that I read in a newspaper, hear on the radio, or see on television a claim that another mountain has been found that is actually ten (or fifty or ten thousand) feet higher than Mount Everest. Indeed, recently, new satellite data convinced a few, just for a while, that a peak neighboring Everest was, in actuality, slightly higher. You and I have never been to Tibet. How do we know if these reports are true? What criteria can we use to decide if the information is correct or not? It all comes back to epistemology. How indeed do we know what we think we "know"?

Collecting Information: Seeing Isn't Necessarily Believing

In general, people collect information in two ways:

1. Directly through their own experiences.

2. Indirectly through specific information sources like friends, teachers, parents, books, TV, etc.

People tend to think that number 1—obtaining firsthand information, the stuff they see or experience themselves—is always the best way. This is unfortunately a false assumption because most people are poor observers.

For example, the list of animals alleged to have been observed by people that turn out to be figments of their imaginations is staggering. It is fascinating to read Pliny, a first-century thinker, or Topsell, who wrote in the seventeenth century, and see detailed accounts of the nature and habits of dragons, griffins, unicorns, mermaids, and so on (Byrne 1979). People claimed to have seen these animals, gave detailed descriptions, and even drew pictures of them. Many folks read their books and believed them.

Some of the first European explorers of Africa, Asia, and the New World could not decide if some of the native people they encountered were human beings or animals. They sometimes depicted them with hair all over their bodies and even as having tails.

Neither are untrained observers very good at identifying known, living animals. A red or "lesser" panda escaped from the zoo in Rotterdam, Holland, in December 1978. Red pandas are very rare animals and are indigenous to India, not Holland. They are distinctive in appearance and cannot be readily mistaken for any other sort of animal. The zoo informed the press that the panda was missing, hoping the publicity would alert people in the area of the zoo and aid in its return. Just when the newspapers came out with the panda story, it was found, quite dead, along some railroad tracks adjacent to the zoo. Nevertheless, over one hundred sightings of the panda *alive* were reported to the zoo from all over the Netherlands *after* the animal was obviously already dead. These reports did not stop until several days after the newspapers announced the discovery of the dead panda (van Kampen 1979). So much for the absolute reliability of firsthand observation.

Collecting Information: Relying on Others

When we explore the problems of secondhand information, we run into even more complications. Now we are not in place to observe something firsthand; we are forced to rely on the quality of someone else's observations, interpretations, and reports—as with the question of the height of Mount Everest. How do we know what to believe? This is a crucial question that all rational people must ask themselves, whether talking about medicine, religion, archaeology, or anything else. Again, it comes back around to epistemology; how do we know what we think we know, and how do we know what or whom to believe?

Science: Playing by the Rules

There are ways to knowledge that are both dependable and reliable. We might not be able to get to absolute truths about the meaning of existence, but we can figure out quite a bit about our world—about chemistry and biology, psychology and sociology, physics and history, and even prehistory. The techniques we are talking about to get at knowledge that we can feel confident in—knowledge that is reliable, truthful, and factual—are referred to as *science*.

In large part, science is a series of techniques used to *maximize* the probability that what we think we know really reflects the way things are, were, or will be. Science makes no claim to have all the answers or even to be right all of the time. On the contrary, during the process of the growth of knowledge and understanding, science is often wrong. The only claim that we do make in science is that if we honestly, consistently, and vigorously pursue knowledge using some basic techniques and principles, the truth will eventually surface and we can truly know things

about the nature of the world in which we find ourselves.

The question then is, What exactly is science? If you believe Hollywood, science is a mysterious enterprise wherein old, white-haired, rather eccentric bearded gentlemen labor feverishly in white lab coats, mix assorted chemicals, invent mysterious compounds, and attempt to reanimate dead tissue. So much for Hollywood. Scientists don't have to look like anything in particular. We are just people trying to arrive at some truths about how the world and universe work. While the application of science can be a slow, frustrating, all-consuming enterprise, the basic assumptions we scientists hold are really very simple. Whether we are physicists, biologists, or archaeologists, we all work under four underlying principles. These principles are quite straightforward, but equally quite crucial.

1. There is a real and knowable universe.

2. The universe (which includes stars, planets, animals, and rocks, as well as people, their cultures, and their histories) operates according to certain understandable rules or laws.

3. These laws are immutable—that means they do not, in general, change depending on where you are or "when" you are.

4. These laws can be discerned, studied, and understood by people through careful observation, experimentation, and research.

Let's look at these assumptions one at a time.

There Is a Real and Knowable Universe

In science we have to agree that there is a real universe out there for us to study—a universe full of stars, animals, human history, and prehistory that exists whether we are happy with that reality or not.

The Universe Operates According to Understandable Laws

In essence, what this means is that there are rules by which the universe works: stars produce heat and light according to the laws of nuclear physics; nothing can go faster than the speed of light; all matter in the universe is attracted to all other matter (the law of gravity).

Even human history is not random but can be seen as following certain patterns of human cultural evolution. For example, the development of complex civilizations in Egypt, China, India/Pakistan, Mesopotamia, Mexico, and Peru was not based on random processes (Lamberg-Karlovsky and Sabloff 1979; Haas 1982). Their evolution seems to reflect similar general patterns. This is not to say that all of these civilizations were identical, any more than we would say that all stars are identical. On the contrary, they existed in different physical and cultural environments, and so we should expect that they be different. However, in each case the rise to civilization was preceded by the development of an agricultural economy. In each case, civilization was also preceded by some degree of overall population increase as well as increased population density in some areas (in other words, the development of cities). Again, in each case we find monumental works (pyramids, temples), evidence of long-distance trade, and the development of mathematics, astronomy, and methods of record keeping (usually, but not always, in the form of writing). The cultures in which civilization developed, though some were unrelated and independent, shared these factors because of the nonrandom patterns of cultural evolution.

The point is that everything operates according to rules. In science we believe that, by understanding these rules or laws, we can understand stars, organisms, and even ourselves.

The Laws Are Immutable

That the laws do not change under ordinary conditions is a crucial concept in science. A law that works here, works there. A law that worked in the past will work today and will work in the future.

For example, if I go to the top of the Leaning Tower of Pisa today and simultaneously drop two balls of unequal mass, they will fall at the same rate and reach the ground at the same time, just as they did when Galileo performed a similar experiment in the seventeenth century. If I do it today, they will. Tomorrow, the same. If I perform the same experiment countless times, the same thing will occur because the laws of the universe (in this case, the law of gravity) do not change through time. They also do not change depending on where you are. Go anywhere on the earth and perform the same experiment—you will get the same results (try not to hit any pedestrians or you will see some other "laws" in operation). This experiment was even performed by U. S. astronauts on the moon. A hammer and a feather were dropped from the same height, and they hit the surface at precisely the same instant (the only reason this will not work on earth is because the feather is caught by the air and the hammer, obviously, is not). We have no reason to believe that the results would

be different anywhere, or "any-when" else.

If this assumption of science, that the laws do not change through time, were false, many of the so-called historical sciences, including prehistoric archaeology, could not exist.

For example, a major principle in the field of historical geology is that of *uniformitarianism*. It can be summarized in the phrase, "the present is the key to the past." Historical geologists are interested in knowing how the various landforms we see today came into being. They recognize that they cannot go back in time to see how the Grand Canyon was formed. However, since the laws of geology that governed the development of the Grand Canyon have not changed through time, and since these laws are still in operation, they do not need to. Historical geologists can study the formation of geological features today and apply what they learn to the past. The same laws they can directly study operating in the present were operating in the past when geological features that interested them first formed.

The present that we can observe is indeed the "key" to the past that we cannot. This is true because the laws or rules that govern the universe are constant—those that operate today operated in the past. This is why science does not limit itself to the present, but makes inferences about the past and even predictions about the future (just listen to the weather report for an example of this). We can do so because we can study modern, ongoing phenomena that work under the same laws that existed in the past and will exist in the future.

This is where science and theology are often forced to part company and respectfully disagree. Remember, science depends on the constancy of the laws that we can discern. On the other hand, advocates of many religions, though they might believe that there are laws that govern things (and which, according to them, were established by a Creator), usually (but not always) believe that these laws can be changed at any time by their God. In other words, if God does not want the apple to fall to the ground, but instead, to hover, violating the law of gravity, that is precisely what will happen. As a more concrete example, scientists know that the heat and light given off by a fire results from the transformation of mass (of the wood) to energy. Physical laws control this process. A theologian, however, might agree with this ordinarily, but feel that if God wants to create a fire that does not consume any mass (like the "burning bush" of the Old Testament), then this is exactly what will occur. Most scientists simply do not accept this assertion. The rules are the rules. They do not change, even though we might sometimes wish that they would.

The Laws Can Be Understood

This may be the single most important principle in science. The universe is knowable. It may be complicated, and it may take years and years to understand even apparently simple phenomena. However, little by little, bit by bit, we expand our knowledge. Through careful observation and objective research and experimentation, we can indeed know things.

So, our assumptions are simple enough. We accept the existence of a reality independent of our own minds, and we accept that this reality works according to a series of unchanging laws or rules. We also claim that we can recognize and understand these laws or at least recognize the patterns that result from these universal rules. The question remains then: how do we do science—how do we explore the nature of the universe, whether our interest is planets, stars, atoms, or human prehistory?

The Workings of Science

We can know things by employing the rules of logic and rational thought. Scientists—archaeologists or otherwise—usually work through a combination of the logical processes known as *induction* and *deduction*. The dictionary definition of induction is "arguing from specifics to generalities," while deduction is defined as the reverse, arguing from generalities to specifics.

What is essential to good science is objective, unbiased observations—of planets, molecules, rock formations, archaeological sites, and so on. Often, on the basis of these specific observations, we induce explanations called *hypotheses* for how these things work.

For example, we may study the planets Mercury, Venus, Earth, and Mars (each one presents specific bits of information). We then induce general rules about how we think these inner planets in our solar system were formed. Or, we might study a whole series of different kinds of molecules and then induce general rules about how all molecules interact chemically. We may study different rock formations and make general conclusions about their origin. We can study a number of specific prehistoric sites and make generalizations about how cultures evolved.

Notice that we cannot directly observe planets forming, the rules of molecular interaction, rocks being made, or prehistoric cultures evolving. Instead, we are inducing general conclusions and principles concerning our data that seem to follow logically from what we have been able to observe.

This process of induction, though crucial to science, is not enough. We need to go beyond our induced hypotheses by testing them. If our induced hypotheses are indeed valid—that is, if they really represent the actual rules according to which some aspect of the universe (planets, molecules, rocks, ancient societies) works—they should be able to hold up under the rigors of scientific hypothesis testing.

Observation and suggestion of hypotheses, therefore, are only the first steps in a scientific investigation. In science we always need to go beyond observation and hypothesizing. We need to set up a series of "if . . . then" statements; "if" our hypothesis is true "then" the following deduced "facts" will also be true. Our results are not always precise and clearcut, especially in a science like archaeology, but this much should be clear—scientists are not just out there collecting a bunch of interesting facts. Facts are always collected within the context of trying to explain something or in trying to test a hypothesis.

As an example of this logical process, consider the health effects of smoking. How can scientists be sure that smoking is bad for you? After all, it's pretty rare that someone takes a puff on a cigarette and immediately drops dead. The certainty comes from a combination of induction and deduction. Observers have noticed for about three hundred years that people who smoked seemed to be more likely than people who did not to get certain diseases. As long ago as the seventeenth century, people noticed that habitual pipe smokers were subject to tumor growths on their lips and in their mouths. From such observations we can reasonably, though tentatively, induce a hypothesis of the unhealthfulness of smoking, but we still need to test such a hypothesis. We need to se up "if . . . then" statements. If, in fact, smoking is a hazard to your health (the hypothesis we have induced based on our observations), then we should be able to deduce some predictions that must also be true. Sure enough, when we test specific, deduced predictions like

1. Smokers will have a higher incidence than nonsmokers of lung cancer

2. Smokers will have a higher incidence of emphysema

3. Smokers will take more sick days from work

4. Smokers will get more upper respiratory infections

5. Smokers will have diminished lung capacity

6. Smokers will have a shorter life expectancy

we see that our original, induced hypothesis—cigarette smoking is hazardous to your health—is upheld.

That was easy, but also obvious. How about an example with more mystery to it, one in which scientists acting in the way of detectives had to solve a puzzle in order to save lives? Carl Hempel (1966), a philosopher of science, provided the following example in his book *The Philosophy of Natural Science.*

The Case of Childbed Fever

In the 1840s things were not going well at the Vienna General Hospital, particularly in Ward 1 of the Maternity Division. In Ward 1 more than one in ten of the women brought in to give birth died soon after of a terrible disease called "childbed fever." This was a high death rate even for the 1840s. In one year 11.4 percent of the women who gave birth in Ward 1 died of this disease. It was a horrible situation and truly mystifying when you consider the fact that in Ward 2, another maternity division in the *same* hospital at the *same* time, only about one in fifty of the women (2 percent) died from this disease.

Plenty of people had tried their hand at inducing some possible explanations or hypotheses to explain these facts. It was suggested that more women were dying in Ward 1 due to "atmospheric disturbances," or perhaps it was "cosmic forces." However, no one had really sat down and considered the deductive implications of the various hypotheses—those things that would necessarily have been true if the proposed, induced explanation[s] were in fact true. No one, that is, until a Hungarian doctor, Ignaz Semmelweis, attacked the problem in 1848.

Semmelweis made some observations in the maternity wards at the hospital. He noted some differences between Wards 1 and 2 and induced a series of possible explanations for the drastic difference in the mortality rates. Semmelweis suggested:

1. Ward 1 tended to be more crowded than Ward 2. The overcrowding in Ward 1 was the cause of the higher mortality rate there.

2. Women in Ward 1 were from a lower socioeconomic class and tended to give birth lying on their backs, while in Ward 2 the predominant position was on the side. Birth position was the cause of the higher mortality rate.

3. There was a psychological factor involved; the hospital priest had to walk through Ward 1 to administer the last rites to dying patients in other wards. This sight so upset some women already weakened by the ordeal of childbirth that it contributed to their deaths.

4. There were more student doctors in Ward 1. Students were rougher than experienced physicians in their treatment of the women, unintentionally harming them and contributing to their deaths.

These induced hypotheses all sounded good. Each marked a genuine difference between Wards 1 and 2 that might have caused the difference in the death rate. Semmelweis was doing what most scientists do in such a situation; he was relying on creativity and imagination in seeking out an explanation.

Creativity and imagination are just as important to science as good observation. But being creative and imaginative was not enough. It did not help the women who were still dying at an alarming rate. Semmelweis had to go beyond producing possible explanations; he had to test each one of them. So, he deduced the necessary implications of each:

1. If hypothesis 1 were correct, then cutting down the crowding in Ward 1 should cut down the mortality rate. Semmelweis tried precisely that. The result: no change. So the first hypothesis was rejected. It had failed the scientific test; it simply could not be correct.

2. Semmelweis went on the test hypothesis 2 by changing the birth positions of the women in Ward 1 to match those of the women in Ward 2. Again, there was no change, and another hypothesis was rejected.

3. Next, to test hypothesis 3, Semmelweis rerouted the priest. Again, women in Ward 1 continued to die of childbed fever at about five times the rate of those in Ward 2.

4. Finally, to test hypothesis 4 Semmelweis made a special effort to get the student doctors to be more gentle in their birth assistance to the women in Ward 1. The result was the same; 10 or 11 percent of the women in Ward 1 died compared to about 2 percent in Ward 2.

Then, as so often happens in science, Semmelweis had a stroke of luck. A doctor friend of his died, and the way he died provided Semmelweis with another possible explanation for the problem in Ward 1. Though Semmelweis's friend was not a woman who had recently given birth, he did have precisely the same symptoms as did the women who were dying of childbed fever. Most importantly, this doctor had died of a disease just like childbed fever soon after accidentally cutting himself during an autopsy.

Viruses and bacteria were unknown in the 1840s. Surgical instruments were not sterilized, no special effort was made to clean the hands, and doctors did not wear gloves during operations and autopsies. Semmelweis had another hypothesis; perhaps the greater number of medical students in Ward 1 was at the root of the mystery, but not because of their inexperience. Instead, these students, as part of their training, were much more likely than experienced doctors to be performing autopsies. Supposing that there was something bad in dead bodies and this something had entered Semmelweis's friend's system through his wound—could the same bad "stuff" (Semmelweis called it "cadaveric material") get onto the hands of the student doctors, who then might, without washing, go on to help a woman give birth? Then, if this "cadaveric material" were transmitted into the woman's body during the birth of her baby, this material might lead to her death. It was a simple enough hypothesis to test. Semmelweis simply had the student doctors carefully wash their hands after performing autopsies. The women stopped dying in Ward 1. Semmelweis had solved the mystery.

Science and Nonscience: The Essential Differences

Through objective observation and analysis, a scientist, whether a physicist, chemist, biologist, psychologist, or archaeologist, sees things that need explaining. Through creativity and imagination, the scientist suggests possible hypotheses to explain these "mysteries." The scientist then sets up a rigorous method through experimentation or subsequent research to deductively test the validity of a given hypothesis. If the implications of a hypothesis are shown not to be true, the hypothesis must be rejected and then it's back to the drawing board. If the implications are found to be true, we can uphold or support our hypothesis.

A number of other points should be made here. The first is that in order for a hypothesis, whether it turns out to be upheld or not, to be scientific in the first place, it must be testable. In other words, there must be clear, deduced implications that can be drawn from the hypothesis and then tested. Remem-

ber the hypotheses of "cosmic influences" and "atmospheric disturbances"? How can you test these? What are the necessary implications that can be deduced from the hypothesis, "More women died in Ward 1 due to atmospheric disturbances"? There really aren't any, and therefore such a hypothesis is not scientific—it cannot be tested. Remember, in the methodology of science, we ordinarily need to:

1. Observe

2. Induce general hypotheses or possible explanations for what we have observed

3. Deduce specific things that must also be true if our hypothesis is true

4. Test the hypothesis by checking out the deduced implications

If there are no specific implications of a hypothesis that can then be analyzed as a test of the validity or usefulness of that hypothesis, then you simply are not doing and cannot do "science."

For example, suppose you observe a person who appears to be able to "guess" the value of a playing card picked from a deck. Next, assume that someone hypothesizes that "psychic" ability is involved. Finally, suppose the claim is made that the "psychic" ability goes away as soon as you try to test it (actually named the "shyness effect" by some researchers of the paranormal). Such a claim is not itself testable and therefore not scientific.

Beyond the issue of testability, another lesson is involved in determining whether an approach to a problem is scientific. Semmelweis induced four different hypotheses to explain the difference in mortality rates between Wards 1 and 2. These "competing" explanations are called *multiple working hypotheses.* Notice that Semmelweis did not simply proceed by a process of elimination. He did not, for example, test the first three hypotheses and—after finding them invalid—declare that the fourth was necessarily correct since it was the only one left that he had thought of.

Some people try to work that way. A light is seen in the sky. Someone hypothesizes it was a meteor. We find out that it was not. Someone else hypothesizes that it was a military rocket. Again this turns out to be incorrect. Someone else suggests that it was the Goodyear Blimp, but that turns out to have been somewhere else. Finally, someone suggests that it was the spacecraft of people from another planet. Some will say that this must be correct, since none of the other explanations panned out. This is nonsense. There are plenty of other possible explanations. Eliminating all of the explanations *we* have been able to think of except one (which, perhaps, has no testable implications) in no way allows us to uphold that final hypothesis. . . .

It's like seeing a card trick. You are mystified by it. You have a few possible explanations: the magician did it with mirrors, there was a helper in the audience, the cards were marked. But when you approach the magician and ask which it was, he assures you that none of your hypotheses is correct. Do you then decide that what you saw was an example of genuine, supernatural magic? Of course not! Simply because you or I cannot come up with the right explanation does not mean that the trick has a supernatural explanation. We simply admit that we do not have the expertise to suggest a more reasonable hypothesis.

Finally, there is another rule to hypothesis ranking and testing. It is called *Occam's Razor* or *Occam's Rule*. In essence it says that when a number of hypotheses are proposed through induction to explain a given set of observations, the simplest hypothesis is probably the best.

Take this actual example. During the eighteenth and nineteenth centuries, huge, buried, fossilized bones were found throughout North America and Europe. One hypothesis, the simplest, was that the bones were the remains of animals that no longer existed. This hypothesis simply relied on the assumption that bones do not come into existence by themselves, but always serve as the skeletons of animals. Therefore, when you find bones, there must have been animals who used those bones. However, another hypothesis was suggested: the bones were deposited by the Devil to fool us into thinking that such animals existed (Howard 1975). This hypothesis demanded many more assumptions about the universe than did the first: there is a Devil, that Devil is interested in human affairs, he wants to fool us, he has the ability to make bones of animals that never existed, and he has the ability to hide them under the ground and inside solid rock. That is quite a number of unproven (and largely untestable) claims to swallow. Thus, Occam's Razor says the simpler hypothesis, that these great bones are evidence of the existence of animals that no longer exist—in other words, dinosaurs—is better. The other one simply raises more questions than it answers.

The Art of Science

Don't get the impression that science is a mechanical enterprise. Science is at least partially an art. It is much more than just observing the results of experiments.

It takes great creativity to recognize a "mystery" in the first place. In the apocryphal story, countless apples had fallen from countless trees and undoubtedly conked the noggins of multitudes of stunned individuals who never thought much about it. It took a fabulously creative individual, Isaac Newton, to even recognize that herein lay a mystery. Why did the apple fall? No one had ever articulated the possibility that the apple could have hovered in midair. It could have moved off in any of the cardinal directions. It could have gone straight up and out of sight. But it did not. It fell to the ground as it always had, in all places, and as it always would. It took great imagination to recognize that in this simple observation (and in a bump on the head) rested the eloquence of a fundamental law of the universe.

Further, it takes great skill and imagination to invent a hypothesis in this attempt to understand why things seem to work the way they do. Remember, Ward 1 at the Vienna General Hospital did not have written over its doors, OVERCROWDED WARD or WARD WITH STUDENT DOCTORS WHO DON'T WASH THEIR HANDS AFTER AUTOPSIES. It took imagination first to recognize that there were differences between the wards and, quite importantly, that some of the differences might logically be at the root of the mystery. After all, there were in all likelihood many, many differences between the wards: their compass orientations, the names of the nurses, the precise alignment of the windows, the astrological signs of the doctors who worked in the wards, and so on. If a scientist were to attempt to test all of these differences as hypothetical causes of a mystery, nothing would ever be solved. Occam's Razor must be applied. We need to focus our intellectual energies on those possible explanations that require few other assumptions. Only after all of these have been eliminated, can we legitimately consider others. As summarized by that great fictional detective, Sherlock Holmes:

> It is of the highest importance in the art of detection to be able to recognize, out of a number of facts, which are incidental and which are vital. Otherwise, your energy and attention must be dissipated instead of being concentrated.

Semmelweis concentrated his attention on first four, then a fifth possible explanation. Like all good scientists he had to use some amount of what we can call "intuition" to sort out the potentially vital from the probably incidental. Even in the initial sorting we may be wrong. Overcrowding seemed a very plausible explanation to Semmelweis, but it was wrong nonetheless.

Finally, it takes skill and inventiveness to suggest ways for testing the hypothesis in question. We must, out of our own heads, be able to invent the "then" part of our "if . . . then" statements. We need to be able to suggest those things that must be true if our hypothesis is to be supported. There really is an art to that. Anyone can claim there was a Lost Continent of Atlantis, but often it takes a truly inventive mind to suggest precisely what archaeologists must find if the hypothesis of its existence were indeed to be valid.

Semmelweis tested his hypotheses and solved the mystery of childbed fever by changing conditions in Ward 1 to see if the death rate would change. In essence, the testing of each hypothesis was an experiment. In archaeology, the testing of hypotheses often must be done in a different manner. There is a branch of archaeology called, appropriately enough, "experimental archaeology" that involves the experimental replication and utilization of prehistoric artifacts in an attempt to figure out how they were made and used. In general, however, archaeology is largely not an experimental science. Archaeologists more often need to create "models" of some aspect of cultural adaptation and change. These models are simplified, manipulable versions of cultural phenomena.

For example, James Mosimann and Paul Martin (1975) created a computer program that simulated or modeled the first human migration into America some 12,000 years ago. By varying the size of the initial human population and their rate of growth and expansion, as well as the size of the big-game animal herds in the New World, Mosimann and Martin were able to test their hypothesis that these human settlers caused the extinction of many species of game animals. The implications of their mathematical modeling can be tested against actual archaeological and paleontological data.

Ultimately, whether a science is experimentally based or not makes little logical difference in the testing of hypotheses. Instead of predicting what the results of a given experiment must be if our induced hypothesis is useful or valid, we predict what new data we must be able to find if a given hypothesis is correct.

For instance, we may hypothesize that long-distance trade is a key element in the development of civilization based upon our analysis of the ancient Maya. We deduce that if this is correct—if this is, in fact, a general rule of cultural evolution—we must find large quantities of trade items in other parts of the world where civilization also developed. We might further deduce that these items should be found in contexts that denote their value and importance to the society (for example, in the burials of leaders). We must then determine the validity of our predictions and, indirectly, our hypothesis by going out and conducting more research. We need to excavate sites belonging to other ancient civilizations and see if they followed the same pattern as seen for the Maya relative to the importance of trade.

Testing a hypothesis certainly is not easy. Sometimes errors in testing can lead to incorrectly validating or rejecting a hypothesis. Some of you may have already caught a potential problem in Semmelweis's application of the scientific method. Remember hypothesis 4? It was initially suggested that the student doctors were at the root of the higher death rate in Ward 1, because they were not as gentle in assisting in birthing as were the more experienced doctors. This hypothesis was not borne out by testing. Retraining the students had no effect on the mortality rate in Ward 1. But suppose that Semmelweis had tested this hypothesis instead by removing the students altogether prior to their retraining. From what we now know, the death rate would have indeed declined, and Semmelweis would have concluded incorrectly that the hypothesis was correct. We can assume that once the retrained students were returned to the ward (gentler, perhaps, but with their hands still dirty) the death rate would have jumped up again since the students were indeed at the heart of the matter, but not because of their presumed rough handling of the maternity patients.

This should point out that our testing of hypotheses takes a great deal of thought and that we can be wrong. We must remember: we have a hypothesis, we have the deduced implications, and we have the test. We can make errors at any place within this process—the hypothesis may be incorrect, the implications may be wrong, or the way we test them may be incorrect. Certainty in science is a scarce commodity. There are always new hypotheses, alternative explanations, and more deductive implications to test. Nothing is ever finished, nothing is set in concrete, nothing is ever defined or raised to the level of religious truth.

Beyond this, it must be admitted that scientists are, after all, ordinary human beings. They are not isolated from the cultures and times in which they live. They share many of the same prejudices and biases of other members of their societies. Scientists learn from mentors at universities and often inherit their perspectives. It often is quite difficult to go against the scientific grain, to question accumulated wisdom, and to suggest a new approach or perspective.

For example, when German meteorologist Alfred Wegener hypothesized in 1912 that the present configuration of the continents resulted from the breakup of a single inclusive landmass and that the separate continents had "drifted" into their current positions (a process called *continental drift*), most rejected the suggestion outright. Yet today, Wegener's general perspective is accepted and incorporated into the general theory of *plate tectonics.*

Philosopher of science Thomas Kuhn (1970) has suggested that the growth of scientific knowledge is not neatly linear, with knowledge simply building on knowledge. He maintains that science remains relatively static for periods and that most thinkers work under the same set of assumptions—the same *paradigm.* New ideas or perspectives, like those of Wegener or Einstein, that challenge the existing orthodoxy, are usually initially rejected. Only once scientists get over the shock of the new ideas and start testing the new frameworks suggested by these new paradigms are great jumps in knowledge made.

That is why in science we propose, test, tentatively accept, but never prove a hypothesis. We keep only those hypotheses that cannot be disproved. As long as an hypothesis holds up under the scrutiny of additional testing through experiment and/or is not contradicted by new data, we accept it as the best explanation so far. Some hypotheses sound good, pass the rigors of initial testing, but are later shown to be inadequate or invalid. Others—for example, the hypothesis of biological evolution—have held up so well (all new data either were or could have been deduced from it) that they will probably always be upheld. We usually call these very well supported hypotheses *theories.* However, it is in the nature of science that no matter how well an explanation of some aspect of reality has held up, we must always be prepared to consider new tests and better explanations.

We are interested in knowledge and explanations of the universe that work. As long as these explanations work, we keep them. As soon as they cease being effective because new data and tests show them to be incomplete or misguided, we discard them and seek new ones. In one sense, Semmelweis was wrong after all, though his explanation worked at the time—he did save lives through its application. We now know that there is nothing inherently bad in "cadaveric material." Dead bodies are not the cause of childbed fever. Today we realize that it is a bacteria that can grow in the flesh of a dead body that can get on a doctor's hands, infect a pregnant woman, and cause her death. Semmelweis worked in a time before the existence of such things was known. Science in this way always grows, expands, and evolves.

Science and Archaeology

The study of the human past is a science and relies on the same general logical processes that all sciences do. Unfortunately, perhaps as a result of its popularity, the data of archaeology have often been used by people to attempt to prove some idea or claim. Too often, these attempts have been bereft of science.

Archaeology has attracted frauds and fakes. Myths about the human past have been created and popularized. Misunderstandings of how archaeologists go about their tasks and what we have discovered about the human story have too often been promulgated. As I stated . . . my purpose is to describe the misuse of archaeology and the non-scientific application of the data from this field . . .

"EPISTEMOLOGY:
HOW YOU KNOW WHAT YOU KNOW"

Kenneth Feder

1) What are the two ways people generally collect information? Why or why aren't they generally effective? Give examples from the article and American culture.

2) What are the four major rules concerning the operation and functioning of science?

3) How did Semmelweiss exemplify how science should be conducted? What innovations did he institute and what possible pitfalls could he have encountered in his experiments?

4) How can errors creep into scientific methodology?

5) Define the following terms and give an example: multiple working hypotheses, Occam's Razor, paradigm.

6) Consider a popular belief (UFOs, Atlantis, Bigfoot, etc.) that you are interested in or find a fascinating possibility. Using science's rules of functioning, how would you go about dispassionately examining this belief?

SECTION TWO

Fieldwork Among the Familiar and the Strange

Kenya, Land of My Fathers: A Time Traveler in Kenya

Chapurukha M. Kusimba

Thirty-five years ago, I was born and given the name Cullen, in honor of an Irishman who was then my father's boss at the Kilembe mines in Uganda. My parents were from western Kenya, but I spent the first five years of my life in Uganda, where Father had found work as a civil engineer. After the two neighboring nations failed to resolve the labor migration crisis, Kenyans were forced to leave Uganda, and we settled in Father's village of Kaptola, where my parents had a modest two-bedroom house. This is where my two brothers, my sister, and I first became acquainted with our extended family. Having been born and raised in Uganda, we spoke Luganda, Lutoro, and some English, but none of our family's mother tongue, Lubukusu. Mother and Father decided that we should spend some time in the village to learn the ways of our people.

Our home was about one hundred yards from my grandparents' huge, six-bedroom house, which always seemed to be a beehive of activity. Here, in the evenings after school and dinner, all the grandchildren gathered to complete their homework, listen to Bible stories or fairy tales, sing traditional and Christian hymns, and, quite often, take refuge from irritated parents. For the next twelve years, in the great house that Grandfather built and Grandmother managed, I and my expanding family of cousins and siblings were raised. We were growing up in a recently independent and fast-changing society, little realizing that our generation enjoyed a unique link to the past.

Occasionally, one of us would bring home an arrowhead or stone tool, and our grandparents would patiently explain how people lived in former times. The Bukusu, to which I belong, are a Bantu-speaking people and inhibit the area around Mount Elgon on the Kenya-Uganda border. Traditionally, the Bukusu lived in large fortress villages, farming and grazing cattle in scattered meadows. They were surrounded by the Nilotic-speaking Iteso, Sabaot, and Nandi; by other Bantu groups; and by the Ndorobo, who were hunter-gathers. In times of peace and prosperity, these peoples engaged in trade and intermarried. In times of famine, they competed for land and stole from one another's herds. Skirmishes, raids, and counterraids were somehow accepted as a way of life.

Born in 1904, Grandfather was a skilled hunter, wonderful teacher, and excellent farmer. He became a Quaker in 1916 and was one of the first local missionaries to set up a meetinghouse among the pastoral Sabaot people of western Kenya. Our grandparents made it clear that we were in one way or another connected with our neighbors, including the hunter-gatherers, who brought us baskets, mats, dried meats, honey, and dried bamboo shoots in exchange for grains (mostly millet, sorghum, and maize).

Grandfather spoke all the languages of his neighbors, among whom he preached the Quaker message of peace and brotherhood. Few Kenyans can now speak more than four indigenous languages, in addition to English and Kiswahili. That people were traditionally multilingual is testimony to the interactions that existed among them. At the time I was growing up, however, the history of African groups was little known, and what we were taught in school was that African cultures were static until European missionaries and colonists arrived in the late nineteenth century.

Kenyan peoples that I learned about in childhood included the Swahili of the coast, whose Arab ties and history as slave traders gave them a less than favorable reputation. Grandfather remembered that Swahili caravans used to stop and trade in western Kenya on their way to Uganda. On one such visit, Grandfather, then five years old, approached one of the Swahili men, borrowed his rifle, and carried the heavy object for a few minutes to the amazement of all those present. One Swahili man declared, *Huyu mtoto ana nguvu kama ya simba*, "This child is as powerful as a lion." Grandfather then got the nickname Kusimba, or Big Lion, a name that he later formalized.

The history of the Swahili also came up when I accompanied Grandfather on a hunting expedition on the slopes of Mount Elgon. There I saw many rockshelters and caves, some with paintings. Because we were learning in school that ancient people used to live in caves, I asked Grandfather whether our people lived in some of them. His response was that people took refuge in the mountains and caves from the slave trade and slavery, which continued at least into the 1881s. He explained that Islamic Swahili people from the coast would attack whole villages and take people away. He also said that one of our ancestors, who had been engaged as a porter by Swahili traders when Grandfather was a young man, had never returned. It was widely believed that he had been taken into slavery. Even in my own childhood there were stories of lost children who were believed to have suffered a similar fate, and the books we used in school were replete with images of caravans led by ferocious, bearded Arab and Swahili men, wielding whips over emaciated slaves tied together and carrying ivory to the coast.

Grandfather's stories helped me understand that the cultural diversity of African people preceded European colonization; that trade, friendships, and alliances among different communities led to the exchange of ideas, information, and often genes. At the same time, Grandfather laid much of the blame for the destruction of East African societies on the slave trade and slavery. As a Quaker and a product of a missionary school, he laid that blame on the Muslim peoples of the coast.

When I got older, I began to learn about the Swahili firsthand. In 1984, I was in a group of one hundred students from Kenyatta University in Nairobi who traveled to the coast to see historical and archeological sites. I was greatly impressed by the great palace and main mosque at Gede (Gedi), built more than 700 years ago. Our guides attributed this and other significant sites to seafaring Arabs and Arabized Persians who came to East Africa to trade and to colonize the coast. Archeologists and historians thought that although these seafaring people intermixed with Africans, their coastal settlements developed in isolation from the up-country African settlements that surrounded them and with which they traded. In the words of archeologist Neville Chittick, then director of the British Institute of Eastern Africa, the coastal settlements were economically dependent on Africa but "it was seawards that they faced, looking out over the great maritime region constituted by the Indian Ocean."

This view did not seem convincing to me, and I determined to delve into the question of Swahili origins. I returned to Mombasa to begin archeological research in the autumn of 1986. There I met Mohammed Mchulla, a curatorial assistant in the department of archeology at the Fort Jesus Museum. Mohammed invited me to live with his family—his wife, Maimuna, and their two young boys, Abubakr and Abdillatif. Over the next ten months, before I left

for graduate school in the United States, Mohammed's house was my home away from home, and I have returned every year since. Through this personal contact, I have been helped to understand Swahili society today and have enjoyed enlightening conversations with sages, poets, midwives, blacksmiths, potters, boat makers, tourist guides, and friends.

The resources of the Swahili coast, which extends from Somalia through Kenya, Tanzania, Mozambique, Madagascar, and the Comoros, have attracted many different peoples. Although most coastal inhabitants speak Kiswahili, a Bantu language, other ethnic groups also inhabit the area, including the hunter-gatherer Dahalo, Waata, and Boni (Sanye); the pastoral Orma and Somali; and the agricultural Malakote, Pokomo, and Mijikenda. To understand the roots of Swahili culture requires more than sorting through all these groups. Five hundred years of colonization also have to be unscrambled. This includes conquest by the Portuguese, who first rounded the Cape of Good Hope in search of a trade route to India; rule by the Omani Arabs, who followed in the eighteenth century after the coast enjoyed a brief period of independence; and finally, occupation by the Western European industrial powers, which met in Berlin in 1884 and partitioned Africa.

Influenced in part by local explanations of Swahili origins and by the abundance of Arabic loan words, the colonizing European intellectual community was convinced that Swahili peoples, especially the elite, were not African, even when they grudgingly accepted that Kiswahili was a Bantu language. All the monuments found in East Africa were assigned to various foreign societies—Phoenicians, Sabaens, Persians, Egyptians, Indians, Omanis—but never to the indigenous Africans. In recent years, however, historians and linguists have begun to question the common assumptions. And since 1980 several major archeological excavations and more than ten doctoral research projects have been carried out, mostly by African archeologists, that have shed new light on the complex origins and development of the Swahili states.

For an archeologist, understanding a place that has seen so many political changes can be a nightmare. But a chronology of the Swahili coast has been constructed based upon radiocarbon dates, coins, imported ceramics, and local pottery. The earliest sites that have been excavated date to the second century A.D. These finds suggest that coastal people lived in village communities, where they fished, farmed, kept domestic animals (chickens, donkeys, camels), and smelted and forged iron. Shards of Partho-Sassanian ware at some of these sites suggest that Egyptians and Ethiopians would round the Horn to trade with communities along the Somali coast. Such contact is mentioned in *Periplus of the Erythraean Sea*, written about A.D. 50, and Claudius Ptolemy's second-century *Geography*.

In the absence of earlier sites, archeologists speculate that the coast was settled sometime between 500 B.C. and A.D. 1. Based on linguistic evidence, Derek Nurse and Thomas Spear believe that Bantu-speaking people spread to the coast from what is now Zaire. The rivers and sea yielded fish and shellfish; the forested floodplains could be cleared, providing both fertile farmland and wood fuel for smelting and forging the region's abundant iron ore; and the clay deposits in the swamps were suitable for pottery making.

Chris Ehret and other linguists suggest that when the Bantu speakers arrived on the coast, the ancestors of present-day Eastern Cushites, Somali, Boni, and Aweera inhabited the hinterland and may also have been rapidly settling along the northern coast of Kenya and Somalia. The Cushites were mostly hunter-gatherers and nomadic pastoralists. Interactions among the various groups, each exploiting specific resources, would have promoted friendships, alliances, gift exchanges, barter, and occasional skirmishes.

Sites dating from the eighth century on are better known, and among their artifacts are local cowries and shell beads, evidence of trade with neighboring and interior groups by such craft specialists as potters, iron-workers, shell bead makers, and boat and canoe builders. By the ninth century, the annual monsoon winds were bringing foreign merchants bearing cloth, clothing, ceramics, and beads in exchange for ivory, rhino horns, hides and skins, ebony, ostrich feathers, ambergris, *bêche-de-mer*, copal, iron, gold—and slaves. As shown by archeologist Mark Horton, Islamic influence began to leave a mark in the ninth century, when a timber mosque was built at Shanga. But Horton found no evidence of foreign settlement at the site in terms of burials or monumental architecture.

Between 1000 and 1200, trade between the coast and the interior, Madagascar, and the Middle East increased. Along the length of the coast, pots were traded for sorghum, millet, rice, and other cereals. Pots, cowrie shells, shell beads, textiles, and cereals were exchanged with hinterland peoples up the rivers for honey, cattle, hides, ghee, and such luxuries as gold, copper, and ivory. Cereals, especially rice, were among the export items from East Africa, bringing in such maritime trade goods as beads and ceramics (primarily from India and China). According to a twelfth-century account by the Arab geographer

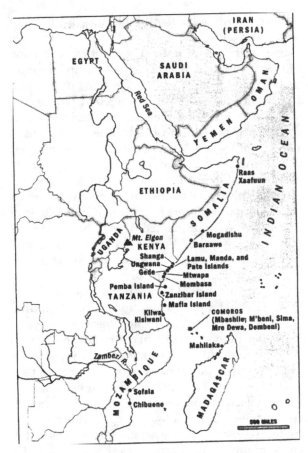

Major archeological sites and historic cities of the Swahili civilization have long been attributed to traders and colonists from the Middle East and elsewhere overseas. New research is helping to clarify the indigenous contributions to East African coastal settlement.

Idrisi, Indians preferred iron from East Africa over their own because of its malleability. (Galu, a village site I excavated, produced the world's oldest crucible steel, a high-carbon steel dated to the seventh century. Before the Galu discoveries, crucible steel was known only from tenth-century India, Sri Lanka, and Arabia.)

As the population grew and settlements became more permanent, an emerging elite began to exercise control over resources, crafts, and trade. By 1300, Islam had become a widespread part of coastal culture. Islam provided a connection between the local elite and other Muslim elites and traders that helped catapult the East African coast into international commerce. The next two centuries witnessed the importation of Chinese porcelain, Islamic pottery, glass beads, and other trade goods. At the same time, local manufacturing surged, not only of pottery and iron but also of new products, notably cotton and kapok clothing.

While early inhabitants built their dwellings of wattle and daub or unfired mud brick on a wooden frame, buildings of unfired mud brick with coral mortar foundations and of coral blocks in lime mortar began to appear after 1200. The buildings, including distinct mosques, were clustered by type of construction, suggesting that place of residence was determined by wealth, social status, and perhaps religious affiliation. Many of the elite, including merchants and political leaders, interred their dead in monumental tombs that show ranking among the townspeople. Nineteenth-century accounts by missionaries and explorers suggest that individuals of lower rank were prohibited from wearing daggers and silk dresses, building coral houses, learning to read the Koran, and buying and displaying expensive jewelry and porcelain.

The civilization of East Africa reached its zenith between 1300 and 1500. Many towns, including Mogadishu, Pate, Lamu, Mombasa, Kilwa, and Mahilaka, burgeoned into major cosmopolitan centers. Traders and merchants began to wrest more political and economic power from the farmers, fishers, potters, and ironworkers. They forged alliances and connections outside the community through contracts (including intermarriage) with potential trading partners and, in general, were the ones to welcome innovations. As the coast became more involved in trade, more and more people from the interior and abroad settled among the coastal people, creating a society that was dynamic, tolerant, and enterprising.

The question that intrigues scholars who study these developments is the extent to which Swahili civilization was an indigenous phenomenon. The vital role of local production and trade with interior African peoples argues for a strong indigenous basis. In contrast, foreign influence is represented in the spread of Islam. The identity of the Swahili elite is harder to ascertain. Nevertheless, important clues suggest that the intermediary between the hinterland and the foreign merchants was an indigenous business community.

In *Islamic Architecture on the East African Coast* (1966), British archeologist Peter Garlake examined the structures generally regarded as evidence of a Middle Eastern or Arabic colonial presence. He concluded that in basic features, such as construction techniques, ornamental and decorative detail, and composition and planning of mosques and domestic buildings, Swahili architecture evolved from local patterns. Also suggestive of the indigenous identity of coastal elites are fourteenth- and fifteenth-century tombs with circular, rectangular, or polygonal pillars and paneled façades. Called phallic pillars by the locals, they are decorated with porcelain bowls and Arabic scripts, often citations from the Koran. Unknown in the Middle East, these structures are widespread among the Oromo of Somalia and Kenya, where they symbolize manhood and show that those interred are men.

Dutch anthropologist A. H. J. Prins has argued that the traditional Swahili system of land tenure would have established a land-owning elite among the original settlers and their descendants, enabling them to control vast tracts of land, labor, and goods through a council of elders. According to their system, virgin land that an ancestor had cleared and walled in for cultivation was inherited and owned communally by patrilineal descendants. The landowners could thus levy taxes on commoners and immigrants; forge patronage relationships that provided labor for fishing, craft production, and other enterprises; and deny immigrants from the interior and abroad the right to own land.

Whatever the nature of the elite, Swahili civilization as a whole was never politically unified. When the Portuguese arrived in 1500, the region put up little organized resistance. The conflict was unlike any that East Africans had experienced. Instead of occasional raids, this conquest saw the burning and destruction of whole villages, with the vanquished often taken wholesale into slavery. Many of these people were shipped to Portuguese colonies in the New World or sold to other European and Arab slavers. Local as well as foreign mercantile traders lost control of the Indian and Red Seas and stopped coming to East Africa. Long-established trade relationships between the coast and hinterland were destabilized.

Colonization brought increased immigration of Europeans, Arabs, and Asians into East Africa. Swahili towns were composed of numerous and diverse clans claiming different ethnic origins, ranging from the African mainland, the Arabian Peninsula, Persia, India, Portugal, and the Far East. Members of the former elite, no longer in a position of control, conspired against one another, allying with colonizers through marriage and becoming political puppets. Those who revolted were defeated and hanged or took refuge in the hinterland in hill fortresses.

The loss of independence and freedom drove many coastal people to seek the safety of the interior. This period of separation must have fostered cultural, linguistic, and ethnic differentiation between coastal and hinterland peoples. The exile continued until slavery was abolished at the end of the nineteenth century. Then, many coastal peoples and others began to move more freely and to reestablish alliances. After some sixteen generations, they had a lot to relearn, including an understanding of cultural ties. In present-day Kenya, centered on the national capital of Nairobi, there is a tendency to regard the Swahili as an alien people. Unfavorable stereotypes of them as lazy urbanites who neglect their rich lands are being used to justify land grabbing and destruction of coastal archeological sites.

This summer marks the final season of my excavations at Mtwapa, a coastal settlement nine miles north of Mombasa. Inhabited from 1100 to 1750, it was, at its height in the fifteenth century, a port town with several wards, each with its own wells, mosques, and cemeteries. Imported beads, textiles, and iron tools passed through Mtwapa in exchange for such hinterland products as cereals, ivory, rhino horns, iron, hides, and skins. Salinization of the wells, to-

gether with the Portuguese conquest of the region and a southward expansion of the Oromo, eventually led to abandonment of the town, whose ruins cover about nine acres. My next project, beginning this fall, is to survey and excavate sites in the hinterland of Mtwapa in order to understand their relationship to the coastal settlement.

I hope my work will help unravel the myths that exclude the Swahili from participation in Kenya's post-colonial national identity. Grandmother may think I'm a well-paid gravedigger, but I have managed to convince some of the folks back home that the Swahili are our brothers. Grandfather passed on in 1982 but, as an ancestor, continues to inspire my work.

"KENYA, LAND OF MY FATHERS: A TIME TRAVELER IN KENYA"

Chapurukha Kusimba

1) Who were the Swahili, and what were their importance in eastern African history?

2) What were African students taught about the early history and prehistory of eastern Africa?

3) What political, cultural, economic, and ideological reasons were behind the European interpretation of remains and sites in eastern Africa?

4) What were the earliest dates of settlement in eastern Africa, and what type of lifestyle did the earliest settlers of the region practice?

5) What groups were in contact with each other through eastern African prehistory and history? What impact did they have on the settlement of the region?

6) What cultural changes occurred in the last 100 years as a result of European colonization of eastern Africa?

7) How has archaeological research changed our ideas regarding eastern African history?

ARE ETHNOGRAPHIES "JUST SO" STORIES?

E. Paul Durrenberger

Some anthropologists think that ethnographies are "just so" stories, not necessarily to be believed as true. I don't agree. Here is why.

Skarp-Hedin leapt across the river, kept his footing as he hit the ice on the other side, went into a glide, and swooped down on Thrain, swinging an axe to split his head open to the jaw bone and spill Thrain's back teeth onto the ice. Skarp-Hedin didn't even slow down. One man threw a shield at him, but he jumped up and over it and just kept on going. Then Skarp-Hedin's four brothers came running up and killed three of Thrain's friends.

They let four of the young people who were in Thrain's group go because Skarp-Hedin couldn't bring himself to kill them. (Skarp-Hedin and his brothers were irritated at Thrain and his followers for insulting them.) Later on, the young men Skarp-Hedin didn't want to kill helped burn Skarp-Hedin and his brothers and father and mother in their house, but not before Skarp-Hedin had gouged out one man's eye with Thrain's back tooth, which he had saved from that day on the ice.

This story could be from a tabloid newspaper you see at the checkout counter at the grocery store or from a slasher movie. But it isn't. Here is another story.

There is a beautiful girl named Helga. When she is twelve, her father takes in a boy of the same age who doesn't get along with his own father. Helga and the boy, Gunnlaug, fall madly in love with each other. When Gunnlaug turns eighteen he goes abroad to make his name and fortune, and Helga's father agrees that he won't make her marry anyone else for three years. Gunnlaug travels all over northern Europe composing poems for kings and raiding and pillaging. Because of a dispute over poetry he makes a lifelong enemy of another poet, named Hrafn. Gunnlaug gets delayed, and by the time he gets home more than the three years have passed and his enemy has married Helga.

Their families won't let them kill each other in a duel, so they agree to fight it out somewhere else. Gunnlaug manages to visit Helga a few times and gives her a cloak that a king had given him. He and Hrafn travel around until finally they meet, have a long and bloody fight, and both die. Helga now has no husband and no boyfriend. Her father finds another poet for her to marry, and she has some children with this man but never really loves him because she can never get her first love, Gunnlaug, out of her mind. Finally, she catches an epidemic disease. One day she lays her head in her husband's lap, has someone get the cloak Gunnlaug had given her, and dies holding it.

Are these true stories? Nobody knows. They are stories that Icelanders wrote in the thirteenth century as part of their sagas about things that were supposed to have happened two or three hundred years before. The first is from Njal's saga and the second is from Gunnlaug's saga.[1] Nobody even knows who wrote the sagas. All we know is that they were written in Icelandic. If these slasher-romances aren't true stories—and nobody can tell if they are true—why should we pay attention to them, especially in anthropology?

Whatever else these stories are, they are cultural artifacts, just as much as a 1965 Chevy, a hand axe, or an episode of *Days of Our Lives* is a cultural artifact. If we want to learn about a culture, we study its artifacts, especially the ones that say something about social relations and the culture itself. But if someone made up the stories, what can they tell us about the culture or the society?

The imagination cannot go beyond culture. All of us are limited by our cultures. Our cultures define who we are and how we are, what we do, what we think and how we think. So, if you work this equation backward, you can learn a lot about a culture from looking at its artifacts, especially artifacts such as literature that talk about the culture itself.

We learn, for instance, that Icelandic people would kill each other over an insult, or even an imagined insult. We learn that they traveled abroad, raided, traded, made poetry, and fell in love. We learn that fathers could make daughters get married against their will, and many other details of the culture of medieval Iceland.

These are stories in books, and I like them as stories as well as for what they can tell us about medieval Iceland. I believe that we can use fiction for ethnography. If you want to learn about people, read their stories and you will see their culture reflected in the authors' imaginations. This is one of the things Ruth Benedict did in her perceptive study of Japanese culture "at a distance," *The Chrysanthemum and the Sword*.[2] This is what you do in your literature classes. Read Shakespeare's plays and you see a different culture. The manufactured parts of stories are names and events; the culturally-given parts are motivations, emotions, judgments, social relations, and settings. To be good, fiction has to be true. The reason we can use fiction for ethnography is that everyone's imagination is a product of his or her culture, a reflection of the culture, so we can see the culture through the fictions.

The wrenching part of anthropology, what some people call culture shock, is being in places where people are doing things that we cannot imagine. You cannot imagine something you have never heard about or seen or done. But all of a sudden there you are, as anthropologist Bronislaw Malinowski was in the second decade of the twentieth century, in a canoe with a bunch of men blowing smoke and making magic to make things work out right.[3] The reason you are on this dangerous voyage in the middle of the ocean in a dugout canoe is that these men want to trade some shell bracelets for some necklaces on another island. To you it is all some kind of costume jewelry, but to them every individual piece has a history and a value. Their sense of prestige hangs on the trades they make, just as a medieval Icelander's prestige hung on never tolerating an insult, or yours hangs on the kind of car you drive, your credit rating, the clothes you wear, the music you listen to, who you date, and how you smell.

Blowing smoke and making magic to get a canoe across the ocean does not make sense to us. But it made sense to Trobriand Islanders when Malinowski was there early in the twentieth century. It was beyond his imagination, but it was an ordinary part of Trobriand culture.

Sometimes it is even more wrenching to come back to your own country and see that everything you thought was "just the way people do things" is really just another culture, another kind of imaginary construct that doesn't make that much sense.

When you think about it, many of the things we take for granted are pretty silly. Think about money, for example. Paper? Backed by the U.S. government? The only reason we can use money is that we all agree to believe that it has value. These days you can't even trade it for silver or gold, and when you think about it, what is the use of gold except for making wire and jewelry? Money is an incredible leap of the imagi-

nation, but an everyday part of our culture. And it gets even weirder than that. There are a lot of people who make a living just by pushing money from one place to another. And even stranger, they don't even push the actual money; they just enter figures in computers and things happen, and for this they make a nice living—making fictions of fictions. Stocks and bonds are stranger yet. You can take whole courses on how this stuff works in your school of business or economics department; you can learn all of the esoteric language and how to make a living doing this kind of magic. You can get a degree in it. It might seem strange to think of getting a B.A. in magic, but that's what business schools do. To anthropologists, it is just another kind of blowing smoke.

When people's assumptions are different from ours, we don't understand their motives, judgments, or sense of propriety. That is where anthropology comes in—trying to understand other people as well as ourselves.

So everything is a cultural artifact. That is one of the important lessons of anthropology. But if everything is a cultural artifact, isn't anthropology just another cultural artifact, like money, a '65 Chevy, a soap opera, or an Icelandic saga?

Whatever you can say about sagas, soap operas, and anthropology, a '65 Chevy will run. If it doesn't you can fix it so it will. There is a bottom line with some things: They work or they don't. You can try teleportation all you want, but if you want to get some place fast you will buy an airplane ticket. Airplanes work. So do computers. Cars, computers, and airplanes are all the result of scientific knowledge. So scientific knowledge must be "culture-free," right?

Wrong. Even science is a cultural artifact—something we make up, something we imagine. How do we know that? Because science changes from time to time and place to place. European science used to tell us that the earth was at the center of the universe and the sun went around it. European scientists didn't record any new stars. They couldn't. God made the heavens and the earth as they were and they did not change. Everyone knew that. If you saw what you thought was a new star, it was just one you had missed before. The Chinese, on the other hand, were looking at the heavens for signs and portents. They did not assume the heavens were changeless; they were looking for changes, and they saw and recorded new stars that astronomers today classify as novas.

Then an astrologer with strange religious ideas, a man named Copernicus, had the idea that the sun was at the center of the system. Everyone thought he was nuts until it turned out he could make a calendar that kept track of holidays better than the

Ptolemaic system could. Easter stayed in the spring and Christmas stayed in the winter instead of straying all over the seasons. The Church wanted a consistent calendar, so they liked this calendar and the rest of the solar system came in on its coat tails. Evidence? There wasn't any evidence one way or the other. In terms of observations you could make at the time, the Copernican system didn't work any better than the old Ptolemaic one that put the earth at the center of everything. Facts did not determine the choice. Imagination—culture—is stronger than facts.

But people who navigated with the Ptolemaic system could get where they wanted to go. It worked. It probably couldn't get them to the moon, but it could get them from Europe to America or Asia and that is what counted in those days. It will work as well today as it did then for navigation—as long as you don't leave our planet. The point is that just because something works does not necessarily mean that the ideas it is based on are correct. Even the pragmatic test of "working" is not always a good guide to truth. So what is left?

The answer is uncomfortable, but one that you might as well get accustomed to: Nothing is left. Everything we can think of, including science, is a cultural artifact. We cannot escape that. Culture is part of our being just as surely as is walking on two feet and talking and having an opposable thumb. It is built and bred into us and has been part of our evolutionary history since we walked out of Olduvai gorge or wherever we originated in our homeland in Africa.

What we try to do in anthropology is to move beyond our own cultures and understand other cultures. We try to do that in a scientific way. So what kind of artifact is science? It strives for reliable and valid knowledge. Valid means that we observe and measure what we think we are observing and measuring. Do Scholastic Aptitude Tests or entrance examinations really predict your college grades? If they do, they are valid. What do grades measure? Reliability means that anyone else would see and describe the same things if they did the same things. Science is cultural because the very terms for judging reliability and validity are cultural, thus anthropology is a cultural artifact.

This is not surprising when you think about it. But some anthropologists were very surprised when they figured it out. A long time ago Aristotle wrote about rhetoric. These anthropologists discovered that all arguments are rhetorical, that they are all cultural artifacts. They discovered that Malinowski used rhetoric—that he was a writer. They acted like this was a big discovery and were very proud of themselves for making it, like the character in Moliere's play who learns that he has been speaking prose all his life.

In 1922, Malinowski said he was constructing interpretations of the kula, the trading of necklaces and shell arm bands; he made the analogy to a physicist constructing a theory from experimental data that everyone can understand but that falls into place when the physicist makes a consistent interpretation, a story. Malinowski was implying that he, like the physicist (a scientist), was constructing interpretations to help people understand things.[4]

In 1973, Clifford Geertz said he discovered that anthropological writings are interpretations, cultural artifacts, something anthropologists make, and he said they were fictions because they are cultural constructs.[5] (You should read some of Geertz's writings, just because anthropologists talk about him a lot. But be warned that Geertz gets confusing. If you find yourself scratching your head and wondering what he means, don't worry. He writes as if he wants to confuse you. And so he does.) He went on to say that these fictions are not untrue; they are just cultural artifacts, something someone makes, and in that sense they are just like any other kind of cultural artifact.

About ten years later, James Clifford and George Marcus got some anthropologists and other people together to talk about these things, and published a book of their essays in 1986.[6] In the introduction, Clifford discusses the idea of ethnographies as fiction, something made, and says they are not false, just incomplete—not unreal, just culturally determined. Some of the words he and the other anthropologists use are "irony," "hegemonic," "discourse," "trope," "interpretation," "hermeneutics," "subjectivity," "conflate" "elide" and "privilege" (as a verb).

Some of these anthropologists call themselves postmodernists. Don't worry if you haven't figured out exactly what that means; they don't want you to, so you are not likely to. Think of it as more of a riddle than a question, or a zen koan whose answer you aren't supposed to understand anyway. The difference is that a zen master will promise you enlightenment if you stick with it and think about the riddle. Enlightenment is another cultural construct. But the postmodernists only promise more confusion. They are in the business of making confusion, not trying to understand it. When they pose you a riddle, if you know it, you know it, and if not, then you are in outer darkness. I am telling you that outer darkness is an "OK" place to be, and that we have to remember now and then to ask whether the emperor has any clothes.

In 1990, Katherine Hales wrote a book about chaos theory.[7] She had studied chemistry and then

English, so she knew something about scientific subjects as well as literature. Talking about post-modernists in literature, she asked about what she called the political economy of their discipline, the political and economic conditions of the people who write literary criticism. If there is only one correct view, she pointed out, these people would be out of business in no time flat. But if there are many equivalent views, none any better than the others, then they can keep on cranking out literary criticism and debating about how to do it until the cows come home. Maybe it is the same for postmodernism in anthropology.

Geertz recognizes the problem. You cannot be systematic about interpretations; if you can't be systematic, you can't evaluate them. It's like trying to figure out how to get an "A" in a course if nobody will tell you how you are being graded. Nobody wants to talk about how to grade interpretations. So they are all equally good. Listen to Geertz:

> For a field of study which, however timidly (though I, myself, am not timid about the matter at all), asserts itself to be a science, this just will not do. There is no reason why the conceptual structure of a cultural interpretation should be any less formulable, and thus less susceptible to explicit canons of appraisal, than that of, say, a biological observation or a physical experiment.

So far so good, and we think Geertz is right on track, but now comes the punch line to his joke:

> . . . no reason except that the terms of which such formulations can be cast are, if not wholly nonexistent, very nearly so. We are reduced to insinuating theories because we lack the power to state them.[8]

Allow me to interpret. It would be nice to know how to grade interpretations, but we don't know how. So we don't. Instead of having theories, we guess.

If all stories are equivalent, how can we choose among them? Comparing personal interpretations is fundamentally undemocratic because, as Geertz suggested, the way to choose is to yield to the authority of the person who presents the interpretation. This person presents the interpretation and he or she is . . . what? The most powerful? The loudest? The most fashionable? However, while Geertz's suggestion at first looks very liberal—it seems to say "entertain every point of view"—it really means "take my word for it and don't be critical or ask questions." On the other hand, if all interpretations are equally legitimate, then they might as well all be fiction.

If fiction can be ethnography and ethnography is fiction, can there be fictional ethnographies? There can be and there are, and it is something anthropologists talk about and even argue about. Maybe the

most famous of these are the writings of Carlos Castaneda, who started with *The Teachings of Don Juan, A Yaqui Way of Knowledge*, which was published in 1968.[9] This was such a success that he went on to publish several others in the same vein. For a while there was a debate about whether Castaneda's books were "true."

Some people pointed out that he must have copied from well-known books about shamans and mysticism because of parallels in the texts. Others argued that the correspondences were universals of shamanic experience. Richard De Mille collected a number of assessments of Castaneda's work in 1980.[10] De Mille distinguishes between validity and authenticity. Validity means that a story corresponds to what we think we know, similar to the idea of validity for judging scientific work. New stars were not valid to early European astronomers, but they were to Chinese astronomers because of their different systems of reference—frameworks for validity, which are culturally variable. Authenticity means whether the events happened the way the stories say they did.

Did Skarp-Hedin really chop Thrain's teeth out of his head on the ice? The story is valid because it matches what we know about medieval Iceland and other such societies, but we don't know if it is authentic. Were Galileo's telescopic observations of the heavens accurate (authentic)? Check them for yourself. Anyone can do it. Science is democratic; it doesn't hide or confuse things.

Were Castaneda's stories authentic? It is more difficult to determine whether he really knew Don Juan. It isn't as simple as repeating an experiment or observation.

Because there are many authentic and valid ethnographic reports in libraries and books, De Mille suggested that people can use them to concoct valid but inauthentic reports. When you write a term paper, you cite your sources and do not pretend that you are the one who studied diet in China or marriage customs in India or religion in Peru. You and your professor are probably equally glad just to have the paper handed in by the due date without a five-year delay for you to go to the place, learn the language, and do the study yourself. You would have to take an incomplete for half a decade. That is what books are good for. But they require honest use. You get an "F" on your term paper if you plagiarize—another one of those cultural things.

When you read an ethnography, how do you know it is true? How do you know the author didn't make it up, as Castaneda did? The main reason is that the writer says, "I was there; this is based on my experience, on what I saw and heard." That experience is the writer's authority, the reason to believe what the writer says. But that is what Castaneda said to claim ethnographic authority, and he was not writing ethnography. In the 1986 book that Clifford and Marcus edited is a piece by Mary Louise Pratt of Stanford's Spanish and Portuguese Department. Pratt points out that you can write an accurate account of life in another culture without ever having been there.[11] Ruth Benedict did. And I have never been to medieval Iceland, but I wrote a book about it.[12] Pratt wonders why there was a big flap in anthropology journals over a book, by Florinda Donner, *Shabono*, published in 1982.[13] Was it fiction based on ethnographies and other sources like Castenada's works, or was it ethnography?

Pratt sees the threat to anthropologists in the missing link, the "being there" that gives ethnographers the "authority" to say they have given you an authentic account. I think the use of the word "authority" for this meaning is interesting, because an appeal to authority, in a somewhat different sense, is the only way to judge stories that are not scientific.

Pratt goes on to talk about how anthropologists establish that they were there, that their accounts are authentic. This is what all scientists do. Galileo said he looked through a telescope and this is what he saw. His authority, his claim to authenticity, came from his having looked through the telescope. If you don't believe him, you can read other books by other people who have looked through telescopes, look at their photos or drawings, or look through a telescope yourself. If other people cannot see the same things, the observations are not reliable. And so it is for ethnography.

Pratt says that ethnographic writing is boring. How, she wonders, could such interesting people doing such interesting things produce such dull books? Boredom, of course, is self-generated. It isn't in what we see but in how we respond to it. Have you ever tried to explain why you were fascinated by an experiment you did in chemistry lab to someone who was so bored with science that he didn't even want to discuss it? If people are bored with something, we can't change their minds about it. It's like what they say about trying to teach pigs to sing. It is a waste of your time and it irritates the pig. People of the English persuasion have tried to explain cricket to me, but I would just as soon watch paint dry.

I must confess that I find some art and some ethnography boring and some exciting. I never could get into *Gravety's Rainbow*, though my wife swears by it. I know Joyce's *Ulysses* is a great work, but I can't get into it. Or Jane Austen. But I once spent an afternoon absorbed in an ethnography of Timbuktu.

Fiction writers are obliged to try not to bore their readers; ethnographers can be irritatingly indifferent to their audience and use the most atrocious obfuscatory language. Among the most obfuscatory and boring writers of modern anthropology, by the way, are those who discovered that they were writing rhetoric. Richard de Mille suggests that Castaneda perpetrated his hoaxes because the competition was too great in the fiction market. Castaneda's stories are short on plot, lack detail, have unconvincing characters who never develop and who show stereotyped emotions, and have nothing in the way of human relations. That is not good fiction—it would never sell—but it makes pretty good reading as fact because readers love supposedly true adventures, even if they aren't well written.

In fiction, the ideas of truth are a little different, and that is why Pratt didn't understand the big flap about authenticity in anthropology. John Gardner, in his book about writing, *The Art of Fiction*,[14] suggests that telling truth in fiction can mean one of several things: being factually correct, being coherent so that it does not feel like lying, or affirming a moral truth about human existence. Like Pratt, he considers authenticity to be trivial, except in creating an appearance of truth that makes a story interesting and compelling (what literary people call "verisimilitude"). He regards validity—making the story fit a cultural framework—as more important. Universal morality he appreciates as the highest form of truth, the goal of art.

This highest truth, as any anthropologist will tell you, is cultural. But reality is just there. Science is the job of trying to match the two. Skarp-Hedin was affirming a truth when he chopped out Thrain's teeth, but his actions would not be considered quite so praiseworthy today. Skarp-Hedin would wind up pleading insanity and hoping to get committed to an asylum rather than death row. But to know that, we have to know something about our culture and other cultures; and to know those things, we have to describe and understand them; and to do that, we have to tell truth as best we can, as Galileo did. Other people and their actions, thoughts, words, and deeds are realities that anthropologists try to understand.

Ethnographers, if they are honest and authentic, must be willing to say, "If you don't believe our stories you can go there yourself and see for yourself." They have to believe that if you do what they did you will see the same things. So the stories to establish authenticity are more than just figures of speech or rhetorical tactics or ploys—tropes, as they say—or they are no less so than any other such rhetoric of any scientific report. And to say that everything is a trope is about as enlightening as to say that we speak in prose. Sometimes people do go and check others' work, and sometimes, though not all the time, it leads to disputes about who was using the better telescope because different people may present equally valid and equally authentic but different pictures of what they saw.

Try it out sometime. You and two of your friends each get cameras and all go to an event like a wedding or a carnival or a graduation—anything at all. Then compare the pictures you took. You all will have been at the same place with the same people, but I will bet that you each took different pictures to emphasize different things. This is one reason different anthropologists can tell different stories—they concentrate on different things. (This may be what was at stake in the differences between Oscar Lewis and Robert Redfield in their understandings of Mexican peasant life.)[15] On the other hand, maybe you went to different weddings and one was in Texas and the other in New Jersey. Or maybe you are comparing pictures from this year's wedding with your grandfather's wedding. There can also be differences of time and location.

The more precisely you can tell people what you did, the better they can try to see things the way you saw them. That is the reason anthropologists have to spend some time on methodology—talking about how they know what they are talking about (to establish reliability), as well as theory. Methodology is the framework for validity.

If everything is a cultural construct and all ethnographic accounts are stories like any other kind of science, does it make any difference whether we make them up in libraries or in some foreign place? Isn't one story as good as another?

Remember that inauthentic ethnographies depend on authentic ones. The only reason people can make up ethnography in a library is that someone did the real job of description before. Without that kind of aid they could not move beyond the imaginative limits of their own culture and would have to write poor fiction rather than fake ethnography.

How you judge a story depends on what you want it for. If its only job is to amuse you, then popular television writing will win over any academic or scientific writing any day of the week. That is what makes popular writing and television popular. Maybe that is why academic writers are so poorly paid. If you are trying to get from Europe to America or Asia, or from the earth to the moon, you need a different kind of story. If you want the kind of story that makes a computer work, you don't ask how amusing it is, you ask how well it works.

And so it is for understanding other cultures and your own culture. That which leaves you with the most authentic and valid account is the best ethnography. That is the ethnography upon which you can

base a sound search for those higher truths. Ask anyone who has tried to understand your culture and its moral truths. Talk to some foreign students as they are getting used to American ways and see what they tell you. You will be surprised at what surprises them.

One young woman confided to me her amusement on hearing at an orientation session that Americans were very conscious of smells in their love lives. She laughed as she regaled me with stories she had heard and this whole new dimension of social relations she had never thought about before. In the United States, that is the foundation for a whole neurosis and the industry based on it. While Icelanders think Americans silly to bathe every day, Thai think Americans uncouth for bathing only once a day.

When you see yourself through others' eyes, you never see what you thought you would see, what you see through your own eyes. Watching yourself in a video is an alienating experience. You don't look like you thought you would. The person holding the camera didn't see things the way you saw them.

Horace Miner wrote an essay called "Body Ritual among the Nacirema," which was published in 1958 in the *American Anthropologist*.[16] "Nacirema" is "American" spelled backwards. In the article he describes how Americans brush their teeth as he imagines an anthropologist might describe this ritual. It seems strange because he puts it in a different context than we do when we brush our teeth. So ethnographic accounts often have an air of strangeness about them to the people they describe. Different people see things differently—that is one of the great lessons of anthropology. Texans, for instance, didn't much like Michener's treatment of their state in his novel. But Texans didn't like Ferber's *Giant* either. Only a Texan, they argue, can really understand the uniqueness of that people and that land. Anything that doesn't agree with our own self images, anything that doesn't confirm the rightness of our own prejudices and opinions, we are likely to dismiss as wrongheaded at worst or innocent fiction at best. Texans say they are heirs to a proud historical tradition, while others see this kind of attitude as boorish, ethnocentric bigotry.

If you are an athlete and your coach tells you how to improve your stroke, your serve, the swing of your golf club, your gait when you are running, or how to hold the bat to hit the ball, you can view the tapes, concede that you don't look to others as you imagined you did, and listen to your coach's advice. Your game will improve. Or you can insist that your view is the only right one and suffer the consequences. It is your choice. It is the same in music, writing, art, computer science, engineering . . . you name it. And it is our choice. We may not like what de Toqueville said about America, but it might help us to listen, whether we like the story or not, whether it is amusing or not.

Three of my favorite writers died on motorcycles. One of them, C. Wright Mills, was a sociologist. He wrote that ordinary people felt they were living in traps because of large social forces beyond their control. To understand a person's life or the history of his or her society, you have to understand both together.[17] Another, John Gardner, wrote fiction and also wrote about writing fiction. He wrote that fiction seeks out truth. We cannot sort universals into moral codes, but fiction interests us because it helps us learn how the world works, how we and all other human beings can resolve conflicts we share, what values we agree with, and what the moral risks are. He said that a writer who cannot distinguish truth from a peanut-butter sandwich can't write good fiction.[18] The third, T. E. Lawrence, wrote something that was sociology, fiction, history, and autobiography as well.[19] All three of these men met the same end. Maybe we should learn to wear helmets when we get on motorcycles.

Some of my favorite writers are still alive. Halldor Laxness is an Icelandic novelist who wrote with such precision that I once despaired that he left nothing for anthropologists to do—regarding Iceland, at least.[20] Like Texans, Icelanders didn't much like his writing, until he won a Nobel prize. Then it was OK because foreigners thought it was good. Richard Condon wrote the definitive work on economics in his novel *Money Is Love*.[21] Miles Richardson is an anthropologist who captured what it is to be an anthropologist.[22]

Richardson talks about how he became an anthropologist and how anthropologists accuse each other of every imaginable sin. He wonders how to explain such accusations when they contrast so with the image of anthropologists as people who are sympathetic to differences. He talks about doing fieldwork and the conditions of fieldwork—that we have to drop the idea that the world is the same as it was for Malinowski seventy years ago. We have to accept the contemporary world on its own terms. When we do this, we can begin to see clearly, we can listen carefully, and we can hear what we must. There are different ways to listen, as there are different ways to take photographs. We can be detached; we can be revolutionaries, bureaucrats, apologists. There are a lot of ambiguities because of the differences in power among people and among peoples and countries.

How can we get anything out of this enterprise besides a bunch of equally good if not equally entertaining "just-so" stories? Richardson says that there is another way to think of anthropology—something like what Gardner had in mind for writers: They are myth-tellers, people who stand on the edge of the society in the outer darkness, away from the hot glow of the campfires that comfort us, and tell the myth of humanity with skill and passion. We cannot falsify what we are. We work with all the pieces of the puzzles we have: what we can develop, what our predecessors developed, what our students are developing. We try to understand it all. We stand between the most and the least powerful social orders and feel the tensions. To tell the story well, Richardson says, we need the passion of the radical, the detachment of the scientist, and the practicality of the liberal. That is our job, he concludes—to tell the human story, to tell it well, to tell it truly.

But why does Richardson call it a myth, this story of our selves and our fellow humans? Isn't it a "just-so" story, along with all the other myths science banishes with its valid and reliable analyses? He calls the story of humanity a myth not because it is untrue but because it reaches for that higher truth that Gardner spoke of. Such myths are true. Anthropology tells those stories, and it is up to us to tell them well and truly.

Notes

1. Anonymous, *Njal's Saga*, trans. Magnus Magnusson and Hermann Pálsson (New York: Penguin, 1960); Anonymous, *The Saga of Gunnlaugur Snake's Tongue with an Essay on the Structure and Translation of the Saga*, trans E. Paul Durrenberger and Dorothy Durrenberger (Rutherford, NJ: Fairleigh Dickinson University Press, 1992).

2. Ruth Benedict, *The Chrysanthemum and the Sword* (Boston: Houghton Mifflin, 1946).

3. Bronislaw Malinowski, *Argonauts of the Western Pacific: An Account of Native Enterprise and Adventure in the Archipelagoes of Melanesian New Guinea* (Prospect Heights, IL: Waveland Press, 1984; originally published in 1922).

4. Ibid.

5. Clifford Geertz, *The Interpretation of Cultures* (New York: Basic Books, 1973).

6. James Clifford and George E. Marcus, eds., *Writing Culture: The Poetics and Politics of Ethnography* (Berkeley: University of California Press, 1986).

7. Katherine N. Hayles, *Chaos Bound: Orderly Disorder in Contemporary Literature and Science* (Ithaca: Cornell University Press, 1990).

8. Geertz, *The Interpretation of Cultures*, p. 24.

9. Carlos Castaneda, *The Teachings of Don Juan: A Yaqui Way of Knowledge* (Berkeley: University of California Press, 1968).

10. Richard De Mille, *The Don Juan Papers: Further Castaneda Controversies* (1980; reprint Belmont, CA: Wadsworth Publishing, 1992).

11. Mary Louise Pratt, "Fieldwork in Common Places," in James Clifford and George E. Marcus, eds., *Writing Culture: The Poetics and Politics of Ethnography* (Berkeley: University of California Press, 1986), pp. 27–50.

12. E. Paul Durrenberger, *The Dynamics of Medieval Iceland: Political Economy and Literature* (Iowa City: University of Iowa Press, 1992).

13. Florinda Donner, *Shabono: A True Adventure in the Remote and Magical Heart of the South American Jungle* (New York: Laurel Books, 1982).

14. John Gardner, *The Art of Fiction* (New York: Alfred A. Knopf, 1984).

15. Robert Redfield, *Tepoztlán, a Mexican Village: A Study of Folk Life* (Chicago: University of Chicago Press, 1930); Oscar Lewis, *Life in a Mexican Village: Tepoztlán Restudied* (Urbana: University of Illinois Press, 1951).

16. Horace Miner, "Body Ritual among the Nacirema," *American Anthropologist* 58 (1956): 503–507.

17. C. Wright Mills, *The Sociological Imagination* (New York: Oxford University Press, 1959).

18. Gardner, *The Art of Fiction*.

19. T. E. Lawrence, *The Seven Pillars of Wisdom: A Triumph* (Garden City, NY: Doubleday, 1938).

20. Halldor Laxness, *Salka Valka*, trans. F. H. Lyon (London: George Allen & Unwin Ltd., 1936); Halldor Laxness, *Independent People* (New York: Alfred A. Knopf, 1946).

21. Richard Condon, *Money Is Love* (New York: Dial Press, 1975).

22. Miles Richardson, *Cry Lonesome and Other Accounts of the Anthropologist's Project* (Albany: State University of New York Press, 1990).

Suggested Readings

Condon, Richard. *Money Is Love*. New York: Dial Press, 1975. A novel that treats the mysteries of money and economic systems. Many of Condon's other novels are equally interesting.

Durrenberger, E. Paul. *The Dynamics of Medieval Iceland: Political Economy and Literature*. Iowa City: University of Iowa Press, 1992. Discusses the relationships between politics, economics, and literature in medieval Iceland.

Geertz, Clifford. *The Interpretation of Cultures*. New York: Basic Books, 1973. Not a very good book, definitely not well written, but anthropologists talk about it a lot. Read it some time if you want to see what they are talking about.

Hayles, Katherine N. *Chaos Bound: Orderly Disorder in Contemporary Literature and Science*. Ithaca: Cornell University Press, 1990. Discusses chaos theory.

Kuhn, Thomas S. *The Copernican Revolution: Planetary Astronomy in the Development of Western Thought*. New York: Vintage Books, 1957. Accessible discussion of astronomy in European cultures. Shows how Ptolemaic astronomy made sense with the observations they had at that time and how sun-centered theories made no more sense than earth-centered ones. This is a good portrayal of the relationship between facts and theories and how ideas about astronomy influenced other areas of thought. Kuhn later wrote the influential book *Structure of Scientific Revolutions*. Chicago: University of Chicago Press, 1962.

Malinowski, Bronislaw. *Argonauts of the Western Pacific: An Account of Native Enterprise and Adventure in the Archipelagoes of Melanesian New Guinea*. 1922; reprint Prospect Heights, IL: Waveland Press, 1984. Better than you might guess as a book just to read and a classic of anthropology. Good summer vacation book.

Mills, C. Wright. *The Sociological Imagination*. New York: Oxford University Press, 1959. Mills is a good writer. His work is generally accessible, no nonsense, to the point, sensible, and necessary reading for anyone going on in anthropology or any social science.

Richardson, Miles. *Cry Lonesome and Other Accounts of the Anthropologist's Project*. Albany: State University of New York Press, 1990. The best account of what it is like to be an anthropologist.

"ARE ETHNOGRAPHIES 'JUST-SO' STORIES?"

E. Paul Durrenberger

1) What is a cultural artifact? How is anthropology possibly a cultural artifact?

2) Is science a culture-free enterprise? Why or why not?

3) What does the author and western science mean by the terms validity, reliability, and authenticity?

4) How do anthropologists establish the validity and authenticity of their research?

5) What is "myth" and what purpose does it serve in all cultures?

6) Why does the author call anthropologists "myth tellers"? What does he mean by this expression?

7) Define and discuss an American or western myth. How would you interpret that myth in the light of Durrenberger's article?

THE MAKING OF A
CROSS-CULTURAL RESEARCHER

Carol R. Ember

As long as I can remember, I have always believed that if you work hard enough and, even more important, think hard enough, you can answer any research question you can dream up. I suppose that makes me a perennial optimist, a quality that I am perfectly comfortable with. If anyone tells me that there is no answer or that the answer is just too complicated, I might try to find an answer just to be ornery. In asking myself to reflect on my own research career—why I got interested in the things I got interested in, how one idea led to another—I have to go back to some of my beginnings. I do not believe that what you choose to do in research is simply a matter of what you are trained to do. Why do we choose certain fields anyway? Why do we gravitate toward certain teachers or certain styles of research? I think a lot of it has to do with your personality—the kinds of conflicts and concerns you grow up with.

I grew up in a household comfortable with science and math. My mother was a math major in college and was one of a few women in the country to be an actuary (a person who computes insurance rates). My father was a high school physics teacher, and later a creator of science educational materials and a science writer. Throughout junior high and high school it never occurred to me to be anything other than a physical or biological scientist of some kind.

Like many of my generation, I was deeply concerned about the state of the world, which seemed threatened by overpopulation, poverty, and nuclear annihilation. Unlike some of my friends who blamed science for some of these ills—particularly the invention of nuclear weapons—I was quite sure that scientific knowledge was not responsible. Even then I realized that humans were the ones putting scientific knowledge to bad uses. I was determined to put science to good use, so I made up my mind to work on the twin problems of overpopulation and hunger. I reasoned that if we could figure out how plants created food, we could manufacture enough to feed the world. In retrospect, this was very naive reasoning, but it pushed me toward the study of biochemistry and photosynthesis. (We now know that the world's farmers can easily grow enough food for everybody with current technology—the reasons food doesn't get to everybody are social, not biological reasons!)

A few things happened to me around the same time while I was a student at Antioch College, to cause me to rethink what I wanted to do. One thing was organic chemistry. I had been doing fine in theoretical chemistry, but I didn't do well in organic. Another thing was I happened to take a tour of the Kettering laboratory devoted to plant research. I vividly remember my dismay when I walked down a corridor full of cubicles and I was told that all those people were working on explaining photosynthesis. How could that be? That was what I was going to do. (Obviously, I didn't want much company!) I also was taking a course called "Marriage and the Family" because I had to take some social science. I found it very exciting. The professor (Toyomasa Fuse), who was Japanese, not only introduced us to variation in customs around the world, he also told us quite a bit about how he reacted to being in the United States. But the thing that really boggled my mind is that students in the class would ask questions about why different people had different customs and Fuse would say that we had some ideas, but we didn't really know. Now this may strike many of you as strange, but a field where very little was known struck me as a marvelous field to go into. It was not the known that intrigued me—it was the unknown.

Although many of my friends and relatives thought the transition I was making extraordinary, it didn't seem like that much of a transition to me. Most of the people I took courses from in the sociology/anthropology department emphasized that there were patterns out there in human behavior and there were methods to test ideas (theories) about why humans did what they did. This was certainly still doing science. But it wasn't until I took courses from Melvin Ember that I had a really clear idea of what I wanted to do. He introduced me to evolutionary and ecological theory as well as to the cross-cultural research strategy, the systematic testing of theories against information from a sample of societies around the world. The sociology/anthropology department was a tough department. We actually had to do a research thesis to graduate. For my thesis I decided to test some of the ideas put forward in George Peter Murdock's book *Social Structure* about why some societies were matrilocal (couples live with or near the wife's parents) or patrilocal (live with or near the husband's parents). In Murdock's view, residence was the key to understanding much of kinship and social organization, since residence put together a particular group of kin (usually related males or related females).[1] From that time on, I have retained a strong interest in social organization, primarily pursuing that interest with Melvin Ember; he and I got married five years after I graduated from Antioch.

I really liked anthropology, but I started my graduate work in sociology at Cornell. In retrospect, I realized that I tried to stay away from anthropology because I knew I would be expected to do fieldwork for my Ph.D., and I was petrified of doing so. I was very shy, so much so that in college I did not utter a word in class. So how could I possibly go somewhere where I did not know anybody, did not know the language, and get all my information by talking to people? But when I kept trying to take anthropology courses for sociology credit, I realized that I could not avoid anthropology—I would just have to get over my fears if I wanted to do what I really loved.

The next year I got to work as a research assistant for John Whiting at Harvard. John and Bea Whiting, my mentors at Harvard, had also been students of George Peter Murdock at Yale, as Melvin Ember had also been, but later. Although the Whitings had done cross-cultural work, by the time I first knew them they had moved primarily into comparative fieldwork projects—first the Six Cultures project and then the Child Development Research Project in Kenya. Since their primary interests lay in psychological processes (and its effects on culture), they had decided to study those processes by doing comparative field studies. Their project in Kenya was ongoing, and they asked me to go there and work among the Luo of western Kenya.

I was still petrified, but how could I say I wouldn't go? It was not possible to refuse the offer. So I went. As it turned out, it was one of the best things that happened to me. The outcome could have been different, but I somehow found courage in the field. The people there were extremely hospitable, and I found that I could talk after all (indeed, some might say that I haven't stopped since)!

There is little or no systematic research on where ideas come from. Sometimes they come from serendipity (unexpected findings or observations), but I also suspect they come from the things that concern us in our lives. For example, I started out to do a demographic study of polygyny in the Luo community I was working in—I was going to get baseline information on the population (age and sex structure) and then do a computer simulation of how polygyny worked. But after completing a community-wide census I realized that I could not possibly do the study because in this community there were twice as many boys born as girls over a period of ten years. How could I use those numbers as a baseline? I realized that the skewed sex-ratio might be just a temporary fluctuation, because it was a small community of about three hundred. In small groups, the ratios could be temporarily uneven by chance. (Indeed, it turned out that the sex-ratio was more even in the next five years.) After briefly being upset that I had to junk my whole project, I asked myself what difference this skewed sex-ratio made, and I realized that in spite of a strong stated preference for boys and girls to do different kinds of work, an awful lot of boys were assigned girls' work.

This gave me a new idea—could I use this to study the effects on boys of doing girls' work? Might it turn out that the sex-stereotyped work that children are traditionally assigned accounts for some of the differences we think are "naturally" boy/girl differences? If boys who do girls' work are more like girls in their behavior, then perhaps the tasks they do account for the differences, not the fact that they are boys.

Was this really serendipity at work? Yes, there was an unexpected snag which caused me to rethink my project. But of all the alternative things I could have thought of, it was probably not chance that led me to this project. When I was growing up, I was very attuned to appropriate gender roles, because I was often not doing what others thought I should do. I played with blocks and trucks, not dolls, and I was called a "tomboy." I took math and science and I was very good at them, even though boys said girls couldn't do those things. I didn't care what the boys said and I tried to prove them wrong. So, when the boys said that girls couldn't do chemistry, I was one of two girls to take college chemistry in high school. I even won a chemistry medal. But did I really not care what the boys said? I think my research shows that I did care. In Kenya, I couldn't study girls doing boys' work because there were too few girls, but I don't think my interest in boys doing girls' work was accidental! Over the years I have continued to be interested in gender differences and roles and the attitudes of males and females toward each other.

Changing thesis topics in the field was not so easy. For one thing, I couldn't do a literature review before I started the new project. For another, it made sense to do behavior observations of children, but I hadn't had formal training in doing them. I was fortunate that I had a strong background in research design and statistics (mostly from sociology and psychology) before I went to the field; I also was fortunate to have the Whitings, who could help me plan those behavior observations, 250 miles away in Nairobi.

At any rate, changing course in midstream worked out just fine. I decided to train Luo assistants to do observations of children because I didn't know the language and culture well enough. How would I know that when a child said to a boy, "You look like your mother" that this was a terrible insult? The biggest problem in doing observations after you figure out what you want to observe is getting children (and their parents) used to the observers so that the observed behave naturally. It took a full three months to get children and parents used to observers coming to the house. I despaired sometimes that we would never finish the observations; I didn't want to count "unnatural" behavior as observations. Finally, one day one of my assistants came back from a day of observations very distressed. "The children treated me just like a piece of furniture!" he exclaimed. When I asked him what he meant he said that they were touching his pen and clipboard as if they were toys and they weren't respectful. (Children would ordinarily keep more distance from adults.) He may have been dismayed, but I was delighted because I knew then that the children were ignoring the observers. So we could finally begin!

Most people assume that "laws" emerge from looking at the world. But all the time that my observers observed and translated their sentences into a standard behavior observation language, and I reviewed all the observations each night, I didn't have a clue that I would find anything I was looking for! It wasn't until a year or so later when I systematically counted and compared various acts of social behavior (for example, the proportion of time boys were aggressive to other people, as compared with boys who did girls' work and as compared with girls) that the patterns emerged. And they were clear and statistically significant! When I took all those social behaviors for which Luo boys were significantly different from girls as a starting point, and I compared the two sets of boys with girls, boys who did girls' work were *in the middle* between other boys and girls. Even when I discounted the times they were working and just looked at play times, the same patterns held!

It seems that the boys learned to behave differently in the course of their chores and that these behaviors generalized to other times. Babysitting is a good example. To do a good job babysitting, you have to be attentive to the baby and try to give it what it needs. Aggression is not appropriate behavior because a baby is vulnerable. Indeed, boys who babysit a lot are less aggressive than other boys, even when they are playing.[2] To be sure, we cannot be certain that the work was the cause of the shift in behavior, since I did not study the boys before they did girls' work. But it did not seem likely that these boys chose girls' work, because I could predict that a boy would be assigned girls' work just from knowing that he didn't have an older sister at home. Of course, as is always true in correlational research, something else besides task assignment may explain the findings.

People have often asked me why I didn't go back to my fieldwork site and do a restudy. Are the men who did girls' work back then different now from other men? While such a project in theory would be very worthwhile, I was only able originally to complete observations on a total of twenty-eight children (eighteen of them males). When I calculate the chances of finding the men now, I probably wouldn't find enough to make the project feasible. But that's probably not the only reason I didn't go back. I discovered that my real passion in research is to try to use the mountain of data out there *already* collected by anthropologists to test theories and discover relationships. And so I became a cross-cultural researcher.

Although there are all sorts of methods to learn, the fundamental strategy of cross-cultural comparisons is really very simple.[3] First, you start out with a research question. It could be a "why" question like: "Why in some societies do married couples usually live with or near the wife's parents (matrilocally) and in others with or near the husband's parents (patrilocally)?" Second, you need at least one theory that suggests an answer to the question. Usually, at least to start out, researchers look to what other people in the profession have suggested in the way of theories. In my case, for my undergraduate thesis, I started with a traditional explanation—that economic contribution would likely determine residence. If women contributed the most to subsistence, parents would want their daughters to remain after marriage; if men contributed the most, parents would want their sons to stay near home.[4] Third, you try to test that theory by selecting a sample of societies from around the world, designing measures of the presumed causes and effects, and looking to see if they are significantly related (in the statistical sense). If the theory is correct, economic contribution should significantly *predict* marital residence. The reasoning here is that if economic contribution is the cause and residence is the result, the two should generally be correlated with each other.

Although a correlation cannot prove that a predictor is a cause, the lack of a correlation is very damaging to the theory that says it is. Thus, cross-cultural research provides a way of eliminating theories that don't generate correct predictions. That is what happened in my first cross-cultural test. The theory sounded great, but it didn't predict correctly—in a worldwide sample of societies, patrilocal and matrilocal societies were not significantly different with respect to which gender contributed the most to subsistence! Other factors that might enhance the status of men versus women didn't work either. For instance, more warlike societies are not more likely to be patrilocal than matrilocal.[5] And foragers who depend a lot on hunting (almost always done by men) are not more likely to be patrilocal.[6]

In short, the specific theory (about economic contribution) and the more general theory (about factors that enhance the status of men) just weren't helping to explain residential variation. The important thing though is to *test* all ideas, no matter how plausible they sound; no theory is so plausible that we should believe it in the absence of testing. So what did we do then?

There were really two choices. We could say we found out something important (that economic contribution did *not* predict residence) and stop there.[7] Or, we could persist until we found a new theory that predicted well. I think there is a very fine line between being stupidly stubborn and creatively persistent. You really never know which you are being! If you never discover anything that works, you might be stupidly stubborn. When you find something, you think your effort was creatively persistent. Anyway, we persisted; it turns out that we eventually happened onto something that suggested a new way of looking at residence.

I say "happened onto" on purpose because we were frankly just playing with the data when we discovered that when warfare was frequent there was a significant relationship between residence and subsistence contribution (but there was no relationship when warfare was occasional or absent). But why were we looking at this relationship when it didn't predict before? You could say we were being stubborn because we still thought that economic contribution had some influence on residence! We just shifted our thinking to the possibility that some other condition was masking (or hiding) the influence of economic contribution. Anyway, we were not at all sure what this finding meant, but we started to ask how warfare might affect both residence and gender division of labor. This led to some new questions. Might conditions of war determine who (females or males) do the most subsistence work? Do different

kinds of fighting relate to different kinds of residence? Now we started to get somewhere.

In those days, when anthropologists talked about subsistence work, they just tended to count food-getting outside the home (agriculture, hunting, herding, gathering, fishing). I didn't think about it then, but it was a male bias to do so because work closer to home (like threshing, grinding, and cooking) usually is not counted. So, when we looked for data about work we also focused on outside the home. We did realize that women spend a lot of time in household work and childcare, so we wondered why in many societies (not most) they also did most of the subsistence work. We thought that it might be because men were pulled off work because of war. Someone had to do the work; if not the men, it had to be women. As it turned out, when there are no specialist armies or labor to be hired (or coerced in slavery), women do most of the "outside the home" work when war occurs during the time work has to be done. But as we looked more at war, we began to see that matrilocal societies and patrilocal societies fight differently. Matrilocal societies almost never fight within the society; patrilocal societies usually do. Now, although we can't know what people in other societies were thinking, it seems likely that if you were a parent and you fought with communities down the road, you would be very reluctant to have your son leave home to go and live with his wife in what may very well be an enemy village! You would probably want your most loyal protectors at home, regardless of whether or not they did most of the subsistence work. Thus, we ended up predicting that when war occurs within the society, parents will opt for patrilocality regardless of the division of labor. But, if war is only with other societies (purely external), then economic considerations will become important because sons-in-law as well as sons could loyally defend against intruders who come from another society.

Our theory, which fits the cross-cultural evidence, suggests that warfare considerations take precedence over economic ones when warfare is purely external. Matrilocality seems to occur with purely external war *and* women contributing a great deal to subsistence.[8]

After this work on matrilocal and patrilocal residence, I turned to questions about other aspects of social organization. Why do some societies allow couples to live with either the husband's or wife's parents (bilocal residence)? Is there a typical pattern of social organization for hunter-gatherers? What explains variation in hunter-gatherer residence?[9] Why do some societies have unilineal descent groups (where the group is formed by those who trace descent only through *either* males or females), and why do some societies typically live in extended family households (two or more families related by blood)?[10]

What was striking about our work on social organization was how many aspects of life seemed to be predicted by some aspect of warfare. If war was the key to understanding, then it was not surprising that our research sooner or later had to shift back to war. Eventually it did, but not right away. Before returning to war, I did some work on other things that puzzled me.

When I first read the material coming out of Highland New Guinea ethnography, I was flabbergasted by the reports of men thinking that sex with women was dangerous and could cause them to become ill or even die! What must life for women be like in such societies? Women spend most of their lives living patrilocally, in the villages into which they marry. How could it be that their husbands think they are polluting and dangerous (and their sons eventually grow up to think so, too)? Unfortunately, I can only imagine how women must feel; we don't know much about what women think because men's beliefs are the ones mostly described in ethnography. Even so, such beliefs need explanation! What struck me particularly was that the things that New Guinea men said were similar to what people in other places sometimes say. I once looked at some sex manuals written in the 1920s in the United States. Many of them implied that too much sex can make a man unsuccessful and dull his wits! Boxers, wrestlers, and football players are supposed to avoid women the night before a game. Why?

I first looked for explanations that came out of comparisons by New Guinea anthropologists. One explanation was that beliefs in sexual danger were common in those societies where men married women from enemy villages (war again!). Another was that beliefs about sex being dangerous were more common where there is population pressure; if you can get men to believe that sex is dangerous, they probably won't be as interested—after all, abstinence is the most effective method of birth control!

Because I believe that a good explanation should be universal—that is, apply to most if not all places in the world, not just to one region like New Guinea—I decided to do a worldwide cross-cultural test of two theories suggested by New Guinea ethnographers, plus two psychological theories about psychic conflicts in boys who, when young, slept exclusively with their mothers. Since few societies have the negative attitudes toward sex with women that are found in New Guinea, I decided to rate the degree to which sex with women is thought of as having negative versus positive consequences in each society studied. In most studies I have done, there is generally

no support for the traditional explanations; this was the only study where all four tested theories were supported by significant results.[11]

Most of the time I have at least a few research ideas that I want to pursue next, but since things always take longer than I anticipate, I usually feel slightly guilty that I haven't gotten to them yet. I never realized how normal this feeling was until after I had my second child. I distinctly remember feeling so tired that I thought I would never have a creative idea again. This is really frightening to a researcher! My two-year-old wasn't eating any meat, so I started browsing in health food stores to turn up some suitable nonmeat protein. I bought something called "wheat berries" which I tried to cook like rice, but found (two burned pots and hours later) that the "berries" were still hard as rocks. So I thought that maybe that's why women in intensive agricultural societies, where cereal grains are usually grown, couldn't do that much agriculture compared to men. (I remembered the finding that women's contribution to agriculture declines relative to men's with intensive agriculture.) To make cereal grains, which are stored in their dry state, edible, you either have to grind them for hours so they can cook fast, or you have to soak and/or boil them for hours. With all that food preparation work, women might be at the limit of what they can do. It was amazing how quickly my depression lifted. I had an idea!

I decided that I could investigate how much time women in intensive agricultural societies spent preparing food and doing other household chores compared to women in horticultural societies. I realized relatively quickly that ethnographers don't generally provide good time estimates. So, I turned to another source—time allocation studies. I was fortunate that some time allocation studies had already been collected for another purpose[12] and I was able to reanalyze the data as soon as I was able to determine what kind of agriculture the society had. These data were very interesting indeed! As it turned out, women in intensive agricultural societies did not do less than women in horticultural societies—they did about four and a half hours a day, seven days a week! Not an inconsiderable amount! But there was an enormous increase in household work, about three hours more a day than horticultural women had; intensive agricultural women worked about eleven hours a day, seven days a week. So they could hardly do more agricultural work! I also found that intensive agricultural women also had more children than horticultural women (that could keep you busy, as I was well aware)![13] I will probably always be especially proud of this piece of research, just because coming up with the idea for it meant so much to me at the time.

I haven't mentioned it yet, but writing a textbook is an important part of my life and my research. The first edition came out in 1973 and we will soon (as of the time this was written) be starting to work on the eighth edition.[14] It takes an enormous chunk of my time—roughly one year out of every three. Although I like to think the textbook will help inspire at least some students to consider a career in anthropology, it is really hard to gauge that kind of influence since people rarely tell us about it. But writing the textbook is important to me for other reasons. For one thing, I need to read more widely in all areas of anthropology than I might do otherwise. For another, reviewing a field that is not my specialty can give me ideas about research that might not have occurred to me.

One line of research we undertook was clearly inspired by writing the textbook. When we wrote up theories about why all human societies had marriage, we were very dissatisfied because none of the theories was supported by other than anecdotal evidence. We realized that it was difficult to test a theory about a universal aspect of human societies because *any other* universal might plausibly account for it. For example, what if I said that humans had marriage because they were bipedal (two-legged walkers). You might say that this was a ridiculous theory. But how could you say that this theory is less supported by the evidence than any other theory pointing to a universal, for example, the theory that marriage exists because human babies have the longest period of infant dependency, so mothers need help in raising their young?

The problem for testing is that none of the presumed "causes"—bipedalism or long dependency—can be taken away, so we can't see if the effect (marriage) disappears. This suggested to us that we should do a study where there wasn't universality. We could compare species of animals that varied in whether they had male-female bonding (the biological term for "marriage"). So we decided to systematically compare mammal and bird species to see if any of the conventional theories about humans predicted for other animals. None of them did, not even the idea about long infant dependency. In fact, animals with the longest infant dependencies tend to be the least likely to have male-female bonding. But we were able to come up with a theory that does seem to apply, namely that bonding will develop when mothers' feeding requirements interfere with their baby-tending.[15]

It seems that if you ask whether a female can care for and feed herself and take care of a baby at the same time, you can predict male-female bonding. Most birds have young in a nest, but there is no food there. If they go away to get food, the eggs or young babies will likely be eaten. As our theory predicts, most birds need male-female bonding, and most bird species have it. Not too many mammals have bonding. But many, like grazing or browsing animals (deer, gazelles, horses) have no problem feeding themselves and their young. The young animals move (and even run) shortly after birth and travel alongside (and nurse from the mother) as she moves. Most primates eat leaves, seeds, and fruits, and the young baby clings to its mother as she moves; so most of them should not need bonding. Indeed, most primates lack bonding. So why should human primates be different from most of their primate relatives? We suggest that bonding for humans was favored by natural selection when they began to depend more on meat-eating (hunting or scavenging), which cannot be done while tending babies and/or when humans (particularly females) lost their body hair, which would have made it difficult for females to forage for themselves while carrying babies.[16] Hopefully, our theory about "marriage" will be tested further. I doubt, however, that we would have thought of it if we did not work on a textbook.

I eventually came back to my interest in war and peace. It was not just because so much of our work on social organization pointed to the influence of war. I always had a deep interest, which went back to my high school days, in trying to prevent war. It took me awhile to realize that research could be brought to bear on important social problems. After all, how can you make something go away if you don't really understand why it occurs in the first place? So, we decided to undertake a comprehensive study of war and aggression, testing theories about why some societies fight more than others. There were a lot of theories to test. Our gut feeling was that people must be fighting over access to resources, not just for revenge, or over love triangles, or because of other minor disputes. So we spent considerable time trying to figure out how to measure from ethnographies whether people had problems with resources.

We ended up looking at three different kinds of problems. One was the presence of chronic shortages or chronic hunger. The second was the incidence of famines in a twenty-five-year period. The third was the incidence of natural disasters that destroyed food supplies in a twenty-five-year period. As it turned out, resource problems were very predictive of more war, but only a certain kind of resource problem. We were surprised that chronic food shortages in a society did not predict that the society would fight more. But shortages that occurred unpredictably, only every once in a while, did! Moreover, people with a history of unpredictable disasters seem to fight not just when they are short but all the time. Where people are always afraid of a terrible drought or other disaster, even though they did not actually have one recently, they fight constantly. We began to think that it was the *fear* of disasters, rather than the actuality of them, that motivated people to try to take resources from others. Despite the fact that many in anthropology think that war is not often about resources, we found that in most unpacified societies land is usually taken from the defeated in war and in almost all societies other resources (e.g., animals) are taken. So it seems that people, when they go to war, may be trying to protect themselves ahead of time from disasters that they expect but cannot predict. While this idea does not clearly apply to modern nations, an extension of it might. Modern nations are not just dependent on food. They also depend on trade routes and markets and access to nonfood resources like oil.[17]

With a political scientist, Bruce Russett, we also began to investigate whether a finding from cross-national studies (systematic comparisons of nations) might apply to the kinds of societies we study. That finding, which is quite robust cross-nationally, is that democratic nations do not fight with each other. Mind you, democratic nations do not fight less than other nations. The finding is just about which nations they fight! If there really is universality here—that something about democracy lessens the likelihood of fighting with other democracies—we ought to find evidence for this proposition in the societies anthropologists generally study.

To test this idea against societies in the cross-cultural record, however, required us to figure out how to transform the predictions to fit that record. Democracy as ideology is not an appropriate term for most societies anthropologists describe. And what is the analog to international war? We decided that we could study the degree to which adults participated in decision-making in the local community; and, since most societies are not organized politically beyond the local community, we could study the degree to which fighting takes place between communities (internal war). If each community within a society is quite participatory, then they should not be likely to fight with each other. However, if they are not very participatory, then more fighting should occur among them. And that indeed is the case! It appears that more political participation and more tolerance for dissent predict less internal war in the ethnographic record, just as democracy predicts less international war with other democracies in the recent historical record.[18]

Where to now? As always, one question leads to others. As I said at the outset, what interested me about anthropology was how much we need to know. Our ignorance is still enormous. What could be more exciting?

Notes

1. George Peter Murdock, *Social Structure* (New York: Macmillan, 1949), p. 201ff.

2. The results of this project are largely described in Carol R. Ember, "Feminine Task Assignment and the Social Behavior of Boys," *Ethos* 1 (1973): 424–439.

3. A simple review of how to do a cross-cultural study can be found in Carol R. Ember and Melvin Ember, *Guide to Cross-Cultural Research Using the HRAF Archive* (New Haven, CT: Human Relations Area Files, 1988). A more advanced treatment of cross-cultural research can be found in "Cross-Cultural and Comparative Research: Theory and Method," in the special issue of *Behavior Science Research* 25 (1991).

4. References to the authors who put forward this idea can be found in Melvin Ember and Carol R. Ember, "The Conditions Favoring Matrilocal versus Patrilocal Residence," in Melvin Ember and Carol R. Ember, *Marriage, Family, and Kinship: Comparative Studies of Social Organization* (New Haven, CT: HRAF Press, 1983), p. 152; originally in *American Anthropologist* 73 (1971): 571.

5. Ember and Ember, "The Conditions Favoring Matrilocal versus Patrilocal Residence," p. 164.

6. Carol R. Ember, "Residential Variation among Hunter-Gatherers," in Melvin Ember and Carol R. Ember, *Marriage, Family, and Kinship: Comparative Studies of Social Organization* (New Haven, CT: HRAF Press, 1983), p. 284; originally in *Behavior Science Research* 10 (1975): 199–227.

7. When I refer to "we" in this piece, I am referring to reasoning and research carried out with Melvin Ember.

8. Ember and Ember, "The Conditions Favoring Matrilocal versus Patrilocal Residence"; see also Carol R. Ember, "An Evaluation of Alternative Theories of Matrilocal versus Patrilocal Residence," in Melvin Ember and Carol R. Ember, *Marriage, Family, and Kinship: Comparative Studies of Social Organization* (New Haven, CT: HRAF Press, 1983), p. 200; originally published in *Behavior Science Research* 9 (1974): 135–149.

9. Suggested answers to these questions can be found in Carol R. Ember and Melvin Ember, "The Conditions Favoring Multilocal Residence"; Carol R. Ember, "Myths about Hunter-Gatherers"; and Carol R. Ember, "Residential Variation among Hunter-Gatherers," all in Melvin Ember and Carol R. Ember, *Marriage, Family, and Kinship: Comparative Studies of Social Organization* (New Haven, CT: HRAF Press, 1983).

10. Research on extended families and unilineal descent was undertaken with Burton Pasternak and Melvin Ember. Burton Pasternak, Carol R. Ember, and Melvin Ember, "On the Conditions Favoring Extended Family Households," *Journal of Anthropological Research* 32 (1976): 109–123; Carol R. Ember, Melvin Ember, and Burton Pasternak, "On the Development of Unilineal Descent," *Journal of Anthropological Research* 30 (1974): 69–94. Both reprinted in Melvin Ember and Carol R. Ember, *Marriage, Family, and Kinship: Comparative Studies of Social Organization* (New Haven, CT: HRAF Press, 1983).

11. Carol R. Ember, "Men's Fear of Sex with Women: A Cross-Cultural Study," *Sex Roles* 4 (1978): 657–678.

12. Wanda Minge-Klevana, "Does Labor Time Decrease with Industrialization? A Survey of Time Allocation Studies," *Current Anthropology* 21 (1980): 279–287.

13. Carol R. Ember, "The Relative Decline in Women's Contribution to Agriculture with Intensification," *American Anthropologist* 85 (1983): 285–304.

14. Carol R. Ember and Melvin Ember, *Anthropology*, 7th ed. (Englewood Cliffs, NJ: Prentice Hall, 1993); Carol R. Ember and Melvin Ember, *Cultural Anthropology*, 7th ed. (Englewood Cliffs, NJ: Prentice Hall, 1993).

15. Melvin Ember and Carol R. Ember, "Male-Female Bonding: A Cross-Species Study of Mammals and Birds," in Melvin Ember and Carol R. Ember, *Marriage, Family, and Kinship: Comparative Studies of Social Organization* (New Haven, CT: HRAF Press, 1983), pp. 36–64; originally published in *Behavior Science Research* 14 (1979): 37–56.

16. Ibid.

17. Carol R. Ember and Melvin Ember, "Resource Unpredictability, Mistrust, and War: A Cross-Cultural Study," *Journal of Conflict Resolution* 36 (1992): 242–262.

18. Carol R. Ember, Melvin Ember, and Bruce Russett, "Peace between Participatory Polities: A Cross-Cultural Test of the 'Democracies Rarely Fight Each Other' Hypothesis," *World Politics* 44 (1992): 573–599.

Suggested Readings

"Cross-Cultural and Comparative Research: Theory and Method." Special issue of *Behavior Science Research* 25 (1991): 1–270. This volume is devoted to state of the art reviews of the various types of cross-cultural research.

Ember, Carol R. "A Cross-Cultural Perspective on Sex Differences." In Ruth H. Munroe, Robert L. Munroe, and B. B. Whiting, eds. *Handbook of Cross-Cultural Human Development*. New York: Garland STPM Press, 1981, pp. 531–580. A critical review of theory and research about what we think we know, as well as what we do not yet know about gender differences in behavior and role.

Ember, Carol R., and Melvin Ember. *Anthropology and Cultural Anthropology*, 7th ed. Englewood Cliffs, NJ: Prentice Hall, 1993. These two textbooks present an overview of what we think we know and do not know in the various fields of anthropology.

Ember, Carol R., and Melvin Ember. "Resource Unpredictability, Mistrust, and War: A Cross-Cultural Study." *Journal of Conflict Resolution* 36 (1992): 242–262. A report of recent research on warfare that focuses on the possible effects of resource problems.

Ember, Carol R., Melvin Ember, and Bruce Russett. "Peace between Participatory Polities: A Cross-Cultural Test of the 'Democracies Rarely Fight Each Other' Hypothesis." *World Politics* 44 (1992): 573–599. This study takes a cross-national finding and translates it into a cross-cultural test. The proposition appears to fit both the ethnographic record and the recent historical record.

Ember, Melvin, and Carol R. Ember, *Marriage, Family, and Kinship: Comparative Studies of Social Organization*. New Haven, CT: HRAF Press, 1983. This collection contains most of my work and that of Melvin Ember (singly and jointly) on social organization. Most chapters evaluate theory, test theory cross-culturally, and suggest new explanations when necessary.

"The Making of a Cross-Cultural Researcher"

Carol R. Ember

1) What is cross-cultural research and what are its general goals?

2) What are the fundamental strategies of cross-cultural research?

3) Where was Ember's first field work, and what hypotheses did she investigate? What methodological approaches did she employ?

4) What did Ember suggest was the relationship between residence patterns, subsistence, and warfare?

5) What correlations did Ember find between men's fear of women and sex in New Guinea and elsewhere in the world? Compare Ember's work to the Herdt article "Rituals of Manhood" included in this reader.

6) What dimensions of human behavior did Ember examine on her studies of war and aggression?

SECTION THREE

Solving Human Problems

RACE WITHOUT COLOR

Jared Diamond

Science often violates simple common sense. Our eyes tell us that the Earth is flat, that the sun revolves around the Earth, and that we humans are not animals. But we now ignore that evidence of our senses. We have learned that our planet is in fact round and revolves around the sun, and that humans are slightly modified chimpanzees. The reality of human races is another commonsense "truth" destined to follow the flat Earth into oblivion. The commonsense view of races goes somewhat as follows. All native Swedes differ from all native Nigerians in appearance: there is no Swede whom you would mistake for a Nigerian, and vice versa. Swedes have lighter skin than Nigerians do. They also generally have blond or light brown hair, while Nigerians have very dark hair. Nigerians usually have more tightly coiled hair than Swedes do, dark eyes as opposed to eyes that are blue or gray, and fuller lips and broader noses.

In addition, other Europeans look much more like Swedes than like Nigerians, while other peoples of sub-Saharan Africa—except perhaps the Khoisan peoples of southern Africa—look much more like Nigerians than like Swedes. Yes, skin color does get darker in Europe toward the Mediterranean, but it is still lighter than the skin of sub-Saharan Africans. In Europe, very dark or curly hair becomes more common outside Scandinavia, but European hair is still not as tightly coiled as in Africa. Since it's easy then to distinguish almost any native European from any native sub-Saharan African, we recognize Europeans and sub-Saharan Africans as distinct races, which we name for their skin colors: whites and blacks, respectively.

What could be more objective?

As it turns out, this seemingly unassailable reasoning is not objective. There are many different, equally valid procedures for defining races, and those different procedures yield very different classifications. One such procedure would group Italians and Greeks with most African blacks. It would classify Xhosas—the South African "black" group to which President Nelson Mandela belongs—with Swedes rather than Nigerians. Another equally valid procedure would place Swedes with Fulani (a Nigerian "black" group) and not with Italians, who would again be grouped with most other African blacks. Still another procedure would keep Swedes and Italians separate from all African blacks but would throw the Swedes and Italians into the same race as New Guineans and American Indians. Faced with such differing classifications, many anthropologists today conclude that one cannot recognize any human races at all.

If we were just arguing about races of nonhuman animals, essentially the same uncertainties of classification would arise. But the debates would remain polite and would never attract attention outside the halls of academia. Classification of humans is different "only" in that it shapes our views of other peoples, fosters our subconscious differentiation between "us" and "them," and is invoked to justify political and socioeconomic discrimination. On this basis, many anthropologists therefore argue that even if one *could* classify humans into races, one should not.

To understand how such uncertainties in classification arise, let's steer clear of humans for a moment and instead focus on warblers and lions, about which we can easily remain dispassionate. Biologists begin by classifying living creatures into species. A species is a group of populations whose individual members would, if given the opportunity, interbreed with individuals of other populations of that group. But they would not interbreed with individuals of other species that are similarly defined. Thus all human populations, no matter how different they look, belong to the same species because they do interbreed and have interbred whenever they have encountered each other. Gorillas and humans, however, belong to two different species because—to the best of our knowledge—they have never interbred despite their coexisting in close proximity for millions of years.

We know that different populations classified together in the human species are visibly different. The same proves true for most other animal and plant species as well, whenever biologists look carefully. For example, consider one of the most familiar species of bird in North America, the yellow-rumped warbler. Breeding males of eastern and western North America can be distinguished at a glance by their throat color: white in the east, yellow in the west. Hence they are classified into two different races, or subspecies (alternative words with identical meanings), termed the myrtle and Audubon races, respectively. The white-throated eastern birds differ from the yellow-throated western birds in other characteristics as well, such as in voice and habitat preference. But where the two races meet, in western Canada, white-throated birds do indeed interbreed with yellow-throated birds. That's why we consider myrtle warblers and Audubon warblers as races of the same species rather than different species.

Racial classification of these birds is easy. Throat color, voice, and habitat preference all vary geographically in yellow-rumped warblers, but the variation of those three traits is "concordant"—that is, voice differences or habitat differences lead to the same racial classification as differences in throat color because the same populations that differ in throat color also differ in voice and habitat.

Racial classification of many other species, though, presents problems of concordance. For instance, a Pacific island bird species called the golden whistler varies from one island to the next. Some populations consist of big birds, some of small birds; some have black-winged males, others green-winged males; some have yellow-breasted females, others gray-breasted females; many other characteristics vary as well. But, unfortunately for humans like me who study these birds, those characteristics don't vary concordantly. Islands with green-winged males can have either yellow-breasted or gray-breasted females, and green-winged males are big on some islands but small on other islands. As a result, if you classified golden whistlers into races based on single traits, you would get entirely different classifications depending on which trait you chose.

Classification of these birds also presents problems of "hierarchy." Some of the golden whistler races recognized by ornithologists are wildly different from all the other races, but some are very similar to one another. They can therefore be grouped into a hierarchy of distinctness. You start by establishing the most distinct population as a race separate from all other populations. You then separate the most distinct of the remaining populations, and separating distinct populations or groups of populations as races or groups of races. The problem is that the extent to which you continue the racial classification is arbitrary, and it's a decision about which taxonomists disagree passionately. Some taxonomists, the "splitters," like to recognize many different races, partly for the egotistical motive of getting credit for having named a race. Other taxonomists, the "lumpers," prefer to recognize few races. Which type of taxonomist you are is a matter of personal preference.

How does that variability of traits by which we classify races come about in the first place? Some traits vary because of natural selection: that is, one form of the trait is advantageous for survival in one area, another form in a different area. For example, northern

hares and weasels develop white fur in the winter, but southern ones retain brown fur year-round. The white winter fur is selected in the north for camouflage against the snow, while any animal unfortunate enough to turn white in the snowless southern states would stand out from afar against the brown ground and would be picked off by predators.

Other traits vary geographically because of *sexual* selection, meaning that those traits serve as arbitrary signals by which individuals of one sex attract mates of the opposite sex while intimidating rivals. Adult male lions, for instance, have a mane, but lionesses and young males don't. The adult male's mane signals to lionesses that he is sexually mature, and signals to young male rivals that he is a dangerous and experienced adversary. The length and color of a lion's mane vary among populations, being shorter and blacker in Indian lions than in African lions. Indian lions and lionesses evidently find short black manes sexy or intimidating; African lions don't.

Finally, some geographically variable traits have *no* known effect on survival and are invisible to rivals and to prospective sex partners. They merely reflect mutations that happened to arise and spread in one area. They could equally well have arisen and spread elsewhere—they just didn't.

Nothing that I've said about geographic variation in animals is likely to get me branded a racist. We don't attribute higher IQ or social status to black-winged whistlers than to green-winged whistlers. But now let's consider geographic variation in humans. We'll start with invisible traits, about which it's easy to remain dispassionate.

Many geographically variable human traits evolved by natural selection to adapt humans to particular climates or environments—just as the winter color of a hare or weasel did. Good examples are the mutations that people in tropical parts of the Old World evolved to help them survive malaria, the leading infectious disease of the old-world tropics. One such mutation is the sickle-cell gene, so-called because the red blood cells of people with that mutation tend to assume a sickle shape. People bearing the gene are more resistant to malaria than people without it. Not surprisingly, the gene is absent from northern Europe, where malaria is nonexistent, but it's common in tropical Africa, where malaria is widespread. Up to 40 percent of Africans in such areas carry the sickle-cell gene. It's also common in the malaria-ridden Arabian Peninsula and southern India, and rare or absent in the southernmost parts of South Africa, among the Xhosas, who live mostly beyond the tropical geographic range of malaria.

The geographic range of human malaria is much wider than the range of the sickle-cell gene. As it happens, other antimalarial genes take over the protective function of the sickle-cell gene in malarial Southeast Asia and New Guinea and in Italy, Greece, and other warm parts of the Mediterranean basin. Thus human races, if defined by antimalarial genes, would be very different from human races as traditionally defined by traits such as skin color. As classified by antimalarial genes (or their absence), Swedes are grouped with Xhosas but not with Italians or Greeks. Most other peoples usually viewed as African blacks are grouped with Arabia's "whites" and are kept separate from the "black" Xhosas.

Antimalarial genes exemplify the many features of our body chemistry that vary geographically under the influence of natural selection. Another such feature is the enzyme lactase, which enables us to digest the milk sugar lactose. Infant humans, like infants of almost all other mammal species, possess lactase and drink milk. Until about 6,000 years ago most humans, like all other mammal species, lost the lactase enzyme on reaching the age of weaning. The obvious reason is that it was unnecessary—no human or other mammal drank milk as an adult. Beginning around 4000 B.C., however, fresh milk obtained from domestic mammals became a major food for adults of a few human populations. Natural selection caused individuals in these populations to retain lactase into adulthood. Among such peoples are northern and central Europeans, Arabians, north Indians, and several milk-drinking black African peoples, such as the Fulani of West Africa. Adult lactase is much less common in southern European populations and in most other African black populations, as well as in all populations of east Asians, aboriginal Australians, and American Indians.

Once again races defined by body chemistry don't match races defined by skin color. Swedes belong with Fulani in the "lactase-positive race," while most African "blacks," Japanese, and American Indians belong in the "lactase-negative race."

Not all the effects of natural selection are as invisible as lactase and sickle cells. Environmental pressures have also produced more noticeable differences among peoples, particularly in body shapes. Among the tallest and most long-limbed peoples in the world are the Nilotic peoples, such as the Dinkas, who live in the hot, dry areas of East Africa. At the opposite extreme in body shape are the Inuit, or Eskimo, who have compact bodies and relatively short arms and legs. The reasons have to do with heat loss. The greater the surface area of a warm body, the more body heat that's lost, since heat loss is directly proportional to surface area. For people of a given weight, a long-limbed, tall shape maximizes surface area, while a compact, short-limbed shape minimizes

it. Dinkas and Inuit have opposite problems of heat balance: the former usually need desperately to get rid of body heat, while the latter need desperately to conserve it. Thus natural selection molded their body shapes oppositely, based on their contrasting climates.

(In modern times, such considerations of body shape have become important to athletic performance as well as to heat loss. Tall basketball players, for example, have an obvious advantage over short ones, and slender, long-limbed tall players have an advantage over stout, short-limbed tall players. In the United States, it's a familiar observation that African Americans are disproportionately represented among professional basketball players. Of course, a contributing reason has to do with their lack of socioeconomic opportunities. But part of the reason probably has to do with the prevalent body shapes of some black African groups as well. However, this example also illustrates the dangers in facile racial stereotyping. One can't make the sweeping generalization that "whites can't jump," or that "black's anatomy makes them better basketball players." Only certain African peoples are notably tall and long-limbed; even those exceptional peoples are tall and long-limbed only on the average and vary individually.)

Other visible traits that vary geographically among humans evolved by means of sexual selection. We all know that we find some individuals of the opposite sex more attractive than other individuals. We also know that in sizing up sex appeal, we pay more attention to certain parts of a prospective sex partner's body than to other parts. Men tend to be inordinately interested in women's breasts and much less concerned with women's toenails. Women, in turn, tend to be turned on by the shape of a man's buttocks or the details of a man's beard and body hair, if any, but not by the size of his feet.

But all those determinants of sex appeal vary geographically. Khoisan and Andaman Island women tend to have much larger buttocks than most other women. Nipple color and breast shape and size also vary geographically among women. European men are rather hairy by world standards, while Southeast Asian men tend to have very sparse beards and body hair.

What's the function of these traits that differ so markedly between men and women? They certainly don't aid survival: it's not the case that orange nipples help Khoisan women escape lions, while darker nipples help European women survive cold winters. Instead, these varying traits play a crucial role in sexual selection. Women with very large buttocks are a turn-on, or at least acceptable, to Khoisan and Andaman men but look freakish to many men from other parts of the world. Bearded and hairy men readily find mates in Europe but fare worse in Southeast Asia. The geographic variation of these traits, however, is as arbitrary as the geographic variation in the color of a lion's mane.

There is a third possible explanation for the function of geographically variable human traits, besides survival or sexual selection—namely, no function at all. A good example is provided by fingerprints, whose complex pattern of arches, loops, and whorls is determined genetically. Fingerprints also vary geographically: for example, Europeans' fingerprints tend to have many loops, while aboriginal Australians' fingerprints tend to have many whorls.

If we classify human populations by their fingerprints, most Europeans and black Africans would sort out together in one race, Jews and some Indonesians in another, and aboriginal Australians in still another. But those geographic variations in fingerprint patterns possess no known function whatsoever. They play no role in survival: whorls aren't especially suitable for grabbing kangaroos, nor do loops help bar mitzvah candidates hold on to the pointer for the Torah. They also play no role in sexual selection: while you've undoubtedly noticed whether your mate is bearded or has brown nipples, you surely haven't the faintest idea whether his or her fingerprints have more loops than whorls. Instead it's purely a matter of chance that whorls became common in aboriginal Australians, and loops among Jews. Our rhesus factor blood groups and numerous other human traits fall into the same category of genetic characteristics whose geographic variation serves no function.

You've probably been wondering when I was going to get back to skin color, eye color, and hair color and form. After all, those are the traits by which all of us members of the lay public, as well as traditional anthropologists, classify races. Does geographic variation in those traits function in survival, in sexual selection, or in nothing?

The usual view is that skin color varies geographically to enhance survival. Supposedly, people in sunny, tropical climates around the world have genetically dark skin, which is supposedly analogous to the temporary skin darkening of European whites in the summer. The supposed function of dark skin in sunny climates is for protection against skin cancer. Variations in eye color are also supposed to enhance survival under particular conditions, though no one has ever proposed a plausible hypothesis for how those variations might actually enhance survival.

Alas, the evidence for natural selection of skin color dissolves under scrutiny. Among tropical peoples, anthropologists love to stress the dark skins of African blacks, people of the southern Indian peninsula, and New Guineans and love to forget the pale skins of Amazonian Indians and Southeast Asians living at the same latitudes. To wriggle out of those paradoxes, anthropologists then plead the excuse that Amazonian Indians and Southeast Asians may not have been living in their present locations long enough to evolve dark skins. However, the ancestors of fair-skinned Swedes arrived even more recently in Scandinavia, and aboriginal Tasmanians were black-skinned despite their ancestors' having lived for at least the last 10,000 years at the latitude of Vladivostok.

Besides, when one takes into account cloud cover, peoples of equatorial West Africa and the New Guinea mountains actually receive no more ultraviolet radiation or hours of sunshine each year than do the Swiss. Compared with infectious diseases and other selective agents, skin cancer has been utterly trivial as a cause of death in human history, even for modern white settlers in the tropics. This objection is so obvious to believers in natural selection of skin color that they have proposed at least seven other supposed survival functions of skin color, without reaching agreement. Those other supposed functions include protection against rickets, frostbite, folic acid deficiency, beryllium poisoning, overheating, and overcooling. The diversity of these contradictory theories makes clear how far we are from understanding the survival value (if any) of skin color.

It wouldn't surprise me if dark skins do eventually prove to offer some advantage in tropical climates, but I expect the advantage to turn out to be a slight one that is easily overridden. But there's an overwhelming importance to skin, eye, and hair color that is obvious to all of us—sexual selection. Before we can reach a condition of intimacy permitting us to assess the beauty of a prospective sex partner's hidden physical attractions, we first have to pass muster for skin, eyes, and hair.

We all know how those highly visible "beauty traits" guide our choice of sex partners. Even the briefest personal ad in a newspaper mentions the advertiser's skin color, and the color of skin that he or she seeks in a partner. Skin color, of course, is also of overwhelming importance in our social prejudices. If you're a black African American trying to raise your children in white U.S. society, rickets and overheating are the least of the problems that might be solved by your skin color. Eye color and hair form and color, while not so overwhelmingly important as skin color, also play an obvious role in our sexual and social preferences. Just ask yourself why hair dyes, hair curlers, and hair straighteners enjoy such wide sales.

You can bet that it's not to improve our chances of surviving grizzly bear attacks and other risks endemic to the North American continent.

Nearly 125 years ago Charles Darwin himself, the discoverer of natural selection, dismissed its role as an explanation of geographic variation in human beauty traits. Everything that we have learned since then only reinforces Darwin's view.

We can now return to our original questions: Are human racial classifications that are based on different traits concordant with one another? What is the hierarchical relation among recognized races? What is the function of racially variable traits? What, really, are the traditional human races?

Regarding concordance, we *could* have classified races based on any number of geographically variable traits. The resulting classifications would not be at all concordant. Depending on whether we classified ourselves by antimalarial genes, lactase, fingerprints, or skin color, we could place Swedes in the same race as either Xhosas, Fulani, and Ainu of Japan, or Italians.

Regarding hierarchy, traditional classifications that emphasize skin color face unresolvable ambiguities. Anthropology textbooks often recognize five major races: "whites," "African blacks," "Mongoloids," "aboriginal Australians," and "Khoisans," each in turn divided into various numbers of sub-races. But there is no agreement on the number and delineation of the sub-races, or even of the major races. Are all five of the major races equally distinctive? Are Nigerians really less different from Xhosas than aboriginal Australians are from both? Should we recognize 3 or 15 sub-races of Mongoloids? These questions have remained unresolved because skin color and other traditional racial criteria are difficult to formulate mathematically.

A method that could in principle overcome these problems is to base racial classification on a combination of as many geographically variable genes as possible. Within the past decade, some biologists have shown renewed interest in developing a hierarchical classification of human populations—hierarchical not in the sense that it identifies superior and inferior races but in the sense of grouping and separating populations based on mathematical measures of genetic distinctness. While the biologists still haven't reached agreement, some of their studies suggest that human genetic diversity may be greatest in Africa. If so, the primary races of humanity may consist of several African races, plus one race to encompass all peoples of all other continents. Swedes, New Guineans, Japanese, and Navajo would then belong to the same primary race; the Khoisans of southern Africa would constitute another primary race by themselves; and African "blacks" and Pygmies would be divided among several other primary races.

As regards the function of all those traits that are useful for classifying human races, some serve to enhance survival, some to enhance sexual selection, while some serve no function at all. The traits we traditionally use are ones subject to sexual selection, which is not really surprising. These traits are not only visible at a distance but also highly variable; that's why they became the ones used throughout recorded history to make quick judgments about people. Racial classification didn't come from science but from the body's signals for differentiating attractive from unattractive sex partners, and for differentiating friend from foe.

Such snap judgments didn't threaten our existence back when people were armed only with spears and surrounded by others who looked mostly like themselves. In the modern world, though, we are armed with guns and plutonium, and we live our lives surrounded by people who are much more varied in appearance. The last thing we need now is to continue codifying all those different appearances into an arbitrary system of racial classification.

"RACE WITHOUT COLOR"

Jared Diamond

1) What is "race" from both the vernacular and scientific meanings of the word?

2) Why do humans classify the world, including other peoples?

3) What does Diamond suggest are possible reasons that physical human traits vary?

4) What alternate ways does Diamond suggest "races" could be defined? What unusual combinations can you define in this manner?

5) What does Diamond suggest are the reason(s) that human skin color varies across the world?

6) How do "common sense" classifications and knowledge contribute to modern human problems surrounding "race" in this country and around the world?

JAPANESE ROOTS

Jared Diamond

Unearthing the origins of the Japanese is a much harder task than you might guess. Among world powers today, the Japanese are the most distinctive in their culture and environment. The origins of their language are one of the most disputed questions of linguistics. These questions are central to the self-image of the Japanese and to how they are viewed by other peoples. Japan's rising dominance and touchy relations with its neighbors make it more important than ever to strip away myths and find answers.

The search for answers is difficult because the evidence is so conflicting. On the one hand, the Japanese people are biologically undistinctive, being very similar in appearance and genes to other East Asians, especially to Koreans. As the Japanese like to stress, they are culturally and biologically rather homogeneous, with the exception of a distinctive people called the Ainu on Japan's northernmost island of Hokkaido. Taken together, these facts seem to suggest that the Japanese reached Japan only recently from the Asian mainland, too recently to have evolved differences from their mainland cousins, and displaced the Ainu, who represent the original inhabitants. But if that were true, you might expect the Japanese language to show close affinities to some mainland language, just as English is obviously closely related to other Germanic languages (because Anglo-Saxons from the continent conquered England as recently as the sixth century A.D.). How can we resolve this contradiction between Japan's presumably ancient language and the evidence for recent origins?

Archeologists have proposed four conflicting theories. Most popular in Japan is the view that the Japanese gradually evolved from ancient Ice Age people who occupied Japan long before 20,000 B.C. Also widespread in Japan is a theory that the Japanese descended from horse-riding Asian nomads who passed through Korea to conquer Japan in the fourth century, but who were themselves—emphatically—not Koreans. A theory favored by many Western archeologists and Koreans, and unpopular in some circles in Japan, is that the Japanese are descendants of immigrants from Korea who arrived with rice-paddy agriculture around 400 B.C. Finally, the fourth theory holds that the peoples named in the other three theories could have mixed to form the modern Japanese.

When similar questions of origins arise about other peoples, they can be discussed dispassionately. That is not so for the Japanese. Until 1946, Japanese schools taught a myth of history based on the earliest recorded Japanese chronicles, which were written in the eighth century. They describe how the sun goddess Amaterasu, born from the left eye of the creator god Izanagi, sent her grandson Ninigi to Earth on the Japanese island of Kyushu to wed an earthly deity. Ninigi's great-grandson Jimmu, aided by a dazzling sacred bird that rendered his enemies helpless, became the first emperor of Japan in 660 B.C. To fill the gap between 660 B.C. and the earliest historically documented Japanese monarchs, the chronicles invented 13 other equally fictitious emperors. Before the end of World War II, when Emperor Hirohito finally announced that he was not of divine descent, Japanese archeologists and historians had to make their interpretations conform to this chronicle account. Unlike American archeologists, who acknowledge that ancient sites in the United States were left by peoples (Native Americans) unrelated to most modern Americans, Japanese archeologists believe all archeological deposits in Japan, no matter how old, were left by ancestors of the modern Japanese. Hence archeology in Japan is supported by astronomical budgets, employs up to 50,000 field-workers each year, and draws public attention to a degree inconceivable anywhere else in the world.

Why do they care so much? Unlike most other non-European countries, Japan preserved its independence and culture while emerging from isolation to create an industrialized society in the late nineteenth century. It was a remarkable achievement. Now the Japanese people are understandably concerned about maintaining their traditions in the face of massive Western cultural influences. They want to believe that their distinctive language and culture required uniquely complex developmental processes. To acknowledge a relationship of the Japanese language to any other language seems to constitute a surrender of cultural identity.

What makes it especially difficult to discuss Japanese archeology dispassionately is that Japa-

interpretations of the past affect present behavior. Who among East Asian peoples brought culture to whom? Who has historical claims to whose land? These are not just academic questions. For instance, there is much archeological evidence that people and material objects passed between Japan and Korea in the period A.D. 300 to 700. Japanese interpret this to mean that Japan conquered Korea and brought Korean slaves and artisans to Japan; Koreans believe instead that Korea conquered Japan and that the founders of the Japanese imperial family were Korean.

Thus, when Japan sent troops to Korea and annexed it in 1910, Japanese military leaders celebrated the annexation as "the restoration of the legitimate arrangement of antiquity." For the next 35 years, Japanese occupation forces tried to eradicate Korean culture and to replace the Korean language with Japanese in schools. The effort was a consequence of a centuries-old attitude of disdain. "Nose tombs" in Japan still contain 20,000 noses severed from Koreans and brought home as trophies of a sixteenth-century Japanese invasion. Not surprisingly, many Koreans loathe the Japanese, and their loathing is returned with contempt.

What really was "the legitimate arrangement of antiquity"? Today, Japan and Korea are both economic powerhouses, facing each other across the Korea Strait and viewing each other through colored lenses of false myths and past atrocities. It bodes ill for the future of East Asia if these two great peoples cannot find common ground. To do so, they will need a correct understanding of who the Japanese people really are.

Japan's unique culture began with its unique geography and environment. It is, for comparison, far more isolated than Britain, which lies only 22 miles from the French coast. Japan lies 110 miles from the closest point of the Asian mainland (South Korea), 190 miles from mainland Russia, and 480 miles from mainland China. Climate, too, sets Japan apart. Its rainfall, up to 120 inches a year, makes it the wettest temperate country in the world. Unlike the winter rains prevailing over much of Europe, Japan's rains are concentrated in the summer growing season, giving it the highest plant productivity of any nation in the temperate zones. While 80 percent of Japan's land consists of mountains unsuitable for agriculture and only 14 percent is farmland, an average square mile of that farmland is so fertile that it supports eight times as many people as does an average square mile of British farmland. Japan's high rainfall also ensures a quickly regenerated forest after logging. Despite thousands of years of dense human occupation, Ja-

pan still offers visitors a first impression of greenness because 70 percent of its land is still covered by forest.

Japanese forest composition varies with latitude and altitude: evergreen leafy forest in the south at low altitude, deciduous leafy forest in central Japan, and coniferous forest in the north and high up. For prehistoric humans, the deciduous leafy forest was the most productive, providing abundant edible nuts such as walnuts, chestnuts, horse chestnuts, acorns, and beechnuts. Japanese waters are also outstandingly productive. The lakes, rivers, and surrounding seas teem with salmon, trout, tuna, sardines, mackerel, herring, and cod. Today, Japan is the largest consumer of fish in the world. Japanese waters are also rich in clams, oysters, and other shellfish, crabs, shrimp, crayfish, and edible seaweeds. That high productivity was a key to Japan's prehistory.

From southwest to northeast, the four main Japanese islands are Kyushu, Shikoku, Honshu, and Hokkaido. Until the late nineteenth century, Hokkaido and northern Honshu were inhabited mainly by the Ainu, who lived as hunter-gatherers with limited agriculture, while the people we know today as Japanese occupied the rest of the main islands.

In appearance, of course, the Japanese are very similar to other East Asians. As for the Ainu, however, their distinctive appearance has prompted more to be written about their origins and relationships than about any other single people on Earth. Partly because Ainu men have luxuriant beards and the most profuse body hair of any people, they are often classified as Causasoids (so-called white people) who somehow migrated east through Eurasia to Japan. In their overall genetic makeup, though, the Ainu are related to other East Asians, including the Japanese and Koreans. The distinctive appearance and hunter-gatherer lifestyle of the Ainu, and the undistinctive appearance and the intensive agricultural lifestyle of the Japanese, are frequently taken to suggest the straightforward interpretation that the Ainu are descended from Japan's original hunter-gatherer inhabitants and the Japanese are more recent invaders from the Asian mainland.

But this view is difficult to reconcile with the distinctiveness of the Japanese language. Everyone agrees that Japanese does not bear a close relation to any other language in the world. Most scholars consider it to be an isolated member of Asia's Altaic language family, which consists of Turkic, Mongolian, and Tungusic languages. Korean is also often considered to be an isolated member of this family, and within the family Japanese and Korean may be more closely related to each other than to other Altaic languages. However, the similarities between Japanese and Korean are confined to general grammatical features and about 15 percent of their basic vocabularies, rather than the detailed shared features of grammar and vocabulary that link, say, French to Spanish; they are more different from each other than Russian is from English.

Since languages change over time, the more similar two languages are, the more recently they must have diverged. By counting common words and features, linguists can estimate how long ago languages diverged, and such estimates suggest that Japanese and Korean parted company at least 4,000 years ago. As for the Ainu language, its origins are thoroughly in doubt; it may not have any special relationship to Japanese.

After genes and language, a third type of evidence about Japanese origins comes from ancient portraits. The earliest preserved likenesses of Japan's inhabitants are statues called haniwa, erected outside tombs around 1,500 years ago. Those statues unmistakably depict East Asians. They do not resemble the heavily bearded Ainu. If the Japanese did replace the Ainu in Japan south of Hokkaido, that replacement must have occurred before A.D. 500.

Our earliest written information about Japan comes from Chinese chronicles, because China developed literacy long before Korea or Japan. In early Chinese accounts of various peoples referred to as "Eastern Barbarians," Japan is described under the name Wa, whose inhabitants were said to be divided into more than a hundred quarreling states. Only a few Korean or Japanese inscriptions before A.D. 700 have been preserved, but extensive chronicles were written in 712 and 720 in Japan and later in Korea. Those reveal massive transmission of culture to Japan from Korea itself, and from China via Korea. The chronicles are also full of accounts of Koreans in Japan and of Japanese in Korea—interpreted by Japanese or Korean historians, respectively, as evidence of Japanese conquest of Korea or the reverse.

The ancestors of the Japanese, then, seem to have reached Japan before they had writing. Their biology suggests a recent arrival, but their language suggests arrival long ago. To resolve this paradox, we must now turn to archeology.

The seas that surround much of Japan and coastal East Asia are shallow enough to have been dry land during the ice ages, when much of the ocean water was locked up in glaciers and sea level lay at about 500 feet below its present measurement. Land bridges connected Japan's main islands to one another, to the Russian mainland, and to South Korea. The mammals walking out to Japan included not only the ancestors of modern Japan's bears and monkeys but also ancient humans, long before boats had been invented. Stone tools indicate human arrival as early as half a million years ago.

Around 13,000 years ago, as glaciers melted rapidly all over the world, conditions in Japan changed spectacularly for the better, as far as humans were concerned. Temperature, rainfall, and humidity all increased, raising plant productivity to present high levels. Deciduous leafy forests full of nut trees, which had been confined to southern Japan during the ice ages, expanded northward at the expense of coniferous forest, thereby replacing a forest type that had been rather sterile for humans with a much more productive one. The rise in sea level severed the land bridges, converted Japan from a piece of the Asian continent to a big archipelago, turned what had been a plain into rich shallow seas, and created thousands of miles of productive new coastline with innumerable islands, bays, tidal flats, and estuaries, all teeming with seafood.

That end of the Ice Age was accompanied by the first of the two most decisive changes in Japanese history: the invention of pottery. In the usual experience of archeologists, inventions flow from mainlands to islands, and small peripheral societies aren't supposed to contribute revolutionary advances to the rest of the world. It therefore astonished archeologists to discover that the world's oldest known pottery was made in Japan 12,700 years ago. For the first time in human experience, people had watertight containers readily available in any desired shape. With their new ability to boil or steam food, they gained access to abundant resources that had previously been difficult to use: leafy vegetables, which would burn or dry out if cooked on an open fire; shellfish, which could now be opened easily; and toxic foods like acorns, which could now have their toxins boiled out. Soft-boiled foods could be fed to small children, permitting earlier weaning and more closely spaced babies. Toothless old people, the repositories of information in a preliterate society, could now be fed and live longer. All those momentous consequences of pottery triggered a population explosion, causing Japan's population to climb from an estimated few thousand to a quarter of a million.

The prejudice that islanders are supposed to learn from superior continentals wasn't the sole reason that record-breaking Japanese pottery caused such a shock. In addition, those first Japanese potters were clearly hunter-gatherers, which also violated established views. Usually only sedentary societies own pottery: what nomad wants to carry heavy, fragile pots, as well as weapons and the baby, whenever time comes to shift camp? Most sedentary societies elsewhere in the world arose only with the adoption of agriculture. But, the Japanese environment is so productive that people could settle down and make pottery while still living by hunting and gathering. Pottery helped those Japanese hunter-gatherers exploit their environment's rich food resources more than 10,000 years before intensive agriculture reached Japan.

Much ancient Japanese pottery was decorated by rolling or pressing a cord on soft clay. Because the Japanese word for cord marking is *jomon*, the term Jomon is applied to the pottery itself, to the ancient Japanese people who made it, and to that whole period in Japanese prehistory beginning with the invention of pottery and ending only 10,000 years later. The earliest Jomon pottery, of 12,700 years ago, comes from Kyushu, the southernmost Japanese island. Thereafter, pottery spread north, reaching the vicinity of modern Tokyo around 9,500 years ago and the northernmost island of Hokkaido by 7,000 years ago. Pottery's northward spread followed that of deciduous forest rich in nuts, suggesting that the climate-related food explosion was what permitted sedentary living.

How did Jomon people make their living? We have abundant evidence from the garbage they left behind at hundreds of thousands of excavated archeological sites all over Japan. They apparently enjoyed a well-balanced diet, one that modern nutritionists would applaud.

One major food category was nuts, especially chestnuts and walnuts, plus horse chestnuts and acorns leached or boiled free of their bitter poisons. Nuts could be harvested in autumn in prodigious quantities, then stored for the winter in underground pits up to six feet deep and six feet wide. Other plant foods included berries, fruits, seeds, leaves, shoots, bulbs, and roots. In all, archeologists sifting through Jomon garbage have identified 64 species of edible plants.

Then as now, Japan's inhabitants were among the world's leading consumers of seafood. They harpooned tuna in the open ocean, killed seals on the beaches, and exploited seasonal runs of salmon in the rivers. They drove dolphins into shallow water and clubbed or speared them, just as Japanese hunters do today. They netted diverse fish, captured them in weirs, and caught them on fishhooks carved from deer antlers. They gathered shellfish, crabs, and seaweed in the intertidal zone or dove for them. (Jomon skeletons show a high incidence of abnormal bone growth in the ears, often observed in divers today.)

Among land animals hunted, wild boar and deer were the most common prey. They were caught in pit traps, shot with bows and arrows, and run down with dogs.

The most debated question about Jomon subsistence concerns the possible contribution of agriculture. Many Jomon sites contain remains of edible plants that are native to Japan as wild species but also grown as crops today, including the adzuki bean and green gram bean. The remains from Jomon times do not clearly show features distinguishing the crops from their wild ancestors, so we do not know whether these plants were gathered in the wild or grown intentionally. Sites also have debris of edible or useful plant species not native to Japan, such as hemp, which must have been introduced from the Asian mainland. Around 1000 B.C., toward the end of the Jomon period, a few grains of rice, barley, and millet, the staple cereals of East Asia, began to appear. All these tantalizing clues make it likely that Jomon people were starting to practice some slash-and-burn agriculture, but evidently in a casual way that made only a minor contribution to their diet.

Archeologists studying Jomon hunter-gatherers have found not only hard-to-carry pottery (including pieces up to three feet tall) but also heavy stone tools, remains of substantial houses that show signs of repair, big village sites of 50 or more dwellings, and cemeteries—all further evidence that the Jomon people were sedentary rather than nomadic. Their stay-at-home lifestyle was made possible by the diversity of resource-rich habitats available within a short distance of one central site: inland forests, rivers, seashores, bays, and open oceans. Jomon people lived at some of the highest population densities ever estimated for hunter-gatherers, especially in central and northern Japan, with their nut-rich forests, salmon runs, and productive seas. The estimate of the total population of Jomon Japan at its peak is 250,000—trivial, of course, compared with today, but impressive for hunter-gatherers.

With all this stress on what Jomon people did have, we need to be clear as well about what they didn't have. Their lives were very different from those of contemporary societies only a few hundred miles away in mainland China and Korea. Jomon people had no intensive agriculture. Apart from dogs (and perhaps pigs), they had no domestic animals. They had no metal tools, no writing, no weaving, and little social stratification into chiefs and commoners. Regional variation in pottery styles suggests little progress toward political centralization and unification.

Despite its distinctiveness even in East Asia at

that time, Jomon Japan was not completely isolated. Pottery, obsidian, and fishhooks testify to some Jomon trade with Korea, Russia, and Okinawa—as does the arrival of Asian mainland crops. Compared with later eras, though, that limited trade with the outside world had little influence on Jomon society. Jomon Japan was a miniature conservative universe that changed surprisingly little over 10,000 years.

To place Jomon Japan in a contemporary perspective, let us remind ourselves of what human societies were like on the Asian mainland in 400 B.C., just as the Jomon lifestyle was about to come to an end. China consisted of kingdoms with rich elites and poor commoners; the people lived in walled towns, and the country was on the verge of political unification and would soon become the world's largest empire. Beginning around 6500 B.C., China had developed intensive agriculture based on millet in the north and rice in the south; it had domestic pigs, chickens, and water buffalo. The Chinese had had writing for at least 900 years, metal tools for at least 1,500 years, and had just invented the world's first cast iron. Those developments were also spreading to Korea, which itself had had agriculture for several thousand years (including rice since at least 2100 B.C.) and metal since 1000 B.C.

With all these developments going on for thousands of years just across the Korea Strait from Japan, it might seem astonishing that in 400 B.C. Japan was still occupied by people who had some trade with Korea but remained preliterate stone-tool-using hunter-gatherers. Throughout human history, centralized states with metal weapons and armies supported by dense agricultural populations have consistently swept away sparser populations of hunter-gatherers. How did Jomon Japan survive so long?

To understand the answer to this paradox, we have to remember that until 400 B.C., the Korea Strait separated not rich farmers from poor hunter-gatherers, but poor farmers from rich hunter-gatherers. China itself and Jomon Japan were probably not in direct contact. Instead Japan's trade contacts, such as they were, involved Korea. But rice had been domesticated in warm southern China and spread only slowly northward to much cooler Korea, because it took a long time to develop cold-resistant strains of rice. Early rice agriculture in Korea used dry-field methods rather than irrigated paddies and was not particularly productive. Hence early Korean agriculture could not compete with Jomon hunting and gathering. Jomon people themselves would have seen no advantage in adopting Korean agriculture, insofar as they were aware of its existence, and poor

Korean farmers had no advantages that would let them force their way into Japan. As we shall see, the advantages finally reversed suddenly and dramatically.

More than 10,000 years after the invention of pottery and the subsequent Jomon population explosion, a second decisive event in Japanese history triggered a second population explosion. Around 400 B.C., a new lifestyle arrived from South Korea. This second transition poses in acute form our question about who the Japanese are. Does the transition mark the replacement of Jomon people with immigrants from Korea, ancestral to the modern Japanese? Or did Japan's original Jomon inhabitants continue to occupy Japan while learning valuable new tricks?

The new mode of living appeared first on the north coast of Japan's southwesternmost island, Kyushu, just across the Korea Strait from South Korea. There we find Japan's first metal tools, of iron, and Japan's first undisputed full-scale agriculture. That agriculture came in the form of irrigated rice fields, complete with canals, dams, banks, paddies, and rice residues revealed by archeological excavations. Archeologists term the new way of living Yayoi, after a district of Tokyo where in 1884 its characteristic pottery was first recognized. Unlike Jomon pottery, Yayoi pottery was very similar to contemporary South Korean pottery in shape. Many other elements of the new Yayoi culture were unmistakably Korean and previously foreign to Japan, including bronze objects, weaving, glass beads, and styles of tools and houses.

While rice was the most important crop, Yayoi farmers introduced 27 new to Japan, as well as unquestionably domesticated pigs. They may have practiced double cropping, with paddies irrigated for rice production in the summer, then drained for dry-land cultivation of millet, barley, and wheat in the winter. Inevitably, this highly productive system of intensive agriculture triggered an immediate population explosion in Kyushu, where archeologists have identified far more Yayoi sites than Jomon sites, even though the Jomon period lasted 14 times longer.

In virtually no time, Yayoi farming jumped from Kyushu to the adjacent main islands of Shikoku and Honshu, reaching the Tokyo area within 200 years, and the cold northern tip of Honshu (1,000 miles from the first Yayoi settlements on Kyushu) in another century. After briefly occupying northern Honshu, Yayoi farmers abandoned that area, presumably because rice farming could not compete with the Jomon hunter-gatherer life. For the next 2,000 years, northern Honshu remained a frontier zone, beyond which the northernmost Japanese island of Hokkaido and its Ainu hunter-gatherers were not even considered part of the Japanese state until their annexation in the nineteenth century.

It took several centuries for Yayoi Japan to show the first signs of social stratification, as reflected especially in cemeteries. After about 100 B.C., separate parts of cemeteries were set aside for the graves of what was evidently an emerging elite class, marked by luxury goods imported from China, such as beautiful jade objects and bronze mirrors. As the Yayoi population explosion continued, and as all the best swamps or irrigable plains suitable for wet rice agriculture began to fill up, the archeological evidence suggests that war became more and more frequent: that evidence includes mass production of arrowheads, defensive moats surrounding villages, and buried skeletons pierced by projectile points. These hallmarks of war in Yayoi Japan corroborate the earliest accounts of Japan in Chinese chronicles, which describe the land of Wa and its hundred little political units fighting one another.

In the period from A.D. 300 to 700, both archeological excavations and frustratingly ambiguous accounts in later chronicles let us glimpse dimly the emergence of a politically unified Japan. Before A.D. 300, elite tombs were small and exhibited a regional diversity of styles. Beginning around A.D. 300, increasingly enormous earth-mound tombs called *kofun*, in the shape of keyholes, were constructed throughout the former Yayoi area from Kyushu to North Honshu. *Kofun* are up to 1,500 feet long and more than 100 feet high, making them possibly the largest earth-mound tombs in the world. The prodigious amount of labor required to build them and the uniformity of their style across Japan imply powerful rulers who commanded a huge, politically unified labor force. Those *kofun* that have been excavated contain lavish burial goods, but excavation of the largest ones is still forbidden because they are believed to contain the ancestors of the Japanese imperial line. The visible evidence of political centralization that the *kofun* provide reinforces the accounts of *kofun*-era Japanese emperors written down much later in Japanese and Korean chronicles. Massive Korean influences on Japan during the *kofun* era—whether through the Korean conquest of Japan (the Korean view) or the Japanese conquest of Korea (the Japanese view)—were responsible for transmitting Buddhism, writing, horseback riding, and new ceramic and metallurgical techniques to Japan from the Asian mainland.

Finally, with the completion of Japan's first chronicle in A.D. 712, Japan emerged into the full light of history. As of 712, the people inhabiting Japan were at last unquestionably Japanese, and their language (termed Old Japanese) was unquestionably ancestral to modern Japanese. Emperor Akihito, who reigns today, is the eighty-second direct descendant of the emperor under whom that first chronicle of A.D. 712 was written. He is traditionally considered the 125th direct descendant of the legendary first emperor, Jimmu, the great-great-great-grandson of the sun goddess Amaterasu.

Japanese culture underwent far more radical change in the 700 years of the Yayoi era than in the ten millennia of Jomon times. The contrast between Jomon stability (or conservatism) and radical Yayoi change is the most striking feature of Japanese history. Obviously, something momentous happened at 400 B.C. What was it? Were the ancestors of the modern Japanese the Jomon people, the Yayoi people, or a combination? Japan's population increased by an astonishing factor of 70 during Yayoi times: What caused that change? A passionate debate has raged around three alternative hypotheses.

One theory is that Jomon hunter-gatherers themselves gradually evolved into the modern Japanese. Because they had already been living a settled existence in villages for thousands of years, they may have been preadapted to accepting agriculture. At the Yayoi transition, perhaps nothing more happened than that Jomon society received cold-resistant rice seeds and information about paddy irrigation from Korea, enabling it to produce more food and increase its numbers. This theory appeals to many modern Japanese because it minimizes the unwelcome contribution of Korean genes to the Japanese gene pool while portraying the Japanese people as uniquely Japanese for at least the past 12,000 years.

A second theory, unappealing to those Japanese who prefer the first theory, argues instead that the Yayoi transition represents a massive influx of immigrants from Korea, carrying Korean farming practices, culture, and genes. Kyushu would have seemed a paradise to Korean rice farmers, because it is warmer and swampier than Korea and hence a better place to grow rice. According to one estimate, Yayoi Japan received several million immigrants from Korea, utterly overwhelming the genetic contribution of Jomon people (thought to have numbered around 75,000 just before the Yayoi transition). If so, modern Japanese are descendants of Korean immigrants who developed a modified culture of their own over the last 2,000 years.

The last theory accepts the evidence for immigration from Korea but denies that it was massive. Instead, highly productive agriculture may have enabled a modest number of immigrant rice farmers to reproduce much faster than Jomon hunter-gatherers and eventually to outnumber them. Like the second theory, this theory considers modern Japanese to be slightly modified Koreans but dispenses with the need for large-scale immigration.

By comparison with similar transitions elsewhere in the world, the second or third theory seems to me more plausible than the first theory. Over the last 12,000 years, agriculture arose at not more than nine places on Earth, including China and the Fertile Crescent. Twelve thousand years ago, everybody alive was a hunter-gatherer; now almost all of us are farmers or fed by farmers. Farming spread from those few sites of origin mainly because farmers outbred hunters, developed more potent technology, and then killed the hunters or drove them off lands suitable for agriculture. In modern times European farmers thereby replaced native Californian hunters, aboriginal Australians, and the San people of South Africa. Farmers who used stone tools similarly replaced hunters prehistorically throughout Europe, Southeast Asia, and Indonesia. Korean farmers of 400 B.C. would have enjoyed a much larger advantage over Jomon hunters because the Koreans already possessed iron tools and a highly developed form of intensive agriculture.

Which of the three theories is correct for Japan? The only direct way to answer this question is to compare Jomon and Yayoi skeletons and genes with those of modern Japanese and Ainu. Measurements have now been made of many skeletons. In addition, within the last three years molecular geneticists have begun to extract DNA from ancient human skeletons and compare the genes of Japan's ancient and modern populations. Jomon and Yayoi skeletons, researchers find, are on the average readily distinguishable. Jomon people tended to be shorter, with relatively longer forearms and lower legs, more wide-set eyes, shorter and wider faces, and much more pronounced facial topography, with strikingly raised browridges, noses, and nose bridges. Yayoi people averaged an inch or two taller, with close-set eyes, high and narrow faces, and flat browridges and noses. Some skeletons of the Yayoi period were still Jomon-like in appearance, but that is to be expected by almost any theory of the Jomon-Yayoi transition. By the time of the *kofun* period, all Japanese skeletons except those of the Ainu form a homogeneous group, resembling modern Japanese and Koreans.

In all these respects, Jomon skulls differ from those of modern Japanese and are most similar to those of modern Ainu, while Yayoi skulls most resemble those of modern Japanese. Similarly, geneticists attempting to calculate the relative contributions of Korean-like Yayoi genes and Ainu-like Jomon genes to the modern Japanese gene pool have concluded that the Yayoi contribution was generally dominant. Thus, immigrants from Korea really did make a big contribution to the modern Japanese, though we cannot yet say whether that was because of massive immigration or else modest immigration amplified by a high rate of population increase. Genetic studies of the past three years have also at last resolved the controversy about the origins of the Ainu: they are the descendants of Japan's ancient Jomon inhabitants, mixed with Korean genes of Yayoi colonists and of the modern Japanese.

Given the overwhelming advantage that rice agriculture gave Korean farmers, one has to wonder why the farmers achieved victory over Jomon hunters so suddenly, after making little headway in Japan for thousands of years. What finally tipped the balance and triggered the Yayoi transition was probably a combination of four developments: the farmers began raising rice in irrigated fields instead of in less productive dry fields; they developed rice strains that would grow well in a cool climate; their population expanded in Korea, putting pressure on Koreans to emigrate; and they invented iron tools that allowed them to mass-produce the wooden shovels, hoes, and other tools needed for rice-paddy agriculture. That iron and intensive farming reached Japan simultaneously is unlikely to have been a coincidence.

We have seen that the combined evidence of archeology, physical anthropology, and genetics supports the transparent interpretation for how the distinctive-looking Ainu and the undistinctive-looking Japanese came to share Japan: the Ainu are descended from Japan's original inhabitants and the Japanese are descended from more recent arrivals. But that view leaves the problem of language unexplained. If the Japanese really are recent arrivals from Korea, you might expect the Japanese and Korean languages to be very similar. More generally, if the Japanese people arose recently from some mixture, on the island of Kyushu, of original Ainu-like Jomon inhabitants with Yayoi invaders from Korea, the Japanese language might show close affinities to both the Korean and Ainu languages. Instead, Japanese and Ainu have no demonstrable relationship, and the relationship between Japanese and Korean is distant. How could this be so if the mixing occurred a mere 2,400 years ago? I suggest the following resolution of this paradox: the languages of Kyushu's Jomon residents and Yayoi invaders were quite different from the modern Ainu and Korean languages, respectively.

The Ainu language was spoken in recent times by the Ainu on the northern island of Hokkaido, so Hokkaido's Jomon inhabitants probably also spoke an Ainu-like language. The Jomon inhabitants of Kyushu, however, surely did not. From the southern tip of Kyushu to the northern tip of Hokkaido, the Japanese archipelago is nearly 1,500 miles long. In Jomon times it supported great regional diversity of subsistence techniques and of pottery styles and was never unified politically. During the 10,000 years of Jomon occupation, Jomon people would have evolved correspondingly great linguistic diversity. In fact, many Japanese place-names on Hokkaido and northern Honshu include the Ainu words for river, *nai* or *betsu*, and for cape, *shiri*, but such Ainu-like names do not occur farther south in Japan. This suggests not only that Yayoi and Japanese pioneers adopted many Jomon place-names, just as white Americans did Native American names (think of Massachusetts and Mississippi), but also that Ainu was the Jomon language only of northernmost Japan.

That is, the modern Ainu language of Hokkaido is not a model for the ancient Jomon language of Kyushu. By the same token, modern Korean may be a poor model for the ancient Yayoi language of Korean immigrants in 400 B.C. In the centuries before Korea became unified politically in A.D. 676, it consisted of three kingdoms. Modern Korean is derived from the language of the kingdom of Silla, the kingdom that emerged triumphant and unified Korea, but Silla was not the kingdom that had close contact with Japan in the preceding centuries. Early Korean chronicles tell us that the different kingdoms had different languages. While the languages of the kingdoms defeated by Silla are poorly known, the few preserved words of one of those kingdoms, Koguryo, are much more similar to the corresponding Old Japanese words than are the corresponding modern Korean words. Korean languages may have been even more diverse in 400 B.C., before political unification had reached the stage of three kingdoms. The Korean language that reached Japan in 400 B.C., and that evolved into modern Japanese, I suspect, was quite different from the Silla language that evolved into modern Korean. Hence we should not be surprised that modern Japanese and Korean people resemble each other far more in their appearance and genes than in their languages.

History gives the Japanese and the Koreans ample grounds for mutual distrust and contempt, so any conclusion confirming their close relationship is likely to be unpopular among both peoples. Like Arabs and Jews, Koreans and Japanese are joined by blood yet locked in traditional enmity. But enmity is mutually destructive, in East Asia as in the Middle East. As reluctant as Japanese and Koreans are to admit it, they are like twin brothers who shared their formative years. The political future of East Asia depends in large part on their success in rediscovering those ancient bonds between them.

"JAPANESE ROOTS"

Jared Diamond

1) What are the four common theories regarding the origin of the Japanese people and culture? What are their possible strengths and weaknesses?

2) What is the Japanese origin myth, and how has it affected recent and modern Japanese history?

3) How do the following lines of evidence support or contradict each other—genetics, linguistic affiliation, Chinese/Korean/Japanese records, archaeology?

4) Discuss the basic outlines of Japanese prehistory, considering the following areas: the peopling of Japan; the nature of Jomon Culture and its differences from other cultures of similar complexity; the Yayoi Period and theoretical explanations for its florit; how does evidence (skeletal, linguistic, genetic) from Korea and Japan support or contradict the theories about the Yayoi Period?

5) Which theories about the origins of the Japanese people and the Yayoi Period do the Japanese prefer? Are the reasons for these preferences mainly scientific or cultural?

Law, Custom, and Crimes Against Women: The Problem of Dowry Death in India

John Van Willigen and V.C. Channa

This routinely reported news story describes what in India is termed a "bride-burning" or "dowry death." Such incidents are frequently reported in the newspapers of Delhi and other Indian cities. In addition, there are cases in which the evidence may be ambiguous, so that deaths of women by fire may be recorded as kitchen accidents, suicides, or murders. Dowry violence takes a characteristic form. Following marriage and the requisite giving of dowry, the family of the groom makes additional demands for the payment of more cash or the provision of more goods. These demands are expressed in unremitting harassment of the bride, who is living in the household of her husband's parents, culminating in the murder of the woman by members of her husband's family or by her suicide. The woman is typically burned to death with kerosene, a fuel used in pressurized cook stoves, hence the use of the term "bride-burning" in public discourse.

Dowry death statistics appear frequently in the press and parliamentary debates. Parliamentary sources report the following figures for married women 16 to 30 years of age in Delhi: 452 deaths by burning for 1985; 478 for 1986 and 300 for the first six months of 1987 (Bhatia 1988). There were 1,319 cases reported nationally in 1986 (Times of India, January 10, 1988). Police records do not match hospital records for third degree burn cases among younger married women; far more violence occurs than the crime reports indicate (Kumari 1988).

There is other violence against women related both directly and indirectly to the institution of dowry. For example, there are unmarried women who commit suicide so as to relieve their families of the burden of providing a dowry. A recent case that received national attention in the Indian press involved the triple suicide of three sisters in the industrial city of Kanpur. A photograph was widely published showing the three young women hanging from ceiling fans by their scarves. Their father, who earned about 4000 Rs. [rupees] per month, was not able to negotiate marriage for his oldest daughter. The

grooms were requesting approximately 100,000 Rs. Also linked to the dowry problem is selective female abortion made possible by amniocentesis. This issue was brought to national attention with a startling statistic reported out of a seminar held in Delhi in 1985. Of 3000 abortions carried out after sex determination through amniocentesis, only one involved a male fetus. As a result of these developments, the government of the state of Maharashtra banned sex determination tests except those carried out in government hospitals.

The phenomenon of dowry-death presents a difficult problem for the ethnologist. Ethnological theory, with its residual functionalist cast, still does not deal effectively with the social costs of institutions of what might be arguably referred to as custom gone bad, resulting in a culturally constituted violence syndrome.

This essay examines dowry and its violent aspects, and some of the public solutions developed to deal with it in India. Our work consists of a meta-analysis of some available literature. We critique the legal mechanisms established to regulate the cultural institution of dowry and the resultant social evils engendered by the institution, and argue that policies directed against these social evils need to be constructed in terms of an underlying cause rather than of the problem itself. We consider cause, an aspect of the problem infrequently discussed in public debate. As Saini asserts, "legal academicians have shown absolutely no interest in the causal roots of dowry as practiced in contemporary India" (1983:143).

The Institution

Since ancient times, the marriage of Hindus has required the transfer of property from the family of the bride to the family of the groom. Dowry or *daan dehej* is thought by some to be sanctioned by such religious texts as the *Manusmriti*. Seen in this way, dowry is a religious obligation of the father of a woman and a matter of *dharma* (religious duty) whereby authority over a woman is transferred from her father to her husband. This transfer takes different forms in different communities in modern India (Tambiah 1973). In public discussion, the term "dowry" covers a wide range of traditional payments and expenses, some presented to the groom's family and others to be retained by the bride. Customs have changed through time. The financial burdens of gifts and the dowry payments per se are exacerbated by the many expenses associated with the marriage celebration itself, but dowry payment is especially problematic because of its open-ended nature. As Tambiah notes, "marriage payments in India usually comprise an elaborate series of payments back and forth between the marrying families" and "this series extends over a long period of time and persists after marriage" (1973:92). Contemporary cases such as the death of Mrs. Sunita, often revolve around such continued demands.

A daughter's marriage takes a long time to prepare and involves the development of an adaptive strategy on the part of her family. An important part of the strategy is the preparation for making dowry payments; family consumption may be curtailed so as to allow accumulation of money for dowry. Seeing to marriage arrangements may be an important aspect of retirement planning. The dowries that the family receives on behalf of their sons may be "rolled over" to deal with the daughter's requirements. Families attempt to cultivate in both their sons and daughters attributes that will make them more attractive in marriage negotiations. Many things besides dowry are considered in negotiations: "non-economic" factors have demonstrable effect on the expectations for dowry and the family's strategy concerning the dowry process.

Education is a variable to be considered in the negotiation process. Education of young women is somewhat problematic because suitable husbands for such women must also be college educated. The parents of such young men demand more dowry for their sons. A consideration in sending a young woman to college will therefore be her parents' capacity to dower her adequately so as to obtain an appropriate groom. In any case, education is secondary to a man's earning power and the reputation of a woman's family. Education is, however, important in the early stages of negotiation because of the need to coordinate the level of the education of the men and women. Education qualifications are also less ambiguously defined than other dimensions of family reputation. Physical attractiveness is a consideration, but it is thought somewhat unseemly to emphasize this aspect of the decision.

Advertisements in newspapers are used for establishing marriage proposals (Aluwalia 1969, Niehoff 1959, Weibe and Ramu 1971), but contacts are more typically established through kin and other networks. Some marriages may be best termed "self-arranged," and are usually called "love marriages." In these cases, young men and women may develop a relationship independent of their families and then ask that negotiations be carried out on their behalf by family representatives.

Analysis of matrimonial advertisements shows some of the attributes considered to be important. Listed in such advertisements are education, age, income and occupation, physical attributes, *gotra* (a kind of unilineal descent group) membership, family background, place of residence, personality features, consideration of dowry, time and type of marriage, and language.

Consideration of dowry and other expenditures are brought out early in the negotiations and can serve as a stumbling block. Dowry negotiations can go on for some time. The last stage is the actual "seeing of the groom" and the "seeing of the bride," both rather fleeting encounters whose position at the end of the process indicates their relative lack of importance.

Marriage is a process by which two families mutually evaluate each other. The outcome of the negotiations is an expression of the relative worth of the two persons, a man and a woman, and, by extension, the worth of their respective families. This estimation of worth is expressed in marriage expenditures, of which dowry is but a part. There are three possible types of expenditures: cash gifts, gifts of household goods, and expenditures on the wedding celebration itself. The cash gift component of the dowry goes to the groom's father and comes to be part of his common household fund. The household goods are for use by the groom's household, although they may be used to establish a separate household for the newlyweds. When separate accommodations are not set up, the groom's family may insist that the goods do not duplicate things they already have.

Dates for marriages are set through consideration of horoscopes; horoscopy is done by professional astrologers (*pandits*). This practice leads to a concentration of marriage dates and consequent high demand for marriage goods and services at certain times of the year. During marriage seasons, the cost of jewelry, furniture, clothes, musicians' services and other marriage related expenditures goes up, presumably because of the concentration of the demand caused by the astrologers.

The expenditures required of the woman's family for the wedding in general and the dowry in particular are frequently massive. Paul reports, for a middle-class Delhi neighborhood, that most dowries were over 50,000 Rs. (1986). Srinivas comments that dowries over 200,000 Rs. are not uncommon (1984).[1]

Ethnological Theories About Dowry

Dowry had traditionally been discussed by ethnologists in the context of the functionalist paradigm, and much theorizing about dowry appears to be concerned with explaining the "contribution" that the institution makes to social adaptation. The early theoretician Westermarck interpreted dowry as a social marker of the legitimacy of spouse and offspring, and as a mechanism for defining women's social roles and property rights in the new household (Westermarck 1921:428). Murdock suggests that dowry may confirm the contract of marriage (1949). Dowry is interpreted by Friedl as a means to adjust a woman to her affinal home as it rearranges social relationships including the social separation of the man from his parents (1967). Dowry payments are public expressions of the new relationship between the two families, and of the social status of the bride and groom.

Dowry is seen in the social science literature as a kind of antemortem or anticipated inheritance by which a widow is assured of support, and provision for her offspring (Friedl 1967; Goody 1973, 1976). It transfers money to where the women will be and where they will reproduce; as a result, resources are also placed where the children will benefit, given the practice of patrilineal inheritance of immovable, economically valuable property like farm land.

In India, dowry is also seen as an expression of the symbolic order of society. According to Dumont, dowry expresses the hierarchal relations of marriage in India and lower status of the bride (Dumont 1957). The amount of dowry given is an expression of prestige. The capacity to buy prestige through dowry increases the potential for social mobility (Goody 1973). Dowry is a kind of delayed consumption used to demonstrate or improve social rank (Epstein 1960).

There is a significant discontinuity between discussions of dowry in the ethnological theory and in public discourse. Certainly the dowry problem does appear in the writing of contemporary ethnologists, but it is simply lamented and left largely uninterpreted and unexplained.

The Extant Solutions To The Problem

The Dowry Prohibition Act of 1961, as amended in 1984 and 1986, is the primary legal means for regulating the dowry process and controlling its excesses. The laws against dowry are tough. Dowry demand offenses are "cognizable" (require no warrant) and nonbailable, and the burden of proof is on the accused. There are, in fact, convictions under the law.

The act defines dowry as "any property of valuable security given or agreed to be given either directly or indirectly—(a) by one party to a marriage to the other party to a marriage; or (b) by parents of either party to a marriage or by any other person, to either party to the marriage or to any other person" (Government of India 1986:1). The act makes it illegal to give or take dowry, "If any person after the commencement of this act, gives or takes or abets the giving or taking of dowry, he shall be punishable with imprisonment for a term which shall not be less than five years; and with fine which shall not be less than fifteen thousand rupees or the amount of the value of such dowry which ever is more" (Government of India 1986:1). While this section unambiguously prohibits dowry, the third section allows wedding presents to be freely given. Thus the law does not apply to "presents which are given at the time of marriage to the bride (without demand having been made in that behalf)" (Government of India 1986:1). Identical provisions apply to the groom. Furthermore, all such presents must be listed on a document before the consummation of the marriage. The list is to contain a brief description and estimation of the value of the gifts, name of presenting person, and the relationship that person has with the bride and groom. This regulation also provides "that where such presents are made by or on the behalf of the bride or any other person related to the bride, such presents are of a customary nature and the value thereof is not excessive having regard to the financial status of the person by whom, or on whose behalf, such presents are given" (Government of India 1986:2). Amendments made in 1984 make it illegal for a person to demand dowry with the same penalty as under the earlier "giving and taking" provision. It was also declared illegal to advertise for dowry, such an offense being defined as not bailable, with the burden of proof on the accused person.

This legislation was coupled with some changes in the Indian Penal Code that legally established the concept of "dowry death." That is, "where the death of a woman is caused by any burns or bodily injury or occurs otherwise than under normal circumstances within seven years of her marriage and it is shown that soon before her death she was subjected to cruelty or harassment by her husband or any relative or her husband for, or in connection with, any demand for dowry, such death shall be called 'dowry death,' and such husband or relative shall be deemed to have caused her death" (Government of India 1987:4). The Indian Evidence Act of 1871 was changed so as to allow for the presumption of guilt under the circumstances outlined above. Changes in the code allowed for special investigation and reporting procedures of deaths by apparent suicide of women within seven years of marriage if requested by a relative. There were also newly defined special provisions for autopsies.

To this point, however, these legal mechanisms have proved ineffective. According to Sivaramayya, the "act has signally failed in its operation" (1984:66). Menon refers to the "near total failure" of the law (1988:12). A similar viewpoint is expressed by Srinivas, who wrote, "The Dowry Prohibition Act of 1961 has been unanimously declared to be an utterly ineffective law" (1984:29).

In addition to the legal attack on dowry abuses, numerous public groups engage in public education campaigns. In urban settings, the most noteworthy of these groups are specialized research units such as the Special Cell for Women of the Tata Institute of Social Sciences (Bombay), and the Center for Social Research (New Delhi). Also involved in the effort are private voluntary organizations such as the Crimes Against Women Cell, Karmika, and Sukh Shanti.

These groups issue public education advertising on various feminist issues. The anti-dowry advertisement of the Federation of Indian Chambers of Commerce and Industry Ladies Organization exemplifies the thrust of these campaigns. In the following advertisement, which was frequently run in the winter of 1988 in newspapers such as the Times of India, a photograph of a doll dressed in traditional Indian bridal attire was shown in flames.

> Every time a young bride dies because of dowry demands, we are all responsible for her death. Because we allow it to happen. Each year in Delhi hospitals alone, over 300 brides die of third degree burns. And many more deaths go unreported. Most of the guilty get away. And we just shrug helplessly and say, "what can we do?" We can do a lot.
>
> Help create social condemnation of dowry. Refuse to take or give dowry. Protest when you meet people who condone the practice. Reach out and help the girl being harassed for it. Act now.
>
> Let's fight it together.
>
> As parents, bring up educated, self-reliant daughters. Make sure they marry only after 18. Oppose dowry; refuse to even discuss it. If your daughter is harassed after marriage stand by her.
>
> As young men and women, refuse marriage proposals where dowry is being considered. As friends and neighbors, ostracize families who give or take dowry. Reach out to help victims of dowry harassment.

> As legislators and jurists, frame stronger laws. Ensure speedy hearings, impose severe punishments. As associations, give help and advice. Take up the challenge of changing laws and attitudes of society. Let us all resolve to fight the evil. If we fight together we can win.
> SAY NO TO DOWRY.

Also engaged in anti-dowry work are peasant political action groups such as Bharatiya Kisan Union (BKU). BKU consists of farmers from western Uttar Pradesh whose political program is focused more generally on agricultural issues. The group sponsored a massive 25-day demonstration at Meerut, Uttar Pradesh, in 1988. The leadership used the demonstration to announce a social reform program, most of it dealing with marriage issues. According to news service reports, "The code of social reforms includes fixing the maximum number of persons in a marriage party at 11, no feasts relating to marriage and no dowry except 10 grams of gold and 30 grams of silver" (Times of India, February 11, 1988). Buses plying rural roads in western Uttar Pradesh are reported to have been painted with the slogan "The bride is the dowry." Private campaigns against dowry occur in the countryside as well as among the urban elites, although it is likely that the underlying motivations are quite different.

Policy Analysis

Our argument is based on the assumption that social problems are best dealt with by policies directed at the correction of causative factors, rather than at the amelioration of symptoms. While current legal remedies directly confront dowry violence, the linkage between cause and the problematic behavior is not made. Here we develop an argument consisting of three components: women's access to production roles and property; delocalization of social control; and economic transformation of society. The pattern of distribution of aspects of the institution of dowry and its attendant problems is important to this analysis. Although dowry practices and the related crimes against women are distributed throughout Indian society, the distribution is patterned in terms of geography, caste rank, socioeconomic rank, urban/rural residence, and employment status of the women. In some places and among some people there is demonstrably more violence, more intensity of dowry practices, and more commitment to dowry itself. Much of the distributional data are problematic in one way or another. The most frequent problem is that the studies are not based on national samples. Furthermore, the interpretation of results is often colored by reformist agendas. There is a tendency to deemphasize differences in frequency from one segment of the population to another so as to build support of dowry death as a general social reform issue. Nevertheless, while the data available for these distributions are of inconsistent quality, they are interpretable in terms of our problem.

Women's Access to Production Roles and Property

Dowry violence is most frequent in north India. Some say that it is an especially severe problem in the Hindi Belt (i.e., Uttar Pradesh, Haryana, Punjab, Delhi, Bihar) (Government of India 1974:75). It is a lesser, albeit increasing problem in the south. There is also a north/south difference in the marriage institution itself. To simplify somewhat, in the north hypergamy is sought after in marriage alliances, in which case brides seek grooms from higher rank descent groups within their caste group (Srinivas 1984). In the south, marriages are more typically isogamous.

The literature comparing north and south India indicates important contrasts at both the ecological and the institutional levels. Based on conceptions developed by Boserup (1970) in a cross-cultural comparative framework on the relationship between the farming system and occupational role of women, Miller (1981) composed a model for explaining the significant north-south differences in the juvenile sex ratio [the ratio of males to females ten years of age and below]. The farming systems of the north are based on "dry-field plow cultivation," whereas in the south the farming systems are dominated by "swidden and wet-rice cultivation" (Miller 1981:28). These two systems make different labor demands. In the wet rice or swidden systems of the south, women are very important sources of labor. In the north, women's involvement in agricultural production is limited. According to Miller, women in the north are excluded from property holding and receive instead a "dowry of movables." In the south, where women are included in the production activities, they may receive "rights to land" (Miller 1981:28). In the north, women are high-cost items of social overhead, while in the south, women contribute labor and are more highly valued. In the north there is a "high cost of raising several daughters" while in the south there is "little liability in raising several daughters." There is thus "discrimination against daughters" and an "intense preference for sons" in the north, and "appreciation for daughters" and "moderate preference for sons" in the south. Miller thus explains the unbalanced-toward-males juvenile sex ratios of the north and the balanced sex ratios of the south (Miller 1981:27–28). The lower economic value of women in the north is expressed in differential treatment of children by sex. Females get less food, less care, and less attention, and therefore they have a higher death rate. In general the Boserup and Miller economic argument is consistent with Engles's thesis about the relationship between the subordination of women and property (Engels 1884, Hirschon 1984:1).

Miller extended her analysis of juvenile sex ratios to include marriage costs (including dowry), female labor participation, and property owning, and found that property owning was associated with high marriage costs and low female labor force participation, both of which were associated with high juvenile sex ratios. That is, the death rate of females is higher when marriage costs are high and women are kept from remunerative employment. Both of these patterns are associated with the "propertied" segment of the population (Miller 1981: 156–159). Her data are derived from the secondary analysis of ethnographic accounts. The literature concerning the distribution of dowry practices and dowry death is consistent with these results.

Miller's analysis shows a general pattern of treatment of females in India. Their access to support in various forms is related to their contribution to production (Miller 1981). This analysis does not explain the problem of dowry violence, but it does demonstrate a fundamental pattern within which dowry violence can be interpreted.

The distribution of dowry varies by caste. In her study of dowry violence victims in Delhi, Kumari found that members of the lower ranking castes report less "dowry harassment" than do those in higher ranking castes (Kumari 1988:31). These results are consistent with Miller's argument since the pattern of exclusion of women from economic production roles varies by caste. Women of lower castes are less subject to restrictions concerning employment outside the realm of reproduction within the household. These women are often poor and uneducated, and are subject to other types of restrictions.

In the framework of caste, dowry practices of higher caste groups are emulated by lower caste groups. This process is known as "Sanskritization" and it may relate to the widely held view that dowry harassment is increasing in lower ranking castes. Sanskritization is the process by which lower ranked caste groups attempt to raise their rank through the emulation of higher rank castes. The emulation involves discarding certain behaviors (such as eating meat or paying bride price) and adopting alternatives (Srinivas 1969). Attitudinal research shows that people of the lower socio-economic strata have a greater commitment to dowry than do those of higher strata (Hooja 1969, Khanna and Verghese 1978, Paul 1986). Although the lower and middle classes are committed to dowry, the associated violence, including higher death rates, is more typically a middle class problem (Kumari 1988).

Employment status of women has an effect on dowry. In her survey of dowry problems in a south Delhi neighborhood, Paul (1986) found that the amount of dowry was less for employed middle class women than it was for the unemployed. This pattern is also suggested by Verghese (1980) and van der Veen (1972:40), but disputed by others (Murickan 1975). This link is also manifested among tribal people undergoing urbanization. Tribal people, ranked more toward the low end of the social hierarchy, typically make use of bride price (i.e., a payment to the bride's family) rather than dowry (Karve 1953). As these groups become more integrated into national life, they will shift to dowry practices to emulate high castes while their women participate less in gainful employment (Luthra 1983). Croll finds a similar relationship in her analysis of post-revolutionary China. She says, "it is the increased value attributed to women's labor which is largely responsible for the decline in the dowry" (1984:58).

Both Kumari (1988) and Srinivas (1984) developed arguments based on non-economic factors. Kumari in effect indicated that if dowry could be explained in economic terms, marriage would be simply a calculation of the value of a woman: if the value were high, bride price would be paid, and if the value were low, dowry transactions would occur. This formulation was presented as a refutation of Madan's dowry-as-compensation argument (Kumari 1988). We agree that reducing this practice to purely economic terms is an absurdity. The argument is not purely economic, but it is certainly consistent with a cultural materialist perspective (Harris 1979) in which symbolic values are shaped by an underlying material relationship that is the basis for the construction of cultural reality.

Delocalization of Social Control

Dowry violence is more frequent in cities (Saini 1983). Delhi has the reputation of having a high frequency of problems of dowry (Srinivas 1984:7). The urban-rural distribution pattern may be a manifestation of the effects of the delocalization of dowry. Dowry, when operative in the relationships among local caste groups in related villages, was to an extent self-regulating through caste *panchayats* (councils) and by the joint families themselves. These groups easily reach into peoples' lives. By contrast, the national level laws have inadequate reach and cannot achieve regulation. While in some areas caste groups continue to function to limit abuses, these groups are less effective in urban settings. Population movements and competition with state level social control mechanisms limit the effectiveness of self-regulation. A government commission study of women's status argues "that because of changed circumstances in which a son generally has a separate establishment and has a job somewhere away from home, the parents cannot expect much help from him, and so they consider his marriage as the major occasion on which their investment in his education can be recovered" (Government of India 1974:74). These views are consistent with the research results reported by Paul, who demonstrates that dowry amounts are higher among people who have migrated to Delhi and those who live in nuclear families, because the families in general and the women in particular are less subject to social constraints (Paul 1986). New brides do not seem to have adequate support networks in urban settings.

Economic Transformation of Society

The custom of dowry has been thrown into disarray by inflationary pressures. The consumer price index for urban non-manual workers has increased from its reference year of 1960 value of 100 to 532 for 1984–85 (Government of India 1987). The media of dowry exchange have changed dramatically because of the increasing availability of consumer goods. It has become increasingly difficult to prepare for giving dowry for a daughter or sister. Sharma argues that, in part, dowry problems are caused by rapid change in the nature of consumer goods which made it no longer possible to accumulate gift goods over a long period as the latest styles in material goods could not be presented (1984:70–71).

The current regime of individual dowry seeking and giving is constituted as a kind of rational behavior. That is, it is achieved through choice, is consistent with certain values, and serves to increase someone's utility. There are a number of things sought by the groom's family in these transactions. Wealth and family prestige are especially important. The family prestige "bought" with marriage expenditures, which is relevant to both the bride and groom's side in the transaction, is no doubt very much worth maximizing in the Indian context. From the perspective of the bride's family, dowry payments involve trading present consumption for future earning power for their daughter through acquiring a groom with better qualities and connections. In a two-tier, gender segregated, high unemployment, inflationary economy such as that of India, one can grasp the advantage of investing in husbands with high future earning potential. It is also possible to argue that in societies with symbolic mechanisms of stratification, it is expected that persons will attempt to make public displays of consumption in order to improve their overall performance and so to take advantage of the ambiguities of the status hierarchy system. The demand for both symbolic goods and future earnings is highly elastic. Family connections, education, and wealth seem especially important in India, and they all serve as hedges against inflation and poverty. With women having limited access to jobs and earning lower pay, it is rational to invest in a share of the groom's prospects. If you ask people why they give dowry when their daughters are being married they say, "because we love them." On the other hand, grooms' families will find the decision to forgo dowry very difficult.

Summary

The distributional data indicate that the relationship between the way females are treated in marriage and their participation in economic production is consistent with Miller's development of the Boserup hypothesis. It is assumed that the pattern of maltreatment of females has been subject to various controls operating at the levels of family, caste, and community. Urbanization reduces the effectiveness of these mechanisms, thus increasing the intensity of the problem. This trend is exacerbated by the economic transformations within contemporary Indian society. It is our viewpoint that policies developed to reduce dowry-related violence will fail if they do not increase the economic value of women.

The criminalization of dowry may have been a politically useful symbol, but it has not curtailed the practice. As dowry is attacked, the state has not adequately dealt with the ante-mortem inheritance aspect of the custom. If dowry continues to provide a share of the family wealth to daughters before the death of the parents, then legally curtailing the practice is likely to damage the economic interests of women in the name of protecting them. One might argue that the primary legal remedy for the dowry problem actually makes it worse because it limits the transfer of assets to women. Perhaps this is why research on attitudes toward dowry indicates a continued positive commitment to the institution (Mathew 1987). India is a society in which most people (most particularly the elite) have given and received dowry; most people are even today giving and taking dowries. Declaring dowry a crime cre-ates a condition in which the mass of society are technically criminals. The moral-legal basis of society suffers, and communal, parochial, and other fissiparous forces are encouraged.

To be effective, anti-dowry legislation must make sure that the social utility provided by dowry practices be displaced to practices that are less problematic, and that the apparent causes of the practice be attacked. To do so would mean that attempts to eradicate the social evils produced by the dowry institution need to be based on an examination of women's property rights so as to increase their economic access. Traditional Hindu customs associated with inheritance give sons the right from birth to claim the so-called ancestral properties. This principle is part of the Mitakshara tradition of Hindu law, which prevails throughout India except in Bengal, Kerala, Assam, and northern parts of Orissa. These properties are obtained from father, paternal grandfather, or paternal great-grandfather. According to Sivaramayya (1984:71), "The Hindu Succession Act (the law which controls inheritance) did not abrogate this right by birth which exists in favor of a son, paternal grandson and paternal great grandson. The availability of the right in favor of these male descendants only is a discrimination against daughters." The right is derived from ancient texts. According to Tambiah (1973:95), the Dharmasastras provide that it is "essentially males who inherit the patrimony while women are entitled to maintenance, marriage expenses and gifts." While the Hindu Succession Act abrogates much traditional law, it specifically accepts the principle of male birth right to the property of the joint family. That is, "When a male Hindu dies after the commencement of the Act, having at the time of death an interest in a Mitakshara coparcenary property, his interest in the property shall devolve by survivorship upon the surviving members of the coparcenary and not in accordance with this Act" (Government of India 1985:3). The Hindu Succession Act in its most recent form provides for the intestate or testamentary inheritance of a female of a share of the family property. Yet the prior right of males at birth is not abrogated. Hindu males own a share of the family rights at birth; females can inherit it. Testamentary succession overrides the principle of intestate succession, and therefore the interests of females can be usurped simply by writing a will. The other procedures for a female to renounce an interest in family property are very simple. Moreover, according to Sivaramayya (1984:58), "no specific formality is required for the relinquishment of the interest beyond the expression of a clear intention to that effect." Instruments of relinquishment can be and are forged.

The ante-mortem inheritance function of dowry has been eroded or perhaps supplanted by transfer of goods to the grooms' family for their consumption and the expression of the so-called prestige of the family. Indeed social science commentary on dowry in India suggests that this aspect of dowry is relatively unimportant in any case because only a small portion of the total marriage expenditure is under the bride's control. There is evidence that even the clothing and ornaments and other personal property of the bride are being usurped (Verghese 1980). Implementation of a gender-neutral inheritance law as advocated by the Government of India Committee on the Status of Women may serve to increase the economic value of women in general, while it serves as an alternative to the ante-mortem inheritance aspect of dowry. Since dowry constitutes a kind of ante-mortem inheritance, it is logical to change the inheritance laws in conjunction with the restrictions on dowry behavior. Sisters as well as brothers need to have a share in the family wealth from birth, and that right should be associated with legal procedures that increase the difficulty of alienation of property rights. There is no question that such a procedure would serve to erode the stability of the patrilineal family by diluting its economic base.

The Government of India has passed legislation such as the Hindu Succession Act (1955) and the Hindu Adoption and Maintenance Act (1956), both of which inter-alia provide for a woman's right of inheritance from her father. For example, under the Adoption and Maintenance Act, a woman has a claim of rights of maintenance from her husband's father in case she is widowed. Moreover, she has the right to claim inheritance from her deceased husband's estate. In spite of these changes, inheritance provisions are quite different for males and females. The Chief Justice of the Supreme Court of India, Honorable Mr. Justice Y. V. Chandrachud wrote that in spite of changes, "some inequalities like the right of birth in favor of a son, paternal grandson and paternal great grandson still persist" (1984:vii). Provision of females with equal rights to inherit ancestral property from birth, or from a bequest, or at the death may reduce dowry problems. Furthermore, property that is allowed to remain in the name of the deceased for any length of time, as is frequently the case in India, should revert to the state. As it stands, property may remain in the name of a deceased ancestor, while his descendants divide it informally among themselves.

The establishment of a gender-neutral inheritance law represents a significant shift in public policy. We argue that there is a link between pro-male property laws and violence toward women. While we assert this position, we also need to recognize that the property laws give coherence and stability to an essential Indian institution, the joint family. The Mitakshara principle of male inheritance rights is both a reflection and a cause of family solidarity. Modifying this principle in an attempt to reduce violence toward women could have a deleterious effect on family coherence. In addition, the fundamental nature of these institutions makes it inconceivable that there would be substantial resistance to these changes. Yet if one considers this issue in historic terms, it is apparent that during the 20th century, legal change is in the direction of gender neutrality, a process that started with the Hindu Law of Inheritance (Amendment) Act (1929) and the Hindu Succession Act (1956), and continues through judicial decisions to the present (Diwan 1988:384). As Diwan notes in reference to the changes brought by the Hindu Succession Act of 1956, "the Mitakshara bias towards preference of males over females and of agnates over cognates has been considerably whittled down" (1988:358). Such change is not easy. The changes brought with the Hindu Succession Act in 1956 were achieved only after overcoming "stiff resistance from the traditionalists" (Government of India 1974:135). The same report states, "The hold of tradition, however, was so strong that even while introducing sweeping changes, the legislators compromised and retained in some respects the inferior position of women" (Government of India 1974:135). It must be remembered that the texts that are the foundations of contemporary law include legislation (such as the Hindu Succession Act itself), case law, and religious texts, so that the constitutional question is also a question for religious interpretation, despite the constitutional commitment to secularism.

We are advocating further steps toward gender neutrality of the inheritance laws so that women and men will receive an equal share under intestate succession, and have an equal chance to be testamentary heirs. The law should thus be gender-neutral while still permitting a range of decisions allowing property to stay in a male line if the holder of the property so chooses. The required social adjustment could be largely achieved through the decisions of a family, backed by the power of the state. Families could express their preferences, but the state would not serve to protect the economic interests of males. The process could involve the concept of birthright as well as succession at death. We do not choose to engage those arguments, but do point out that the rapid aging of the Indian population may suggest that a full abrogation of the Mitakshara principle of birthright would be the best social policy because doing so would give older people somewhat greater control over their property in an economy virtually devoid of public investment in social services for older people (Bose and Gangrade 1988, Sharma and Dak 1987).

There are precedents for such policy at the state level. In Andhra Pradesh, the Hindu Succession Act was amended to provide for a female's birthright interest in the Mitakshara property. In Kerala, the Mitakshara property concept was legally abrogated altogether. Other gender asymmetries in the laws of India need to be attacked. The overall goal of policy should be to increase the economic value of women.

Ethnological theory directs our attention to social recognition of marriage and property transfer as functionally important features of the institution. The state can provide a means of socially recognizing marriage through registration and licensure. The law expresses no explicit preference for traditional marriage ritual, and it is possible to have a civil marriage under the provisions of the Special Marriage Act (1954) through registration with a magistrate. Nevertheless, this system co-exists parallel with the traditional system of marriage, which is beyond the reach of state control. Other marriages may be registered under this act if the persons involved so choose, and if a ceremony has been carried out. These special marriages are an alternative to an unregistered marriage.

We conclude that a useful mechanism for state control of dowry problems is the establishment of universal marriage registration, which does not exist at the present time. Marriage registration is also called for by the first Round Table on Social Audit of Implementation of Dowry Legislation (Bhatia 1988), which may serve to provide some monitoring of dowry abuses and perhaps to manifest the state's interest in an effective marriage institution. It would be naive to assume that such a policy would be widely honored, but as it is, low-income persons do not get married because they do not have the resources for marriage under the traditional non-state controlled regime. There are numerous reform groups that organize mass marriage ceremonies of village people so as to help them escape the burden of marriage expenditures. The point is that compliance is a large problem even under current circumstances.

In conclusion, we feel that the causes of the dowry problems are a product of the low economic value of women, loss of effective social control of abuse through delocalization, and pressures caused by economic transformation. The traditional family, caste group, and community controls which have been reduced in effectiveness should be replaced by state functions. The foundation of state control is universal marriage registration and licensure. The impact of the economic value of women on the problem is indicated by the transition from bride price to dowry among tribal people. It is also associated with a reduction in the extent of gainful employment and lower dowry amounts demonstrated for employed women. A broad program to increase the economic value of women would be the most useful means of dealing with the problem of dowry. Further restrictions on dowry without providing for a radically different property right for females is probably not in the interests of Indian women, since dowry represents ante-mortem inheritance. This underlying paradox may explain the commitment to dowry revealed in attitudinal research with Indian women, even though it is also an important feminist issue. The alternatives include the abolition of the legal basis for the joint family as a corporate unit as has been done in Kerala, or the legal redefinition of the joint family as economically duolineal, as has occurred in Andhra Pradesh.

Note

1. For purposes of comparison, a mid-career Indian academic might be paid 60,000 Rs. per year.

References Cited

Aluwalia, H. 1969. Matrimonial Advertisements in Panjab. *Indian Journal of Social Work* 30:55–65.

Bhatia, S. C. 1988. Social Audit of Dowry Legislation. Delhi: Legal Literacy Project.

Bose, A. B., and K. D. Gangrade. 1988. *The Aging in India, Problems and Potentialities.* New Delhi: Abhinav.

Boserup, Ester. 1970. *Women's Role in Economic Development.* New York: St. Martin's Press.

Chandrachud, Y. V. 1984. Foreword. In *Inequalities and the Law.* B. Sivaramayya, ed. Pp. iv–vi. Lucknow: Eastern Book Company.

Croll, Elisabeth. 1984. The Exchange of Women and Property: Marriage in Post-revolutionary China. In *Women and Property—Women as Property.* Renee Hirschon, ed. Pp. 44–61. London/New York: Croom Helm/St. Martin's Press.

Diwan, Paras. 1988. *Modern Hindu Law, Codified and Uncodified.* Allahabad: Allahabad Law Agency.

Dumont, Louis. 1957. *Hierarchy and Marriage Alliance in South Indian Kinship.* London: Royal Anthropological Institute.

Engles, Fredrich. 1884. *The Origin of Family, Private Property and the State.* New York: International.

Epstein, T. Scarlett. 1960. Peasant Marriage in South India. *Man in India* 40:192–232.

Friedl, Ernestine. 1967. *Vasilika, A Village in Modern Greece*. New York: Holt, Rinehart and Winston.

Goody, Jack. 1973. Bridewealth and Dowry in Africa and Eurasia. In *Bridewealth and Dowry*. Jack Goody and S. J. Tambiah, eds. Pp. 1–58. Cambridge: Cambridge University Press.

_____, 1976. *Production and Reproduction, A Comparative Study of the Domestic Domain*. Cambridge: Cambridge University Press.

Government of India. 1974. *Towards Equality: Report of the Committee on the Status of Women*. New Delhi: Government of India, Ministry of Education and Social Welfare.

_____. 1985. The Hindu Succession Act. New Delhi: Government of India.

_____. 1986. The Dowry Prohibition Act, 1961 (Act No. 28 of 1961) and Connected Legislation (as on 15th January, 1986). New Delhi: Government of India.

_____. 1987. *India 1986, A Reference Manual*. Delhi: Ministry of Information and Broadcasting.

Harris, Marvin. 1979. *Cultural Materialism: The Struggle for a Science of Culture*. New York: Random House.

Hirschon, Renee. 1984. Introduction: Property, Power and Gender Relations. In *Women and Property—Women as Property*. Renee Hirschon, ed. Pp. 1–22. London/New York: Croom Helm/St. Martin's Press.

Hooja, S. L. 1969. *Dowry System in India*. New Delhi: Asia Press.

Karve, Irawati. 1953. *Kinship Organization in India*. Bombay: Asia Publishing.

Khanna, G. and M. Verghese. 1978. *Indian Women Today*. New Delhi: Vikas Publishing House.

Kumari, Ranjana. 1988. Practice and Problems of Dowry: A Study of Dowry Victims in Delhi. In *Social Audit of Dowry Legislation*. S. C. Bhatia, ed. Pp. 27–37. Delhi: Legal Literacy Project.

Luthra, A. 1983. Dowry Among the Urban Poor, Perception and Practice. *Social Action* 33:207.

Mathew, Anna. 1987. Attitudes Toward Dowry. *Indian Journal of Social Work* 48:95–102.

Menon, N. R. Madhava. 1988. The Dowry Prohibition Act: Does the Law Provide the Solution or Itself Consti-

tute the Problem? In *Social Audit of Dowry Legislation*. S. C. Bhatia, ed. Pp. 11–26. Delhi: Legal Literacy Project.

Miller, Barbara D. 1981. *The Endangered Sex, Neglect of Female Children in Rural North India*. Ithaca, NY: Cornell University Press.

Murdock, George P. 1949. *Social Structure*. New York: Macmillan.

Murickan, J. 1975. Women in Kerala: Changing Socio-economic Status and Self Image. In *Women in Contemporary India*. A. de Souza, ed. Pp. 73–95. Delhi: Manohar.

Niehoff, Arthur H. 1959. A Study of Matrimonial Advertisements in North India. *Eastern Anthropologist* 12: 37–50.

Paul, Madan C. 1986. *Dowry and the Position of Women in India. A Study of Delhi Metropolis*. New Delhi: Inter India Publishers.

Saini, Debi. 1983. Dowry Prohibition Law, Social Change and Challenges in India. *Indian Journal of Social Work* 44(2):143–147.

Sharma, M. L. and T. Dak. 1987. *Aging in India, Challenge for the Society*. Delhi: Ajanta Publications.

Sharma, Ursula. 1984. Dowry in North India: Its Consequences for Women. In *Women and Property—Women as Property*. Renee Hirshcon, ed. Pp. 62–74. London/New York: Croom Helm/St. Martin's Press.

Sivaramayya, B. 1984. *Inequalities and the Law*. Lucknow: Eastern Book Company.

Srinivas, M. N. 1969. *Social Change in Modern India*. Berkeley, CA: University of California Press.

_____. 1984. *Some Reflections on Dowry*. Delhi: Oxford University Press.

Tambiah, S. J. 1973. Dowry and Bridewealth and the Property Rights of Women in South Asia. In *Bridewealth and Dowry*. Jack Goody and S. J. Tambiah, eds. Pp. 59–169. Cambridge: Cambridge University Press.

van der Veen, Klaus W. 1972. *I Give Thee My Daughter—A Study of Marriage and Hierarchy Among the Anavil Brahmins of South Gujarat*. Assen: Van Gorcum.

Verghese, Jamila. 1980. *Her Gold and Her Body*. New Delhi: Vikas Publishing House.

Weibe, P. O. and G. N. Ramu. 1971. A Content Analysis of Matrimonial Advertisements. *Man in India* 51:119–120.

Westermarck, Edward. 1921. *The History of Human Marriage*. London: MacMillan and Co.

"Law, Custom, and Crimes Against Women: The Problem of Dowry Death in India"

John Van Willigen and V.C. Channa

1) What is a dowry? What legal, social, economic, and religious purposes does it serve?

2) What is a "dowry death"? How do such deaths occur?

3) Why does the Indian government downplay the problem of "dowry death" in India?

4) What current legal remedies are in place to combat the problem of "dowry death"? Are they effective?

5) What social solutions do the authors argue for to help reduce or eliminate dowries and "dowry deaths"?

SECTION FOUR

Subsistence and Economics

Yanomamö: Varying Adaptations of Foraging Horticulturalists

Raymond B. Hames

The documentation of behavioral variation in cultural anthropology is key to scientific description and explanation. Early ethnographers were content to describe typical patterns of behavior to give readers an idea of what was expected or customary in a given culture. In order to understand variation in cultural practices, anthropologists who are engaged in cross-cultural comparison use individual societies as data points or exemplars of particular traits. While comparative or cross-cultural approaches have been enormously productive, they are not the only useful approach to a scientific understanding of cultural variation. Within each society, individuals or even whole regions may vary enormously in how they conduct their social, economic, and political lives. Accurately documenting this intracultural variation and attempting to associate it with explanatory factors is an important alternative approach. This is not to say that intracultural comparisons are superior to or in competition with cross-cultural approaches. In fact, I would expect them to complement each other. For example, one might demonstrate cross-culturally that warfare is strongly associated with a particular environmental variable. This then might lead us to test that proposition within a particular cultural group if that environmental variable had enough variation.

The goal of this chapter is to describe variation in Yanomamö economic activities at cross-cultural, regional, and individual comparative levels. I will first compare Yanomamö horticultural adaptation to other horticultural groups. The striking finding here is that compared to other horticulturalists the Yanomamö spend an enormous amount of time in the foraging activities of hunting, gathering, and fishing. In many ways they behave like hunters and gatherers, peoples without agriculture. I will then turn to a regional comparison of Yanomamö economic adaptations by comparing how highland and lowland Yanomamö adapt to the rain forest. Here we will find that highland Yanomamö are much more dedicated to a sedentary horticultural life than lowland Yanomamö. Finally, I will turn to an analysis of individual Yanomamö to describe how sex and age determine the division of labor and the amount of time that individuals work.

Demography, Geography, and Environment

The Yanomamö are a tribal population occupying the Amazonian border between Venezuela and Brazil. In Venezuela, the northern extension of the Yanomamö is delimited to the north by headwaters of the Erebato and Caura rivers, east along the Parima mountains, and west along the Padamo and Mavaca in a direct line to the Brazilian border. In Brazil, they concentrate themselves in the headwaters of the Demini, Catrimani, Araca, Padauari, Urari Coera, Parima, and Mucajai rivers. In both countries the total area inhabited by the Yanomamö is approximately 192,000 square kilometers. Dense tropical forest covers most of the area. Savannas are interspersed in forests at high elevations. In general, the topography is flat to gently rolling, with elevations ranging from 250 to 1,200 meters.

Area Exploited

The area village members exploit in the course of their economic activities is probably best characterized as a *home range*. Home ranges differ from territories because they are not defended, but like territories they tend to be used exclusively by a single group. This exclusiveness is not determined by force but by the following simple economic considerations. Important food resources tend to be evenly distributed in the tropical forest. When Yanomamö establish a new village they intensively exploit and deplete resources near the village. Through time, they must travel greater distances where higher return rates compensate for greater travel costs needed to reach areas of higher resource density. At a certain point they will begin to reach areas that are exploited by neighboring villages and if they were to travel still further they would begin to enter areas close to neighboring villages that have been depleted. At this point, it is not economic to travel further since the costs of gaining resources increases (more travel time) while resource density decreases. Thus the borders of home ranges are established with some overlap with the home ranges of adjacent villages. The point to understand here is that a village has near-exclusive use of its home range but that exclusivity is determined by economic factors and not by aggression or threat of aggression.[1]

Where warfare is intensive home ranges may become more like territories if enemy villages are neighbors. In such cases exclusive use of an area is maintained through aggression or threat of aggression. However, it is difficult to determine what is being defended. It may be that the Yanomamö want to keep enemies out of their foraging areas so that they may hunt and gather without the worry of meeting a raiding party; or it may be that a powerful village decides to press its advantage over a weaker neighbor by expanding its range into a neighbor's area to monopolize all the resources in the area. The way in which Yanomamö verbally rationalize their reasons for warring complicates this matter further. Yanomamö may claim that they go to war in order to avenge an insult, a previous killing, an abduction of a woman, or the illness-causing spells cast by a neighboring shaman. Therefore, Yanomamö explain war in terms of vengeance for harm caused by an enemy. The problem here is that neighboring villages invariably have members who have done one or more of the above to a neighbor or a neighbor's ancestor. Why some past wrongs are ignored or acted upon may be determined by economic (territorial) and political factors (opponent's strength or perceived threat). Further complexities of Yanomamö warfare are described in the section on conflict below.

We have little comparative data on sizes of the home ranges of Yanomamö villages. Differences in home range may be the result of ecological differences in resource density or the distribution of neighboring villages. The limited data we have indicate that home ranges vary from three hundred to seven hundred square kilometers, roughly a circular area with a radius of ten to fifteen kilometers. This radius is approximately the distance one can easily walk through the forest in less than a day.

Demography and Settlement Pattern of Yanomamö Villages

Although ethnographers have done extensive and excellent demographic research on some Venezuelan and Brazilian Yanomamö, a complete census for Venezuelan and Brazilian Yanomamö is lacking. Current estimates are 12,500 and 8,500 Yanomamö in Venezu-

ela and Brazil, respectively, for a total of 21,000. However, the figures for Brazil may be significantly less because of epidemics and white-Yanomamö fighting caused by incursions of Brazilian gold miners starting about 1987. I discuss this problem later. In Venezuela and Brazil there are approximately 363 villages ranging in size from 30 to 90 residents each. But some Venezuelan villages in the Mavaca drainage may reach two hundred or more. Napoleon A. Chagnon[2] provides evidence that warfare intensity is associated with village size: where warfare is intense, villages are large. People are forced to associate in large villages both to deter attackers and enable themselves to mount effective counterattacks. Population density ranges from about 6.7 square kilometers per person to 33.5 square kilometers per person.

Anthropologists consider stable settled life one of the important consequences of the agricultural revolution. Although the Yanomamö are agriculturists, villages are unstable in duration, location, and membership. A typical Yanomamö village (shabono) has the shape of a giant circular "lean-to" with a diameter of fifty meters or more depending on the number of people living in the village. Each house or apartment section of a village has a roof and back wall but no front or side walls. Individual family lean-tos are joined in a circle. When a Yanomamö sits in his hammock and looks left or right he sees his next door neighbor; if he looks straight ahead he sees a broad plaza and the dwellings of neighbors on the other side of the village. A village structure rarely lasts more than a few years before the roof thatch begins to rot and the entire village becomes filled with vermin. On such occasions, a new village may be constructed adjacent to the old one.

Aside from the reasons stated above, Yanomamö villages are relocated about every five years because of economic and political considerations.[3] The practice of shifting cultivation forces the Yanomamö to use extensive tracts of land. This is because garden land is used for only two to three years and then abandoned to the encroaching forest. Through time gardens become increasingly distant from the village. When gardens or easily accessible garden land become too distant, the village may move several kilometers to be in the midst of good garden land. Raiding provides a political cause for village relocation. When a village is repeatedly raided by a more powerful enemy, the entire village may be forced to relocate. Such moves are designed to put as much distance as possible between themselves and an enemy and may cause great privation due to loss of easy access to productive gardens.

Highland and Lowland

There is good reason to suspect that there are fundamental differences in environmental quality for Yanomamö who occupy highland and lowland elevations. Defining a precise boundary between the highlands and lowlands is impossible at this point. However, I tentatively define highland populations as villages found in areas higher than 500 to 750 meters of elevation and occupying areas of highly dissected and hilly terrain with small fast flowing streams and occasional savannas. The lowland environment is flatter with slowly moving, larger streams and rivers. This highland-lowland distinction appears to have important implications for the fundamental economic activities of gathering, hunting, fishing, and agriculture.

General ecological research provides considerable evidence that plant biomass and diversity decrease with increases in altitude. Detailed ethnographic research on the Yanomamö points to a similar conclusion. For example, ethnobotanical research by Lizot[4] shows a greater variety of edible plants are available to lowland groups, more plants are restricted to lowland environments, and, on average, more edible plants are available on a monthly basis for lowland groups. In addition, the cultural geographer William Smole[5] notes a decrease in edible plants with increasing elevation. Although it cannot be positively concluded that gathering is more productive in lowland areas since plants differ enormously in food value, processing costs, density, and seasonal availability, available data show that the rate of return in gathering wild forest resources is much greater in lowland than in highland areas.[6]

It is well established that fish are more abundant and larger in the wider, slower moving rivers in lower elevations.[7] A comparison of sites reveals that groups living along large streams or rivers consume twice as much fish and other aquatic prey (frogs, caimans, and crabs).[8] In addition, these lowland groups gain fish at efficiencies two to three times higher than highland groups.[9]

The evidence on game density is less direct. However, it is my impression (based on Yanomamö statements and direct observation) and that of other Yanomamö researchers[10] that game animals are much less abundant in higher elevations. In terms of kilograms of game killed per hour of hunting, Colchester shows that the highland Sanema Yanomamö hunt much less efficiently than lowland Yanomamö.[11] Since both highland and lowland groups use the same bow and arrow technology and are equally adept hunters, it can be concluded that the greater hunting success of lowlanders is the result of greater game densities in the lowlands. A review of the ecological and biogeographical literature on altitude and animal biomass gradients suggests that huntable biomass declines with increasing elevation.[12]

We have no convincing comparative data to indicate significant differences between highland and lowland areas for agricultural pursuits. Agricultural productivity is a complex interplay of many factors such as soil quality, quantity and distribution of rain, and temperature extremes. It is clear, as I show below, that there are significant differences in garden size corresponding to a highland and lowland divide. What is not clear, however, is whether these differences are the result of environmental, economic, or socio-political factors to be discussed below.

Yanomamö Economics

Economically, the Yanomamö, along with most other tribal peoples living in the tropics, are classified as shifting cultivators because most of their dietary calories come from horticulture. However, a significant amount of time is allocated to the foraging activities of hunting, gathering, and fishing. In fact, as we shall see later, the Yanomamö allocate more time to foraging activities than they do to agriculture. Their dedication to foraging is greater than any other Amazonia group and any other horticultural group that we know of.[13] Given this huge investment in foraging activities it might be more accurate to refer to the Yanomamö as "foraging horticulturalists." In this section I describe the basic productive components of the Yanomamö economy.

Technology

Until the mid-1950s the Yanomamö relied on a locally produced "stone age" technology, which was dependent on local, non-metal resources. For example, axes were made of stone, knives of bamboo, fish hooks of bone, and pots of clay. Since that time much of their traditional technology has been replaced by steel cutting tools (machetes and axes), aluminum pots, and other industrial items given or traded to the Yanomamö primarily by missionaries. The main impact of such introductions has been to reduce labor time and increase Yanomamö dependence on non-Yanomamö to satisfy these new needs.[14] In many instances the Yanomamö no longer possess the skills to make or use traditional technology such as clay pots or fire drills.

Gardening

In shifting cultivation, forest is cleared with machetes, axes, and fire. The newly opened forest is then planted with plantains, root crops (manioc, sweet potatoes, and taro) and a large variety of plants that serve as relishes, medicines, and technology sources. After about two to three years of cultivation, the garden is abandoned to the encroaching forest. In most years Yanomamö add to the size of a current garden by clearing adjacent forest. As yields begin to diminish and weeding becomes time consuming, they cease to work old areas of the garden and let them naturally revert to scrub and, later, to forest. Men do nearly all the heavy work involved in clearing, such as slashing the undergrowth and felling large forest trees. Men and women work together to plant the garden and women are responsible for the nearly daily trips to the garden to harvest and weed.

There is considerable variation, as Figure 1 clearly indicates, in the amount of land under cultivation per capita in Yanomamö villages. Per-capita land cultivated in highland villages averages five times as much as in lowland villages, a difference that is statistically significant. There are at least two possible ecological and economic explanations for these differences. Garden land may not be as fertile in higher elevations, or basic crops may not be as productive because of the cooler temperatures in highland areas.15 As a result, highlanders are forced to increase garden size to produce the same quantity of plantains as lowlanders. A second reason to cultivate less land in lowland areas is that foraging success (efficiency) is greater in lowland areas, therefore lowlanders may gain a larger fraction of their diet from foraging, which lessens their dependence on garden food.

There is a basic contrast in subsistence crops relied upon by highland and lowland groups that may have far reaching consequences in helping us understand their economic differences. Lowland groups rely on plantains and bananas as the basic subsistence crop while some highland groups rely more heavily on manioc, a very productive root crop. Where either crop is a staple, it contributes up to forty percent or more of all dietary calories. This difference leads us to ask why some highland groups depend on manioc and what impact dependence on one or the other has on the overall Yanomamö economy. Colchester suggests that manioc is a recent introduction from neighboring groups such as the Ye'kwana.[16] Where manioc has been introduced the Yanomamö have taken it up because it appears to be a forty percent more efficient source of calories than plantains. However, this alleged advantage may disappear since the comparative data on efficiency do not consider processing costs. Some varieties of manioc become poisonous ("bitter") soon after harvesting and must be detoxified. In addition, many varieties require a laborious process of peeling, grating, and baking before consumption. Plantains, in contrast, are easily peeled and quickly cooked by roasting or boiling. Chagnon makes an opposite argument by suggesting that manioc was aboriginal with the Yanomamö and it was replaced by plantains (an Old World crop introduced by the Spanish more than four hundred years ago) because plantains were a more efficient producer of calories.[17] Unfortunately, neither Colchester or Chagnon have quantitative data to back

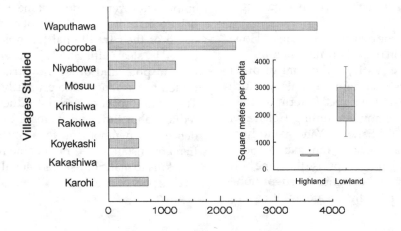

Figure 1
Garden Land Per-Capita (m²) in Nine Villages, and Low-land /Highland Contrasts

up their claims. Clearly, relatively simple research could help settle this issue.

Whether or not manioc or plantains are ancient or recent introductions, dependence on one or the other may have a strong impact on the Yanomamö economy. The key issue here is not one of efficiency but of reliable and predictable yield. Tropical forest peoples tend to rely on crops that can be harvested over a long time. In contrast to temperate horticulturalists, many tropical peoples who grow root crops or plantains do not harvest their entire field during a single harvest period and do not store the crop to tide them through seasons when crop growth is impossible or risky. Instead, tropical cultivators stagger-plant throughout the year so that what is needed can be harvested from the field every few days or week. For example, one can harvest manioc six, twelve, or eighteen or more months after it is planted. This allows the manioc cultivator considerable flexibility in insuring a steady and reliable yield. Plantains, in contrast, have much less flexibility. Although Yanomamö attempt to stagger-plant plantains to gain a reliable weekly or half-weekly yield, a variety of environmental factors thwart this strategy. Dry spells can hasten maturation while prolonged wet spells slow maturation. Also, heavy winds that accompany violent thunderstorms may blow down plantains with heavy maturing racemes (bunches). Yanomamö can salvage blown down bunches of plantains (if they're close to maturation) by hanging them in the village. When the plantains ripen there will be a momentary glut of food, but there will be a lack of plantains in the near future when they would have otherwise matured.

Heavy dependence on plantains by lowland groups may help us to understand their greater reliance on gathering compared to manioc producing highland groups. Since plantains are far less reliable than manioc, lowland Yanomamö may be forced to gather because of periodic underproduction of plantains. Evidence consistent with this idea is presented in Table 1. The only highland group on which we have time allocation (Sanema, in the table) shows that the average adult spends only twenty-six minutes each day gathering, which is the lowest figure in the table and fully one-half of the average time allocated to this task in lowland villages.

If manioc is more reliable than plantains we must ask why plantain-growing lowlanders do not grow more manioc than they currently do. Since lowland gathering is about twice as efficient as highland gathering, it may mean that unreliable plantain production is buffered by highly productive gathering. Since the overall work effort for the highland Sanema is essentially identical to the average level of work for lowland villages (see the Total column in Table 1), I suggest that this is clear evidence that plantain gardening coupled with a high reliance on gathering causes no discernible hardship in overall work effort.

Foraging

Foraging is the simple extraction of resources from the environment without any attempt to modify the

Table 1
Time Allocation in Eight Yanomamö Villages (Minutes per Day)[25]

Village	Hunt	Fish	Garden	Gather	Cook	Manufacture	Misc	Total	Source
Bisaasi	83	86	29	51	42	43	33	367	2
Hasubë	65	19	40	100	ND	ND	ND	[a]	4
Koyekashi	42	85	85	66	26	36	17	357	3
Krihi	32	108	32	54	26	58	65	375	2
Mishi	13	109	81	53	37	149	17	459	1
Rakoi	12	109	44	24	27	68	76	360	2
Sanema	70	15	52	26	59	118[b]	ND	350	5
Toropo	61	56	43	55	41	69	35	359	1
Yanomami	38	40	38	45	54	52	84	357	2
Mean	50	64	45	52	37	62	49	359	

Sources: 1 = Hames, 1989; 2 = Hames, b; 3 = Lhermillier, 1974; 4 = Good, 1989; 5 = Colchester, 1984. ND = no data.

[a] total not given because of incomplete data

[b] technology and maintenance activities are combined and column mean ignores these figures

environment (as agriculture does) to increase the yield of that which is harvested. Hunting, gathering, and fishing are the basic foraging activities. Foraging is the most ancient technique humans use to exploit the environment and an adaptation that humans share with all other animals. What is interesting about Yanomamö foraging is the large amount of time they allocate to it. As time allocation statistics in Table 1 indicate, Yanomamö allocate more than twice as much time to foraging as they do to gardening.

Given the amount of time the Yanomamö spend foraging on a daily basis, the term foraging horticulturalists might be an apt designation for their economic adaptation to the tropical forest. The logic of this designation is further reinforced by the Yanomamö practice of *waiyumö*, or trekking. Trekking is camping in the forest and subsisting mostly by foraging. It usually occurs in the dry season when there is an abundance of forest fruit and the dryness makes walking and camping out pleasant. The probable motivation behind most trekking is to save travel time by taking advantage of abundant vegetable resources distant from the village. However, trekking may also be stimulated by a shortage of garden food or the presence of powerful enemies. If the latter is the cause, then trekking is an adaptation designed for concealment against enemies. Treks may last a week to more than a month and normally include all village members. Dependence on wild resources is not total, since young men are sent from forest camps to gardens to harvest plantains if the wild resources are scarce.

Hunting

Hunting is the main source of dietary protein for the Yanomamö. As we shall later see in the time allocation statistics, hunting is essentially a male activity with important social and ritual functions. Bows and arrows, which measure approximately two meters in length, are the main weapons of the hunt. The long arrow is not accurate beyond about thirty meters. This is of little significance in dense tropical forest where it is rare to have a clear shot at a greater distance.[18] Skills in locating game and stalking it to a short distance are abilities that differentiate good from poor hunters. Game sought ranges from 1-kilogram birds, to 25-kilogram peccaries, and to the occasional 175-kilogram tapir (the largest terrestrial animal in South America). Yanomamö quivers contain large lancelotate (spear shaped) tips for big game, poisoned pencil-shaped tips for monkeys, and harpoon points for birds and small terrestrial game. Because arrows are two meters long a hunter can carry

no more than three arrows on a hunt; however, hunters carry a case which contains a repair kit of thread, resin, and a hand tool to repair damaged arrows.

Although most hunting is done by individuals or pairs, organized group hunts occur under two important circumstances. If a hunter discovers a herd of white-lipped peccaries (a distant relative of the pig weighing twenty to thirty kilograms), he carefully notes the location and immediately returns to the village to alert other hunters who return to cooperatively hunt the herd. To prepare for a feast *(reahu)* organized hunting parties travel great distances and may continuously hunt for a week in order to amass a large quantity of game to provide high quality meals for visiting allies on a variety of social occasions (reahu and *braiai* rituals). During these excursions hunters especially seek highly esteemed game, such as peccaries, turkey-like birds, and monkeys.

Gathering

The harvesting of wild plant resources is an activity that includes all ages and sexes and is commonly organized by families and groups of families. Important resources include honey, palm fruits, brazil nuts, palm heart, and cashew fruit. Men specialize in the risky task of climbing trees to shake loose fruit or to sever fruit-laden branches. The peach palm is especially important. It is planted in gardens but it only begins to yield several years after a garden has been abandoned and it continues to bear for a decade or more. The Yanomamö assert that peach palms are owned by those who planted them and it is not uncommon for disputes to arise over ownership. With the exception of the peach palm, the Yanomamö make little or no effort to harvest fruit trees or palms so they may be harvested on a sustained basis. The Yanomamö fell small, fruit-ladened trees to make harvesting easier, but never such forest giants as Brazil nut or cashew trees because of the enormous labor required.

Fishing

Most Yanomamö villages occupy areas between major rivers that are crossed by small streams. Fish found here are seldom larger than a few kilograms. Nevertheless, fishing is widely and avidly pursued by all ages and sexes, especially in the dry season through hand catching, stream poisoning, and archery. In the dry season small streams begin to shrink, leaving fish in large ponds or cutoffs. The Yanomamö will use a vegetable poison to stun fish and cause them to rise to the surface where they can be grabbed or shot with a miniature bow and arrow. Women sometimes will jointly push a long, broad palm frond through the water to herd fish towards a bank where they can be trapped.

Marriage and Family

Yanomamö marriage rules prescribe that marriage partners ought to be cross-cousins. Ideally, mates are double cross-cousins, a result of the practice of sister exchange. Soon after their first menses, women typically marry men in their early twenties. Although women are required to reside in their husband's village after marriage (patrilocal marriage), a husband must initially live with his in-laws for several years and work diligently for them, performing what is known as bride service. This requirement may be relaxed for high status males. Polygyny (a man having more than one wife) is permitted; ten to twenty percent of all males at any time are polygynists. Ideally, polygynists marry sisters (sororal polygyny) since the Yanomamö believe that sisters get along better. If a woman's husband dies she may be required to marry his brother (levirate marriage) and if a man's wife dies he may claim her sister as a bride (sororate marriage). Men and women average 2.8 marital partners during their lifetime, with about 75 percent of those marriages ending as a result of divorce with the balance as a result of death of one of the partners.[19]

Monogamous or polygynous nuclear families are the rule among the Yanomamö. Deviations from this pattern occur when aged parents live closely associated with married children or when newlyweds dwell with one or the other's parents. Each family has a garden or gardens and is responsible for basic subsistence activities.

Political Organization

Each Yanomamö village is an autonomous political entity, free to make war or peace with other villages. Coalitions between villages are important: nevertheless, such coalitions tend to be fragile and ephemeral. Although the Yanomamö are an egalitarian people, age, sex, and personal accomplishments are important in status differentiation. Yanomamö men acquire high status through valor in combat, accomplished oratory, and expertise in shamanism. However, high status cannot be inherited—it must be earned. Mature men dominate positions of political authority and religious practice. Local descent groups play important roles in regulating marriages and settling disputes within the village.

The village headman is the dominant political leader and comes from the largest local patrilineage (a kin group whose members trace descent through male relatives). When a village is large or when two local descent groups are approximately equal in size, a village may have several headmen. The headman must rely on demonstrated skills in settling disputes, representing the interests of his lineage, and successfully dealing with allies and enemies. Styles of leadership vary: some headmen lead through practiced verbal skills while others resort to bullying. Concerted action requires the consensus of adult males. However, an individual is free to desert collective action if it suits him.

Villages range in size from about forty residents to more than two hundred. As a village increases in size it has a tendency to break into two groups of approximately equal size, which form new villages. As villages become large, kinship relationships become weaker and village headmen are less able to amicably settle disputes.[20] In addition, local resources tend to be more quickly depleted, which causes an increase in work effort.[21] However, if warfare is intense village members are more likely to realize the value of large size as a deterrent against enemies and are more likely to tolerate irksome co-villagers and increased work loads.

Social Control

Conflicts typically arise from accusations of adultery, failure to deliver a betrothed woman, personal affronts, stinginess, or thefts of coveted garden crops such as tobacco and peach palm. For men, if such conflicts move past a boisterous shouting match, a variety of graded, formal duels may occur. If a fight becomes serious, respected men may intervene to cool tempers and prevent others from participating. Frequently, duels end in a draw, which allows each contestant to preserve his dignity. For women, dueling is rare. Instead, a direct attack is made by the aggrieved woman using hands and feet or makeshift weapons.

Conflict

Warfare between villages is endemic among the Yanomamö. While the initial cause of a conflict may be frequently traced to a sexual or marital issue, conflicts are self-perpetuating since the Yanomamö lack any formal mechanisms to prevent aggrieved parties from exacting the amount of vengeance or counter-vengeance they deem sufficient once a conflict has started. The primary vengeance unit is the lineage, but coresident non-kin have some obligation to assist, since coresidence with a feuding faction is seen as implicit support of the faction by the faction's enemies. Most combat is in the form of stealthy raids. The goal is to quickly kill as many of the enemy as possible (who are frequently found on the outskirts of the other village engaging in mundane activities), abduct nubile women if possible, and return quickly home. While the primary goal is to kill mature men and their kin believed to be responsible for a previous wrong, unrelated co-villagers may be killed if there is no safe opportunity to kill primary targets. Endemic warfare has a profound effect on politics and settlement size and location. Each village needs at least one allied village it can call upon for assistance if it is overmatched by a more powerful enemy; and village size and distance between villages tend to increase with the intensity of conflict. Peace between villages may develop if conflict has remained dormant for a long period and there is a mutual need for an alliance in the face of a common enemy. It begins with a series of ceremonially festive visits. If old antagonisms do not flare, visits may lead to joint raids and intermarriage between villages that strongly solidify an alliance. Proximity of missions and government agencies has had little impact on warfare.

Major Changes

Over the last twenty years most Yanomamö have become totally dependent on outside sources of axes, machetes, aluminum cooking pots, and fish hooks and line. These metal goods have replaced much of their stone-age technology. Most of these items have come from missionaries as gifts and wages. Through mission-organized cooperatives, the Yanomamö recently have begun to market baskets and arrows and some agricultural products.

Missionary presence has also distorted the traditional Yanomamö settlement pattern. Yanomamö attempt to gain easy access to mission outposts by moving their villages near a mission. As a result, the normal spacing of about a day's walk between villages has diminished dramatically. For example, around the Salesian mission at Mavaca there are five villages and numerous small settlements with a total population of about nine hundred people within one day's walk. This population density is unprecedented for the Yanomamö and has led to severe depletion of wild resources. In addition, a significant fraction of that population no longer lives in traditional round communal villages but rather in small settlements of two to three houses occupied by a few

families. Despite these changes, missionaries have failed to gain significant numbers of Yanomamö converts to Christianity. The Yanomamö have enormous pride in their culture and have strong doubts about the authenticity or superiority of Christian beliefs.

However, the greatest change and threat to the Yanomamö are the thousands of Brazilian gold miners who have infiltrated Yanomamö territory in Brazil and who have again (July 1993) illegally entered into Venezuela and this time killed seventeen men, women, and children. The situation in Brazil is similar to the situation in the United States in the 1800s when whites expanded into the lands of Native Americans. Miners bring epidemics of measles and influenza that lead to high mortality rates among the Yanomamö. Gold processing pollutes streams with mercury, killing fish and ruining a village's water supply. And open warfare between miners and Yanomamö has killed numerous Yanomamö and disrupted village life.[22]

Time Allocation

In the West, we tend to think of work as something done away from the home for forty hours a week. In subsistence-based tribal populations this sort of definition is as inadequate for them as it is for us. While it is true that the Yanomamö, for example, leave the village to travel to garden, forest, and stream to acquire resources, much work takes place in the village. But the same thing is true in the West. Driving to work, mowing the lawn, shopping for food, washing clothes, and all those other household chores that must be done are not what we would call leisure time activities. We do these tasks to maintain our material well-being. I believe that most of us would define leisure time activities as including dining out, going to the movies, visiting friends, and playing sports. Therefore, one can define work as all those other activities we must do in order to maintain or enhance our material existence. Clearly, adults in the West work more than forty hours per week if we use this expansive definition of work. Researchers who have investigated time allocated to work in the West show that urban European and North Americans work on average 55 to 65 hours per week, or 7.8 to 9.3 hours per day, seven days a week.[23]

Table 1 presents time allocation data for adults in eight Yanomamö villages on a basic set of work activities. The table reveals that the Yanomamö work about 6 hours per day (360 minutes) or 42 hours per week. This is significantly less than the fifty-five to sixty-six hours of work in modern societies. Furthermore, if we compare Yanomamö and related simple tropical horticulturalists to other types of economies (hunters and gatherers, pastoralists, agriculturists, etc.) we find that they are among the most leisured people in the world.[24]

Although Table 1 shows little variation in overall labor time (mean 359, SD 7.88), there is considerable variation among villages in time allocated to various subsistence tasks. Much of the variation can be attributed to local conditions such as the season in which the researcher collected the data, the degree to which a village is associated with missionaries, or special environmental conditions. Nevertheless, the only highland site, Sanema, shows some interesting patterns. This village allocates the third-most time to gardening, the least time to fishing, the second-least amount of time to gathering, and the second-most amount of time to hunting. Gathering and gardening times are probably related, as I suggested earlier. Since the density of wild sources of plant food is lower in the highlands, foraging is not as productive, which leads highlanders to spend more time gardening. Related to this is the higher reliability of manioc gardening, which makes gathering less of an important alternative source of vegetable foods. Another way of expressing the contrasting dependence on foraging (hunting, gathering, and fishing) and gardening in highland and lowland locales is to note that the highland population spends the least amount of time foraging and has the lowest ratio of foraging time to gardening time (2.13:1.0 compared to a mean of 4.43:1.0 for the lowlanders).[25]

The extremely low amount of time highlanders allocate to fishing and the relatively high amount of time they allocate to hunting are also related. High-

landers do little fishing because of difficulties exploiting steep and narrow highland streams. Since fishing and hunting are the only ways of gaining sufficient high quality protein to the diet and fishing is unprofitable, highlanders are forced to hunt more intensively.

Division of Labor

As Figure 2 indicates, women spend significantly more time in cooking, fishing, gathering, and in child care than men do, while men spend more time hunting than women. From what we know about the division of labor cross-culturally these differences in time allocation are not surprising. In all cultures hunting is either predominately or wholly a male activity. Although the data indicate that Yanomamö women do almost no hunting, some qualifications are necessary. Yanomamö women occasionally accompany men on hunting forays to act as spotters and assist in the retrieval of game. Rarely do they ever make kills while with men. However, they occasionally make fortuitous kills of their own while gathering or fishing. Such kills are made without the use of bows and arrows.

Although the data show no significant difference between men and women in gardening there are important differences in garden tasks performed. Men almost exclusively do the heavy work of felling large trees, slashing the undergrowth, and burning the resulting debris prior to planting. Both sexes share in planting, while the daily tasks of weeding and harvesting fall almost exclusively to women. The pat-

Figure 2
Male and Female Time Allocation to Basic Economic Tasks

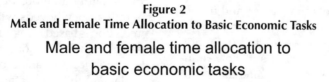

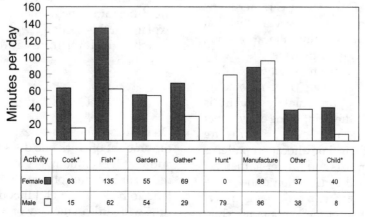

Activity	Cook*	Fish*	Garden	Gather*	Hunt*	Manufacture	Other	Child*
Female ■	63	135	55	69	0	88	37	40
Male ☐	15	62	54	29	79	96	38	8

* Statistically significant difference at 0.05 level or better

tern of men doing tasks which are dangerous and/ or take them far from home is consistent with Judith Brown's model of the division of labor.[26] Brown suggests that women tend to dominate tasks that are compatible with simultaneous child care. Such tasks are not dangerous, can be accomplished near to home, and can be interrupted and resumed with no loss of efficiency.

While Brown's model usefully captures much of the variation in the division of labor among the Yanomamö and other groups, it does not explain why women who are post-menopausal or otherwise unencumbered with intensive child care do not, for example, engage in hunting or tree felling. For dangerous and arduous activities such as tree felling, it is probable that models that focus on physical strength differences may be useful. Or perhaps task linkages are required to complement Brown's model.[27] However, lack of female participation in hunting may require yet another explanation. Hunting is a highly skilled activity that is not easily learned and requires frequent practice to maintain proficiency. On average, little Yanomamö boys spend sixty to eighty minutes per day playing with bows and arrows and spotting, tracking, and stalking small birds and other tiny game near the village. It may be the case that women don't hunt because they never acquired the skills necessary to become proficient hunters.

The question of whether men or women work more can only be answered if we have a reasonable definition of work. Generally, economic anthropologists define work as all of those activities required to directly maintain and enhance survival and reproduction. Thus, it includes rather obvious activities such as the provisioning and preparing of food, construction and repair of tools and shelter, and the acquisition and management of fuel (or firewood, in the case of the Yanomamö). If we use this definition of work, Yanomamö women work about twelve minutes per day more than men, but the difference is not statistically significant. This finding is rather interesting since in the vast majority of horticultural tribal populations on which we have time allocation data, women work significantly more than men.[28] The only societies in which men work significantly more than women are hunters and gatherers. That Yanomamö men and women work approximately equally is therefore consistent with the point made earlier: that they can be best characterized as foraging horticulturalists since their time allocation patterns fall between horticulturalists and hunter-gatherers.

Some may consider this definition unnecessarily restrictive because it ignores a task that is critical for the long-term survival of the Yanomamö: child care. The tropical forest harbors many sources of en-vironmental trauma that are very dangerous to infants and small children. Inside and outside the village there are stinging and biting insects, dangerous plant spines, and poisonous plants, snakes, and insects. Infants and small children are protected from these threats by being carried in slings much of the time and actively watched when they are set down.[29] While caring for infants and small children in this way may be pleasurable, it is also exhausting and difficult. And recall that I defined work as those things we do to enhance or maintain our physical well-being. Just as the Yanomamö labor to provide food for their children, they also physically care for them. In order to assess the impact of child care on overall labor time differences, I must restrict my analysis to data I collected on four Yanomamö villages (Mishimishimaböwei, Rakoiwä, Krihisiwä, and Bisaasi) since none of the other studies collected child care data. When I include direct child care activities (carrying, feeding, nursing, holding, etc.),[30] female work time increases by forty-three minutes per day while male work time increases by only eight minutes per day. If child care activities are added to conventionally defined labor, then Yanomamö women work more than men.

Status and the Allocation of Labor

The Yanomamö, like all people, exhibit strong individual differences in the amount of labor they perform that are independent of sex. Factors such as age, number of dependents, and marital status should logically help us to understand much of the variation. For example, one would expect that a married couple with numerous dependent children to labor more than newlyweds with no dependents. Such a prediction is based on a number of assumptions, such as each family is wholly responsible for supplying its economic needs and economic resources are freely available. While this latter assumption is correct for the Yanomamö, the former is suspect, as I will later explain. In this section I will examine the degree to which age determines individual labor time allocation.

Child Labor Trends

On the basis of our own experiences we expect that the amount of work one does will increase with age and that it eventually begins to diminish when one retires or becomes physically incapacitated. We also tend to believe that childhood should be a carefree time with little in the way of work responsibilities— a time for play, exploration, and learning. An examination of Yanomamö time allocation data will allow us to evaluate all of these ideas; and, since the Yanomamö are relatively typical representatives of the tribal world, we can get a sense of whether our Western experience is in any way typical over the history of humankind.

Figure 3 shows the amount of time children from ages five through eighteen allocate to labor time activities.[31] As can be easily seen, labor time does generally increase with age of the child. The rate of increase is uneven only because of small sample sizes in some of the age groups. Over the chart I have superimposed adult male and female labor time. You will note in this graph that adult females work significantly more (421 min./day) than males (372 min./day). These figures differ from the ones given earlier in the ten-village comparison because they derive from the four villages I studied. I use this smaller data set here because it is the only one broken down by age. As the figure indicates, boys and girls begin to achieve adult labor time levels by the time they become teenagers.

The data presented seem to indicate that childhood is brief and children are quickly recruited into the family work force. To some extent these figures are an artifact of the method I used to collect time allocation data. If I could not observe someone when I was sampling behavior, I had to rely on reports of what they were doing. For example, someone would tell me that all the members of a particular family were in the forest gathering wild palm nuts or weeding the garden. When I was able to accompany fami-

lies on their economic activities I found that children did work but not as hard or as constantly as adults: they worked about forty to eighty percent as much as adults when, for example, a garden was being weeded. Nevertheless, the data tell us something important about work and family life that provides a strong contrast to what occurs in the urban West. Yanomamö children work alongside their parents and are important to the household economy. The family unit does not separate in the morning; children and adults do not go their separate ways to school and work only to rejoin each other in the evening. "School" for a Yanomamö child is in the context of the family economy where they learn how to hunt, gather, garden, fish, and perform all the other activities necessary for them to become competent adults.

Adult Labor Trends

If we extend the analysis of time allocated to work across the entire life span we expect to see labor time increase to a point then decrease. This pattern, an inverted U-shaped curve, is evident for both men and women in Figure 4. However, the shapes of the curves are quite different. Male allocation of labor time begins at a lower level but increases rapidly until it peaks around age thirty-five and then rapidly decreases thereafter. Females, in contrast, begin at initially higher levels, ascend more slowly to a peak at age fifty and then decrease their efforts much more slowly. The last point is rather interesting since the curve shows that women at ages thirty and sixty work about the same amount of time. The factors that account for these patterns are quite complex. Women engaged in active child care (for example, nursing) work less than women who are not.[32] This fact probably accounts for female labor time peaking after menopause. Male labor time decreases quite rapidly after age thirty-five, but I am not sure why the rate of decrease is so much greater than for women. There are two interrelated possibilities. Since males have higher rates of mortality than women at all ages they may also have higher rates of decrepitude than women that is, their ability to do physically demanding labor may decrease more rapidly. Related to this trend is that as men become older they work more at relatively sedentary tasks such as manufacturing and the gardening tasks of weeding and harvesting, and work significantly less in hunting and clearing new gardens.

Figure 3
Labor Time of Children

Labor Time of Children

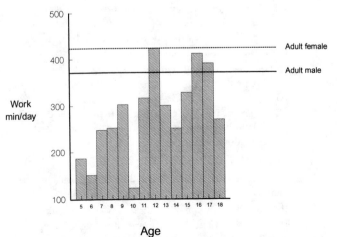

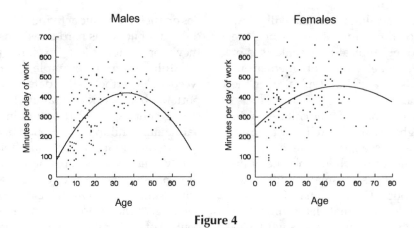

Figure 4
Work over the Life Span

Conclusion

Since 1975 when Allen Johnson reintroduced anthropologists to methods for measuring time allocation,[33] studies of how people use their time have become increasing popular among anthropologists. In this chapter I have attempted to show some of the uses to which time allocation can be put by showing how it can elucidate fundamental ethnographic problems in intracultural variation. I showed that differences in environment between lowland and highland Yanomamö lead to differences in the allocation of time to basic economic activities. We found that highland groups are much more tied to agricultural pursuits because of a lack of high-quality foraging resources. In the area of the sexual division of labor we found that men and women work nearly the same amount of time but allocate their efforts much differently. In addition, we found that if child care activities are included in labor time, then women work significantly more than men. Finally, I showed that time allocation patterns show significant patterns associated with age. Both boys and girls are quickly absorbed into the family's labor pool and adult male labor effort peaks earlier and declines more quickly than it does for women.

In closing I should note that time allocation studies are not simply restricted to the documentation of variation in work effort. Researchers now use the method to quantify patterns of social interaction such as how much time husbands and wives spend together, the size and composition of play groups among children, and patterns of cooperation among co-villagers. So long as ethnographers are interested in quantitative measures of variation in social life we can expect that time allocation studies will play a central role.

Notes

1. R. Hames, "The Settlement Pattern of a Yanomamö Population Bloc," in R. Hames and W. Vickers, eds., *Adaptive Responses of Native Amazonians* (New York: Academic Press, 1983), pp. 192–229.

2. N. Chagnon, *Studying the Yanomamö* (New York: Holt, Rinehart & Winston, 1974).

3. N. Chagnon, *Studying the Yanomamö*; R. Hames, "The Settlement Pattern of a Yanomamö Population Bloc."

4. J. Lizot, *Les Yanomami Centrau* (Paris: Editions de L'Ecole des Hautes Etudes en Sciences Sociales, 1984), p. 54, Table 2.

5. W. Smole, *The Yanoama Indians: A Cultural Geography* (Austin: University of Texas Press, 1976).

6. M. Colchester, "Rethinking Stone Age Economics: Some Speculations Concerning the Pre-Columbian Yanoama Economy," *Human Ecology* 12 (1984): 291–314.

7. M. Goulding, *The Fishes and the Forest* (Berkeley: University of California Press, 1980).

8. G. Saffirio and R. Hames, "The Forest and the Highway," in K. Kensinger and J. Clay, eds., *Working Papers on South American Indians #6 and Cultural Survival Occasional Paper #11*, joint publication (Cambridge, MA: Cultural Survival, 1983), pp. 1–52.

9. R. Hames, "Time, Efficiency, and Fitness in the Amazonian Protein Quest," *Research in Economic Anthropology* 11 (1989): 43–85. Anthropologists measure the efficiency of subsistence activities in kilograms of food gained per hour of work, or kilocalories of food gained per kilocalorie of work.

10. W. Smole, pp. 81 and 227.

11. M. Colchester, p. 300, Table 2; Hames, "Time, Efficiency, and Fitness in the Amazonian Protein Quest," p. 64, Table 6.

12. J. Eisenberg, "The Density and Biomass of Tropical Mammals," in M. Soule and B. Wilcox, eds., *Conserva-*

tion Biology: An Evolutionary-Ecological Perspective (Sunderland, MA: Sinauer Associates, 1980), pp. 35–55; J. Eisenberg, M. O'Connell, and V. August, "Density, Productivity, and Distribution of Mammals in the Northern Neotropics," in J. Eisenberg, ed., *Vertebrate Ecology in the Northern Neotropics* (Washington DC: Smithsonian Institution Press, 1979), pp. 187–207.

13. R. Hames, "Time, Efficiency, and Fitness in the Amazonian Protein Quest."

14. R. Hames, "A Comparison of the Efficiencies of the Shotgun and Bow in Neotropical Forest Hunting," *Human Ecology* 7 (1979): 219–252.

15. Data on Yanomamö garden size is from the following sources: E. Fuentes, "Los Yanomami y las plantas silvestres," *Antropologica* 54 (1980): 3–138; Smole, *The Yanamo Indians*, pp. 36–37; J. Lizot, "Economie Primitive et Subsistence: Essai sur Le Travail et L'alimentation Chez les Yanomami," *Libre* 4 (1980): 69–113; and J. Lizot, "La Agricultural Yanomami," *Anthropologica* 53 (1980): 3–93. Information on cultivated bananas and plantains can be found in N.W. Simmonds, *The Evolution of Bananas* (London: Longmans & Green, 1979).

16. M. Colchester, p. 301.

17. N. Chagnon, *Yanomamö, the Fierce People* (New York: Harcourt Brace Jovanovich, 1992).

18. R. Hames, "A Comparison of the Efficiencies of the Shotgun and Bow in Neotropical Forest Hunting."

19. T. Melancon, "Marriage and Reproduction among the Yanomamö of Venezuela" (Ph.D. diss., Pennsylvania State University, 1982). Cross-cousins are offspring of siblings of the opposite sex. For example, your father's sister's children are your cross-cousins and so are your mother's brother's children. Double cross-cousin marriage is set up when two men marry one another's sisters. The Yanomamö prescribe that the offspring of such unions should marry. These people are double cross-cousins because (using the male as an example) a male is marrying a woman who is simultaneously his father's sister's daughter and his mother's brother's daughter.

20. N. Chagnon, *Yanomamö, the Fierce People.*

21. R. Hames, "The Settlement Pattern of a Yanomamö Population Bloc."

22. N. Chagnon, *Yanomamö: The Last Days of Eden* (New York: Harcourt Brace Jovanovich, 1993); N. Chagnon, "Covering Up the Yanomamö Massacre," *New York Times,* October 23, 1993; see also Saffirio and Hames, on the impact of road construction on Yanomamö economy, and N. Chagnon and T. Melancon, "Reproduction, Epidemics, and the Number of Kin in Tribal Populations: A Case Study," in N. Keyfitz, ed., *Population and Biology: a Bridge between Two Disciplines* (Liege: Ordina Editions, 1984), pp. 147–167, on the effects of epidemics spread by whites.

23. R. Hames, "Time, Efficiency, and Fitness in the Amazonian Protein Quest." Adult labor time is the average of male and female labor time.

24. Sources for time allocation data in Table 1 are as follows: Colchester, p. 299; K. Good, "Yanomami Hunting Patterns: Trekking and Garden Relocation as an Adaptation to Game Availability in Amazonia, Venezuela" (Ph.D. diss., University of Florida, 1989); Hames, "Time, Efficiency, and Fitness in the Amazonian Protein Quest"; A. Lhermillier and N. Lhermillier, "Vie Economique et Sociale d'une Unite Familliale Yanomami" (thesis, L'Ecole Pratique des Hautes Etudes, 1974); Lizot, "Economie Primitive et Subsistence."

25. Ibid.

26. J. Brown, "A Note on the Division of Labor," *American Anthropologist* 72 (1970): 1073–1078.

27. G. P. Murdock and C. Provost, "Factors in the Division of Labor by Sex: A Cross-Cultural Analysis," *Ethnology* 12 (1973): 206–212; M. Burton and D. White, "Sexual Division of Labor in Agriculture," *American Anthropologist* 86 (1984): 568–583. In their task linkage model Burton and White show that the sex that begins a task that has a series of steps is more likely to complete the subsequent steps. For example, if women harvest food they are more likely to perform the processing and storage tasks that immediately follow harvesting.

28. R. Hames, "Time, Efficiency, and Fitness in the Amazonian Protein Quest."

29. R. Hames, "Variation in Paternal Care among the Yanomamö," in B. Hewlett, ed., *The Father's Role: Cultural and Evolutionary Perspectives* (Chicago: Aldine de Gruyter, 1992), pp. 85–110.

30. Ibid.

31. The data reported here on the division of labor, male and female labor time, and child labor time are taken from data I collected in the villages of Mishimishimaböwei-teri, Rakoiwä-teri, Bisaasi-teri, and Krihisiwä-teri in 1986 and 1987. The data set consists of seventy-three adult females and seventy-six adult males. Adults are defined as anyone over the age of fifteen years who is married or has been married.

32. Ibid.

33. A. Johnson, "Time Allocation in a Machiguenga Community," *Ethnology* 14 (1975): 301–310. See also the continuing series of studies of time allocation, in various societies, that are published by the Human Relations Area Files.

Suggested Readings

Biocca, E. Yanoama: *The Narrative of a White Girl Kidnapped by Amazonian Indians.* New York: E.P. Dutton, 1970. Helena Valero was captured by Brazilian Yanomamö when she was twelve years old. This book is the exciting account of her capture, problems in adjusting to Yanomamö social life, marriage to several Yanomamö men, and eventual release to missionaries.

Chagnon, N. *Yanomamö: The Fierce People.* 4th ed. New York: Holt, Rinehart & Winston, 1992. This is perhaps the most popular ethnography written in the last several decades. It is an introductory yet detailed ethnography of the Yanomamö with a special focus on kinship, social organization, and politics.

_____. *Yanomamö: The Last Days of Eden.* New York: Harcourt Brace Jovanovich, 1993. A more personal and accessible account of the Yanomamö than Chagnon's standard ethnography listed above. It presents a lucid picture of what it is like to do fieldwork with the Yanomamö and some contemporary problems faced by the Yanomamö.

Early, J., and J. Peters. *The Population Dynamics of the Mujacai Yanomamö.* New York: Academic Press, 1991.

This monograph describes Brazilian Yanomamö with a special emphasis on demography in relation to social organization. In addition, it presents a novel explanation of mother-in-law avoidance by the son-in-law, a moderately common cross-cultural phenomenon.

Lizot, J. *Tales of the Yanomami: Daily Life in the Venezuelan Forest.* Cambridge: Cambridge University Press, 1985. Jacques Lizot is a French social anthropologist who has worked with the Yanomamö for nearly two dozen years. He presents vignettes of Yanomamö life in novelistic fashion with stories of romance, vengeance, politics, shamanism, and women's lives.

"Yanomamö: Varying Adaptations of Foraging Horticulturalists"

Raymond B. Hames

1) Who are the Yanomamö and where do they live?

2) Define the Yanomamö in terms of their marriage/kinship patterns, systems of social control, political organization, and other social institutions.

3) Define the differences, in terms of topography, available resources, soil productivity, forest cover, and other factors, between the highland and lowland environments of the Yanomamö.

4) In general, what are the various components of the Yanomamö economic system, and how does it vary between the lowlands and the highlands?

5) What resources are emphasized in both zones, and what economic, environmental, and human factors affect these differences?

KALAHARI SAN:
SOMETIME HUNTER-GATHERERS

Edwin N. Wilmsen

The San peoples who live in and around the Kalahari Desert in southern Africa speak several languages belonging to a larger linguistic family called Khoisan, all of which have many click sounds among their consonants. The term *Khoisan* is composed of two words, *khoi* and *san*.[1] The first word is derived from khoe, which means simply "people" in one large division of Khoisan languages, while *san* can mean either "aboriginal people" or "people poor in livestock who must forage for food" in those same languages. This distinction came to be solidified in both popular and academic thinking as marking a real difference between "Khoi" peoples (called Hottentot in the past) who were comparatively wealthy herders and "San" peoples (often called Bushmen in the past) who were hunter-gatherers.[2] Thus, San is not like most other ethnographic terms, which are intended to name a particular group that might be thought to have a common ancestry or history. Instead, the peoples ethnographically classified as San speak at least ten mutually unintelligible languages plus a number of distinct dialects today; in addition, several other languages are no longer spoken. Although described as foragers in the ethnographic literature, these peoples have (as we shall see) engaged in a wide range of economic and social practices, the development of which can be traced through the past two thousand years. We will need to look into those years in order to place these peoples in their social and cultural context.

Some anthropologists paint a very different picture of Kalahari San than I portray here. In order not to be hopelessly confused by this, you need to be aware that a debate about the ethnographic status of these peoples (and, more generally, contemporary hunter-gatherers all over the world) is now going on in anthropology. There are two facets to this debate. One is simply about the history of these peoples and the extent to which they have been engaged with or isolated from other peoples, especially during the last couple of centuries or so. The other facet is connected to a broader concern that is also currently being discussed by anthropologists; this has to do with how we represent other peoples to a Euroamerican audi-

ence, such as students like yourself. In the specific case of the Kalahari San, this second facet includes the question of the extent to which these peoples may be represented as living examples of prehistoric hunter-gatherers on a lower, or more primary, level of cultural evolution than ourselves. Ethnographers who believe the Kalahari San are such examples argue that these peoples had remained, until as late as 1970, relatively isolated from other, non-San peoples—not totally isolated, of course, but enough to avoid outside influences that would change their hunter-gatherer status. In effect, these ethnographers argue that these peoples had little recognizable history and thus feel justified in paying it scant attention. Other anthropologists, of whom I am one, argue to the contrary that far from having been isolated, Kalahari San were actively engaged with their neighbors throughout history and, therefore, this history has a strong bearing on the contemporary appearance of a few of these peoples as hunter-gatherers. We maintain that they are not primal hunter-gatherers at all but are very poor rural people who forage on the fringes of the Kalahari economy because through the unfolding of the social-economic history of the region they are denied access to a more comfortable place in its current social formation.[3]

Before looking at this history, we must consider the distribution and composition of the Khoisan language family and its speakers. There may be one hundred thousand Khoisan-speakers living today; about fifty thousand are ethnographically classified as San. There are three major divisions of this language family—northern (!Kung), central (Khoe), and southern (Twi)—each with a distinct grammatical structure and vocabulary. !Kung has five dialects of which the best known is Zhu|oasi (abbreviated Zhu or Ju),[4] which is also the name of the people made anthropologically famous by the ethnographies of Lorna Marshall[5] and Richard Lee[6] and by John Marshall's film *The Hunters*. Khoe has the greatest number of speakers and the greatest number of currently spoken languages, including Nama—the language of all Khoi herders in Namibia—and Cape Khoi, once spoken by herders over all of western

South Africa but now confined to a few communities near the Orange River; some Khoe languages are not mutually intelligible. Only one Twi language is still spoken, in southern Botswana; those formerly spoken in South Africa have died out.

Peoples who speak these languages are now found only in southern Angola, northern Namibia, and most of Botswana, with a handful in adjacent parts of Zambia and Zimbabwe. While this is a large area (nearly twice the size of Texas), they once occupied a much larger portion of the southern African subcontinent. In the eighteenth century, the first Europeans to enter the region found Khoisan peoples in the entire western half of southern Africa from its tip at the Cape of Good Hope almost to the mouth of the Congo River (an area not quite as large as the continental United States). Archaeological and linguistic evidence shows that about two thousand years ago the ancestors of these peoples lived throughout the entire southern subcontinent below the Zambezi River.

A Short Social History of Southern Africa

An overview of the mosaic of southern African history that brought about these changes will help to locate the San peoples of the Kalahari in their contemporary political and social context. Over two thousand years ago, Khoisan peoples seem to have been the only human inhabitants of this region and had developed a variety of hunting-fishing-gathering economies adapted to its highly diverse local ecologies. Then, about or slightly before two thousand years ago, cattle and sheep were introduced from sources in the north and incorporated into local Khoisan foraging economies. Very little is known about how this took place or who was involved, but we can be confident that Khoe-speakers played an important role because the basic pastoral vocabulary of most southern African herders, including Bantu, is Khoe in origin.

Bantu peoples began moving down from central Africa shortly after this initial introduction of livestock. Small groups of families were the main, if not sole, units of movement. With them, they brought horticulture—sorghum, millet, cowpeas, and melons—and goats, as well as iron and copper metallurgy. Relations between these incoming Bantu and indigenous Khoisan must have involved considerable mutual exchange; Bantu peoples added cattle-keeping to their economies while Khoisan acquired metals, field crops, and goats (all Khoisan languages incorporate Bantu goat terms). But material items

were not the sole elements of exchange. In the eastern half of the subcontinent, the Bantu-Khoisan distinction became increasingly blurred through amalgamation of the peoples themselves. We cannot pinpoint details of the means by which this took place so long ago, but we can be confident that some form of kinship extension associated with marriage between Bantu and Khoisan persons was a key factor. Such marriages, and non-marital matings as well, must have been very common, perhaps preferred, because genetic studies have demonstrated that today people who speak the Bantu languages Kizulu, Isixhosa, and Sindebele[7] have about equal proportions of Khoisan and Bantu ancestry; indeed, this ancestry is praised in the poems that recount the oral histories of these peoples. These languages themselves (and Sesotho to a lesser extent), while Bantu in structure and lexicon, incorporate many click consonants and a large vocabulary (especially in the domain of animal husbandry) from Khoisan sources. The fact that Bantu languages, though radically altered, continued to be spoken while Khoisan was not and Bantu social forms became the norm for all suggests that Bantu-speakers, though increasingly absorbing Khoisan persons and cultural elements into their social formation, were politically hegemonic in the eastern region and Bantu ideology was more highly valued there. Thus, in this eastern region peoples, economies, and languages had long merged to such an extent that when Europeans arrived there were no peoples or languages there that could be called Khoi or San and no economies that could be called hunter-gatherer.

The social history of the western half of the subcontinent is similar in outline, but there are important differences. Bantu peoples arrived at roughly the same time bringing essentially the same economic suite; they encountered Khoisan pastro-foragers who probably spoke !Kung languages in Angola and Khoe languages farther south in the Kalahari of Botswana-Namibia. But here similarities give way to differences, the most salient being that Khoisan-speaking peoples continued to live everywhere in this western region right up to the time Europeans arrived (and, as mentioned above, all peoples who speak Khoisan languages today still live here). Also, with the exception of G|wi and G||ana peoples who live in the central Kalahari, peoples who speak Khoe languages in Angola, Botswana, and Namibia are genetically and physically indistinguishable from their Bantu neighbors and until recently Khoe social forms were predominant in this area. This is strong evidence that, in contrast to the east, during the early centuries of association ideological values and political power were the prerogatives of Khoe peoples and Bantu were drawn into Khoe social networks through marriage and other kinds of mating alliances (these are described in the section on kinship) rather than the reverse. Other than this, the early history of Bantu-Khoisan relations in the west is not so well known. The Bantu language, Shiyei, incorporates a large click inventory of Khoisan origin and, therefore, the Wayei people of the Okavango Delta must have a long history of intimate association with Khoisan peoples. These peoples along with speakers of the western-Bantu Herero group of languages (Otji-herero, Oshivambo, and others)[8] are the only southern African peoples who employ Bantu pastoral terminology, which implies a different economic history in the region for them.

Part of that history seems to be linked to the establishment of Portuguese trading entrepôts on the Atlantic coast between Congo and Luanda in the sixteenth century. These ports vigorously stimulated ancient trade networks stretching into the interior by offering a wide variety of European goods (cloth, clothing, glass beads, guns, pots and pans, tobacco, sugar, coffee, and tea), which rapidly gained the status of necessities in local economies. This set off intensive activity to supply the commodities demanded by the Portuguese in return: ivory, diamonds, hides, cattle, and, later, slaves. In the process, the indigenous social landscape was disrupted and another period of population movements was set in motion; some peoples moved to escape marauders and slavers, some to take advantage of newly opened economic opportunities. Oral histories place the movement of Herero peoples from Angola into Botswana-Namibia during this time and there are suggestions that Zhu then moved down as well (I shall return to this). In the eighteenth and nineteenth centuries, other Europeans—and Americans and Canadians—opened southern routes to trade through South Africa, and in so doing stimulated similar needs and precipitated similar upheavals.

The subsequent colonial history of the region, particularly that of South Africa and Namibia, is filled with bloody atrocities, many involving the massacre of Khoisan peoples—especially those called Bushmen. Because of this, it is often said that these peoples played no further role in the development of southern African history but instead defended an isolated independence from it. Another common belief is that Khoisan peoples were almost entirely exterminated in the colonial encounter; this is true for the mountain and high plains areas of South Africa, but happily not elsewhere. This has led to the romantic notion that, as one writer put it, only in the great wasteland of the Kalahari can a last living remnant of their authentic remains be found; people who think

this way are usually looking for what they believe to be "pure" primitive Bushman hunter-gatherers.[9]

The chronicle of genocide, though grim, is only partly true; large numbers of Khoisan people, perhaps the majority, were incorporated into newly emerging groups. We have already seen that the people who speak Kizulu and Isixhosa as well as some others classified as Bantu have about equal proportions of Khoisan and Bantu ancestry; there are perhaps ten million of these descendants of eastern Khoisan forebears living today. More recently, at the end of the nineteenth century a group of people came to be identified as "Coloured" in South Africa; although they speak Afrikaans[10] rather than a Khoisan language, they are descendants of mainly western Khoisan ancestors who since the seventeenth century had had intimate association with Bantu and Europeans, as well as the Malayans whom the Dutch imported into the Cape as slaves. There are four million of these people today.

The Kalahari in the Nineteenth Century

We now have the necessary historical background to focus more closely on the Kalahari itself. As the nineteenth century began, Khoe-speaking peoples continued to occupy by far the largest part of the Kalahari, as they had done for millennia. But now these Khoe peoples shared most of the region with others who today are collectively known as Bakgalagadi.[11] These peoples had come into the Kalahari at least by 1600 (this date is derived from analysis of oral histories) and most likely much earlier; since then Khoe and Kgalagadi have maintained close economic and social ties, including a considerable amount of marriage.[12] The economy practiced by all these peoples is called pastro-foraging; in this economic system, hunting and gathering remain important but livestock are also kept, small numbers in poorly watered areas and vast herds on the better ranges. The southern African suite of crops—sorghum, millet, melons, and cowpeas—is grown.[13] In the Okavango Delta-Lake Ngami-Botletli River belt, Khoe and Wayei added intensive fishing and aquatic plant harvesting to this pastro-foraging economy.

Around 1750, Bantu-speaking Tswana peoples began moving up from the south; at that time, these peoples were not very different in most economic and political respects from the Khoe and Kgalagadi peoples they met in the Kalahari. All were organized in small extended family groups under a local leader; groups were composed of thirty to forty households with no more than about three hundred persons in total; associations with other groups were maintained through marriage alliances; identity distinctions of the kind we call "tribal" or "ethnic" were apparently not very important, if they existed at all, judging by the many inter-group marriages recorded in genealogies collected from descendants of the people of this time. A later *kgosi* (chief) of Batswana[14] said of the relations among Bantu and Khoe peoples, "There was in those times no question of overlordship of one people over another. It was simply a mutual understanding; at that time we had no strength by which we could force them to become our servants."[15]

This relative social equality came to an end early in the nineteenth century. European goods were then filtering up in greater quantity to the southern margins of the Kalahari from the South African trading ports, and the Kalahari had become the major source of ivory and ostrich feathers, because the animals that produced these goods had been slaughtered almost to extinction farther south in order to meet the European demand. This demand accelerated until in the 1860s and 1870s about three thousand elephants were killed every year in the Kalahari. Enormous profits were realized from the ivory produced. Ostrich feathers were even more profitable, selling in London for as much as $1,000 per pound.[16] Batswana, whose lands straddled the area between European traders and Kalahari commodities, were ideally situated to exploit the trade. The Tswana kgosi, Khama III, had an annual income from these sources and his huge cattle herd of £3,000 in the 1870s; this would have made him a millionaire in modern terms. Khama was able to extract this large income because of the enormous growth of the Tswana *merafe* (polities);[17] whereas his grandfather had been leader of about three hundred pastro-foragers who were not very different from peoples classified ethnographically as Bushmen today, Khama was head of a state with more than thirty thousand people and considered himself a king on a par with Queen Victoria.[18] Khama's cousin, Sechele, ruled an equally large Tswana *morafe* and controlled most of the Kalahari.

This is an astonishing social transformation to have taken place in hardly more than half a century; we must look briefly at how it happened. Doing so will help explain how some San peoples were reduced to a state of rural poverty that made them appear to ethnographers in the 1950s and 1960s to be simple hunter-gatherers.

In 1826, Kgari (a kgosi of one of the small Tswana groups described above) strengthened his position by establishing what is called the *kgmelo* (milk-jug) system; in essence, he decreed that half of all products produced by people under his control belonged to the kgosi—half of every jug of milk (hence the name), one tusk of every elephant, five of every ten feathers, and so on. He also assigned his *dikgosana* (male relatives) the task of overseeing the collection of this tribute and allowed them to keep a part for themselves; it was thus in the interests of dikgosana to collect as much tribute as possible. To do so they recruited hunters from all surrounding groups, Khoe and Kgalagadi as well as Tswana; these hunters produced almost all the ivory and feathers for the trade.

Cattle were important in this system. They were lent out by the dikgosana to the hunters under conditions of patronage called *mafisa*, in which the recipient becomes a client of the cattle owner and assumes not only the responsibility to manage the patron's herd properly but also the obligation to support the patron's wider economic and political interests. Failure on the client's part to perform to the patron's satisfaction results not only in the withdrawal of the mafisa cattle but also the forfeiture of the client's animals. Failure could be simply the production of too little ivory, and as elephants became scarce, this happened frequently. This could, and often did, lead to the client's impoverishment. Batswana elites gained thereby a degree of control over Khoe and Kgalagadi as well as poor Tswana peoples' economic lives.

This economic control was translated into political control as the trade intensified. Dikgosana made sure that they remained the only channel through which commodities could be passed to the kgosi and on to the traders; this meant that Khoe and Kgalagadi hunters had very little direct access to traders and soon were forced to hand over both tusks and all feathers to dikgosana, for they had no other market. But in the 1850s this was not yet the case: in a passage that reveals the nature of earlier indigenous trade, a European trader named Chapman wrote, "My Bushmen begged me to shoot an ostrich, as they were collecting black feathers to adorn the heads of Ndebele warriors"; as Chapman wanted the white feathers popular in Europe, he and his "Bushmen" struck a mutually beneficial deal.[19] Eventually, as kgamelo strengthened elite power, European goods filtered back exclusively through the same dikgosana channels. The kgosi kept the most and best for himself, and dikgosana allowed only a few less valuable items (mainly tobacco and some glass beads) to pass further down the line. This rapidly strengthened the class structure inherent in the social division between chiefly and commoner members of a group (the word kgosi in fact is derived from the same root as the word for wealth), and by mid-nineteenth century a new class, *malata* (serfs), had come into being, composed almost entirely of Khoe and Kgalagadi peoples. However, by no means were all of these latter people reduced to serf status; many had previously become Tswana through marriage, concubinage, and the recruitment of whole groups to meet the growing labor needs of the expanding merafe.[20]

Only those whose labor was not needed were not recruited. For the most part, they were in the most desert-like parts of the Kalahari farthest from developing centers. These people were usually dispossessed of cattle, both *mafisa* and their own, and necessarily relied more heavily on foraging than did others. This was the first step to San hunter-gatherer poverty. Until the 1870s, however, even these people retained a significant degree of economic leverage as the primary producers of the wealth that enriched their Tswana masters. Ten years after the ostrich-feather deal, one of Chapman's companions recorded this scene of San bargaining power: "There has been a game of diplomacy between Chapman and the Batswana all the morning, the object of the latter being to persuade the Bushmen to bring the tusks of Chapman's elephants to them, or at least within their power."[21]

The "Bushmen" who were negotiating terms with both Batswana and Europeans in this scene were Khoe peoples living in the Ngamiland district of northwestern Botswana (an area about the size of New Jersey). The great majority of place names in this district as well as in adjacent Namibia are, even today, Khoe. Khoe peoples continue to live in the eastern and southern parts of Ngamiland and farther west in Namibia; but in a narrow strip along the border, most of the San inhabitants today are !Kung-speaking Zhu. A German geographer, Siegfried Passarge, who worked in this area between 1896 and 1898 and wrote the first ethnography of San peoples, thought that this indicated that Zhu were relatively recent immigrants into a country formerly occupied by Khoe;[22] evidence is accumulating which suggests he was right. The move probably has its roots in the upheavals in the sixteenth and seventeenth centuries that followed the establishment of Portuguese trading ports on the Congo-Luanda coast. As I have already said, the indigenous social landscape was severely disrupted by this trade, especially after the demand for slaves became great. In the scramble to supply the trade or to escape slavers, many peoples migrated. The Khoisan peoples of northern Angola, who we may be sure spoke a !Kung language, were displaced 250 miles southward into the middle of the country where they live today. Zhu lived too far south and east to be subject to heavy slaving predation, and as the Portuguese did not reach southern Angola until the late 1840s they were well placed to take advantage of economic opportunities newly opened by the trade.[23] Archaeological evidence shows that glass beads and implements made from blast-furnace iron (made only in Europe and America at that time) were widespread in Ngamiland and northern Namibia beginning in the seventeenth century; these, along with new introductions of native pottery, mark these emigrants from the north.

Then in 1795, Batswana moved into the area and within fifty years had subjugated the Khoe and Wayei who lived around the Okavango Delta; Batswana generally refer to these peoples as *Makoba* (note the *ma* prefix), which means "menial people." Shortly after 1860, they extended their hunting and herding range westward. A Tswana man described their relations with the Zhu living there: "We just ruled them . . . it was good that they were so afraid of us, because if they had tried to fight, we would have slaughtered them."[24] A Zhu man portrayed the encounter this way: "They put us under the carrying yoke. We had to carry the meat that they shot . . . and a line of porters would carry bales of *biltong* (dried meat strips) back to Tsau."[25] Batswana also brought Zhu persons back to work on their cattle posts, and sent cattle out to the waterholes to be tended by Zhu.

The Atlantic slave trade also came into the area sometime in the early nineteenth century, although by no means as disastrously as farther north. Oral histories describe the social context in which this trade took place:

> They bought Kxoé children with bundles of goods. Sometimes a grandfather-headman sold his nephews to the Mbari, sometimes the son of his older sister, sometimes of his younger sister. Also a father exchanged his son for woven cloth from Mbari men. If he had no slave available he gathered the Kxoé men; they hunted children and women and took them back to their place.[26]

The texts specifically include Zhu among those captured; Zhu in turn captured Kxoé children to sell to the Mbari agents of the Portuguese. We have evidence that substantiates this native oral history. In 1865, a group of European traders organized a posse to avenge the murder of one of their partners by Ovambo; among the avenging party were twenty "Bushmen (almost surely Zhu) willing enough to fight the Ovambos who make slaves of them."[27]

Commodity trade, nevertheless, was far more important. Carl Hugo Hahn, one of the first Europeans in northern Namibia, gives a clear indication of the extent of Khoisan participation in this trade in 1850:

> At the lowest estimate I can make, fifty to sixty tons of copper ore must go yearly to Ondonga. Bushmen are so jealous of this trade, that to this day they have not allowed strangers to see the places where they dig. . . . Other Bushmen pre-

pare salt from saltpans in the form of sugarloaves and bring them to Ondonga to sell, from where they go on to other tribes.[28]

As in the east, ivory and ostrich feathers were the most valuable items as far as Europeans were concerned and many came to get them; about four hundred of the three thousand elephants killed annually in the Kalahari as a whole during the 1860s and 1870s came from the comparatively small area we are now discussing, most of them killed by Khoe and Zhu. Lee justly remarks that Zhu "recall the period with a great deal of affection as a time of intense social activity and economic prosperity."[29] Although the intensity diminished in the 1880s, a degree of trade continued, almost exclusively in hides and pelts. This caused a German soldier who patrolled the Namibian side of Zhu country in 1912 to remark that on the Botswana side "modern culture is established. Our neighbors [Batswana and British] have ensconced trade relations with the Bushmen."[30] Zhu participated actively in this trade, as they had in previous generations; this gave them a degree of economic security no longer enjoyed by Khoe peoples.

The First Half of the Twentieth Century

Several traumatic changes coincided in the mid-1880s: elephants were wiped out in the Kalahari, so there was no more ivory; ostrich feathers went out of fashion in Europe and ostrich farms were established at the Cape, so Kalahari feathers became worthless. The economic vitality that had attracted hundreds of Euroamerican traders to the Kalahari and engaged almost every one of its inhabitants collapsed. The heyday of hunting had passed; the activity and prosperity of the previous quarter-century was over. Kalahari labor thus lost its value in the Kalahari. As a result, San—Khoe and !Kung alike—lost the little bargaining power they still retained. This was the second step to San hunter-gatherer poverty.

At the same time that hunting collapsed, however, gold and diamonds were discovered in South Africa; a modern capitalist economy was quickly established to exploit these riches and soon dominated the subcontinent. The colonies surrounding South Africa rapidly became what has been called a labor reserve, sending men as needed to work the mines. Kalahari labor found a new market. To meet these capitalist conditions, Khama abolished the kgamelo system and decreed that San were no longer serfs; dikgosi of the other Tswana merafe quickly followed his lead. They did this in order to free San labor from

attachment to any fixed place and to make it more flexibly available to Botswana. This was necessary because Tswana men of all classes were eager to reserve the money wages paid by the mines for themselves. To do so they, of course, had to leave their families and go to the mines; although this brought in money for the family (very little in actual fact), it left a labor vacuum on cattle-posts and farms. This labor was replaced mainly by San (and some Kgalagadi) men who were not allowed to go to the mines until the 1950s. These men and their families were permitted to drink some of the milk of the cattle they tended and eat some of the grains they harvested for their employers, but they were paid very low wages, or none at all. Almost all had to supplement their diet by foraging.

Those who found cattle-post and farm employment were, however, comparatively well off. Relatively few found such employment. The reason is that it takes fewer herders to manage a hundred cattle than it takes hunters to kill one elephant. Furthermore, the tusks of an elephant, when one could be found,[31] were in the 1890s worth only about a third their value of twenty years earlier; in the world economic depression of the 1930s and the 1940s war years, they were worth nothing at all. In addition, a hunter's family contributes nothing to commodity production, while a herder's family—even children as young as five—make substantial contributions to cattle-post production and thus eliminate the need to hire many men. A herd owner had little incentive to accommodate more families than necessary. Most San, many Kgalagadi, and some Tswana families were now without direct means to participate in regional economies. They were relegated to the more difficult ecological zones of the Kalahari where they fell deeper and deeper into subsistence foraging, which had become a condition of poverty in the overall social-economic structure of the subcontinent. This was the final step to San hunter-gatherer poverty. It is a condition from which people constantly aspire to escape.

Social Organization of Kalahari Subsistence Foraging

Land Tenure

Security of land tenure is as important for men who hunt and women who gather as it is for those who herd cattle and grow crops. For this reason, Kalahari San peoples long ago developed ways for assuring that individual persons would acquire such security at birth and retain it throughout life. This is done through rules of kinship inheritance and extensions of these rules through marriage; thus, we will have to look at these rules in order to understand San relations to land. But first I shall outline these relations to land themselves.

All Kalahari San peoples construct very similar land tenure institutions, so all may be considered together. At birth, a San person inherits land rights from both parents; these rights will be those that each parent had in turn inherited at birth. So a San acquires the right to the land of each grandparent; and since every person has four grandparents, every San acquires rights to four areas of land—two from the father's parents and two from the mother's parents. These areas of land are the only ones a San person is entitled to use and to pass on to his/her children. This kind of socially sanctioned security in land is called tenure; the Zhu word for an area of land held in tenure is *n!ore* and the Khoe languages have words derived from the same root (for example, G|wi *n!usa*). A person's primary tenure is the place where he/she was born, usually this will be the place where that person will spend most of his/her life and identify with; for example, a Zhu person born at a waterhole called *CaeCae* will say, "My n!ori is CaeCae." Generational continuity is invoked to validate a claim; a Khoe man asserted, "This is my place—I was born here, and my father and my father's father were born here."[32] Entitlements to other inherited tenures may be retained by visiting relatives in each and exchanging gifts with them; I shall return to this in a moment. Upon marriage, a San person gains rights to use the spouse's tenures, but entitlement to this land is passed to the couple's children only through the spouse.

It should be apparent that a San person gains entitlement to land only through a network of social relations with other persons in the same group. Land, itself, is not inherited, but rights to its use is acquired by being born into a specific social group. What Silberbauer has said of G|wi, "the link between the individual and territory is derived from the bond between community and land,"[33] applies to all Kalahari San in this respect. Membership in that social group carries a set of reciprocal obligations among all the members, including the responsibility for management of the group's land. This means no San "owns" land in the sense of being able to give or sell it to someone else. Rather, the group is the corporate owner of its land; entitlement to use this land is vested in all members of the group. This corporate relation to land is marked in the G|wi girl's puberty ceremony, when the young woman's mother says to her, "this is the country of all of us, and of you; you will always find food here."[34] Among Zhu, members

of such a group are called *n!ore kausi* (owners of a country); these people refer to themselves as "those who have each other" while members of a Khoe group, the Naro, say they are "owned" by their grandparents.[35]

Kinship and Marriage

Unlike land tenure institutions, Khoe and !Kung peoples have different kinship systems; the differences lie mainly in the areas of terminology (what a person calls a specific kind of relative, for example, a cousin) and the way in which kinship is extended to persons who were not born into the same group. But these different terminological systems are employed to achieve very similar sociological results with regard to land and its use. I shall only present the important points here.

All !Kung-speaking peoples separate lineal kin (those descended from the same set of great-grandparents) from collaterals (kin descended from siblings of those great-grandparents). They also use a single term for all cousins of the same sex and another term for cousins of the opposite sex. Thus, a Zhu woman calls all her female cousins *!u!naa* and all her male cousins *txu*, while a man calls his female cousins txu and his male cousins !u!naa. Notice that both use the same terms but apply them reciprocally according to the sex of individuals; because opposite sex cousins are preferred marriage partners, txu can be said to mean "marriageable person." The term !u!naa (literally, "big name") is also applied to same-sex grandparent (by a woman to her grandmother and by a man to his grandfather); when applied to a grandparent it means "name giver" and when to a cousin "name sharer." This is because a Zhu person receives the name of a same-sex grandparent or someone sociologically equivalent, and the same set of names is passed through many generations of a family line; these are the people who have each other. As Lorna Marshall was told by Zhu at NyaeNyae, "We name our children for our people. Those people [their collaterals] name their children for their own people."[36] Among these people, persons of the opposite sex with the same grandparents (second cousins) or same great-grandparents (third cousins) are preferred marriage partners. We shall see why in a moment.

In contrast, all Khoe peoples use one term for the children of their father's sisters and mother's brothers (cross cousins); they use a different term for the children of their father's brothers and mother's sisters (parallel cousins) and this is the same term they use for their own siblings. No distinction between the sexes is made. In the G⏐wi case, these terms are *n⏐⏐odi* (cross cousin) and *gjibaxu* (parallel cousin/sibling). The latter term has no separate meaning, but Barnard translates *n⏐⏐odi-ku* as "grandrelatives to each other;" people in this relationship are marriageable.[37]

Both Zhu and G⏐wi—more broadly, !Kung and Khoe—kinship and marriage practices, while substantially different from each other, produce very similar local descent groups, which are able to perpetuate themselves and their associated claims to land over many generations. Within this incorporative structure of kinship the corporate unity of San land holding is handed down from one generation to the next. In response to the question, "Is it good and just to say that people live in a defined country?", a Zhu elder replied, "If a person stays with his relatives; if a person separates from his relatives it is not right to call that place his."[38]

Property right transfers that occur when people marry are, accordingly, largely matters of reshuffling priorities among latent claims by members of a descent consort. This is because the new married pair will already, as children of their related parents, hold a set of entitlements in common (because they have a grandparental and/or great-grandparental sibling pair in common). Any proper marriage will unite entitlement strands through one parent of the bride and one of the groom; a more desirable marriage will unite strands through each parent of the couple. Marriage strategy is directed toward bringing about this more desirable condition, which strengthens individual security of tenure and consequently local descent group solidarity.

To the extent that the strategy is successfully employed by sibling sets from generation to generation, kinship ties are strengthened for individuals and group solidarity is passed on from grandparental through parental to current sibling sets. San brideservice, in which the man lives with his wife's family and contributes to its economy for a period of years, is crucial to the operation of this system; it can be seen as a form of marriage payment that mediates the conflicts over land which inevitably occur among mutually interdependent groups. Brideservice resolves the question of personal status and locates a marriage union with its offspring within the structure of relations between persons and places through the transferal of property and rights in land that takes place first between the families of bride and groom and later between their parents and their children.

Property and Exchange Networks

The transferal of property begins with negotiations and gift-giving between principals to a future marriage, primarily future coparents-in-law. This process may extend over a period of many years and begins to take more concrete form with the establishment of a new household located in association with the woman's parents. The period of brideservice is measured in terms of offspring, its conditions being satisfied when two or more children have been born to the union. Among Zhu, children born during this period in the woman's n!ore will have that locality as their primary country; Khoe follow a similar practice. This confers lifelong mutual obligations between persons in the woman's family and her children, and on the descendants of those children so long as kinship obligations are met.

During the period of service in the Zhu wife's home n!ore, rights in husband's n!ore are kept open by visiting his primary kin who reside there and participating with them in production from their mutually possessed land. This revalidates entitlements through production relations; visitors who stay for longer than a couple of days are expected to contribute to the food supply. After the period of brideservice, if household residence changes to husband's n!ore, rights in wife's n!ore are kept open by visiting her kin who remain there. Such visiting is undertaken not only to enjoy each other's company but to assure n!ore inheritance by children during the lifetime of the parents. Frequent visits are necessary because there are conflicts over rights and without participation in a n!ore threats to withdraw them may become serious. Thus, fights are common during visits; nearly seventy percent of all homicides occur when families are together and a high proportion of the fights and murders occurs between in-laws. These risks are counterbalanced by the need to keep options open through fulfillment of obligations to participate actively in social relations to land.

Exchange networks play important integrative roles in this social-spatial structure, but only Zhu and Naro have developed formal exchange systems, called *haro* and *kamane* respectively. In haro individuals engage in a form of linked-partner exchange; sixty-two percent of haro partners are traceable to same grandparents and eighty-two percent to same great-grandparents.[39] Given the marriage preference, these people will be contiguous, consanguineal relatives among whom are potential as well as actual marriage partners. It is this group of people who form the stable set of descendant tenure holders; they are the *n!ore kausi,* those who have generationally continuous, inherent entitlement of tenure in their land. A high proportion of the exchange they engage in is associated with marriage negotiations designed to insure continuity into the future. *Kamane* works in much the same way and appears to have been adopted by Naro, the only Khoe-speaking people who have such a system, from Zhu, who have been their neighbors and trading partners for several generations.

The Politics of Production

Sharing and Taking

It is in the politics of implementing this strategy that relations of production are created. Negotiations for and legitimation of marriage ties are important in this creative process; they occupy much of the time and energy of descent group elders. Elders are hierarchically dominant—particularly fathers and parents-in-law—and have a defined right to an extra portion of the production of their descent group. Part of that extra portion is the right to arrange marriages, a right that carries with it increased access to material and social resources. This is the reason why Zhu parents strive diligently to reserve for themselves this potentially onerous right, which leads to the fights and homicides just noted. Zhu kinship is thus the product of strategies oriented toward the satisfaction of material and symbolic interests organized by reference to a determinate set of economic and social conditions. It emerges as relationships that can be read in different ways by participants in them. Zhu relations of production are structured in the engagement of this kinship practice with the economic sphere.

No local descent group can independently reproduce itself within the parochial limits of a single n!ore. For this reason a significant number of marriage ties are negotiated with strategically placed collateral in-laws in adjacent and nearby *n!oresi.* Adults with mature children choose to gain strength through intensified haro and other forms of cooperation in specific n!ore areas. While finding spouses in those n!oresi for their children, the person with the broadest social influence is likely to be most effective in arranging marriages. To facilitate cooperation and strengthen influence, productive partnerships between first cousins are passed on from parents to children. Such inheritance accounts for forty-five percent of the haro links of Zhu individuals and these links are the most secure and long-lasting of all partnerships, some of them spanning many generations. Now, first cousins of one's parents are the parents of one's preferred marriage partner; maintaining good relations with them increases the chances of obtaining a desirable marriage partner from them. Haro exchanges between parties to these partnerships begin in childhood. They intensify in the parental generation during the period of marriage negotiations, solidify during the period of bride-service, and devolve incrementally upon the next generation. Thus, haro partnerships are inheritances that provide a person with working keys to the future.

Wealth, Status, and Leadership

The impartability of descent group land is assured by the cooperation of homesteads in the negotiation of proper marriages, that is, those marriages that protect the undivided inheritance of that land. Marriage negotiations, therefore, are not the simple prerogatives of single families but involve numbers of senior members of an entire group. Without strong control of marriage the impartability of descent group land inheritance could not be perpetuated. Some kin units are able to retain or expand family land at the expense of politically weaker fractions of the social formation; they are able to do so because a concept of unequal possession is inherent in Zhu ideology. That contrast is expressed in the contrast between "wealthy person" *(xaiha)* and "poor person" *(gaakhòe)*; xaiha is also the term for "chief" or leader of a group. Inequality between the statuses of wealthy and poor persons tends to be enhanced because those who can regularly produce a surplus have a broader sphere of haro.[40] As we have seen, a broader sphere of exchange partners is associated with enhanced political influence, that is, of power.

The basis for wealth resides in n!ore entitlements and the productive benefit that that entails; these entitlements are inherited by all members of a descent group. But it is apparent that leadership positions are passed through a smaller subset of families within the n!ore entitlees. All leaders at CaeCae are descendants of several generations of the same families. Lee describes the basis of power of these leaders: "Because his kin ties to past n!ore owners gave Tsau a strong claim to legitimacy, he did not elicit from his own people the same degree of hostility and criticism that other !Kung leaders suffered when they tried to deal with outsiders."[41] Also clearly, xaihasi are able to mobilize labor and to extract a surplus product. The CaeCae leader and his extended family were the beneficiaries of the ivory and feather trade in the nineteenth century, and it is these families who recall the prosperity of that heyday of the hunters with affection. These same families were able to appropriate for themselves the cattle-post positions that became available after hunting prosperity collapsed. This is visible today in the economy of CaeCae: although they are only forty-five percent of the population, these families own ninety percent of the cattle kept by Zhu in this place; they receive eighty-eight percent of the wages paid there; and they kill and consume sixty percent of the animals hunted in the area. Their success in hunting is due primarily to their ability to invest in horses, which allow them to range widely after the few large animals remaining from nineteenth-century depletion. Poor persons are forced to hunt small animals on foot; and people displaced from other n!orisi have no rights to the land and are not allowed to hunt at all.

This has led to conflicting perceptions among Zhu over what constitutes a "proper" marriage. On the one hand are the wealthy who say that to marry properly is to marry as was proper in the past; these people have secure entitlement in place. Their strategy aims to retain the advantage accruing in entitlement; it results in protection of the undivided inheritance of descent group land. On the other are the poor who insist that one marries anyone other than kin; these people have lost entitlement to any land. Their strategy seeks to gain entrance to entitled entities; these families constantly seek alliances with a large productive group so as to acquire a stronger base for developing reciprocal obligations. These conflicting perceptions are rooted in convergent interests of persons who find themselves in contrasting circumstances and are expressions of strategy options sought to fulfill those interests. These relations have been defined in a particular history of political struggle over access to land resources and their products and to the attendant power conferred by recognized legitimate entitlement to manipulate the disposal of these products. This structure is inherent in Zhu social relations and has not been imposed by external forces in recent decades.

Present conditions of political and economic asymmetry visible at CaeCae are, of course, a result of the colonial era and its aftermath, that is, of the particular modern history of the region. But particular histories engage underlying structures to produce visible results, and these structures—while not deterministic in the sense that the conjunction of certain variable events will have a fixed outcome—do structure the outcome in terms of their own logic. For example, if Zhu ideology were in fact egalitarian, its structural logic would distribute entitlements and leadership positions among individuals on an unbiased, perhaps random, basis. Yet, the evidence

demonstrates that quite the opposite is the case. Clearly, n!orekausi homesteads reproduce the conditions of their exclusive entitlements, and those families from which the leader is drawn reproduce the conditions of their dominance. These fundamental conditions of class reproduction are endemic in Zhu social relations.

If, nonetheless, to even careful observers, Zhu, along with all Kalahari San, appear superficially classless today, it is because they are incorporated as an underclass in a wider social formation that includes Tswana, Herero, and the other peoples of the region whose coordinated history in the last two millennia we have scanned. A crucial moment in this history occurred in the nineteenth century colonial encounter when dynamic interaction between the solidarities evoked by kinship and the status inequalities of political organization facilitated the slipping of collateral branches of descent lines into commoner status and of impoverished individuals and families into servitude. Thus, in the political economy of the Kalahari we cannot speak of social relations particular to San or Tswana or any other separate cultural entity; the peoples' histories are too interlocked for that. It was precisely in form of the cattle-post system that the chiefs could extract labor from subordinates and initiate the conditions of rural poverty that prevail today.

Current Rural Poverty

These conditions force some people into subsistence foraging. A pattern of San cattle ownership similar to that of rural Botswana as a whole has emerged—fewer than a third of the families in a language group own any cattle at all and, in 1981, cattle-owning San families had on average five head as compared to twenty for all rural Botswana. Typically less than ten percent of these families own more than half of all animals held by their group; among these, a very few have entered the middle-class ranks of rural Botswana. But for the average San cash income was $10 per adult per year in 1980; those families with a cattlepost wage earner were a bit better off with $25 per adult, which can be translated as $50 per average family of five. When income in kind is added (foraged food, clothing gifts, etc.) an adjusted income of $180 was attained. The poverty level at the time was $250 for such a family, and the average family income for the country as a whole was just over $600. Thus, most San families with wage earners—roughly fourteen percent of all families—fell within the lowest ten percent of income level and did not reach the minimum considered necessary for the bare essentials of life. And this bare existence was available only to those with cattle and/or a wage paying job. Those without such assets foraged and scavenged and had no disposable income at all. Many of these people have left their home tenures to seek employment on the fringes of towns. Some have been successful. These inequities in the overall political economy are shared by all the rural poor of Botswana regardless of their group identification. They reproduce the structural deprivation of a rural underclass deprived of a market for its labor. These inequities are the modern legacy of the history of progressive deprivation we have witnessed, buttressed by a prejudice that assigns to San an ethnographic bewilderment when confronted by the present. In the 1990s, San peoples have begun to organize to overcome this legacy. A first step toward the realization of their aspirations leads away from a fascination with a fixed forager image, a fascination that sets the present of peoples so labeled out of focus and circumscribes any vision of their future.

Notes

1. The term was coined in 1930 by anthropologist Isaac Schapera, in his book *The Khoisan Peoples of South Africa* (London: Routledge) to distinguish these languages and their speakers from the other broad family of indigenous languages, called Bantu, spoken in southern Africa. Neither Khoisan nor Bantu refer to any specific language or people; rather, they are classifying terms useful for designating sets of languages which may sound quite different when spoken today but which can be shown to have common origins in the distant past—just as the term Indo-European links mutually unintelligible English, German, and Greek (and many more languages) to a common origin different from that of other European languages such as Basque and Finnish.

2. Richard Elphick's *Kraal and Castle: KhoiKhoi and the Founding of White South Africa* (New Haven, CT: Yale University Press, 1977) is the trailblazing work in modern Khoisan studies; Elphick documents the falsity of this distinction.

3. Richard Lee is the most articulate advocate of the relative isolation of Kalahari San; his book *The Dobe !Kung* (New York: Holt, Rinehart & Winston, 1984) is a readable presentation of this point of view. Very good statements of the historical integration position can be found in papers by Carmel Schrire, "Wild Surmises on Savage Thoughts," James Denbow, "Prehistoric Herders and Foragers of the Kalahari: The Evidence for 1500 Years of Interaction," and Robert Gordon, "The !Kung in the Kalahari Exchange: An Ethnohistorical Perspective," all in Carmel Schrire, ed., *Past and Present in Hunter Gatherer Studies* (Orlando,

FL: Academic Press, 1984), pp. 1–26, 175–194, 195–224. My book, Land Filled with Flies: A Political Economy of the Kalahari (Chicago: University of Chicago Press, 1989) is probably too long and complicated for beginning students, but Chapter 3, "The Past Recaptured," and Chapter 4, "The Past Entrenched," retell the dynamic history of the region, much of it in the words of the actors themselves.

4. The click consonants are written |, ||, ≠, and !; the sounds these signs represent do not occur in any European language, although many of us use something like them to "talk" to our cats and horses. They are made by clicking the tongue against the teeth and palate.

5. Lorna Marshall, *The !Kung of NyaeNyae* (Cambridge, MA: Harvard University Press, 1976).

6. Richard Lee, *The !Kung San: Men, Women, and Work in a Foraging Society* (Cambridge: Cambridge University Press, 1979).

7. Bantu (also an academically coined term) languages add prefixes to noun roots to modify their meanings; for example, the locative prefix, *bo*, designates "place of" as in Botswana ("place of Tswana people"). Here the prefixes are *ki, isi, sin*, and in the next sentence, *se*; these modify the roots *zulu, xhosa, debele*, and *sotho* (each meaning *people* in some sense) to mean "language of Zulu people" and so forth.

8. The prefixes *shi, otji*, and *oshi* all mean "language of" the people specified by the roots *yei, herero*, and *ambo*; *wa* is the plural applied to people who speak Shiyei.

9. Laurens van der Post, *The Lost World of the Kalahari* (New York: William Morrow, 1958). A similarly idealist notion of people preserving in isolation a remnant of authentic primitive humanity motivated ethnographic research on Kalahari San peoples in the 1950s and 1960s. John Yellen, "The Integration of Herding into Prehistoric Hunting and Gathering Economies," in Martin Hall and Graham Avery, eds., *Frontiers: Southern African Archaeology Today* (Cambridge: Cambridge University Press), p. 54, expresses this motivation well: "This San group has been used as a kind of narrow and opaque window to the Pleistocene." Lee, *The Dobe !Kung*, pp. 1–2, gives it fuller expression: "The !Kung San of the Kalahari Desert, fierce and independent, unknown to the outside world until recently…[were important because] our ancestors had evolved as foragers…thus the study of the surviving foragers—[the San and others]—had much to teach us."

10. Euroamericans think of Afrikaans as the language of South African whites (those who call themselves Afrikaners or Boers). But the language actually evolved as a mixture of Dutch (mainly), French, Portuguese, Malay, and Cape Khoi spoken by many people in Cape Colony; it thus became as much the native language of blacks as of whites.

11. This is also a cover term (plural prefix *ba*, root *kgalagadi*) for a number of peoples who speak a set of closely

related Bantu languages; it means simply "people of the Kalahari."

12. Gary Okihiro, "Hunters, Herders, Cultivators, and Traders: Interaction and Change in the Kgalagadi, Nineteenth-Century" (Ph.D. diss., University of California at Los Angeles, 1976).

13. The most readily available ethnographies of a Khoe people are George Silberbauer's *Hunter and Habitat in the Central Kalahari Desert* (Cambridge: Cambridge University Press, 1981) and Jiro Tanaka's *The San Hunter-Gatherers of the Kalahari: a Study in Ecological Anthropology,* David Hughes, trans. (Tokyo: University of Tokyo Press, 1980). Both focus on G⏐wi and G⏐⏐ana peoples who conform most closely to Euroamerican Bushman stereotypes; that is, they are relatively short, have comparatively light-brown skin color, and tend to hunt and gather more than do other Khoe. Alan Barnard, in *Hunters and Herders of Southern Africa: a Comparative Ethnography of the Khoisan Peoples* (Cambridge: Cambridge University Press, 1992), provides a valuable synthesis of much of the literature on all Khoe peoples; this would be an excellent work to consult for ethnographic details.

14. Batswana are the ruling people of Botswana and so will be referred to frequently.

15. This was part of testimony given in the 1930s by Tshekedi Khama to a British commission investigating charges of Tswana enslavement of Khoisan peoples (see Wilmsen, *Land Filled with Flies,* p. 97).

16. The extent to which the "remote" Kalahari was a part of world trade is neatly illustrated here; ivory was wanted to make piano keys and billiard balls. Pianos and billiards were newly fashionable playthings of the European middle class, which was then growing rapidly in numbers and wealth. Ostrich feathers were high fashion ornaments on women's hats and bustles.

17. The Tswana word *morafe* (plural, *merafe*), is usually translated "tribe" but I prefer "polity" as a translation that avoids a connotation of primitiveness and to stress that these are as fully developed as are any other political organizations.

18. Q. Neil Parsons, "The Economic History of Khama's Country in Botswana, 1844–1930," in Robin Palmer and Q. Neil Parsons, eds., *The Roots of Rural Poverty in Central and Southern Africa* (Berkeley: University of California Press, 1977), pp. 113–143.

19. This passage is from James Chapman's diary, *Travels in the Interior of Africa, 1849–1863,* Edward Tabler, ed. (Cape Town: Balkema, 1971), vol. 1, p. 143, and is quoted in *Land Filled with Flies,* p. 117.

20. It was recruitment of all sorts of peoples, not an impossibly high birth rate, that brought about the rapid expansion of the Tswana merafe.

21. Thomas Baines, *Explorations in South-West Africa* (London: Longman-Green, 1864), p. 409; quoted in Land Filled with Flies, p. 118.

22. Siegfried Passarge, *Die Buschmänner der Kalahari* (Berlin: Dietrich Reimer, 1907). I am currently preparing a translation, that will be published by the University of Michigan Press.

23. Zhu have a strong tradition of trading, both to maintain their social networks and for exchanging goods (see Polly Wiessner, "Hxaro: A Regional System of Reciprocity for the Reduction of Risk among the !Kung San" [Ph.D. diss., University of Michigan, 1977]), and their language has a rich vocabulary concerned with trade.

24. Lee, *The !Kung San,* p. 77.

25. Ibid., p. 78. Tsau was the Tswana capitol on the Delta.

26. Oswin Köhler, *Die Welt der Kxoé Buschleute* (Berlin: Dietrich Reimer, 1989), p. 425. A vivid description of the experience of a person captured into slavery is found in Joseph Miller, *Way of Death* (Madison, WI: University of Wisconsin Press, 1988).

27. P. Serton, *The Narrative and Journal of Gerald McKiernan in South West Africa, 1874–1879* (Cape Town: Van Riebeck Society, 1954), p. 167.

28. Carl Hugo Hahn, "Neueste Deutsche Forschungen in Süd-Afrika," *Petermann's geographische Mitteilungen* 8 (1967): 285.

29. Jacqueline Solway and Richard Lee, "Foragers, Genuine or Spurious? Situating the Kalahari San in History," *Current Anthropology* 31 (1990): 116.

30. *Deutsches Kolonialblatt* 23 (1912): 530–541. Ein Erkundungsritt in das Kaukau-Veld, von Hauptmann Müller.

31. It has been estimated that no more than two hundred elephants remained in all Botswana in 1900; remember that during the 1860s and 1870s about three thousand had been killed every year. The latest wildlife census indicates that there are now about sixty-eight thousand in the country.

32. Elizabeth Cashdan, "Property and Social Insurance among the G⏐⏐ana," paper presented at Second International Conference on Hunting and Gathering Societies, Quebec City, 1980.

33. Silberbauer, *Hunter and Habitat,* p. 99.

34. Ibid., p. 151.

35. See my paper, "Those Who Have Each Other: Land Tenure of San-Speaking Peoples," in Edwin Wilmsen, ed., *We are Here: Politics of Aboriginal Land Tenure* (Berkeley: University of California Press, 1989), pp. 43–67, and Barnard, *Hunters and Herders,* p. 146.

36. Marshall, *The !Kung of NyaeNyae,* p. 340.

37. Barnard, *Hunters and Herders,* p. 111.

38. Wilmsen, *Land Filled with Flies,* p. 180.

39. Wiessner, "Hxaro," p. 119.

40. Ibid., p. 224.

41. Lee, *The !Kung San,* p. 350.

Suggested Readings

Bernard, Alan. *Hunters and Herders of Southern Africa.* Cambridge: Cambridge University Press, 1992. A very good synthesis of ethnographies of all Khoisan groups.

Lee, Richard. *The Dobe !Kung.* New York: Holt, Reinhart & Winston, 1984. The standard classic ethnography of one San group.

Pratt, Mary Louise. "Scratches on the Face of the Earth, or, What Mr. Barrow Saw in the Land of the Bushmen," in Henry Lewis Gates Jr., ed., *Race, Writing, and Difference.* Chicago: University of Chicago Press, 1985, pp. 119–143. An excellent critique of classic San ethnographies.

Schrire, Carmel. "An Enquiry into the Evolutionary Status and Apparent Identity of San Hunter-Gatherers." *Human Ecology* 8 (1980): 9–32. The first use of historical material in San ethnography.

Wilmsen, Edwin. "The Ecology of Illusion: Anthropological Foraging in the Kalahari." *Reviews in Anthropology* 10 (1983): 9–20. A critical review of the four major modern classics of San ethnography.

"KALAHARI SAN:
SOMETIME HUNTER-GATHERERS"

Edwin N. Wilmsen

1) What are the two major opposing views regarding the Kalahari San as a viable ethnographic reality?

2) What was the social history of the Khoisan peoples in relationship to the other peoples in southern Africa prior to the arrival of the Europeans?

3) According to Wilmsen, how did the *kgmelo* (milk-jug) economic system contribute to the reduction of some San peoples to a state of rural poverty?

4) How did hunting and changes in fashion trends in Europe contribute to the marginalization of some San in the Kalahari Desert?

5) How did the introduction of a modern capitalistic economic system based on mining and wage labor contribute further to the marginalization of the San?

6) Discuss current San culture in terms of land tenure, kinship/marriage, property/exchange systems, and other social institutions. How close are these to the traditional systems practiced by the San?

VARIATION IN ECONOMY

Richard E. Blanton

Social scientists and historians have described many different kinds of economies that have evolved since the end of the ice age. These range from small-scale systems in which economic action was primarily a reflection of kinship ties and other personal relations, to larger, more commercialized economies that have developed in several world areas over the last several thousand years, in which economic transactions included those between anonymous buyers and sellers engaged in market transactions. The heavily commercialized modern economies of the capitalist nations are the product of this general evolutionary trend toward more and more elaborate market systems. However, in spite of the pervasive influence of European capitalism and its offshoots in today's world, there remain substantial cross-cultural differences in economic systems.

Comparative research has the goal of explaining this cross-cultural variation, as well as long-term change, in economy. This goal is realizable only through the development of a set of concepts and methods applicable in a wide range of sociocultural and historical settings, and this task has proven quite challenging. However, over a period of more than fifty years, social scientists have made substantial progress in cross-cultural economic understanding.[1]

Production, Distribution, and Consumption

While specific features of economic systems vary considerably from society to society and have changed substantially over time, all societies are comparable from an economic perspective. People everywhere develop both the technologies and the institutional arrangements to carry out the related processes of production, distribution (i.e., the allocation of goods and services among members of society), and consumption. Taken together, the patterned arrangement of behaviors in the contexts of production, distribution, and consumption constitute the economic system of society. Understanding systems of production, distribution, and consumption may help us understand other aspects of society and culture, including quality of life, economic inequality,

political change, technological change, and economic development, among a myriad of other possible topics. Production, distribution, and consumption are the central themes of economic analyses, whether applied to our society or cross-culturally, although different schools of economic thought may emphasize one or another domain of economic action.[2]

Because production, distribution, and consumption are found in all societies, it would seem to follow that cross-cultural comparison of economic systems would be a relatively straightforward and focused analytical task. Instead, the study of variation in economy is an endeavor that severely challenges the cross-cultural researcher. A vexing problem faces those social scientists whose interests lead them into the domain of cross-cultural economic study, namely: To what extent may we apply our western (i.e., capitalist) economic theory in noncapitalist societies? Superficially, the answer to this question seems obvious. Because many features of capitalist economic systems are not found in other sociocultural settings, they have limited value for cross-cultural comparison. Institutions like stock markets and incorporated firms are unique to the capitalist economies, and so theories about their behavior clearly cannot be applied elsewhere.

The real difficulty in conducting cross-cultural economic analysis resides at a deeper level. The persistent problem in cross-cultural comparison is found in how we view the nature of the economic behavior of individuals. In the so-called "neoclassical" economic theories developed in the capitalist nations since the latter nineteenth century,[3] it is assumed that "economizing" behavior involves the making of rational economic choices among alternatives, given limited material and human resources (i.e., making prudent choices between ends, given a scarcity of means).

In the economic behavior assumed by the "economizing" theoretical framework, costs and benefits are assessed in measurable quantities in order to arrive at optimal solutions to problems faced in production, distribution, and consumption. In firms, for example, this means identifying an optimal combination of inputs to production (land, labor, and capital), in order to maximize profit. In households, it involves consuming an optimal mix of goods and services that will maximize consumer utilities (i.e., satisfactions such as health and material well-being). This does not mean that all individuals and institutions are carefully and objectively engaging in economizing behavior at all times. But, to the degree possible (given the limited information available to economic actors, and given that cultural values may at times constrain optimization), an economizing theory is thought to provide a powerful means for explaining cross-cultural and temporal variation in economy. Further, it is argued that this kind of rational, calculative behavior, when elaborated to its fullest extent, is the basis for the development and functioning of the strongly commercialized economic system of capitalism.[4]

In anthropology, cultural materialists such as Marvin Harris make use of a similar utilitarian theory.[5] In this approach, sociocultural change as a general process in all human societies is seen as the outcome of choices that provide primarily material and environmental adaptive benefits. But critics of utilitarian theories argue that economizing behavior is particular to the western, strongly commercialized, capitalist economies, and that economic theories developed in this particular sociocultural milieu should not be applied elsewhere.[6] This difference of theoretical orientation has produced a split in economic anthropology between those who see possibilities for the broad use of an economizing theory and those who reject it as a tool of comparative analysis. "Formalist" economic anthropologists[7] argue that there are advantages to a broadly-applied "economizing" theory, while the "substantivist" camp argues that non-capitalist systems are best understood through the study of local institutions of production, distribution, and consumption peculiar to particular times and places.[8] Substantivists argue that comparative economic inquiry should be primarily a factual, historical, descriptive endeavor, rather than part of a theoretically-inspired economic science.

The central difficulty of cross-cultural economic study is captured in the formalist-substantivist argument. Is the economizing approach ethnocentric, or is it a powerful tool for cross-cultural economic analysis? The formalist-substantivist debate has had a beneficial outcome for cross-cultural research in that it has prompted much thought and writing, as well as problem-oriented research. As a result, we have a much better understanding of these issues now than when they were first brought to light over fifty years ago, although issues surrounding the applicability of western economic science in other societal settings have not been entirely resolved. Advances in cross-cultural study of economy can be summarized by viewing differences and similarities in economies in terms of three facets of human behavior as seen in sociocultural context, namely: (1) the cross-cultural applicability of the concept of rationality, (2) the degree of "embeddedness" of economy in society and culture, and (3) the distinction made between exchanges involving "gifts" and "commodities."

A Cross-Cultural Perspective on Economic Rationality

Are market economies, especially capitalism, the most commercialized of them all, more rational than the economies of foragers, tribal societies, or early civilizations? This is an exceedingly difficult question to answer because rationality is an intricate and difficult concept for cross-cultural consideration.[9] The difficulty is that no particular aspect of behavior, of society, or of culture can be considered rational in any absolute sense, nor is it meaningful to compare whole sociocultural systems as being more or less rational overall. The degree of rationality is always relative to the situation at hand, and any aspect of human activity that one may consider will exhibit both rational and irrational dimensions.

The rationality of economizing behavior that operates in capitalist institutions such as firms, and which figures prominently in western economic theory, is a particular dimension of rationality in which prudent choices produce utilitarian benefits such as profits. In this conceptualization, utilitarian benefits are realized within the context of a particular bounded social entity, such as a firm or household. But this is only one type of rationality that one might consider. What about situations in which desired ends involve more than utilitarian benefits? And what if the rationality of the social entity in question is viewed in its larger societal and environmental context? An American farm, for example, may prudently deploy an optimal combination of land and capital (chemicals and farm machinery), according to the dictates of accepted capitalist practice, in order to maximize profit. But, as a consequence of these optimizing practices, the farmer may pollute ground water and surface water with fertilizer and pesticide residues. These external environmental consequences, which eventually constitute a cost to society in terms of a degraded environment, are not taken into consideration in assessing the farm's profitability. Is this rational? Yes, but only in the limited, bounded, economizing sense that is typical of western economic analysis. When viewed from a larger perspective of the farm in nature and society, there is a strong element of irrationality at play, which economic science chooses to ignore. In fact, if capitalist farms did aim to minimize environmental impacts, they might not be profitable.[10]

Anthropologists studying western-inspired agricultural development programs in the less developed countries have often pointed to similar kinds of unanticipated social and environmental costs resulting from the use of a narrow economizing approach to farm management and technology.[11] For example, when Latin American peasants are removed from their land in order to convert it to commercial cattle grazing for export, is this rational behavior? The cattle ranches can become successful commercial enterprises, and the export of beef improves a country's balance of payments. These are both rational outcomes when counted in economistic terms. However, the benefits of capitalist farming often accrue to only a small number of wealthy landowners, while the peasantry removed from their land experiences a declining standard of living.[12] Again, from a narrow perspective of the economic maximization of a capitalist enterprise, cattle ranching in cases like these is rational, but there are at the same time unaccounted external costs of social disruption and poverty in society, viewed more broadly. Thus rationality is always situational, not absolute.

The economic rationality assumed in economizing theory and cultural materialism is also misleading in that it assumes a primarily utilitarian focus of human action (i.e., that choice will aim at outcomes that maximize primarily material benefits). But human strategizing may aim at many possible outcomes, including power and social standing, even when, as a result, material benefits may not be realized. In the "big-man" societies of tribal Highland New Guinea, for example, large numbers of pigs are fattened for eventual distribution in elaborate giveaway (prestational) events that establish the prestige of a big-man and his faction.[13] But the great effort—and garden produce—that goes into pig-keeping does not necessarily provide a substantial nutritional benefit to the human population.[14] In this kind of situation, animal husbandry is better understood in terms of the dynamics of the prestige system than in terms of nutritional utility, and to employ an assumption of narrow utilitarian rationality here would be misleading.[15]

At present, the best tactic for cross-cultural economic study may require that the researcher take a tentative, exploratory view of economic rationality that can make use of a well-developed economic theory, while not making overly-strong assumptions about its general cross-cultural applicability. That is, rather than either assuming that people will or will not engage in utilitarian economizing, research can proceed by using the expectations of economizing theory as a set of predictions against which to compare the actual behavior observed; thus, economizing theory may be regarded as a "model," (i.e., an analytical tool), not an assumption about what people will tend to do. In this way, the researcher can infer the degree to which economically rational choice constitutes an explanation for a given cultural practice. Deviations from the theoretically expected outcomes indicate that the behavior in question must be understood in other than economizing terms.

An elaborate theory in economic geography—"central-place theory"—provides an example of model-building inquiry. This theory makes possible predictions about the optimal spatial distribution of retail centers (towns and cities with retailing activities) in a region, assuming economizing behavior—for example, when retailers optimize the locations of retail outlets, and when their customers minimize travel costs in their shopping trips.[16] The theory applies to all commercialized regions (regions with market economies), including regions containing peasant market systems.[17]

Research based on central-place theory can generate predictions about the ideal locations of communities with retail functions, against which to compare their actual distribution in a region. Deviations from the expected locations lead the analyst to make inferences about factors in society that distort economically optimal spatial distributions of centers—for example, commercial monopolies or political policies that limit the free movement of market participants.[18] The consequences of such deviations in regional systems are important, since they may lead to less than optimal market structure, and this, in turn, may preclude full commercial participation and perpetuate marked wealth differences in different zones of a regional economic system.[19] In a similar vein, a rapidly growing literature is evaluating the degree of applicability to non-capitalist civilizations of theories pertaining to the nature of international economic relations in the capitalist world-economy.[20] One of the preliminary findings of this fascinating new research direction is that the unequal economic development of cores and peripheries in large-scale, multi-cultural economic systems is a process that can be traced back thousands of years.[21]

The Embedded Economy

One fruitful strategy for cross-cultural analysis of economy is to ask the question: To what degree are

similar researchers fill the sometimes conflicting roles of academic writers, field researchers, advisors to development agencies, and representatives of indigenous peoples whose lives are being fundamentally altered, not always beneficially, by development projects and other forces of modernization. Developing improved theory through cross-cultural comparative study and historical study is not only important for its own sake, but is needed to better cope with the problems presented by a rapidly changing world.

Notes

1. These developments are summarized in Sutti Ortiz, ed., *Economic Anthropology: Topics and Theories* (Lanham, MD: University Press of America, 1983); and in Stuart Plattner, ed., Economic Anthropology (Stanford: Stanford University Press, 1989).

2. Marxists, for example, emphasize social relations of production, as discussed in Alice Littlefield and Hill Gates, eds., *Marxist Approaches in Economic Anthropology* (Lanham, MD: University Press of America, 1991). Those who borrow from standard or "neoclassical" economic analysis often emphasize distribution or consumption; see, for example, Carol A. Smith, "Exchange Systems and the Spatial Distribution of Elites: The Organization of Stratification in Agrarian Societies," in Carol A. Smith, ed., *Regional Analysis, Volume II: Social Systems* (New York: Academic Press, 1976), pp. 309–374.

3. See, for example, Eric Roll, *A History of Economic Thought* (London: Faber and Faber, 1938), Chapters 7 and 8.

4. This argument is elaborated in Max Weber, *General Economic History* (New York: Collier Books, 1966), and *Economy and Society,* ed. Guenther Roth and Claus Wittich (Berkeley: University of California Press, 1978). A useful summary of Weber's theory of capitalism is presented by Randall Collins, "Weber's Last Theory of Capitalism: A Systematization," *American Sociological Review* 45 (1980): 925–942.

5. Marvin Harris, *Cultural Materialism* (New York: Random House, 1979).

6. See, for example, Marshall Sahlins, *Culture and Practical Reason* (Chicago: University of Chicago Press, 1976).

7. See, for example, Harold K. Schneider, *Economic Man: The Anthropology of Economics* (New York: The Free Press, 1974).

8. The substantivist position was laid out by Karl Polanyi, *The Great Transformation* (New York: Rinehart, 1944); and by Karl Polanyi, Conrad Arensberg, and Harry Pearson, eds., *Trade and Market in the Early Empires* (New York: The Free Press, 1957). The status of the formalist-substantivist debate is summarized in Edward E. LeClair, Jr., and Harold K. Schneider, eds.,

Economic Anthropology: Readings in Theory and Analysis (New York: Holt, Rinehart and Winston, 1968); see also Stuart Plattner, "Introduction," in Stuart Plattner, ed., *Economic Anthropology* (Stanford: Stanford University Press, 1989), pp. 1–20.

9. Useful comments on the current status of concerns with rationality are found in Sutti Ortiz, "Introduction," in Sutti Ortiz and Susan Lees, eds., *Understanding Economic Process* (Lanham, MD: University Press of America, 1992), pp. 3–7.

10. Bob Holmes, "Can Sustainable Farming Win the Battle of the Bottom Line?" *Science* 260 (1993): 1893–1895.

11. Richard W. Franke, "Miracle Seeds and Shattered Dreams," *Natural History* 83 (1974).

12. See, for example, James D. Nations and Daniel I. Komer, "Indians, Immigrants, and Beef Exports: Deforestation in Central America," *Cultural Survival Quarterly* 2 (1982): 8–12.

13. See, for example, Andrew Strathern, *The Rope of Moka: Big-Men and Exchange in Mount Hagen, New Guinea* (Cambridge: Cambridge University Press, 1971).

14. Paula Brown, *Highland Peoples of New Guinea* (Cambridge: Cambridge University Press, 1978), pp. 51–60.

15. Richard E. Blanton and Jody Taylor, "Patterns of Exchange and the Social Production of Pigs in Highland New Guinea: Their Relevance to Questions about the Origin and Evolution of Agriculture," *Journal of Archaeological Research* 3 (1995): 113–145.

16. A recent summary of central-place theory is found in Stuart Plattner, "Markets and Marketplaces," in Stuart Plattner, ed., *Economic Anthropology* (Stanford: Stanford University Press, 1989), pp. 171–208.

17. See description of late Imperial China in G. William Skinner, "Cities and the Hierarchy of Local Systems," in G. William Skinner, ed., *The City in Late Imperial China* (Stanford: Stanford University Press, 1977), pp. 275–351.

18. I used this method to better comprehend the nature of Aztec imperial strategies in the late prehispanic Basin of Mexico, in Richard E. Blanton, "The Basin of Mexico Market System and the Growth of Empire," in Frances F. Berdan, Richard E. Blanton, Elizabeth Boone, Mary Hodge, Michael Smith, and Emily Umberger, eds., *Aztec Imperial Strategies* (Washington, D. C.: Dum-barton Oaks, in press).

19. See, for example, Carol Smith's analysis of the system of central places in Western Guatemala, in Carol A. Smith, "Causes and Consequences of Central-Place Types in Western Guatemala," in Carol A. Smith, ed., *Regional Analysis, Volume I: Economic Systems* (New York: Academic Press, 1976), pp. 255–302.

20. The most widely-used version of the theory is found in Immanuel Wallerstein, *The Modern World-System: Capitalist Agriculture and the Origins of the European World-Economy in the Sixteenth Century* (New York: Academic Press); a recent summary of ideas about how the theory may be applied in noncapitalist contexts is

found in Christopher Chase-Dunn and Thomas D. Hall, eds., *Core/Periphery Relations in Precapitalist Worlds* (Boulder, CO: Westview Press, 1991).

21. Andre Gunder Frank, "Bronze Age World-System Cycles," *Current Anthropology* 34 (1993): 383–429.

22. Embeddedness is usefully discussed in Mark Granovetter, "Economic Action and Social Structure: The Problem of Embeddedness," *American Journal of Sociology* 91 (1985): 481–510; Mark Granovetter, "The Nature of Economic Relations," in Sutti Ortiz and Susan Lees, eds., *Understanding Economic Process* (Lanham, MD: University Press of America, 1992), pp. 21–37.

23. Granovetter, "The Nature of Economic Relations," pp. 21–22.

24. See Dennis Wrong, "The Oversocialized Conception of Man in Modern Sociology," *American Sociological Review* 29 (1961): 183–196; Granovetter, "The Nature of Economic Relations," p. 22.

25. Samuel L. Popkin, *The Rational Peasant: The Political Economy of Rural Society in Vietnam* (Berkeley: University of California Press, 1979).

26. See, for example, Frank Cancian, "Economic Behavior in Peasant Communities," in Stuart Plattner, ed., *Economic Anthropology* (Stanford: Stanford University Press, 1989), pp. 127–170.

27. Granovetter, "The Nature of Economic Relations," p. 32.

28. There is a large literature on exchange in comparative economic study; here I follow the lead provided by C. A. Gregory, *Gifts and Commodities* (New York: Academic Press, 1982).

29. Although the comparative values of items in reciprocal gift exchange transactions may weakly reflect supply-demand forces (i.e., price formation), as in the example in Marshall Sahlins, *Stone Age Economics* (Chicago: Aldine-Atherton, 1972), Chapter 6.

30. Frederic L. Pryor, *The Origins of the Economy: A Comparative Study of Distribution in Primitive and Peasant Economies* (New York: Academic Press, 1977), pp. 34–36. Sahlins's concept of "generalized reciprocity," like Malinowski's "pure gift," is an altruistic transaction that creates none or only a vague sense of return obligation: See, for example, Sahlins, *Stone Age Economics*, pp. 193–194; Bronislaw Malinowski, *Argonauts of the Western Pacific* (London: Routledge and Kegan Paul, 1922), pp. 177–180; Jonathan Parry, "The Gift, The Indian Gift, and the 'Indian Gift'," *Man (New Series)* 21 (1986): 453–473.

31. Even altruistic exchanges are assumed to involve some expectation of a future benefit in Oded Stark, "Nonmarket Transfers and Altruism," in Sutti Ortiz and Susan Lees, eds., *Understanding Economic Process* (Lanham, MD: University Press of America, 1992), pp. 9–20; Annette B. Weiner, "Reproduction: A ReplacePlattner, Stuart, ed. *Economic Anthropology*. Stanford: Stanford University Press, 1989. An up-to-date textbook exploring many aspects of contemporary economic anthropology.

32. Strathern, The Rope of Moka; Marilyn Strathern, "Qualified Value: The Perspective of Gift Exchange," in Caroline Humphrey and Stephen Hugh-Jones, eds., Barter, Exchange, and Value: An Anthropological Approach (Cambridge: Cambridge University Press, 1992), p. 170; Gregory, Gifts and Commodities, p. 19.

33. Mayfair Yang points to the pervasiveness of the gift economy (Guanxi) of modern China, in Mayfair Yang, "The Gift Economy and State Power in China," Comparative Studies in Society and History 31 (1989): 25–54.

34. See a description of the competitive exchange events referred to as "tournaments of value," in Arjun Appadurai, The Social Life of Things: Commodities in Cultural Perspective (Cambridge: Cambridge University Press, 1986), p. 21.

35. See, for example Blanton and Taylor, "Patterns of Exchange and the Social Production of Pigs in Highland New Guinea"; and Brian Hayden, "Nimrods, Piscators, Pluckers, and Planters: The Emergence of Food Production," Journal of Anthropological Archaeology 9 (1990): 31–69; see also Sahlins, Stone Age Economics, Chapter 3.

36. This argument is developed in S. N. Eisenstadt, The Political Systems of Empires: The Rise and Fall of the Historical Bureaucratic Societies (New York: The Free Press, 1969); Richard E. Blanton, "Factors Underlying the Origin and Evolution of Market Systems," in Sutti Ortiz, ed., Economic Anthropology: Topics and Theories (Lanham, MD: University Press of America, 1983), pp. 51–66.

Suggested Readings

Appadurai, Arjun, ed. The Social Life of Things: Commodities in Cultural Perspective. Cambridge: Cambridge University Press, 1986. Develops a useful cross-cultural approach to exchange, commodities, and the determination of value.

Chase-Dunn, Christopher, and Thomas D. Hall, eds. Core/Periphery Relations in Precapitalist Worlds. Boulder, CO: Westview Press, 1991. Explores the usefulness of applying a modified world-systems theory in precapitalist civilizations.

Douglas, Mary, and Baron Isherwood. The World of Goods: Toward an Anthropology of Consumption. New York: W. W. Norton, 1979. Develops a theory of consumer behavior applicable cross-culturally.

Ortiz, Sutti, ed. Economic Anthropology: Topics and Theories. Lanham, MD: University Press of America, 1983. A collection of papers from the first meeting of the Society for Economic Anthropology that represents the recent state of the art of economic anthropology, including the status of the Formalist-Substantivist debate.

Plattner, Stuart, ed. Economic Anthropology. Stanford: Stanford University Press, 1989. An up-to-date textbook exploring many aspects of contemporary economic anthropology.

Schneider, Harold K. Economic Man: The Anthropology of Economics. Salem, WI: Sheffield, 1989. A reissue of the original 1974 publication, this book is one of the classic sources for a Formalist economic anthropology. It is highly readable and is still useful as an introductory source.

"VARIATION IN ECONOMY"

Richard E. Blanton

1) Blanton suggests that all societies can be cross-culturally compared in terms of production, distribution, and consumption. He then asks to what extent can we apply western economic theory to the analysis of non-western cultures. How does he answer his own question?

2) What is the "economizing" theoretical framework and how has it been employed in anthropology to analyze non-western economies?

3) What is economic rationality and can such a concept be employed in dealing with economic systems, even though no particular aspect of human behavior is absolutely rational?

4) What does Blanton mean by an "embedded economy"?

5) What are the different types of exchange relationships that occur in all cultures?

SECTION FIVE

Realities of Gender

NEW WOMEN OF THE ICE AGE

Heather Pringle

The Black Venus of Dolní Vestonice, a small, splintered figurine sensuously fashioned from clay, is an envoy from a forgotten world. It is all soft curves, with breasts like giant pillows beneath a masked face. At nearly 26,000 years old, it ranks among the oldest known portrayals of women, and to generations of researchers, it has served as a powerful—if enigmatic—clue to the sexual politics of the Ice Age.

Excavators unearthed the Black Venus near the Czech village of Dolní Vestonice in 1924, on a hillside among charred, fractured mammoth bones and stone tools. (Despite its nickname, the Black Venus is actually reddish—it owes its name to the ash that covered it when it was found.) Since the mid-nineteenth century, researchers had discovered more than a dozen similar statuettes in caves and open-air sites from France to Russia. All were cradled in layers of earth littered with stone and bone weaponry, ivory jewelry, and the remains of extinct Ice Age animals. All were depicted naked or nearly so. Collectively, they came to be known as Venus figurines, after another ancient bare-breasted statue, the Venus de Milo. Guided at least in part by prevailing sexual stereotypes, experts interpreted the meaning of the figurines freely. The Ice Age camps that spawned this art, they concluded, were once the domain of hardworking male hunters and secluded, pampered women who spent their days in idleness like the harem slaves so popular in nineteenth-century art.

Over the next six decades, Czech archeologists expanded the excavations at Dolní Vestonice, painstakingly combing the site square meter by square meter. By the 1990s they had unearthed thousands of bone, stone, and clay artifacts and had wrested 19 radiocarbon dates from wood charcoal that sprinkled camp floors. And they had shaded and refined their portrait of Ice Age life. Between 29,000 and 25,000 years ago, they concluded, wandering bands had passed the cold months of the year repeatedly at Dolní Vestonice. Armed with short-range spears, the men appeared to have been specialists in hunting tusk-wielding mammoths and other big game, hauling home great mountains of meat to feed their dependent mates and children. At night men feasted on mammoth steaks, fed their fires with mammoth bone, and fueled their sexual fantasies with tiny figurines of women carved from mammoth ivory and fired from clay. It was the ultimate man's world.

Or was it? Over the past few months, a small team of American archeologists has raised some serious doubts. Amassing critical and previously overlooked evidence from Dolní Vestonice and the neighboring site of Pavlov, Olga Soffer, James Adovasio, and David Hyland now propose that human survival there had little to do with manly men hurling spears at big-game animals. Instead, observes Soffer, one of the world's leading authorities on Ice Age hunters and gatherers and an archeologist at the University of Illinois in Champaign-Urbana, it depended largely on women, plants, and a technique of hunting previously invisible in the archeological evidence—net hunting. "This is not the image we've always had of Upper Paleolithic macho guys out killing animals up close and personal," Soffer explains. "Net hunting is communal, and it involves the labor of children and women. And this has lots of implications."

Many of these implications make her conservative colleagues cringe because they raise serious questions about the focus of previous studies. European archeologists have long concentrated on analyzing broken stone tools and butchered big-game bones, the most plentiful and best preserved relics of the Upper Paleolithic era (which stretched from 40,000 to 12,000 years ago). From these analyses, researchers have developed theories about how these societies once hunted and gathered food. Most researchers ruled out the possibility of women hunters for biological reasons. Adult females, they reasoned, had to devote themselves to breast-feeding and tending infants. "Human babies have always been immature and dependent," says Soffer. "If women are the people who are always involved with biological reproduction and the rearing of the young, then that is going to constrain their behavior. They have to provision that child. For fathers, provisioning is optional."

To test theories about Upper Paleolithic life, researchers looked to ethnography, the scientific description of modern and historical cultural groups. While the lives of modern hunters do not exactly duplicate those of ancient hunters, they supply valuable clues to universal human behavior. "Modern ethnography cannot be used to clone the past," says Soffer. "But people have always had to solve problems. Nature and social relationships present problems to people. We use ethnography to look for theoretical insights into human behavior, test them with ethnography, and if they work, assume that they represent a universal feature of human behavior."

But when researchers began turning to ethnographic descriptions of hunting societies, they unknowingly relied on a very incomplete literature. Assuming that women in surviving hunting societies were homebodies who simply tended hearths and suckled children, most early male anthropologists spent their time with male informants. Their published ethnographies brim with descriptions of males making spears and harpoons and heaving these weapons at reindeer, walruses, and whales. Seldom do they mention the activities of women. Ethnography, it seemed, supported theories of ancient male big-game hunters. "When they talked about primitive man, it was always 'he,'" says Soffer. "The 'she' was missing."

Recent anthropological research has revealed just how much Soffer's colleagues overlooked. By observing women in the few remaining hunter-gatherer societies and by combing historical accounts of tribal groups more thoroughly, anthropologists have come to realize how critical the female half of the population has always been to survival. Women and children have set snares, laid spring traps, sighted game and participated in animal drives and surrounds—forms of hunting that endangered neither young mothers nor their offspring. They dug starchy roots and collected other plant carbohydrates essential to survival. They even hunted, on occasion, with the projectile points traditionally deemed men's weapons. "I found references to Inuit women carrying bows and arrows, especially the blunt arrows that were used for hunting birds," says Linda Owen, an archeologist at the University of Tübingen in Germany.

The revelations triggered a volley of new research. In North America, Soffer and her team have found tantalizing evidence of the hunting gear often favored by women in historical societies. In Europe, archeobotanists are analyzing Upper Paleolithic hearths for evidence of plant remains probably gathered by women and children, while lithics specialists are poring over stone tools to detect new clues to their uses. And the results are gradually reshaping our understanding of Ice Age society. The famous Venus figurines, say archeologists of the new school, were never intended as male pornography: instead they may have played a key part in Upper Paleolithic

rituals that centered on women. And such findings, pointing toward a more important role for Paleolithic women than had previously been assumed, are giving many researchers pause.

Like many of her colleagues, Soffer clearly relishes the emerging picture of Upper Paleolithic life. "I think life back then was a hell of a lot more egalitarian than it was with your later peasant societies," she says. "Of course the Paleolithic women were pulling their own weight." After sifting through Ice Age research for nearly two decades. Soffer brings a new critical approach to the notion—flattering to so many of her male colleagues—of mighty male mammoth hunters. "Very few archeologists are hunters," she notes, so it never occurred to most of them to look into the mechanics of hunting dangerous tusked animals. They just accepted the ideas they'd inherited from past work.

But the details of hunting bothered Soffer. Before the fifth century B.C., no tribal hunters in Asia or Africa had ever dared make their living from slaying elephants; the great beasts were simply too menacing. With the advent of the Iron Age in Africa, the situation changed. New weapons allowed Africans to hunt elephants and trade their ivory with Greeks and Romans. A decade ago, keen to understand how prehistoric bands had slaughtered similar mammoths, Soffer began studying Upper Paleolithic sites on the Russian and Eastern European plains. To her surprise, the famous mammoth bone beds were strewn with cumbersome body parts, such as 220-pound skulls, that sensible hunters would generally abandon. Moreover, the bones exhibited widely differing degrees of weathering, as if they had sat on the ground for varying lengths of time. To Soffer, it looked suspiciously as if Upper Paleolithic hunters had simply camped next to places where the pachyderms had perished naturally—such as water holes or salt licks—and mined the bones for raw materials.

Soffer began analyzing data researchers had gathered describing the sex and age ratios of mammoths excavated from four Upper Paleolithic sites. She found many juveniles, a smaller number of adult females, and hardly any males. The distribution mirrored the death pattern other researchers had observed at African water holes, where the weakest animals perished closest to the water and the strongest farther off. "Imagine the worst time of year in Africa, which is the drought season," explains Soffer. "There is no water, and elephants need an enormous amount. The ones in the worst shape—your weakest, your infirm, your young—are going to be tethered to that water before they die. They are in such horrendous shape, they don't have any extra energy to go anywhere. The ones in better shape would wander off slight distances and then keel over farther away. You've got basket cases and you've got ones that can walk 20 feet."

To Soffer, the implications of this study were clear. Upper Paleolithic bands had pitched their camps next to critical resources such as ancient salt licks or water holes. There the men spent more time scavenging bones and ivory from mammoth carcasses than they did risking life and limb by attacking 6,600-pound pachyderms with short-range spears. "If one of these Upper Paleolithic guys killed a mammoth, and occasionally they did," concedes Soffer dryly, "they probably didn't stop talking about it for ten years."

But if Upper Paleolithic families weren't often tucking into mammoth steaks, what were they hunting and how? Soffer found the first unlikely clue in 1991, while sifting through hundreds of tiny clay fragments recovered from the Upper Paleolithic site of Pavlov, which lies just a short walk from Dolní Vestonice. Under a magnifying lens, Soffer noticed something strange on a few of the fragments: a series of parallel lines impressed on their surfaces. What could have left such a regular pattern? Puzzled, Soffer photographed the pieces, all of which had been unearthed from a zone sprinkled with wood charcoal that was radiocarbon-dated at between 27,000 and 25,000 years ago.

When she returned home, Soffer had the film developed. And one night on an impulse, she put on a slide show for a visiting colleague, Jim Adavasio. "We'd run out of cable films," she jokes. Staring at the images projected on Soffer's refrigerator, Adovasio, an archeologist at Mercyhurst College in Pennsylvania and an expert on ancient fiber technology, immediately recognized the impressions of plant fibers. On a few, he could actually discern a pattern of interlacing fibers—weaving.

Without a doubt, he said, he and Soffer were gazing at textiles or basketry. They were the oldest—by nearly 7,000 years—ever found. Just how these pieces of weaving got impressed in clay, he couldn't say. "It may be that a lot of these [materials] were lying around on clay floors," he notes. "When the houses burned, the walked-in images were subsequently left in the clay floors."

Soffer and Adovasio quickly made arrangements to fly back to the Czech Republic. At the Dolní Vestonice branch of the Institute of Archeology, Soffer sorted through nearly 8,400 fired clay pieces, weeding out the rejects. Adovasio made positive clay casts of 90. Back in Pennsylvania, he and his Mercyhurst

colleague David Hyland peered at the casts under a zoom stereomicroscope, measuring warps and wefts. Forty-three revealed impressions of basketry and textiles. Some of the latter were as finely woven as a modern linen tablecloth. But as Hyland stared at four of the samples, he noted something potentially more fascinating: impressions of cordage bearing weaver's knots, a technique that joins two lengths of cord and that is commonly used for making nets of secure mesh. It looked like a tiny shred of a net bag, or perhaps a hunting net. Fascinated, Soffer expanded the study. She spent six weeks at the Moravian Museum in Brno, sifting through the remainder of the collections from Dolní Vestonice. Last fall, Adovasio spied the telltale impressions of Ice Age mesh on one of the new casts.

The mesh, measuring two inches across, is far too delicate for hunting deer or other large prey. But hunters at Dolní Vestonice could have set nets of this size to capture hefty Ice Age hares, each carrying some six pounds of meat, and other furbearers such as arctic fox and red fox. As it turns out, the bones of hares and foxes litter camp floors at Dolní Vestonice and Pavlov. Indeed, this small game accounts for 46 percent of the individual animals recovered at Pavlov. Soffer, moreover, doesn't rule out the possibility of turning up bits of even larger nets. Accomplished weavers in North America once knotted mesh with which they captured 1,000-pound elk and 300-pound bighorn sheep. "In fact, when game officials have to move sheep out west, it's by nets," she adds. "You throw nets on them and they just lie down. It's a very safe way of hunting."

In many historical societies, she observes, women played a key part in net hunting since the technique did not call for brute strength nor did it place young mothers in physical peril. Among Australian aborigines, for example, women as well as men knotted the mesh, laboring for as much as two or three years on a fine net. Among native North American groups, they helped lay out their handiwork on poles across a valley floor. Then the entire camp joined forces as beaters. Fanning out across the valley, men, women, and children alike shouted and screamed, flushing out game and driving it in the direction of the net. "Everybody and their mother could participate," says Soffer. "Some people were beating, others were screaming or holding the net. And once you got the net on these animals, they were immobilized. You didn't need brute force. You could club them, hit them any old way."

People seldom returned home empty-handed. Researchers living among the net-hunting Mbuti in the forests of Congo report that they capture game every time they lay out their woven traps, scooping up 50 percent of the animals encountered. "Nets are a far more valued item in their panoply of food-producing things than bows and arrows are," says Adovasio. So lethal are these traps that the Mbuti generally rack up more meat than they can consume, trading the surplus with neighbors. Other net hunters traditionally smoked or dried their catch and stored it for leaner times. Or they polished it off immediately in large ceremonial feasts. The hunters of Dolní Vestonice and Pavlov, says Soffer, probably feasted during ancient rituals. Archeologists unearthed no evidence of food storage pits at either site. But there is much evidence of ceremony. At Dolní Vestonice, for example, many clay figurines appear to have been ritually destroyed in secluded parts of the site.

Soffer doubts that the inhabitants of Dolní Vestonice and Pavlov were the only net makers in Ice Age Europe. Camps stretching from Germany to Russia are littered with a notable abundance of small-game bones, from hares to birds like ptarmigan. And at least some of their inhabitants whittled bone tools that look much like the awls and net spacers favored by historical net makers. Such findings, agree Soffer and Adovasio, reveal just how shaky the most widely accepted reconstructions of Upper Paleolithic life are. "These terribly stilted interpretations," says Adovasio, "with men hunting big animals all the time and the poor females waiting at home for these guys to bring home the bacon—what crap."

In her home outside Munich, Linda Owen finds other faults with this traditional image. Owen, an American born and raised, specializes in the microscopic analysis of stone tools. In her years of work, she often noticed that many of the tools made by hunters who roamed Europe near the end of the Upper Paleolithic era, some 18,000 to 12,000 years ago, resembled pounding stones and other gear for harvesting and processing plants. Were women and children gathering and storing wild plant foods?

Most of her colleagues saw little value in pursuing the question. Indeed, some German archeologists contended that 90 percent of the human diet during the Upper Paleolithic era came from meat. But as Owen began reading nutritional studies, she saw that heavy meat consumption would spell death. To stoke the body's cellular engines, human beings require energy from protein, fat, or carbohydrates. Of these, protein is the least efficient. To burn it, the body must boost its metabolic rate by 10 percent, straining the liver's ability to absorb oxygen. Unlike carnivorous animals, whose digestive and metabolic systems are well adapted to a meat-only diet, humans who consume more than half their calories as lean meat will die from protein poisoning. In Upper Paleolithic times, hunters undoubtedly tried to round out their diets with fat from wild game. But in winter, spring, and early summer, the meat would have been very lean. So how did humans survive?

Owen began sifting for clues through anthropological and historical accounts from subarctic and arctic North America. These environments, she reasoned, are similar to that of Ice Age Europe and pose similar challenges to their inhabitants. Even in the far north, Inuit societies harvested berries for winter storage and gathered other plants for medicines and for fibers. To see if any of the flora that thrived in Upper Paleolithic Europe could be put to similar uses, Owen drew up a list of plants economically important to people living in cold-climate regions of North America and Europe and compared it with a list of species that botanists had identified from pollen trapped in Ice Age sediment cores from southern Germany. Nearly 70 plants were found on both lists. "I came up with just a fantastic list of plants that were available at that time. Among others, there were a number of reeds that are used by the Eskimo and subarctic people in North America for making baskets. There are a lot of plants with edible leaves and stems, and things that were used as drugs and dyes. So the plants were there."

The chief plant collectors in historical societies were undoubtedly women. "It was typically women's work," says Owen. "I did find several comments that the men on hunting expeditions would gather berries or plants for their own meals, but they did not participate in the plant-gathering expeditions. They might go along, but they would be hunting or fishing."

Were Upper Paleolithic women gathering plants? The archeological literature was mostly silent on the subject. Few archeobotanists, Owen found, had ever looked for plant seeds and shreds in Upper Paleolithic camps. Most were convinced such efforts would be futile in sites so ancient. At University College London, however, Owen reached a determined young archeobotanist, Sarah Mason, who had analyzed a small sample of charcoal-like remains from a 26,390-year-old hearth at Dolní Vestonice.

The sample held more than charcoal. Examining it with a scanning electron microscope. Mason and her colleagues found fragments of fleshy plant taproots with distinctive secretory cavities—trademarks of the daisy and aster family, which boasts several species with edible roots. In all likelihood, women at Dolní Vestonice had dug the roots and cooked them into starchy meals. And they had very likely simmered other plant foods too. Mason and her colleagues detected a strange pulverized substance in the charred sample. It looked as if the women had either ground plants into flour and then boiled the results to make gruel or pounded vegetable material into a mush for their babies. Either way, says Soffer, the results are telling. "They're stuffing carbohydrates."

Owen is pursuing the research further. "If you do look," she says, "you can find things." At her urging, colleagues at the University of Tübingen are now analyzing Paleolithic hearths for botanical remains as they unearth them. Already they have turned up more plants, including berries, all clearly preserved after thousands of years. In light of these findings, Owen suggests that it was women, not men, who brought home most of the calories to Upper Paleolithic families. Indeed, she estimates that if Ice Age females collected plants, bird eggs, shellfish, and edible insects, and if they hunted or trapped small game and participated in the hunting of large game—as northern women did in historical times—they most likely contributed 70 percent of the consumed calories.

Moreover, some women may have enjoyed even greater power, judging from the most contentious relics of Ice Age life: the famous Venus figurines. Excavators have recovered more than 100 of the small statuettes, which are crafted between 29,000 and 23,000 years ago from such enduring materials as bone, stone, antler, ivory, and fired clay. The figurines share a strange blend of abstraction and realism. They bare prominent breasts, for example, but lack nipples. Their bodies are often minutely detailed down to the swaying lines of their backbones and the tiny rolls of flesh—fat folds—beneath their shoulder blades, but they often lack eyes, mouths, and any facial expression. For years researchers viewed them as a male art form. Early anthropologists, after all, had observed only male hunters carving stone, ivory, and other hard materials. Females were thought to lack the necessary strength. Moreover, reasoned experts, only men would take such loving interest in a woman's body. Struck by the voluptuousness of the small stone, ivory, and clay bodies, some researchers suggested they were Ice Age erotica, intended to be touched and fondled by their male makers. The idea still lingers. In the 1980s, for example, the well-known American paleontologist Dale Guthrie wrote a scholarly article comparing the postures of the figurines with the provocative poses of *Playboy* centerfolds.

But most experts now dismiss such contentions. Owen's careful scouring of ethnographic sources, for example, revealed that women in arctic and subarctic societies did indeed work stone and ivory on occasion. And there is little reason to suggest the figurines figured as male erotica. The Black Venus, for example, seems to have belonged to a secret world of ceremony and ritual far removed from everyday sexual life.

The evidence, says Soffer, lies in the raw material from which the Black Venus is made. Clay objects sometimes break or explode when fired, a process called thermal-shock fracturing. Studies conducted by Pamela Vandiver of the Smithsonian Institution have demonstrated that the Black Venus and other human and animal figurines recovered from Dolní Vestonice—as well as nearly 2,000 fired ceramic pellets that litter the site—were made from a local clay that is resistant to thermal-shock fracturing. But many of the figurines, including the celebrated Black Venus, bear the distinctive jagged branching splinters created by thermal shock. Intriguingly, the fired clay pellets do not.

Curious, Vandiver decided to replicate the ancient firing process. Her analysis of the small Dolní Vestonice kilns revealed that they had been fired to temperatures around 1450 degrees Fahrenheit—similar to those of an ordinary hearth. so Vandiver set about making figurines of local soil and firing them in a similar earthen kiln, which a local archeological crew had built nearby. To produce thermal shock, she had to place objects larger than half an inch on the hottest part of the fire; moreover, the pieces had to be so wet they barely held their shape.

To Vandiver and Soffer, the experiment—which was repeated several times back at the Smithsonian Institution—suggests that thermal shock was no accident. "Stuff can explode naturally in the kiln," says Soffer, "or you can make it explode. Which was going on at Dolní Vestonice? We toyed with both ideas. Either we're dealing with the most inept potters, people with two left hands, or they are doing it on purpose. And we reject the idea that they were totally inept, because other materials didn't explode. So what are the odds that this would happen only with a very particular category of objects?"

These exploding figurines could well have played a role in rituals, an idea supported by the location of the kilns. They are situated far away from the dwellings, as ritual buildings often are. Although the nature of the ceremonies is not clear, Soffer speculates that they might have served as divination rites for discerning what the future held. "Some stuff is going to explode. Some stuff is not going to explode. It's evocative, like picking petals off a daisy. She loves me, she loves me not."

Moreover, ritualists at Dolní Vestonice could have read significance into the fracturing patterns of the figurines. Many historical cultures, for example, attempted to read the future by a related method called scapulimancy. In North America, Cree ceremonialists often placed the shoulder blade, or scapula, of a desired animal in the center of a lodge. During the ceremonies, cracks began splintering the bone: a few of these fractures leaked droplets of fat. To Cree hunters, this was a sign that they would find game if they journeyed in the directions indicated by the cracks.

Venus figurines from other sites also seem to have been cloaked in ceremony. "They were not just something made to look pretty," says Margherita Mussi, an archeologist at the University of Rome–La Sapienza who studies Upper Paleolithic figurines. Mussi notes that several small statuettes from the Grimaldi Cave carvings of southern Italy, one of the largest troves of Ice Age figurines ever found in Western Europe, were carved from rare materials, which the artists obtained with great difficulty, sometimes through trade or distant travel. The statuettes were laboriously whittled and polished, then rubbed with ocher, a pigment that appears to have had ceremonial significance, suggesting that they could have been reserved for special events like rituals.

The nature of these rites is still unclear. But Mussi is convinced that women took part, and some archeologists believe they stood at the center. One of the clearest clues, says Mussi, lies in a recently rediscovered Grimaldi figurine known as Beauty and the Beast. This greenish yellow serpentine sculpture portrays two arched bodies facing away from each other and joined at the head, shoulders, and lower extremities. One body is that of a Venus figurine. The other is a strange creature that combines the triangular head of a reptile, the pinched waist of a wasp, tiny arms, and horns. "It is clearly not a creature of this world," says Mussi.

The pairing of woman and supernatural beast, adds Mussi, is highly significant. "I believe that these women were related to the capacity of communicating with a different world," she says. "I think they were believed to be the gateway to a different dimension." Possessing powers that far surpassed others in their communities, such women may have formed part of a spiritual elite, rather like the shamans of ancient Siberia. As intermediaries between the real and spirit worlds, Siberian shamans were said to be able to cure illnesses and intercede on behalf of others for hunting success. It is possible that Upper Paleolithic women performed similar services for their followers.

Although the full range of their activities is unlikely ever to be known for certain, there is good reason to believe that Ice Age women played a host of powerful roles—from plant collectors and weavers to hunters and spiritual leaders. And the research that suggests those roles is rapidly changing our mental images of the past. For Soffer and others, these are exciting times. "The data do speak for themselves," she says finally. "They answer the questions we have. But if we don't envision the questions, we're not going to see the data."

"NEW WOMEN OF THE ICE AGE"

Heather Pringle

1) What are Venus figurines, and what is the traditional interpretation of their use and meaning in prehistoric societies?

2) How did incomplete or inaccurate ethnographic data on historic and modern hunter-gatherer groups contribute to the traditional reconstruction of the sociopolitical and economic organization of prehistoric hunter-gatherer groups?

3) How has recent ethnographic research contributed to a new understanding of the roles of women in prehistory?

4) How has recent archaeological research contributed to a different understanding of the role of hunting in paleolithic societies?

5) Referring back to the Durrenberger article ("Are Ethnographies 'Just-So' Stories?"), have cultural mores and ideas within western culture in the last seven decades influenced how the archaeological record has been interpreted in regard to prehistoric gender roles? Why or why not?

6) What lines of evidence have been employed to construct new theories regarding the use and meaning of Venus figurines in Paleolithic societies?

RITUALS OF MANHOOD: MALE INITIATION IN PAPUA NEW GUINEA

Gilbert H. Herdt

Sambia are a mountain-dwelling hunting and horti-cultural people who number some 2,000 persons and inhabit one of New Guinea's most rugged terrains. The population is dispersed through narrow river valleys over a widespread, thinly populated rain for-est; rainfall is heavy; and even today the surround-ing mountain ranges keep the area isolated. Sambia live on the fringes of the Highlands, but they trace their origins to the Papua hinterlands; their culture and economy thus reflect a mixture of influences from both of those areas. Hunting still predominates as a masculine activity through which most meat protein is acquired. As in the Highlands, though, sweet po-tatoes and taro are the staple crops, and their culti-vation is for the most part women's work. Pigs are few, and they have no ceremonial or exchange sig-nificance; indigenous marsupials, such as possum and tree kangaroo, provide necessary meat prestations for all initiations and ceremonial feasts (cf. Meigs 1976).

Sambia settlements are small, well-defended, mountain clan hamlets. These communities comprise locally based descent groups organized through a strong agnatic idiom. Residence is patrivirilocal, and most men actually reside in their father's hamlets. Clans are exogamous, and one or more of them to-gether constitute a hamlet's landowning corporate agnatic body. These men also form a localized warriorhood that is sometimes allied with other ham-lets in matters of fighting, marriage, and ritual. Each hamlet contains one or two men's clubhouses, in addition to women's houses, and the men's ritual life centers on their clubhouse. Marriage is usually by sister exchange or infant betrothal, although the lat-ter form of prearranged marriage is culturally pre-ferred. Intrahamlet marriage is occasionally more fre-quent (up to 50 percent of all marriages in my own hamlet field site) than one would expect in such small segmentary groupings, an involutional pattern weak-ened since pacification.

Sambia male and female residential patterns dif-fer somewhat from those of other Highlands peoples. The nuclear family is an important subunit of the hamlet-based extended family of interrelated clans.

A man, his wife, and their children usually cohabit within a single, small, round hut. Children are thus reared together by their parents during the early years of life, so the nuclear family is a residential unit, an institution virtually unknown to the Highlands (Meggit 1964; Read 1954). sometimes this unit is ex-panded through polygyny, in which case a man, his cowives, and their children may occupy the single dwelling. Girls continue to reside with their parents until marriage (usually near the menarche, around fifteen to seventeen years of age). Boys, however, are removed to the men's clubhouse at seven to ten years of age, following their first-stage initiation. There they reside exclusively until marriage and cohabitation years later. Despite familial cohabitation in early childhood, strict taboos based on beliefs about men-strual pollution still separate men and women in their sleeping and eating arrangements.

Warfare used to be constant and nagging among Sambia, and it conditioned the values and mascu-line stereotypes surrounding the male initiatory cult. Ritualized bow fights occurred among neighboring hamlets, whose members still intermarried and usu-ally initiated their sons together. At the same time, though, hamlets also united against enemy tribes and in staging war parties against them. Hence, warfare, marriage, and initiation were interlocking institu-tions; the effect of this political instability was to re-inforce tough, strident masculine performance in most arenas of social life. "Strength" (*jerundu*) was—and is—a pivotal idea in this male ethos. Indeed, strength, which has both ethnobiological and behav-ioral aspects, could be aptly translated as "maleness" and "manliness." Strength has come to be virtually synonymous with idealized conformity to male ritual routine. Before conquest and pacification by the Aus-tralians, though, strength had its chief performative significance in one's conduct on the battlefield. Even today bitter reminders of war linger on among the Sambia; and we should not forget that it is against the harsh background of the warrior's existence that Sambia initiate their boys, whose only perceived pro-tection against the inconstant world is their own un-bending masculinity.

Initiation rests solely in the hands of the men's secret society. It is this organization that brings the collective initiatory cycle into being as jointly performed by neighboring hamlets (and as constrained by their own chronic bow fighting). The necessary feastcrop gardens, ritual leadership and knowledge, dictate that a handful of elders, war leaders, and ritual experts be in full command of the actual staging of the event. Everyone and all else are secondary.

There are six intermittent initiations from the ages of seven to ten and onward. They are, however, constituted and conceptualized as two distinct cultural systems within the male life cycle. First-stage (*moku*, at seven to ten years of age), second-stage (*imbutu*, at ten to thirteen years), and third-stage (*ipmangwi*, at thirteen to sixteen years) initiations—bachelorhood rites—are collectively performed for regional groups of boys as age-mates. The initiations are held in sequence, as age-graded advancements; the entire sequel takes months to perform. The focus of all these initiations is the construction and habitation of a great cult house (*moo-angu*) on a traditional dance ground; its ceremonialized building inaugurates the whole cycle. Fourth-stage (*nuposha*: sixteen years and onward), fifth-stage (*taiketnyi*), and sixth-stage (*moondangu*) initiations are, conversely, individually centered events not associated with the confederacy of interrelated hamlets, cult house, or dance ground. Each of these initiations, like the preceding ones, does have its own ritual status, social role, and title, as noted. The triggering event for the latter three initiations, unlike that for the bachelorhood rites, is not the building of a cult house or a political agreement of hamlets to act collectively but is rather the maturing femininity and life-crisis events of the women assigned in marriage to youths (who become the initiated novices). Therefore, fourth-stage initiation is only a semipublic activity organized by the youths' clansmen (and some male affines). Its secret purificatory and other rites are followed by the formal marriage ceremony in the hamlet. Fifth-stage initiation comes at a woman's menarche, when her husband is secretly introduced to additional purification and sexual techniques. Sixth-stage initiation issues from the birth of a man's wife's first child. This event is, de jure, the attainment of manhood. (The first birth is elaborately ritualized and celebrated; the next three births are also celebrated, but in more truncated fashion.) Two children bring full adulthood (*aatmwunu*) for husband and wife alike. Birth ceremonies are suspended after the fourth birth, since there is no reason to belabor what is by now obvious: a man has proved himself competent in reproduction. This sequence of male initiations forms the basis for male development, and it underlies the antagonistic tenor of relationships between the sexes.

It needs stating only once that men's secular rhetoric and ritual practices depict women as dangerous and polluting inferiors whom men are to distrust throughout their lives. In this regard, Sambia values and relationships pit men against women even more markedly, I think, than occurs in other Highlands communities (cf. Brown and Buchbinder 1976; Meggitt 1964; Read 1954). Men hold themselves as the superiors of women in physique, personality, and social position. And this dogma of male supremacy permeates all social relationships and institutions, likewise coloring domestic behavior among the sexes (cf. Tuzin 1980 for an important contrast). Men fear not only pollution from contact with women's vaginal fluids and menstrual blood but also the depletion of their semen, the vital spark of maleness, which women (and boys, too) inevitably extract, sapping a man's substance. These are among the main themes of male belief underlying initiation.

The ritualized simulation of maleness is the result of initiation, and men believe the process to be vital for the nature and nurture of manly growth and well-being. First-stage initiation begins the process in small boys. Over the ensuing ten to fifteen years, until marriage, cumulative initiations and residence in the men's house are said to promote biological changes that firmly cement the growth from childhood to manhood. Nature provides male genitals, it is true; but nature alone does not bestow the vital spark biologically necessary for stimulating masculine growth or demonstrating cold-blooded self-preservation.

New Guinea specialists will recognize in the Sambia belief system a theme that links it to the comparative ethnography of male initiation and masculine development: the use of ritual procedures for sparking, fostering, and maintaining manliness in males (see Berndt 1962; Meigs 1976; Newman 1964, 1965; Poole 1981; Read 1965; Salisbury 1965; Strathern 1969, 1970). Sambia themselves refer to the results of first-stage collective initiation—our main interest—as a means of "growing a boy"; and this trend of ritual belief is particularly emphatic.

Unlike ourselves, Sambia perceive no imminent, naturally driven fit between one's birthright sex and one's gender identity or role.[1] Indeed, the problem (and it is approached as a situation wanting a solution) is implicitly and explicitly understood in quite different terms. The solution is also different for the two sexes: men believe that a girl is born with all of the vital organs and fluids necessary for her to attain reproductive competence through "natural" maturation. This conviction is embodied in cultural perceptions of the girl's development beginning with the sex assignment at birth. What distinguishes a girl *(tai)* from a boy *(kwulai'u)* is obvious: "A boy has a penis, and a girl does not," men say. Underlying men's communications is a conviction that maleness, unlike femaleness, is not a biological given. It must be artificially induced through secret ritual; and that is a personal achievement.

The visible manifestations of girls' fast-growing reproductive competence, noticed first in early motor coordination and speech and then later in the rapid attainment of height and secondary sex traits (e.g., breast development), are attributed to inner biological properties. Girls possess a menstrual-blood organ, or *tingu*, said to precipitate all those events and the menarche. Boys, on the other hand, are thought to possess an inactive tingu. They do possess, however, another organ—the *kere-ku-kereku*, or semen organ—that is thought to be the repository of semen, the very essence of maleness and masculinity; but this organ is not functional at birth, since it contains no semen naturally and can only store, never produce, any. Only oral insemination, men believe, can activate the boy's semen organ, thereby precipitating his push into adult reproductive competence. In short, femininity unfolds naturally, whereas masculinity must be achieved; and here is where the male ritual cult steps in.

Men also perceive the early socialization risks of boys and girls in quite different terms. All infants are closely bonded to their mothers. Out of a woman's contaminating, life-giving womb pours the baby, who thereafter remains tied to the woman's body, breast milk, and many ministrations. This latter contact only reinforces the femininity and female contamination in which birth involves the infant. Then, too, the father, both because of postpartum taboos and by personal choice, tends to avoid being present at the breast-feedings. Mother thus becomes the unalterable primary influence; father is a weak second. Sambia say this does not place girls at a "risk"—they simply succumb to the drives of their "natural" biology. This maternal attachment and paternal distance clearly jeopardize the boys' growth, however, since nothing innate within male maturation seems to resist the inhibiting effects of mothers' femininity. Hence boys must be traumatically separated—wiped clean of their female contaminants—so that their masculinity may develop.

Homosexual fellatio inseminations can follow this separation but cannot precede it, for otherwise they would go for naught. The accumulating semen, injected time and again for years, is believed crucial for the formation of biological maleness and masculine comportment. This native perspective is sufficiently novel to justify our using a special concept for aiding description and analysis of the data: masculinization (Herdt 1981:205 ff). Hence I shall refer to the overall process that involves separating a boy from his mother, initiating him, ritually treating his body, administering homosexual inseminations, his biological attainment of puberty, and his eventual reproductive competence as masculinization. (Precisely what role personal and cultural fantasy plays in the negotiation of this ritual process I have considered elsewhere: see Herdt 1981: chaps. 6, 7, and 8.)

A boy has female contaminants inside of him which not only retard physical development but, if not removed, debilitate him and eventually bring death. His body is male: his tingu contains no blood and will not activate. The achievement of puberty for boys requires semen. Breast milk "nurtures the boy," and sweet potatoes or other "female" foods provide "stomach nourishment," but these substances become only feces, not semen. Women's own bodies internally produce the menarche, the hallmark of reproductive maturity. There is no comparable mechanism active in a boy, nothing that can stimulate his secondary sex traits. Only semen can do that; only men have semen; boys have none. What is left to do, then, except initiate and masculinize boys into adulthood?

Note

1. I follow Stroller (1968) in adhering to the following distinctions: the term *sex traits* refers to purely biological phenomena (anatomy, hormones, genetic structure, etc.), whereas *gender* refers to those psychological and cultural attributes that compel a person (consciously or unconsciously) to sense him- or herself, and other persons, as belonging to either the male or female sex. It follows that the term *gender role* (Sears 1965), rather than the imprecise term *sex role*, refers to the normative set of expectations associated with masculine and feminine social positions.

References

Berndt, R. M. 1962. *Excess and Restraint: Social Control among a New Guinea Mountain People.* Chicago: University of Chicago Press.

Brown, P., and G. Buchbinder (eds.). 1976. *Man and Woman in the New Guinea Highlands.* Washington, D.C.: American Anthropological Association.

Herdt, G. H. 1981. *Guardians of the Flutes: Idioms of Masculinity.* New York: McGraw-Hill.

Meggitt, M. J. 1964. Male-female relationships in the Highlands of Australian New Guinea. In *New Guinea: The Central Highlands*, ed. J. B. Watson, *American Anthropologist*, 66, pt. 2 (4):204–224.

Meigs, A. S. 1976. Male pregnancy and the reduction of sexual opposition in a New Guinea Highlands society. *Ethnology* 15 (4):393–407.

Newman, P. L. 1964. Religious belief and ritual in a New Guinea society. In *New Guinea: The Central Highlands*, ed. J. B. Watson, *American Anthropologist* 66, pt. 2 (4):257–272.

_____. 1965. *Knowing the Gururumba*. New York: Holt, Rinehart and Winston.

Poole, F. J. P. 1981. Transforming "natural" woman: female ritual leaders and gender ideology among Bimin-Kuskumin. In *Sexual Meanings*, ed. S. B. Ortner and H. Whitehead. New York: Cambridge University Press.

Read, K. E. 1954. Cultures of the Central Highlands, New Guinea. *Southwestern Journal of Anthropology* 10 (1):1–43.

_____. 1965. *The High Valley*. London: George Allen and Unwin.

Salisbury, R. F. 1965. The Siane of the Eastern Highlands. In *Gods, Ghosts, and Men in Melanesia*, P. Lawrence and M. J. Meggitt, pp. 50–77, Melbourne: Melbourne University Press.

Sears, R. R. 1965. Development of gender role. In *Sex and Behavior*, ed. F. A. Beach, pp. 133–163. New York: John Wiley and Sons.

Stoller, R. J. 1968. *Sex and Gender*. New York: Science House.

Strathern, A. J. 1969. Descent and alliance in the New Guinea Highlands: some problems of comparison. Royal Anthropological Institute, *Proceedings*, pp. 37–52.

_____. 1970. Male initiation in the New Guinea Highlands societies. *Ethnology* 9 (4):373–379.

Tuzin, D. F. 1980. *The Voice of the Tambaran: Truth and Illusion in Ilahita Arapesh Religion*. Berkeley, Los Angeles, and London: University of California Press.

"Rituals of Manhood: Male Initiation In Papua New Guinea"

Gilbert H. Herdt

1) Outline Sambia culture based on information from the article: economics, social and political organization, and other facets of life.

2) How do warfare, marriage, and male initiation rites operate as interlocking institutions in Sambia culture?

3) What is the purpose of male initiation rites? How many stages do the Sambia employ in the rite to reach their goal of adult male status for the boys?

4) How do Sambia men's attitudes towards women and sex contribute to the operation and cultural understanding of the purpose of the initiation rites?

5) How do the Sambia explain their understanding of the biological basis of maleness and femaleness, and how does it affect their behavior?

THE BRUTALIZING OF WOMEN

Jan Goodwin

Even though women in the United States have yet to achieve parity with men when it comes to paychecks or power, our circumstances are ideal when compared with women around the world. And increasingly, we do compare—as news comes into our living rooms from the most far-flung corners of the globe. Unfortunately, much of that news has made us familiar with cultures and governments that are oppressive and even brutal to women.

The often terrible lot faced by many women abroad literally hits home when families immigrate to the United States and bring their customs with them. Nine years ago, in New York City, a Chinese immigrant killed his wife for being unfaithful; after he argued that in his culture the act would have been justified because his shame was so great, he was given only probation. Last November, in Lincoln, NE, a father arranged a double wedding for his two daughters, respectively 13 and 14 years old, to two men, 28 and 34 years old. All the men were recent emigrants from Iraq, where such child marriages are not uncommon among Muslims. When authorities found out, they arrested the father and charged him with child abuse; the grooms were charged with sexual assault of a minor.

Another case that horrified many is that of Fauziya Kasinga, who fled to the United States three years ago at age 17 to escape the ritual of female genital mutilation (FGM), which is still practiced in her homeland of Togo. The ritual involves cutting off a girl's clitoris, and sometimes also the labia minora and majora; in extreme cases the sides are then stitched together, leaving only a tiny opening. One hundred and thirty million girls and women worldwide have undergone this agonizing procedure (often without anesthesia and under unsanitary conditions); some will die from complications. Survivors suffer chronic infection and pain.

Twenty-eight African nations and some minority groups in the Middle East and Asia still practice FGM, believing that it prevents promiscuity among women. A woman's chance of marrying, which in many countries is still her only route to economic survival, depends on whether she has undergone FGM. In a number of places, the price a girl fetches as a bride is higher the smaller her vaginal opening has been made.

A Philadelphia judge initially rejected Kasinga's bid for political asylum. She was jailed for 16 months, during which time women's rights activists launched a highly publicized campaign for her freedom. She was released and finally granted asylum last June, and her case established a legal precedent for FGM as grounds for political asylum.

What follows are examples of barbarism from three other countries. More voices need to be raised against these practices, so that one day they can be stopped.

— *Nepal* —
Sentenced For Having A Stillbirth

Twenty-nine-year-old Thirtha Maya Baral has been in Central Jail in Nepal's capital, Katmandu, for three years and still has another seven to serve. Her crime: giving birth to a stillborn baby. "It was my third baby," she says through tears. "I was alone when I went into labor. My husband was working abroad. The delivery was long and hard. No one came to assist me. When the baby was finally born, it was very small, and dead."

Four days later, police, tipped off by neighbors who'd known she was pregnant, came and arrested her. No medical opinion was sought, and the only evidence against her was the accusation of the neighboring family, who did not tell the police they were involved in an angry land dispute with Thirtha's husband. She had no lawyer and was quickly found guilty.

Since being jailed, she has not seen her 12-year-old son and 10-year-old daughter, who have been left to survive on the streets alone. Had they been with her at the time of her arrest, they would have been taken with her, but now she does not even have the bus fare it would take to bring them to her cell. "This is the worst," she says, "not knowing how my children are doing."

Nepal has some of the most spectacular scenery on Earth, including Mount Everest, but it also has the most severe prohibitions against abortion on the planet, forbidding it even in cases of rape, incest, or when a woman's life is medically endangered. *Garbhabat*, or destruction of life, is the official abortion charge, but the law also covers infanticide and child abandonment.

Tragically, it is also used against women whose babies are stillborn or who have miscarriages. Women found guilty of garbhabat often have their property confiscated, making them vulnerable to accusations from vengeful or greedy relatives or neighbors who use the law to effect a property or land grab. Police and prosecutors are also known to be bribed into bringing such charges, and in other cases, women are beaten into confessions. But this is rarely necessary in a land where rural women can't afford doctors or lawyers, and where the word of an influential accuser is usually taken on faith.

Jyoti (name changed), 41, has already spent more than a quarter of her life in jail. Widowed two decades ago, she was unable to remarry since Nepalese law requires her to remain faithful to her husband, even after his death. She followed custom and lived with her in-laws. Forced to become her father-in-law's concubine, she became pregnant, and was made to have an abortion. Word leaked—possibly the abortionist talked—and Jyoti was arrested.

"Her father-in-law was among her public accusers, although in private he told her to accept the blame and he would get her out of jail within a month or two," says women's health and welfare activist Roshan Karki. "But eleven years have passed, and she hasn't heard from her in-laws."

Neither Thirtha nor Jyoti's children are with them in jail, but many women's children are. When women are imprisoned, families encourage husbands to divorce and remarry, and traditionally, those children are not accepted by a new spouse. In Central Jail last year, there were 15 children, ranging in age from 2 to 15, effectively "serving" lengthy sentences with their mothers. There are 73 prisons in the country, all of which usually have children living in them under horrendous conditions: crumbling, flea- and rat-infested cells, inadequate food, bedding, and clothing, and no basic health care and schooling.

Anti-garbhabat activists say the situation is made graver by Nepal's extreme poverty and high birth rate—the government's birth control program reaches only 21 percent of women, in part because of limited funding. "Eighty percent of women of reproductive age are severely anemic because of poor diet and simply aren't able to carry their babies to term," says Aruna Upreti, M.D., a maternal and child-care specialist in Katmandu. "Compounding this is the lack of physicians in much of the country, and the practice of women giving birth unaided. Under conditions like these, is it any wonder that babies are frequently born dead, and women too easily accused of garbhabat?"

— *Pakistan* —
Arrested For Being Raped

In rape cases in the United States, only recently have courts stopped blaming the victim, or believing "she must have asked for it." But in Pakistan, not only is a rape victim rarely believed, frequently she is also arrested and jailed, even if she is a child.

Majidah Abdullah was 11 years old when she was abducted and repeatedly raped by her father's employers. He owed money he was unable to repay, so he was punished by having his daughter abused. When the family tried to bring rape charges, the girl was thrown in jail.

In Pakistan, *zina*, or sex outside of wedlock—which includes rape as well as adultery—is a crime. For married women, the maximum sentence is death by stoning. For single women, the punishment is up to 100 lashes and up to ten years' imprisonment. Technically, men can also be charged with zina, but with a simple denial, they can go free.

In Pakistani courts under Islamic law, the judge has the discretion to reject the victim's account and that of any female witness; in such cases, there must be four adult males, "Muslims of good repute," who are witnesses—an unfair standard since few men of good repute would stand by and watch a rape take place. Then the tables are cruelly turned: A woman's complaint of rape is considered a confession of illicit sexual intercourse; a subsequent pregnancy is also evidence against her. Although common law, whose standards of evidence are less stringent, can also be applied, activists say that in practice few cases go that route.

Such was the case of Safia Bibi. She was 16 when she was raped by her employer and his son, and she became pregnant. Her father reported the assaults, but a judge acquitted both men since Safia's family could not produce four male witnesses. Yet Safia's pregnancy was deemed proof of fornication.

Her harsh sentence—a three-year jail term, a public flogging, and a fine—struck a chord with Pakistan's women's rights activists, particularly in view of the fact that she has a disability: She is nearly blind. When their campaign on her behalf was reported by foreign media, the teenager was freed.

Eleven-year-old Majidah was less fortunate. While her attackers went free, she spent several years in jail without a court hearing until her plight was discovered by Asma Jahangir, a human rights activist. Jahangir was able to get Majidah released on bail, but the girl says her life is over. Since it's well known that she's no longer a virgin, her chances of marriage are virtually nil, which means that she becomes a social outcast.

According to Jahangir, some 60 percent of women in Pakistan's jails are there on charges of zina, many after being raped. Once in custody, about 70 percent are physically and/or sexually abused again by the police or prison guards, according to War Against Rape, a Pakistani human rights organization.

It appalls activists that this law exists in a country that has twice elected Benazir Bhutto its prime minister. Educated at Radcliffe and Oxford, Bhutto had promised to reform the law. But needing the backing of religious leaders who support such anti-woman laws, she never followed through. Her government was recently overthrown.

"For Bhutto, this was clearly not a priority, and there is not enough of a will in the country," says Surita Sandosham, head of Equality Now, a New York City-based human rights organization. "Nothing will change," she says, "without international pressure."

— *Thailand* —
Sold Into Sexual Slavery

The California travel agency brochure could not be more explicit: SEX TOURS TO THAILAND, REAL GIRLS, REAL SEX, REAL CHEAP. THESE WOMEN ARE THE MOST SEXUALLY AVAILABLE IN THE WORLD. DID YOU KNOW YOU CAN ACTUALLY BUY A VIRGIN GIRL FOR AS LITTLE AS $200?

What the ad copy doesn't say is that these "virgin girls" are children who have been kidnapped or sold into Thai brothels. They average 15 customers a day, and are beaten if they don't cooperate. On Phuket Island in 1984, a popular resort for foreigners in southern Thailand, five prostitutes burned to death when a fire broke out in a brothel; they had been chained to their beds to prevent their escape.

Because Thailand has one of the highest AIDS rates in the world, virgins net a higher price for sex traffickers; but given that men can refuse to wear condoms, and the girls' immature bodies make them more vulnerable to tissue tears, HIV infection in brothels is rampant.

Lin-Lin was just 13 when a visitor to her village in Burma told her father he could find the girl work as a domestic. Her impoverished family accepted the offer. But the man was in fact a sex-trade agent, and Lin-Lin was taken to a brothel and sold. (In other cases, the families know the fate their daughters face, but are too poor and without options to refuse.) Two years later, Lin-Lin is HIV-positive—though the brothel does not reveal this to customers.

Brothels are illegal in Thailand, but owners have little fear of arrest. The industry generates $3 billion annually in tourism, and therefore the sex trade, says Human Rights Watch, is protected by graft-taking police and a government that looks the other way.

A 1993 Human Rights Watch report points out that the United States gives Thailand $4 million a year to control the traffic in narcotics but nothing to stop sex trafficking. "The United Nations needs to be very aggressive in fighting this modern form of slavery," says Dorothy Thomas, director of the women's rights project at Human Rights Watch in New York City.

Only recently did it become a felony in the United States for Americans to engage in sex with minors on tours abroad, or for American tour operators to promote such trips. But because of lax enforcement, experts say that American men continue to go abroad and sexually prey on children.

"THE BRUTALIZING OF WOMEN"

Jan Goodwin

1) Compare and contrast problems faced by women in the United States with women in other countries. How do they compare on an ideological, economic, and legal basis?

2) Why is rape seen as a crime *of* women, rather than a crime *against* women, under Islamic law in Pakistan?

3) How does western tourism contribute to the problems of female exploitation, prostitution, and the spread of disease in Thailand and Southeast Asia?

SECTION SIX

Religion and Religious Specialists

THE ABOMINATIONS OF LEVITICUS

Mary Douglas

Defilement is never an isolated event. It cannot occur except in view of a systematic ordering of ideas. Hence any piecemeal interpretation of the pollution rules of another culture is bound to fail. For the only way in which pollution ideas make sense is in reference to the total structure of thought whose keystone, boundaries, margins and internal lines are held in relation by rituals of separation.

To illustrate this I take a hoary old puzzle from biblical scholarship, the abominations of Leviticus, and particularly the dietary rules. Why should the camel, the hare and the rock badger be unclean? Why should some locusts, but not all, be unclean? Why should the frog be clean and the mouse and the hippopotamus unclean? What have chameleons, moles and crocodiles got in common that they should be listed together?

[To help follow the argument the reader is referred to Deuteronomy XIV and Leviticus XI using the text of the New Revised Standard Translation.]

• • •

All the interpretations given so far fall into one of two groups: either the rules are meaningless, arbitrary because their intent is disciplinary and not doctrinal, or they are allegories of virtues and vices. Adopting the view that religious prescriptions are largely devoid of symbolism, Maimonides said:

> The Law that sacrifices should be brought is evidently of great use . . . but we cannot say why one offering should be a lamb whilst another is a ram, and why a fixed number of these should be brought. Those who trouble themselves to find a cause for any of these detailed rules are in my eyes devoid of sense. . . .

• • •

Any interpretations will fail which take the Donots of the Old Testament in piecemeal fashion. The only sound approach is to forget hygiene, aesthetics, morals and instinctive revulsion, even to forget the Canaanites and the Zoroastrian Magi, and start with the texts. Since each of the injunctions is prefaced by the command to be holy, so they must be explained by that command. There must be contrariness between holiness and abomination which will make over-all sense of all the particular restrictions.

Holiness is the attribute of Godhead. Its root means "set apart," What else does it mean? We should start any cosmological enquiry by seeking the principles of power and danger. In the Old Testament we find blessing as the source of all good things, and the withdrawal of blessing as the source of all dangers. The blessing of God makes the land possible for men to live in.

God's work through the blessing is essentially to create order, through which men's affairs prosper. Fertility of women, livestock and fields is promised as a result of the blessing and this is to be obtained by keeping covenant with God and observing all His precepts and ceremonies (Deut. XXVIII, 1–14). Where the blessing is withdrawn and the power of the curse unleashed, there is barrenness, pestilence, confusion. For Moses said:

> But if you will not obey the voice of the Lord your God or be careful to do all his commandments and his statutes which I command you to this day, then all these curses shall come upon you and overtake you. . . . (Deut. XXVIII, 15–24)

From this it is clear that the positive and negative precepts are held to be efficacious and not merely expressive: observing them draws down prosperity, infringing them brings danger. We are thus entitled to treat them in the same way as we treat primitive ritual avoidances whose breach unleashes danger to men. The precepts and ceremonies alike are focussed on the idea of the holiness of God which men must create in their own lives. So this is a universe in which men prosper by conforming to holiness and perish when they deviate from it. If there were no other clues we should be able to find out the Hebrew idea of the holy by examining the precepts by which men conform to it. It is evidently not goodness in the sense of an all-embracing humane kindness. Justice and moral goodness may well illustrate holiness and form part of it, but holiness embraces other ideas as well.

Granted that its root means separateness, the next idea that emerges is of the Holy as wholeness and completeness. Much of Leviticus is taken up with stating the physical perfection that is required of things presented in the temple and of persons approaching it. The animals offered in sacrifice must be without blemish, women must be purified after childbirth, lepers should be separated and ritually cleansed before being allowed to approach it once

---

171

they are cured. All bodily discharges are defiling and disqualify from approach to the temple. Priests may only come into contact with death when their own close kin die. But the high priest must never have contact with death.

• • •

He must be perfect as a man, if he is to be a priest.

This much reiterated idea of physical completeness is also worked out in the social sphere and particularly in the warriors' camp. The culture of the Israelites was brought to the pitch of greatest intensity when they prayed and when they fought. The army could not win without the blessing and to keep the blessing in the camp they had to be specially holy. So the camp was to be preserved from defilement like the Temple. Here again all bodily discharges disqualified a man from entering the camp as they would disqualify a worshipper from approaching the altar. A warrior who had had an issue of the body in the night should keep outside the camp all day and only return after sunset, having washed. Natural functions producing bodily waste were to be performed outside the camp (Deut. XXIII, 10–15). In short the idea of holiness was given an external, physical expression in the wholeness of the body seen as a perfect container.

• • •

Other precepts develop the idea of wholeness in another direction. The metaphors of the physical body and of the new undertaking relate to the perfection and completeness of the individual and his work. Other precepts extend holiness to species and categories. Hybrids and other confusions are abominated.

Lev. XVIII

23. *And you shall not lie with any beast and defile yourself with it, neither shall any woman give herself to a beast to lie with it: it is perversion, . . .*

The word "perversion" is a significant mistranslation of the rare Hebrew word *tebhel*, which has as its meaning mixing or confusion. The same theme is taken up in Leviticus XIX, 19.

You shall keep my statutes. You shall not let your cattle breed with a different kind; you shall not sow your field with two kinds of seed; nor shall there come upon you a garment of cloth made of two kinds of stuff.

All these injunctions are prefaced by the general command:

Be holy, for I am holy.

We can conclude that holiness is exemplified by completeness. Holiness requires that individuals shall conform to the class to which they belong. And holiness requires that different classes of things shall not be confused.

Another set of precepts refines on this last point. Holiness means keeping distinct the categories of creation. It therefore involves correct definition, discrimination and order. Under this head all the rules of sexual morality exemplify the holy. Incest and adultery (Lev. XVIII, 6–20) are against holiness, in the simple sense of right order. Morality does not conflict with holiness, but holiness is more a matter of separating that which should be separated than of protecting the rights of husbands and brothers.

Then follows in Chapter XIX another list of actions which are contrary to holiness. Developing the idea of holiness as order, not confusion, this list upholds rectitude and straight-dealing as holy, and contradiction and double-dealing as against holiness. Theft, lying, false witness, cheating in weights and measures, all kinds of dissembling such as speaking ill of the deaf (and presumably smiling to their face), hating your brother in your heart (while presumably speaking kindly to him), these are clearly contradictions between what seems and what is. This chapter also says much about generosity and love, but these are positive commands, while I am concerned with negative rules.

We have now laid a good basis for approaching the laws about clean and unclean meats. To be holy is to be whole, to be one; holiness is unity, integrity, perfection of the individual and of the kind. The dietary rules merely develop the metaphor of holiness on the same lines.

First we should start with livestock, the herds of cattle, camels, sheep and goats which were the livelihood of the Israelites. These animals were clean inasmuch as contact with them did not require purification before approaching the Temple. Livestock, like the inhabited land, received the blessing of God. Both land and livestock were fertile by the blessing, both were drawn into the divine order. The farmer's duty was to preserve the blessing. For one thing, he had to preserve the order of creation. So no hybrids, as we have seen, either in the fields or in the herds or in the clothes made from wool or flax. To some extent men covenanted with their land and cattle in the same way as God covenanted with them. Men respected the first born of their cattle, obliged them to keep the Sabbath. Cattle were literally domesticated as slaves. They had to be brought into the special order in order to enjoy the blessing. The differences between cattle and the wild beasts is that the wild beasts have no covenant to protect them. It is possible that the Israelites were like other pastoralists who do not relish wild game. The Nuer of the South Sudan, for instance, apply a sanction of disapproval of a man who lives by hunting. To be driven to eating wild meat is the sign of a poor herdsman. So it would be probably wrong to think of the Israelites as longing for forbidden meats and finding the restrictions irksome. Driver is surely right in taking the rules as an *a posteriori* generalisation of their habits. Cloven hoofed, cud chewing ungulates are the model of the proper kind of food for a pastoralist. If they must eat wild game, they can eat wild game that shares these distinctive characters and is therefore of the same general species. This is a kind of casuistry which permits scope for hunting antelope and wild goats and wild sheep. Everything would be quite straightforward were it not that the legal mind has seen fit to give ruling on some borderline cases. Some animals seem to be ruminant, such as the hare and the hyrax (or rock badger), whose constant grinding of their teeth was held to be cud-chewing. But they are definitely not cloven-hoofed and so are excluded by name. Similarly for animals which are cloven-hoofed but are not ruminant, the pig and the camel. Note that this failure to conform to the two necessary criteria for defining cattle is the only reason given in the Old Testament for avoiding the pig; nothing whatever is said about its dirty scavenging habits. As the pig does not yield milk, hide nor wool, there is no other reason for keeping it except for its flesh. And if the Israelites did not keep pig they would not be familiar with its habits. I suggest that originally the sole reason for its being counted as unclean is its failure as a wild boar to get into the antelope class, and that in this it is on the same footing as the camel and the hyrax, exactly as is stated in the book.

After these borderline cases have been dismissed, the law goes on to deal with creatures according to how they live in the three elements, the water, the air and the earth. The principles here applied are rather different from those covering the camel, the pig, the hare and the hyrax. For the latter are excepted from clean food in having one but not both of the defining characters of livestock. Birds I can say nothing about, because, as I have said, they are named and not described and the translation of the name is open to doubt. But in general the underlying principle of cleanness in animals is that they shall conform fully to their class. Those species are unclean which are imperfect members of their class, or whose class itself confounds the general scheme of the world.

To grasp this scheme we need to go back to Genesis and the creation. Here a three-fold classification unfolds, divided between the earth, the waters and the firmament. Leviticus takes up this scheme and allots to each element its proper kind of animal life. In the firmament two-legged fowls fly with wings. In the water scaly fish swim with fins. On the earth four-legged animals hop, jump or walk. Any class of creatures which is not equipped for the right kind of locomotion in its element is contrary to holiness. Contact with it disqualifies a person from approaching the Temple. Thus anything in the water which has not fins and scales is unclean (XI, 10–12). Nothing is said about predatory habits or of scavenging. The only sure test for cleanness in a fish is its scales and its propulsion by means of fins.

Four-footed creatures which fly (XI, 20–26) are unclean. Any creature which has two legs and two hands and which goes on all fours like a quadruped is unclean (XI, 27). Then follows (v. 29) a much disputed list. In some translations, it would appear to consist precisely of creatures endowed with hands instead of front feet, which perversely use their hands for walking: the weasel, the mouse, the crocodile, the shrew, various kinds of lizards, the chameleon and mole (Danby, 1933), whose forefeet are uncannily hand-like. This feature of this list is lost in the New Revised Standard Translation which used the word "paws" instead of hands.

The last kind of unclean animal is that which creeps, crawls or swarms upon the earth. This form of movement is explicitly contrary to holiness (Lev. XI, 41–44). Driver and White use "swarming" to translate the Hebrew *shérec*, which is applied to both those which teem in the waters and those which swarm on the ground. Whether we call it teeming, trailing, creeping, crawling or swarming, it is an indeterminate form of movement. Since the main animal categories are defined by their typical movement, "swarming" which is not a mode of propulsion proper to any particular element, cuts across the basic classification. Swarming things are neither fish, flesh nor fowl. Eels and worms inhabit water, though not as fish; reptiles go on dry land, though not as quadrupeds; some insects fly, though not as birds. There is no order in them. Recall what the Prophecy of Habacuc says about this form of life:

> For thou makest men like the fish of the sea, like crawling things that have no ruler. (I. v. 14)

The prototype and model of the swarming things is the worm. As fish belong in the sea so worms belong in the realm of the grave, with death and chaos.

The case of the locusts is interesting and consistent. The test of whether it is a clean and therefore edible kind is how it moves on the earth. If it crawls it is unclean. If it hops it is clean (XI, v. 21). In the Mishnah it is noted that a frog is not listed with creeping things and conveys no uncleanness (Danby, p 722). I suggest that the frog's hop accounts for it not being listed. If penguins lived in the Near East I would expect them to be ruled unclean as wingless

WORLDS OF THE SHAMAN

WHAT IS A SHAMAN?

Piers Vitebsky

Flying above the earth to the spirit world or descending into the underworld; being stripped to a skeleton, reassembled, and reborn; fighting evil spirits and sorcerers; and protecting their people from famine and disease—these are powers commonly claimed by shamans throughout the world. The word *shaman*, sometimes erroneously used interchangeably with sorcerer or medicine man, comes from the language of the Evenk, a small group of Tungus-speaking hunters and reindeer herders in Siberia. In the strictest sense, it refers to a practitioner who can will his or her spirit to leave the body and journey to upper or lower worlds.

Shamanic beliefs do not constitute a single religion or doctrinal system, although worldwide shamanic traditions approach reality and human experience in similar ways. In shamanic thinking, every element of the world around us, whether human, animal, tree, or rock, is imbued with spirits. Spirits are conscious, often anthropomorphic, and can also be interpreted as representing the essences that underlie surface appearances.

Events in the spirit world are believed to be intimately connected to everyday occurrences, particularly in the realm of human health and fertility. By entering a trance state and allowing his or her soul to venture into other worlds, the shaman can seek out the underlying causes of mundane events, and then fight, beg, or cajole the spirits to intervene in the affairs of the living.

A shaman's soul-journeys are thought to take place within a layered cosmology, with the earth at the center of various upper and lower worlds. Illness is often ascribed to the kidnapping of a patient's soul by spirits. When a fisherman in the Peruvian Amazon is seduced by a freshwater mermaid, his soul must be rescued by a mestizo shaman whose soul travels along the river bottom. In Sulawesi, Indonesia, when a patient's soul wanders off into the sky, the Wana shaman pursues it in a spirit canoe that can traverse the heavens. Many traditional Inuit communities believed that the supply of marine mammals was controlled by a female water spirit who punished people for moral lapses by withholding the animals. One of the most daunting tests of a great shaman was to travel down to the sea floor to persuade the spirit to release the seals and whales into the hunters' path again.

Shamanic power is usually acquired through difficult initiations, ordeals believed to be imposed by the spirits. The accomplished shaman generally acquires "spirit helpers," with whom he is thought to associate. These may be gods or ancestors but are commonly the spirits of powerful, agile, or cunning animals. Often they enable the shaman to turn into one of these creatures or take on its attributes—flying into the sky in the form of a hawk or diving into the water as a fish. Such powers remain elusive and—as the need for spirit helpers suggests—always partly outside the range of the shaman's unaided abilities. Acquired with difficulty, shamanic powers can be lost again in battles with spirit enemies or through failure to perform the rituals properly.

Shamanic religion may date from the time of the earliest known Paleolithic drawings, which were made some 30,000 years ago by our hunting ancestors. Although many of these cave and rock paintings are of animals, some show humans wearing animal masks and other motifs suggestive of shamanic practices. Even today, belief in shamans seems strongest in societies that rely on hunting and gathering. In the absence of a priestly class, individuals believe they can communicate directly with gods and spirits. Agricultural societies seem somewhat inimical to shamans because of their more institutionalized forms of religion. In our own times, shamans have been widely persecuted and their activities suppressed by secular governments and by the major established religions. Yet, because shamanic thinking is flexible and adaptable, it often persists even in complex urban societies.

Although outside observers have called them madmen or charlatans, within their own cultures shamans are viewed as a combination of priest, doctor, social worker, and mystic. Eighteenth-century anthropologists and travelers encountered shamans in the Arctic and subarctic; throughout Siberia, Lapland, Tibet, and Mongolia; and among the Inuit of North America. Shamanic cultures are also widespread among rain forest tribes of South America, particularly in Amazonia, and throughout Southeast Asia.

Since he or she must often deal with illness, malevolence, and death, the shaman is often concerned with matters that are dark and dangerous. A youngster may dread being called by the spirits to follow the shamanic path, and some strenuously resist at first. Rather than seeing them as mad, their clients believe that shamans have extraordinary insight into the cosmic processes governing health, food supply, and fertility. After painful initiations, a shaman is entrusted with looking over the edge of the abyss without falling in, and returning with help for the people of this world.

DIALOGUES WITH THE DEAD

Piers Vitebsky

Almost every day among the Sora, a jungle tribe in eastern India, the living conduct dialogues with the dead. A shaman, usually a woman, serves as an intermediary between the two worlds. During a trance, her soul is said to climb down terrifying precipices to the underworld, leaving her body for the dead to use as their vehicle for communication. One by one the spirits speak through her mouth. Mourners crowd around the shaman, arguing vehemently with the dead, laughing at their jokes, or weeping at their accusations.

To prepare her for the important position of intermediary, a future shaman is visited in childhood dreams by helper spirits, who are said to turn her soul into a monkey to enable her to clamber down to the underworld. Later, the Sora believe, she learns to make this journey at will during a trance. She marries a helper spirit, bears spirit children, and makes a second home in the underworld, which she visits every time she dreams or goes into a trance.

According to Sora thinking, death is not the end of existence, but merely another phase. After death one becomes a powerful spirit with contradictory motives. On the one hand, the dead nourish their living descendants by infusing their growing crops with their own "soul force." In aggressive moods, however, they may "eat" their relatives' souls and cause in them the same illness to which the deceased succumbed.

At funerals and in divinations to diagnose the cause of illness, people stage dialogues to interrogate the dead about where they are—the landscape, the sky, or the underworld. A spirit that is trying to harm the living is presumed to be in a bad place. The relatives will then try to persuade it to move or offer a sacrificial animal as a substitute for the sick person under attack.

My research has revealed several stages of emotional involvement between living Sora and their dead. Those who died recently are considered the most dangerous because they still retain an intense

attachment—often expressed as hostility—to the living. When speaking with the recently dead, people can become extremely distressed, as pity for the dead is mixed with fear for their own safety. Someone who has been dead for some time—a second stage of detachment—is no longer so threatening or aggressive. People who have been dead for many years arouse no strong feelings and (speaking through a shaman) bestow their names on their descendants' children.

Finally, the deceased dies a second death in the underworld and becomes a butterfly, bereft of human memories. As the dead drift inexorably away from the living toward butterflyhood, they become increasingly inaccessible and unknowable. In that form, souls are believed to become characterless and beyond the reach of dialogue.

Sora shamans appear to heal physical illness by helping the bereaved to manage painful and guilty memories about the dead. Healing is thought to occur only through dialogue, not merely from the passage of time. While the shaman goes on her soul journey to the underworld, the bereaved or ailing client also makes an inner journey of discovery. The mourners heal themselves by exploring and modifying the deceased's pain and hostility.

Emphasis on a "talking cure" seems similar to many Western therapies, but with a crucial difference. We may speak to our dead in one-sided conversations, but the Sora expect responses. Without the shaman's intervention, there could be no dialogue and thus no healing. Both systems, I believe, are based on the same insight: that intense emotional attachment gives rise to memories that have the power to cause illness. In Western therapies, however, the memories of a grieving patient are considered isolated and subjective, while Sora memories of the dead are made "objective" by social dialogue. The whole Sora community moves toward a consensus as it traces the dead person's shifting states of mind on a shared psychic landscape.

While the traditional Sora religion met certain psychological and social needs very well, it is proving inadequate for a younger generation that is being exposed to rapid social change. Many of today's youngsters—the first generation to attend school—have joined the Baptist church, believing that the affiliation will help them gain access to mainstream society.

The older Sora know that after they die, their Baptist children will not talk to them or feed them with sacrifices. While some young Baptists extoll the benefits of their new religion, others confess to a gnawing uncertainty. "Maybe my father is with Jesus, or maybe he's in the underworld," said one, "but we can't know because we don't speak with him anymore."

SOVIET SUPERPOWERS

Marjorie Mandelstam Balzer

In the Siberian Far East, a story told by the Sakha (Yakut) people recounts how some of their shamans escaped Soviet jails: they simply turned into birds and flew away. The Sakha elder Somogotto recalled that one revered curer, Nikon, was arrested as part of the Soviet persecution of shamanic practitioners. Handcuffed to a policeman, the unprotesting shaman was led to the courthouse. But when they got there, instead of an old shaman, there was just a piece of tree branch handcuffed to the policeman, whom the magistrate accused of being drunk.

For the past ten years, I have collected many such tales of the powers of shamans, their prowess as curers and wiliness in the face of state-led persecution. These tales have not only helped to keep shamanic traditions alive in the Sakha Republic (Yakutia), they have also become a vital source of ethnic identity and resistance to absorption by the dominant Russian culture. Despite centuries of suppression and ridicule by church and state, some ancient worldviews are being reintegrated into the chaotic post-Soviet debates.

The shaman Konstantin of the Abyi region and two others captured by local officials reportedly were released after they made an entire roomful of Party functionaries believe they saw wild bears and snow inside a Young Communist League hall.

The legendary woman shaman Alykhardaakh is said to have bested Sakha Soviet authorities, whom she invited to her cabin for a seance. After dancing and drumming herself into a trance, she called forth water, and the men's ankles were submerged. Then she called forth a large fish, which she caught in her hands. Finally, she asked the officials to remove their pants and hold their male organs. The men, caught in this embarrassing position when she emerged from her trance, vowed never to bother her again.

The thrust of many of these popular stories is that even when shamans were jailed, at least some of them were spiritually more powerful than their captors and could transcend victimization. Such exuberant tales can lead a listener to romanticize the Soviet period, but the reality of ideology-driven repression was bleak. By the 1930s, most shamans were barely able to function. Soviet propaganda against "kulak-shamans" played to villagers' mixture of fear, distrust, and admiration of shamans. Practitioners were accused of political subversion and of being frauds who conned people out of goods, savings, animals, and even their daughters. Villagers who were converts to Communism collected shamans' drums for public burning, and shamans were pressed to donate their cloaks and paraphernalia to museums. One gray-bearded villager told me that when he was a boy, a local Communist activist invited the school-children to help him burn nine drums he had seized. The large, white drum of Tokoyeu, the most powerful local shaman, "jumped out of the fire three times" and had to be replaced each time. The drum burner died a horrible death soon after—but not before begging Tokoyeu for help and forgiveness.

Going into trance without a drum was difficult, but not impossible, for the few shamans who continued to practice. The elderly Marfa Zamorshikova recalled a desperate situation from her childhood, when her younger brother was ill and screaming in pain. Her mother summoned Matrena, an old woman "known for doing things that the shamans had done." To make a proper diagnosis, Matrena took up a frying pan in lieu of a drum and beat it with a wooden spoon. While in a trance, she announced that someone in the family had killed a big animal, whose spirit had entered the sick child. Four days later, after the boy had died, his father returned from a successful hunt. The family accepted the spirit possession interpretation of the child's illness and were resigned to his fate (*d'ylkha*), which derived from forces larger than themselves.

Like Matrena, some women in remote villages were able to cure in secret, while men with high-profile reputations went to jail. Authorities sometimes resorted to various pretexts for arrest, when a curer's true "crime" was shamanic practice. Still more insidious was the post-World War II Soviet policy of having shamans diagnosed as insane. Labeled as "schizophrenics," they were institutionalized and kept in a twilight of sedation. Fear of such treatment, perhaps even more than of jail, kept some from practicing. One black-leather-jacketed, motorcycle-driving young man, grandson of Tokoyeu, tearfully told me of the drugs he was given to silence the spirit voices he had heard from childhood. Recently, he has turned to traditional curers who may help him heed those voices and become a shaman himself.

Many Sakhas perceive modern medicine as being cold and bureaucratic, while shamans practice in a setting of intense, personal concern for the individual patient. Shamanic cures of cancer, gallstones, diabetes, infertility, and other common ailments are widely accepted. One popular story making the rounds is that of a young male shaman from the Viliuisk region, a protégé of Nikon, who cured a Soviet-trained Russian woman doctor of cancer. With a distrust of Soviet hospitals born of first-hand experience, the woman is said to have commissioned secret seances and postponed a risky operation. Later she was gratified to learn her tumor had disappeared.

A successful symbol of a revitalized merging of the old and new is a Moscow-trained surgeon, Aleksandra Chirkova, daughter of the shaman Konstantin. As head doctor of the huge Abyi region, she has incorporated aspects of shamanic seances, human X-ray vision, dream analysis, individual therapy, and herbal medicine into her hospital programs.

Some Sakha intellectuals are wary of the current swing toward folk medicine, fearful of a new wave of charlantry among those who call themselves "extrasenses," mixing Russian and Sakha curing traditions. Most Sakhas consider only five shamans, from different indigenous groups, to be genuine, and even their authenticity is hotly debated. Few patients have completely forsaken modern medicine. But many Sakhas are finding a new cultural pride and confidence in the emergence of shamans from the underground.

Shamanic functions have been reinforced and reinterpreted in new contexts. One female shaman reputedly used spirit power to fix a broken bus on the way to a meeting with Native American visitors. Another has built a reputation for finding stolen cars, and others have helped police find missing persons. One environmental activist is also a healer, building on a shamanic theme of harmony with nature gained through telepathy, meditation, and spirit propitiation.

A Sakha cultural revival movement called Kut-Sur (Heart-Soul-Mind-Reason) has drawn upon ancient shamanic concepts and rites. Kut-Sur members rejoiced in 1990 when, at their urging, the major Sakha midsummer shamanic celebration of renewal and fertility, *yhyakh*, became a republic holiday. Members stress a renewed respect for the power of spirits, the power of certain words, and the curative benefits of prayer.

Some healers have joined in private practices or in an Association of Folk Medicine, founded in 1990 and headed by the shaman-historian-extrasense Vladimir Kondakov. Although past Sakha shamans rarely worked together, his teams of curers are welcomed in many villages. Kondakov exhorts spiritual seekers and patients to climb a hill at sunrise and "let the first rays of the sun and the first songs of birds give you strength and energy. . . . As the sun rises, so shall you fly higher."

Another team of folk healers, led by Klavdia Maksimova and Petr Sleptsov, has organized group seances, using drumming and a jaw harp (*khomus*) to produce cures, stimulate artistic creativity, and open the "shamanic third eye" of intuition and spirit power. In 1995, I watched twenty patients as they danced and went into trances in a field to the resonating twang of the *khomus*. Some of the participants, who had appeared incapacitated during earlier sessions, now moved joyously, with animal and bird movements. A few rolled on the ground. They laughed and feasted and prayed to the fire spirit, closing with the drawing of solar energies toward their chests. "I am well," they chanted, "I am Sakha. I am here, in and with this land."

THE SHAMAN'S APPRENTICE

Laurel Kendall

Uijongbu, Republic of Korea, September 1989: Chini's dank little rented room and her pale, emaciated figure reflect the hardship suffered by someone who is destined to serve the spirits. The gods and ancestors will torment Chini until she becomes a shaman. Today, experienced shamans will dress her in the costumes of various spirits and coach her until she bursts into inspired words and actions. When Chini's "gates of speech" are finally opened, when she can give divinations in the spirits' own words, clients will seek her out and she will be able to earn a living as a shaman.

Although held in low esteem, the work of a shaman may offer the only hope for thirty-two-year-old Chini, who has so far failed at everything she has tried. Raised in poverty and married to an abusive drunk, she fled her marriage and was forced to leave her two small children behind. Drifting from one menial job to another, she began to hear the spirits' voices, urging her to leave her tasks and run outdoors. "But of course, once I got outside, there wasn't anyone there," she says with a faint smile. Her bizarre behavior earned her two visits to a mental hospital.

Whenever Chini had her fortune told, the shamans insisted that she was destined to be a shaman, that she must accept her fate and be initiated into the profession. Chini's mother and sister were appalled at first, but eventually they supported Chini's apprenticeship and went deep into debt to pay for her initiation *kut*.

A *kut* is a ceremony in which shamans—clothed as gods and ancestors and inspired by dancing to loud, percussive music—become hosts to the spirits. In an initiation *kut*, the apprentice shaman does this for the first time. Early in her ceremony, Chini must balance on an earthen water jar and deliver an oracle. Speaking through Chini, the god known as the Buddhist Sage announces that an intrusive spirit is blocking the way. Then Chini says no more.

The shamans first cajole the spirits, then coach and finally scold their apprentice, berating her for letting her thoughts wander. In mounting desperation, they tell her that the spirits will not move her tongue for her, that performing inspired speech, "whether or not the spirits have made you into a shaman," is more constructive than her stage fright and stony silence.

As the shamans see it, Chini's gates of inspired speech are blocked by an obstinate spirit, but at another level they recognize that Chini is blocked because she cannot clear her mind, opening herself to feelings and losing herself in performance. She does not heed the impulse to clothe herself in a particular spirit's costume, a vehicle of that spirit's presence and power. She does not weep or shout insults, but resists the emotional release and surrender that would bring on the force of the spirits.

Kim Pongsun, the "spirit mother" in charge of Chini's initiation, tries to identify the troublesome spirit. She divines that the culprit is Chini's dead sister, a pockmarked maiden who took her own life at age nineteen. Kim Pongsun now claims that the dead sister was herself a destined shaman. Once installed in Chini's shrine as Princess Hogu, the sister will assist Chini as a potent guardian spirit.

But even when she is clothed in the robes of this new spirit, Chini can't find inspiration. As a last resort, the shamans dress Chini in the gold satin robe of the Heavenly King, since no intrusive spirit would dare to block the high king's path. Swaying on her feet, eyes vacant, a smile on her lips, Chini proclaims the presence of the Heavenly King, then lapses again into silence.

Kim Pongsun castigates the spirits whose painted images hang above Chini's altar, calling them heartless for insisting on a *kut* and then failing to uphold their part of the bargain. She threatens to tear them off the wall and burn them up.

At last, the apprentice seems ready to speak for Princess Hogu. Kim Pongsun urges Chini on, using a now-familiar formula: "If there's a costume the spirit wants to wear, then put it on! Jump and keep shouting out the spirit's commands. That's what we mean by the true words of the spirits—shout out what the spirits have to tell us. That's what it's all about." The shamans pound cymbals, drum, and gong as Chini reaches for Princess Hogu's robe. Kim Pongsun shouts, "You must cry your heart out. Then everything will burst out!"

Sobbing convulsively, Chini covers her tear-streaked face with Princess Hogu's fan and—in the person of the dead sister—laments her pitiful situation, forced to become a shaman. The dead girl calls for her mother and pours out wrenching words that could be Chini's own:

> Mother! Mother! I wanted so much to be beautifu,
> Mother . . . I'll help my little sister as a shaman.
> Mother, I want your blessing, but you don't respond.
> Mother, how many times I've called you! . . .
> When my mother raised me she wasn't able to give

> us decent food. I'm full of pity for Chini.
> How can it be helped,
> Mother? . . . That's why I've come.

Tears trickle down the mother's wrinkled face. Chini's sister and sister-in-law are weeping in the corner. The shamans wipe away their own tears. Chini gives a round of divinations, staggers drunkenly through her performance of Princess Hogu's praise song, and collapses in a bow in front of her altar.

Although the apprentice has made progress, the outcome of the *kut* is still uncertain. But for the brief, cathartic encounter with her dead sister, Chini's performance has been limited, her divinations commonplace and unremarkable.

The next day—after much coaxing, encouragement, and scolding—Chini undertakes the most difficult ordeal of her *kut*. She climbs six feet to the top of a makeshift edifice and balances on the blades of a fodder-chopper. There she proclaims the presence of the Knife-Riding General, who is one of the most powerful spirits in her pantheon. But she gives no divinations, and when she descends from the blades, she speaks no more.

Chini ends her *kut* deep in debt and not yet empowered to work as a shaman. She has failed, the shamans acknowledge, because she is too self-conscious and inhibited.

Discouraged, Chini breaks off the apprenticeship with her spirit mother and disappears. Her unsuccessful initiation and failed apprenticeship are common in the world of Korean shamans. Although disappointed by Chini's defection, Kim Pongsun is philosophical:

> Look at it this way. It isn't as if anyone can become a successful shaman right when they get the calling. They must make a great effort and change completely. If it happened automatically, then wouldn't everyone be making their living as a shaman? Everyone has their moment, and all things happen in their season. If this time the spirits vacillated, then by and by the time can come when they will make her into a successful shaman.

OBJECTS OF POWER

Allen Wardwell

Beset by European-American culture and law, the Northwest Coast tradition of shamanism died out early this century, but not before being recorded by such linguists, anthropologists, and collectors as Franz Boas, John Swanton, George Hunt, and George T. Emmons. Among the Tlingit, Tsimshian, Haida, and other peoples, shamans could be men or women.

They often lived the life of ascetics, away from villages and everyday affairs, and their hair was long and uncut. Accompanied by tales of encounters with helpful and malevolent spirits, journeys to the land of the dead, acquisition of animal languages, and flights to the moon and stars, shamans were fantastic figures. But they were also remembered as human beings, and the masks, rattles, and other objects they used are a reminder of the vital ritual role they played in the life of their people.

Death of a Shaman

In about 1890, the Tlingit shaman Tek-'ic felt it was time to die. His brother had recently passed away, and Tek-'ic realized no one would succeed him as shaman or care for his remains. According to his niece's account, Tek-'ic decided to have himself photographed on the steps of his house in Yakutat Bay. He then called in the members of his clan, who sang spirit songs. Afterward they took him out to the clean sand beach to cut his long hair. He died that same day, and following the custom for shamans, his remains were placed in a grave house above ground. About ten years later, the desiccated body was buried in the ground by a Tlingit convert to Christianity who did not want its spirit powers to cause someone else to become a shaman.

AMAZON GRACE

Kenneth Good

Among the Yanomami of the Amazon forest of Venezuela and Brazil, the normal chatter in the communal house is pierced almost every afternoon by the bellows of the village shaman beginning his chant. It is an all-in-one sermon about the world, a lecture on life's meaning, an explanation of cultural and social origins. As small children dart playfully between the support posts, and men and women roast plantains, weave cotton, repair arrows, or lie back in their hammocks talking, the melodious chanting of the man who is a leader, curer, and defender against evil spirits is a reassuring sound. It engenders a feeling that all is well, that this most important man is in good humor and in control of the all-pervading spirits.

At other times, the sound of the shaman brings village life almost to a standstill. This is when he chants to cure the sick or dying, to make whole a child whose soul has escaped the body and left him or her vulnerable to dangerous forces. Then women weep or sometimes wail, and everyone feels a combination of anger and sorrow.

As an adolescent, Rinawe spent innumerable afternoons sitting in the semicircle of Yanomami elders, participating in shamanic sessions. To experience the supernatural world, he took *ebene*, hallucinogenic snuff made from psychoactive plants and blown through three-foot-long bamboo tubes into each nostril. When he was no more than fifteen, he felt the calling to become a shaman himself and began to practice chants, rhythms, and struts, at first on his own and later with a few other young men as an audience. Eventually, he was taken seriously by the senior shamans, who guided his chanting.

Now the crucial time has come for Rinawe to be initiated. For this he must present himself as a worthy host to the spirits. Day after day he sits on the ground in the communal house, his legs extended in front of the headman's section, taking large doses of *ebene* and repeating the phrases chanted by the master shaman. As the spirits, summoned and encouraged by the master, approach Rinawe, the youth is overcome and falls prostrate on his back. A village mate props him up and holds him steady as the shaman blows more drugs into him and continues with his instruction.

After five days of taking *ebene*, and almost no food or water, Rinawe is emaciated and covered with dried mucus, *ebene*, and soil. He is so weak that he appears barely conscious, and his repetitions of the shaman's phrases are almost inaudible. Will the spirits come? Will they accept him? Or will they flee, depriving him of his hopes of becoming a shaman? Some women begin to cry in fear for Rinawe's life and from compassion for his ordeal. Even one of the men sitting close to the participants begins to sob.

Rinawe survives the ordeal, and on the seventh morning the shamans decide the time has come for the crucial rite. They leave for the forest, where they cut a young tree to make a seven-foot ceremonial pole. Decorated along its length with feathers, the pole is called the rock, or rock outcrop; it is the place where the spirits live. The spirits that swarm around it must be guided to the new shaman.

With great ceremony and thunderous shouts, two shamans decorated with feathers carry the pole into the village clearing. As the entire community watches, they move toward the initiate, crouching and swinging their arms to drive off the malevolent spirits that seek to interfere. Finally they plant the pole in the ground between Rinawe's legs. *Pei!*—"It is done!" The master shaman grasps Rinawe's head and tilts it forward to touch the ceremonial mast, the rock, the dwelling of the spirits; and thus Rinawe enters the venerable realm of the shaman.

NEW SPIRITS FOR OLD

Shoefoot (Bautista Cajicuwa), as told to Kenneth Good and Mark Ritchie

Until their first contact with outsiders, about fifty years ago, the Yanomami Indians of Venezuela led an isolated existence in the Amazon rain forest. Once these Indians became known to the outside world, anthropologists wanted to study them, and missionaries sought to win their minds and souls. Within a few decades, the Yanomami have been exposed not only to new technologies but also to new "spirits."

Although communal life in the jungle can be pleasant—replete with laughter, friendship, and family—there is also a full measure of paranoia, sickness, and violence. Malaria remains rampant, food is often scarce, and vengeance raids are a fact of life. Shamans often tell their people that the cause of a relative's illness or death is a malevolent spirit sent by someone in a neighboring village. Wars of retaliation are commonly carried out with clubs and bows and arrows. During such tension-filled times, people are afraid to venture out of their villages alone, even to hunt or draw water from the river.

In the early 1960s, a Yanomami shaman and village leader known as Shoefoot, tired of living in fear and seeing people killed, felt betrayed by his spirits. Then he met Joe Dawson and his family, independent Evangelical missionaries from the United States, who convinced him to follow a foreign spirit that would help him find peace. In September 1996, Shoefoot, then sixty-five years old, visited the American Museum of Natural History, along with Joe Dawson's son Gary (Keleewa) and writer Mark Ritchie, who had told Shoefoot's story in his book Spirit of the Rain Forest. *Kenneth Good, an anthropologist who speaks fluent Yanomami, attended as an independent observer for this magazine. During the interview, Good was convinced of the sincerity of Shoefoot's conversion, although it is unique in his twelve years' experience of living with the Yanomami. The following is Shoefoot's statement:*

When I was a little boy, I used to sit in my hammock across from the communal dwelling and listen to the village shamans chant, calling out to the spirits. Everyone held these men in awe: they guided the community, controlled the spirits, and understood all things in life. I watched them blow *ebene* powder into each other's nostrils through long, hollow reeds. This potent drug is made from several jungle plants; it makes strong men's heads snap backward, but then it helps them talk to spirits. One day, I thought, I will become one of the village shamans, as the *hekura* (forest spirits) were already speaking to me.

When I was about fifteen, my father, a shaman himself, called on me to carry on this solemn service to the community. He said the village needed more powerful shamans, because it had so many enemies. Following him and his older brothers, I began to inhale *ebene* and chant. After several years of training, I was publicly initiated into the world of the *hekura*. Various spirits came to make a home within my chest.

Many sick and dying people were brought to my hearth to be healed. I inhaled the drug, called up the spirits, and tried to drive away those who came to do harm. Some of the sick recovered, but many died, because the spirits of the forest are powerful. When someone died, their relatives would cremate the body and drink the ashes. And they would ask me who was the evil shaman from another village who had caused their misfortune. Sometimes I would understand who it was who had done this, so I would call the men to take up clubs and arrows and raid the village where the evil shaman lived. We would kill as many men as we could, rape the women, and take some back to our village. Then we knew we might be raided ourselves, so I would advise everyone to move out into the forest on a trek of many days to escape the dangers. When a soul was stolen, I would try to send my spirits to retrieve it, but usually without success. I took great amounts of *ebene* so I could see the spirits and magically travel to far places and find them.

When I began my own family, I planted a garden and hunted to feed my children. Many times others would bring sick children, and I would take my drug and chant to cure them. At some times, very many got sick at once, and I was chanting and taking the drug all day and night. But young and old died anyway, and I doubled my efforts to heal until I was exhausted. When food was scarce in the village, I led trekking parties into the forest in search of fruits and berries. I was strong and respected as one who guided his community, and I received the largest portions of meat after a hunt.

As the years went on, the responsibilities of a shaman weighed heavier and heavier upon me. I was tired. So many sick and dying. I could not cure them, no matter how hard I tried. So many threats to my village. People were raiding and killing one another. I could not protect them. Often there were food crises. I took more and more *ebene* to get assistance from the spirits, but my mind began to play tricks. Instead of help, my spirits left me with nothing but worry and fear. Sometimes I was so confused I wanted to escape into the forest, but I never ran off. Some men got lost in the spirit world when they took the drug; many ran into the jungle and were never heard from again. Now and then, one of them was found dead. I was strong, but I was thinking I wasn't strong enough to go on like this.

A visitor from another village told me about foreign people, *nabas*, who had come to live on the river.

One older couple had a son called Keleewa, who talks and hunts just like us, because he grew up in a Yanomami village. We call him "the white Yanomami." Keleewa and his father told me of a big spirit that could help us, one that was friendly and not desiring death and destruction. I began to think about this peaceful new spirit, and pretty soon after, my spirits got jealous and gave me bad dreams. They said they were afraid I would abandon them and that they would kill me if I tried. When I stopped taking *ebene* and turned to the spirit of the *nabas*, I was happy to see that it was stronger than my forest spirits. They became afraid and went away. They didn't tell me to kill people or lead raids anymore. Instead, the new spirit told me to stop fights whenever I could.

I became calm in my mind and my fear went away. I no longer hated anyone or wanted to cause their death. My old spirits were happy whenever someone died, and they kept telling the shamans to stir up more violence. We thought we had power over these spirits, but they really had the power over us— causing our own people to die. Even when we shamans were chanting and taking *ebene* and looking content, there was turmoil inside, for our spirits kept telling us to kill. Some men lost all control when they took the drug, sometimes even killing their own wives and children.

Today I no longer live in fear and I'm a friend to everyone. We have ended our feuds and stopped the killing. Now that we are living in a bigger, more secure village, we are able to devote ourselves to growing more food; we have some cattle, and we have better homes to protect ourselves from the mosquitoes. The *nabas* told us that malaria comes from mosquitoes, not from evil shamans, and we have changed our belief. Some of us have learned to look at blood slides under Keleewa's microscope and tell what kind of malaria someone has. Our population at Honey Village is growing, while many others are decreasing. The new spirit freed me from the fear I had all the time. Today my people are better off and at peace.

ON THE PEYOTE ROAD

Mike Kiyaani, as told to
Thomas J. Csordas

Most Americans know peyote only as a cactus containing an illegal psychotropic substance, but to some 250,000 American Indian adherents of the peyote religion, it is a sacrament and a spirit. To live according to its inspiration is to follow the peyote road of personal dignity and respect for nature and for other people. Those recognized as having the ability to lead others along this path are known as "road men." Mike Kiyaani, who underwent his own long

apprenticeship, is such a road man. Now seventy-seven, Kiyaani is a Navajo who first used peyote in the late 1940s, after returning to his native Arizona as an honored veteran of military service. He had served in an elite Marine unit, along with other Navajos who used their complex native language to communicate sensitive information— a code that defied penetration.

The peyote religion, formally institutionalized as the Native American Church, was introduced to the Navajos in the 1930s by members of several Plains Indian tribes. Its practices and spirituality differ from those of the traditional Navajo religion, although both are fundamentally concerned with healing. Traditional Navajo medicine men—Kiyaani's own father was one—lead ceremonies known as chants. Lasting as long as nine consecutive nights, chants involve prayers in the form of songs, specific acts by the healer and patient, and the creation of potent visual symbols such as sand paintings. A peyote ceremony, in contrast, is a prayer meeting during which peyote is eaten by participants under the leadership of a road man. Combining singing, drumming, and prayers, the ceremony typically lasts one night, from dusk to dawn.

Assembled in a tepee or hogan, the participants focus their prayers on an altar or fire place. In the style learned by Mike Kiyaani, the centerpiece of the fire place is a crescent of heaped-up earth on which rests a special cactus button known as the chief peyote. The road man cherishes his chief peyote and may pass it down through several generations. Kiyaani concentrates on his chief peyote and the fire place to facilitate his dialogue with nature. He says that whereas white people talk directly to God, the humble prefer going through the intermediary of nature—the air and the sunshine, which are God's creations. Kiyaani is not a shaman who takes spirit flights to other worlds but a healer who prays through the elements of nature in which, for him, God already resides.

Mike Kiyaani's mentor was Truman Dailey, an Oto Indian who instructed him not to imitate Plains Indian ways but to take the medicine home and adapt its use to the Navajo culture and way of life. For Dailey, the elements of the altar represent parts of the eagle, which is sacred to his clan. Kiyaani stresses the Navajo understanding of corn as a symbol of growth and life. He performs the traditional corn pollen blessing, sprinkling some grains to make a path that corresponds to the peyote road. He also uses a song learned from his father that metaphorically connects the prayer meeting to the growth of the life-giving corn plant.

Navajo adherents of the peyote religion once faced opposition from their own tribal government, which decreed the religion illegal in 1940 and did not move for tolerance until 1966. Only in 1994 did the federal government adopt a law that guarantees the right of American Indians to practice the peyote religion. Mike Kiyaani remains deeply concerned that, against the background of a long struggle for freedom of religion, the use of peyote be protected for its importance in healing, spirituality, and identity. He has traveled widely to describe his work to audiences of health care professionals, and on the reservation his reputation as a road man keeps him in great demand by Navajos who travel considerable distances to seek his assistance.—T.J.C.

I'm a Navajo veteran—World War II, Navajo Code Talker, wounded in action. My clan is Salt Clan. I got my name from Kiyaani; that's my grandfather's clan. When I came back from the war, I was a sick man. There was something wrong with my mind, something wrong all over my body. No pain, but I felt kind of lousy. My father had died in 1944, and I guess that's what got into me. One man I got acquainted with took me to Oklahoma. I met this man Truman Dailey there, and he noticed my condition. He said, "You take this peyote," and gave me a twenty-five-pound flour sack filled with Mexican dry peyote. I took that back home.

During that time I was way up there where nobody lives, herding sheep, and I used peyote. Just a little bit during the day, every day. It seemed like it went all through my system. Then one particular day I felt like eating, and I had fifty buttons. In about another hour and a half, I ate another fifty buttons—maybe four times, fifty buttons. At midnight everything started coming. My life seemed to be coming to an end. That's the way the medicine showed me, but I still kept on eating until morning. Everything began coming out different. There was a lot of sagebrush out there, and everything was too beautiful. But every time I looked to the peyote, it wasn't pleasant to look at.

Then toward noon I looked for that peyote, and now I saw it was real pure, real white. It kind of talked to me, "Your body is like that, your body is pure. Now you don't need treatment, you're a well man. You wanted to get well, now you're well." I understood it to be that way. At that time I sure cried. I was all right then. After that I was pretty much on the go most of the time performing ceremonies for sick people. I kind of experimented with the peyote eating, how it works, how it can heal.

At the start of the ceremony, I don't know what's ailing the patient, but when you take some peyote into your system, the peyote affects you, and then you kind of know. A lot of people just say, "I'm sick," that's all. They don't know exactly what's bothering them. But peyote does wonderful things. My patient eats peyote. He has peyote in his system. Peyote is in my system, too. He's talking; then I kind of know. I kind of see things, what's wrong in that way. It's the peyote that shows me things. It's my patient talking his mind—the way he talks, the way he expresses

himself. It might be his action in there that's kind of unusual; that tells me. But I don't watch him directly, I keep my eyes on the fire all the time.

I say, "You come to me, and I want you to help yourself; whatever it is that's bothering your mind, whatever it is you think that's bothering your health, get your mind off of it. You get on to this medicine, this fire place, this singing that you hear, the prayers that you are hearing in here, which are all for you. The people sitting here, they're talking for you. They're singing for you. Everybody wants you to get well. Whatever's bothering you—maybe it's an evil, maybe it's that lightning struck near you, maybe something else. Get your mind off of it." He might have a hard time [from nausea] through the peyote effect, but that's going to help him. That's the time he's going to figure out what's wrong, why he's sick.

I go outside for a special ceremony at midnight. I get my bone whistle out. Some medicine men take their flashlight out there or maybe take somebody with them out there. I don't do those things. I'd rather be in the dark, praying by myself. A lot of Navajos, while they're out there, they see something, visualize something. I don't look for those things. But I might be hearing that the patient's mind is bothered by witchcraft or maybe some lightning struck that might be affecting his body, his mind.

Peyote. You eat it and it goes through your body, your blood veins, your flesh, your bone, your brain, and we talk to this peyote. And this peyote goes through all the patient's blood veins, goes to his brain, brain vessel; it seems like we talk to the peyote like that. Talking with nature; that's all it is. Whatever you do, peyote knows it, nature knows it. Whatever is wrong inside here, nature knows it. The Almighty knows it, so there's no way you can get away from this peyote, from this Almighty, from nature. If at some place you get off the road, then you notice it. Then you come back and pray. You go back to the Almighty, back to peyote. You get back on the road.

The spirit peyote came up among the Navajo people on a very hard road. But peyote found its way here, and so you see it has some kind of power. It found its way into the Navajo people, into the Navajo hogan, into the heart. Where the heart is, this peyote goes in there. So I want this thing to go on, this peyote religion, peyote worship. It's something for Indians who are humble. Just like in the Bible—it says the meek shall inherit the earth.

Now I'm worried the white man is going to go for it. That's what they usually do. That's what we don't want to happen. I don't think it's for the white people. This natural herb peyote is used by Native Americans with more sincerity. Indian people are more serious in their mind, in their heart, in the way they worship. Just let the Indians have it, let the Indians use it the way they want it, just natural. Our identity is there.

A DIFFERENT DRUMMER

Michael Harner

While on an anthropological expedition to the Peruvian Amazon for the American Museum of Natural History in 1960–1961, I lived for the better part of a year in a village of Conibo Indians on a remote lake near the lower Río Tamaya. After I had spent months in a relatively futile effort to learn about their spiritual beliefs, the Conibo finally advised me that there was only one way to learn, and that was to take *ayahuasca*, the consciousness-changing brew their shamans used to reach the hidden worlds of the spirits. *Ayahuasca* is a boiled mixture that contains a particular species of *Banisteriopsis* vine, along with one or more other components, such as *Psychotria* leaves or the leaves of another species of *Banisteriopsis*.

At the time I first took the brew, I was unacquainted with psychedelics. Timothy Leary was only just having his first psychedelic experience, and knowledge of LSD was not yet a part of American culture. I also believed myself to be an atheist. I was simply taking the *ayahuasca* potion in the interests of anthropology because participant observation is one of the cornerstones of serious research.

The Conibo were right, for when I finally drank the potion one night, the results astonished me. Not only did I enter amazingly real, unknown worlds, but in later describing them to a Conibo shaman, I discovered he was already familiar with them, even volunteering details I had not yet had a chance to tell him. I realized anthropology had underestimated the seriousness of shamanic knowledge and that I had entered a reality far deeper than human culture.

The same shaman encouraged me to continue to work with *ayahuasca* so that I could become initiated into full-fledged shamanic practice. As we worked night after night in an altered state of consciousness, I learned much more about the nonordinary worlds of the shaman, especially that in them one can find and merge with compassionate spiritual powers to help heal the sick and suffering of our ordinary world. I also learned techniques of shamanic divination, methods of obtaining spiritual anwers to difficult questions.

Following this experience, I received similar initiations into Amazonian shamanism from the Untsuri Shuar (Jívaro) people of eastern Ecuador, with whom I had previously lived for a year as an ethnographer. I also started to search the cross-cultural literature, expecting to find evidence of the use of indigenous psychedelics in shamanism worldwide. I eventually concluded, however, that the Amazonians' use of psychedelics was a minority practice. The much more common method to enter the shaman's altered state of consciousness was monotonous percussive sound, achieved especially through drumming.

With experimentation, I learned what the shamans already knew; monotonous drumming, in a frequency of four to seven beats per second, was another valid doorway to the other reality. This "sonic driving" is in approximately the same frequency range as the brain's own theta waves, and its effectiveness is probably partly due to its stimulation of the brain in that range. Compared with drugs, such drumming was also safe, and its effects were short term.

My research among the Inuit of the Canadian Arctic and the peoples of the Northwest Coast of North America reinforced my conclusion that most of the world's shamans use drums or other percussion instruments as "horses" or "canoes" that transport them into the hidden reality of the spirits. Among the Sami (Lapps) of northern Scandinavia, who retained shamanism longer than any other culture in Europe, a few households still have what they call the magic drum. Doing research in the Soviet Union, I learned that the truly professional Siberian shamans generally employed only the drum, even when the psychedelic mushroom *Amanita muscaria* was locally available and was being used by others.

With the shaman's drum, I was able to continue my practice of shamanism in the United States. I lectured on the subject, in and outside of my university teaching, and inevitably, others asked me to introduce them to the practice of shamanism. Thus I began to teach shamanic healing and divination work, first to one or two people at a time, and then, by the mid-1970s, in workshops for groups of students at New Age learning centers such as California's Esalen Institute.

Continuing cross-cultural research, fieldwork, and personal experimentation led me to the fundamental principles of shamanic practice, which I found to be basically the same among indigenous peoples, whether in Siberia, Australia, southern Africa, or North and South America. This "core shamanism," as I call it, is what I taught. Instead of imitating the practices of some ethnic group, my students were able to build on these bare bones of practical shamanic knowledge to fit their own culture. With this basis, the spirits became their teachers—the classic way for shamans to acquire most of their knowledge.

Shamans probably played an important role in European societies from at least the Upper Paleolithic, but this heritage was virtually destroyed in the Middle Ages and early Renaissance by the Church and the Inquisition. Such persecution was common in most of the major civilizations, East and West, because the shamans' ongoing journeys to the gods tended to undermine the authority of state religions. With this in mind, I gave up my university career in 1987 and founded the Foundation for Shamanic Studies, whose purpose is to help Westerners recover this lost shamanic heritage and to help indigenous peoples revive and preserve their own shamanic practices.

Recently, for example, a team from the foundation traveled to the central Asian republic of Tuva (part of the Russian Federation) at the invitation of its president, to help revive shamanism, which had been outlawed there—with the death penalty for practitioners—during the period of Communist domination. In cooperation with the remaining Tuvan shamans, the team performed numerous public healings, demonstrating that shamanism and shamanic healing were valued in America and compatible with modern life. At the conclusion of our visit, the president announced that thereafter shamanism would be respected on a par with Buddhism and Christianity.

In the United States, Europe, and elsewhere, more and more people are learning the practice of shamanism, including health care professionals seeking a more holistic approach. Shamanism has always been done in conjunction with the application of plant remedies, bone setting, and other healing practices. It is not an "alternative" method but a complementary one that looks after the spiritual side of healing.

Much has happened since the shamans introduced me to hidden spirit worlds thirty-six years ago. For me, entering these worlds has transformed my understanding of reality and added great meaning to existence. To the question you often hear today, "Is this all there is?" I can answer with assurance, "No, there is far more than one can even imagine."

DESPERATELY SEEKING REDEMPTION

Diane Bell

Writing for the *Lakota Times* in 1991, Avis Little Eagle summed up the growing anger of many indigenous peoples concerning the practices of self-styled New Age shamans. Throughout the 1980s, the American Indian Movement had protested, picketed, and passed resolutions condemning those individuals and institutions that packaged Indian sweat lodges, vision quests, shamanic healing, and sun dances for the spiritually hungry. Two years later, at the Parlia-

ment of the World's Religions in Chicago, the Dakota, Lakota, and Nakota Nations issued a Declaration of War Against Exploiters of Lakota Spirituality.

This theme has been developed by a number of Native American writers and activists. Ward Churchill, in *Fantasies of the Master Race* (1992), calls the exploiters "plastic medicine men" and cites them as evidence of the continuing genocidal colonization of Native Americans. Poet-anthropologist Wendy Rose writes of "white shamanism" as a form of cultural imperialism, and feminist Andrea Smith, in her article "For All Those Who Were Indian in a Former Life," calls these "wannabes" to account. Echoing the defiant stand taken in the nineteenth century by the Lakota and Cheyenne over the Black Hills, these activists insist that their "spirituality is not for sale."

Lynn V. Andrews, the Los Angeles-based author of the highly successful *Medicine Woman* trilogy says, "I write of my own experience. I am not an anthropologist." The books, workshops, and promotional tours of this self-proclaimed shaman, however, have been cited as a prime example of the appropriation and commercialization of indigenous peoples' spirituality. According to Andrews, the teachings of her Canadian spiritual guide, a "Native American medicine woman" named Agnes Whistling Elk, include Lakota, Cree, and Hopi terms and concepts. Such eclecticism deeply troubles many Native Americans, who see the mixing and matching of different traditions from different tribes as an assault on the integrity of the extremely personal and specific ties of kin and country that underpin their beliefs and practices. In addition, Andrews writes of being introduced into the Sisterhood of the Shields, a secret organization of forty-four women from different Native American tribes. Andrews's loyal readers, however, are not deterred. Over and over, as I research the appeal of these texts, I hear, "I don't care if it's not true; it speaks to me."

In *Mutant Message Down Under*, Marlo Morgan—a self-described alternative health care provider from Kansas City—describes her 2,000-mile trek across the burning deserts of Australia with a hitherto unknown tribe of Aborigines she calls the Real People. She claims she must keep the location of their "opal cave" secret for fear that the government might imprison them or blow up their sacred site. Australian Aborigines have protested that her book is, at best, nonsense and, at worst, a violation of their law. HarperCollins lists her book as fiction, but Morgan continues to lecture on the Real People as though they were real. Although exposés have appeared in the American and Australian media, this best-seller has reached millions of readers, many of whom report, "It changed my life."

In both Morgan's book and Andrews's *Crystal Woman*, Aboriginal life is simple. Neither author (unlike ethnographers whose careful work rarely reaches a general audience) finds the need to grapple with the intricacies of kinship and land-based relations among Aboriginal groups. Both authors avoid the complexities of local languages, and the books' spiritual folks frequently communicate by telepathy or by giggling and winking their way through the stories. Andrews's meeting with the Sisterhood of the Shields takes place in a native "village" near a brook in the middle of the arid Australian desert. At this unlikely site, she meets with her Native American Sisters, as well as with female Aborigines. In reality, no group of people could travel for a thousand miles through Australia without having to negotiate access through the territories of many other groups. (But how convenient for government authorities if this were true! Relocation policies would be perfectly acceptable because one piece of land would be as good as the next to the Aborigines.)

Enraged that a gullible public was consuming these misrepresentations—and that yet again exotic stereotypes of Aborigines were obscuring the gritty realities of the lives of many of these peoples—Robert Eggington, coordinator of the Dumbartung Aboriginal Corporation (Western Australia), led a group of Aboriginal elders to Los Angeles in January 1996 to protest Morgan's book and a planned film. Morgan responded to the protest in a radio interview reported in the *Weekend Australian*. "I'm terribly sorry," she said, "and my sincere apologies to any Australian Aboriginal person if I have offended them in any way . . . please read this book . . . with an open mind and see if there is anything, anything at all that is derogatory."

Morgan's and Andrews's readers often tell me that these books offer a vision of a world in which all life forms coexist in physical and spiritual harmony; where one person's journey can undo centuries of abuse; where women are wise; where, despite differences in language, history, geography, economic status, and personal skills, we are all one. Here is community, meaning, belonging—all the connectedness for which the self-absorbed, postindustrial, fragmented individual yearns. I certainly agree that we should be open to wisdom from a range of sources, but must we suspend all critical faculties in the process? It matters that the beliefs and practices of Native Americans and Australian Aborigines have been put through a cultural blender. It matters that the stories of those engaged in ongoing struggles for their very lives are marginalized, and that these representations of indigenous peoples are romantic and ahistorical. Morgan and Andrews shroud their "native teachers" in mystery while telling us that they hold the keys to true and authentic ways of knowing.

Marketers of neo-shamanic books and workshops claim that indigenous wisdom is part of our common human heritage. By sharing such knowledge, the argument goes, together we can save the planet. But is this sharing or a further appropriation? There is a bitter irony in turning to indigenous peoples to solve problems of affluent urbanites. In the midst of the wealth of first-world nations, most native peoples endure appalling health problems, underemployment, and grinding poverty. A philosophy of reverence for the earth rings hollow in the reality of toxic waste dumps and nuclear testing on native lands. As Inès Talamantez, of the University of California, Santa Barbara, says: "If the impulse is for respect and sharing, then come stand with us in our struggles for religious freedoms and the return of skeletal remains and against hydroelectric dams and logging roads."

We anthropologists, too, have been part of the problem. Too often our power to define "the other" has displaced and silenced indigenous voices. Here, I am not speaking *for* indigenous peoples; rather I am turning the anthropological gaze on Western cultures so that we may understand why so many individuals seek healing, meaning, and spiritual answers in the lives of peoples whose lands and lives have been so devastated by Western colonialism.

"WORLDS OF THE SHAMAN"

Various

---

1) What *is* a shaman?

2) Define the necessary qualities one must have to be a shaman.

3) What various paths can one take to achieve the position and status of a shaman?

4) What role(s) or job(s) does a shaman generally undertake in his/her society?

5) How have state-level societies, particularly the USSR, viewed shamans and shamanistic belief systems?

6) What trends in American society, both religious and secular, have contributed to the trend of Americans turning to "traditional" shamanistic systems of belief for answers to their spiritual problems?

7) How do individuals in "traditional" societies view this shamanistic trend in American culture?

ANCIENT ALTERED STATES

Mary Roach

"Here's a real nice sheep getting killed," says archeologist Dave Whitley, pointing at a rock. Whitley is not hallucinating. Step up to the rock and a carving can be seen: a horned sheep and a man with a bow and arrow, a petroglyph made by a Shoshone some 1,500 years ago.

The Shoshone was the one hallucinating. He was a shaman, Whitley says, who came here to this canyon in the Mojave Desert in California on a vision quest. The bighorn sheep was his spirit guide. "Killing the sheep" is a metaphor for entering the supernatural through a hallucinogenic trance.

You can see why Whitley has taken some grief in his day. For 30 years the prevailing theory about petroglyphs like this one has been that they were all about hunting. The assumption was that Native Americans believed that making art of their prey would magically cause the creatures to materialize in abundance. On the surface, the hunting-magic explanation seemed to make sense. Of some 100,000 petroglyphs in the canyons of the Coso Mountain range, 51 percent are bighorn sheep and 13 percent are male humans. For a long time no one bothered to question it.

Trouble is, the Shoshones didn't eat much sheep. "We looked at 10,000 bones, and precisely 1 was a bighorn," says Whitley, tossing back a wool serape. If not for the serape, you would be hard-pressed to divine the man's vocation. Ruddy-cheeked and plaid-clad, he could as easily be out here hunting chukar or mending downed fences. "If they were going to make rock art out of what they were eating," he adds, "there'd be bunnies all over the rock." Though Whitley spends most of his time running a cultural resource management consultancy in his hometown of Fillmore, California, his background is in research and academics, at UCLA (where he still teaches) and at the Rock Art Research Unit of the University of the Witwatersrand in Johannesburg, South Africa.

What sets Whitley and a handful of his colleagues apart is a willingness to stray from the ordinary precepts of archeology into the hinterlands of anthropology and psychology. Whitley turned to ethnographies of the Shoshone and Paiute tribes that inhabited the Coso Range—a string of small mountains lying east of the Sierra Nevada—from as early as A.D.

1200 to the end of the last century. Ethnographies are detailed descriptions of the lives of people in traditional cultures, gleaned from interviews and the observations of field anthropologists.

From ethnographic materials, Whitley learned that the places shamans made rock art were held to be portals to the supernatural; cracks and caves in the rock were interpreted literally as openings to the beyond. The art itself—carved with chunks of quartz—is said to depict visions that came to the shamans in their trances. The bighorn sheep is referred to as the spirit guide specific to rainmaking. One ethnographic source cited shamans who traveled from as far away as Utah to these canyons in their quest for rain.

With an average annual rainfall of about four inches, the Mojave Desert seems an unlikely setting for rainmaking activities. This is a landscape of dust and desolation, a sere, scrubby chenille of sage and saltbush. Joshua trees point spiky mascara-wand limbs this way and that, invariably at nothing. Sheep Canyon, where we are hiking, is a dry riverbed.

"It does seem odd," allows Whitley, "until you realize that Native American shamanic rituals subscribe to the principle of symbolic inversion." Where the natural world is dry, its supernatural counterpart is the opposite.

Why didn't archeologists bother to check the ethnographies before? "Partly," says Whitley, "there's this perception that prehistory has to be interpreted on its own terms. If we go to the ethnography, then we're assuming that the past was like the near present, and then what's the point of doing archeology? There's a deeply embedded presupposition that archeologists maintain, and that is that because things change over time, time causes things to change." Which isn't always true. Shamanic rituals have persisted unchanged for centuries.

The other part of the story is that few archeologists had any real interest in pinning down the origins and meaning of rock art. Whitley was the first American archeologist to do a dissertation interpreting rock carvings (the technical term is petroglyphs; rock paintings are pictographs). There has been a tendency among archeologists to regard the study of ritual and belief as less scientific and less relevant than the study of technology and subsistence. "It's that bumper sticker: 'He who dies with the most toys wins,'" Whitley says. "Which is, to me, a very shallow, materialistic view of human culture."

To illustrate his point, Whitley gives the example of Australian Aborigines. "You can take a line from the center of Australia out to the coast, and you can plot on that line a series of different aboriginal cultures. And if you look at the complexity of their kinship system and the complexity of their technology and tools, what you see is a perfect inverse relationship." Coastal groups have a complex technology and tend to use a lot of tools. In the middle of Australia, it's more like it is in the Cosos. "Those guys are running around near to buck naked, surviving only on their wits, yet they have this kinship system that is mind-bogglingly complex. And it structures every aspect of their social life. Now what is more important, this complex cognitive mental construct or the kind of tools these folks made?"

Whitley stops talking and directs his gaze at my hiking boot. "You're standing on a sheep."

The art of the Coso Mountains is not all sheep and stick-legged men with feathers and horns. High above Whitley's head is a circle filled in with grid lines, like a flattened fly's eye. Across the canyon, a sine wave snakes across a boulder. Beside it is an arc of nested curves, like a fragment of a mammoth fingerprint. Abstract patterns are everywhere among the boulders—grids, hatch marks, zigzags, curves, spirals. They're trippy, doodley, devoid of any recognizable meaning. For years, archeological theories about these markings amounted to guesswork. Maps? Menstrual calendars? Solstice observatories? Forget about it. Let's go dig up a hogan.

There is another place you can reliably see these images, and that is inside your head. In the 1960s, neuropsychologists began cataloging the visual imagery of altered states of consciousness. Subjects given LSD or mescaline would lie on mattresses, describing their visions into researchers' tape recorders. The first stage of the hallucinogenic experience—whether brought on by drugs, sensory deprivation, fasting, or rhythmic movement—is characterized by recurring geometric patterns, known variously as "phosphenes" or "entoptics." The seven most common categories strike a familiar chord: grids, parallel lines, dots, zigzags, nested curves, meanders, and spirals.

Whitley wasn't the first to notice parallels between this abstract imagery and that of rock art. In the 1950s, a German neuropsychologist named Max Knoll noted similarities between electrically stimulated (and, later, LSD-induced) patterns that appeared in his subjects' visual fields and common abstract patterns in southern African rock art. In a 1970 article in *Scientific American*, psychologist Gerald Oster highlighted "phosphenelike figures" in prehistoric cave drawings.

One of the first archeologists to come on board was David Lewis-Williams, professor of cognitive archeology and director of the Rock Art Research Unit at the University of the Witwatersrand. Lewis-Williams found examples of the seven common entopic patterns throughout the ancient rock art of the San bushmen. He also found evidence in the ethnographies that San shamans went into trances, both to heal and to make rain, and that they recorded their trance visions on the rock to preserve them. (Coso Shoshones believed that if they forgot their visions, they would die—powerful incentive to jot them down.) Lewis-Williams's "neuropsychological model" for interpreting rock art incorporated not only abstract images but also the representational images that occur in the later stages of trance.

The Shoshone and Paiute shamans didn't, as is often assumed, take peyote or jimsonweed. Their route to trance was a combination of exceptionally strong native tobacco, lack of sleep, sensory deprivation (the canyons here are mute as tombs), and fasting.

Somewhat surprisingly, given his interests, Whitley himself has never tried hallucinogenic drugs. "What I do do is, I interview archeological field crews a lot." He did experience entoptics once, when someone ran a heavy dolly over his foot. "Pow! Entoptics. Just like the cartoonists draw around someone's head when the safe lands on his toe. Those guys are keyed in to it."

Cartoonists aren't the only artists keyed in to entoptics and altered states. Whitley says Wassily Kandinsky, revered tribal elder of abstract art, wrote a paper in a psychological journal in 1881 about the entoptics that preface a migraine. Whitley also says Kandinsky studied shamanism and the role of the subconscious in art, and that this influenced his transition from figurative to abstract art. "His paintings are full of entoptic forms."

Entoptic means "within the eye." It's believed that these geometric patterns derive from the optic system itself. In some instances, says Whitley, "you're basically seeing what's in your eyeball." Retinal blood vessels and "floaters"—the faint squiggly lines that meander across the vision field—may be the anatomic inspiration for dots and meandering line entoptics. Concentric circles, spirals, and grids are probably generated by neurons firing in the visual cortex and the retina.

In the second stage of altered states imagery, the mind steps in and tries to make sense of the doodlings set before it. This is something minds do: they decode visual input, matching it against the memory banks of stored experience. If a match is made, the image is recognized. How the brain interprets an entoptic depends on the state of the brain's owner. "The same ambiguous round shape," wrote psychologist M. J. Horowitz in *Hallucinations: Behavior, Experience, and Theory* in 1975, ". . . can be 'illusioned' into an orange (if the subject is hungry), a breast (if he is in a state of heightened sexual drive), a cup of water (if he is thirsty), or an anarchist's bomb (if he is hostile or fearful)." Or a bighorn sheep body if he's a shaman on a rainmaking vision quest.

By way of demonstration, Whitley leads me to a carving of a bighorn that is more horn than sheep. Three parallel arcs span the length of the sheep, rainbowlike, from its head to its tail. Whitley identifies the entoptic: "Nested or catenary curves." The size of the horns, and the fact that there are three, not two, suggests the curves appeared first, and the shaman then interpreted them as horns.

A few hundred yards down the canyon, Whitley points out a fantastical creature, like something from one of those split-page children's books in which the giraffe's head is on the monkey's body, with kangaroo legs. The figure sports bird-talon feet, an upright humanoid body, and big, downward-curling horns.

This is an example of Stage 3 of Lewis-Williams's neuropsychological model: the full-blown vision. The shamans didn't think of it as a vision. To them it was a parallel reality; they had entered the realm of the supernatural. The literature on altered states of consciousness describes the sensory changes involved. According to Lewis-Williams, "This shift to iconic imagery is also accompanied by an increase in vividness. Subjects stop using similes to describe their experiences and assert that the images are indeed what they appear to be."

The man with the horns is the shaman himself, in his own vision, entering the supernatural and "shape shifting" into his spirit guide. The original assumption about the horns was that they were a hunting disguise. Which makes sense until you think about it. "It'd be way too heavy," observes Whitley. "Besides, the Native Americans have systematically denied this."

The talons in place of the shaman's feet could be part of a common metaphor for entering the supernatural: flight. (Many petroglyphs of therianthropes—beings part animal and part human—also have wings in place of arms.) This probably ties in with the feeling of floating up and out of one's body, as often happens during the third stage of a mind-bending altered state.

"Here's a guy with six fingers on one hand," says Whitley. "Clearly not a normal individual." Again, it fits with the literature on altered states of consciousness. Imagined extra digits are a common hallucination.

The humanoid figures that aren't busy turning into sheep are busy shooting them with bows and arrows. In the mythology of the Native American cultures of the Far West, death is the most prevalent metaphor for entering the supernatural. (At this point, according to Whitley, the shaman has become his spirit guide and the two are considered interchangeable.) Whitley cites the example of Coyote, the shaman character of myth, who begins many of his adventures by dying or being killed, whereupon all manner of supernatural events ensue. On a physiological level, the metaphor makes sense. Consider what can happen to a person who enters a trance: his eyes roll back into his head, he may go limp and lose consciousness, he may bleed from the nose. Whitley has shown me examples here today of bighorn sheep with lines coming from their noses.

Beside the horned shaman is a shaman with what appear to be truncated golf clubs or perhaps musical quarter notes protruding from his head. Whitley insists they're California quail topknot feathers. They do look a lot like the bobbing doohickey you see on these birds' heads, but to link this to the flight metaphor strikes me as a bit of a reach.

As it turns out, it might have nothing to do with flight metaphors. Rain shamans, Whitley explains, wore a distinctive headdress festooned with quail head feathers. Know your ethnographies.

Not all petroglyphs fit the neuropsychological model of rock art. The Hopi carved clan symbols on rocks during pilgrimages. Northern Plains tribes decorated the landscape with symbolic renderings of their war exploits. The carving on the standing stone in front of us fits no established categories. Whitley has no idea who made it, or why. It says, "$E = mc^2$."

Given that this canyon sits within the million acres of supersecret labs and missile ranges known as China Lake Naval Air Weapons Station, it was most likely military personnel. Even if the carving were a sheep, Whitley wouldn't have been fooled into believing it was carved by early Native Americans. He can eyeball a petroglyph and tell, by the degree to which the carved areas have darkened, approximately how old it is. Out little theory of relativity inscription is, relatively speaking, brand-new. The etching still appears white. After about 500 years, a "brown crud," as Whitley puts it, begins to become visible. The crud, known in academic circles as rock varnish, derives from microbes on the rock surfaces. The microbes metabolize manganese in the dust that lands on the rock, and metabolites accrete on the rock's surface. Over time, different trace elements leach out from the varnish at different rates. By calculating what's leached out and how much, chronometricians can get an idea of how long the varnish has been there, and from that, the carving's age. This can be compared with the results of radiocarbon-dating of organic materials such as lichen and pollen that are trapped on the carving as the varnish accumulates on top of them. Neither method is especially precise, but the combination suffices to pin the date to within a few hundred years.

While the oldest Coso petroglyphs may have been made as long as 16,500 years ago, the overwhelming majority fall in the neighborhood of less than 1,500 years old. Whitley has a theory to explain the sudden flurry of shamanism in the region. An examination of the archeological record around this time shows a dramatic increase in abandonment of villages in the region. The likely reason: The area was being sucked dry by a major drought some 800 years ago. Hence the unprecedented upsurge in rainmaking endeavors.

In a bizarre display of symbolic meteorologic inversion, rain clouds have appeared overhead. Against the gathering gray, a dozen Canada geese fly in perfect V formation, as though under orders from the base commander.

The rock art of the Coso Range is by no means the oldest in the world. The famed Lascaux and Chauver cave paintings of France date, respectively, from 15,000 and 30,000 years ago. As anthropologists had yet to materialize 30,000 years ago, no ethnographies exist for these peoples. Partly because of this, European rock art archeologists were slow to warm to the shamanistic, neuropsychological model. The skepticism may also have had to do with the European separation of archeology and anthropology; they're not, as they typically are in the States, part of the same academic department.

In 1992, Whitley brought French archeologist Jean Clottes, the world-renowned scholar of Paleolithic cave paintings, out to the Mojave and did his pitch. Clottes wasn't easily swayed. Though the rock art of France and Spain most certainly includes the classic entoptic patterns, Clottes saw too many other images that didn't fit.

"Over the next two to three years," says Whitley, "I brought him back to the Cosos again, and he started reading the ethnographic texts." Eventually Clottes crossed the divide. Whitley knew he had him when Clottes called him up in 1995 after the discovery of the famed Chauvet cave. "He said to me, 'There's a therianthrope here!'"

It's easy to buy the entoptics portion of the theory; the similarities between the rock art and the hallucination descriptions in the neuropsychology papers are too striking to dismiss. Less clear are the Stage 3 visions. What's odd is the uniformity of the Coso shamans' hallucination. The vast majority of the estimated 100,000 images found in the Coso Range fall into one of six categories: bighorn sheep (51 percent), humans (13 percent), other animals (5 percent), weapons (2.4 percent), medicine bags (1.3 percent), and geometric (entoptic) designs (26 percent). Yet the hallucinations of nonshamanic drug-induced trance are limitlessly diverse. Whitley's answer to this is that the shamans may have been practicing some form of "lucid dreaming." With the help of special glasses that flash lights when the eyes begin the characteristic movements of REM sleep, lucid dreamers achieve a borderline level of consciousness that allows them to watch their dreams like movies and, it's said, even influence the plots and direct their outcomes. The ethnographies say nothing of this practice. However, as Whitley points out, that doesn't mean it didn't occur. "This may," he says, "be an example of rock art supplementing the body of ethnographic knowledge."

Back at the mouth of the canyon, a vision appears out of the mist: four wild horses running abreast, manes rippling like white water. As abruptly as they appeared, they wheel and vanish again into the fog. A comment about the four horses of the Apocalypse prompts a raised eyebrow from Whitley. "Some horses got left behind when the military evicted the homesteaders here." Some things are less symbolic than they appear. And some aren't.

"ANCIENT ALTERED STATES"

Mary Roach

1) What was the traditional anthropological/archaeological interpretation of the meaning of petroglyphs recorded in the Mojave Desert?

2) What supposition have archaeologists traditionally made about the relationship between historic or modern ethnographic data and archaeological research?

3) How have recent reinterpretations of ethnographic data and archaeological research cast doubt on the traditional interpretations of the meanings of petroglyphs?

4) Why has archaeology tended to disregard or avoid the study of religious belief and ritual?

5) What connections has Dave Whitley drawn between Mojave Desert petroglyphs and the hallucinogenic trances that shamans often enter into?

6) What is entoptics, and how does it relate to the study and interpretation of petroglyphs?

RITUALS OF THE MODERN MAYA

Angela M.H. Schuster

The murmur of chanting filled the Church of San Juan Chamula; the fragrance of pine needles crushed underfoot mingled with the scent of candles and burning copal incense. Pilgrims moved slowly from station to station, beseeching saints for health, wealth, and luck in love. An elderly woman had come with a shaman bearing fresh eggs and a chicken. Egg in hand, the shaman traced the woman's body several times, praying aloud as he worked. He then broke the egg into a bowl, the pattern of its yolk revealing the affliction. With further incantations and offerings, the shaman "transferred" the illness to the chicken, which he then sacrificed by breaking its neck. A three-foot-tall Colonial period polychrome figure of John the Baptist stood near the altar, dressed in layers of embroidered garments—tokens of gratitude from those whom he had helped. Patron saint of this Tzotzil Maya church in highland Chiapas, Mexico, the Baptist was responsible for bringing rain and ensuring the fertility of crops and animals. Had he assumed the mantle of Chak, the Classic period water god?

Despite Catholic trappings, the rites I witnessed in 1996 were rooted deep in antiquity. In recent years, archaeologists and anthropologists have opened a dialog with those who practice the old ways, and are coming to realize just how much Precolumbian ritual has survived. "Considering that 500 years have elapsed since the Spanish Conquest," says Harvard University ethnologist Evon Z. Vogt, "I am impressed with the ending nature of Classic Maya religious concepts and beliefs."

In the Chol town of Tila, in highland Chiapas, Nicholas Hopkins and Kathryn Josserand of Florida State University have documented the cult of a "Black Christ" known as the Señor de Tila, an amalgam of Christ and Ik'al, a Precolumbian cave-dwelling earth deity. Each January and June, tens of thousands of pilgrims come to the town to seek the support of the Señor de Tila, who is venerated both in the local church and in a nearby rock-shelter, which contains a large soot-blackened stalagmite believed by townspeople to be a representation of Christ. According to local tradition, Ik'al is a manifestation of "Earth Owner," the master of souls who holds the key to health and wealth and must be petitioned and re-warded through prayers and sacrifice. "For the people of Tila," says Hopkins, "the Precolumbian idea of making sacrifices to ensure the well-being of one's family and loved ones echoes Christ's giving of his life to pay for the sins of the world."

"Modern Maya see little conflict in merging the two faiths," says Robert M. Laughlin, an anthropologist with the Smithsonian Institution who has lived among the Tzotzil of Zinacantan for more than 30 years. "It is common on feast days for a procession to begin at the Church of San Lorenzo with a mass for Christ the Sun God and his mother the Moon Goddess, and then proceed to a nearby hill for the veneration of ancestors and Maya gods, including Chauk, an earth and water deity."

Dark, secretive, and full of exotic geological formations, caves have played a key role in Mesoamerican religion for more than 3,000 years, serving as portals to the Otherworld—the realm of deities, demons, and ancestors. There are more than 25 known painted caves in the Maya world, the earliest being Loltún in Yucatán, whose paintings have been dated to the Late Preclassic, ca. 300 B.C. James Brady of George Washington University has documented the continued veneration of Naj Tunich, a two-mile-long painted cave in the southeastern Petén region of Guatemala. Naj Tunich began attracting pilgrims early in the first century B.C., when stone platforms were erected just inside the cave's entrance. Offerings such as ceramics and jadeite pendants were deposited atop platforms adjacent to several large stalagmite columns. The majority of the cave's painted inscriptions, some 40 in all, were executed during the seventh and eighth centuries.

Three verbs associated with pilgrimage—*hul* (to arrive), *pak* (to return), and *il* (to see or witness events at a foreign place)—pervade the Naj Tunich texts, according to Andrea Stone of the University of Wisconsin, Milwaukee, who has studied the inscriptions. The presence of emblem glyphs from a number of cities suggests that the cave was used by people living throughout the region. One inscription notes that lords from the Lowland Maya city of Caracol, 30 miles to the north, performed a *k'ak' kuch*, or "burning" ritual in the cave in A.D. 744. Burning incense may have served to appease local gods and guarantee safe passage for dignitaries traveling through foreign territory. Brady and his team have recovered potsherds encrusted with the charred resin of the copal palm spanning the entire Classic period (ca. A.D. 250-900), attesting the prolonged practice of such rites.

Today's pilgrims, mostly from the Kekchi villages of Tanjoc and Alta Verapaz, ten to 15 miles away, come to the cave before the rainy season, which begins in late May and early June, to burn incense and light candles to ensure a good harvest. "Though some ritual aspects have certainly changed," adds Brady, noting the singing of Christian hymns and the participation of women, "cave worship continues to figure prominently in Maya religion."

According to Vogt, there are five classes of sacred topography among the Tzotzil of Zinacantan—*vits* (mountains), *ch'en* (holes in the ground such as caves), *hap 'osil* (mountain passes), *ton* (rocks), and *te'* (trees)—geographic features rife with spirit activity. "For Zinacantecos," says Vogt, "mountains are the most important features on the landscape, being places of contact between heaven and earth." The veneration of mountains, he believes, stretches deep into the Precolumbian past, serving as the impetus behind the building of pyramids. "Pyramids are artificial mountains," says Harvard University epigrapher David Stuart, "both represented by the glyph *wits*" (the Classic period form of the Tzotzil word *vits*). According to Stuart, there are numerous references to buildings as mountains in the epigraphic record, perhaps the best example being temple 22 on the Copán acropolis. "The building is actually labeled 'mountain,' its doorway, the gaping maw of the earth monster, a metaphor for a cave," he says. "One would have entered the 'cave' of temple 22 to converse with the ancestral spirits, surely in association with all sorts of ritual activities, including incense burning and bloodletting."

As caves and mountains occur together in the landscape, both serve as doorways to the Otherworld. To journey through them and return alive, however, requires the special talent of a shaman. In antiquity, Maya kings interceded with the gods and ancestors on behalf of their cities. Today, in many Maya communities, mayors and healers are one and the same, responsible for their people's physical and spiritual health. "Shamans are specialists in ecstasy, a state of mind that allows them to move freely beyond the ordinary world—beyond death itself—to deal directly with the gods, demons, ancestors, and other unseen but potent things that control the world of the living," says David Freidel of Southern Methodist University in Dallas, who has participated in shamanic rites at a *ch'a-chak* or "bring rain" ceremony in Yucatán. "When we began our summer field season at Yaxuná in 1989," recalls Freidel, "the nearby community was in the midst of a crisis. A severe drought had destroyed two plantings and measures were needed to ensure the success of a third." With the help of the villagers, Don Pablo, the local shaman, built an altar of young saplings, baby corn plants, and hanging gourds—a portal between this world and the next through which he could summon *chakob*, or rain gods. For three days, he chanted and prepared offerings of corn bread, incense, stewed meats, and honey wine. "At the climax of the ceremony," says Freidel, "Don Pablo, aided by copious amounts of aguardiente, a sugarcane brandy, entered a trance state in which he remained for more than ten hours. It is in sleep, whether a trance or dream state, that Maya spirits communicate with shamans. Shortly after the ceremony, we heard the deep rumble of thunder. Had the *chakob* heard the shaman's prayers?"

According to Freidel, such an altar, known as a *ka'an te'* or "wooden sky," represents the cosmos. The leafy green saplings, tied together several feet above the table's center, symbolize the arching of the Milky Way across the night sky. Thirteen gourds suspended from the saplings represent the constellations of the Maya zodiac. The building of the *ka'an te'* can be traced back as early as the Classic period, from which there are depictions on several stone vases, including one from Escuintla in southwestern Guatemala.

Shamans are also traditional healers—bone setters, mid-wives, and herbalists. The most skilled are the *h'men,* doctor-priests who treat the minds, bodies, and souls of villagers. For the Maya, physical and spiritual health are one and the same. According to the late Mopán Maya *h'men* Don Elijio Panti, ailments could be brought on by a restless soul or profaned gods and ancestors. To cure an illness took not only prescribed remedies but spiritual reconciliation.

Among the Quiché of highland Guatemala, says Barbara Tedlock, a State University of New York, Buffalo, anthropologist and trained shaman-priest, "some illnesses can even be a call to serve gods and ancestors." There are six such illnesses—snake, horse, twisted stomach, dislocated bone, inebriation, and money loss—all of which incapacitate the patient. To cure them requires becoming a daykeeper, one who burns incense and offers prayers at shrines on designated days of the *tzolkin,* the 260-day sacred calendar.

The Quiché believe that when great shamans die, their souls congregate at lineage shrines where they worshipped during their lives. As the shamans' souls accumulate, the shrines—known as *warab'alja,* literally "sleeping places"—are endowed with increasing power. Each lineage group has four such shrines built in the form of small stone boxes where prayers are offered on specific calendar days and to commemorate births, deaths, marriages, plantings, and harvests.

"These shrines are also used to demarcate lands owned by a lineage group," says Dennis Tedlock, also a trained Quiché shaman-priest. "When a property is sold in the Quiché region, new landowners remember previous landowners in prayers at recently acquired shrines. The location of each shrine is dictated by the landscape, there being a distinct preference for mountains, caves, lakes, and springs."

Linda Schele of the University of Texas at Austin believes that *warab'alja* is a derivation of the Classic Maya phrase *waybil*, which also means "sleeping house." *Waybilob* are well known from Classic period sites. In 1989 John Pedro Laporte of Guatemala's Instituto de Antropologia e Historia was excavating a large compound of houses and came across just such a shrine embedded in a later altar platform. An open-sided stone box, the structure was filled with burnt offerings. Two particularly fine miniature stone shrines, labeled *waybil* in hieroglyphs, were found in a cache behind structure 33 at the Classic Maya city of Copán in Honduras.

By studying modern Maya religious practices, archaeologists and anthropologists are beginning to gain critical insight into rites often depicted in ancient Maya art. "We still have much to learn about Classic Maya religious practices," says Vogt, "but the progress made so far is astounding. The next decade promises to bring even more discoveries as scholars continue their cooperative work on Maya culture."

"RITUALS OF THE MODERN MAYA"

Angela M. H. Schuster

---

1) How are Roman Catholic and ancient Maya beliefs combined in a syncretic way in modern Maya religion?

2) What role do caves play in Maya religion, both prehistoric and modern?

3) How can modern Maya religious rituals give us insights into the prehistoric belief systems of the Maya?

4) Define and discuss the sacred religious topography of the Tzotzil.

5) In what ways are this article and Holloway's article on Bolivian miners ("Working the Devil's Mines") similar? What points of agreement and disagreement can you find in such a comparison?

SECTION SEVEN

Symbolic Expression

THE CREATION OF THE UNIVERSE

Steven H. Gale

For centuries Ife was the principal city of the Yoruba people. Located in the southwest corner of Nigeria, it was also a sacred city. "The Creation of the Universe" describes how the universe, life, and human beings were created.

At the beginning of time the universe consisted only of the sky, the water, and marshland. Olorun, the most powerful and wisest of the gods, was the creator of the sun and the ruler of the sky. Olokun was the ruler of the waters and the marshes. Even though her kingdom contained no plants, animals, or human beings, Olokun was happy with it. Unfortunately, Obatala, one of Olorun's favorites, was not pleased.

"The world would certainly be more interesting if living things inhabited it," he said to Olorun. "What can we do so that Olokun's kingdom can be inhabited? What she needs is mountains, forests, and fields."

"Well," Olorun answered, "I agree that mountains, forests, and fields would be better than water alone, but how would it be created?"

"With your permission, I will create the solid land."

Olorun gladly gave Obatala permission to create the solid land. Obatala immediately went to see Orunmila, Olorun's oldest son, a god with the gift of being able to foresee the future.

"Olorun has given me permission to create solid land where now only water and marshland exist," he said to Orunmila. "Will you teach me how to do this so that I can then populate the world with living things?"

"I will be happy to, Obatala. You must first obtain a golden chain that is long enough to reach from the sky to the water. You must then take a snail's shell and fill it with sand. Next you must place the snail's shell, a white hen, a black cat, and a palm nut in a bag. When you have done this, you must carry them down to the marshland by way of the chain."

Obatala immediately went to find the goldsmith. The goldsmith agreed to make such a chain, but he did not have enough gold on hand to complete the task. So, Obatala went to all of the gods and asked them for the gold that they possessed so that the chain could be made. Because the gods agreed that Obatala's project was a worthy one, they gave him

their golden necklaces, bracelets, and rings. Still, according to the goldsmith, Obatala had not collected enough gold to make a chain of sufficient length to reach from the sky to the water. He returned to the goldsmith anyway, and he asked the smith to fashion a chain as long as possible with what gold they had and to put a hook at the end of it.

When the chain was readied, Obatala and Orunmila hooked one end of it to the edge of the sky, and Orunmila gave Obatala the sand-filled snail shell, the white hen, the black cat, and the palm nut to put into a bag, which he slung over his shoulder. Obatala then began to climb down the golden chain.

When he had climbed down about half the length of the chain, Obatala realized that he was leaving the world of light and entering the world of twilight. Still he continued to climb down. When he reached the end of the chain, he was still far above the ocean, much too high to jump safely.

As he was wondering what to do, he heard Orunmila's voice call out from above. "Obatala," he said, "use the sand in your snail shell."

Obatala did as Orunmila dictated. He pulled the snail shell out of his bag and poured the sand into the water.

"Now free the white hen."

Obatala again obeyed Orunmila's command. The white hen fluttered down to land upon the sandy waters. She immediately began to scratch at the sand, scattering it far and wide. Wherever the grains of sand landed, dry land was created, the largest piles becoming hills.

Seeing the dry land grow high beneath him, Obatala let go of the golden chain and fell the short distance to the earth. The place where he landed he named Ife. He looked around and saw that the ground stretched as far as the horizon in every direction that he could see, but it was still barren.

Now Obatala dug a hole in the ground and buried the palm nut. He had barely shoveled the last handful of dirt over the nut when a palm tree began growing out of the buried nut. The tree quickly reached its full height and grew more palm nuts, which dropped upon the land and grew into mature trees before his eyes. Obatala took the bark from the trees and built a house. He gathered palm leaves and made a thatched roof for the house. When he went inside his new house, Obatala took the black cat out of the bag, and he settled down with the cat as his companion.

After some time, Olorun wondered how Obatala was doing, so he asked one of his servants, Chameleon, to go down the golden chain to visit Obatala. When the Chameleon saw Obatala, he said, "Olorun, the ruler of the sky, has asked me to find out how you are doing."

"Tell Olorun that the land and vegetation that I created are quite nice, but it is always twilight here and I miss the brightness of the sky world."

The Chameleon returned to Olorun and told him what Obatala had said. Olorun was so pleased with Obatala's effort that he said, "I will create the sun." He then did just that, and every day the sun's light and warmth poured down upon Obatala and his creations.

A great deal more time passed, and Obatala found that he was still not satisfied. "As much as I love my black cat," he said, "I think that I need another kind of companionship. Perhaps it will be good for me to populate this world with creatures more like myself."

Obatala set about to accomplish this task. He began digging in the soil, and he gathered together bits and pieces of clay that stuck together. Taking this clay, Obatala created small figures shaped like himself. This endeavor proved to be very tiring, and soon Obatala decided to take the juice from the palm trees to make palm wine. As tired as he was, he drank more of the wine than he realized, and soon he was drunk.

When Obatala began making the clay figures again, the effects of the wine made him a little clumsy. As a result, the figures that he created were not as well made as those that he had fashioned earlier. Some of the new figures had arms that were too short or legs of uneven length or a curved back, although Obatala's senses were so dulled from the drink that he did not notice that these figures were not perfect.

After he had created a large number of clay figures, Obatala called up to Olorun: "Olorun, I have created clay figures to populate my world and be companions to me, but they are devoid of life. Of all of the gods, you are the only one who can bestow life. I ask that you do this so that I may spend the rest of my life with companions who are like me."

Once more Olorun was pleased to do what Obatala asked. The sky god breathed life into the clay figures, which became living human beings. As soon as the figures were endowed with life, they saw Obatala's hut, and they began to build homes for themselves all around it. Thus was the first Yoruba village created. That village was called Ife, and it still exists today.

Obatala was very pleased with his work. Then, as the effects of the palm wine wore off, he saw that some of the people whom he had created were not perfect, and he promised that he would never drink palm wine again and that he would devote himself to protecting those who suffered because of his drunkenness. This is how Obatala became the protector of those who are born deformed.

The people whom Obatala had created needed food, so they began to work the earth. Since iron did not yet exist, Obatala presented his people with a copper knife and a wooden hoe, which they used to raise grain and yams. Ife slowly turned from a village into a city as the people prospered.

Seeing that his work on earth was done and having grown tired of being the ruler of Ife, Obatala climbed back up the golden chain to the sky. From that time afterward, he spent half of his time in the sky and half of his time in Ife.

When he was living in his home in the sky, Obatala told all of the other gods about the things that he had created on earth. Many of the gods were excited by his tales, and they decided to travel to the earth to live among the clay figures called human beings that Obatala had created. Before they left the sky, however, Olorun called them together and said, "Because you are gods, you must remember that you have certain obligations to the human beings. Among other things, you must listen to their prayers and help them when they need help." To each of the gods Olorun assigned a specific task that he or she would be responsible to fulfill on the earth.

Unfortunately, when he created the Yoruba world, Obatala had not consulted with Olokun, the ruler of the sea, and she became quite angry. She felt that he, a sky god, had usurped her power by changing a large portion of her domain and by assuming rulership over that kingdom. She thought long and hard, and finally she decided upon a plan that she felt would bring her revenge for Obatala's insulting actions.

One day, after Obatala had returned to the sky, Olokun brought together the great waves of her ocean world and flung them one after another across the land that Obatala had created. Before long the land was completely flooded and only marshland remained. The palm trees that Obatala had grown, the yams that the people had planted, and even most of the people themselves were washed away from the soil and drowned. The people who still lived called out to Obatala for help, but the noise of the waves was so great that he could not hear them.

The people found Eshu, the messenger god who had come to live among them, and asked him to carry their plea for help to Obatala and Olorun. Eshu told them to prepare a sacrifice to go along with their message in order to make sure that the great sky gods would listen to their plea, and he asked for a sacrifice for himself in return for his service. The people sacrificed a goat to Obatala and a white chicken to Eshu, and Eshu climbed back up the golden chain to tell Obatala about the flood.

Obatala was overwhelmed when he heard about the floods. He did not know how to deal with Olokun. Orunmila, after hearing about the destruction that the waves had brought to the land that Obatala had created said that he would make the water withdraw. Orunmila climbed down the golden chain and used his vast power to make the waves return to the water. The marshland dried and the people pled with Orunmila to stay with them and protect them from Olokun. While Orunmila had no desire to remain in the Yoruba world, he agreed to teach both the gods and the humans who lived there how to foretell the future and how to control the forces that they could not see. Then he climbed back up to his home in the sky, though like Obatala before him, he felt a kinship with the Yoruba people and he often returns to their world to see how they are doing.

Olokun was not defeated yet, however. She decided to make another attempt to show that she was the equal of the ruler of the sky. A skilled weaver and dyer of cloth, Olokun challenged Olorun to a weaving contest.

Olorun knew that Olokun was the best weaver ever, yet he knew that he could not avoid her challenge, so he determined to accept it without actually undergoing the test. He called Chameleon and ordered him to go to Olokun with his reply: "Olorun, the ruler of the sky, greets Olokun, the ruler of sea. Olorun asks that Olokun show his messenger, Chameleon, samples of the cloth that she has woven so that Chameleon can judge her skill. If Chameleon determines that the cloth that Olokun has woven is as beautiful as she claims, then Olorun will gladly engage in the contest."

Chameleon traveled down the golden chain to Olokun's abode, where he delivered Olorun's message. Olokun was pleased by Olorun's reply, and she put on a bright green skirt made from material that she had woven and dyed; amazingly, Chameleon turned the same color as the skirt. Olokun then put on a bright orange skirt; amazingly, again, Chameleon changed to the color of the garment. Next Olokun put on a bright red skirt; once more, Chameleon became the color of the skirt. For the rest of the day, Olokun put on the brightly colored skirts that she had woven. Each time Chameleon turned into the exact color of the skirt that she was wearing. By the end of the day, Olokun was ready to give up. She thought to herself that if even Olorun's messenger could duplicate the bright colors of her finest fabrics, surely the greatest of the gods could easily beat her in the contest. Therefore, she told Chameleon, "Tell Olorun, your master and the ruler of the sky, that Olokun, the ruler of the sea, sends her greetings. Tell him that I acknowledge his superiority in all things, including weaving." Thus it was that peace was restored between Olorun, the ruler of the sky, and Olokun, the ruler of the sea, and that order again returned to the universe.

"The Creation of the Universe"

Steven H. Gale

1) Discuss examples of ways in which the ordering and organization of the universe portray gender divisions among the Yoruba.

2) How is the contest between Olurun, the ruler of the sky, and Olokun, the ruler of the waters and the marshes, a metaphor for gender relations?

3) What implications for male dominance and female subordination can be deduced from the story?

IN THE FIELD: MANDE BLACKSMITHS

Patrick R. McNaughton

Blacksmiths in sub-Saharan Africa occupy confusing social spaces, as if they lived in two conflicting dimensions. They are at once glorified and shunned, feared and despised, afforded special privileges and bounded by special interdictions. To western observers, the status of smiths in African societies seems enigmatic, and most authors, from the earliest colonial officers and missionaries to contemporary scholars, have felt hard pressed to make sense of it. A statement of the dilemma is provided by anthropologist Laura Makarius:

> The status of the blacksmith in tribal societies poses one of the most puzzling problems of anthropology. By a strange paradox, this noted craftsman, whose bold and meritorious services are indispensable to his community, has been relegated to a position outside the place of society, almost as an "untouchable." Regarded as the possessor of great magical powers, held at the same time in veneration and contempt, entrusted with duties unrelated to his craft or to his inferior social status, that make of him performer of circumcision rites, healer, exorcist, peace-maker, arbiter, counselor, or head of a cult, his figure in what may be called the "blacksmith complex," presents a mass of contradictions.[1]

In the vast savanna lands of the Western Sudan among the large group of societies that speak Mande languages, there is a third dimension to this problem: here, the Mande blacksmiths are also important artists, making most of their culture's wood and iron sculpture. This art, along with the other things they do, gives smiths important roles in everyone else's professional, social, and spiritual lives, thereby putting them in a surprisingly prominent position, given their enigmatic status.

How can artists fill so many other roles, and how do these other roles influence their art? This book seeks a preliminary answer to these questions. Exploring the principal roles of the Mande smiths, it shows that their work as artists is enhanced, in a sense even made possible, by their activities as technicians, healers, sorcerers, and mediators. At the same time it demonstrates that all the work they do is aimed at shaping the environments and the individuals around them, while their social status both enhances their work and is the result of it.

Officers and missionaries of the colonial era were the first to write at length about Mande culture. Early in this century, Father Joseph Henry described the sculpture types. Over the next few decades, Maurice Delafosse, Louis Tauxier, Charles Monteil, and Henri Labouret provided useful materials on the culture. Around mid-century the French anthropologists Marcel Griaule, Germaine Dieterlen, Salonge de Ganay, Viviana Pâques, and Zacharie Ligers examined various aspects of the culture and cosmology, while Carl Kjersmeier and F. H. Lem assembled fine collections of sculpture. More recently, Mary Jo Arnoldi, Charles Bird, Sarah Brett-Smith, James T. Brink, George E. Brooks, Gerald Anthony Cashion, Kate Ezra, Barbara E. Frank, Bernhard Gardi, Kathryn L. Green, Pascal James Imperato, John William Johnson, Martha B. Kendall, Peter Weil, and Dominique Zahan have made valuable contributions to the literature. Since the early decades of this century, west African scholars, including Youssouf Cissé, Bokar N'Diaye, Massa Makan Diabaté, Mamby Sidibé, and Moussa Travélé, have also published materials that greatly enrich our understanding of Mande culture. Still, the corpus of Mande sculpture is large, and its contexts are complex. It will take many more scholars and many more studies before we may claim a systematic understanding of the culture.

I went to the Republic of Mali as a Ford Foreign Area Research Fellow in 1972–1973 and returned for the summer of 1978, with hopes of learning about traditional black smiths. I knew what the literature told us: that the Mande smiths were also sculptors and that they possessed much notoriety as sorcerers. I had also read that they were casted and in some measure looked down upon. In actual fact, I knew little about these artists and their roles in society, because only a small percentage of the scholarly literature addressed them directly. By extension, then, I realized that I also knew little about the motivations and intentions of their art.

The majority of my time that first year was spent in small towns between Bamako and Bougouni, just east of the Niger River. I also made some brief excursions: north to the area around the town of Banamba; east to the areas around Ségou, Markala, and San; south through Sikasso; and west on the roads to Sibi and Kita. In 1978 I visited San, but spent most of my time in the Mande Plateau near Bamako.

In the early months I traveled from one town to another, asking youngsters and elders where I might find blacksmiths. In every town I was introduced to at least one and sometimes several. I watched them work and asked them questions. I saw many of them on a regular basis, and some, including Dramane Dunbiya, Magan Fane, and Sedu Traore, I visited quite often. I also saw a good deal of Seydou Camara. He was born a smith and maintained a forge in his hometown in the Wasoulou region of southern Mali, but he had found that he loved music and so gave up smithing to become one of Mali's most renowned hunters' bards. He was extremely knowledgeable about the institution of smithing, and he provided me with a great deal of information. His nephew, Bourama Soumaoro, was also very knowledgeable, and, though I saw less of him, he too helped me greatly.

Ultimately, I found myself in a causal way apprenticed to the blacksmith Sedu Traore, and, while maintaining my contacts with the others, I worked with Sedu constantly. Sedu was from the southernmost region of the Bèlèdougou area north of Bamako. His father, in later life, had built a small blacksmiths' hamlet at the top of the Mande Plateau, which afforded a magnificent view of the great plains astride the Niger River. But I met Sedu in a town south of Bamako, where we spent most of our time together. I began to work intensely with him just before he became busy in the planting season with tool making and repairing, and, since his sons were all grown up and on their own, he let me spend many hours developing my technique on the bellows. Occasionally, Sedu had me try my hand at wood carving. More occasionally, I sat behind his anvil with a hammer in my hand, trying to make red-hot iron move the way Sedu did. The results of these enterprises were dismal but instructive; they made clear the depth of skill and acumen good sculpting requires of its practitioners.

Clients often came to Sedu, to have old tools repaired or new tools made. But they also came with requests for soothsaying, amulet-making, medical diagnoses and treatment, and general advice on all kinds of problems. I watched and listened and learned a great deal. When we were alone, working wood or iron, we talked for hours about every aspect of blacksmithing, from sculpting to sorcery. Sedu explained the importance of knowledge to every aspect of his trade. He related to me the experiences of his youth and what they had meant to his development as a smith. He discussed the usefulness of travel for the acquisition of wisdom, the importance of attaining genuine expertise, and the equal importance of maintaining a good name. He often discussed the rudiments of herbal and occult lore and the ethics that smiths should apply in their manipulation. He explained the tensions that develop regularly in communities as individuals negotiate their lives, families negotiate their community positions, and communities address an array of problems from the socialization of their youth to the inhibition of anti-social forces in the human and spiritual environments. He made the role of smiths in all these problems quite clear to me, and other smiths I talked to corroborated his account.

Sedu was generally fond of company, and so we visited a lot and were visited in turn. Dramane Dunbiya, the senior smith in Sedu's town, was a frequent companion with a wealth of information. So were several other community smiths with whom Sedu associated. A commonality of interests binds smiths together, and they tend to maintain extensive networks of friendship and communication. Therefore, Sedu and I traveled often and rather widely. I had a car, and we took full advantage of it to visit his fellow smiths in distant towns as well as his clients, his hunting companions, and other friends. He knew people everywhere, and I was pleased to be his chauffeur, because in these gregarious contexts I learned a great deal about smiths, their clients, and their cosmos.

When my informal apprenticeship began, Sedu marked me with a small white bead he hung around my neck. He passed a piece of string through it, which he knotted as he chanted. The bead was a special blacksmiths' device, used to announce membership in the profession and to protect the wearer from the unpleasant occult activities of others. For me it became a passport and an agent of transformation. Everywhere I went, both with and without Sedu Traore, people knew its meaning and accepted me on different terms from those they had applied before. Just once I used the bead avariciously. Back in Bamako at the main cloth market I had long been negotiating with a recalcitrant vendor over the price of a fine piece of cloth. He wanted to charge me the tourist price and I would not pay it. Finally one day I noticed a middle-aged woman watching us from an adjacent table, and I concluded that she was my vendor's boss. I marched straight over to her and, pointing to my bead, indicated that I was not a tourist. The fine piece of cloth instantly became mine.

The bead initiated a fundamental change in what people perceived me to be. Mande smithing is steeped in beliefs about the manipulation of nature's most powerful forces. The act of working iron and the myriad other acts that blacksmiths undertake embed them in a dangerous atmosphere of energies that we would define as occult or supernatural. My bead became the first link in a chain of protection from these forces. Gradually, Sedu gave me more amulets and some of his own tools; through these devices, Sedu and his colleagues believed, I gradually acquired the energies needed by someone who expected to spend much time in the intimate company of blacksmiths and their forges. I was not born a smith. But they made me resemble one closely enough to do my work.

The dimension of power that blacksmiths inhabit is matched by an equally important dimension of secrecy. The profession floats on a sea of secret expertise that outsiders have no right to learn about. My developing status as an informal apprentice began to make up in large measure for my foreign nature. Yet, I made plain from the start that I was doing research, with the goal of writing up whatever they would permit me to share with Westerners wanting to learn about Mande smiths. It was made equally plain to me that I would learn only what I was worthy of and only what they believed would do no harm. In fact, I learned what any beginning Mande apprentice might learn: the Mande principles of secrecy but not the secrets. Sedu, the other smiths of his community, and the elders who governed it were extremely careful about what I could be told, but they told enough for me to build a sound picture of their world.

I also made a point of interviewing Mande citizens who were not blacksmiths, both before and after I wore the bead that Sedu gave me. As a result, I acquired an idea of how the general Mande populace perceives the smiths. Nevertheless, my perceptions, as presented in this book, are aligned more closely with those of the blacksmiths than with those of the general population.

Most of my research assistants and colleagues were not smiths, and I enjoyed many hours of talk with them. They were quite different from one another, and quite different from the smiths. Chiekna Sangare was a teacher in Mali's public school system. Possessed of an open mind and a great curiosity, he had nevertheless known very little about blacksmiths until he began spending time in their forges with me. Abdulaye Sylla worked with the Ministry of Education as a curator at the National Museum in Bamako. He was quite knowledgeable about art and took a great interest in efforts to preserve and explain it. Dugutigi Traore was a farmer who came to Bamako with the hope of discovering another line of work. I met him through my friend Adbulaye Sissoko and decided it might be helpful to work with him for a while and watch his responses to smiths. Sissoko was

himself born a smith, but he made a living welding and repairing all types of vehicles. He also owned several trucks that carried trade goods to Mauritania and elsewhere. He was an amateur inventor, and at one point he built and ran a restaurant-nightclub on the banks of the Niger River. Although I never really worked with him, we spent much time together and he provided me with many insights. Sekuba Camara was also born a smith; he was the son of the hunters' bard Seydou. Rather than practice smithing, however, or taking up the hunters' harp like his father, Sekuba was a student aspiring to teach or to work for the Ministry of Education. Having been raised in the Wasoulou as a smith, he knew a great deal about the many enterprises of smiths. In the summer of 1978, when I returned to Mali for a second visit, I spent much of the time with Sekuba, transcribing, translating, and interpreting blacksmith songs sung by his father.

Finally, there was Kalilou Tera, who was finishing his degree at Mali's École normale supérieure when I encountered him working with Charles Bird at Indiana University in the summer of 1977. We had many discussions that summer and then worked together in Mali during the summer of 1978. I found his depth and clarity of understanding to be invaluable. He was the son of a well known ascetic Muslim and the grandson of an equally well-known marabout. But he believed in the value of Mande traditional religion and wanted to know as much as possible about Mande beliefs and practices. All his life he had talked with elders. He had acquired as a result a sense of Mande civilization as supple and complex as the culture itself.

Note

1. Makarius 1968:25. Cline 1937:114–139 and Barnes 1980:8–13 summarize much of the literature on the status of smiths in African cultures.

References

Barnes, Sandra T. 1980 *Ogun: An Old God for a New Age. Occasional Papers in Social Change*, 3. Philadelphia: Institute for the Study of Human Issues.

Cline, Walter Buchanan 1937 *Mining and Metallurgy in Negro Africa*. Menasha, Wisconsin: George Banta Publishing.

Makarius, Laura 1968 *The Blacksmith's Taboos: From the Man of Iron to the Man of Blood*. Diogenes 62 (Summer):25–48.

"IN THE FIELD: MANDE BLACKSMITHS"

Patrick R. McNaughton

1) Discuss the contradictory roles of the Mande blacksmith.

2) How is social status linked to the role of the blacksmith in Mande society?

3) Discuss the role of supernatural forces in Mande blacksmithing.

RADIANCE FROM THE WATERS: MENDE FEMININE BEAUTY

Sylvia Ardyn Boone

Beauty and Goodness

Mende expect women to be beautiful, graceful, delicate, curvaceous, pretty, clean, fresh, perfumed, groomed, adorned. And Mende expect women to be good, kind, sweet, patient, gentle, modest, loving, helpful, cheerful, honest, understanding. A beautiful girl must be a good girl, and goodness alone can make a girl beautiful. The Mende word *nyande* means both to be good and to be beautiful, to be nice—character, looks, and comportment refracting and overlapping. In any discussion of the physical aspects of beauty, before very long somebody would say: "but no one can be beautiful if she doesn't have a fine character." If I could make any distinction in the answers it would be that older men were the most precise and detailed in their descriptions of the physical, while older women held that comportment and character are more important. And so the Mende community, like all human societies, struggles to harmonize the short-term physical desires of the men for sexual contact with the longer-range goals of the women for family life, and with the sustained goals of the community for progeny and prosperity.

Toward these wider ends, older women train young girls in good behavior, discipline young women to their serious responsibilities, and themselves serve as examples of high morals and ethical behavior. In the larger sense, the mind of the Mende is concerned with questions of ethics and morality; the guiding ideology is moral rather than religious or scientific. The *hale* [men's and women's societies] formed by the Mende all have in part or full the intention of upholding the moral standards of the community. Considering this overwhelmingly moralistic cast to Mende thought, it is no surprise that beauty, too, is judged for its goodness.

The dangers of beauty are an outcome of its extraordinary impact and power—a beautiful girl can become arrogant, her pride turn to narcissism. One oft-told tale on the subject of beauty concerns a chief's daughter who is the most beautiful girl in the land.[1] When it comes time for her to marry, she declares she will marry only the most handsome man, one as good-looking as herself. Her father brings her proposals from wealthy, important men of the area, but she refuses them all. Then a most handsome man, resplendently dressed, presents himself at the chief's court. After inspection he is found to be perfect in every detail, without scar or flaw. The girl welcomes him as her husband, only to discover in the marriage chamber that he has removed his disguise of physical perfection and has resumed his true form of an *ndili*-python.[2] She cries out for help but is ignored, as the serpent swallows her whole. Here, the perils of youthful willfulness and the misuse of attractiveness conferred by beauty connect with implications of nonproductive autoeroticism.[3] The punishment for such social crimes is violent death, the python doing the job of removing the offender from the community.

Beauty is closely inspected all the time to make sure it is good. Mende fear that beauty will blind the eye to some evil that hides within. Many beautiful women resent the fuss made about them and feel they are unjustly harassed and harshly treated. Their beauty serves to draw attention to them and excite added criticism from their superiors. People seem to expect the best but fear the worst. Lovers may be tough with her, declaring that the girl may have used her looks to impress other men, but that *he* is not going to be taken in. Others feel bothered for minor infractions interpreted by their families as signs that they may become lazy or irresponsible and try to slide by on looks alone. One woman expressed bitterness about all this. She was nagged and punished all her life, she complained. Though she lived in town and was a bright pupil interested in a career in nursing, missionary teachers made her marry very young for fear that she could not resist urban pressures and would become a concubine or a prostitute. "This beauty, this beauty, what did all this beauty ever get me!"

A more positive illustration of Mende reflections on beauty lies in their interest in transcendence of the physical to an even greater *nyande* [i.e. beauty] through art. Mende declare that any girl with a beautiful voice is a beautiful girl: she may be quite ordinary to look at, but if she can sing well she will be considered lovely by any man in town. As we have already observed, "Beauty as a quality seems to emerge from a certain quantitative threshold" (Memel-Fotê 1968:52). We have seen how it works in physiological terms, but it also seems to apply to what Mende call delicate, *yéngèlé*, performances: artistic activities depending on wit, skill, talent, dedication, practice. Everybody in a Mende community is taught the rudiments of musical performance, singing, dancing, playing an instrument. But when a woman goes beyond the ordinary to become the soloist, not the chorus, this transcendence of the ordinary is called Beauty, and transfigures its owner into an Object of Beauty, a beauty that has all the allure and impact of physical beauty, and is even on a higher plane because it is derived from the "goodness"—pleasure-giving, group-forming—of fine performance.

Mende assume that a beautiful exterior enshrines the most useful something. It is a big disappointment for something to be beautiful to look at but not good, not useful, not fine. A "good thing" must be efficacious, do its job well. Part of the goodness can only be judged in its performance of the task for which it was created or fashioned. A good thing is utilitarian and is well-suited to fulfilling a useful purpose. In almost every discussion of beauty, someone would say how awful it is if a pretty girl is lazy or does not have a fine character. Mende call this *nyande gbama*, empty beauty, *gbama* meaning "for nothing, in vain" (Innes 1969:17). *Nyande gbama* refers to many of the functional and moral issues. It is *gbama* for a good-looking girl to be rude, insolent, disrespectful. It is *gbama* for her to be nonfunctional in the community: "She can't work, can't cook, can't dance, can't sing—of what use is she?" It is *gbama* to be poor, low status, living in coarse company although because of your looks you would be welcomed among those of refinement and prestige. It is beauty wasted. Beauty without a dimension of goodness is hollow, without substance, a deception.

Certainly the most serious *gbama* is barrenness. There can be no more horrible deception than that the beautiful girl—so sought after since childhood, so fought over by relatives, Sande, [i.e. women's society] and suitors—should, finally married, prove incapable of having children. It is a blow to the community, a vile mockery of all that they hold sacred. Beauty, in Mende thought, "is required to aid, it is called upon to participate and is a participant in the efficacy of the object. . . . The more beautiful the object, the better it accomplishes its affectively desired, imaginatively dreamed, technically hoped-for effect" (Memel-Fotê 1968:57). The irreducible, primary function of a woman is to bear children. For beauty to be

associated with sterility brings sad musings of "how can beautiful people not be good."[4]

If we look closely at the Mende words for beauty and goodness, we will see them overlapping, intersecting, and blending into a Möbius strip of meanings. *Nyande* is the word for beauty and *kpekpe* is the word for goodness.[5] Nyande can go off in the direction of describing the physical, the external, so it relates to prettiness, desirable body shape, admirable skin, hair, or eyes, and other physical attributes. In speaking of any one of these features for each of which there is a definite canon of beauty, *nyande* stands for the fulfillment of that canon. Thus *nyande yama*, "beautiful eyes," means the eyes are big, round, prominent, bright, and expressive. *Nyande nyini*, "beautiful breasts," means the breasts are low, firm, thick, covering the entire chest area; and so on.

Kpekpe relates to worth in the utility of objects and the behavior of human beings. For instance, *kpatoi kpekpe-ngò*, "the cutlass is good," means that it is comfortable to hold, useful to work with, performs well the job for which a cutlass is designed. Also, though, it is nothing else but a cutlass, doing the cutlass job.[6] When referring to people, the goodness of *kpekpe* means a person is kind-hearted, helps you, gives you gifts. As with objects, this is an appreciation based on the disposal of the object or the person to offer its services for your benefit.

In talking of objects, *nyande* can also express utility. However ugly-looking a cutlass may be, Mende can also say, "*Kpatoi nande-ngò*," meaning that the cutlass is beautiful because it is indeed a cutlass, a functional object, and not just a piece of useless, worthless junk. In a way, the two words are interchangeable; however, *nyande-ngò* is a more gentle use of the language. *Nyande* is broader, implying that the thing in question is comprehensively good, and includes a positive evaluation of both its looks and its usefulness.

When describing human beings, at a more abstract level, the two words converge at a point—the point of kindness and generosity. *Ngi kpekpe-ugò*—"He is good, he is *kind*, he is *generous*." *Ngi hinda nyande-ngò*—"His ways are fine, he is *kind*, he is *generous*." At the highest level of Mende conceptualization, beauty and goodness meet to express a sympathetic interest in the welfare of others and a warm-hearted readiness to give.[7]

Beauty as a Historical Fact

As beauty is physical and metaphysical, it is also "an historical fact."[8] By interviewing some thirty persons over the age of sixty-five, each of whom had been trained by an old grandmother or aunt, I was able to obtain information about beauty in a time span of about one hundred and twenty-five years. It was quickly evident that a young girl in 1885 was judged by the same standards as her counterpart in 1985! If Mende canons appear to have been so static for such a long time, I do not believe it is due to isolation or xenophobia. Although Mende culture has matured in small rural farming communities, like all West African peoples, Mende have extensive contact with neighboring groups. Since the people with whom Mende have mingled hold to similar views, ethnic interaction has probably served only to reinforce the existing Mende standards.[9] And, since beauty is body-based, and since all bodies resemble each other and the same features constantly recur over time, they are seen to have the permanence of nature itself as a manifestation of God.

Properly speaking, Mende people were never colonized (they were governed by the British as a protectorate), and they do not feel themselves the victims of cultural rape. The British colonial presence and its exploitation of mineral and farming resources served in part to introduce a number of innovations into Mende life that offered a new set of opportunities and challenges. Through it all, beauty, as an aspect of the "absorptive" Mende culture, managed to pick out what it needed and thus enhance the aesthetic qualities that are valued. So now for the first time beauty can be faked by makeup or flattering clothes. Short, thin hair can be augmented by hairpieces and covered by wigs, a flat chest enlarged by falsies, a fallen bust line uplifted by a brassiere, brows thickened with a pencil, and a healthy glow applied with makeup. Islamic styles for women made popular by *haja* has meant a beauty of clothing and adornment rather than of face and body; these voluminous robes, veils, and jewelry give older women more opportunity for glamor and elegance.

When Mende say that "before" beauty was "natural," they are saying several things. The remark goes back to a time when a virgin stood naked before the criticisms of the community, then the sole arbiter of taste but now only one of several. The release of many girls from this evaluation marks the outside influences that have brought upset to all sectors of Mende life. The vast majority of Mende girls who live in the villages still maintain the same lifestyles, but town girls, schoolgirls, and the chiefs' daughters are freer, less subject to the decisions of elders. Among the elders themselves, before, a woman in her fifties or sixties was sought after as a love-partner only if she had the prestige of being an artist or a Sowei. Now another group of mature women have attained social prominence and sexual desirability: the rich wives and mothers of the new political and governmental elite, whose prestige is based on money rather than, as it had been for women before, on service to the community. In Mendeland, as elsewhere in the world, "beauty changes."

Notes

1. I term "oft-told-tales" those stories I was told repeatedly by Mende who liked me and wanted to help me understand Mende ways. They are all tales of supernatural, mysterious happenings that are said to happen in different places at different times. Among them: (1) The Sande initiates turned to stone; (2) The relative who visits from afar and then you hear the next day that he died last week; (3) The orphan girl whose Sande tuition is mysteriously paid and she graduates and marries the president; (4) The beautiful girl who is a bed-wetter; (5) The pond you drink from which makes you return to that spot; (6) The *Tingoi* who brings a particular man great riches. These stories never appear in collections of folktales, and they do not seem to fit into any standard form. "Mende literature comprises many forms including prayers to the dead (*ngo gbia*), ritual slogans addressed to dancing spirits, dream (*kibalo*) narrations, fictitious tales (*dómé njele*), myths and legends (*njia wova; njepe wowa*), place puzzles (*hoboi*), proverbs and riddles (*sale*), and songs (*ngule*)." They are perhaps closest to *njia wova*, since such a narrative "recounts actual events, . . . may be told to an individual" (Kilson 1976:17). The question is whether or not they "recount actual events." Under the guidance of my preceptors I have come to see that they encapsulate Mende thought and, like moral tales, "are used for the socialization of the young, and therefore embody the mores of the society (Innes 1964:15). Mende kindly saw me as a "child Mende" who needed to be socialized. The lessons these "oft-told-tales" teach and the way they function in the life of the community would be the topic of an interesting paper.

2. This is not the natural python so revered by Mende cultists, but the vampire *ndili*, "a mythical creature in the shape of a python that is believed to attack children at night" (Innes 1969:95). The *ndili* is a complicated notion of evil; discussed by Harris and Sawyerr 1968:77–79, 118, 122; and by Little 1967:231.

3. The very perfection of her suitor should have warned the girl that he was not a normal human being, but a monster. This tale is an admonition to be suspicious of perfect beauty; Mende are sure that the very loveliest girls, for example, have serious, secret physical flaws. There is a prevalent notion that what can be seen may be fine, but what is completely hidden, the genitals, may be amiss in some way. Or a girl may have scars from infections that are covered by the long lappa. Three different men told me of encountering girls whose public and private parts were all exquis-

ite, only to find that they were bed-wetters.

4. This is real dilemma to Mende. rather like a western Christian brought up with a sense of guilt and retribution who questions "why innocent babies die." Both sets of speculations are unanswerable and express the layman's confusion about the ethical bases of the world he lives in.

5. In Innes: "*Kpekpe*—goodness, generosity; be good, be generous" (1969:57). "*Nyande*—be nice, be good looking, good, beauty, good looks . . . *Ngi wie hinda nyandengɔ̀*—he is good, kind" (p. 118).

6. "No matter how important its artistic content may be, the making of a garment, a uniform, an ornament, a piece of jewelry, or a tool is subordinated to its function, its efficacy. Any adjunctions whose only purpose would be beauty [ornament] are excluded insofar as it would overburden or hamper proper utilization of the object" (Memel-Fotê 1968:57).

7. Again, I am grateful especially to the Bo preceptor and to the Mme. K. compound for their patient and lucid explanations of Mende aesthetic and moral concepts.

8. Susan Sontag, "Beauty, How Will It Change Next?" *Beauty in Vogue* (London), Autumn/Winter 1975, p. 86.

9. The comparisons Memel-Fotê has made of fourteen different cultures indicates their considerable agreement in aesthetic matters (1968:47–56).

References

Harris, W. T., and Harry R. Sawyer 1968 *The Springs of Mende Relief and Conduct.* Freetown: Sierra Leone University Press.

Innes, Gordon 1964 *Some Features of Theme and Style of Mende Folktales.* Sierra Leone Language Review, no. 3.

_____ . 1969 *A Mende-English Dictionary.* Cambridge: Cambridge University Press.

Kilson, Marion De B. 1976 *Royal Antelope and Spider: West African Mende Tales.* Cambridge, Massachusetts: The Press of the Langdon Associates.

Little, Kenneth 1967 *The Mende Chiefdoms of Sierra Leone.* In P. M. Kaberry and C. D. Forde, eds., *West African Kingdoms in the Nineteenth Century.* London: Oxford University Press.

Memel-Fotê, Harris 1968 *The Perception of Beauty in Negro African Culture. In Colloquium on Negro Art, Dakar, First World Festival of Negro Arts.* Paris: Présence Africaine.

Sontag, Susan 1975 B*eauty, How Will It Change Next? Beauty in Vogue.* London. Autumn/Winter.

"RADIANCE FROM THE WATERS: MENDE FEMININE BEAUTY"

Sylvia Ardyn Boone

1) Discuss the symbolic significance of beauty among the Mende.

2) Discuss the similarities and differences between physical beauty and inner beauty as perceived by the Mende.

Yekuana Myths of the Origins of Artifacts

David M. Guss

In writing about the nature of origin myths in tribal societies, Mircea Eliade calls attention to what he refers to as an underlying "paradisiac syndrome" (1960:63). He claims that tribal man periodically reenacts these myths in rituals and festivals in order to return (the "eternal return") to the conditions that existed at the time of the Beginning, *in illo tempore*. Characterized by a lack of division between Heaven and Earth, an unimpaired communication between animals and humans, and the absence of both death and physical want, these myths satisfy, however fleetingly, man's endless "nostalgia for Paradise, the longing to recover the Eden-like state of the Ancestor" (ibid.:45). To simply tell them allows one to participate in the eternal state of abundance they evoke. The performance of these myths provides for the sanctification of the event or object for which they are being sung. By introducing the original celestial models upon which the structures of the culture are based, man magically reenters the sacred space of creation that produced them. For Eliade, this immersion into the mythic space of the sacred is the result of a profound need to regularly regenerate Time. Unlike the linear historicity of profane time, that of the sacred mythic is cyclical, requiring annual renewal. For those who set their clocks by this cyclical Time, it is the only one worth recording; hence Eliade's conclusion that the desire for paradise, as represented by the sacred myth, is in essence a desire for the real or, as he states it, "an ontological nostalgia": "In short, through the reactualization of his myths, religious man attempts to approach the gods and to participate in *being*; the imitation of paradigmatic divine models expresses at once his desire for sanctity and his ontological nostalgia" (1959:106).

While the Yekuana have various origin myths that conform to Eliade's "paradisiac syndrome"—such as the *Adaha ademi hidi* for the garden and the *Atta ademi hidi* for the house—they also have many others which do not. Among the latter are myths describing the origin of such objects of daily use as canoes, weapons, instruments, and baskets. Although the action described in such narratives clearly takes place in a mythic time when animals and humans could still communicate, it is far removed from the idyllic era of the Beginning. Gone now are Wanadi [a Yekuana creator-being who brought the First People to earth] and the other culture heroes with whom he created the first structures. Humans, called So'to or Yekuana, are already a well-defined group, and though they still interact with other species, it is an interaction fraught with danger and hostility. Led mainly by shamans, they succeed in obtaining the objects necessary for culture by either waging war or deceiving those who already possess them. As such, the models these myths portray are not the cosmogonic ones of annual renewal, but rather the cultural ones of daily creation. As the origin myths of objects made daily, they describe the daily making of culture. The access to the sacred which they provide is not reserved for special occasions, but is translated into the everyday creation of culture itself.

Whereas the myths of Wanadi's initial deeds explain the creation of the dualities extant in the world today, the myths describing the origin of man-made artifacts attempt to resolve them. The world they take place in is already deeply divided. Humans, surrounded by the forces of negativity and darkness, are barely able to exist. Hostile tribes of blood-thirsty monsters prey upon them from all sides. To emerge from this state of vulnerability and degradation, humans must both defeat these enemies and gain control of the secret weapons that give them their power. It is not enough to merely vanquish "death;" humans must incorporate it into their very being if they are to survive. This then is the message repeated in myth after myth: Culture is a medium of synthesis through which the noncultural—darkness, death, rawness, poison—is converted into it to reproduce the whole. As such, these myths of origin serve as the perfect para digms of transformation, symbolically de picting the daily operation of culture. The action they describe is inevitably one of movement from darkness to light, from chaos to order, from cannibal to human. In some instances it is not even necessary to return to the mythic era of the First People. For example, one brief account of the making of the first canoe describes how the Yekuana derived this skill from the Kariña or Caribs. A fierce tribe of cannibals (from whom the English word derives), these people preyed upon the Yekuana until their destruction at the hands of the Spanish at the end of the eighteenth century:

> Before they didn't know. The Yekuana didn't know how to make canoes. They learned from the Kariña. The Kariña know a lot. They really did things well. The Yekuana didn't know.
>
> When the Kariña had a twelve-meter tree, they cut ten canoes from it! They didn't throw the in side away like we do. They didn't waste it. First they carved one canoe, very carefully. Then another and another and another, until they got down to the biggest one at the bottom. The Yekuana just throw all that away and make one canoe.
>
> The first Yekuana to learn how to make canoes was a man who married a Kariña girl. One day his father-in-law sent him out to make five canoes from one tree.
>
> He didn't know how. The Yekuana didn't know how to make canoes. When the father-in law came to see the work, there were only three canoes. He asked, "Why aren't you working? What are you doing just standing there?" And so he struck the Yekuana across the side of the head and killed him.

While this tale is a somewhat abbreviated one set within a historical context, it nevertheless conforms to the structure of metaphor underlying the origin myths of other cultural artifacts. In it the Yekuana are a defenseless group, possessing none of the skills available to other beings. Portrayed as cannibals, these other groups are able to dominate the Yekuana so long as they maintain their monopoly on the special skill attributed to them. The source of their power is equated with death, either as a weapon or a poison. In the story of the first canoe, it is the boy's contact with canoe-making that must be seen as the cause of his death. In the following myth explaining the origin of the drum (*samhuda*), the parallel between death and artifact is even more explicit:

> Before, when they didn't have it, the drum was a different shape. It was pointed and could run right through a person like a sword. The people didn't know what *samhuda* was then. They said, "They have it over there. Let's go see."
>
> So they went to the village where they had the drum. And they asked to see it. And the chief said, "OK." But first he told them to line up in a long row, like this (indicating single-file formation).
>
> Then he went in and got it and came up to the first one, like this. And he stuck it right in, himself. Not thrown, himself! And he ran it

through all of them, the whole row. And he killed them all.

> Later on, other Yekuana stole that drum. I don't know how. They stole it. That was a long time ago. Before me . . . Before there was Simón. Before there was González (the oldest singers in the village). It was pointed . . . like a *yaribaru*.[1]

In order to create culture, as represented by the material forms that constitute it such as canoes and drums, one must be able to integrate into it the wild and untamed. As the Yekuana recognize, this demands much more than simple technical expertise. With every object possessing an invisible double of incalculable power, humans must be able to control the unseen as well as the seen when negotiating the conversion of wild objects into domestic ones. The ritual performance that accompanies every technical activity guarantees that the incorporation of this potentially dangerous new and foreign will not be disruptive. The material transformation of any object—such as tree to drum or animal to food—must be accompanied as well by a spiritual transformation realigning its symbolic structure with that of the human world into which it is being integrated. It is this humanization process, so fundamental to every material activity, that is the real subject of these myths of origin. By recounting how each object was retrieved from the forces of darkness beyond the ordered world of the *atta*, they become models for the process of transformation by which culture itself is created. The story they tell of the dangerous acquisition of forms from their nonhuman (that is, cannibal) owners is the same one reenacted daily by the Yekuana of today.

While culture may be said to represent the controlled and safe, it is nevertheless completely composed of elements that come from without. In this sense, its genius is its ability to successfully mediate between the world of nature and itself, to make whole what is fragmented and divisive. To fail in this mediation results in a form of reverse transformation by which the human is converted back into the animal. And indeed there are many stories recounting how people have been overcome by animals, disappearing into their world forever. Often these stories of reverse transformation are the result of some broken taboo—a menstruating woman stolen by anaconda while bathing in a river, an impure hunter kidnapped by armadillo while sleeping alone in the forest (Guss 1985:55 passim). All of these stories are dominated by the same tension that exists in the myths of the origins of artifacts—the conflict of two opposing forces, each determined to transform the other into itself. It is due to this conflict that the animals and other beings in these stories are inevitably characterized as cannibals or "people of Odosha." Referred to as *odokato* (from Odosha plus the suffix *-ato*, "people") or *chuttakomo*, "the people of the bush" (*chutta*, "bush," *komo*, "people"), these beings form a direct opposition to the world of the So'to or humans. In order for humans to continue as an organized species, however, this opposition must be synthesized daily, with "the people of the bush" regularly transfigured into usable, safe, detoxified forms.

The fact that culture depends on elements wrested from the nonhuman (Odos hankomo) for its continued reproduction has been alluded to by several scholars as a determining factor in various mythologies. Eliade claims that the central myth of many paleo-agricultural people focuses on a ritual killing from which both agriculture and the underworld developed. Referring to these sacrificed tuber gods as *demas*, he writes that "the edible plant is not given by Nature: it is a product of an assassination, because that is how it was created at the beginning of time . . . So that the vegetable world may continue, man must kill and be killed" (1960:46). And in one of his earliest structuralist studies, Lévi-Strauss, after stating that "the basic problem in Pueblo mythology is in discovering a mediation between life and death," concludes that "death has to be come integrated so that agriculture can exist" ([1955]1979:193). In both of these examples the origin myth is seen as an act of appropriation from the underworld, a means by which culture renews itself through union with the anti-cultural or Death. For the Yekuana such myths are not relegated to agriculture alone. They exist wherever cultural forms are organized to resolve the basic conflict of dualities inherent within them. Among the best examples of these myths is that of the origin of the *waja tomennato*, the "painted" *waja* baskets woven daily by the men. The following version of this myth was not narrated by a man, however, but by the eldest woman singer in the village of Parupa on the Paragua River. First told to me in 1977, the version that follows is an interlinear translation of another telling by the same singer during a visit six years later:

A long time ago
I'm going to tell a little bit about a long time ago
about how the Warishidi were a long time ago[2]
I don't know that much but I'll try and tell anyway

A long time ago Warishidi ate many
Then Warishidi ate a So'to
There was a So'to killed
The people went out to hunt
There were two who were found
One man ran off

fleeing
He hid in an armadillo hole
Kadamaadi fled from them because he was afraid
He fled because he was afraid of Warishidi
Then that one who fled screamed for help
"They're biting me"
"They're biting me" (very slowly)
So when he screamed the other hid
He (the hidden one) was looking at the other one
Nothing
There was nothing left
They carried off the two arms
They carried the two arms up in the trees
and just sat there
Warishidi
That's the way Warishidi used to be

Now listen

The other brother   Adamaadi
CALLED EVERYONE TOGETHER
They called all the people
They called every person
Ihuruña[3]
They called Ihuruña
They called all the So'to together
To avenge themselves
To avenge themselves with curare
Many people came together
Just as many as the Warishidi
Just as many Warishidi as there were
were there people together
Then each one took his place
There were as many as there are trees in the forest

It was like a huge breeze
when the Warishidi came sweeping down upon the
*   So'to*
They shot   shot   shot   shot   shot
*   (very softly)*
Now the Warishidi fell
They thought they would eat So'to
That there was just one of them
Now there are none
They fell   fell   fell   fell   (softly)
That's how it was
like that
Now there were just a few
Now there were almost none
Now the Warishidi were completely gone
That's the way it went right up to the chief
Because they killed all the rest
They killed all the rest right up to the chief
It was the Warishidi who made the war
That's really the way it was

Now they had to kill the chief
Now they went up there
They went up there
They shot   shot   shot
There he was now
There he was
Now he appeared
He actually lived in Mount Ihani[4]
That's where they came from
Where they came from before
That's where they were born
That Ihani was the house where they lived
Okay   Now Waña Kasuwai appeared
He was an enormous monster
with great huge chakara
the size of suitcases[5]
Now he hung his kungwa up from a branch
He hung it up there before he fell
When they shot him it was hanging up there like that
And he fell and died
Now then they were all gone those Warishidi
Those Warishidi were all gone
Because their chief was dead now too
Now there were none left
They were really through

Now they got down his kungwa
They took down Waña Kasuwai's kungwa
Then the looked to see what was inside
"What does he have in here?"
thinking about what was inside
Very small waja
There were miniature waja inside there[6]
Well they were all there
Mawadi asadi   Awidi
All of them
That's the way they discovered that
That's the way all those things were found out
The So'to saw all those things there
and learned how to make them

Now then
Woroto Sakedi showed it
Woroto Sakedi did it   (very softly)

And so if it wasn't for that we
wouldn't have all this
None of this would exist
if it wasn't for that
The people wouldn't have learned about that
if that hadn't of happened
And so they went and learned all this
If not for that
we wouldn't have had to do anything
Yes that's the way it is

Well that's what they say
You know that now there are taboos
that today there are prohibitions
Because that wasn't created by people
Odosha invented all that

A woman who has just given birth
who's just had a child
can't put cassava in the waja
She can't put anything in the painted ones
The ahachito hato   the new woman
she can't put anything inside either
It's forbidden for her to put anything
inside the painted ones
That's why the ahachito hato don't use painted waja
That's what they say

Well now let's see
That's the way I remember it
the way I recall it   remember hearing it
Now I don't know how it is today
Those   those young ones who are out there
      yelling
yelling and playing out there
I don't know what those young ones will say in my
      place[7]
Well now it's not very long
not very long
It's really rather short
very short
But that's why Warishidi is dangerous
Because he ate people
Yes Warishidi is still dangerous
That's all I have to say
That's it
Everything

Like the monkeys in many traditions throughout the world, the Warishidi of this story are symbols of chaos and immorality. Closer to humans than any other animal, monkeys are nevertheless radically different, a fact that may account for their common opposition to the norms of culture (see Ohnuki-Tierney 1987). As has already been noted, Iarakuru, the weeping capuchin (*Cebus* sp.) is held responsible for introducing the night into the Yekuana world, thereby explaining his close association with all that is dark (de Civrieux 1980:24). Equally identified with these negative forces is Warishidi who, belying his name of "spider monkey," is a large, muscular animal, with a prehensile tail over three feet long. In the above myth he is described as a fierce cannibal who at one time devoured humans. His chief, in addition, is closely identified with the Devil as his name, Waña Kasuwai (a variant of Kahushawa or Odosha), makes clear. In other versions of this myth, Waña Kasuwai is described as even more monstrous, enormous and hairy with blood gushing from his mouth and two huge shaman's pouches (*chakara*) slung across his chest like bandoliers. The defeat of the Warishidi, creatures of chaos and death, represents the victory of culture over nature. Yet, as already stated, it is not enough for culture to simply vanquish nature. It must also integrate it if it is to continue to reproduce itself.

As in the other myths of the origins of artifacts, the source of power of the Yekuana's enemies is not discarded after their victory, but is transformed into an essential element of their culture. The ability of the foreign and dangerous to destroy is neutralized and converted into a usable object. The memory of these objects' origins is not only recorded in myths, however. It is incorporated into the very design of the objects themselves. By simply manufacturing an artifact one repeats the message encoded in the story of its origin. The organization of its parts reiterates the same synthesis through which all of culture is created. Just as its origin myth successfully resolves the opposition between nature and culture, so too does the construction of the artifact itself. The safe integration of the wild and toxic into a harmonious whole is now restated as a compositional achievement. In the case of the "painted" *waja*, the designs woven into them memorialize not only the history of their origin but also the integrative process that that history represents.

Notes

1. The *yaribaru* is a slender, double-pronged weapon carved from a single piece of hardwood (see pl. 22). An interesting variation of the drum origin story recounts how the first *samhuda* was borrowed from the Warishidi monkeys. After using the drum's hypnotic beat to put a group of visiting enemies to sleep, the Yekuana slew them.

2. Known as *marimonda* in Spanish and "long-haired spider monkey" in English, the Warishidi (*Ateles belzebuth*), one of the New World's largest primates, travel in multi-male groups and subsist on a diet of fruit (Tello 1979:52).

3. Literally meaning "the Headwater Place," Ihuruña is the homeland of the Yekuana. Its name is derived from its dramatic location at the headwaters of several Orinoco tributaries that include the Padamo, Kuntinamo, Erevato, Ventuari, and Caura. In some versions of this tale, other tribes join with the Yekuana in their battle against the Warishidi. However, when the *kungwa* is opened and its contents divided, the tribes use their new powers to wage war upon one another. In these variations the tale is also used to explain the origin of war and the enmity between the tribes.

4. A small mountain sometimes referred to as Mount Marimonda, Mount Ihani is located in the uppermost headwaters of the Caura and Ventuari rivers near the Brazilian border. It should not be confused with Mount Warishidi, in which the Erevato has its source.

5. Normally a small leather pouch in which shamans store magic remedies, the *chakara* of this tale are described as *kungwa* baskets "the size of suitcases." Although the use of the word *medetta*, from the Spanish *maleta*, is used with some humor here, it emphasizes the enormous shamanic powers that Waña Kasuwai must possess to own *chakara* of this size.

6. In some versions of this tale the *waja* miniatures are referred to as "snapshots," a description that is not surprising, since the waja contained in the *kungwa* are meant to be *muestras* or "samples." The Yekuana term used here for these small baskets is *waja nakomokwa*.

7. Commenting upon the tradition itself, the story teller wonders whether young people will still tell *Watunna* when they are as old as she is. "What will they say when they are my age?" she ponders. Such musings are not unique to this story but are part of a lengthy, self-reflexive "sign-off" common to many of the tales told by this narrator.

References

De Civrieux, Marc. 1980. *Watunna: An Orinoco Creation Cycle.* Edited and translated by David M. Guss. San Francisco: North Point Press.

Eliade, Mircea 1959 *The Sacred and the Profane.* New York: Harper & Row.

_____ 1960 *Myths, Dreams, and Mysteries.* New York: Harper & Row.

Guss, David M.1980 *Watunna: An Orinoco Creation Cycle.* San Francisco: North Point Press.

_____. 1981 *The Selected Poetry of Vicente Huidobro.* New York: New Directions.

_____. 1985 *The Language of the Birds: Tales. Texts, and Poems of Interspecies Communication.* San Francisco: North Point Press.

_____ . 1986 *Five Meters of Poems.* Santa Barbara: Turkey Press.

Levi-Strauss, Claude 1979 [1955] "The Structural Study of Myth." In William A. Lessa and Evon Z. Vogt, eds., *Reader in Comparative Religion*, 4th ed. New York: Harper & Row.

Ohnuki-Tierney, Emiko 1987 *The Monkey as Mirror: Symbolic Transformations in Japanese History and Ritual.* Princeton, New Jersey: Princeton University Press.

Tello, Jaime 1979 *Mamiferos de Venezuela.* Caracas: Fundacion La Salle de Ciencias Naturales.

"YEKUANA MYTHS OF THE ORIGINS OF ARTIFACTS"

David M. Guss

1) According to the story of the myths, what contradictions exist in the Yekuana world?

2) What societal tensions were the Yekuana myths supposed to resolve?

3) What is the role of myths in Yekuana life?

4) What humanization processes were objects (artifacts) subjected to and why?

5) What is significant about "The Story of the First Canoe"? Relate it to the Yekuana attitudes towards life.

6) What does the story about the "painted" waja baskets woven daily by men reveal?

7) What did the Yekuana intend to teach the world through their myths?

8) What interpretations of the Yekuana myths were offered by the author?

SECTION EIGHT

Politics: Who Gets
What, When, and How

FROM EGALITARIANISM TO KLEPTOCRACY

Jared Diamond

In 1979, while I was flying with missionary friends over a remote swamp-filled basin of New Guinea, I noticed a few huts many miles apart. The pilot explained to me that, somewhere in that muddy expanse below us, a group of Indonesian crocodile hunters had recently come across a group of New Guinea nomads. Both groups had panicked, and the encounter had ended with the Indonesians shooting several of the nomads.

My missionary friends guessed that the nomads belonged to an uncontacted group called the Fayu, known to the outside world only through accounts by their terrified neighbors, a missionized group of erstwhile nomads called the Kirikiri. First contacts between outsiders and New Guinea groups are always potentially dangerous, but this beginning was especially inauspicious. Nevertheless, my friend Doug flew in by helicopter to try to establish friendly relations with the Fayu. He returned, alive but shaken, to tell a remarkable story.

It turned out that the Fayu normally lived as single families, scattered through the swamp and coming together once or twice each year to negotiate exchanges of brides. Doug's visit coincided with such a gathering, of a few dozen Fayu. To us, a few dozen people constitute a small, ordinary gathering, but to the Fayu it was a rare, frightening event. Murderers suddenly found themselves face-to-face with their victim's relatives. For example, one Fayu man spotted the man who had killed his father. The son raised his ax and rushed at the murderer but was wrestled to the ground by friends; then the murderer came at the prostrate son with an ax and was also wrestled down. Both men were held, screaming in rage, until they seemed sufficiently exhausted to be released. Other men periodically shouted insults at each other, shook with anger and frustration, and pounded the ground with their axes. That tension continued for the several days of the gathering, while Doug prayed that the visit would not end in violence.

The Fayu consist of about 400 hunter-gatherers, divided into four clans and wandering over a few hundred square miles. According to their own account, they had formerly numbered about 2,000, but their population had been greatly reduced as a result of Fayu killing Fayu. They lacked political and social mechanisms, which we take for granted, to

achieve peaceful resolution of serious disputes. Eventually, as a result of Doug's visit, one group of Fayu invited a courageous husband-and-wife missionary couple to live with them. The couple has now resided there for a dozen years and gradually persuaded the Fayu to renounce violence. The Fayu are thereby being brought into the modern world, where they face an uncertain future.

Many other previously uncontacted groups of New Guineans and Amazonian Indians have similarly owed to missionaries their incorporation into modern society. After the missionaries come teachers and doctors, bureaucrats and soldiers. The spreads of government and of religion have thus been linked to each other throughout recorded history, whether the spread has been peaceful (as eventually with the Fayu) or by force. In the latter case it is often government that organizes the conquest, and religion that justifies it. While nomads and tribespeople occasionally defeat organized governments and religions, the trend over the past 13,000 years has been for the nomads and tribespeople to lose.

At the end of the last Ice Age, much of the world's population lived in societies similar to that of the Fayu today, and no people then lived in a much more complex society. As recently as A.D. 1500, less than 20 percent of the world's land area was marked off by boundaries into states run by bureaucrats and governed by laws. Today, all land except Antarctica's is so divided. Descendants of those societies that achieved centralized government and organized religion earliest ended up dominating the modern world. The combination of government and religion has thus functioned, together with germs, writing, and technology, as one of the four main sets of proximate agents leading to history's broadest pattern. How did government and religion arise?

Fayu bands and modern states represent opposite extremes along the spectrum of human societies. Modern American society and the Fayu differ in the presence or absence of a professional police force, cities, money, distinctions between rich and poor, and many other political, economic, and social institutions. Did all of those institutions arise together, or did some arise before others? We can infer the answer to this question by comparing modern societies at different levels of organization, by examining written accounts or archaeological evidence about past societies, and by observing how a society's institutions change over time.

Cultural anthropologists attempting to describe the diversity of human societies often divide them into as many as half a dozen categories. Any such attempt to define stages of any evolutionary or developmental continuum—whether of musical styles, human life stages, or human societies—is doubly doomed to imperfection. First, because each stage grows out of some previous stage, the lines of demarcation are inevitably arbitrary. (For example, is a 19-year-old person an adolescent or a young adult?) Second, developmental sequences are not invariant, so examples pigeonholed under the same stage are inevitably heterogeneous. (Brahms and Liszt would turn in their graves to know that they are now grouped together as composers of the romantic period.) Nevertheless, arbitrarily delineated stages provide a useful shorthand for discussing the diversity of music and of human societies, provided one bears in mind the above caveats. In that spirit, we shall use a simple classification based on just four categories—band, tribe, chiefdom, and state—to understand societies.

Bands are the tiniest societies, consisting typically of 5 to 80 people, most or all of them close relatives by birth or by marriage. In effect, a band is an extended family or several related extended families. Today, bands still living autonomously are almost confined to the most remote parts of New Guinea and Amazonia, but within modern times there were many others that have only recently fallen under state control or been assimilated or exterminated. They include many or most African Pygmies, southern African San hunter-gatherers (so-called Bushmen), Aboriginal Australians, Eskimos (Inuit), and Indians of some resource-poor areas of the Americas such as Tierra del Fuego and the northern boreal forests. All those modern bands are or were nomadic hunter-gatherers rather than settled food producers. Probably all humans lived in bands until at least 40,000 years ago, and most still did as recently as 11,000 years ago.

Bands lack many institutions that we take for granted in our own society. They have no permanent single base of residence. The band's land is used jointly by the whole group, instead of being partitioned among subgroups or individuals. There is no regular economic specialization, except by age and sex: all able-bodied individuals forage for food. There are no formal institutions, such as laws, police, and treaties, to resolve conflicts within and between bands. Band organization is often described as "egalitarian": there is no formalized social stratification into upper and lower classes, no formalized or hereditary leadership, and no formalized monopolies of information and decision making. However, the term "egalitarian" should not be taken to mean that all band members are equal in prestige and contribute equally to decisions. Rather, the term merely means that any band "leadership" is informal and acquired through qualities such as personality, strength, intelligence, and fighting skills.

My own experience with bands comes from the swampy lowland area of New Guinea where the Fayu live, a region known as the Lakes Plains. There, I still encounter extended families of a few adults with their dependent children and elderly, living in crude temporary shelters along streams and traveling by canoe and on foot. Why do peoples of the Lakes Plains continue to live as nomadic bands, when most other New Guinea peoples, and almost all other peoples elsewhere in the world, now live in settled larger groups? The explanation is that the region lacks dense local concentrations of resources that would permit many people to live together, and that (until the arrival of missionaries bringing crop plants) it also lacked native plants that could have permitted productive farming. The bands' food staple is the sago palm tree, whose core yields a starchy pith when the palm reaches maturity. The bands are nomadic, because they must move when they have cut the mature sago trees in an area. Band numbers are kept low by diseases (especially malaria), by the lack of raw materials in the swamp (even stone for tools must be obtained by trade), and by the limited amount of food that the swamp yields for humans. Similar limitations on the resources accessible to existing human technology prevail in the regions of the world recently occupied by other bands.

Our closest animal relatives, the gorillas and chimpanzees and bonobos of Africa, also live in bands. All humans presumably did so too, until improved technology for extracting food allowed some hunter-gatherers to settle in permanent dwellings in some resource-rich areas. The band is the political, economic, and social organization that we inherited from our millions of years of evolutionary history. Our developments beyond it all took place within the last few tens of thousands of years.

The first of those stages beyond the band is termed the tribe, which differs in being larger (typically comprising hundreds rather than dozens of people) and usually having fixed settlements. However, some tribes and even chiefdoms consist of herders who move seasonally.

Tribal organization is exemplified by New Guinea highlanders, whose political unit before the arrival of colonial government was a village or else a close-knit cluster of villages. This political definition of "tribe" is thus often much smaller than what linguists and cultural anthropologists would define as a tribe—namely, a group that shares language and culture. For example, in 1964 I began to work among a group of highlanders known as the Foré. By linguistic and cultural standards, there were then 12,000 Foré, speaking two mutually intelligible dialects and living in 65 villages of several hundred people each. But there was no political unity whatsoever among villages of the Foré language group. Each hamlet was involved in a kaleidoscopically changing pattern of war and shifting alliances with all neighboring hamlets, regardless of whether the neighbors were Foré or speakers of a different language.

Tribes, recently independent and now variously subordinated to national states, still occupy much of New Guinea, Melanesia, and Amazonia. Similar tribal organization in the past is inferred from archaeological evidence of settlements that were substantial but lacked the archaeological hallmarks of chiefdoms that I shall explain below. That evidence suggests that tribal organization began to emerge around 13,000 years ago in the Fertile Crescent and later in some other areas. A prerequisite for living in settlements is either food production or else a productive environment with especially concentrated resources that can be hunted and gathered within a small area. That's why settlements, and by inference tribes, began to proliferate in the Fertile Crescent at that time, when climate changes and improved technology combined to permit abundant harvests of wild cereals.

Besides differing from a band by virtue of its settled residence and its larger numbers, a tribe also differs in that it consists of more than one formally recognized kinship group, termed clans, which exchange marriage partners. Land belongs to a particular clan, not to the whole tribe. However, the number of people in a tribe is still low enough that everyone knows everyone else by name and relationships.

For other types of human groups as well, "a few hundred" seems to be an upper limit for group size compatible with everyone's knowing everybody. In our state society, for instance, school principals are likely to know all their students by name if the school contains a few hundred children, but not if it contains a few thousand children. One reason why the organization of human government tends to change from that of a tribe to that of a chiefdom in societies with more than a few hundred members is that the difficult issue of conflict resolution between strang-

ers becomes increasingly acute in larger groups. A fact further diffusing potential problems of conflict resolution in tribes is that almost everyone is related to everyone else, by blood or marriage or both. Those ties of relationships binding all tribal members make police, laws, and other conflict-resolving institutions of larger societies unnecessary, since any two villagers getting into an argument will share many kin, who apply pressure on them to keep it from becoming violent. In traditional New Guinea society, if a New Guinean happened to encounter an unfamiliar New Guinean while both were away from their respective villages, the two engaged in a long discussion of their relatives, in an attempt to establish some relationship and hence some reason why the two should not attempt to kill each other.

Despite all of these differences between bands and tribes, many similarities remain. Tribes still have an informal, "egalitarian" system of government. Information and decision making are both communal. In the New Guinea highlands, I have watched village meetings where all adults in the village were present, sitting on the ground, and individuals made speeches, without any appearance of one person's "chairing" the discussion. Many highland villages do have someone known as the "big-man," the most influential man of the village. But that position is not a formal office to be filled and carries only limited power. The big-man has no independent decision-making authority, knows no diplomatic secrets, and can do no more than attempt to sway communal decisions. Big-men achieve that status by their own attributes; the position is not inherited.

Tribes also share with bands an "egalitarian" social system, without ranked lineages or classes. Not only is status not inherited; no member of a traditional tribe or band can become disproportionately wealthy by his or her own efforts, because each individual has debts and obligations to many others. It is therefore impossible for an outsider to guess, from appearances, which of all the adult men in a village is the big-man: he lives in the same type of hut, wears the same clothes or ornaments, or is as naked, as everyone else.

Like bands, tribes lack a bureaucracy, police force, and taxes. Their economy is based on reciprocal exchanges between individuals or families, rather than on a redistribution of tribute paid to some central authority. Economic specialization is slight: full-time crafts specialists are lacking, and every able-bodied adult (including the big-man) participates in growing, gathering, or hunting food. I recall one occasion when I was walking past a garden in the Solomon Islands, saw a man digging and waving at me in the distance, and realized to my astonishment that it was a friend of mine named Faletau. He was the most famous wood carver of the Solomons, an artist of great originality—but that did not free him of the necessity to grow his own sweet potatoes. Since tribes thus lack economic specialists, they also lack slaves, because there are no specialized menial jobs for a slave to perform.

Just as musical composers of the classical period range from C. P. E. Bach to Schubert and thereby cover the whole spectrum from baroque composers to romantic composers, tribes also shade into bands at one extreme and into chiefdoms at the opposite extreme. In particular, a tribal big-man's role in dividing the meat of pigs slaughtered for feasts points to the role of chiefs in collecting and redistributing food and goods—now reconstrued as tribute—in chiefdoms. Similarly, presence or absence of public architecture is supposedly one of the distinctions between tribes and chiefdoms, but large New Guinea villages often have cult houses (known as *haus tamburan*, on the Sepik River) that presage the temples of chiefdoms.

Although a few bands and tribes survive today on remote and ecologically marginal lands outside state control, fully independent chiefdoms had disappeared by the early twentieth century, because they tended to occupy prime land coveted by states. However, as of A.D. 1492, chiefdoms were still widespread over much of the eastern United States, in productive areas of South and Central America and sub-Saharan Africa that had not yet been subsumed under native states, and in all of Polynesia. The archaeological evidence discussed below suggests that chiefdoms arose by around 5500 B.C. in the Fertile Crescent and by around 1000 B.C. in Mesoamerica and the Andes. Let us consider the distinctive features of chiefdoms, very different from modern European and American states and, at the same time, from bands and simple tribal societies.

As regards population size, chiefdoms were considerably larger than tribes, ranging from several thousand to several tens of thousands of people. That size created serious potential for internal conflict because, for any person living in a chiefdom, the vast majority of other people in the chiefdom were neither closely related by blood or marriage nor known by name. With the rise of chiefdoms around 7,500 years ago, people had to learn, for the first time in history, how to encounter strangers regularly without attempting to kill them.

Part of the solution to that problem was for one person, the chief, to exercise a monopoly on the right to use force. In contrast to a tribe's big-man, a chief held a recognized office, filled by hereditary right.

Instead of the decentralized anarchy of a village meeting, the chief was a permanent centralized authority, made all significant decisions, and had a monopoly on critical information (such as what a neighboring chief was privately threatening, or what harvest the gods had supposedly promised). Unlike big-men, chiefs could be recognized from afar by visible distinguishing features, such as a large fan worn over the back on Rennell Island in the Southwest Pacific. A commoner encountering a chief was obliged to perform ritual marks of respect, such as (on Hawaii) prostrating oneself. The chief's orders might be transmitted through one or two levels of bureaucrats, many of whom were themselves low-ranked chiefs. However, in contrast to state bureaucrats, chiefdom bureaucrats had generalized rather than specialized roles. In Polynesian Hawaii the same bureaucrats (termed konohiki) extracted tribute *and* oversaw irrigation *and* organized labor corvées for the chief, whereas state societies have separate tax collectors, water district managers, and draft boards.

A chiefdom's large population in a small area required plenty of food, obtained by food production in most cases, by hunting-gathering in a few especially rich areas. For example, American Indians of the Pacific Northwest coast, such as the Kwakiutl, Nootka, and Tlingit Indians, lived under chiefs in villages without any agriculture or domestic animals, because the rivers and sea were so rich in salmon and halibut. The food surpluses generated by some people, relegated to the rank of commoners, went to feed the chiefs, their families, bureaucrats, and crafts specialists, who variously made canoes, adzes, or spittoons or worked as bird catchers or tattooers.

Luxury goods, consisting of those specialized crafts products or else rare objects obtained by long-distance trade, were reserved for chiefs. For example, Hawaiian chiefs had feather cloaks, some of them consisting of tens of thousands of feathers and requiring many human generations for their manufacture (by commoner cloak makers, of course). That concentration of luxury goods often makes it possible to recognize chiefdoms archaeologically, by the fact that some graves (those of chiefs) contain much richer goods than other graves (those of commoners), in contrast to the egalitarian burials of earlier human history. Some ancient complex chiefdoms can also be distinguished from tribal villages by the remains of elaborate public architecture (such as temples) and by a regional hierarchy of settlements, with one site (the site of the paramount chief) being obviously larger and having more administrative buildings and artifacts than other sites.

Like tribes, chiefdoms consisted of multiple hereditary lineages living at one site. However, whereas the lineages of tribal villages are equal-ranked clans, in a chiefdom all members of the chief's lineage had hereditary perquisites. In effect, the society was divided into hereditary chief and commoner classes, with Hawaiian chiefs themselves subdivided into eight hierarchically ranked lineages, each concentrating its marriages within its own lineage. Furthermore, since chiefs required menial servants as well as specialized craftspeople, chiefdoms differed from tribes in having many jobs that could be filled by slaves, typically obtained by capture in raids.

The most distincitve economic feature of chiefdoms was their shift from reliance solely on the reciprocal exchanges characteristic of bands and tribes, by which A gives B a gift while expecting that B at some unspecified future time will give a gift of comparable value to A. We modern state dwellers indulge in such behavior on birthdays and holidays, but most of our flow of goods is achieved instead by buying and selling for money according to the law of supply and demand. While continuing reciprocal exchanges and without marketing or money, chiefdoms developed an additional new system termed a redistributive economy. A simple example would involve a chief receiving wheat at harvest time from every farmer in the chiefdom, then throwing a feast for everybody and serving bread or else storing the wheat and gradually giving it out again in the months between harvests. When a large portion of the goods received from commoners was not redistributed to them but was retained and consumed by the chiefly lineages and craftspeople, the redistribution became tribute, a precursor of taxes that made its first appearance in chiefdoms. From the commoners the chiefs claimed not only goods but also labor for construction of public works, which again might return to benefit the commoners (for example, irrigation systems to help feed everybody) or instead benefited mainly the chiefs (for instance, lavish tombs).

We have been talking about chiefdoms generically, as if they were all the same. In fact, chiefdoms varied considerably. Larger ones tended to have more powerful chiefs, more ranks of chiefly lineages, greater distinctions between chiefs and commoners, more retention of tribute by the chiefs, more layers of bureaucrats, and grander public architecture. For instance, societies on small Polynesian islands were effectively rather similar to tribal societies with a bigman, except that the position of chief was hereditary. The chief's hut looked like any other hut, there were no bureaucrats or public works, the chief redistributed most goods he received back to the commoners, and land was controlled by the community. But on the largest Polynesian islands, such as Hawaii, Tahiti, and Tonga, chiefs were recognizable at a glance by their ornaments, public works were erected by large labor forces, most tribute was retained by the chiefs, and all land was controlled by them. A further gradation among societies with ranked lineages was from those where the political unit was a single autonomous village, to those consisting of a regional assemblage of villages in which the largest village with a paramount chief controlled the smaller villages with lesser chiefs.

By now, it should be obvious that chiefdoms introduced the dilemma fundamental to all centrally governed, nonegalitarian societies. At best, they do good by providing expensive services impossible to contract for on an individual basis. At worst, they function unabashedly as kleptocracies, transferring net wealth from commoners to upper classes. These noble and selfish functions are inextricably linked, although some governments emphasize much more of one function than of the other. The difference between a kleptocrat and a wise statesman, between a robber baron and a public benefactor, is merely one of degree: a matter of just how large a percentage of the tribute extracted from producers is retained by the elite, and how much the commoners like the public uses to which the redistributed tribute is put. We consider President Mobutu of Zaire a kleptocrat because he keeps too much tribute (the equivalent of billions of dollars) and redistributes too little tribute (no functioning telephone system in Zaire). We consider George Washington a statesman because he spent tax money on widely admired programs and did not enrich himself as president. Nevertheless, George Washington was born into wealth, which is much more unequally distributed in the United States than in New Guinea villages.

For any ranked society, whether a chiefdom or a state, one thus has to ask: why do the commoners tolerate the transfer of the fruits of their hard labor to kleptocrats? This question, raised by political theorists from Plato to Marx, is raised anew by voters in every modern election. Kleptocracies with little public support run the risk of being overthrown, either by downtrodden commoners or by upstart would-be replacement kleptocrats seeking public support by promising a higher ratio of services rendered to fruits stolen. For example, Hawaiian history was repeatedly punctuated by revolts against repressive chiefs, usually led by younger brothers promising less oppression. This may sound funny to us in the context of old Hawaii, until we reflect on all the misery still being caused by such struggles in the modern world.

What should an elite do to gain popular support while still maintaining a more comfortable lifestyle than commoners? Kleptocrats throughout the ages have resorted to a mixture of four solutions:

1. Disarm the populace, and arm the elite. That's much easier in these days of high-tech weaponry, produced only in industrial plants and easily monopolized by an elite, than in ancient times of spears and clubs easily made at home.

2. Make the masses happy by redistributing much of the tribute received, in popular ways. This principle was as valid for Hawaiian chiefs as it is for American politicians today.

3. Use the monopoly of force to promote happiness, by maintaining public order and curbing violence. This is potentially a big and underappreciated advantage of centralized societies over noncentralized ones. Anthropologists formerly idealized band and tribal societies as gentle and nonviolent, because visiting anthropologists observed no murder in a band of 25 people in the course of a three-year study. Of course they didn't: it's easy to calculate that a band of a dozen adults and a dozen children, subject to the inevitable deaths occurring anyway for the usual reasons other than murder, could not perpetuate itself if in addition one of its dozen adults murdered another adult every three years. Much more extensive long-term information about band and tribal societies reveals that murder is a leading cause of death. For example, I happened to be visiting New Guinea's Iyau people at a time when a woman anthropologist was interviewing Iyau women about their life histories. Woman after woman, when asked to name her husband, named several sequential husbands who had died violent deaths. A typical answer went like this: "My first husband was killed by Elopi raiders. My second husband was killed by a man who wanted me, and who became my third husband. That husband was killed by the brother of my second husband, seeking to avenge his murder." Such biographies prove common for so-called gentle tribespeople and contributed to the acceptance of centralized authority as tribal societies grew larger.

4. The remaining way for kleptocrats to gain public support is to construct an ideology or religion justifying kleptocracy. Bands and tribes already had supernatural beliefs, just as do modern established religions. But the supernatural beliefs of bands and tribes did not serve to justify central authority, justify transfer of wealth, or maintain peace between unrelated individuals. When supernatural beliefs gained those functions and became institutionalized, they were thereby transformed into what we term a religion. Hawaiian chiefs were typical of chiefs elsewhere, in asserting divinity, divine descent, or at least a hotline to the gods. The chief claimed to serve the people by interceding for them with the gods and reciting the ritual formulas required to obtain rain, good harvests, and success in fishing.

Chiefdoms characteristically have an ideology, precursor to an institutionalized religion, that buttresses the chief's authority. The chief may either combine the offices of political leader and priest in a single person, or may support a separate group of kleptocrats (that is, priests) whose function is to provide ideological justification for the chiefs. That is why chiefdoms devote so much collected tribute to constructing temples and other public works, which serve as centers of the official religion and visible signs of the chief's power.

Besides justifying the transfer of wealth to kleptocrats, institutionalized religion brings two other important benefits to centralized societies. First, shared ideology or religion helps solve the problem of how unrelated individuals are to live together without killing each other—by providing them with a bond not based on kinship. Second, it gives people a motive, other than genetic self-interest, for sacrificing their lives on behalf of others. At the cost of a few society members who die in battle as soldiers, the whole society becomes much more effective at conquering other societies or resisting attacks.

The political, economic, and social institutions most familiar to us today are those of states, which now rule all of the world's land area except for Antarctica. Many early states and all modern ones have had literate elites, and many modern states have literate masses as well. Vanished states tended to leave visible archaeological hallmarks, such as ruins of temples with standardized designs, at least four levels of settlement sizes, and pottery styles covering tens of thousands of square miles. We thereby know that states arose around 3700 B.C. in Mesopotamia and around 300 B.C. in Mesoamerica, over 2,000 years ago in the Andes, China, and Southeast Asia, and over 1,000 years ago in West Africa. In modern times the formation of states out of chiefdoms has been observed repeatedly. Thus, we possess much more information about past states and their formation than about past chiefdoms, tribes, and bands.

Protostates extend many features of large paramount (multivillage) chiefdoms. They continue the increase in size from bands to tribes to chiefdoms. Whereas chiefdoms' populations range from a few thousand to a few tens of thousands, the populations of most modern states exceed one million, and China's exceeds one billion. The paramount chief's location may become the state's capital city. Other population centers of states outside the capital may also qualify as true cities, which are lacking in chiefdoms. Cities differ from villages in their monumental public works, palaces of rulers, accumulation of capital from tribute or taxes, and concentration of people other than food producers.

Early states had a hereditary leader with a title equivalent to king, like a super paramount chief and exercising an even greater monopoly of information, decision making, and power. Even in democracies today, crucial knowledge is available to only a few individuals, who control the flow of information to the rest of the government and consequently control decisions. For instance, in the Cuban Missile Crisis of 1963, information and discussions that determined whether nuclear war would engulf half a billion people were initially confined by President Kennedy to a ten-member executive committee of the National Security Council that he himself appointed; then he limited final decisions to a four-member group consisting of himself and three of his cabinet ministers.

Central control is more far-reaching, and economic redistribution in the form of tribute (renamed taxes) more extensive, in states than in chiefdoms. Economic specialization is more extreme, to the point where today not even farmers remain self-sufficient. Hence the effect on society is catastrophic when state government collapses, as happened in Britain upon the removal of Roman troops, administrators, and coinage between A.D. 407 and 411. Even the earliest Mesopotamian states exercised centralized control of their economies. Their food was produced by four specialist groups (cereal farmers, herders, fishermen, and orchard and garden growers), from each of which the state took the produce and to each of which it gave out the necessary supplies, tools, and foods other than the type of food that this group produced. The state supplied seeds and plow animals to the cereal farmers, took wool from the herders, ex-

changed the wool by long-distance trade for metal and other essential raw materials, and paid out food rations to the laborers who maintained the irrigation systems on which the farmers depended.

Many, perhaps most, early states adopted slavery on a much larger scale than did chiefdoms. That was not because chiefdoms were more kindly disposed toward defeated enemies but because the greater economic specialization of states, with more mass production and more public works, provided more uses for slave labor. In addition, the larger scale of state warfare made more captives available.

A chiefdom's one or two levels of administration are greatly multiplied in states, as anyone who has seen an organization chart of any government knows. Along with the proliferation of vertical levels of bureaucrats, there is also horizontal specialization. Instead of konohiki carrying out every aspect of administration for a Hawaiian district, state goverments have several separate departments, each with its own hierarchy, to handle water management, taxes, military draft, and so on. Even small states have more complex bureaucracies than large chiefdoms. For instance, the West African state of Maradi had a central administration with over 130 titled offices.

Internal conflict resolution within states has become increasingly formalized by laws, a judiciary, and police. The laws are often written, because many states (with conspicuous exceptions, such as that of the Incas) have had literate elites, writing having been developed around the same time as the formation of the earliest states in both Mesopotamia and Mesoamerica. In contrast, no early chiefdom not on the verge of statehood developed writing.

Early states had state religions and standardized temples. Many early kings were considered divine and were accorded special treatment in innumerable respects. For example, the Aztec and Inca emperors were both carried about in litters; servants went ahead of the Inca emperor's litter and swept the ground clear; and the Japanese language includes special forms of the pronoun "you" for use only in addressing the emperor. Early kings were themselves the head of the state religion or else had separate high priests. The Mesopotamian temple was the center not only of religion but also of economic redistribution, writing, and crafts technology.

All these features of states carry to an extreme the developments that led from tribes to chiefdoms. In addition, though, states have diverged from chiefdoms in several new directions. The most fundamental such distinction is that states are organized on political and territorial lines, not on the kinship lines that defined bands, tribes, and simple chiefdoms. Furthermore, bands and tribes always, and chiefdoms usually, consist of a single ethnic and linguistic group. States, though—especially so-called empires formed by amalgamation or conquest of states—are regularly multiethnic and multilingual. State bureaucrats are not selected mainly on the basis of kinship, as in chiefdoms, but are professionals selected at least partly on the basis of training and ability. In later states, including most today, the leadership often became nonhereditary, and many states abandoned the entire system of formal hereditary classes carried over from chiefdoms.

Over the past 13,000 years the predominant trend in human society has been the replacement of smaller, less complex units by larger, more complex ones. Obviously, that is no more than an average long-term trend, with innumberable shifts in either direction: 1,000 amalgamations for 999 reversals. We know from our daily newspaper that large units (for instance, the former USSR, Yugoslavia, and Czechoslavakia) can disintegrate into smaller units, as did Alexander of Macedon's empire over 2,000 years ago. More complex units don't always conquer less complex ones but may succumb to them, as when the Roman and Chinese Empires were overrun by "barbarian" and Mongol chiefdoms, respectively. But the long-term trend has still been toward large, complex societies, culminating in states.

Obviously, too, part of the reason for states' triumphs over simpler entities when the two collide is that states usually enjoy an advantage of weaponry and other technology, and a large numerical advantage in population. But there are also two other potential advantages inherent in chiefdoms and states. First, a centralized decision maker has the advantage at concentrating troops and resources. Second, the official religions and patriotic fervor of many states make their troops willing to fight suicidally.

The latter willingness is one so strongly programmed into us citizens of modern states, by our schools and churches and governments, that we forget what a radical break it marks with previous human history. Every state has its slogan urging its citizens to be prepared to die if necessary for the state: Britain's "For King and Country," Spain's "Por Dios y España," and so on. Similar sentiments motivated 16th-century Aztec warriors: "There is nothing like death in war, nothing like the flowery death so precious to Him [the Aztec national god Huitzilopochtli] who gives life: far off I see it, my heart yearns for it!"

Such sentiments are unthinkable in bands and tribes. In all the accounts that my New Guinea friends have given me of their former tribal wars, there has been not a single hint of tribal patriotism, of a suicidal charge, or of any other military conduct carrying an accepted risk of being killed. Instead, raids are initiated by ambush or by superior force, so as to minimize at all costs the risk that one might die for one's village. But that attitude severely limits the military options of tribes, compared with state societies. Naturally, what makes patriotic and religious fanatics such dangerous opponents is not the deaths of the fanatics themselves, but their willingness to accept the deaths of a fraction of their number in order to annihilate or crush their infidel enemy. Fanaticism in war, of the type that drove recorded Christian and Islamic conquests, was probably unknown on Earth until chiefdoms and especially states emerged within the last 6,000 years.

How did small, noncentralized, kin-based societies evolve into large centralized ones in which most members are not closely related to each other? Having reviewed the stages in this transformation from bands to states, we now ask what impelled societies thus to transform themselves.

At many moments in history, states have arisen independently—or, as cultural anthropologists say, "pristinely," that is, in the absence of any preexisting surrounding states. Pristine state origins took place at least once, possibly many times, on each of the continents except Australia and North America. Prehistoric states included those of Mesopotamia, North China, the Nile and Indus Valleys, Mesoamerica, the Andes, and West Africa. Native states in contact with European states have arisen from chiefdoms repeatedly in the last three centuries in Madagascar, Hawaii, Tahiti, and many parts of Africa. Chiefdoms have arisen pristinely even more often, in all of the same regions and in North America's Southeast and Pacific Northwest, the Amazon, Polynesia, and sub-Saharan Africa. All these origins of complex societies give us a rich database for understanding their development.

Of the many theories addressing the problem of state origins, the simplest denies that there is any problem to solve. Aristotle considered states the natural condition of human society, requiring no explanation. His error was understandable, because all the societies with which he would have been acquainted—Greek societies of the fourth century B.C.—were states. However, we now know that, as of A.D. 1492, much of the world was instead organized into chiefdoms, tribes, or bands. State formation does demand an explanation.

The next theory is the most familiar one. The French philosopher Jean-Jacques Rousseau speculated that states are formed by a social contract, a rational decision reached when people calculated their self-interest, came to the agreement that they would be better off in a state than in simpler societies, and voluntarily did away with their simpler societies. But observation and historical records have failed to uncover a single case of a state's being formed in that ethereal atmosphere of dispassionate farsightedness. Smaller units do not voluntarily abandon their sovereignty and merge into larger units. They do so only by conquest, or under external duress.

A third theory, still popular with some historians and economists, sets out from the undoubted fact that, in both Mesopotamia and North China and Mexico, large-scale irrigation systems began to be constructed around the time that states started to emerge. The theory also notes that any big, complex system for irrigation or hydraulic management requires a centralized bureaucracy to construct and maintain it. The theory then turns an observed rough correlation in time into a postulated chain of cause and effect. Supposedly, Mesopotamians and North Chinese and Mexicans foresaw the advantages that a large-scale irrigation system would bring them, even though there was at the time no such system within thousands of miles (or anywhere on Earth) to illustrate for them those advantages. Those farsighted people chose to merge their inefficient little chiefdoms into a larger state capable of blessing them with large-scale irrigation.

However, this "hydraulic theory" of state formation is subject to the same objections leveled against social contract theories in general. More specifically, it addresses only the final stage in the evolution of complex societies. It says nothing about what drove the progression from bands to tribes to chiefdoms during all the millennia before the prospect of large-scale irrigation loomed up on the horizon. When historical or archaeological dates are examined in detail, they fail to support the view of irrigation as the driving force for state formation. In Mesopotamia, North China, Mexico, and Madagascar, small-scale irrigation systems already existed before the rise of states. Construction of large-scale irrigation systems did not accompany the emergence of states but came only significantly later in each of those areas. In most of the states formed over the Maya area of Mesoamerica and the Andes, irrigation systems always remained small-scale ones that local communities could build and maintain themselves. Thus, even in those areas where complex systems of hydraulic management did emerge, they were a secondary consequence of states that must have formed for other reasons.

What seems to me to point to a fundamentally correct view of state formation is an undoubted fact of much wider validity than the correlation between irrigation and the formation of some states—namely, that the size of the regional population is the strongest single predictor of societal complexity. As we have seen, bands number a few dozen individuals, tribes a few hundred, chiefdoms a few thousand to a few tens of thousands, and states generally over about 50,000. In addition to that coarse correlation between regional population size and type of society (band, tribe, and so on), there is a finer trend, within each of those categories, between population and societal complexity: for instance, that chiefdoms with large populations prove to be the most centralized, stratified, and complex ones.

These correlations suggest strongly that regional population size or population density or population pressure has *something* to do with the formation of complex societies. But the correlations do not tell us precisely how population variables function in a chain of cause and effect whose outcome is a complex society. To trace out that chain, let us now remind ourselves how large dense populations themselves arise. Then we can examine why a large but simple society could not maintain itself. With that as background, we shall finally return to the question of how a simpler society actually becomes more complex as the regional population increases.

We have seen that large or dense populations arise only under conditions of food production, or at least under exceptionally productive conditions for hunting-gathering. Some productive hunter-gatherer societies reached the organizational level of chiefdoms, but none reached the level of states: all states nourish their citizens by food production. These considerations, along with the just mentioned correlation between regional population size and societal complexity, have led to a protracted chicken-or-egg debate about the causal relations between food production, population variables, and societal complexity. Is it intensive food production that is the cause, triggering population growth and somehow leding to a complex society? Or are large populations and complex societies instead the cause, somehow leading to intensification of food production?

Posing the question in that either-or form misses the point. Intensified food production and societal complexity stimulate each other, by autocatalysis. That is, population growth leads to societal complexity, by mechanisms that we shall discuss, while societal complexity in turn leads to intensified food production and thereby to population growth. Complex centralized societies are uniquely capable of organizing public works (including irrigation systems), long-distance trade (including the importation of metals to make better agricultural tools), and activities of different groups of economic specialists (such as feeding herders with farmers' cereal, and transferring the herders' livestock to farmers for use as plow animals). All of these capabilities of centralized societies have fostered intensified food production and hence population growth throughout history.

In addition, food production contributes in at least three ways to specific features of complex societies. First, it involves seasonally pulsed inputs of labor. When the harvest has been stored, the farmers' labor becomes available for a centralized political authority to harness—in order to build public works advertising state power (such as the Egyptian pyramids), or to build public works that could feed more mouths (such as Polynesian Hawaii's irrigation systems or fishponds), or to undertake wars of conquest to form larger political entities.

Second, food production may be organized so as to generate stored food surpluses, which permit economic specialization and social stratification. The surpluses can be used to feed all tiers of a complex society: the chiefs, bureaucrats, and other members of the elite; the scribes, craftspeople, and other non-food-producing specialists; and the farmers themselves, during times that they are drafted to construct public works.

Finally, food production permits or requires people to adopt sedentary living, which is a prerequisite for accumulating substantial possessions, developing elaborate technology and crafts, and constructing public works. The importance of fixed residence to a complex society explains why missionaries and governments, whenever they make first contact with previously uncontacted nomadic tribes or bands in New Guinea or the Amazon, universally have two immediate goals. One goal, of course, is the obvious one of "pacifying" the nomads: that is, dissuading them from killing missionaries, bureaucrats, or each other. The other goal is to induce the nomads to settle in villages, so that the missionaries and bureaucrats can find the nomads, bring them services such as medical care and schools, and proselytize and control them.

Thus, food production, which increases population size, also acts in many ways to make features of complex societies *possible*. But that doesn't prove that food production and large populations make complex societies *inevitable*. How can we account for the empirical observation that band or tribal organization just does not work for societies of hundreds of thousands of people, and that all existing large societies have complex centralized organization? We can cite at least four obvious reasons.

One reason is the problem of conflict between unrelated strangers. That problem grows astronomically as the number of people making up the society increases. Relationships within a band of 20 people involve only 190 two-person interactions (20 people times 19 divided by 2), but a band of 2,000 would have 1,999,000 dyads. Each of those dyads represents a potential time bomb that could explode in a murderous argument. Each murder in band and tribal societies usually leads to an attempted revenge killing, starting one more unending cycle of murder and countermurder that destabilizes the society.

In a band, where everyone is closely related to everyone else, people related simultaneously to both quarreling parties step in to mediate quarrels. In a tribe, where many people are still close relatives and everyone at least knows everybody else by name, mutual relatives and mutual friends mediate the quarrel. But once the threshold of "several hundred," below which everyone can know everyone else, has been crossed, increasing numbers of dyads become pairs of unrelated strangers. When strangers fight, few people present will be friends or relatives of both combatants, with self-interest in stopping the fight. Instead, may onlookers will be friends or relatives of only one combatant and will side with that person, escalating the two-person fight into a general brawl. Hence a large society that continues to leave conflict resolution to all of its members is guaranteed to blow up. That factor alone would explain why societies of thousands can exist only if they develop centralized authority to monopolize force and resolve conflicts.

A second reason is the growing impossibility of communal decision making with increasing population size. Decision making by the entire adult population is still possible in New Guinea villages small enough that news and information quickly spread to everyone, that everyone can hear everyone else in a meeting of the whole village, and that everyone who wants to speak at the meeting has the opportunity to do so. But all those prerequisites for communal decision making become unattainable in much larger communities. Even now, in these days of microphones and loud-speakers, we all know that a group meeting is no way to resolve issues for a group of thousands of people. Hence a large society must be structured and centralized if it is to reach decisions effectively.

A third reason involves economic considerations. Any society requires means to transfer goods between its members. One individual may happen to acquire more of some essential commodity on one day and less on another. Because individuals have different talents, one individual consistently tends to wind up with an excess of some essentials and a deficit of others. In small societies with few pairs of members, the resulting necessary transfers of goods can be arranged directly between pairs of individuals or families, by reciprocal exchanges. But the same mathematics that makes direct pairwise conflict resolution inefficient in large societies makes direct pairwise economic transfers also inefficient. Large societies can function economically only if they have a redistributive economy in addition to a reciprocal economy. Goods in excess of an individual's needs must be transferred from the individual to a centralized authority, which then redistributes the goods to individuals with deficits.

A final consideration mandating complex organization for large societies has to do with population densities. Large societies of food producers have not only more members but also higher population densities than do small bands of hunter-gatherers. Each band of a few dozen hunters occupies a large territory, within which they can acquire most of the resources essential to them. They can obtain their remaining necessities by trading with neighboring bands during intervals between band warfare. As population density increases, the territory of that band-sized population of a few dozen would shrink to a small area, with more and more of life's necessities having to be obtained outside the area. For instance, one couldn't just divide Holland's 16,000 square miles and 16,000,000 people into 800,000 individual territories, each encompassing 13 acres and serving as home to an autonomous band of 20 people who remained self-sufficient confined within their 13 acres, occasionally taking advantage of a temporary truce to come to the borders of their tiny territory in order to exchange some trade items and brides with the next band. Such spatial realities require that densely populated regions support large and complexly organized societies.

Considerations of conflict resolution, decision making, economics, and space thus converge in requiring large societies to be centralized. But centralization of power inevitably opens the door—for those who hold the power, are privy to information, make the decisions, and redistribute the goods—to exploit the resulting opportunities to reward themselves and their relatives. To anyone familiar with any modern grouping of people, that's

obvious. As early societies developed, those acquiring centralized power gradually established themselves as an elite, perhaps originating as one of several formerly equal-ranked village clans that became "more equal" than the others.

Those are the reasons why large societies cannot function with band organization and instead are complex kleptocracies. But we are still left with the question of how small, simple societies actually evolve or amalgamate into large, complex ones. Amalgamation, centralized conflict resolution, decision making, economic redistribution, and kleptocratic religion don't just develop automatically through a Rousseauesque social contract. What drives the amalgamation?

In part, the answer depends upon evolutionary reasoning. I said at the outset of this chapter that societies classified in the same category are not all identical to each other, because humans and human groups are infinitely diverse. For example, among bands and tribes, the big-men of some are inevitably more charismatic, powerful, and skilled in reaching decisions than the big-men of others. Among large tribes, those with stronger big-men and hence greater centralization tend to have an advantage over those with less centralization. Tribes that resolve conflicts as poorly as did the Fayu tend to blow apart again into bands, while ill-governed chiefdoms blow apart into smaller chiefdoms or tribes. Societies with effective conflict resolution, sound decision making, and harmonious economic redistribution can develop better technology, concentrate their military power, seize larger and more productive territories, and crush autonomous smaller societies one by one.

Thus, competition between societies at one level of complexity tends to lead to societies on the next level of complexity *if* conditions permit. Tribes conquer or combine with tribes to reach the size of chiefdoms, which conquer or combine with other chiefdoms to reach the size of states, which conquer or combine with other states to become empires. More generally, large units potentially enjoy an advantage over individual small units *if*—and that's a big "if"—the large units can solve the problems that come with their larger size, such as perennial threats from upstart claimants to leadership, commoner resentment of kleptocracy, and increased problems associated with economic integration.

The amalgamation of smaller units into larger ones has often been documented historically or archaeologically. Contrary to Rousseau, such amalgamations never occur by a process of unthreatened little societies freely deciding to merge, in order to promote the happiness of their citizens. Leaders of little societies, as of big ones, are jealous of their independence and prerogatives. Amalgamation occurs instead in either of two ways: by merger under the threat of external force, or by actual conquest. Innumerable examples are available to illustrate each mode of amalgamation.

Merger under the threat of external force is well illustrated by the formation of the Cherokee Indian confederation in the U.S. Southeast. The Cherokees were originally divided into 30 or 40 independent chiefdoms, each consisting of a village of about 400 people. Increasing white settlement led to conflicts between Cherokees and whites. When individual Cherokees robbed or assaulted white settlers and traders, the whites were unable to discriminate among the different Cherokee chiefdoms and retaliated indiscriminately against any Cherokees, either by military action or by cutting off trade. In response, the Cherokee chiefdoms gradually found themselves compelled to join into a single confederacy in the course of the 18th century. Initially, the larger chiefdoms in 1730 chose an overall leader, a chief named Moytoy, who was succeeded in 1741 by his son. The first task of these leaders was to punish individual Cherokees who attacked whites, and to deal with the white government. Around 1758 the Cherokees regularized their decision making with an annual council modeled on previous village councils and meeting at one village (Echota), which thereby became a de facto "capital." Eventually, the Cherokees became literate (as we saw in Chapter 12) and adopted a written constitution.

The Cherokee confederacy was thus formed not by conquest but by the amalgamation of previously jealous smaller entities, which merged only when threatened with destruction by powerful external forces. In much the same way, in an example of state formation described in every American history textbook, the white American colonies themselves, one of which (Georgia) had precipitated the formation of the Cherokee state, were impelled to form a nation of their own when threatened with the powerful external force of the British monarchy. The American colonies were initially as jealous of their autonomy as the Cherokee chiefdoms, and their first attempt at amalgamation under the Articles of Confederation (1781) proved unworkable because it reserved too much autonomy to the ex-colonies. Only further threats, notably Shays's Rebellion of 1786 and the unsolved burden of war debt, overcame the ex-colonies' extreme reluctance to sacrifice autonomy and pushed them into adopting our current strong federal constitution in 1787. The 19th-century unifi-

cation of Germany's jealous principalities proved equally difficult. Three early attempts (the Frankfurt Parliament of 1848, the restored German Confederation of 1850, and the North German Confederation of 1866) failed before the external threat of France's declaration of war in 1870 finally led to the princelets' surrendering much of their power to a central imperial German government in 1871.

The other mode of formation of complex societies, besides merger under threat of external force, is merger by conquest. A well-documented example is the origin of the Zulu state, in southeastern Africa. When first observed by white settlers, the Zulus were divided into dozens of little chiefdoms. During the late 1700s, as population pressure rose, fighting between the chiefdoms became increasingly intense. Among all those chiefdoms, the ubiquitous problem of devising centralized power structures was solved most successfully by a chief called Dingiswayo, who gained ascendancy of the Mtetwa chiefdom by killing a rival around 1807. Dingiswayo developed a superior centralized military organization by drafting young men from all villages and grouping them into regiments by age rather than by their village. He also developed superior centralized political organization by abstaining from slaughter as he conquered other chiefdoms, leaving the conquered chief's family intact, and limiting himself to replacing the conquered chief himself with a relative willing to cooperate with Dingiswayo. He developed superior centralized conflict resolution by expanding the adjudication of quarrels. In that way Dingiswayo was able to conquer and begin the integration of 30 other Zulu chiefdoms. His successors strengthened the resulting embryonic Zulu state by expanding its judicial system, policing, and ceremonies.

This Zulu example of a state formed by conquest can be multiplied almost indefinitely. Native states whose formation from chiefdoms happened to be witnessed by Europeans in the 18th and 19th centuries include the Polynesian Hawaiian state, the Polynesian Tahitian state, the Merina state of Madagascar, Lesotho and Swazi and other southern African states besides that of the Zulus, the Ashanti state of West Africa, and the Ankole and Buganda states of Uganda. The Aztec and Inca Empires were formed by 15th-century conquests, before Europeans arrived, but we know much about their formation from Indian oral histories transcribed by early Spanish settlers. The formation of the Roman state and the expansion of the Macedonian Empire under Alexander were described in detail by contemporary classical authors.

All these examples illustrate that wars, or threats of war, have played a key role in most, if not all, amalgamations of societies. But wars, even between mere bands, have been a constant fact of human history. Why is it, then, that they evidently began causing amalgamations of societies only within the past 13,000 years? We had already concluded that the formation of complex societies is somehow linked to population pressure, so we should now seek a link between population pressure and the outcome of war. Why should wars tend to cause amalgamations of societies when populations are dense but not when they are sparse? The answer is that the fate of defeated peoples depends on population density, with three possible outcomes:

Where population densities are very low, as is usual in regions occupied by hunter-gatherer bands, survivors of a defeated group need only move farther away from their enemies. That tends to be the result of wars between nomadic bands in New Guinea and the Amazon.

Where population densities are moderate, as in regions occupied by food-producing tribes, no large vacant areas remain to which survivors of a defeated band can flee. But tribal societies without intensive food production have no employment for slaves and do not produce large enough food surpluses to be able to yield much tribute. Hence the victors have no use for survivors of a defeated tribe, unless to take the women in marriage. The defeated men are killed, and their territory may be occupied by the victors.

Where population densities are high, as in regions occupied by states or chiefdoms, the defeated still have nowhere to flee, but the victors now have two options for exploiting them while leaving them alive. Because chiefdoms and state societies have economic specialization, the defeated can be used as slaves, as commonly happened in biblical times. Alternatively, because many such societies have inten-sive food production systems capable of yielding large surpluses, the victors can leave the defeated in place but deprive them of political autonomy, make them pay regular tribute in food or goods, and amalgamate their society into the victorious state or chiefdom. This has been the usual outcome of battles associated with the founding of states or empires throughout recorded history. For example, the Spanish conquistadores wished to exact tribute from Mexico's defeated native populations, so they were very interested in the Aztec Empire's tribute lists. It turned out that the tribute received by the Aztecs each year from subject peoples had included 7,000 tons of corn, 4,000 tons of beans, 4,000 tons of grain amaranth, 2,000,000 cotton cloaks, and huge quantities of cacao beans, war costumes, shields, feather headdresses, and amber.

Thus, food production, and competition and diffusion between societies, led as ultimate causes, via chains of causation that differed in detail but that all involved large dense populations and sedentary living, to the proximate agents of conquest: germs, writing, technology, and centralized political organization. Because those ultimate causes developed differently on different continents, so did those agents of conquest. Hence those agents tended to arise in association with each other, but the association was not strict: for example, an empire arose without writing among the Incas, and writing with few epidemic diseases among the Aztecs. Dingiswayo's Zulus illustrate that each of those agents contributed somewhat independently to history's pattern. Among the dozens of Zulu chiefdoms, the Mtetwa chiefdom enjoyed no advantage whatsoever of technology, writing, or germs over the other chiefdoms, which it nevertheless succeeded in defeating. Its advantage lay solely in the spheres of government and ideology. The resulting Zulu state was thereby enabled to conquer a fraction of a continent for nearly a century.

"FROM EGALITARIANISM TO KLEPTOCRACY"

Jared Diamond

1) How do anthropologists define stages of cultural evolutionary development? What are the benefits and pitfalls of such an approach?

2) Define the "band" level of sociopolitical development. How do bands function? Give an example from the reading or from class discussions and material.

3) Define the "tribal" level of sociopolitical development. How do they function? Give an example from the reading or from class discussions and material.

4) Define the "chiefdom" level of sociopolitical development. How do they function? Give an example from the reading or class discussions and material.

5) Compare and contrast the Diamond discussion on chiefdoms with the article on Tlingit chiefdoms in the reader. How does traditional and modern Tlingit culture compare to the generalizations in Diamond's work?

6) Why do chiefdom level societies no longer exist in the modern world?

7) Define the "kleptocracy"/state level of sociopolitical development. How do such organizations function?

8) What solutions have "kleptocrats" used to gain popular support for their positions? Which solution does Diamond seem to think is the most important?

9) Define and discuss the various theories that have been put forward to explain the evolution of state-level societies, including Diamond's discussion of the interrelationship between dense populations, food production, and warfare.

10) What reasons does Diamond suggest to explain why all large societies have complex centralized organizations? Give examples from the article and other material you have read or discussed.

TLINGIT: CHIEFS PAST AND PRESENT

Kenneth Tollefson

Many centuries ago the Tlingit [Tleen·git] Indians of southeastern Alaska—in search of migrating salmon—journeyed down the rivers that connect the interior of North America with the Pacific Ocean. They discovered a forested coastal region with a moderate climate and abundant rainfall. Varieties of fish swarmed in the rivers and bays; shellfish grew plentiful along the sandy beaches; seals, sea lions, and sea otters inhabited the coastal areas; and deer, bears, and goats roamed in the forests and mountains. Numerous offshore islands protected most of the coastline from the wind and waves, providing sheltered coves for fishing and for beaching canoes. Few areas in the world offered a greater natural abundance.

Early historical records suggest a population of some ten thousand Tlingit. However, this early population projection is only an approximation, since an epidemic ravaged the coastal Indians following each of several European contacts—each one claiming many lives.

The Tlingit were divided into fourteen districts, or *kwaans*. Kwaans were composed of several autonomous groups, commonly referred to as clans. A clan is a kinship group that can trace its descent to a founder—either real or mythical. The clan, which contained one or more longhouses, provided the organization of Tlingit economic, social, political, and religious activities. Social identity, group history, cultural education, and social status revolved around the clan. Clans held aboriginal title to hunting lands, shellfish-laden beaches, fishing sites, community longhouses, and sacred artifacts and crests. Clans provided leadership and protection, as well as the settling of disputes. In return, clans demanded unquestioning obedience from their members.

A ranking clan elder is frequently referred to by outsiders as the clan chief—*ashudi huny* in Tlingit. Although the role of clan chief has changed significantly over the past century, clan chiefs continue to serve as political and ceremonial leaders. As such, they command considerable respect. To fully illustrate the sense of continuity in Tlingit society we will compare the lives of two clan elders who lived in different centuries and both represented the central kwaans of Angoon, Hoonah, Klukwan, and Sitka. The older chief, Old Beaver Chief, lived near the end of the nineteenth century, when the Tlingit still retained much of their traditional subsistence culture. The younger chief, Young Beaver Chief, is a present-day seventy-year-old elder, who inherited his great-great-uncle's title of clan head. A comparison of the leadership of these two elders will illustrate many continuities and changes over the past century.

Economy: Continuity and Change

Old Beaver Chief lived in one of the last of the communal longhouses with about six to eight other nuclear families. The chief lived in the back of the longhouse behind the heraldic screen that told the story of the clan. On either side of the house lived his brothers and their families, along with the nephews and their families. Each family was ranked in a descending order from the chief's quarters. A large fireplace was located in the middle of the longhouse to provide heat and light for cooking food, warming the living quarters, and working crafts.

All families in a longhouse, and in a clan, were related through the mother's bloodline, or by matrilineal descent. Women were held in high esteem and were primarily responsible for educating their small children in clan history and stories. So that all could partake of the area's abundance, members of the various longhouses within a clan shared in the ownership of sections of streams, ocean beaches, hunting areas, and off-shore halibut beds. Members of clan longhouses often worked together in gender-segregated parties, harvesting roots and berries in the clearings, gathering shellfish and clams along the tidelands, hunting land and sea mammals that inhabited the forests and waterways, or catching migrating salmon in the small streams that led to the spawning beds.

The annual subsistence cycle in Old Beaver Chief's longhouse consisted of three kinds of activities: tool and craft production, food harvesting, and food preservation. Toolmaking included the manufacture of knives, spears, clubs, canoes, nets, traps, baskets, clothing, shelter, ceremonial artifacts, and other handicrafts. Economic activities were geared to the annual growth cycles of the fauna and flora in the area. Thus, the annual cycle varied among the islands and coastal and upland regions, and from south to north, depending upon local temperature and climate conditions.

The economic year began in March with the spring food-harvesting activities.[1] The following is a monthly analysis of the Tlingit's economic activities:

March:	deep-sea fishing and trapping; shellfish
April:	deep-sea fishing; seaweed, wild fowl, and rabbits
May:	herring roe, roots, and wild rhubarb; processing eulachon oil
June:	bird eggs; hunting, fishing, and berry-picking
July:	salmon migration begins; travel to trading posts
August:	berry-picking, subsistence fishing, and cannery work
September:	family fish camps: catching, cleaning, drying and packing fish
October:	hunting, trading, and ceremonials
November:	feasting and ceremonials
December–February:	fishing, trapping, carving, basketweaving, and repairs; shellfish

Part-time wages were becoming increasingly important around the turn of the nineteenth century. Some of the younger men in Old Beaver Chief's longhouse spent considerable time running their trap lines during the winters. By the 1880s men spent weeks away from the community tending the trap lines, skinning animals, and stretching the hides. Money earned from the sale of furs was used to purchase metal pots, rifles, coffee, sugar, fishing supplies, and other desired items from the expanding number of trading posts in the area. Considerable time was also spent during the winter months in the production of traditional items: weaving mats and baskets, designing ceremonial blankets, working skins, repairing hunting and fishing equipment, shaping spoons, and carving bowls, masks, rattles, and small story poles for sale to tourists.

Old Beaver Chief netted a small fortune from running trap lines, fishing for the canneries, trading with other communities, and selling furs and fish. His clan was large and had access to a considerable area of land with several small streams. Fox, marten, otter, beaver, and other fur-bearing animals were readily available. Whaling, herring, and salmon canneries, in succession, moved into the region and hired many local Tlingit—depleting the local population—and then moved on to more productive areas. Some of this wealth trickled down to the other clan members. In the process, however, these large industries exhausted local resources, forcing the Tlingit to sacrifice their future security for present gain.

During the 1880s six canneries flourished briefly in Chatham Straits at "Pybus Bay, Gambier Bay, Murder Bay, Hawk Inlet, Funter Bay, and Hood Bay."[2] In 1878 the Northwest Trading Company at Killisnoo established a fish-processing plant for whales, herring, and the production of fish fertilizer. The influx of industry contributed to the appearance of steamers, freighters, and tourists. The growing tourist trade opened up a market for selling baskets and small wood carvings. With the decline of the local herring population in Chatham Straits, the Beaver clan traded with the Sitka kwaan for herring roe, the Klukwan kwaan for oulachen oil, the Hoonah kwaan for copper, and the southern tribes for abalone shells. The Beaver clan specialized in raising potatoes and traded them for some of these other products.

Old Beaver Chief increased the wealth of his household through the education of his nephews and the recruitment of talented spouses for them. One nephew became a renowned spirit healer, another nephew became a master carver, while a third nephew became the clan historian. In addition, Old Beaver Chief arranged marriages between members of his clan and the Klukwan kwaan for an expert basketmaker and blanketweaver, another with a trading partner in the Sitka kwaan to tap into the trade coming from the south, and a third with the Bear clan across the straits. Trade from the north and south went through the Sitka kwaan, while interior trade came over the mountains to the Klukwan kwaan. Marriages with these people extended the trade and the wealth to the Angoon kwaan.

As the ranking elder from the ranking longhouse in the Beaver clan, Old Beaver Chief controlled the mouth of the best salmon fishing site in the area. He also served as the manager of the clan's subsistence resources. No hunter was permitted to go sealing or sea otter hunting until the chief determined that the baby seals and sea otters could survive if the adult females were killed in the hunt. The chief usually received part of each nephew's kill or catch. Because Old Beaver Chief had the responsibility for maintaining the high ranking of their clan, the clan placed its wealth at the disposal of the chief, in consultation with the clan elders. He was also the clan manager and spokesperson. The rank and honor of the clan rose and fell with his skills and decisions. Chiefs worked hard to maintain the welfare of the clan.

Young Beaver Chief follows many of the customs and shares many of the clan values that were held by Old Beaver Chief. However, the Tlingit economy has changed from a subsistence-plus-part-time-wage economy to a wage-plus-part-time-subsistence economy. Many of the traditional food resources were seriously depleted. Furthermore, government restrictions frequently placed the Tlingit in a confrontational relationship over the rights to the remaining traditional food resources. They now have to fight legal battles in the courts and legislatures to gain access to these resources. Economic development, pollution, and increased harvesting by commercial fishermen have also taken their toll on subsistence resources.

Young Beaver Chief has made several economic changes in order to maintain his self-sufficiency. In his youth he spent many days in late summer at his family fish camp, catching, cleaning, and smoking salmon for the winter. He used a gaffing hook in the shallow stream to rake in the migrating salmon. The family took only what it needed and then packed up its belongings and returned to its winter village. During the autumn and winter, Young Beaver Chief gathered shellfish along a sheltered beach, hunted deer in the hills, and fished for halibut and other bottom fish in the nearby straits.

As the young chief grew older he encountered growing opposition to subsistence living. School officials required students to be in attendance when school opened in the fall. This meant that the families could no longer go to their fish camps in September to put up fish for the winter. The state fish and game officers sought to extend their controls over sportsmen's hunting and fishing, affecting native subsistence living. Foreign markets opened up for herring eggs and fish roe, contributing to decreasing runs. Fish traps nearly depleted salmon runs in some streams. The state opposed the selling of seaweed and other traditional foods among Native Alaskans. All of these measures undermined the subsistence way of life, making it increasingly difficult for the Tlingits to acquire a majority of their food from traditional sources.

Young Beaver Chief, however, made a good living and was highly respected by his peers. But he had a large clan, and since several of the younger members were having a difficult time obtaining employment, he fed and housed many close relatives in his own home. He owned a new house on a hill overlooking the straits. Snowcapped mountains rose above the water, adding blue, green, and white layers to the horizon. Young Beaver Chief's fishing salary was considerably higher than the average for the United States. His reputation was impeccable, and his home was well equipped. But his family was

large, and his clan was confronting employment problems in addition to the loss of subsistence resources. Therefore, his obligations as clan chief were compounded, and much of his time was spent assisting relatives with economic and domestic problems. Economically, it was the best of times for him, but the worst of times for his clan.

Today Young Beaver Chief has a small smokehouse along the beach in front of the village. He continues to smoke salmon for winter use because he prefers the taste to canned salmon. It is also considered more fashionable among his Tlingit guests. Occasionally, a nephew will shoot a seal for its meat and fur. Its fur is stretched on a wooden rack and tanned for making moccasins or vests. Members of his family pick and can several quarts of berries each year. They gather shellfish most of the year and seaweed in the spring. Herring roe and oulachan oil are still traded, given as gifts, or purchased from Tlingit in Sitka or Klukwan. Recently, Young Beaver Chief retired from commercial fishing. He sold his boat and his native fishing license to a promising young member of his clan.

Social System: Continuity and Change

Originally, Tlingit settlements consisted of one communal longhouse inhabited by a single lineage. As the lineage population increased in these single-lineage villages, the tensions within the community house were compounded and other lineage community houses were added as the need arose to accommodate the growing community, thus creating a "localized clan village." In time another clan, with whom the local clan frequently intermarried, was invited to move in with the local clan for convenience and protection, forming a "localized moiety village." The second clan was always considered to be guests of the original owner-clan. When subsistence resources were severely depleted in the late 1800s many clans moved to one location for survival, creating "consolidated clan villages" or kwaan villages.[3]

Tlingit community houses were constructed out of large timber beams, corner posts, and split planks, had a gabled roof, and were some thirty to forty feet wide and forty or more feet long. The central portion of the house was excavated to a depth of three to six feet, depending upon the size of the house, to accommodate one or more central fire pits and a cooking, eating, working, and entertaining area. Around this central excavation were the sleeping quarters and storage areas, with blankets and mats hung from the ceiling to provide a measure of privacy for the nuclear families. A door facing the beach and a smoke hole in the center of the roof were the only openings in the structure. Air circulated through the front door and out the smoke hole, providing fresh air and ventilation for the fires and the residents.

The Tlingit use the word house, *hit*, in three ways: (1) to refer to the lineage community house in which they were born; (2) to refer to the clan to which they belong; and (3) to refer to the moiety (the word *moiety* means one-half) to which their clan belongs. For example, if a person stated that he was from the Copper-Plate House *Tina Hit*, a knowledgeable Tlingit would know that he belonged to the Frog clan located in Sitka, which was classified under the Raven moiety. The Tlingit Nation is divided into two complementary moieties—Raven *Laayneidee* and Eagle *Shangookeidee*. Clans and moieties are both exogamous. Consequently, women from the Raven clans marry men from the Eagle clans and vice versa.

This system of exchange among the clans kept them dependent upon one another for spouses. It opened lines of diplomacy among participating groups, and it provided a means for exchanging a variety of goods and services. The moiety system created socio-political alignments that shared common crests of identity (Raven or Eagle) and kinship ties of rights and duties. Marriage rules and ceremonial services perpetually reinforced this alliance between the moieties. Few social or political events could legitimately be held without the assistance of the other moiety. The men and women of the opposite moiety performed much of the work in giving weddings, conducting funerals, constructing longhouses, carving ceremonial artifacts, weaving Chilkat blankets, inaugurating chiefs, bestowing names and titles, and similar services.

Persons were not only differentiated according to their household, clan, and moiety, but also according to class. The class system developed as some families acquired greater wealth through production, trade, and ceremonial exchanges. Every Tlingit was conscious of belonging to a social class. A Tlingit belonged to either (1) the high class—*anyaddi*; (2) the commoner class—*kanachideh*; (3) the low class—*nitckakaku*; or (4) the classless category of slaves—*gux*.[4] Social class was significant in Tlingit society because it determined with whom one played as a child, to whom one was married as a youth, and to whom one sent invitations to attend potlatches as an adult. High- and low-class children were not permitted to play together for fear that a low-class child might severely injure a child of a higher class and would not be able to provide proper compensation. Marriages were arranged within one's social class to promote stability and security. Only high-class people were invited to other villages for potlatches, because they were financially able to participate in the exchange of wealth items.

It was not sufficient to be born high class. High class was not only dependent upon family affiliation but also upon social conformation. That is, a "high class" individual was expected to conform to the proper behavior of a Tlingit—to speak softly to promote peace, to select one's words carefully to avoid insulting another, to treat an elder respectfully, to eat slowly to avoid the appearance of gluttony, and to conduct one's self wisely to demonstrate a disciplined lifestyle. Those who did not conform to this standard of behavior were branded as belonging to the low class. Such persons were to be pitied for their bad manners, their loose tongues, and their social ignorance.

Tlingit education focused upon the mastery of oral tradition. A strong emphasis was put on the capacity for memorization. Youths were told stories to be repeated at a later time. Individuals who possessed the best memories were given advanced instruction and selected to be the village historians. Youths were constantly under the surveillance of their elders, who guided each individual into the area of service in which he or she could make the greatest contribution to the household. If an individual demonstrated a certain aptitude toward becoming a hunter, a fisherman, a wood carver, or a spirit doctor, the person would be sent to the uncle who specialized in that area of expertise to work as an apprentice. The elder attempted to develop the youth to his or her potential and to thus strengthen the economic and political base of the household.

During prepuberty, sons were removed from their mothers and transferred to their maternal uncles to receive a rigorous apprenticeship in clan life and subsistence living. Maternal uncles were strict in the education of their nephews. Uncles had absolute control over these nephews. No nephew would dare question an uncle's order or request. (Old Beaver Chief was selected at an early age to receive a more extensive training than the other young men, due to his membership in the high class and his mental and athletic abilities.) Uncles educated their maternal nephews to eventually replace themselves as clan elders. Nephews served their uncles for many years and in return inherited their possessions.

The Tlingit sought to instill in their youth the cultural values of "bravery, fortitude, industry, thrift, and pride in family and clan."[5] To attain these goals the uncles subjected the nephews to a rigorous physical-fitness program generally referred to as "warrior's school." The physical training involved certain techniques designed to strengthen the youths and enable them to develop resistance to pain. They were taught to come to the defense of the women and the wealth of their clan with all their might and never to back down to anyone or beg for mercy, even if they were critically wounded. Women were also taught to be strong and followed their men into battle, killing the wounded who had sought to attack their families.

Daily dips in the sea at dawn were required regardless of the weather. A handful of saltwater was occasionally swallowed. It made the weak vomit and strengthened the strong. These doses of saltwater were gradually increased to condition the youth to life on the sea. Following the cold plunge, elders whipped the aspiring warriors with spruce branches to stimulate circulation and develop tolerance for pain. Youths reported that they had to brace themselves during these lashings to keep from being knocked off their feet.

Young women also experienced an extended time of education at the onset of puberty. They were instructed in personal hygiene, social etiquette, cultural values, clan history, and domestic skills. A girl was considered to be fortunate if she had a grandmother to guide her through the puberty rite. Confinement began with her first menses and lasted from a few weeks up to a year or more, depending upon the rank of the participating girl. A primary reason for this seclusion related to the plethora of responsibilities of becoming a mature woman. The girl was reminded that she had come into the possession of a new creative power and was told to guard it carefully and use it wisely. She was told that some men prey on young women only to rob them of their virtue and then discard them.

The grandmother, assisted by the mother and clan aunts, instructed the pubescent youth in matters concerning sexual reproduction and prenatal and postnatal care. She was taught how to care for her body during and following pregnancy and at what times to refrain from sexual intercourse. The female puberty ritual included the use of symbols and taboos to impress upon the girl the mystery and sacredness of her reproductive powers. For example, she was forbidden to scratch her body with her fingernails because it was considered to be sacred, especially during her seclusion. She was required to demonstrate a successful level of ability to sew clothes, weave baskets, tan hides, and prepare food, as well as a knowledge of clan history and crests. She needed to know specific stories and songs because they were tantamount to deeds to property, since title to land and food resources were related to stories and songs concerning their discovery and use.

A girl was married soon after the completion of her puberty rite, at which time she left her community house, and often her village. Therefore, it was imperative that she be able to demonstrate to the satisfaction of her peers that she had the knowledge and skills necessary to function in the adult world. She would be the repository of her clan heritage and customs for her future children. The continuity of her clan depended primarily upon her ability to pass it on to the next generation.

The household head, or one of his designated elders, conducted occasional evening classes covering household migrations, history, songs, dances, and forms of ceremonial speech. Speakers used illustrations during their ceremonial speeches to allude to historical events, cultural leaders, and clan stories. Since the value placed on respect precluded directness in public speaking, numerous figures of speech and allusions were employed to refer indirectly to a particular incident. In a funeral potlatch, for example, a speaker might mention that the sorrow of his group has been "licked away." This statement would have little meaning to the uninformed listener. However, to a knowledgeable Tlingit, this statement would call to remembrance the story of "The Sad Boy." It seems that once there was a sadness in a boy that no shaman could cure. As a last resort, the uncle said, "Let's take him to the Island of the Wolves." So they got a large canoe and took him to the Island of the Wolves. After they landed on the island all the wolves came down to greet them and began to lick the boy. Gradually, his sadness subsided as the wolves kept licking away his sadness. When the spokesman for the mourning group referred to their sorrow being "licked away," he meant that the sympathy and support that the other moiety had shown had, in effect, dissipated their sorrow.

Old Beaver Chief married according to traditional customs. That is, as a teenager he married a female of equal rank from his father's Bear clan (patrilateral cross-cousin). His marriage was arranged by the elders of the two clans. Personal choice was largely irrelevant in his decision. Criteria were based upon rank, class, family, physical appearance, personal characteristics and abilities, and lineage needs. An old Tlingit adage states, "Choose your equal in caste for a lifemate, and your children shall rejoice over their birth."

Once a bride was taken into a clan she was treated as a functioning member of it. She was expected to work hard and contribute to its wealth and security and in exchange was given security and companionship. If her husband happened to be killed or otherwise die, a younger brother or a nephew would take her in marriage. To refuse to marry a widow would have been interpreted by her natal household as a denigration of the widow and a grave insult to her clan. Once a bride became part of a community house, she could expect the members to care for her as long as they lived.

Community house living required many people to co-exist with very little personal space. Many societies provided a social safety valve for potentially disruptive relationships in the form of avoidance. Among the Tlingit, a son-in-law could not converse with his mother-in-law, even if they resided under the same roof. Communication had to be conducted through a third person. Because grandmothers, mothers, and grandchildren belonged to the same lineage and clan, mothers-in-law often had conflicting loyalties with those of a son-in-law. Old Beaver Chief never spoke to his mother-in-law as long as he lived, even though they resided in the same house for much of his life. Biological brothers and sisters avoided one another even though it was the sister's responsibility to look after her brother both before and after marriage. Whenever a brother entered a room his sister, if present, left immediately.[6]

The Tlingit had a concern for the attainment of rank and its proper social response. People needed to know who was ranked above and below them so that they could respond in the appropriate manner and thus avoid social disgrace. Rank was based upon wealth and privilege. The groups that migrated first to the coast and selected the best settlements had access to better resources. Therefore, they could amass more wealth and were accorded higher rank. Oberg[7] observed that the stronger clans usually controlled the area of the kwaan's watershed that was nearest their villages and contained greater resources, while the weaker clans harvested less convenient areas with fewer resources or waited until the more powerful clans completed their communal needs and then harvested their own needs.[8]

Names were the property of the lineages and clans. They were ranked in a clan in a descending order from the name of the chief down to the least of the low class. At certain potlatches the chief or his appointee would call out the names of the clan in rank order, and each member would step forward at the appropriate time to acknowledge that name and its rank in the hierarchy of the clan. Hence, the ranking of clan names was a very public phenomenon. When Tlingit met, one of the first concerns was to inquire as to their Tlingit names. Since each name was ranked by clan, a knowledgeable Tlingit could discern the longhouse, the clan, the moiety, and the rank of the person who owned the name. This meant that most Tlingit knew the relative rank of hundreds, sometimes thousands, of names and the rank that went along with each name. Those ranked above you

were frequently addressed as grandfather/grandmother and those below you as grandson/granddaughter.[9] Deference prescribed social behavior. A person of higher rank was treated with respect and responded by showing graciousness to those of lower rank. The rank of a person was also important in matching up persons in marriage and in determining appropriate persons to kill in peace settlements. If a member of one clan accidentally or deliberately killed a person from another clan, the two councils of clan elders met to select an individual of equal rank to be executed to even the scales of social justice and restore peace between the clans. This seemed a better solution than warfare, in which many persons could be killed.

Lineage, clan, class, and rank continue to be valued and applied within Tlingit society, but on a lesser scale. Names are still bestowed by clan elders, and their rank is still important for contemporary social standing. However, the social intensity of names has become somewhat diminished because much of the social life of the contemporary Tlingit is lived in the social milieu of the dominant society. Marriages between the moieties is still viewed as the ideal, but many marriages are with non-Tlingit or with Tlingit who have lost or ignored their clan and moiety affiliation. Still, some of these non-Tlingit spouses are adopted into the opposite moiety of the spouse. Moiety marriages, within the more isolated Tlingit communities, continue to be practiced. In marriages in which the moiety principle is missing, the spouses feel less comfortable attending potlatches.

The life of Young Beaver Chief illustrates some of the changes that have occurred in modern Tlingit life. He was born in what some have called the most traditional Tlingit village in Alaska, and thus has always been aware of his lineage, household, and clan affiliation. He grew up speaking the native language, attending potlatches, gathering subsistence resources, listening to Tlingit stories, and learning the customs of the elders. Because he was born into the highest-ranking household in the village and was a good learner, Young Beaver Chief received much attention from his maternal aunts and uncles and so emerged as an adult well versed in Tlingit culture.

Young Beaver Chief was born into a box-shaped western-style clan house with a large living room, kitchen, and storage area downstairs and bedrooms upstairs. The large living room was used for hosting clan gatherings, entertaining guests, and holding wakes for deceased members of the clan. The several families who lived in a clan house shared the kitchen facilities and the storage area. Any member of a clan could live in the clan house if he or she had nowhere else to go. Clan houses provided safety nets for their members as they made the transition from communal longhouses to nuclear-style homes. Most of the clan houses have since fallen into disrepair due to their age—the trend being toward single-family dwellings due to the availability of government loans for the construction of new homes.

The boys of Young Beaver Chief's generation continued to rise early in the morning for the traditional dip in the cold, icy waters of Alaska. Like their fathers and uncles, the young boys were also whipped with spruce boughs and had to fight with other boys in the village (to learn self-defense) and listen to long lectures from their elders. The boys of this generation, however, never lived in community longhouses with their maternal uncles as their great-great-uncles did. Nevertheless, Young Beaver Chief joined his uncle's fishing crew as a teenager and spent the next several summers under his uncle's tutelage, learning about the fishing industry as well as receiving an advanced education in clan and tribal culture.

After dating others in his youth Young Beaver Chief eventually married a member of the Bear clan, much as his ancestors had done for decades. But he broke with tradition by selecting his own bride rather than having her selected for him by his elders. He did check with his grandparents to see if his selection conformed to the boundaries of tradition.

Weddings within the Beaver Village were usually held in either the Presbyterian or Russian Orthodox Church. Weddings were conducted in English, because the Alaskan Territorial Government specified that Tlingit marriages were to be performed by legally accepted religious or civil authorities. Since Young Beaver Chief belonged to a ranking family, his clan sponsored a wedding potlatch for the new couple. As in traditional potlatches, the clans within the Eagle Moiety performed many of the detailed tasks of putting on a wedding and presented gifts to the newlyweds. In return, the clans within the Raven Moiety reciprocated by distributing gifts and money to the invited guests and those who contributed to the wedding ceremony and subsequent potlatch preparations. Less prosperous families deferred sponsoring a wedding potlatch. Instead, they waited to be included as part of the next moiety potlatch, which was usually held in the autumn after the fishing season. During these moiety potlatches a clan could transact its affairs and receive public confirmation. Clan members were given Tlingit names, memorials were held for deceased relatives, and wedding gifts were exchanged. Gifts would include money, household items, clothing, personal items, and foodstuffs.

Young Beaver Chief and his wife lived in the Beaver clan house for many years. Young Beaver Chief served as the caretaker of the house to keep it in repair and ready for clan use. Later, he purchased a newly constructed home with government assistance. He spent his working years as a fisherman, using cannery boats, and eventually bought a boat of his own. Since retirement, he enjoys the view of the mountains, the forest, and the sea from his large picture window. Whenever relatives experience economic hardships, they seek out the assistance of Young Beaver Chief and frequently spend short periods of time living with him until they can get on their feet again.

Political System: Continuity and Change

As clan populations increased they divided into lineage households, in which all residents were directly related to a common descendant. The administrative structure of a Tlingit lineage household was organized around a core of matrilineal, married male members who formed a council. In smaller lineage households the council also included older nephews. This core of males served much like a board of trustees to oversee the property and ceremonial rights of the group. The eldest brother, or otherwise qualified male, was acknowledged by the members as the administrator of the lineage household's resources and labor, as well as the spokesperson for the membership. The lineage household was largely self-sufficient and autonomous. For all practical purposes the household was self-governing and dispensed its own system of justice. The household head, in consultation with his council of elders, provided the executive, legislative, judicial, and diplomatic services of their community longhouse government.[10]

The leader of a lineage household was selected with great care in order to assure the appointment of the best-qualified candidate. Some of the criteria used in the selection were as follows: (1) high birth; (2) personal accomplishments; (3) ability to work with people; (4) success in making decisions under pressure; (5) performance in acquiring and managing wealth; and (6) knowledge of traditional culture. It was customary for leadership within the longhouse to be handed down from older to younger brother or from uncle to nephew. Some individuals declined the position while others were skipped over in order to select a more-qualified member.

As a general rule the Tlingit waited until a nephew was over thirty-five years of age before they would select him to head a community household. It was believed that by that age the personality was sufficiently stabilized to permit a reasonable evaluation of his character. The selection process began when the uncle and his wife started to watch the nephews as they were being educated. When the uncle died, the honor student among the nephews would marry the uncle's widow. She might be seventy, and he might be much younger. The older wife would then train the nephew while she looked for an honor student (who was a virgin) among her nieces to replace her when she died. After the older wife's death the nephew would inherit one-half of his uncle's wealth and the rest of the members would divide the other half.

As the population increased new community houses were constructed to accommodate the people. Each community house shared the same kind of political organization, with the exception that the ranking lineage household leader, *hitsati*, became the clan spokesperson, ashudi huny, for all the local longhouses in that clan village. A hitsati, by virtue of his office, also served on the village clan council. Community houses were ranked so the Tlingit system of deference existed between the leaders and members of the longhouses. One elder stated that when the clan council of chiefs met and made a decision "then that [was] the way it [was] to be."[11]

By 1912 the Tlingit population had dipped to an historic low of some five thousand persons. The Tlingit people had lost control of most of their economic resources, were denied their civil rights—including voting and holding title to property—and had been placed under a system in which they had no representation. Thus, the clans had little wealth or resources to use in hosting potlatches. Nevertheless, hosts were still expected to enhance clan honor through lavish gift-giving. When hosts were no longer able to finance these clan responsibilities, local groups had to join together and pool their resources. Two options existed: They could either scale down their expectations or restructure their potlatching system to enable hosts to recruit more people with a greater amounts of wealth. The Tlingit chose the latter option.

Consequently, in 1912 the Tlingit changed from a clan-host-guest relationship to a moiety-host-guest relationship.[12] This structural change in potlatching was facilitated by a corresponding community nucleation process in which the declining resources of a clan's subsistence region forced some local clans to move to more productive areas for survival. Generally, the various clans moved to the most productive subsistence area within the kwaan to form consolidated clan villages.[13] The effort to protect their interests from nonnative settlers also contributed to a growing movement, based upon the concept of brotherhood, to unite to fight for their civil rights and re-

sources. Nucleation of the former clan villages, along with the political opposition from nonnatives, contributed to the need for greater cooperation among the clans. This resulted in the consolidation of clans in hosting potlatches.

The loss of economic resources and political autonomy led the Tlingit to new ways of conducting their public affairs. Some Tlingit leaders asked McAfee, a Presbyterian minister in Juneau, what they should do to resolve their grim political situation. He advised them "to organize into a society and through solidarity work to achieve the good for themselves, and the territory . . . they desired."[14] Ten Alaskan native leaders met in Sitka in 1912 and organized the Alaska Native Brotherhood (ANB) to focus upon unity and brotherhood. These concepts of unity and brotherhood influenced the way potlatches were conducted by uniting clans to form a moiety-host-guest relationship. Brotherhood and unity were stressed within the moiety, while individual and clan ranking was retained to preserve the integrity of the localized clans.

In the nineteenth century the emphasis in potlatches was on autonomous clans that met and conducted their political affairs in a neutral arena. Only people of rank and wealth were invited to intercommunity potlatches, which lasted for several days or weeks. Potlatches were conducted in the Tlingit language and accompanied by much drama, dancing, and symbolism. Clans sat in different sections of a longhouse to indicate their identity and autonomy. Traditional wealth items—such as spruce root baskets, choice animal furs, shell, canoes, carved bowls, and other Tlingit items, as well as money—were distributed to the guests.

During most of the twentieth century, however, the emphasis in potlatches has been on the unity of the moiety in which the member clans pool their resources to host a potlatch. Virtually all members of the opposite moiety within the local community are invited to attend these potlatches, regardless of their rank. These potlatches usually last only one night, beginning about 5:00 in the evening and ending about 5:00 in the morning—"before the Raven crows." Most guests come in street clothes, and the potlatch is conducted in both the English and the Tlingit languages. Much of the wealth at these potlatches is distributed in the form of money, divided among all the assembled guests. The guests with rank and standing in the community still receive more than the average guest does, but they also contribute more whenever they serve as hosts. Rarely are the traditional forms of wealth given in present-day potlatches.

This change in potlatching does not mean that the Tlingit have become less political. Rather, it signifies that they modify and change their institutions to survive in a changing political environment. It signifies that the Tlingit political process has become more complex. While traditional obligations of lineage, clan, and moiety have decreased in intensity and commitment, new responsibilities have been added during the twentieth century, due to two new institutions. First, the 1912 initiation of the ANB, with its concerns for citizenship and brotherhood, enabled the Tlingit to obtain their civil rights in the 1920s and to address new social issues, such as discrimination, poverty, and education. The ANB stressed the use of the English language, education, and majority rule in contrast to the former rule of the chiefs. The ANB continues to struggle with the economic and social conditions of living as a minority within a dominant society. In 1929 the ANB began a land-claims issue, which was settled by Congress in the Alaska Native Claims Settlement Act of December 18, 1971. The act granted some forty million acres of land and one billion dollars to Alaskan Natives.

This act authorized the formation of village and regional corporations to supervise the land and money to be given by the federal government to clear up the land titles of Alaska that had been in limbo since Russia sold Alaska to the United States. Native corporations enabled the Tlingit to select their own leaders, to develop their own resources, and to chart their own futures. These corporations are supervised under government rules and regulations. They are intended not only to be profit-making institutions, but also to serve certain community needs of their stockholders.

It is not inconceivable for a Tlingit elder to attend a village corporation meeting in the morning, an ANB meeting in the afternoon, and a potlatch feast in the evening. Thus, his political activities in one day include three very diverse yet complementary institutions that serve to advance the interests of the Tlingit people. Consequently, the present political process has a three-pronged institutional approach to sustain a measure of their ethnic identity, to establish their social continuity, and to enhance their financial security.

Religious System: Continuity and Change

The Tlingit explanation of the world begins in a mythical Garden of Eden located somewhere near the headwaters of the Nass River. Tlingit refer to the creator as Kah-shu-goon-yah, the deity in the beginning, who was highly respected and who had a sacred name that was never mentioned above a whisper. However, Tlingit folklore focused upon a less distant past when the world of mythical creatures, animating spirits, and cultural institutions originated, lived, and expressed themselves through their words and works.

These spirits were believed to inhabit lakes, streams, swamps, trees, rocks, birds, animals, mountains, the sun, the sea, and the moon. Humans could use these resources if they took care to pay proper respect to the spirits that inhabited them. The Tlingit believed that these spirits would punish those who failed to respect them by causing temporary blindness in future hunts and scarcity of animals, contributing to food shortages. Birds and animals were believed to be endowed with understanding and could comprehend what people said. Therefore, individuals were taught to talk circumspectly at all times so that the creature would not overhear any disrespectful words and retaliate.[15]

The Tlingit offered prayers of thanksgiving to the creatures before going on hunting or fishing expeditions, explaining to the targeted creature what they were going to do and why they wanted to do it. They told the creature that they needed food for their families and that they would take only what they needed. The Tlingit believed that killing animals just for their furs would result in punishment by the spirit of the affected creature. Consequently, the Tlingit watched in horror and anticipation of pending doom as the early Europeans slaughtered their sea mammals.

The Tlingit's intense respect for nature was heightened by rigorous physical discipline. For example, prior to the autumn hunting season, hunters fasted and meditated. They drank seawater along with freshwater to purge their bodies, to lose excess weight, and to clear their mental perception. They concentrated upon the forces of nature, the problems of securing sufficient food supplies, and the strategy to be used to obtain them. Individuals would sit for hours on the rocks along some scenic section of the beach and absorb the sights and sounds of the tidelands while they meditated on the weather, nature, and the meaning of their existence. All things were believed to have a reason for being. Rain, fog, and thunder had a reason for being. Thunder in the early spring was believed to signify that there would be good weather in the summer. Late thunder in the autumn was a sign of a long winter. Even the ocean waves and rocks held meaning for the Tlingit.

The Tlingit believed in the availability of supernatural power. The word for spirits, *yek*, indicates a distributive or a collective nature and can be classified into sky, land, and water spirits. Spirit power was thought to be readily available. It was revealed or manifested through animals, objects, or individuals and could be used for either good or evil. Spirits assisted seekers who properly purified themselves and who summoned them by use of the drum and rattle. These spirit powers were believed to assist individuals in curing the sick, in achieving success in warfare, in acquiring wealth, or in performing ceremonial rites.[16]

All Tlingit had two spirits: (1) an active earthly spirit, Ka-too, and (2) an immortal spirit, Ka-yah-ha-ko. Individual accomplishments were defined in terms of spirit power. Krause[17] suggests that an individual's acquired spirit power, Tu-kina-jek, would desert an unclean or evil person. Anyone could go alone into the woods and, by means of fasting, praying, and meditation, seek spirit power. Accomplishments of life were attributed to the assistance of spirit power. De Laguna[18] suggests that an individual's name defined his social rank and also "embodied" his soul. Spirit power seemed to reinforce the social hierarchy because high-class people sought and received high-class names and low-class people sought and received low-class names.

Community households were permeated with a sacred atmosphere. Animals and objects were believed to be inhabited by animating spirits. It was necessary to show animals respect in order to succeed in life. In return, the spirit of animals might offer needed assistance. The Tlingit looked to animals for signs, omens, and spiritual guidance. For example, a frog, a beaver, or a bear might lead a Tlingit to a desirable site. In recognition of that assistance, a household's affiliated clan would claim that animal as its crest. It would then be adopted as the sacred symbol of their identity and the clan households, in turn, would use that crest to represent both its members and their belongings.

Each clan had its own spirit doctor, or *ich*. Spirit doctors wielded considerable power and were held in high regard. They were reputed to be able to heal the sick, predict the future, communicate with other spirit doctors, find food in times of scarcity, give counsel during times of war, battle hostile evil forces, locate lost hunters and fishermen, detect the presence of evil, and teach moral living. Spirit doctors lived a very austere and disciplined lifestyle. They spent many weeks in rigorous physical procedures to cleanse the spirit and prepare the mind for an encounter with a supernatural spirit. After receiving the power, spirit doctors continued to spend several weeks each year alone in the forest, fasting and meditating, seeking wisdom and direction for their clan. Spirit doctors never cut their hair, frequently observed periods of sexual continence, and always followed special food restrictions.

While every family possessed a basic knowledge of healing herbs, spirit doctors possessed a superior knowledge of herbal medicines and had access to powerful spirits. A Tlingit sought the assistance of a spirit doctor when home remedies proved to be ineffective. Every individual had a spirit helper, but only the spirit doctor had direct contact with several spirits. Spirit doctors served their communities during times of crises when the uncertainties of life forced the people to turn to other sources of assistance, such as the supernatural. Thus, spirit doctors interceded between the natural and the supernatural forces, confronted evil and suffering, and defended the good in life. No clan dared to be without recourse to its own spirit doctor whom its members could trust.

The Tlingit believed in two sources of power in the universe—good and evil. They also believed that one would progressively become the source of power to which one committed oneself. The Tlingit sought to appease evil spirits and to call upon good spirits for aid. Spirit doctors spent much of their life seeking good spirit power for the preservation and welfare of the community. Spirit doctors taught people to help, rather than to hate. The Tlingit word for hate, *kan*, means "to boomerang." Tlingit believed that hate was self-destructive. Spirit doctors sought beneficent powers to help people, while witches sought malevolent powers to harm people. One of the duties of a spirit doctor was to expose witches.

Spirit doctors occupied a socially acceptable position, while witches occupied a socially unacceptable position in the Tlingit social structure. It was believed that spirit doctors sought good for society while witches were evil and sought to harm society. Spirit doctors performed public ceremonies to cure diseases while witches held private ceremonies to cause diseases. Spirit doctors practiced rigorous self-restraint while witches practiced unrestrained passion. Spirit doctors represented the best in society while witches represented the worst. Consequently, when discovered, witches were hunted down, tortured to obtain a confession, and sometimes killed. Tlingit continue to go into the woods to seek spirit power, and a very few still seek the special power of a spirit doctor. In April 1994 a Tlingit clan buried one of its members who had been training for years to be a spirit doctor. It was considered to be a great loss to the community.

The following story further explains the distinction of the spirit doctor: A youth in Sitka spent some time living along a local stream and meditating. One day he saw what he thought was the spirit of the stream. He asked an elder to help him in his spirit quest. The elder inquired if he was on drugs or had been drinking. The youth replied, "No." The elder pressed the youth concerning his motive for seeking power and told the youth that Indians seek spirit power to make them better persons. The elder commented that a spirit doctor's motive for seeking spirit power was for assisting people, not for assaulting them. In a few days the youth was out of his tree house and working at a job.[19]

The Tlingit believed in immortality. At death, it was believed, the spirit of the deceased traveled to one of the various levels of heaven, depending upon the person's moral conduct on earth. Good people went to heaven, *Kiwa-a*, a realm of happiness. Moral delinquents went to dog heaven, *Ketl-kiwa*, a realm of misery. Life on earth and in heaven was perceived as a continuous cycle. Death was viewed as the prelude to the other world, while birth was viewed as the reentrance into this world. Individuals remained in the other world for a period of time, and then were born anew into this world. People were consoled at the death of a relative with the promise that the deceased would soon return to this world again. Relatives, in anticipation of the return of loved ones, looked for physical marks of identification on babies in order to properly identify the ancestor's reappearance.[20]

Young Beaver Chief includes sacred roots in traditional ceremonies, as well as in the rites of the Russian Orthodox and the Presbyterian Churches. Many Tlingit combine some of the beliefs of the past with those of the present. Young Beaver Chief will participate in a Sunday morning service in the Presbyterian Church and read Holy Scripture, attend a funeral in the Russian Orthodox Church on a Friday afternoon and kiss the icons of the past, and then on Friday evening feed the spirit of the deceased at a funeral potlatch, according to traditional custom.

Young Beaver Chief has recorded many stories, customs, and genealogies to pass on to future generations. Youths receive most of their education in public schools that stress book learning, with an emphasis on note-taking rather than on rote memory. Consequently, Tlingit youth have concentrated less on memory development than their elders once did. Today's Tlingit youth rely more on modern means for preserving the past, such as tape recorders, videotapes, and printed pages. Their elders view this as a necessary adaptation to a change in learning skills.

The net result of living in two cultures, a dominant culture and a minority culture, provides both cultural gains and losses. The Tlingit population, educational levels, and income have increased considerably. One recent potlatch was given by a single host clan much like it was done before 1912, when clans possessed sufficient numbers and resources to sponsor their own potlatch. This particular potlatch was in excess of thirty-two thousand dollars. The talk of most of the guests at this potlatch was that they had never seen this type of potlatch in their lifetime. In some areas the clans are increasing traditional cultural participation in such events as the single potlatch, while in others, such as speaking Tlingit, there is a decrease in usage.

Summary

While the Tlingit culture experienced considerable changes over the past century, they also retained an essential core of values, symbols, and institutions. This cultural core seems to have provided them with a sense of freedom to revise their symbolic code in the process of adapting to rapid change, while also contributing to ethnic continuity and distinctiveness.

The subsistence economy plus a part-time-wage economy of the last century has evolved into a wage economy plus a part-time-subsistence economy in the present. Subsistence foods are becoming increasingly difficult to obtain due to commercial depletion and government regulations. The more remotely dispersed native communities have greater access to native foods, and therefore depend more on them than urban Tlingit. Nevertheless, dried and smoked seafood, wild game, and herbs are praised and prized by most Tlingit for their taste and ethnic symbolism.

Tlingit socio-political institutions changed (1) from communal households to nuclear households; (2) from emphasizing interclan marriages and potlatches to practicing intermoiety marriages and potlatches; (3) from single-clan and moiety-village organization to nucleated kwaan villages; (4) from speaking Tlingit language to speaking both English and Tlingit; (5) from exclusive Tlingit host-guest potlatches to more open Tlingit and non-Tlingit potlatches; (6) from the elders selecting a spouse to personal selection of a spouse; and (7) from eight plus days of potlatching to one night of potlatching.

The Tlingit incorporated Christian values and symbols into their traditional culture, including the concept of brotherhood, the modification of traditional customs, and the interpretation of aboriginal stories. Stories of the flood, the strong man, and traditional teachings on moral behavior are compared with the Noah story, the Samson story, and the Ten Commandments. The Tlingit continue to present a plate of food to feed the spirits of the ancestors. They continue to collect herbal medicines and to seek spirit power. The Tlingit are in the process of constructing a synthesis of traditional, modern, and Christian values and symbols into their ethnic version of contemporary culture.

Notes

1. Kalervo Oberg, *The Social Economy of the Tlingit Indians* (Seattle, WA: University of Washington Press, 1973), pp. 65–78.

2. C. H. Rosenthal, Robert A. Henning, Barbara Olds, R.N. De Armond, eds., "Admirality . . . Island in Contention," *Alaska Geographic* 1 (Summer 1973): 57.

3. Kenneth D. Tollefson, "Northwest Coast Village Adaptations: A Case Study," *Canadian Journal of Anthropology* 3 (1982): 19–29.

4. Ronald L. Olson, "Social Structure and Social Life of the Tlingit in Alaska," *Anthropological Records* 26 (1967): 48.

5. Ronald L. Olson, "Channeling of Character in Tlingit Society," *Personal Character and Cultural Milieu*, 3rd ed. (1956): 679.

6. Robert J. Peratrovich, Jr., *Social and Economic Structure of the Henya Indians* (M.A. thesis, University of Alaska, 1959), p. 114.

7. Kalervo Oberg, *The Social Economy of the Tlingit Indians* (Ph.D. diss., Department of Anthropology, University of Chicago, 1937), p. 121.

8. John R. Swanton, "Social Conditions, Beliefs, and Linguistic Relationship of the Tlingit Indians," *Bureau of American Ethnology, Annual Report 26* (1908): 425.

9. Samuel L. Stanley, *Historical Changes in Tlingit Social Structure* (Ph.D. diss., University of Chicago, 1958), p. 49.

10. George Ramos and Elaine Ramos, *Yakutat History* (Sitka, AK: Sheldon Jackson College, 1973), p. 4.

11. Kenneth D. Tollefson, "Northwest Coast Village Adaptations. A Case Study," *Canadian Journal of Anthropology* 3 (1982): 23.

12. Kenneth D. Tollefson, "A Structural Change in Tlingit Potlatching," *The Western Canadian Journal of Anthropology* 7 (1977): 16–27

13. Kenneth. D. Tollefson, "Northwest Coast Village Adaptations: A Case Study," *Canadian Journal of Anthropology* 3 (1982): 26.

14. *The Alaska Fisherman* 8, no. 8 (1931).

15. John R. Swanton, "Social Conditions, Beliefs, and Linguistic Relationship of the Tlingit Indians," *Bureau of American Ethnology, Annual Report 26* (1908): 454-458.

16. Robert J. Peratrovich, Jr., *Social and Economic Structure of the Henya Indians* (M.A. thesis, University of Alaska, 1959), p. 105.

17. Aurel Krause, *Die Tlinkit-Indianer*, Jena H. Costenoble (1956). Published in English as: *The Tlingit Indians*, trans. Erna Gunther (Seattle: University of Washington Press, 1970), pp. 199–210.

18. Frederica de Laguna, *Under Mount Saint Elias: The History and Culture of the Yakutat Tlingit* (Washington, D.C.: Smithsonian Institution Press, 1972), p. 187.

19. Kenneth D. Tollefson, *The Cultural Foundation of Political Revitalization among the Tlingit* (Ph.D. diss., University of Washington, 1976), p. 163.

20. Frederica de Laguna, "Childhood among the Yakutat Tlingit," in M.E. Spiro, ed., *Context and Meaning in Cultural Anthropology* (New York, NY: The Free Press, 1965), p. 5.

Suggested Readings

De Laguna, Frederica. *Under Mount Saint Elias: The History and Culture of the Yakatat Tlingit*. Washington, D.C.: Smithsonian Institution Press, 1972. A recent ethnography on the northern Tlingit.

Kan, Sergli. *Symbolic Immortality: The Tlingit Potlatch of the Nineteenth Century*. Washington, D.C.: Smithsonian Institution Press, 1989. An analysis of the Tlingit mortuary complex as it relates to the social organization of the tribe.

Krause, Aurel. *The Tlingit Indians*. Seattle: University of Washington Press, 1956. A general ethnography collected in the 1880s.

Oberg, Kalervo. *The Social Economy of the Tlingit Indians*. Seattle: University of Washington Press, 1973. Describes the socio-political organization of the Klukwan Tlingit.

Tollefson, Kenneth. "Tlingit Acculturation: An Institutional Perspective," *Ethnology* 23 (1984): 229–247. A comparative political analysis of the Tlingit in 1880, 1930, and 1980.

"TLINGIT: CHIEFS PAST AND PRESENT"

Kenneth Tollefson

1) What do early historic records and ethnographic research suggest about the traditional organization of Tlingit society?

2) Old Beaver Chief represented the last of old Tlingit society. What traditional economic activities did he and his people pursue, and what western economic pursuits began making inroads into the economy in the late 19th century?

3) How did Young Beaver Chief accommodate modern economic pursuits into his economic life?

4) What changes occurred in village size and organization, kinship structure, class structure and social ranking, educational patterns, political structure, religious beliefs, and other patterns of Tlingit life between the time of Old Beaver Chief and Young Beaver Chief?

HAITIANS: FROM POLITICAL REPRESSION TO CHAOS

Robert Lawless

Haiti may be regarded as a predatory state run by an elite class that extorts its living from the masses. The institutional structures of government do not operate for the benefit of the people as a whole. Rather, the government largely serves the elite. Directly and indirectly, members of the elite depend on the government to make their living. Thus, in order to earn and increase their incomes, members of the elite have to stay in power. All members of the elite, however, cannot be in control at the same time, and so individuals, families, and groups must make alliances with those who manage the agencies of government.

The political repression seen in the succession of arrests, torture, and gross violations of human rights in Haiti represents the efforts of the elite to maintain itself economically at the direct expense of the poor. Their loss of power would result not only in the loss of control and prestige but also in the loss of income.

It is my view that the long Duvalier reign from 1957 to 1986 destroyed the traditional balance among the competing members of the elite and raised both the degree of violence of the state against the people and the techniques of stealing from the people to their highest levels in Haitian history. For example, although the Central Bank maintained a minimum of integrity and kept the Haitian currency tied to the U.S. dollar, all other state units and agencies were absolutely personal sources of household income for the Duvaliers and their cohorts. After the downfall of the Duvaliers in February 1986 the machinery of political repression had no traditional channels for its expression and devolved into a chaotic situation with no conventional, indigenous solutions currently in sight (as of the time of this writing in Spring 1994).

Laying the basis for such a thesis requires some knowledge of basic information about Haiti and also some knowledge of the history of Haiti.

Introduction

Located in the Caribbean Sea just fifty-four miles (ninety kilometers) southeast of Cuba and part of the Greater Antilles, Haiti shares the island of Hispaniola with the Dominican Republic. Taking up the western third of the island, Haiti contains about 11,100 square miles (27,750 square kilometers)—approximately the size of Maryland. Its topography varies from a few flat, semiarid valleys to some densely forested, deeply dissected mountains and many semi-denuded, gently sloping mountains. About one third of Haiti is at an elevation between 660 and 1,650 feet (200 and 500 meters) above sea level and about two thirds is divided into three mountain ranges with the highest elevation, the La Selle Peak, at about 8,840 feet (2,680 meters).

The average annual temperature falls somewhere between 75 and 81 degrees Fahrenheit (24 and 27 celsius). The major changes in temperature are caused by changes in elevation. Starting at the capital of Port-au-Prince with an altitude of 130 feet (40 meters) and a mean temperature of 79, a perspiring person can walk up to nearby Petionville at an elevation of 1,320 feet (400 meters) and experience a mean temperature of 76, and the same person can continue up the road to an elevation of 4,785 feet (1,450 meters) at the vegetable center of Kenscoff with a quite enjoyable mean annual temperature of 65 degrees Fahrenheit.

Demographic information is difficult to come by, but an educated estimate would put the total population at about 6.5 million. Port-au-Prince has about 1.25 million people, and the second largest city, Cap-Haitien, has maybe 70,000. The important regional cities such as Les Cayes, Gonaives, Port-de-Paix, Jacmel, Jeremie, St. Marc, and Hinche have populations of only ten thousand to fifty thousand at the most. Probably about eighty percent of the Haitian population lives in rural areas and subsists through farming.

Outsiders have traditionally misunderstood the language situation of Haiti. It has often been stated that the elite speaks French, and the masses speak some sort of degraded version of French called *patois* or Creole. Anthropological linguists wring their hands in despair at such notions. All languages that have been in use for more than a couple of generations are structurally and functionally complex enough to handle all the descriptive, emotional, and expressive needs of the people speaking the particular language. The language of Haiti, the language spoken by *all* Haitians, is properly referred to as Haitian Creole. For much of the modern history of Haiti, however, the official language of government, business, and education has been French, even though only about eight percent of the people speak French consistently. The reason for the usage of French is that members of the educated elite have found that they can exclude the masses from competing for scarce jobs by requiring knowledge of the French language for positions in government and business.

The contrast between "Blacks" and "mulattoes" is a salient theme in Haitian history. A nineteenth- century writer, for example, pointed out that color distinctions were extremely important and he included an appendix with charts on color types in the Haitian population.[1] Even Leslie Manigat, a political science professor who was briefly president of Haiti in 1988, spoke in the mid-1960s at North American universities in terms of these color distinctions, saying:

> On the one hand, there has been the light-skinned elite, claiming to be ideologically liberal, in reality, politically autocratic, economically conservative, socially sectarian, and culturally pro-European. When in power, this elite has represented the interests of the urban, moneyed oligarchy. Against its traditional hegemony, on the other hand, there has been a coalition led by the dark-skinned elite. Although socially progressive because of the need to maintain solidarity with the middle classes and masses through the common denominator of color, this coalition was also politically autocratic, ideologically authoritarian, economically quasi-traditional, and culturally nationalistic.[2]

The "color issue" was nonexistent in the election campaigns leading up to the November 1987 aborted elections, in which Manigat was originally a minor candidate. Almost all families in Haiti can claim members whose skin color ranges from light to dark, but the idea of a society divided into a small sophisticated, Westernized mulatto segment and a large dangerous, Africanish Black segment does benefit some groups. In particular, the traditional power elite gains an advantage by presenting this picture of Haiti to the white world, that is, the mulatto elite can claim outside help in its efforts to rule the unruly masses.

Despite its political difficulties Haiti is internationally famous for its art and literature. In the 1940s Haiti burst into the consciousness of the art world with an astonishing display of paintings. Her artists justly deserved the worldwide attention they received for their so-called primitive or naive art.

Haitian writers initially focused on concepts of negritude foreshadowing the black power and anti-colonial post-World War II movements. Haiti's literary production is even more amazing in light of the high rate of illiteracy, probably around eighty-five percent. Fewer than half of the rural children attend school, and only about twenty percent of those complete the primary grades. Most of the literature is strikingly indigenous. Voodoo has been a major theme in many of the novels.

The current chaos, however, has closed down the traditional channels for the production of art and literature. Writers had usually depended on bookstores with small print shops to put out limited editions of their works, which were sold by the bookstores. These book stores and print shops have been virtually put out of business through losing their primary customers (because schools have been closed) and through harassment by army and police personnel, who see any printed work as anti-government. Artists had depended largely on the tourist trade to earn a living. The few hardy tourists who were not turned off by the AIDS scare are now thoroughly repulsed by the continuing chaos and perceived lack of safety in Haiti.

Religion

A cementing element of the Haitian population is religion. Although some of the population is nominally Roman Catholic and although Protestant missionaries have made considerable headway in the poorer rural areas of Haiti, the religion of Haiti is still Voodoo, a religion that focuses on contacting and appeasing immediate relatives, such as dead parents and grandparents, and ancestral spirits, who include distant, stereotyped ancestors.

Voodoo is an egalitarian religion with both men and women serving as priests presiding over ceremonies that include divination rites, which are used to find out the course of the future or the causes of various difficulties. It has healing rites in which a Voodoo priest interacts directly with sick people to cure them, propitiatory rites in which food and drink are offered to specific spirits to get into their good graces, and preventive rites in which ancestors are offered sacrifices to help head off any possible future trouble. Indeed, many Voodoo rituals can be seen as healing rites, since many of the rituals are performed at times of sickness and death. Much of Voodoo, then, can be seen as a folk medical system that attributes illness to the work of angry ancestors and that consists of ceremonies performed to appease those ancestors in order to cure illness.

The influence of Voodoo on politics has always been problematic since Voodoo is practiced largely on a household level and has no regional or national connections. Due to its egalitarian ideology, Voodoo has often been the target of repression by the government. Voodoo may, indeed, be the one aspect of Haitian life surviving quite well through the current period of chaos.

Health

Voodoo healers are a major part of the medical system of Haiti, though Western medicine has been available to the urban elite for several decades and is, indeed, available from a few rural clinics. For the most part, however, health and healing for poorer Haitians is handled by herb medicine, bone setters, injectionists, Voodoo rituals, and by a rich body of folk knowledge. The poorer masses, nevertheless, suffer many health problems of malnutrition and disease. The daily per capita food consumption is estimated at sixteen hundred calories, and measles, diarrhea, and tetanus kill many children before they reach their teens.

Tuberculosis is Haiti's most devastating disease, followed closely by malaria, influenza, dysentery, tetanus, whooping cough, and measles. Eye problems are endemic, with the chief causes of blindness being cataracts, scarring of the cornea, and glaucoma.

A ninety-two-page study released in September 1992 by the Permanent Commission on Emergency Aid, which represents over sixty nongovernmental development and democracy organizations in Haiti, said that the death rate has been rising and the health of the population dropping since the September 1991 military coup that ousted the democratically elected government. It also pointed out that there has been a deterioration in state services amounting to a descent into chaos, with the Departments of Public Health and Water totally mismanaged. The supply of drinkable water, for example, has dropped by fifty percent in the cities and twenty percent in the countryside. According to the report, "The situation is extremely critical and just waiting for cholera to strike."[3] Other problems include an increase in garbage in the streets (with only about twenty-five percent of the country's garbage being collected), a rise in the number of preventable illnesses, and a deterioration in mental health.

History

Haitian history is unique among Caribbean nations and, in fact, unique in the world; Haiti's slave uprising was the only one that grew into a modern nation. How Haitians view themselves and how the world views Haiti must always be filtered through the prism of this momentous historical fact.

Slave Beginnings

Haiti became a slave colony of the French after Europeans, mainly the Spaniards, killed off the pre-Columbian Indian population on the island of Hispaniola through murder, diseases, and slavery. Then the Europeans looked toward Africa for the labor they needed to work the farms that were to become enormous sugarcane plantations. In 1502, just ten years after Columbus landed in Haiti, the Spanish governor brought the first black slaves to Hispaniola, and in 1505 sugar cane was introduced to Hispaniola from the Canary Islands. In 1697 Spain recognized France's claim to the western part of Hispaniola, to be known as the French colony of Saint Domingue.

Independence

The brutality and exploitation of the French resulted in many failed slave uprisings until, in August 1791, the slaves managed a major revolt that the plantation owners could not contain. By 1796 white supremacy was at an end, and Black rule was established under the leadership of Toussaint Louverture, a charismatic ex-slave. In 1800 Napoleon sent twenty-eight thousand troops to retake the colony and re-enslave the Blacks, but by late 1803 the Haitians had defeated the French troops. On January 1, 1804, Jean-Jacques Dessalines, Toussaint's successor, proclaimed the independence of Haiti, an event that shocked the white world to its foundations. Haitians further goaded the white world by proclaiming Haiti as a symbol of redemption for the whole African race. For example, the first Haitian constitution designated Haitians of whatever color as "Black" (including those Germans and Poles who had been given Haitian citizenship), opened Haitian citizenship to all persons everywhere of African or Indian descent, and forbade whites to own land.

At the time of the Haitian Revolution fully two thirds of the slaves had been born in Africa. By the end of the revolution virtually all the whites had been eliminated, and there were several massacres of the mulattoes. As a consequence, Haiti was ostracized by the white world. It was not until 1862 that Haiti's most important neighbor, the United States, recognized Haitian independence. Great Britain was one of the few nations that did have early diplomatic relations with Haiti, but it was in the writings of the English racists and anti-abolitionists that Haiti began to get its unwarranted bad press,[4] focusing largely on the savagery of these "African" Haitians and the barbaric practices of Voodoo—especially its alleged ritual cannibalism.

In actuality Haiti represents the only time in history when a slave population on its own suddenly faced the task of organizing a government and an economic system. The press on Haiti, nevertheless, focused almost entirely on the former prosperity of the French system in Saint Domingue in contrast to the poverty, ignorance, and disorder in independent Haiti—just as the press today largely emphasizes the destitution found in Haiti. Such depictions, however, neglect the fact that in colonial Saint Domingue only an extraordinarily small percentage of the population enjoyed the good life—and, indeed, even today only a small percentage of the Haitian population enjoys considerable wealth.

One of the crucial problems facing Haiti immediately after independence concerned access to the land previously owned by the French and how to maintain the agricultural productivity of this land. Initially the Haitian government attempted to reinstate the painful plantation system of colonial Saint Domingue. When these attempts failed because plantations were associated with slavery, land was, for the most part, simply distributed among the ex-slaves. As a result, from sixty to eighty percent of the farmers currently own their own land, though the plots are fragmented and small. The urban-based government has rarely shown a sustained interest in agriculture, and although the state owns land, nobody seems to pay much attention to it and peasants occupy most of it rent-free.

Modern Developments

Except for a brief period between 1915 and 1934 when it was occupied by United States Marines, Haiti has remained self-consciously independent. The twenty-three-year period after the occupation and until the election of François "Papa Doc" Duvalier as president saw increased feelings of nationalism and pride in the African heritage, a growth in trade and political interaction with other Caribbean nations, the development of peasant economic cooperation, the introduction of a progressive income tax, and, especially, the rise of a new Black middle class. In 1957 Duvalier won the presidency with a decisive margin as the self-proclaimed heir to these new developments.

In addition, Haitians have always taken a special interest in the affairs of Blacks throughout the world. In 1859 the Haitian government ordered a

special requiem mass for the death of John Brown, the famous American abolitionist. In that same year the Haitian Secretary of State called for immigration to Haiti by "members of the African race, who groan in the United States" (quoted in DuBois).[5] More than a hundred years later the Duvalier regime declared several days of national mourning after the assassination of Martin Luther King, Jr. And two major thoroughfares in Port-au-Prince are named after John Brown and Martin Luther King, Jr.

Duvalier the Senior

Widely regarded as a tool of the army by some and as a lackey of the U.S. embassy by others, Duvalier, instead, proved to be an extraordinarily astute politician; initially he gained the trust of the indigenous clergy, the peasants and the urban proletariat, and then he brought diverse elements into his circle of advisers, including communists, North Americans, Haitian exiles, taxi drivers, Voodoo priests, and Black power intellectuals. To keep the army in control, he cut its funding and created an alterative volunteer militia loyal only to him, the organization that came to be known as the notorious *tonton-makout*—named after a character in Haitian folklore who stalks bad children and carries them off in his basket.

The first few years of Duvalier's rule were marked by several unsuccessful coups and invasions. In 1958 and 1959 invasions by Haitian exiles were thwarted, and in 1963 Clément Barbot, chief of the tonton-makout, attempted a major coup that was accompanied by a small guerrilla war and a number of bombings and shootings in and around Port-au-Prince. Also in 1963 an attempt was made on the life of Duvalier's children Simone and Jean-Claude. In April of the next year Duvalier declared himself president-for-life, and in August yet another invasion failed. In 1968 the National Palace was bombed but an accompanying invasion fizzled out. Duvalier's reprisals were swift, vicious, and widespread. The result of his campaign of oppression against opponents was increased isolation from the international community, which began to attribute all of Haiti's problems to Duvalier.

During the years of Duvalier's rule thousands of Haitian professionals fled to the United States, Canada, the Bahamas, the Dominican Republic, Venezuela, French Guyana, Africa, and France. During the rule of his son, from 1971 to 1986, thousands more from all classes fled to Florida. The Haitians who left greatly influenced politics back in Haiti. Those who went to the United States tended to have little patience with the traditional French-oriented elite. Haitians of all classes mixed extensively and intensively overseas, and the Duvalier brand of Black nationalism found little support among these upwardly mobile, welfare-conscious Haitian exiles.

Duvalier the Junior

In January 1971, Duvalier announced that his son would succeed him as president-for-life, and in April of that year Duvalier died and was, indeed, succeeded by his nineteen-year-old son, Jean-Claude. The junior Duvalier closely tied the fortunes of Haiti to the United States—a relationship featuring private investments from the United States wooed by such incentives as no customs taxes, a minimum wage kept very low, the suppression of labor unions, and the right of U.S. companies to repatriate profits from their off-shore plants. So, with the help of U.S. government agencies Haiti became economically dependent on its powerful North American neighbor. Also, with the aid of the international lending enterprise Haiti joined the ranks of the debtor nations for the first time in its history. And with the Reagan administration giving five times as much military aid to the dictatorship as had President Carter, the army in Haiti finally regained the power under the junior Duvalier that it had lost under the senior Duvalier.

In addition to the economic exploitation by the United States, Haiti suffered greatly from the oil crises of 1973–1974 and 1980. In addition, Hurricane Allen in 1980 devastated the coffee trees and ruined the production of coffee, one of Haiti's most significant exports.

Initially Jean-Claude did make some progressive changes under pressure from the Carter administration and its emphasis on human rights. By the end of 1979, however, Jean-Claude's administration had slid back toward repression as the Carter administration became occupied with other matters. Correctly reading the incoming Reagan administration's lack of interest in human rights, the Haitian government increased its control of political, press, and labor groups. Immediately following Reagan's election in November 1980, several hundred progressive Haitians were arrested and many were deported.

According to a study of the North American mass media, "The foreign media seemed confused by the attitude of the American government, and, understandably, could not present a clear picture of the enigmatic Jean-Claude. Some journalists, especially Americans, who had written about the hopelessness of François Duvalier's Haiti, began writing about the sudden improvement in Haiti after the death of Papa Doc. Others, especially Haitians, claimed that repression was just as bad under Jean-Claude as it had been under François."[6]

Clearly Jean-Claude was not as politically astute as was his father. Some Haitians have emphasized to me that the beginning of his end was his elaborate wedding in 1980 to Michèle Bennett, the daughter of a mulatto business family. This event alienated many of the Black power followers of his father. At any rate, after fourteen years of rule by a second Duvalier and precious few, if any, economic gains, Haitians reached the end of their patience. In late November 1985 street protests began in towns throughout Haiti, and the violent police responses led to further protests. Despite these attempts at repression, some reshuffling at high levels of government, and a farcical "referendum" that gave Jean-Claude "99.98 percent" of the vote, the second of the Duvaliers could not hang onto power. Just a little over a year later, on the morning of February 7, 1986, Jean-Claude Duvalier fled to France. An era had ended. That morning the streets of Port-au-Prince were full of Haitians with tree branches symbolically sweeping away the evil spirits of the Duvaliers.

Later in the day it was announced that Haiti would be run by an interim government initially composed of a five-member council. Headed by Lt. Gen. Henri Namphy, it was pared down to three members six weeks later. A few days after the ouster of Jean-Claude the council abolished the widely hated tonton-makout, but the interim government did not pursue supporters of Duvalier except under intense public pressure. Namphy and others still in power obviously did not view the end of Duvalier as a revolution signaling the end of authoritarianism in Haiti.

Current Events

For several years Haiti limped along with various forms of the council, all of them inevitably run in one way or another by the army. With assorted groups jockeying for influence Haiti attempted to have presidential and National Assembly elections in November 1987 and presidential and National Assembly (and mayoral) elections in January 1988. Despite the indifference of the council to the public welfare, attempts to form a progressive government continued. The 1987 constitution is, in fact, a good example of an indigenous document created by progressive Haitians to solve the peculiar political problems that have arisen out of Haitian history. It was, of course, produced in opposition to the wishes of the ruling military-dominated council.

The referendum on the constitution, held in March 1987, represented the highest level of political participation by the Haitian general public since the elections that led to the installation of the Duvalier dynasty in 1957. Almost all Haitians that I have talked with regard the twenty-day period leading up to the referendum as the freest political period in living memory and the period in which cultural expressions reached their height. The constitution was published both in French and Creole. Several hundred thousand comic books and posters explaining the constitution were distributed throughout Haiti. Radio stations devoted many hours of their air time to the reading and discussion of the constitution.

After the overwhelming approval of the new constitution, various thugs, including those identified as former tonton-makout, began attacking institutions identified with the new democratic processes, such as radio stations and the elections offices. It seems that these attacks occurred because the military and other elite elements saw the involvement of the masses as a threat to their position, and preferred the appearance of chaos in the hope that they would be called back to power to restore order.

In the ensuing descent into disorder two presidential candidates were killed—one in front of a police station clutching a copy of the constitution. Another candidate refused to campaign because of the lack of police protection. A few days before the elections the polling headquarters was burned down, a popular radio station was set on fire, and arsonists screaming "Long live the army!" destroyed a large open-air market in Port-au-Prince.

On the morning of the November 1987 presidential and National Assembly elections, gunmen roamed the streets of Port-au-Prince firing at those going to vote and invading some voting sites killing several people. Haitians have told me that uniformed soldiers often joined in these attacks. Outside of Port-au-Prince the ballots were rarely delivered because the trucks had been hijacked, usually by soldiers.

At least thirty-four people were killed in these aborted elections, which the council cancelled later in the day. On the very next day a friend in Cap-Haitien wrote to me,

> For many months, November 29, 1987, has stood out in the hearts and minds of Haitians as a day of hope. Yesterday it became a day of deception. Yesterday, we saw, in one day, our hopes and dreams for a democratic and free Haiti crushed. We feel we no longer have a hope that there will be a change in the country.

Another told me in Creole the same day over the telephone, "Kè-m grenn" (My heart is broken).

While the military council tried to control politics, social controls in the streets began breaking down. Starting soon after Duvalier's departure Haitians spoke to me about the lack of control in Port-au-Prince and Cap-Haitien and complained about the unprecedented frequency of crimes in these two largest Haitian cities. During the first week of October 1986 the opening of schools was delayed in Cap-Haitien because of rioting that included the sacking of the CARE warehouse and the main post office.

Personal violence that had been extremely rare in Haiti began occurring. Haitians were shocked by several rapes in Port-au-Prince in February and March 1987. One Haitian told me, "There were people so frustrated by what they saw as a worsening situation here that rioting and burning barricades was their only means of expression." A returning exile is quoted as saying, "We have no work, nothing to live on; the country is in ruins."[7]

After the 1987 elections were undermined by the army and aborted, the 1988 elections were controlled by the army and widely regarded as illegitimate. Leslie Manigat, the president installed from this 1988 election, attempted to finesse the army and was thrown out by the military after four months.

For a couple of years after 1988 there were a series of military coups, and then a legitimate election was held in December 1990. Scheduled first for November 4 and then postponed to December 16, this election was monitored by more than four hundred international observers, including former U.S. President Carter. Jean-Bertrand Aristide won the presidency in a landslide approaching 70 percent of the estimated 75 percent of the two million registered voters who cast ballots, and his election raised expectations both in Haiti and elsewhere in the Caribbean. For example, at Aristide's inauguration Jamaica's prime minister said that he sensed "a very great moment in Caribbean history after all the generations of struggle and tyranny."[8]

Installed in office on February 7, 1991, five years to the day after the end of the Duvalier dictatorship, Aristide was a thirty-seven-year-old charismatic priest who had been active in Haitian human rights movements for many years. At the time of his election he had escaped at least three assassination attempts, one by uniformed soldiers. He has an obvious and perhaps volatile appeal to many segments of the Haitian population, especially the peasantry and the urban poor.

While attempting to reorganize military policy, Aristide was ousted by the army a little over seven months after he took office. The Organization of American States declared the new government to be illegitimate, and in November 1991 the United States imposed an embargo on Haiti demanding that the army allow a democratically elected government to take its place. Aristide has lived since his ouster mostly in the United States negotiating with the United States, the Organization of American States, and various power brokers in Haiti for his return to what can only be some limited form of presidential power.

Part of the current chaos no doubt comes from heightened expectations. After the ouster of the Duvalier regime a very wide variety of urban and rural groups attempted to develop a progressive government. Even peasants in some of the most isolated areas of Haiti came to think of the government not only as the cause of problems (the shortage of drinkable water, for example) but also as the source of possible solutions to such problems.

Haitian Social and Economic Life

Since political repression has traditionally resulted from the elite's exploitation of the rural farmers, an understanding of Haiti must include knowledge about the peasantry. About sixty-five percent of the labor force works in agriculture and only about seven percent in manufacturing (with one percent in construction and twenty-seven percent in other sectors).

The greatest accomplishment of the early Haitian nation was total land reform. Changing the country from a collection of slave-worked plantations to a nation of land-owning Black peasants involved, as I have stated, dividing the land among the former field slaves and their descendants. After these rural farmers received their small subsistence plots they wanted nothing further to do with the government, which they had always seen as being responsive to the slave owners. And, indeed, until very recently—beginning ironically with François Duvalier's efforts to court rural support—they have regarded the government as having little relevance to their lives. Another result of the land reform is that—in striking contrast to the rest of the Caribbean and Latin America—the largely mulatto elite, descended from the former house slaves or freed mulattoes, retreated to the cities and, with no land to their name, made its living from taxing peasant markets and the nation's imports and exports.

Peasant Farmers

In addition to constantly attempting to deflect a parasitical elite, the Haitian farmers face many problems, perhaps the most immediate being how to cope with small, scattered plots that are subdivided each generation. In addition, farmers often denude the land of trees to make charcoal for cooking fuel, lack capital to buy fertilizer, seeds, pesticides, and farm equipment, and are always dealing with increasing soil erosion. Since 1983 farmers have also had to deal with the loss of their major livestock population due to the total pig eradication project carried out by U.S. and international agencies after the discovery of African Swine Fever.

The peasants, however, do endure. Most of the people of Haiti, in fact, can be found living in scattered huts in villages loosely tied together by well-traveled trade routes. They organize their lives around a cluster of households composed of loosely related residents serving a particular Voodoo spirit under the guidance of the oldest male member. In the past there were also regional centers that had considerable importance culturally and commercially. Since the 1915–1934 U.S. occupation, however, Port-au-Prince has become a more important city that now dominates the country.

In his classic study of the peasant farmers of Mirebalais in central Haiti the anthropologist Melville J. Herskovits described a scene that rings true even today more than half a century after his fieldwork there in 1934:

> The small cultivator holds the center of the economic stage. In the main he works his own land, inherited from his father or acquired through purchase.... The life of the Haitian farmer, though hard, is simple and self-contained. With but few exceptions, he supplies all his necessities.... The day's work begins at dawn, the women rising before the men to prepare coffee.... When finished with his breakfast, the farmer goes to his field, where, except for the hottest hours, he works until sundown, his own meal being brought to him at about nine or ten o'clock in the morning. His wife meanwhile occupies herself with her household tasks, pounding grain in her mortar or working in her garden.... On market days she takes the produce of the family's fields to the town to sell. If she has young children, she cares for them while she does her other work, but when they are old enough, they help her about the house if they are girls, or, if boys, go with their father to the garden. From time to time, when house repairs are needed or there are implements to be mended, the man spends a day at home getting these odd jobs done.[9]

Rural Markets

The involvement of Haitian peasants with the wider world is through marketing. And it is women who usually market and make marketing decisions. As Herskovits wrote,

The woman, who is held to be more thrifty than the man, is thus the banker of the family. Her opinion is prized by her husband, and though a man has the legal right to dispose of a horse or a cow or his own land as he desires, in most households nothing would be done until the wife was consulted.[10]

The anthropologist Sidney Mintz has done the pioneering and still the best studies on Haitian markets, and he has pointed out that market women are "as typically Haitian as voodoo."[11] In fact, the market women and the bustling markets scattered all over the Haitian country are the very heart of the Haitian economy. These rural markets fill the roles of banks and warehouses; they operate as a socioeconomic network that moves the goods, as well as the gossip, that the people need in order to live materially and socially.

Haiti's primary products of coffee, sugar, rice, and cocoa have traditionally moved through these rural markets. Many Haitians also engage in part-time craft work, particularly in the manufacture of wood utensils, tools, and furniture. Haiti was, in fact, well-known for its fine mahogany carvings, and most of the products of the industrial arts were aimed at tourists. Due to the AIDS scare, however, the tourist trade declined drastically beginning in the early 1980s and declined to nearly zero following the sociopolitical instability after Duvalier's 1986 ouster.

Nonrural Markets

In recent history there has been a market for products from light manufacturing in Haiti, which has consisted largely of shoes, soap, flour, cement, and domestic oils. The industries owned by foreign interests produced items such as garments, toys, baseballs, and electronic goods almost exclusively for the U.S. market. This small-scale industrialization has, however, always been a minor part of the Haitian economic scene and has not added much to the national economy since the purpose of it is to supply cheap labor that the U.S. corporations can exploit. In addition, the instability of the government since 1986 has resulted in a number of these foreign-owned industries leaving Haiti. Those that had not left before November 1991 did leave during the imposition of the U.S. embargo during that month.

Family and Household

With the men in the fields and the women in the markets it may be stated—at the risk of oversimplification—that men handle the agricultural production and that women handle the produce of agriculture. The men who do the agriculture, however, usually do it for the women. In other words, the women depend on the men to have a product to sell, and the men depend on the women for domestic labor and marketing. The Haitian family structure, then, contains a great deal of gender complementarianism, as well as generational complementarianism; the children are seen as working for the parents. Growing out of these complementary roles and statuses is a complex system of mating, parenting, and day-to-day subsisting that is maintained through a variety of household arrangements.

Herskovits, in his classic anthropological ethnography, made the important clarification that "the word 'family' as employed in Haiti can be understood only in terms of a broader meaning than is given it in Europe and America…; the Haitian 'family' includes a wide range of relatives…on the sides of both parents."[12] It is, in fact, relatively rare that the small group of people contained in a household acts on its own without consulting with a large number of relatives.

The plantation system and the institution of slavery throughout the eighteenth and nineteenth centuries certainly did not encourage slaves to develop a legally recognized family institution, and the urban orientation of the republic reinforced the tendency of the peasants to avoid legal and church marriages. Consequently a wide variety of households exists, such as long-term co-residing couples, unions without formal sanction, couples who do not live together, fathers who do not participate actively in rearing their children, as well as, of course, conventional church weddings. In addition, the same man may simultaneously marry, maintain a consensual union in a second household of which he is the titular head, and conduct one or more relatively stable extraresidential affairs in which the women head the household. Women also may legitimately enter several different kinds of unions. As it turns out, then, children may be born to a married couple, to a married man with another woman, to a couple in a consensual union, to a mother not in union with any man, and so forth.

Due to the great variety of households, inheritance can be a troublesome problem. In general, all children from all the varieties of marriage have equal rights of inheritance, but, in practice, residence, contacts, and personal feelings play important roles. Since both adults and children change residences frequently, children have a variety of temporary residential rights and come into contact with a relatively large number of adults who may discipline and train them. In general, a great deal of emphasis is placed on respect for adults, who are quick to use corporal punishment in enforcing that respect.

Living in Chaos

Current Reports

In March 1993 a student of mine made a trip from Port-au-Prince to the interior regional center of Hinche. The 750-mile trip used to take about 2 hours. Due to the deterioration of the roads in Haiti, however, it took him six hours. Coming into Hinche he was stopped at five different military checkpoints, and he, his driver, and his vehicle were searched at each checkpoint. Hinche itself had no electricity and no running water. The people were afraid to use the water from wells and streams because there was no sewage treatment. He was told many stories of arrests, tortures, and the disappearance of numerous townspeople. He also mentioned to me that, as a sport, soldiers often aimed their jeeps at people in the streets and sped toward them, apparently killing one little girl.

A February 1993 report from the Chicago Religious Task Force Delegation to Haiti stated that a Mennonite Central Committee worker was detained because he carried pamphlets about Haiti Solidarity Week, a celebration scheduled for February 7 through February 13, marking the February 7, 1986, fall of the Duvalier regime and the February 7, 1991, inauguration of Aristide. The worker had to stand by helpless as his Haitian guide was beaten.

The same report noted that Gonaives, a city where Dessalines declared Haitian independence and also a city where the first anti-Duvalier protests took place, was heavily patrolled by the army. Arrests, torture, and violence were rampant there.

In January 1993 representatives from over fifteen international organizations concerned with human rights and refugee issues in Haiti met in Port-au-Prince to attend the International Colloquium on Human Rights. Colloquium participants strongly condemned the human rights violations by the Haitian military regime. The colloquium estimated that since the September 1991 military coup approximately three thousand Haitians have been killed, six thousand injured, forty thousand have fled by boat, and up to four hundred thousand have been internally displaced.

Personal Consequences

A newsletter published in Haiti by a coalition of grassroots democratic movements recently detailed a typical story of a delegate who was elected to the National Assembly in December 1990. Samuel Madistin, the twenty-nine-year-old son of a Protestant minister, was to represent about forty thousand citizens in the Artibonite Valley. After only a few months in office, he found the government taken over by the army. He stated, "Today we are witnessing an unimaginable situation. People are arrested, taken to jail, sometimes beaten to death. They are gravely injured, they lose their eyes, they are forced to eat their excrement. These are all things we have been witnessing for the past twelve months."[13]

In March 1992 when the Assembly convened to vote on the "Washington Accord," a compromise agreement between the legitimate government and the de facto military government, Madistin and others who were going to vote in favor of it were taken out of the Assembly room and beaten by soldiers. Since then Madistin has apparently been blacklisted by the military and is in hiding.

Conclusion

The elite of Haiti has always made its living through their control of the state apparatus, a situation that one contemporary Haitian scholar calls "state fetishism."[14] The new Black middle class,—largely a product, ironically, of François Duvalier's efforts to counter the old, mulatto elite—makes its living from mercantile, capitalist, and service enterprises. For the most part, this middle class has been politically neutral and socially silent throughout the recent upheavals.

Indeed, arguments about governance have mostly involved only a small number of members of the elite class. Although their college experiences may differ, members of the elite pretty much attend the same schools in Haiti and accept the same values. What divides them from the rest of the nation is the extremely unequal allocations of resources between rural regions (including the increasingly slum-like urban fringes) and downtown urban (and outer suburban areas); the elite is wealthy and the rest of the people are poor. Keeping the poor from claiming their fair share of the meager resources is what has led to sociopolitical repression. What divides the elite into seemingly arbitrary, and often competing, segments is their noncooperative efforts to gain individual and familial power.

This competition enjoyed a certain balance throughout most of Haitian history, but the supporting structure began, as we have seen, to collapse under Duvalier policies. At least four factors have recently come together that seem to lead to the chaos: (1) The various group and family elites have become increasingly smaller (with many members living abroad); (2) The resources of Haiti are increasingly limited, rural markets exhausted, and foreign aid virtually shut off; (3) The new Black, politically neutral middle class is trying to tap into these same finite resources (and expecting government services); and (4) The military has been left as the only existing instrument of government (and, for the most part, they neither desire nor are capable of governance).

My expectations for the future of Haiti are both optimistic and pessimistic. Haitians have survived incompetence, corruption, ignorance, the military, the greed of powerful neighbors, and even the machinations of their own elite; most of them will probably survive the current chaos. How long, however, will they have to yearn for their freedom?

Notes

1. John R. Beard, *The Life of Toussaint L'Ouverture: The Negro Patriot of Hayti* (1853; reprint Westport, CN: Negro Universities Press, 1970).

2. Leslie F. Manigat, *Haiti of the Sixties: Object of International Concern* (Washington, D.C.: Washington Center of Foreign Policy Research, 1964), p. 33.

3. Staff Report (Port-au-Prince: CPAU, 1992).

4. James Franklin, *The Present State of Hayti (Santo Domingo): With Remarks on Its Agriculture, Commerce, Laws, Religion, Finances, and Population* (1828; reprint London: Cass, 1971); Charles MacKenzie, *Notes on Haiti: Made During a Residence in that Republic*, 2 vols. (1830; reprint London: Cass, 1971); and Spenser St. John, *Hayti: Or the Black Republic* (London: Smith, Elder, 1884).

5. F. E. DuBois, "Call for Immigration," in James Redpath, ed., *A Guide to Hayti* (1861; reprint Westport, CN: Negro Universities Press, 1970), p. 99.

6. Robert Lawless, *Haiti's Bad Press: Origins, Development, and Consequences* (Rochester, VT: Schenkman, 1992), pp. 160–161.

7. Annick Billard, "Haiti: Hope, Return, Disillusion," *Refugees* 39 (1987): 16.

8. Susana Hayward, "Priest Becomes Haiti's First Freely Elected President," *Gainesville Sun,* February 8, 1991, p. 5A.

9. Melville J. Herskovits, *Life in a Haitian Valley* (New York: Knopf, 1937), pp. 67–68.

10. Ibid., p. 125.

11. Sidney W. Mintz, "Markets in Haiti," *New Society* 26 (1963): 18.

12. Herskovits, *Life in a Haitian Valley,* p. 123.

13. Staff, "Profile," *Haiti Info* 1, no. 2 (1992): 2.

14. Michael-Rolph Trouillot, *Haiti: State against Nation: The Origins and Legacy of Duvalierism* (New York: Monthly Review Press, 1990), p. 9.

Suggested Readings

Aristide, Jean-Bertrand. *In the Parish of the Poor: Writings from Haiti.* Maryknoll, NY: Oris, 1990. A revealing book by the charismatic priest who was popularly elected as president of Haiti.

Bellegarde-Smith, Patrick. *Haiti: The Breached Citadel.* Boulder. CO: Westview, 1990. A brilliant account of modern Haiti by a Haitian-American.

Brown, Karen McCarthy. *Mama Lola: A Vodou Priestess in Brooklyn.* Berkeley: University of California Press, 1991. A sympathetic reading of Voodoo.

Laguerre, Michel S. *Urban Life in the Caribbean: A Study of a Haitian Urban Community.* Cambridge, MA: Schenkman, 1982.

Nicholls, David. *From Dessalines to Duvalier: Race, Colour, and National Independence in Haiti.* Cambridge: Cambridge University Press, 1979. A contemporary account of the ideology of the Haitian elite.

Roumain, Jacques. *Masters of the Dew.* New York: Reynal and Hitchcock, 1944. The most famous novel written by a Haitian.

"HAITIANS: FROM POLITICAL REPRESSION TO CHAOS"

Robert Lawless

1) What significance does skin color play in Haiti in terms of political, economic, and social structure and functioning?

2) What is voodoo, and what purpose does it serve for most Haitians?

3) How has the history of Haiti influenced present-day politics?

4) Who were the Duvaliers and why were they important in Haitian political history?

5) Since the overthrow of the repressive regime, have conditions in Haiti improved?

6) Discuss the role of peasantry in Haitian economic and political life.

SECTION NINE

Family, Marriage, and Kinship

THE DISAPPEARANCE OF THE INCEST TABOO

Yéhudi Cohen

Several years ago a minor Swedish bureaucrat, apparently with nothing better to do, was leafing through birth and marriage records, matching people with their natural parents. To his amazement he found a full brother and sister who were married and had several children. The couple were arrested and brought to trial. It emerged that they had been brought up by separate sets of foster parents and never knew of each other's existence. By a coincidence reminiscent of a Greek tragedy, they met as adults, fell in love, and married, learning of their biological tie only after their arrest. The local court declared their marriage illegal and void.

The couple appealed the decision to Sweden's Supreme Court. After lengthy testimony on both sides of the issue, the court overturned the decision on the grounds that the pair had not been reared together. The marriage was declared legal and valid. In the wake of the decision, a committee appointed by Sweden's Minister of Justice to examine the question has proposed that criminal sanctions against incest be repealed. The committee's members were apparently swayed by Carl-Henry Alstrom, a professor of psychiatry. Alstrom argued that psychological deterrents to incest are stronger than legal prohibitions. The question will soon go to Sweden's Parliament, which seems prepared to follow the committee's recommendation.

Aside from illustrating the idea that the most momentous changes in human societies often occur as a result of unforeseen events, this landmark case raises questions that go far beyond Sweden's (or any other society's) borders. Some people may be tempted to dismiss the Swedish decision as an anomaly, as nothing more than a part of Sweden's unusual experiments in public welfare and sexual freedom.

But the probable Swedish decision to repeal criminal laws against incest cannot be regarded so lightly; this simple step reflects a trend in human society that has been developing for several thousand years. When we arrange human societies along a continuum from the least to the most complex, from those with the smallest number of interacting social groups to those with the highest number of groups, from those with the simplest technology to those with the most advanced technology, we observe that the incest taboo applies to fewer and fewer relatives beyond the immediate family.

Though there are exceptions, the widest extension of incest taboos beyond the nuclear family is found in the least complex societies. In a few societies, such as the Cheyenne of North America and the Kwoma of New Guinea, incest taboos extend to many remote relatives, including in-laws and the in-laws of in-laws. In modern industrial societies, incest taboos are usually confined to members of the immediate household. This contraction in the range of incest taboos is reaching the point at which they may disappear entirely.

The source of these changes in incest taboos lies in changing patterns of external trade. Trade is a society's jugular. Because every group lives in a milieu lacking some necessities that are available in other habitats, the flow of goods and resources is a society's lifeblood. But it is never sufficient merely to encourage people to form trade alliances with others in different areas. Incest taboos force people to marry outside their own group, to form alliances and to maintain trade networks. As other institutions— governments, business organizations—begin to organize trade, incest taboos become less necessary for assuring the flow of the society's lifeblood; they start to contract.

Other explanations of the incest taboo do not, under close examination, hold up. The most common assumption is that close inbreeding is biologically deleterious and will lead to the extinction of those who practice it. But there is strong evidence that inbreeding does not materially increase the rate of maladies such as albinism, total color blindness, or various forms of idiocy, which generally result when each parent carries the same recessive gene. In most cases these diseases result from chance combinations of recessive genes or from mutation.

According to Theodosius Dobzhansky, a geneticist, "The increase of the incidence of hereditary diseases in the offspring of marriages between relatives (cousins, uncle and niece or aunt and nephew, second cousins, etc.) over that in marriages between persons not known to be related is slight—so slight that geneticists hesitate to declare such marriages disgenic." Inbreeding does carry a slight risk. The progeny of relatives include more stillbirths and infant and early childhood deaths than the progeny of unrelated people. But most of these deaths are due to environmental rather than genetic factors. Genetic disadvantages are not frequent enough to justify a prohibition. Moreover, it is difficult to justify the biological explanation for incest taboos when many societies prescribe marriage to one cousin and prohibit marriage to another. Among the Lesu of Melanesia a man must avoid sexual contact with his parallel cousins, his mother's sisters' daughters and his father's brothers' daughters, but is supposed to marry his cross cousins, his mother's brothers' daughters and his father's sisters' daughters. Even though both types of cousins have the same genetic relationship to the man, only one kind is included in the incest taboo. The taboo is apparently a cultural phenomenon based on the cultural classification of people and cannot be explained biologically.

Genetic inbreeding may even have some advantages in terms of natural selection. Each time a person dies of a hereditary disadvantage, his detrimental genes are lost to the population. By such a process of genetic cleansing, inbreeding may lead to the elimination, or at least to reduced frequencies, of recessive genes. The infant mortality rate may increase slightly at first, but after the sheltered recessive genes are eliminated, the population may stabilize. In-breeding may also increase the frequency of beneficial recessive genes, contributing to the population's genetic fitness. In the end, inbreeding seems to have only a slight effect on the offspring and a mixed effect, some good and some bad, on the gene pool itself. This mild consequence hardly justifies the universal taboo on incest.

Another explanation of the incest taboo is the theory of natural aversion, first produced by Edward Westermarck in his 1891 book, *The History of Human Marriage.* According to Westermarck, children reared in the same household are naturally averse to having sexual relations with one another in adulthood. But this theory has major difficulties. First, it has a basic logical flaw: If there were a natural aversion to incest, the taboo would be unnecessary; As James Frazer pointed out in 1910, "It is not easy to see why any deep human instinct should need to be reinforced by law. There is no law commanding men to eat and drink or forbidding them to put their hands in the fire . . . The law only forbids men to do what their instincts incline them to do; what nature itself prohibits and punishes, it would be superfluous for the law to prohibit and punish . . . Instead of assuming, therefore, from the legal prohibition of incest that there is a natural aversion to incest, we ought rather to assume that there is a natural instinct in favor of it."

Second, the facts play havoc with the notion of natural aversion. In many societies, such as the Arapesh of New Guinea studied by Margaret Mead, and the Eskimo, young children are betrothed and raised together; usually by the boy's parents, before the marriage is consummated. Arthur Wolf, an anthropologist who studied a village in northern Taiwan, describes just such a custom: "Dressed in the traditional red wedding costume, the bride enters her future husband's home as a child. She is seldom more than three years of age and often less than a year . . . [The] last phase in the marriage process does not take place until she is old enough to fulfill the role of wife. In the meantime, she and her parents are affinally related to the groom's parents, but she is not in fact married to the groom."

One of the examples commonly drawn up to support Westermarck's theory of aversion is the Israeli *kibbutz,* where children who have been raised together tend to avoid marrying. But this avoidance has been greatly exaggerated. There is some tendency among those who have been brought up in the same age group in a communal "children's house" to avoid marrying one another, but this arises from two regulations that separate young adults from their *kibbutz* at about the age when they might marry. The first is a regulation of the Israel Defense Forces that no married woman may serve in the armed forces. Conscription for men and women is at 18, usually coinciding with their completion of secondary school, and military service is a deeply felt responsibility for most *kibbutz*-reared Israelis. Were women to marry prior to 18, they would be denied one of their principal goals. By the time they complete their military service, many choose urban spouses whom they have met in the army. Thus the probability of marrying a person one has grown up with is greatly reduced.

The second regulation that limits intermarriage on a *kibbutz* is a policy of the federations to which almost all *kibbutzim* belong. Each of the four major federations reserves the right to transfer any member to any other settlement, especially when a new one is being established. These "seeds," as the transferred members are called, are recruited individually from different settlements and most transfers are made during a soldier's third or fourth year of military service. When these soldiers leave the army to live on a *kibbutz,* they may be separated from those they were reared with. The frequency of marriage among people from working-class backgrounds who began and completed school together in an American city or town is probably higher than for an Israeli *kibbutz*; the proclivity among American college graduates to marry outside their neighborhoods or towns is no more an example of exogamy or incest avoidance than is the tendency in Israel *kibbutzim* to marry out.

Just as marriage within a neighborhood is accepted in the United States, so is marriage within a *kibbutz* accepted in Israel. During research I conducted in Israel between 1967 and 1969, I attended the wedding of two people in a *kibbutz* who supposedly were covered by this taboo or rule of avoidance. As my tape recordings and photographs show, it would be difficult to imagine a more joyous occasion. When I questioned members of the *kibbutz* about this, they told me with condescending smiles that they had "heard of these things the professors say."

A third, "demographic," explanation of the incest taboo was originally set forth in 1960 by Wilson Wallis and elaborated in 1959 by Mariam Slater. According to this theory, mating within the household, especially between parents and children, was unlikely in early human societies because the life span in these early groups was so short that by the time offspring were old enough to mate, their parents would probably have died. Mating between siblings would also have been unlikely because of the average of eight years between children that resulted from breast feeding and high rates of infant mortality. But even assuming this to have been true for the first human societies, there is nothing to prevent mating among the members of a nuclear family when the life span is lengthened.

A fourth theory that is widely subscribed to focuses on the length of the human child's parental dependency, which is the longest in the animal kingdom. Given the long period required for socializing children, there must be regulation of sexual activity so that children may learn their proper role. If the nuclear family's members are permitted to have unrestricted sexual access to one another, the members of the unit would be confused about their roles. Parental authority would be undermined, and it would be impossible to socialize children. This interpretation has much to recommend it as far as relationships between parents and children are concerned, but it does not help explain brother-sister incest taboos or the extension of incest taboos to include remote relatives.

The explanation closest to my interpretation of the changes in the taboo is the theory of alliance advocated by the French anthropologist Claude Levi-Strauss, which suggests that people are compelled to marry outside their groups in order to form unions with other groups and promote harmony among them. A key element in the theory is that men ex-change their sisters and daughters in marriage with men of other groups. As originally propounded, the theory of alliance was based on the assumption that men stay put while the women change groups by marrying out, moved about by men like pieces on a chessboard. But there are many instances in which the women stay put while the men change groups by marrying out. In either case, the result is the same. Marriage forges alliances.

These alliances freed early human societies from exclusive reliance on their own limited materials and products. No society is self-sustaining or self-perpetuating; no culture is a world unto itself. Each society is compelled to trade with others and this was as true for tribal societies as it is for modern industrial nations. North America, for instance, was crisscrossed with elaborate trade networks before the Europeans arrived. Similar trade networks covered aboriginal New Guinea and Australia. In these trade networks, coastal or riverline groups gave shells and fish to hinterland people in exchange for cultivated foods, wood, and manufactured items.

American Indian standards of living were quite high before the Europeans destroyed the native trade networks, and the same seems to have been true in almost all other parts of the world. It will come as no surprise to economists that the material quality of people's lives improves to the extent that they engage in external trade.

But barter and exchange do not automatically take place when people meet. Exchange involves trust, and devices are needed to establish trust, to distinguish friend from foe, and to assure a smooth, predictable flow of trade goods. Marriage in the tribal world established permanent obligations and reciprocal rights and privileges among families living in different habitats.

For instance, when a young Cheyenne Indian man decided on a girl to marry, he told his family of his choice. If they agreed that his selection was good, they gathered a store of prized possessions—clothing, blankets, guns, bows and arrows—and carefully loaded them on a fine horse. A friend of the family, usually a respected old woman, led the horse to the tepee of the girl's elder brother. There the go-between spread the gifts for everyone to see while she pressed the suitor's case. The next step was for the girl's brother to assemble all his cousins for a conference to weigh the proposal. If they agreed to it, the cousins distributed the gifts among themselves, the brother taking the horse. Then the men returned to their tepees to find suitable gifts to give in return. Within a day or two, each returned with something roughly equal in value to what he had received. While this was happening, the bride was made beautiful. When all arrangements were completed, she mounted one horse while the return gifts were loaded on another. The old woman led both horses to the groom's camp. After the bride was received, her accompanying gifts were distributed among the groom's relatives in accordance with what each had given. The exchanges between the two families did not end with the marriage ceremony, however; they continued as a permanent part of the marriage ties. This continual exchange, which took place periodically, is why the young man's bridal choice was so important for his entire family.

Marriage was not the only integral part of external trade relationships. Another was ritualized friendship, "blood brotherhood," for example. Such bonds were generally established between members of different groups and were invariably trade partnerships. Significantly, these ritualized friendships often included taboos against marriage with the friend's sisters; sometimes the taboo applied to all their close relatives. This extension of a taboo provides an important key for understanding all incest taboos. Sexual prohibitions do not necessarily grow out of biological ties. Both marriage and ritualized friendships in primitive societies promote economic alliances and both are associated with incest taboos.

Incest taboos force people into alliances with others in as many groups as possible. They promote the greatest flow of manufactured goods and raw materials from the widest variety of groups and ecological niches and force people to spread their social nets. Looked at another way, incest taboos prevent localism and economic provincialism; they block social and economic inbreeding.

Incest taboos have their widest extensions outside the nuclear family in those societies in which technology is least well developed and in which people have to carry their own trade goods for barter or exchange with members of other groups. Often in these small societies, everyone in a community is sexually taboo to the rest of the group. When the technology surrounding trade improves and shipments of goods and materials can be concentrated (as when people learn to build and navigate oceangoing canoes or harness pack animals), fewer and fewer people have to be involved in trade. As this happens, incest taboos begin to contract, affecting fewer and fewer people outside the nuclear family.

This process has been going on for centuries. Today, in most industrial societies, the only incest taboos are those that pertain to members of the nuclear family. This contraction of the range of the taboo is inseparable from the fact that we no longer engage in personal alliances and trade agreements to get the food we eat, the clothes we wear, the tools and materials we use, the fuels on which we depend. Goods are brought to distribution points near our homes by a relatively tiny handful of truckers, shippers, merchants, entrepreneurs, and others. Most of us are only vaguely aware of the alliances, negotiations, and relationships that make this massive movement of goods possible. When we compare tribal and contemporary industrialized societies, the correspondence between the range of incest taboos and the material conditions of life cannot be dismissed as mere coincidence.

Industrialization does not operate alone in affecting the degree to which incest taboos extend beyond the nuclear family. In the history of societies, political institutions developed as technology advanced. Improvements in packaging and transportation have led not only to reductions in the number of people involved in external trade, but also to greater and greater concentrations of decision making in the hands of fewer and fewer people. Trade is no longer the responsibility of all members of a society, and the maintenance of relationships between societies has become the responsibility of a few people—a king and his bureaucracy, impersonal governmental agencies, national and multinational corporations.

To the extent that trade is conducted and negotiated by a handful of people, it becomes unnecessary to use incest taboos to force the majority of people into alliances with other groups. Treaties, political alliances, and negotiations by the managers of a few impersonal agencies have replaced marital and other personal alliances. The history of human societies suggests that incest taboos may have outlived their original purpose.

But incest taboos still serve other purposes. For social and emotional reasons rather than economic ones, people in modern industrial societies still need to prevent localism. Psychological well-being in a diversified society depends largely on the ability to tap different ideas, points of view, life styles, and social relationships. The jugulars that must now be kept open by the majority of people may no longer be for goods and resources, but for variety and stimulation. This need for variety is what, in part, seems to underlie the preference of Israelis to marry outside the communities in which they were born and brought up. The taboo against sex within the nuclear family leads young people to explore, to seek new experiences. In a survey of a thousand cases of incest, Christopher Bagley found that incestuous families are cut off from their society's social and cultural mainstream. Whether rural or urban, he writes, "the family seems to with draw from the general community, and initiates its own 'deviant' norms of sexual behavior, which are contained within the family circle." "Such a family," he continues, "is an isolated cultural unit, relatively untouched by external social norms." This social and cultural inbreeding is the cause of the profound malaise represented by incest.

To illustrate the correspondence between incest and social isolation, let me describe an incestuous family reported by Peter Wilson, an anthropologist. Wilson sketched a sequence of events in which a South American family became almost totally isolated from the community in which it lived, and began to practice almost every variety of incest. The decline into incest began many years before Wilson appeared on the scene to do anthropological research, when the father of five daughters and four sons made the girls (who ranged in age from 18 to 33) sexually available to some sailors for a small sum of money. As a result, the entire household was ostracized by the rest of the village. "But most important," Wilson writes, "the Brown family was immediately cut off from sexual partners. No woman would have anything to do with a Brown man; no man would touch a Brown woman."

The Brown's isolation and incest continued for several years, until the women in the family rebelled—apparently because a new road connecting their hamlet to others provided the opportunity for social contact with people outside the hamlet. At the same time the Brown men began working in new light industry in the area and spending their money in local stores. The family slowly regained some social acceptance in Green Fields, the larger village to which their hamlet belonged. Little by little they were reintegrated into the hamlet and there seems to have been no recurrence of incest among them.

A second example is an upper middle class, Jewish urban American family that was described to me by a colleague. The Erva family (a pseudonym) consists of six people—the parents, two daughters aged 19 and 22, and two sons, aged 14 and 20. Mr. Erva is a computer analyst and his wife a dentist. Twenty-five years ago, the Ervas seemed relatively normal, but shortly after their first child was born, Mr. and Mrs. Erva took to wandering naked about their apartment, even when others were present. They also began dropping in on friends for as long as a week; their notion of reciprocity was to refuse to accept food, to eat very little of what was offered them, or to order one member of their family not to accept any food at all during a meal. Their rationale seemed to be that accepting food was receiving a favor, but

occupying a bed was not. This pattern was accompanied by intense family bickering and inadvertent insults to their hosts. Not surprisingly, most of their friends wearied of their visits and the family was left almost friendless.

Reflecting Bagley's general description of incestuous families, the Ervas had withdrawn from the norms of the general community after the birth of their first child and had instituted their own "deviant" patterns of behavior. They thereby set the stage for incest.

Mr. Erva began to have intercourse with his daughters when they were 14 and 16 years old. Neither of them was self-conscious about the relationship and it was common for the father to take both girls into bed with him at the same time when they were visiting overnight. Mrs. Erva apparently did not have intercourse with her sons. The incest became a matter of gossip and added to the family's isolation.

The Erva family then moved to the Southwest to start over again. They built a home on a parcel of land that had no access to water. Claiming they could not afford a well of their own, the family began to use the bathrooms and washing facilities of their neighbors. In the end these neighbors, too, wanted nothing to do with them.

Mr. and Mrs. Erva eventually separated, he taking the daughters and she the sons. Later the younger daughter left her father to live alone, but the older daughter still shares a one bedroom apartment with her father.

Social isolation and incest appear to be related, and social maturity and a taboo on incest are also related. Within the modern nuclear family, social and emotional relationships are intense, and sexuality is the source of some of the strongest emotions in human life. When combined with the intensity of family life, sexually stimulated emotions can be overwhelming for children. Incest taboos are a way of limiting family relationships. They are assurances of a degree of emotional insularity, of detachment on which emotional maturity depends.

On balance, then, we can say that legal penalties for incest were first instituted because of the adverse economic effects of incestuous unions on society, but that today the negative consequences of incest affect only individuals. Some will say that criminal penalties should be retained if only to protect children. But legal restraints alone are unlikely to serve as deterrents. Father-daughter incest is regarded by many social workers, judges, and psychiatrists as a form of child abuse, but criminal penalties have not deterred other forms of child abuse. Moreover, incest between brothers and sisters cannot be considered child abuse. Some have even suggested that the concept of abuse may be inappropriate when applied to incest. "Many psychotherapists," claims psychologist James McCary in *Human Sexuality*, "believe that a child is less affected by actual incest than by seductive behavior on the part of a parent that never culminates in any manifest sexual activity."

Human history suggests that the incest taboo may indeed be obsolete. As in connection with changing attitudes toward homosexuality, it may be maintained that incestuous relations between consenting mature adults are their concern alone and no one else's. At the same time, however, children must be protected. But questions still remain about how they should be protected and until what age.

If a debate over the repeal of criminal laws against incest is to begin in earnest, as it surely will if the Swedish Parliament acts on the proposed reversal, one other important fact about the social history of sexual behavior must be remembered. Until about a century ago, many societies punished adultery and violations of celibacy with death. When it came time to repeal those laws, not a few people favored their retention on the grounds that extramarital sexual relationships would adversely affect the entire society. Someday people may regard incest in the same way they now regard adultery and violations of celibacy. Where the threat of punishment once seemed necessary, social and emotional dissuasion may now suffice.

References

Bagley Christopher, "Incest Behavior and Incest Taboos," *Social Problems*, Vol. 16, 1969, pp. 505–519.

Birdsell, J.B., *Human Evolution: An Introduction to the New Physical Anthropology*, Rand McNally. 1972.

Bischof, Norbert, "The Biological Foundations of the Incest Taboo," *Social Science Information*, Vol. 11, No. 6, 1972.

Fox, Robin, *Kinship and Marriage*, Penguin Books, 1968.

Slater, Mariam, "Ecological Factors in the Origin of Incest," *American Anthropologist*, Vol. 61, No. 6, 1959.

Wilson, Peter J., "Incest: A Case Study," *Social and Economic Studies*, Vol. 12,1961, pp. 200–209.

"THE DISAPPEARANCE OF THE INCEST TABOO"

Yéhudi Cohen

1) What is the incest taboo, and what relatives does it cover?

2) What are the various theories suggested to explain the origin of the incest taboo, and what are their strengths and weaknesses?

3) Cohen suggests that incest taboos force people to forge alliances. What purposes do such alliances serve in human culture?

4) What are the major problems caused by incest, in Cohen's view?

5) Why does Cohen suggest that the need for the incest taboo is disappearing? Do you agree or disagree with his thesis and conclusions?

NAYARS: TRADITION AND CHANGE IN MARRIAGE AND FAMILY[1]

N. Prabha Unnithan

Anthropologists and sociologists have often remarked on the unique features of marriage and family during the nineteenth century among the Nayars, a caste group who inhabit what is now the state of Kerala in southwestern India.[2] Social scientists describe the Nayars of old as an "exception" to general definitions of marriage and family because sex was separated from economic relations in marriage.[3] Among certain regional Nayar communities, a woman did not have a "regular" husband and a man usually did not help much to support his wife and children. In recent times, however, many changes have taken place that have blurred and even overturned those distinctive features of former domestic life.[4]

In this reading, the Nayars as a group are described in historical, geographic, and cultural terms. The traditional and current forms of Nayar marriage, family, and household arrangements are discussed in detail so that changes that have taken place can be identified. Most of these changes occurred in the late nineteenth and twentieth centuries, and in a final section I discuss the factors that brought change about. I begin, however, with a personal note.

I am a Nayar, but I was born and brought up in Malaysia where my parents had migrated to before the Second World War. Other than the language we spoke at home (Malayalam, the language of Kerala) my childhood and family life in multi-ethnic Malaysia carried no trace of anything systematically different from that of other immigrant families from India (mainly from the states of Tamil Nadu and Andhra Pradesh). On a visit to India as a ten-year-old, it appeared to me that my mother and I were spending more time at her family *taravad* (ancestral home based on descent group), which was described to me as "my home." I preferred my father's place where there were more children of my age but I remember suggestions from my mother's family that I did not "really belong" to my father's family. I thus recall wondering why my two brothers and I were encouraged to identify more with my mother's family and my maternal uncles. At the time, I thought this was be-cause there were more members of my mother's family among those who had migrated to Malaysia.

My first perception of the uniqueness of my heritage came as a college student in other parts of India in the 1970s. Visiting Kerala for extended periods of vacation time, reading a series about the various communities of India (including the Nayars) carried by a leading magazine, *The Illustrated Weekly of India,* and discussing similarities and differences among various states and groups of India with students of anthropology (I was a criminology major) formed my first exposure to the exceptional traditions of the Nayars. What I learned awoke a degree of curiosity that led me to read as much as possible about the Nayars, and to discuss these matters with other Nayars. This interest was sustained and enhanced after coming to the United States. My wife and I discovered we could attract the respectful and fascinated attention of any anthropologist around by merely stating that we were Nayars. However, as a criminologist/sociologist my own background has not been particularly relevant even in semi-autobiographical writing[5] and this is the first time I have explored it professionally. Thus I hope that the combination of familiarity and distance (in both personal and professional senses) that I bring to these issues will help illuminate this fascinating topic.

Kerala and the Nayar

Evans-Pritchard declares, "The people of Kerala in South Western India are amongst the most fascinating ethnic groups of the world. Their traditional claim to anthropological eminence rested on the once flourishing institution of matriliny among the Nayars and a special ritual bond of caste between the Nambudiri Brahmins and the martial Nayars."[6] The Indian state of Kerala where these groups have traditionally lived has a history and culture that "is one of the major streams that have enriched the composite culture of the country."[7]

Kerala is a state that was created in 1956 on the basis of a common language among its inhabitants following the linguistic reorganization of states in India. It immediately gained prominence when in 1957 the local Communist Party was elected to form the state government, the first time that this had happened anywhere in the non-Communist world.[8] Besides for its scenic beauty, in recent times Kerala has attracted attention because of its performance on various indicators of "development." Remarkably, for a state with significant levels of poverty and unemployment, it has achieved high rates of life expectancy and literacy combined with low rates of birth and infant mortality.[9]

Geographically, Kerala consists of "a long fish-shaped land squeezed between"[10] the thickly forested Western Ghats on the east and a 360-mile coastline on the Arabian Sea on the west. The resulting geographic isolation from the rest of the Indian sub-continent and extensive contact with other countries across the seas have facilitated the growth of a distinctive culture. For example, at various times, Christianity, Judaism, and Islam have all found a home in Kerala; and trade with Greek, Roman, and Arab states has been historically documented.

Kerala's geography also provided a religio-mythical rationale for the ritual bond between Nayars and Nambudiris that Evans-Pritchard commented on.[11] Jeffrey describes the creation of Kerala according to Brahminical tradition as resulting from:

> . . . the banishment from India of the god Parasurama. Having nowhere to live, he won the permission of Varuna, the god of the sea, to reclaim all the land within a throw of his axe. Parasurama threw his axe from Cape Comorin to Gokarnam, the sea receded and Kerala was formed. To populate the new area, Parasurama introduced a special race of Brahmins, the Nambudiris, and gave them ownership of all the land and unique customs which prevented their return to the India on the other side of the Western Ghats. Next, he brought Sudras—the Nayars —to act as servants and bodyguards of the Nambudiris. He bestowed on the Nayars the *marumakkattayam* or matrilineal system of family and inheritance, and decreed that Nayars should have no formal marriage and that their women should always be available to satisfy the desires of the Nambudiris.[12]

Jeffrey considers this legend to be an attempt to justify the most important features of the seventeenth century social structure of certain areas of Kerala.[13] Namboodiripad however, dismisses it as "obviously invented" by those who benefited from it.[14] This legend illustrates the point that unlike the caste stratifi-

cation system (based on birth/occupation) of the rest of India the traditional configuration in Kerala had different connotations and consequences. Traditionally, Hindu society has been divided into four major categories. The Brahmins were priests and pursued religious learning; the Kshatriyas were soldiers and kings; the Vaisyas were traders, and the Sudras performed various occupations of service to the castes above them. In Kerala, the Nayars, although Sudras, also carried out the functions of Vaisyas and Kshatriyas.

Before I describe the place of the Nayars in the traditional caste structure of Kerala, one further characteristic of various regions of Kerala needs to be pointed out. In the scholarly literature and based on traditional descriptions, Kerala has been divided into three major geographic/cultural areas: North Kerala, Central Kerala, and South Kerala.[15] Nayar marriage, family and kinship patterns have varied roughly along these regional lines. Politically, during the period of British domination of India, most of North Kerala was directly controlled by the British government in Madras, while Central and South Kerala operated as kingdoms that were (nominally independent) British protectorates.

The traditional Hindu caste system of Kerala, which Puthenkulam refers to as "the citadel of caste rigidity and orthodoxy," came into being around the tenth century and is extremely complicated.[16] Woodcock comments, "There were no less than five hundred castes and sub-castes, divided from each other by rigorous rules against inter-marriage and by an extraordinary pattern of pollution taboos."[17] He goes on to identify the nine principal categories, in descending order, in the caste hierarchy as follows:[18]

1. Brahmins, the priestly caste (originally only Nambudiris, but by extension Brahmins who migrated from neighboring states);
2. Kshatriyas, the rulers (mainly members of a few kingly families of the smaller kingdoms from which Kerala was formed);
3. Ambalavasis, the temple attendants and musicians (believed to be a pre-Brahmin priesthood);
4. Samantans, the local chieftains;
5. Nayars, the traditional warriors and feudal landholders;
6. Kammalans, the artisans and craftsmen (believed to have migrated from the Tamil areas east of the Ghats);
7. Ezhavas, originally those who tapped toddy from palm trees, but subsequently agrarian tenants;
8. Mukkuvans, the fisherman castes; and

9. the "outcastes," such as astrologers, washermen, and agricultural laborers (who toiled under conditions of servitude for the Nayars).

The historical and contemporary significance of Nayars in Kerala can be understood when we consider the following. The Nayars were "simultaneously the backbone of the military system, stratum of the cultivating population and did service to the Brahmin and ruling families."[19] The nominal Kshatriyas and the Samantans identified above are also thought to have originally been Nayars. The Nayars dominated Kerala earlier through force as "a class of professional warriors who developed to a high level the art of swordsmanship, who formed themselves at time of battle into suicide squads"[20] in the service of various kings and local chieftains.[21] More recently, their importance is based on ownership of land and distribution all across Kerala. Historically, the Nambudiri Brahmins were "never more than a thin insecure top crust on society."[22]

Traditional Nayar Marriage, Family, and Kinship Patterns

Rules of descent connect individuals with particular sets of kin because of a presumed common ancestry. Traditionally, Nayars with minor exceptions were matrilineal (*marumakkatayam* or, literally descent traced through sister's children). This meant that in terms of succession the females carried the family name and their children also had claims to family property. In contrast the Nambudiri Brahmins were patrilineal (*makkatayam* or, literally descent traced through own children); males carried the family name and their children were the ones who had claims to the family property.

Among the Nayars, two patterns of marriage and family life have been identified. In Central Kerala and the upper region of South Kerala, the first and (to social scientists) more well-known pattern was practiced. Here, every Nayar girl before puberty underwent a *talikettu-kalyanam* (literally, *tali*-tying ceremony) as part of an elaborate celebration, which Fuller indicates died out in the 1920s.[23] Following a short period of seclusion (supposedly indicating menstruation) a *tali* (a small leaf-shaped locket worn on a string or gold chain) was tied around the girl's neck by an "adult male who is a member of a superior caste, an unrelated member of the same caste, a cross-cousin, an aunt or the shaman of a local goddess."[24] Among Hindus in other parts of India the tali indicated that a woman was married. This ceremony was followed by the girl and the man who tied the tali spending a short time (hours or days) together after which they separated. There were no sexual connotations to this event. A lively debate exists in the anthropological literature as to what the talikettu-kalyanam meant.[25] Recent views appear to be that it should be considered an elaborate prepuberty rite of passage rather than (as previously thought) a form of sham marriage and divorce (between the girl and the man who tied the tali) or a full-dress marriage rehearsal.

Some time following the talikettu-kalyanam, when the female in question had attained maturity, she became eligible to form more or less permanent sexual relationships with other men each known as *sambandham* (literally, alliance). Puthenkulam defines it as "the socially recognized alliance constituting matrimony among matrilineals."[26] The sam-bandham was initiated without elaborate associated ritual. A proposal from either the parents or friends of either sambandham partner was followed by consultations with the *karanavan* (the eldest male who usually was the head) of each ancestral home (taravad). Males eligible to be considered had to be of equivalent or higher caste status. On an auspicious day, the man went in procession to the woman's house followed by a brief ceremony with minimal religious connotations. The couple then spent the night together and the man left for his taravad in the morning. A gift of clothes for the woman was sent by the man's family if this was not a part of the ceremony. A woman could consent to receive several men as sambandham partners with the approval of the head of her taravad although it is highly unlikely a separate ceremony was held each time. The various partners took turns visiting the Nayar woman at night. At the same time, men in that woman's taravad would be visiting their own sambandham partners. The men were also permitted to have more than one sambandham partner but the children of such unions belonged in the mother's taravad. The man and woman in a sambandham partnership did not live together and the man did not have any say in the upbringing of his biological children.

Ceremonial gifts such as clothes, betel-nut as well as hair and bath oil were given by the man to his sambandham partner during important festivals. The only other obligation of the man to his sambandham partner was to acknowledge paternity of his children and to assume a minimal portion of the expenses of the midwife during the delivery. The relationship could be broken off at any time by either partner without any formality.

In attempting to account for this rather unique form of marriage, anthropologists have observed that there is symmetry between the Nayar matrilineal and

Nambudiri Brahmin patrilineal systems. In most Nambudiri *illams* (the equivalent of the Nayar taravads), only the oldest son was allowed to marry (sometimes, and particularly if no male heir was born, he could marry more than one wife) and inherit property so that ancestral land and wealth would not be sub-divided away. Thus, younger Nambudiri men were allowed to form sambandhams with Nayar women who were lower in caste status. At the same time, given the matrilineality of the Nayars, these Nambudiri men had no responsibility towards their biological children or their Nayar sambandham partners. The Nayar taravad in question gained some status in being associated with Brahmins (and by extension, Kshatriya upper castes) although the Nambudiri Brahmin community considered the relationship nothing more than concubinage. This explanation comes close to suggesting that matrilineality was a system imposed on the Nayars by the Nambudiris for the latter's convenience. However, as the Nambudiris were historically a small minority, their ability to impose cultural patterns would have been limited. Further, such an imposition if true could have affected only a small proportion of Nayar families whose female members would be needed as sexual partners.

Fuller suggests that this form of marriage, "developed in response to the problems caused by their [Nayars'] military role."[27] Matrilineality and sambandhams can also be viewed as solving some of the problems of soldiers and mercenaries who had to be away from home for extended periods of time and who could die in battle. This form of marriage "inhibited the development of close attachments between Nayar men and women in their native villages and, at the same time, permitted them sexual access to Nayar women throughout the land."[28]

The second and less well-known pattern of marriage and family life was practiced mainly in North Kerala.[29] Here the talikettu-kalyanam was not considered an important rite although it was carried out. The sambandham relationship was similar to Hindu marriages in other parts of India and was meant to be a stable one. Gough describes the ceremony as follows:

> The giving of the cloth by the husband which marked the start of a sambandham was carried out with ceremony in the girl's ancestral house and was the occasion for a large feast to relatives of both parties. After the marriage had been consummated in the girl's house the couple were ceremonially conducted to the bridegroom's taravad and the girl was formally received into it by her husband's mother and his karanavan's wife.[30]

The man and woman lived together in his matrilineal taravad along with his brothers and all of their children or the woman would live in a separate house with her own children where she would be visited by her husband. In the latter case, the man split his time between both houses. Women who were divorced or widowed moved back to their own taravad where they (and their married sisters who may have been living elsewhere) retained property rights. Divorce and remarriage were permitted but rare.

The two traditional patterns described above are somewhat simplified and not quite as clearcut in terms of regions. Apparently, many local or minor variations—such as preference for cross-cousin sambandham, and a few cases of brothers having a common wife—existed.[31] What did not vary as far as Nayar families were concerned were three features. First, there was matrilineality of descent and inheritance, whereby female members and their (both male and female) children possessed property rights; the children of male members did not have such rights. Second, there was a professed identification with one's own taravad whose members were considered blood relatives (this obviously excluded the father's family who belonged to a different taravad) and were therefore ineligible to marry each other. Finally, a great deal of importance was attached to the whims and wishes of the eldest male karanavan who acted as head, manager as well as representative (in public) of the taravad.[32]

In comparison to other Hindus, the traditional arrangements of Nayars provided relatively greater freedom and status for their female members. Women had a say in consenting to the initiation or termination of marriage relationships. Children, as long as their paternity had been acknowledged, had to be taken care of by their taravad. Property rights were guaranteed for females. A certain amount of respect for women and "intensity of concern for mothers and sisters"[33] as carriers of the taravad name existed among Nayar men. At the same time, under most circumstances all of the above depended on the responsible management of taravad affairs by the karanavan and the good graces of other older males.

Contemporary Nayar Marriage, Family, and Kinship

A number of factors that affected Kerala and its people in the nineteenth and early twentieth centuries (to be discussed in detail later) resulted in the dying out or extreme modification of the ceremonies, marriage patterns, and family relationships described above. In this section, I will describe the current versions of these practices so that a sharp contrast can be made with the traditional forms. The contemporary situation can be summarized as including a decline in identification with the taravad; the expansion and increased importance attached to the sambandham ceremony; and the second also signifying an almost absolute conversion by Nayars to the ideal of a "strong" or stable monogamous marriage.

The Decline of the Taravad

One of Puthenkulam's respondents remarked that with regard to family relationships and descent, Nayars "had left the mother's house but have not yet reached the father's home."[34] This implies that while the transition to a more patrilineal system is ongoing, there continue to linger remnants of identification with matrilineality and the taravad. A number of manifestations of this state of transition can be identified.

The most remarkable of these is the changed nature of property ownership within the taravad. Property used to be held jointly by the taravad and administered by the eldest male in the matrilineal group (the karanavan). It was difficult, though not impossible, for the property to be divided against the wishes of the *karanavan* and older males in the matrilineal family. Historically, in the nineteenth and early twentieth centuries a number of reports and court cases accusing karanavans of financial mismanagement, extravagance, waste and transfer of property on the sly to their own children came up. This led to more legal equality among members of a taravad with regard to property. Now, such property is owned jointly by individual members who may ask for their share of it on attaining adulthood. Puthenkulam notes that given the legal bias towards individual property division, "it is not surprising that the vast majority of Nayar taravads have made use of it and partitioned their taravads."[35] Thus ancestral property that belonged to my own taravad through my maternal grandmother has been subdivided as follows: roughly equally among eleven people, her seven children (my mother, her sister and five brothers) and the four grandchildren of her two daughters (my two brothers, me, and a cousin-sister, who is my mother's sister's surviving daughter). Note that matrilineality continues with the children of female members receiving shares, while those of male members do not. Often even unborn babies of pregnant women are given shares in the property. This arrangement pertains only to taravad property. Obviously, after a few generations of division and sub-division and given

the increasing role of the father in Nayar households, there is not likely to be any matrilineal property left. Individual property owned by a father is now divided equally among his sons and daughters, where previously it would have reverted back to the father's matrilineal taravad.

A second measure of the decline of the taravad can be found in the increased influence of the father in the affairs of his children and the corresponding decrease in that of the karanavan. Or as Puthenkulam puts it, "The father has come to his own and the karanavan has been supplanted."[36] Previously, as noted, children had very little to do with their fathers. They may have not even seen much of him, particularly if he continued to live in his own taravad, and only visited at night. Given the changed pattern of residence and consequent economic arrangements, this is perhaps inevitable. Still, certain attachments to the karanavan and/or mother's brother continue. For example, my older brother spent much of his childhood with one of my maternal uncles who also lived in Malaysia (because better educational facilities were available nearby). My uncle was accepting of his guardianship role, and this was accepted by others in the extended family as "proper."

Finally, consider the current expectation regarding residence following marriage. It is assumed now that the wife will move permanently into her husband's home and live there along with any children that may ensue. In terms of the transitional state of Nayar customs, ironically, the house she moves into may sometimes be his ancestral taravad. A married son may thus bring his wife to live with his parents if he cannot afford a separate home. With employment opportunities mainly in the more urbanized areas of Kerala, elsewhere in India or abroad, the couple is more likely to establish a new residence apart from kin (neolocal residence). Thus, the nuclear family I was a member of (my parents, brothers and myself) lived in Malaysia where my father found employment in rubber plantations in the 1930s. Similarly, my wife, our two children and I live together in the United States. Neither of these middle and late twentieth century living arrangements is looked upon as anything unusual among Nayars today.

However, the influence of the taravad does persist in some matters. First, it continues to be expected and followed that Nayars take their surnames from their mother's side of the nuclear family and often also include their taravad name. Clearly, this is an expectation that I have violated. For purposes of convenience (having spent a large part of my life in patrilineal or bilateral descent societies and not being very good at snappy explanations of my matrilineal heritage) I have taken my father's surname (Unnithan) rather than my mother's (Nair); and I also do not use the name of my taravad (Payanimvilayil). This has led to rather bemused questioning among some of my relatives as to how and when I had turned into an Unnithan!

Second, although supplanted otherwise, the karanavan continues to command formal and deferential respect. For example, it is expected that his nephews and nieces stand, as a mark of respect, in his presence. His formal consent is sought on matters involving younger siblings, nephews and nieces. He is the first to be invited for weddings and often presides over family ceremonies. The honor accorded to the karanavan in contemporary times can be viewed as resulting from a combination of expectations: remnants of the Nayar past and traditional Indian respect for elders.

The Expansion and Importance of the Sambandham

Both Fuller and Puthenkulam suggest that the word sambandham is not in use anymore to describe Nayar marriage, because of what many reformers from within the community felt was its "immoral" connotations.[37] I continue to hear it used, though less often than *vivaham* (originally, the Nambudiri Brahmin word for wedding) and *kalyanam* (literally, ceremony). While the talikettu-kalyanam and associated rituals have all but disappeared, those surrounding the sambandham have expanded. However, in comparison to marriage ceremonies of other Hindu groups, that of the present-day Nayars tends to be very short and simple.

The actual marriage ceremony is the culmination of a number of steps taken in advance that represent a close approximation of what social scientists have described as the "arranged" form of marriage. Marriages based on notions of romantic love do take place but are to a large extent subject to family approval. Marriages are mostly intra-caste, with marriages to upper (including Nambudiris) and lower castes rare. The preference for intra-caste marriage often causes middle-class Nayar families to look for potential partners in places far beyond the local village or district. Photographs of "eligible" young men and women are exchanged utilizing professional matchmakers or friends and relatives to see if there is any interest on either side in a potential sambandham. Horoscopes are matched to consider whether the couple is astrologically compatible. The young man may make a short visit to the woman's home along with his relatives for what is referred to as a *pennukaanal* (liter-

ally, seeing the young woman). Based on the consent of both the young man and woman and their respective families, arrangements are made for the wedding ceremony itself. Often a ceremony that is meant to determine an astrologically auspicious date and time for the marriage ceremony is also held. Invitations are mailed out by both families, or personally handed to close relatives who live nearby. Among some Nayars, wedding invitations are issued in the name of the karanavan, another vestige of the prestige that position once commanded.

Marriage ceremonies may be conducted at the bride's home or in an area built and used for that purpose at a temple nearby. The bridegroom, who arrives in a procession of his family and friends, is greeted at the entrance by members of the bride's family. His feet are washed and he is garlanded. The actual ceremony itself follows and consists of these rites: The couple sit next to each other facing (among other objects that signify auspiciousness and fertility) a pot full of rice and a lighted oil lamp. The couple exchange rings and garlands (previously blessed by placing in front of a temple idol). The bridegroom places and/or ties the tali around the neck of the bride. The bridegroom then gives the bride a piece of cloth (almost always a *saree*). The bride and groom clasp hands and walk around the lighted lamp three times. They are then blessed by elders of both families. The ceremony is followed by a vegetarian feast in which both families participate. As noted above, the bride accompanies the groom to live with his family or (perhaps, later) to a new residence.

Let me point out a few features of contemporary Nayar marriage that indicate continuity and change. In terms of continuity, although a marriage may be solemnized at a temple, religious connotations are still minimal and the ceremony is often conducted by a fellow Nayar in the community. The giving of clothing also survives from the traditional Nayar sambandham ceremony. Tremendous changes can also be detected. The tali-tying rite has been shifted from the talikettu-kalyanam to the sambandham ceremony. The sambandham ceremony itself and the process leading up to it has expanded and taken on features that serve to underline the desirability of monogamy and stability of marriage. In addition, there are now elements suggesting increasing male dominance. For example, the male's family goes to view the bride-to-be and the bridegroom's party is respectfully received at the wedding site. Increasingly, the groom's family demands from the bride's family a "groomprice" or "direct payments to the family of the groom"[38] as a condition of marriage. This was previously unknown among Nayars. Finally, the expansion of rites associated with the sambandham and the receiving of blessings from elders signify the encouraging of stability in the marriage partnership being entered into.

Stable Monogamy as an Ideal

The importance of the sambandham relationship among contemporary Nayars is associated with the promotion of a family ideology based on stable monogamy. Three expressions of this ideal can be found in contemporary marriage and family patterns. The traditional pattern identified in Central Kerala and upper regions of South Kerala involving multiple visiting husbands and relationships with Nambudiri Brahmins is not operative any longer. In its place, Nayars have substituted endogamy (as in restricting the selection of marriage partners from within the caste and sub-caste group) and long-term monogamy. The practice of allowing Nambudiri sambandham partners has also died out. This can be attributed to the cessation of military service as the common occupation of Nayars; to changes within Nambudiri households that allowed all males (not just the oldest) to marry Nambudiri women; and to criticisms from Nayar reformers who berated Nambudiris harshly on their "religious" pretensions in separating sex and responsibility for its consequences (children).

The second aspect of this ideal can be found in the contemporary expectation that a husband and wife be sexually faithful to each other over the period of marriage. Not surprisingly, divorce is strongly discouraged. This focus on sexual exclusivity has also resulted in scrutiny of a potential bride's "character" (premarital virginity) before moving forward with the steps towards an arranged marriage. There is some, though less intense, attention paid to a potential groom's "character."

A third expression of the stable, monogamous family ideal is the rise of essentially neolocal (living apart from kin) nuclear family living arrangements especially when work locations are far away.[39] Biological parents and children live together over a long period of time with the former having responsibility and authority over the latter. In the twentieth century, Nayar men in search of employment (Kerala being a state with high levels of both education and unemployment) have migrated to and lived in other parts of India (e.g., my father-in-law), Southeast Asia (e.g., my father), the Middle East (e.g., my wife's cousin, i.e., her mother's sister's son), and the West (e.g., me). It has become customary and accepted for their wives to live with them and raise their children in nuclear family units. If the couple returns to Kerala, they continue to live together.

It is difficult to find remnants of the old order "weak" marriage ties among the Nayars. It is my observation that in comparison to other Hindu groups, Nayar women have greater degrees of freedom in consenting or turning down potential marriage proposals. Whether this is the result of Nayar traditions or because Nayar women possess relatively high levels of education and are more likely to work outside the home is open to question. Relative to other Hindu women, it also appears that Nayar women may also choose to remain unmarried for longer periods of time. Further, female children are not looked upon with disfavor even in the face of the creeping in of practices such as "groomprice." Billig predicts that these practices "may actually enhance female autonomy and economic independence in Kerala by forcing women even further to pursue educational and career opportunities outside of marriage."[40] If so, given their traditionally higher status, such effects should be more pronounced for Nayar women.

Change Factors in Nayar Marriage and Family Practices

Having identified the traditional and contemporary forms of Nayar marriage and family, let us turn our attention to accounting for some of the influences that have propelled the remarkable changes documented. It is possible to discern factors that can be subsumed under either materialist, ideological or other types of explanation for social change. It should be recognized that any categorization of change factors is somewhat artificial and that causal interactions may exist between them. It is possible to identify three sets of influences—economic, reform movements, and legal—that helped move Nayars away from their traditional patterns of marriage and family.

Economic Influences

Two major economic factors have been identified by observers. The first is the end of the traditional military occupational roles of Nayars. After the British established effective and actual control in the early nineteenth century over the regions that constitute the present Kerala, they demobilized the armies of the local kings and chieftains. The Nayar men who controlled lands that had been given to them earlier by these rulers turned their attention to agriculture and supervision of those who worked for them producing rice, coconuts, pepper, and so on. There was more stability in their lives and more contact of a permanent nature with their sambandham partners, relatives and their biological children. This may have led to greater identification with their family of procreation rather than their family of orientation. This may also be the reason why many men began to ignore traditional norms with regard to property accumulated on their own. Earlier, on a man's death his property reverted to his matrilineal taravad. Instead, many Nayar men wished to transfer such property to their wives and children.

The second of these economic factors is the increasing role of manufacturing and service industry sectors in India, and Kerala in particular. Nayars, given their elite status, had greater opportunities to achieve the educational qualifications needed for these new jobs. At the same time, the last century saw population growth and tough competition from Ezhavas (a lower caste group) and Syrian Christians who were also rapidly "modernizing." These groups also began to aggressively buy up land that Nayar taravads and Nambudiri illams had owned. This resulted in the migration of Nayars (as mentioned earlier) to more urban areas, elsewhere in India and other parts of the world. All this meant that the rural agricultural feudal economy that supported the caste structure and the place of Nayars in it was being dismembered. Puthenkulam observes, "Neither the taravad nor its kinship system or the sambandham could be imagined outside a village set-up. When the village economy crumbled, systems built on it had to follow suit."[41]

Reform Movements

The economic changes should not obscure the importance of reform movements from among the Nayars themselves that agitated for an end to matrilineality and the regularization of sambandham unions. Groups such as the Malayali Sabha and, later, the Nayar Service Society and their leaders were instrumental in developing forceful arguments and agitating to end features of traditional Nayar life of which they disapproved.[42] They disliked the grip of the karanavan on the property and affairs of the younger members of a taravad. The reformers wanted to end what they considered wasteful celebrations such as talikettu-kalyanam. They had nothing but bitter scorn for the "status" associated with sambandhams that involved Nayar women and Nambudiri men, particularly since the latter did not have any further responsibility towards the children they fathered. They also wished for sambandham

relationships to be recognized as legal marriages whereby the husband could leave property accumulated by him during his lifetime to his children.

Fuller suggests that the scathing attacks these reformers launched on the old order through newspapers, books (the first Malayalam novel dealt with Nayars and matrilineality), and speeches, were "undoubtedly . . . due to the spread of Western ideas" most of it through education in English.[43] To this we should also add that Kerala during this period was becoming less isolated from the rest of India. Contacts multiplied with other (mostly patrilineal) Hindu and non-Hindu groups through the migration patterns described above (assisted by the spread of rail travel). In addition, the work of Christian missionaries (who though they may have failed to convert the Nayars were able to instill Christian ideas regarding morality and monogamy) was also among the influences on these reformers. Some observers suggest that cumulatively Nayar reformers was ashamed of their traditional way of life and its implied "immorality" and wished to substitute for it one that had a higher moral tenor. As Aiyappan puts it, "We grew ashamed of our matriliny and this affected even the thinking of scholars. . . ."[44]

Legal Changes

The reformers, perhaps aided by changing economic and political circumstances, were successful in challenging almost every feature of traditional Nayar life that they disapproved of. These legal changes hastened the decline of taravad and matrilineality. In South Kerala, this took the form of two pieces of legislation called the Nair Acts of 1912 and 1925. Although there were significant differences between the two, taken together they had the effect of allowing for the division and bequeathing of individually acquired property to any individual's children, and made the practice of multiple spouses illegal. Similar legislation in Central Kerala enacted in 1920 and 1938 severely curtailed the powers of the karanavan, legalized the sambandham relationship, prohibited multiple spouses, and declared the wife and children of a man as his heirs. Most of North Kerala, which was ruled directly by the British provincial government in Madras, enacted the legislation in 1933 with similar provisions. These laws resulted in the many court cases brought against karanavans alluded to earlier, charging them with mismanagement. It should also be noted that legislation was also brought forward that allowed all Nambudiris to inherit their joint family property and for all Nambudiri men (not just the eldest) to be able to marry. This was the result of efforts from within the Nambudiri community as well, and effectively ended the era of Nayar sambandhams with Nambudiris.

While these pieces of legislation were frontal attacks on the traditional structure, at the same time other laws subverting the economic basis that sustained it were coming into effect. Land reforms that allowed tenants (primarily of the lower castes) to become owners of the lands that they had cultivated for generations began to be enacted in the early twentieth century. As Nayars and to a lesser extent Nambudiris were the landholders, such legislation was clearly inimical to their interests. Related reforms protected tenants from arbitrary eviction and from being required to pay excessive rents. The pace of these reforms picked up considerably after India's independence in 1947, and as a result of a string of communist and leftist governments that have ruled Kerala since 1957. More recent legislation has given existing tenants the right to buy the land they have tilled, banned the creation of new tenancies, and proposed limits on the amount of land that can be owned by any one family.

Political Factors

Although at one time the "dominant caste"[45] of Kerala, Nayars do not occupy elite positions automatically anymore. "The traditional Kerala society in which the caste of a person and the extent of the landed property owned by him determined his standing in the social scale is now a thing of the past."[46] Instead, the disappearance of their patrons (rulers and local chieftains), democratization and preferential policies favoring lower castes (implemented all over India) have eroded the powerful position that Nayars once held. They now have to compete with other groups or form coalitions with them to achieve power, wealth and prestige. Caste, taravad, and matrilineality matter less in the public sphere than what can be gained or lost through interpersonal and intergroup transactions. Thus, while there exist political parties claiming to represent the interests of Nayars, Ezhavas and other caste groups, the major parties in Kerala are shifting coalitions of various castes, classes, and religious groups. The leadership of the government and these parties also varies among all of these groups. The structures that propped up Nayars and their particular way of life have been dismantled, making them, at least politically, not very different from other groups around them.

Conclusion

Under attack from the outside through economic, legal, and political changes and from within through the efforts of Nayar reformers, it is not surprising that the traditional Nayar system of marriage and family that so captivated social scientists began to change. As we have seen, there are a few lingering remnants of their matrilineal past and it has not been replaced by a completely male-dominated system. For example, although matrilineal inheritance has all but disappeared, Nayar women have more to say about their lives than do other Hindu women. Currently, Nayars can best be described as possessing stable, monogamous marriages, with a tendency for families to live with the husband's family or alone.

Notes

1. I gratefully acknowledge the help of Robert Theodoratus with the anthropological literature on the Nayars as well as the comments and clarifications of Gopi Nair and Raman R. Nayar.

2. Kathleen Gough, "Nayar: Central Kerala" and "Nayar: North Kerala," in David M. Schneider and Kathleen Gough, eds., *Matrilineal Kinship* (Berkeley, CA: University of California Press, 1961).

3. Carol R. Ember and Melvin Ember, *Cultural Anthropology,* 7th ed. (Englewood Cliffs, NJ: Prentice Hall, 1993).

4. Kathleen Gough, "Nayar: Central Kerala" and "Nayar: North Kerala," in David M. Schneider and Kathleen Gough, eds., *Matrilineal Kinship* (Berkeley, CA: University of California Press, 1961).

5. N. Prabha Unnithan, "Marginality, Credibility, and Impression Management: The Asian Sociologist in America," *The American Sociologist* 19 (1988): 372–377.

6. Edward Evans-Pritchard, "Foreword," in K. E. Verghese, *Slow Flows the Pampa: Socio-Economic Changes in a Kuttanad Village in Kerala* (New Delhi, India: 1982), p. 5. The Nambudiri Brahmins, engaged in religious occupations were, as we will see, at the top of the caste ladder.

7. A. Sreedhara Menon, *A Survey of Kerala History* (Kottayam, India: National Book Stall, 1967), p. 1.

8. P. M. Mammen, *Communalism vs. Communism: A Study of the Socio-Religious Communities and Political Parties in Kerala, 1892–1970* (Columbia, MO: South Asia Books, 1981).

9. Richard Franke and Barbara Chasin, "Development without Growth: The Kerala Experiment," *Technology Review* (April 1990): 43–51.

10. George Woodcock, *Kerala: A Portrait of the Malabar Coast* (London: Faber and Faber, 1967).

11. Edward Evans-Pritchard, "Foreword."

12. Robin Jeffrey, *The Decline of Nayar Dominance: Society and Politics in Travancore, 1847–1908* (New York: Holmes and Meier, 1976), p. xv.

13. Ibid.

14. E. M. S. Namboodiripad, *Kerala Society and Politics: An Historical Survey* (New Delhi, India: National Book Centre, 1984), p. 25.

15. Kathleen Gough, "Nayar: Central Kerala" and "Nayar: North Kerala," in Christopher J. Fuller, *The Nayars Today* (Cambridge, England: Cambridge University Press, 1976), suggests that there are further differences in the local cultures of the upper and lower regions of South Kerala.

16. J. Puthenkulam, *Marriage and the Family in Kerala: With Special Reference to Matrilineal Castes* (Calgary: University of Calgary, 1977), p. 22.

17. Woodcock, *Kerala: A Portrait of the Malabar Coast*, p. 58.

18. Ibid., pp. 5–69.

19. Namboodiripad, *Kerala Society and Politics*, p. 28.

20. Woodcock, *Kerala: A Portrait of the Malabar Coast*, p. 60.

21. Jeffrey, *The Decline of Nayar Dominance* provides a historical account.

22. Woodcock, *Kerala: A Portrait of the Malabar Coast*, p. 59.

23. Fuller, *The Nayars Today.*

24. A. Aiyappan, *The Personality of Kerala* (Trivandrum, India: University of Kerala, 1982), p. 226.

25. Puthenkulam, *Marriage and the Family in Kerala*, pp. 35–54, summarizes the debate.

26. Ibid., p. 74.

27. Fuller, *The Nayars Today*, p. 121.

28. Ibid., p. 124.

29. Ibid., p. 100.

30. Gough, "Nayar: Central Kerala," and "Nayar: North Kerala," p. 398.

31. Puthenkulam, *Marriage and the Family in Kerala*, pp. 73–117.

32. For a more conventional way of defining matrilineality, see Ember and Ember, *Cultural Anthropology.*

33. Aiyappan, *The Personality of Kerala*, p. 192.

34. Puthenkulam, *Marriage and the Family in Kerala*, p. 216.

35. Ibid., p. 157.

36. Ibid., p. 162.

37. Fuller, *The Nayars Today*; Puthenkulam, *Marriage and the Family in Kerala.*

38. Michael S. Billig, "The Marriage Squeeze and the Rise of Groom-price in India's Kerala State," *Journal of Comparative Family Studies* 23 (1993): 197–216.

39. Gough, "Nayar: Central Kerala" and "Nayar: North Kerala"; Fuller, *The Nayars Today.*

40. Billig, "The Marriage Squeeze," pp. 211–212.

41. Puthenkulam, *Marriage and the Family in Kerala*, p. 245.

42. Jeffrey, *The Decline of Nayar Dominance: Society and Politics in Travancore, 1847–1908.*

43. Fuller, *The Nayars Today*, p. 130.

44. Aiyappan, *The Personality of Kerala*, p. 222.

45. See Jeffrey, *The Decline of Nayar Dominance: Society and Politics in Travancore, 1847–1908.*

46. A. Sreedhara *Menon, A Survey of Kerala History* (Kottayam, India: National Book Stall, 1967), p. 393.

Suggested Readings

Aiyappan, A. *The Personality of Kerala.* Trivandrum, India: University of Kerala, 1982. Based on a series of lectures, it provides some detailed discussion of matrilineality and Kerala in general.

Fuller, Christopher J. *The Nayars Today.* Cambridge, England: Cambridge University Press, 1976. Somewhat argumentative, but provides probably the best account of Nayar traditions and practices.

Jeffrey, Robin. *The Decline of Nayar Dominance: Society and Politics in Travancore, 1847–1908.* New York: Holmes and Meier, 1976. Historical account of changes in South Kerala society at the turn of the twentieth century.

Menon, A. Sreedhara. *A Survey of Kerala History.* Kottayam, India: National Book Stall, 1967. Provides a basic overview of Kerala history from ancient to contemporary times.

Namboodiripad, E.M.S., *Kerala Society and Politics: An Historical Survey.* New Delhi, India: National Book Centre, 1984. Written by a prominent Communist Party leader from Kerala, it attempts to weave Marxist analysis into a discussion of the state's history.

Puthenkulam, J. *Marriage and the Family in Kerala: With Special Reference to Matrilineal Castes.* Calgary: University of Calgary, 1977. Based on survey research, it provides a comprehensive (though unevenly written) discussion of marriage and family practices in Kerala.

Woodcock, George. *Kerala: A Portrait of the Malabar Coast.* London: Faber and Faber, 1967. An impressionistic account of Kerala in the 1960s shortly after its three regions were reconstituted into one state.

"NAYARS: TRADITION AND CHANGE IN MARRIAGE AND FAMILY"

N. Prabha Unnithan

1) What is the traditional caste hierarchy of Kerala State in India, and what role did the Nayar play in this system?

2) What is the *sambandham* marriage pattern found in central and upper South Kerala?

3) What role did the Nayar's traditional profession as mercenaries play in establishing and perpetuating the *sambandham*?

4) What is the taravad, and what is its function in traditional Nayar culture?

5) What changes have occurred in Nayar culture that have reduced the function and cohesion of the taravad?

6) What changes have occurred in Nayar culture to change the functions and role of the *sambandham* in Nayar society?

FAMILY AND HOUSEHOLD: WHO LIVES WHERE, WHY DOES IT VARY AND WHY IS IT IMPORTANT?

Burton Pasternak

And Ruth said: "Entreat me not to leave thee, or to return from following after thee; for whither thou goest, I will go; and where thou lodgest, I will lodge; thy people shall be my people, and thy God my God." (*Ruth*: 1:16)

One consequence of the incest taboo is that people everywhere must find mates outside the immediate family. Since wives and husbands most often live together, one or both must move from the home of their parents. When Ruth married, in accordance with custom she went to live with the family of her husband. Even after his death, as the citation indicates, she remained with her mother-in-law. Why should Ruth have been the one to inconvenience herself? Why didn't her husband leave everything and everyone to join her family? Or, for the sake of fairness, why didn't they simply go off to live independently when they married, as we do?

Because our custom is for married couples to live on their own, we tend to think that ours is the natural way. But in societies where people are more dependent on kin than on employers or government when it comes to making a living, defense, and support in old age, newlyweds more commonly live with or near close relatives.

In most societies (Table 1) custom recommends the way of Ruth—a bride leaves home to live with her husband with or near his family (*patrilocality*). In fewer societies, men live with or near the families of their wives (*matrilocality*), and even less often do couples live with or near *either* set of parents (*bilocality*). Our own preference for independence of the married couple (*neolocality*) is actually rarer still. Nearly as common as neolocality is a custom that has newlyweds live with or near the groom's mother's brother (*avunculocality*). There are even a few societies in which *duolocality* is the preference, where husband and wife live apart after marriage. Although we might imagine still other arrangements, they do not occur. There are no societies in which residence at marriage is with the groom's father's

sister, for example. Why do people marry the way they do, why are some practices more common than others, and what difference does it make if people marry one way rather than another?

TABLE 1: Prevailing Rules of Residence, by Frequency*

Rule of Residence	Percent of All Societies Coded for Residence
Patrilocality	68.5
Matrilocality	13.1
Bilocality	8.5
Neolocality	4.7
Avunculocality	4.3
Duolocality	0.9
Total No. Societies	858

*Sample includes all societies coded for residence in George P. Murdock, Ethnographic Atlas (Pittsburgh: University of Pittsburgh Press, 1967).

Marital Residence: Causes and Consequences

What have we learned about the factors likely to induce people to adopt one residence option rather than another? If we can answer that general question, will we better understand why the majority of societies prefer patrilocal residence? Whatever one might think of male chauvinism, we can hardly suppose that our remote male ancestors, at some regular cave meeting, conspired to inconvenience women, and that the decision then passed from generation to generation and people to people. The mere existence of other practices argues against that. Why, indeed, do some people reject patrilocality?

And why should we care? Because the decision we make on this issue may shape the composition of our families, determining who the insiders and outsiders are. Which kin live together or nearby in turn affects the nature of whatever larger kin groups we might form—and indeed most societies organize functional groups on the basis of descent from a common ancestor. Further, the nature of residence can even influence the status of women and gender relations.

Residence, Family, and Kin Group

If men stay put at marriage, over time the local group comes to include a core of men related through their fathers. If families coalesce into groups based on common descent, they are likely to trace descent through males since only they have a common ancestor. Women are outsiders from different places and blood lines. But if men live with or near the parents of their wives, descent will more likely be traced through women because the men come from different localities and blood lines. Avunculocality, like patrilocality, localizes males (a maternal uncle and his sisters' sons) who are related through their *mothers* rather than their fathers. When avunculocal peoples form descent groups (and most do), they trace descent through *females*.

Because bilocality and neolocality create local groups in which some people are related through females and others through males, these customs are not conducive to tracing descent exclusively through one sex. In bilocal societies people trace descent through either sex, or provide some other basis for organization apart from common descent. Neolocal residence by its nature emphasizes independence of the married couple, and societies with that preference rarely have descent groups of any sort.

Even kinship terms are affected by marital residence because they reflect the kinds of families and descent groups people have. In our own society, for example, we refer to the brothers and sisters of our parents as uncles and aunts, without distinguishing those on our father's and mother's side. Similarly, we distinguish cousins from brothers and sisters without regard to whether they are on our father's or mother's side. But in many more societies people refer to uncle on the father's side as father, and mother's sister as mother. The children of such fathers and mothers are, as we might expect, brothers and sisters.

Such usages are not the product of misunderstanding. Even when paternity is uncertain, people usually know who their mothers are. The terms have sociological rather than purely biological meaning; they signal the presence (or past presence) of extended families and descent groups. Thus, *father* may simply indicate a male in father's generation and descent group, and *mother* can be any woman of mother's generation and descent group, or a woman eligible to marry one of one's fathers.

It is because kinship terms reflect kinship organization that anthropologists are attentive to them. In some cases they may even provide a window on the past. If rule of residence has changed, for example, it may have produced adjustments in family composition and descent but not yet in kinship terms. In that event unexpected terms can provide a hint about forms of organization now superseded.

Residence and the Status of Women

Apart from its impact on family, descent, and kinship terms, there is another reason to be attentive to marital residence, and especially to the circumstances that account for a predominance of patrilocality. So long as women leave their families (and often their communities as well) when they marry, they are considered losses. Their labor and reproductive contributions ultimately belong to others. Patrilocal residence thus has profound implications for the status and well-being of women. There is also cross-cultural evidence suggesting that women enjoy higher status in some respects in matrilocal, matrilineal societies.[1]

In most societies people rely on offspring for care in old age. Rarely can they count on welfare, pensions, or public institutions like old age homes, nursing facilities, or hospices. If marriage transfers daughters to others, parents have little motivation for investing heavily in them. They are more likely to favor sons when it comes to food, attention, and education and, if resources are in short supply, females may even be at higher risk of early death.

Norma Diamond highlighted the problem in a study of early Communist transformation in China.[2] From the outset the Communists had promised to liberate women and break the constraints that the traditional patriarchal family and descent group imposed on modernization. But the Communists fell far short of their goals; their failure was commonly attributed to wrong thinking—to the persistence of "feudal patriarchal ideology." The hope was that enlightened reeducation would correct the situation. Yet, despite many campaigns designed to alter traditional notions, preference for sons has persisted and people still commonly assert that "boys are precious, girls worthless." It is not that they do not want daughters (they do), but sons still constitute "large happinesses," daughters only small ones.

Ultimately, the problem has less to do with ideology than with economic reality. Despite all the transformations—land reform, collectivization, drawing women into the labor force, etc.—the rule of post-marital residence remained unchanged. Ironically, when land was collectivized—transferred from families to collectives and then later to teams, brigades, and communes—the persistence of patrilocality meant that land was still vested in groups of men related through the male line. Despite their concerted attempt to undermine descent groups and to politically emasculate their wealthy leadership, the Communist transformation actually recreated and incorporated *de facto* patrilineal descent groups. Even with recent privatization of the economy, women continue to be losses. Without altering the rule of post-marital residence the situation is unlikely to change in China, and wherever else marriage requires the bride to move. The popularity of patrilocality in human societies is a matter of considerable consequence.

Why One Way Rather Than Another?

What does cross-cultural research tell us about the circumstances that lead people to adopt one residence practice rather than another, and why is patrilocality especially preferred in so many societies? Are we to suppose that it reflects a basic and inevitable human condition—male dominance? Were that the case, wouldn't all societies be patrilocal? As it turns out, moreover, beyond the family itself males are politically dominant in all societies, even in matrilocal and avunculocal ones.

Some have proposed that perhaps the societal propensity for patrilocality reflects the fact that, in most societies, men do most of the subsistence work. Another suggestion has been that the popularity of patrilocality may have something to do with the fact that male activities more often require cooperation, especially where there is a potential for violence. Perhaps that provides a reason for keeping men who know each other and their territory well together.

Cross-cultural research indicates that neither the division of labor by sex nor male cooperation in hunting or war help us predict whether people will be patrilocal or matrilocal. We find no relationship between contribution to subsistence and residence, or between frequency of fighting and likelihood of patrilocality over matrilocality.[3]

How then might we effectively anticipate the likelihood of patrilocality or matrilocality? One suggestion is that we must simultaneously consider the nature of warfare and the division of labor. Indeed, it turns out that where fighting occurs only among people with different cultures and languages (external warfare), the division of labor alone predicts quite well whether patrilocality or matrilocality will prevail. If men contribute most to subsistence the society will be patrilocal; where women contribute most it will be matrilocal. But if people fight among themselves, even occasionally (internal warfare), residence

will likely be patrilocal *regardless of the division of labor.*[4]

Why should the division of labor be relevant when warfare is purely external but not if fighting is internal? Since men normally do the fighting, it may be particularly advantageous to localize them, regardless of the division of labor, if there is a possibility of sudden attack from nearby (more likely with internal warfare). But where the enemy provides earlier warning (more commonly the case with purely external warfare), keeping sons together may be less vital and the division of labor might then be more important.

Perhaps because childbearing and menstruation periodically remove women from labor outside the home, men normally have principal responsibility for crucial tasks that must be completed at specific times. But if fighting periodically requires men to be away when those tasks need doing, women may assume a greater role and localizing them may be preferred. This would explain why matrilocality is so rare—we expect it only in relatively rare situations where we find purely external warfare of a sort that imposes heavier obligations on women.

Internal warfare discourages matrilocality regardless of the division of labor, and there may even be a structural incompatibility between matrilocal residence and internal warfare. Consider some salient characteristics of matrilocal societies. When they form larger kin groups they are likely to trace descent through women. While succession and property pass through females, however, authority is still vested in men (their brothers). Because they play an important authoritative role in matrilocal, matrilineal societies, brothers rarely move far when they marry. The situation is quite different in patrilocal societies, where women are neither channels for descent nor sources of authority. Daughters are dispensable; there is no need for them to remain close after marriage.

Consider now what might happen were neighboring matrilocal communities to begin fighting among themselves. The danger of sudden raids would increase, as would the desirability of keeping brothers together. And since men exercise authority in their sisters' homes and villages even after marriage, they might have to defend a sister's group in a conflict involving members of their own local group! We might well expect people in that situation to change to a post-marital residence option that localizes males rather than females.[5]

There are only two ways that could be accomplished. A matrilocal people without important matrilineal descent groups could simply shift to patrilocality. To do that might be highly destabilizing if they had functional matrilineal descent groups, however. In that case it would be better to find a way to localize males without disturbing the matrilineal descent groups. Only avunculocality meets the need, by localizing men related through the female line.

We can appreciate now why patrilocality is so much more common than matrilocality. Rarely do people fight only externally and never among themselves, and even more rarely is the division of labor matridominant. We can now understand also why avunculocality is even less common than matrilocality. To produce it you would have to confront a matrilocal society with conditions that favor keeping brothers together (like the development of internal warfare), and there would also have to be important matrilineal descent groups. This is an uncommon combination, since matrilocality is not that common. Not all such societies have matrilineal descent, and even fewer will develop internal war.

Thus far we have only discussed factors that might predispose societies to patrilocal or matrilocal residence. But what conditions might favor bilocal or neolocal residence? Comparative research indicates that bilocality results from a recent and dramatic depopulation, which brings local groups or kin groups below optimal size for organizing work.[6] They must reconstitute to survive. So couples may move to the most viable group. Many technologically simpler peoples have found themselves in this position. All too often contact with more developed societies has brought disease and death, and in many instances the victims have found themselves displaced and forced into marginal environments. The linkage between bilocality and depopulation has evolutionary implications. If bilocality is mostly a product of contact, it could be a relatively recent phenomenon, one less familiar to our ancient hunting-gathering ancestors.

The same may be true of neolocality. This is a residential pattern particularly common in complex industrial-commercial societies like our own, where conditions encourage independence of the nuclear family, the conjugal unit consisting of husband, wife, and children.[7] In these societies opportunity is particularistic and the nuclear family is pretty much on its own. Individuals, not families or larger kin groups, find employment. Education and ability are usually more important than kinship when it comes to finding work. When work requires movement, people take their spouses and children along but rarely their brothers and sisters. Many burdens of the extended family in simpler societies—education, defense, welfare, and care of the elderly—pass to public institutions in complex societies.

Family and Household

The rule of post-marital residence influences the form of family as well as its composition. It says something not only about who remains, but also about the kind of families that result. Our own nuclear families are small and simple, but in other societies families are commonly larger and more complex, in part because of the rule of post-marital residence. Neolocality produces independent nuclear families. But by bringing newlyweds to live with or near relatives, the other rules provide greater potential for family extension.

Most societies allow family enlargement through polygamous marriage, but more often extension involves some combination of married couples. In *stem* families, for example, there are two married couples in different generations—parents and a married child. Even more complex are *joint* families, which contain two or more married couples in the same generation. What might encourage such family extension and, apart from the rule of post-marital residence, what factors influence the form of extended family?

The Extended Family and Its Variants

Comparative research indicates that extended families (stem and joint) prevail in more than 50 percent of societies.[8] They are less common in very simple and very complex societies than in mid-range agricultural societies, however. We find them less often among hunter-gatherers or in commercial-industrial-urban contexts than in nonintensive agricultural societies. Various explanations have been offered for this curvilinear relationship between family and societal complexity.[9] According to one view, families are simpler (and kinship in general less important) in urban-industrial contexts for much the same reasons that neolocality becomes more common. Public institutions assume many functions performed by extended families and kin groups in simpler societies, while the economy encourages nuclear family independence. Hunter-gatherers may less often form extended families because their way of life encourages mobility and because food production is limited or stored less often. Families may be more complex in simple agricultural societies because cultivation encourages a sedentary way of life, while land ownership discourages family division.

But there are problems with these speculations, empirical as well as logical. For one thing, while mid-range (nonintensive) agricultural societies are more likely to have extended families (and descent groups) than simple or very complex societies, it is not easy to predict which mid-range societies will have them.

Some hunter-gatherers and some complex societies have them as well, and the curvilinear hypothesis will not anticipate those cases.

If simple societies have extended families less often it is probably not because they cannot produce sufficient food to sustain them. Hunter-gatherers have not always inhabited only the marginal areas in which we now find them, and even contemporary representatives in areas unsuited for cultivation produce enough to support multi-family groups. If they can feed collections of families, why not extended families?

In a demographic sense, cultivators certainly have a greater potential for large, complex families. Hunter-gatherers have lower fertility, perhaps because women cannot leave babies home alone. They carry their infants as they work, nursing on demand, a practice that inhibits the resumption of ovulation and hence conception. Cultivators can leave their infants home in the care of another woman, often a mother-in-law in the same extended family. Nursing is therefore less frequent, birth spacing shorter, and fertility higher. But we cannot conclude that cultivators have larger families simply because they have more children. More offspring could as well translate into more conflict, earlier family division and, therefore, more simple families.

How then can we account for the greater likelihood of extended families in mid-range cultivating societies? Is there some way we might even anticipate which societies are more likely to have them? Cross-cultural evidence suggests that extension is most likely when the various activities of women or men regularly require them to be in two places at once, which is more often the case in cultivating contexts where women tend home and children and also work in fields. Family extension resolves the problem by providing a second woman—a mother-in-law or mother, and/or a sister-in-law or sister. Indeed, task incompatibility effectively predicts which societies of any complexity are more or less likely to have many extended families.[10]

Chinese Clues

Cross-cultural research thus explains why some societies are more likely than others to favor family extension. But we also observe considerable variation within societies. Why are joint families more often found in certain villages than in others? Why do some families resist division longer than others, even in the same community? Why are joint families more common at one time than at another? Focusing on how labor is used may also help us anticipate particular forms of family extension within societies and communities.

Many have noted that joint families are especially common among the wealthy. For example, Nimkoff & Middleton proposed that, cross-culturally, differences in land ownership may be crucial—the more land owned the more family members needed.[11] But why should family extension be necessary if land can be rented out or labor hired? Since many scholars have similarly observed some connection between class and family extension we need to consider, in specific contexts, why the wealthy might be more likely to have joint families than the poor. Further, we should consider cases in which even poor families have them.

Joint families have been highly valued but actually rare in China. There is abundant evidence of a class linkage there; the wealthy achieved the ideal more often than the poor. It is speculated that this is because they had more land and therefore needed more labor, or because the wealthy were better educated and more familiar with Confucian virtues. Their value system thus encouraged family extension. Sons of the wealthy were especially likely to obey their parents, and younger brothers to defer to older brothers. Filial piety delayed family division.

But not all wealthy families were joint, while even some poor ones were. More land does not necessarily demand more *family* labor if workers can be hired or land rented out. Nor can differences in education, ideology, or values really account for joint families, or for the linkage between wealth and their maintenance. However, studies conducted in specific Chinese communities do indicate how specific technological and economic considerations may discourage family division, especially among the wealthy.

Chinese commonly attribute family division to arguments among women, an explanation not without some merit. It is important to keep in mind that, in traditional Chinese contexts, property passes in the male line. It is divided equally among sons, so women have access to it only through husbands and sons. The situation pits mothers-in-law against daughters-in-law and sisters-in-law against each other. It poses a threat to family harmony and, thus, discourages family extension, especially to joint form.

For her well being, that of her children, and even that of her husband, a woman must influence those who control property. When she marries she seeks to assure the loyalty of her husband. Since she will likely outlive him, security in old age will also depend on the control she can exert over her sons. But in that regard she has competition from her daughters-in-law, which is why, in traditional contexts, marriage so often unites people from different communities who have never met. A conjugal bond otherwise formed could more readily constitute a threat to the parent-child bond.

Whereas a mother-in-law has reason to keep her sons together, daughters-in-law have good reason to press for family division, to pull the men apart. Each looks to the interests of her own conjugal unit, her own children. Their interests often do not coincide with those of the parents-in-law. A few hypothetical situations make the contradiction clear.

Mr. Hwong, head of a joint family, decides to send the son of his eldest son to college. The boy is the smartest, most capable of his grandsons, the one most likely to bring rewards to the larger family by virtue of advanced education. But his younger son's wife resents this decision. Why should the labor and resources of her conjugal unit be used to subsidize the well being of people who will eventually be independent? She therefore becomes what the Chinese sometimes call a "pillow ghost." In bed at night she presses her husband to seek a family division.

To take another case, suppose one daughter-in-law has a child while another does not. The childless one might well agitate for family division on the grounds that her labor, and that of her husband, are subsidizing food for an unproductive family member, one who could well depart before matching their contribution. Her position will likely change when she has her own infant and when her nephew is old enough to work a plow. Her sister-in-law will become the pillow ghost then.

Given the potential for conflict that patrilocal residence and patrilineal inheritance provide, it is hardly surprising that, despite the praise lavished upon them, joint families rarely endure long, if they are formed at all. Although most people may spend some part of their lives in such families, at any given time there are likely to be few of them in any Chinese farming village—perhaps not more than five percent of all families. However, in some cases we do find more of them. Why in those villages, or in those families, are the usual centrifugal tendencies repressed? What factors suppress conflict and, thus, delay family division?

In one village, dependence on rainfall rather than canals for irrigation discouraged family division even in poor families by putting a premium on adult male labor.[12] People could break soil and prepare their fields for rice only when it rained and the ground was wet. The work had to be done quickly and, since it rained on all fields at the same time, there was little opportunity for cooperation among families. Only men plowed, so it was important that every family try to have more than one. Under the circumstances

there was good reason to resist the pillow ghost and, in that village, the frequency of joint families was unusually high. This is consistent with our cross-cultural finding that activity incompatibility is likely to encourage family extension.

Confucian virtue had little to do with it. In fact, while there were many joint families, there were also many marriages of a less than filial, virtuous sort. In response to the need for males, parents without adult sons often brought husbands in for their daughters, deviating from the customary and more valued patrilocal pattern. The situation changed later, when there was a reservoir to store water and irrigation canals to deliver it. Access to water could then be controlled and water allocated over a longer period. Families no longer had to accomplish tasks at the same time—in fact they could not do so. Cooperation then became possible and commonplace. From that time, the frequency of joint families and of matrilocal marriages dropped precipitously.

This case indicates yet another way in which the rule of residence, the way marriage is contracted and why, can influence other things we do. Before the shift to canals, matrilocality had demographic effects—compared to patrilocal marriage, and to matrilocal marriage elsewhere, it was here associated with relatively high fertility, low divorce, and relatively infrequent female adoption.

When Chinese deviate from the patrilocal ideal by bringing in a husband for a daughter, they normally do so to ensure family continuity. Matrilocality is most often a resort of poor couples who lack an heir (male) to carry on their family line. The husband, usually also poor, allows his children to take their mother's surname in exchange for access to her family's land. Although poverty has driven him to this concession, people pity him because he has turned his back on his ancestors and married in like a woman, leaving his family and community.

The likelihood of discord and dissatisfaction is great in such marriages. Anticipating that, parents try to find a husband far away, someone their daughter has never seen. It is especially important in such cases to compromise the conjugal bond for the sake of the parent-child bond. That increases the likelihood that a daughter will remain behind with her children even if her husband departs. People therefore anticipate that matrilocal marriages arranged to carry on the family will be fragile, with relatively high divorce rates and perhaps lower fertility.

But in this particular community, where an unusual dependence on rainfall rather than canals put a premium on male labor, matrilocality had little to do with family continuity and much to do with an exaggerated need for labor. These marriages were, therefore, arranged quite differently. Every effort was made to attract a man within the community, possibly a long-term laborer, someone already familiar to their daughter.

Parents were prepared to compromise the parent-child bond here because their intention was to ensure an enduring union—to lock the husband in. If he lived in their village and already knew their daughter he might be less likely to leave. Their daughter would likely be content since marriage did not require that she leave family and community to join strangers elsewhere.

As we might expect, matrilocal marriage had lower divorce rates than patrilocal marriages in this village, and also lower rates than matrilocal marriages in other Chinese villages. Given the familiarity upon which matrilocal marriages were based, it is no surprise that marital fertility (and the rate of premarital conception) was higher than for patrilocally married women. It was also higher than for matrilocally married women in villages where family continuity was the motive. The fertility of these marriages declined, however, once canals reduced the need for males, and matrilocal marriages were once again arranged for more traditional purposes.

The need for male labor also discouraged early female adoption, commonplace in other Chinese villages. Given high infant mortality rates, one could never be certain that a son would survive to adulthood. Better, then, to hold daughters longer as potential lures for matrilocal husbands should the need arise.

This case shows how technology can alter marital residence and the form of family by creating an unusual need for men. Data from another Chinese village illustrates how technology can discourage family division by putting a special premium on the labor of women.[13] When some rice-growing families began to cultivate and process tobacco as a profitable cash crop, most of the work was given to women. The men continued to concentrate on rice. Women picked tobacco leaves as they ripened, carried them to the drying house, regulated fires there day and night, and sorted the leaves when dried. Their skills were so crucial that tobacco growers married only tobacco growers.

While rice farmers had few joint families, those that also cultivated tobacco were almost invariably joint. For them family division created special problems. Which son, for example, would inherit the very profitable drying house, and how would his brothers be compensated? More important, any family division would mean a diversion of female labor from tobacco to separate kitchens, pigs, and child care.

We have seen how technology can delay family division by encouraging men or women to remain together. These two Chinese examples actually illustrate our more general cross-cultural finding—namely, that activity or task incompatibility encourages family extension. In one case a single male could not accomplish on his own all the work that needed to be done, in the other the different tasks of women were at issue.

There are also certain economic conditions, especially characteristic of the wealthy, that may have a similar effect. In the Chinese context, the wealthy have been able to delay family division longer than the poor because they enjoy a greater potential for multienterprise family investment. To the extent that a family invests human and capital resources in different enterprises (i.e., puts its eggs in many baskets), it improves security, ability to withstand economic fluctuations, and long term wealth. Consider the following case: Mr. Lin manages a substantial family estate and heads a joint family consisting of four married sons and their respective children. He lives on the family farm with one son. Another son runs the family brothel in town, one manages the family brick factory, and yet another runs a family trucking firm. The family is invested in a number of enterprises, each of which operates on its own schedule. While the joint family is the minimal corporate kin group, the brothers live apart in different households. That short-circuits some of the conflict that might otherwise emerge were they living together. But there are also powerful economic reasons to avoid family division in this case.

By keeping the family intact, Mr. Lin can shift family labor and capital around in the most profitable way, an advantage that would be lost were his sons to divide. When the crop is brought in, he directs sons and grandsons to help. Men and women are diverted from other family enterprises as needed. Once the crop is in, assuming a good yield, the brothel gets busy. Family members then help there. In winter, during the slack, the brick factory needs workers. Mr. Lin can meet that need as well without having to hire outsiders. He can shift capital, too, from one enterprise to the other, reducing the need to borrow at high rates of interest.

His brothel, very profitable in good years, can be a serious drain on family resources when harvests are poor and farmers less free with their money. A family that can move labor and capital between enterprises is better able to weather fluctuations of this sort. The advantage would be lost were Mr. Lin's sons to divide. Further, it would not be easy to divide the family estate. How does one assess the value of a brothel compared to a brick factory or farm? They have different values, potentials, and risks.

Conclusions

Several lessons emerge from this discussion of marital residence and family. Clearly, how and why people marry the way they do and where they live after marriage are not inconsequential matters of accident. Some practices are more common than others. Cross-cultural research has suggested some conditions that usually favor one pattern over another. The task is of more than casual interest, given that these choices have ramifications elsewhere—they influence the nature of our families and kin groups, have implications for gender relations, and even for demographic performance.

One of our Chinese examples suggests that something will be lost if we think about residence patterns exclusively in terms of general social patterns. It illustrated how, in the Chinese case, matrilocal marriage can be contracted for very different purposes, in dissimilar ways, with varied consequences. Clearly we have much to learn about how technology and economy shape motivation, residence, and family form in particular contexts, and about how these in turn affect demographic behavior.

We learned from these Chinese examples, too, that predicting post-marital residence, or the likelihood and form of family extension in terms of shared values, level of development, or class is not very effective. Consistent with our cross-cultural findings we should, in specific contexts as well, look for technological and/or economic conditions likely to produce task incompatibilities, or that might especially encourage keeping men and/or women together.

The case of Mr. Lin warns us to avoid confusing families and households, especially in complex societies. The minimal corporate kin group or family in his case consisted of several residential units, or households. If we confuse the two we run a serious risk of underestimating the incidence of extended families, especially in complex societies.

An Indian grocery store owner in Hoboken, New Jersey, living with his wife and children, might well be only one segment of a larger family corporation centered in Bombay, India. They may merely be one egg in a basket. The illegal Chinese boat person in New York, whose voyage was paid for by his relatively wealthy family in China, may similarly represent another family investment. If we fail to recognize the connections between households, we may underestimate family complexity and mystify our understanding of family dynamics.

Notes

1. Martin K. Whyte, *The Status of Women in Preindustrial Societies* (Princeton, NJ: Princeton University Press, 1978), pp. 132–134.

2. Norma Diamond, "Collectivization, Kinship, and the Status of Women in Rural China," in Rayna R. Reiter, ed., *Toward an Anthropology of Women* (New York: Monthly Review Press, 1975), pp. 372–395.

3. See Melvin Ember and Carol R. Ember, "Conditions Favoring Matrilocal versus Patrilocal Residence," *American Anthropologist* 73 (1971): 571–594; and William T. Divale, "Migration, External Warfare, and Matrilocal Residence," *Behavior Science Research* 9 (1974): 75–133. However, one study of only hunting-gathering societies does indicate a relationship between division of labor and marital residence. Where men contribute most to subsistence in such societies, residence is more often patrilocal; where women predominate, the rule is more likely to be matrilocal. The matter becomes far more complicated if we include other sorts of societies, however. On hunter-gatherers, see Carol R. Ember, "Residential Variations among Hunters-Gatherers," *Behavior Science Research* 10 (1975): 199–227.

4. Ember and Ember, "Conditions Favoring Matrilocal versus Patrilocal Residence."

5. Melvin Ember, "The Conditions That May Favor Avunculocal Residence," *Behavior Science Research* 9 (1974): 203–209.

6. Some suggest that bilocality reflects sexual equality. Another proposal is that scarce, fluctuating resources encourage greater residential flexibility, and thus bilocality. Although these are reasonable expectations, the ethnographic record indicates that not all bilocal peoples have these characteristics. Depopulation is a better predictor. It accounts for most bilocal cases, and perhaps for the environmental marginality of many of them as well. See Carol R. Ember and Melvin Ember, "The Conditions Favoring Multilocal Residence," *Southwestern Journal of Anthropology* 28 (1972): 382–400.

7. Melvin Ember, "The Emergence of Neolocal Residence," *Transactions of the New York Academy of Sciences* 30 (1967): 291–302.

8. Allan D. Coult and Robert W. Habenstein, *Cross Tabulations of Murdock's World Ethnographic Sample* (Columbia: University of Missouri Press, 1965).

9. Ray Lesser Blumberg and Robert F. Winch, "Societal Complexity and Familial Complexity: Evidence for the Curvilinear Hypothesis," *American Journal of Sociology* 77 (1972): 898–920; M. F. Nimkoff and Russell Middleton, "Types of Family and Types of Economy," *American Journal of Sociology* 66 (1960): 215–225.

10. Burton Pasternak, Carol R. Ember, and Melvin Ember, "On the Conditions Favoring Extended Family Households," *Journal of Anthropological Research* 32, no. 2 (1976): 109–123, reprinted in Melvin Ember and Carol

R. Ember, *Marriage, Family, and Kinship: Comparative Studies of Social Organization* (New Haven: HRAF Press, 1983), pp. 125–150.

11. Nimkoff and Middleton, "Types of Family and Types of Economy."

12. Burton Pasternak, *Kinship and Community in Two Chinese Villages* (Stanford: Stanford University Press, 1972); Burton Pasternak, *Guests in the Dragon: Social Demography of a Chinese District, 1895–1946* (New York: Columbia University Press, 1983).

13. Myron L. Cohen, *House United, House Divided: The Chinese Family in Taiwan* (New York: Columbia University Press, 1976).

Suggested Readings

Pasternak, Burton. *Introduction to Kinship and Social Organization*. Englewood Cliffs, NJ: Prentice-Hall, 1976. General overview with coverage of marital residence and family organization.

Ember, Melvin, and Carol R. Ember. *Marriage, Family, and Kinship: Comparative Studies of Social Organization*. New Haven: HRAF Press, 1983. Collection of cross-cultural studies of variation in social organization, including marital residence and family.

"FAMILY AND HOUSEHOLD: WHO LIVES WHERE, WHY DOES IT VARY, AND WHY IS IT IMPORTANT?"

Burton Pasternak

1) What are the different types of post-marital residence found around the world?

2) How are residence and kinship organization interrelated?

3) What are the possible influences of warfare and the division of labor on a culture's preference for certain residence patterns?

4) What circumstances or factors influence a society to choose bilocality or neolocality as a preferred residence pattern?

5) What is a "joint family" and what practical purposes does it serve for Chinese society?

FAMILY AND KINSHIP IN VILLAGE INDIA

David W. McCurdy

On a hot afternoon in May, 1962, I sat talking with three Bhil men in the village of Ratakote, located in southern Rajasthan, India.[1] We spoke about the results of recent national elections, their worry over a cattle disease that was afflicting the village herds, and predictions about when the monsoon rains would start. But our longest discussion concerned kin—the terms used to refer to them, the responsibilities they had toward one another, and the importance of marrying them off properly. It was toward the end of this conversation that one of the men, Kanji, said, "Now sāb (Bhili for sāhīb), you are finally asking about a good thing. This is what we want you tell people about us when you go back to America."

As I thought about it later, I was struck by how different this social outlook was from mine. I doubt that I or any of my friends in the United States would say something like this. Americans do have kin. We have parents, although our parents may not always live together, and we often know other relatives, some of whom are likely to play important parts in our lives. We grow up in families and we often create new ones if we have children. But we also live in a social network of other people whom we meet at work or encounter in various "outside" social settings, and these people can be of equal or even greater importance to us than kin. Our social worlds include such non-kin structures as companies and other work organizations, schools, neighborhoods, churches and other religious groups, and voluntary associations, including recreational groups and social clubs. We are not likely to worry much about our obligations to relatives with the notable exceptions of our children and grandchildren (middle-class American parents are notoriously child-centered), and more grudgingly, our aging parents. We are not supposed to "live off" relatives or lean too heavily on them.

Not so in Ratakote. Ratakote's society, like many agrarian villages around the world, is kinship-centered. Villagers anchor themselves in their families. They spend great energy on creating and maintaining their kinship system. This actually is not so surprising. Elaborate kinship systems work well in agrarian societies where families tend to be corporate units and where peoples' social horizons are often limited to the distance they can walk in a day.

For the same reasons, families in the United States were also stronger in the past when more of them owned farms and neighborhood businesses.

What may come as a surprise, however, is how resilient and strong Indian kinship systems such as Ratakote's have been in the face of recent economic changes, especially the growth of wage labor. Let us look more closely at the Bhil kinship system, especially at arranged marriage, to illustrate these ideas.

Arranging a Marriage

If there is anything that my American students have trouble understanding about India, it is arranged marriage. They can not imagine sitting passively by while their parents advertise their charms and evaluate emerging nuptial candidates. The thought of living—to say nothing of have sex with—a total stranger seems out of the question to them. In our country, personal independence takes precedence over loyalty to family.

Not so in India. There, arranged marriage is the norm, and most young people, as well as their elders, accept and support the custom. (They often find it sexually exciting, too.) There are many reasons why this is so, but one stands out for discussion here. Marriage constructs alliances between families, lineages, and clans. The resulting kinship network is a pivotal structure in Indian society. It confers social strength and security. People's personal reputations depend on the quality and number of their allied kin. There is little question in their minds about who should arrange marriages. The decision is too important to leave up to inexperienced and impressionable young people.

As an aside I should note that young Indians play a greater part in the process than they used to. Middle class boys often visit the families of prospective brides, where they manage to briefly "interview" them. They also tap into their kinship network to find out personal information about prospects. Young women also seek out information about perspective grooms. Bhils are no exception. They often conspire to meet those to whom they have been betrothed, usually at a fair or other public event where their contact is likely to go unnoticed. If they don't like each other, they will begin to pressure their parents to back out of the arrangement.

The importance of arranging a marriage was brought home to me several times during fieldwork in Ratakote, but one instance stands out most clearly. When I arrived in the village for a short stay in 1985, Kanji had just concluded marriage arrangements for his daughter, Rupani.[2] What he told me about the process underscored the important role kinship plays in the life of the village.

Kanji started by saying that he and his wife first discussed Rupani's marriage the previous year when the girl first menstruated. She seemed too young for such a union then so they had waited nine months before committing to the marriage process. Even then, Rupani was still only 15 years old. Kanji explained that everyone preferred early marriage for their children because young people were likely to become sexually active as they grew older and might fall in love and elope, preempting the arrangement process altogether. Now they figured that the time had come, and they began a series of steps to find a suitable spouse that would eventually involve most of their kin.

The first step was to consult the members of Kanji's *lineage*. Lineage is an anthropological term, not one used by Bhils. But Bhils share membership in local groups of relatives that meet the anthropological definition. Lineages (in this case, (patrilineages) include closely related men who are all descended from a known ancestor. Kanji's lineage consists of his two married brothers, three married sons of his deceased father's brother (his father is also dead), and his own married son when the latter is home. All are the descendants of his grandfather who had migrated to Ratakote many years earlier. He had talked with all of them informally about the possibility of his daughter's marriage before this. Now he called them together for formal approval.

The approval of lineage mates is necessary because they are essential to the marriage process. Each one of them will help spread the word to other villages that Rupani is available for marriage. They will loan money to Kanji for wedding expenses, and when it comes time for the wedding ceremony, they will provide much of the labor needed to prepare food and arrange required activities. Each family belonging to the lineage will host a special meal for the bride (the groom is similarly entertained in his village) during the wedding period, and one or two will help her make offerings to their lineal ancestors. The groom will also experience this ritual.

The lineage also has functions not directly related to marriage. It has the right to redistribute the land

of deceased childless, male members, and it provides its members with political support. It sees to memorial feasts for deceased members. Its members may cooperatively plow and sow fields together and combine their animals for herding.

With lineage approval in hand, Kanji announced Rupani's eligibility in other villages. (Bhils are village exogamous, meaning they prefer to marry spouses from other communities.) Kanji and his lineage mates went about this by paying visits to feminal relatives in other villages. These are kin of the women, now living in Ratakote, who have married into his family. They also include the daughters of his family line who have married and gone to live in other villages, along with their husbands and husbands' kin.

Once the word has been spread, news of prospective candidates begins to filter in. It may arrive with feminal kin from other villages when they visit Ratakote. Or it may come from neighbors who are acting as go-betweens in Ratakote for kin who live in other villages and who seek partners for their children. Either way, a process of evaluation starts. Does the family of the suggested boy or girl have a good reputation? Are they hospitable to their in-laws? Do they meet their obligations to others? What is the reputation of the boy or girl they are offering in marriage? Is he or she tall or short, light or dark, robust or frail, cheerful or complaining, hard working or lazy? What about their level of education? Does the family have sufficient land and animals? Have they treated other sons- and daughters-in-law well?

The most fundamental question to ask, however, is whether the prospective spouse is from the right clan. In anthropology, the term *clan* refers to an aggregate of people who all believe they are descended from a common ancestor. In Ratakote this group is called an *arak*. Araks are named and the names are used as surnames when Bhils identify themselves. Kanji comes from the pargi *arak* and is thus known as Kanji Pargi. There is Lalu Bodar, Naraji Katara, Dita Hiravat, Nathu Airi—all men named for one of the 36 araks found in Ratakote. Women also belong to their father's clan, but unlike many American women who adopt their husband's surname at marriage, they keep their arak name all their lives.

Araks are based on a rule of patrilineal descent. This means that their members trace ancestry through males, only. (Matrilineal descent traces the line through females only, and bilateral descent, which is found in U.S. society, includes both sexes.) Patrilineal descent not only defines arak membership, it governs inheritance. (Sons inherit equally from their fathers in Ratakote; daughters do not inherit despite a national law giving them that right.) It says that the children of divorced parents stay with the father's family. It bolsters the authority of men over their wives and children. It supports the rule of patrilo-cality. It even defines the village view of conception. Men plant the "seeds" that grow into children; women provide the fields in which the seeds germi-nate and grow.

The arak symbolizes patrilineal descent. It is not an organized group, although the members of an arak worship the same mother goddess no matter where they live. Instead it is an identity, an indicator that tells people who their lineal blood relatives are. There are pargis in hundreds of other Bhil villages. Most are strangers to Kanji but if he meets pargis else-where, he knows they share a common blood heri-tage with him.

It is this sense of common heritage that affects marriage. Bhils, like most Indians, believe that clan (arak) mates are close relatives even though they may be strangers. Marriage with them is forbidden. To make sure incest is impossible, it is also forbidden to marry anyone from your mother's arak or your father's mother's arak, to say nothing of anyone else you know you are related to.

This point was driven home to me on another occasion when a neighbor of Kanji's, Kamalaji Kharadi, who was sitting smoking with several other men, asked me which *arak* I belonged to. Instead of letting it go at "McCurdy," I said that I didn't have an *arak*. I explained that Americans didn't have a kin-ship group similar to this, and that was why I had to ask questions about kinship.

My listeners didn't believe me. After all, I must have a father and you get your arak automatically from him. It is a matter of birth and all people are born. They looked at each other as if to say, "We won-der why he won't tell us what his *arak* is?", then tried again to get me to answer. My second denial led them to ask, "OK, then what is your wife's *arak*?" (If you can't get at it one way, then try another.) I answered that she didn't have an *arak* either. This caused a mild sensation. "Then how do you know if you have not married your own relative?", they asked, secretly (I think) delighted by the scandalous prospect.

The third step that occurred during the arrange-ment of Rupani's marriage came after the family had settled on a prospective groom. This step is the be-trothal, and it took place when the groom's father and some of his lineage mates and neighbors paid a formal visit to Kanji's house. When they arrive, Kanji must offer his guests a formal meal, usually slaugh-tering a goat and distilling some liquor for the occa-sion. The bride, her face covered by her sari, will be brought out for a brief viewing, as well. But most of the time will be spent making arrangements—when will the actual wedding take place?; who will check

the couple's horoscopes for fit?; how much will the bride price (also called bride wealth by many anthro-pologists) be?

Bride price (*dapa*) deserves special comment. It is usually a standard sum of money (about 700 ru-pees in 1985), although it may also include silver or-naments or other valuables. The dapa is given by the groom's father and his line to the parents of the bride. Bhils view this exchange as a compensation for the loss of the bride's services to her family. It also pays for a shift in her loyalty.

The exchange points up an important strain on families in patrilineal societies, the transfer of a woman from her natal family and line to those of her husband. This transfer includes not only her person, but her loyalty, labor, and children. Although she al-ways will belong to her father's arak, she is now part of her husband's family, not his.

This problem is especially troublesome in India because of the close ties formed there by a girl and her parents. Parents know their daughter will leave when she marries, and they know that in her husband's house and village, she will be at a disad-vantage. She will be alone, and out of respect for his parents her husband may not favor her wishes, at least in public. Because of this, they tend to give her extra freedom and support. In addition, they recog-nize the strain she will be under when she first goes to live with her new husband and his family. To ease her transition, they permit her to visit her parents frequently for a year or two. They also may try to marry her into a village where other women from Ratakote have married, so that she has some kin or at least supporters.

After her marriage, a woman's parents and espe-cially her brothers find it hard not to care about her welfare. Their potential interest presents a built-in struc-tural conflict that could strain relations between the two families if nothing were done about it.

A solution to this problem is to make the mar-riage into an exchange, and bride price is one result. Bride price also helps to dramatize the change in loy-alty and obligation accompanying the bride's en-trance into her new family.

Bhils have also devised a number of wedding rituals to dramatize the bride's shift in family mem-bership. The bride must cry to symbolize that she is leaving her home. The groom ritually storms the bride's house at the beginning of the final ceremony. He does so like a conquering hero, drawing his sword to strike a ceremonial arch placed over the entrance while simultaneously stepping on a small fire (he wears a slipper to protect his foot), ritually violating the household's sacred hearth. At the end of the wed-ding, the groom, with some friends, engages in a mock battle with the bride's brothers and other young men, and symbolically abducts her. The meaning of this ritual is a dramatic equivalent of a father "giving away the bride" at American weddings.

One additional way of managing possible tension between in-laws is the application of respect behavior. The parents of the bride must always treat those of the groom and their relatives with respect. They must not joke in their presence, and they must use respectful language and defer to the groom's parents in normal conversation. In keeping with the strong patrilineal system, a groom may not accept important gifts from his wife's family except on ritual occasions, such as weddings, when exchange is expected. A groom may help support his own father, but he should not do so with his in-laws. That is up to their sons.

Bride price exchange also sets in motion a life-long process of mutual hospitality between the two families. Once the marriage has taken place, the families will become part of each other's feminal kin. They will exchange gifts on some ritual occasions, open their houses to each other, and, of course, help one another make future marriages.

The Future of Indian Kinship

On our last trip to India in 1994, my wife and I learned that Rupani had delivered three children since her wedding. Kanji had visited them a few months before we arrived, and he said that Rupani was happy and that he had wonderful grandchildren. But he also mentioned that her husband now spent most of his time in the nearby city of Udaipur working in construction there. He sent money home, but his absence left Rupani to run the house and raise the children by herself, although she did so with the assistance of his parents and lineage mates.

Rupani's case is not unusual. Every morning 70 or 80 men board one of the 20 or so busses that travel the road, now paved, that runs through Ratakote to the city. There they wait to be recruited by contractors for day labor at a low wage. If they are successful, gain special skills, or make good connections, they may get more permanent, better-paying jobs and live for weeks at a time in the city.

The reason they have to take this kind of work is simple. Ratakote has more than doubled in population since 1962. (The village had a population of 1,184 in 1963. By 1994 an estimate put the number at about 2,600.) There is not enough land for everyone to farm nor can the land produce enough to feed the growing population, even in abundant years. Work in the city is the answer, especially for householders whose land is not irrigated like Kanji's.

Cash labor has a potential to break down the kinship system that Bhils value so highly. It frees men and women from economic dependence on the family (since they make their own money working for someone else). It takes up time, too, making it difficult for them to attend the leisurely eleven-day weddings of relatives or meet other obligations to kin that require their presence. With cash labor, one's reputation is likely to hinge less on family than on work. For some, work means moving the family altogether. Devaji Katara, one of Kanji's neighbors, has a son who has moved with his wife and children to the Central Indian city of Indore. He has a good factory job there, and the move has kept them together. By doing so, however, he and they are largely removed from the kinship loop.

Despite these structural changes, kinship in Ratakote and for India as a whole remains exceptionally strong. Even though they may live farther away, Bhil sons and daughters still visit their families regularly. They send money home, and they try to attend weddings. They talk about their kin, too, and surprisingly, they continue the long process of arranging marriage for their children.

Perhaps one reason for kinship's vitality is the use to which kinship is put by many Indians. The people of Ratakote and other Indians have never given up teaching their children to respect their elders and subordinate their interests to those of the family. Family loyalty is still a paramount value. They use this loyalty to help each other economically. Family members hire each other in business. They take one another in during hard times. They offer hospitality to each other. Unlike Americans who feel guilty about accepting one-sided help from relatives, Indians look to the future. Giving aid now may pay off with a job or a favor later. Even if it doesn't, it is the proper thing to do.

Instead of breaking up the kinship network, work that takes men and families away from the village has simply stretched it out. An Indian student I know has found relatives in every American city he has visited. He knows of kin in Europe and southeast Asia too. Anywhere he goes he is likely to have relatives to stay with and to help him. When he settles down he will be expected to return the favor. Another Indian acquaintance, who went to graduate school in the United States and who continues to work here, has sent his father thousands of dollars to help with the building of a house. This act, which would surprise many Americans, seems perfectly normal to him.

Kanji is not disturbed by the economic changes that are overtaking the quiet agricultural pace of

Ratakote. I last left him standing in front of his house with a grandson in his arms. His son, who had left the village in 1982 to be a "wiper" on a truck, returned to run the farm. He will be able to meet the family's obligation to lineage and feminal kin. For Kanji, traditional rules of inheritance have pulled a son and, for the moment at least, a grandson, back into the bosom of the family where they belong.

Notes

1. Ratakote is a Bhil tribal village located 21 miles southwest of Udaipur, Rajasthan, in the Aravalli hills. I did ethnographic research in the village from 1961 to 1963, and again in 1985, 1991, and 1993 for shorter periods of time.

2. Kanji and Rupani are not real people. Their experiences are a composite of several life histories.

"FAMILY AND KINSHIP IN VILLAGE INDIA"

David W. McCurdy

1) What is an arranged marriage?

2) Why are arranged marriages the norm in India, and what purposes do such marriages serve?

3) What characteristics do Indian families look for in a potential spouse in arranging marriages for their children?

4) What pressures are being placed on the institutions of marriage and kinship in India, and what problems can these pressures potentially cause?

SECTION TEN

The Old and New in Cultures

CONFRONTING CREATIONISTS

Michael Shermer

Late in his life, Charles Darwin received many letters asking for his views of God and religion. On October 13, 1880, for example, he answered a letter from the editor of a book on evolution and free thought who was hoping to dedicate it to him. Knowing that the book had an antireligious slant, Darwin dissembled: "Moreover though I am a strong advocate for free thought on all subjects, yet it appears to me (whether rightly or wrongly) that direct arguments against christianity & theism produce hardly any effect on the public; & freedom of thought is best promoted by the gradual illumination of men's minds, which follow from the advance of science. It has, therefore, been always my object to avoid writing on religion, & I have confined myself to science" (in Desmond and Moore 1991, p. 645).

In classifying the relationship of science and religion, I would like to suggest a three-tiered taxonomy:

> The *same-worlds model:* Science and religion deal with the same subjects and not only is there overlap and conciliation but someday science may subsume religion completely. Frank Tipler's cosmology (1994), based on the anthropic principle and the eventual resurrection of all humans through a supercomputer's virtual reality in the far future of the universe, is one example. Many humanists and evolutionary psychologists foresee a time when science not only can explain the purpose of religion, it will replace it with a viable secular morality and ethics.

> The *separate-worlds model:* Science and religion deal with different subjects, do not conflict or overlap, and the two should coexist peacefully with one another. Charles Darwin, Stephen Jay Gould, and many other scientists hold this model.

> The *conflicting-worlds model:* One is right and the other is wrong, and there can be no reconciliation between the two viewpoints. This model is predominantly held by atheists and creationists, who are often at odds with one another.

This taxonomy allows us to see that Darwin's advice is as applicable today as it was a century ago. Thus, let us be clear that refuting creationists' arguments is not an attack on religion. Let us also be clear

that creationism is an attack on science—all of science, not just evolutionary biology—so the counterarguments presented in this chapter are a response to the antiscience of creationism and have nothing whatsoever to do with antireligion. If creationists are right, then there are serious problems with physics, astronomy, cosmology, geology, paleontology, botany, zoology, and all the life sciences. Can all these sciences be wrong in the same direction? Of course not, but creationists think they are, and, worse, they want their antiscience taught in public schools.

Creationists and religious fundamentalists will go to absurd lengths to protect their beliefs from science. The Summer 1996 issue of the National Center for Science Education's *Reports* notes that in Marshall County, Kentucky, elementary school superintendent Kenneth Shadowen found a rather unique solution to a vexing problem with his fifth- and sixth-graders' science textbooks. It seems that the heretic textbook *Discovery Works* claimed that the universe began with the Big Bang but did not present any "alternatives" to this theory. Since the Big Bang was explained on a two-page spread, Shadowen recalled all the textbooks and glued together the offending pages. Shadowen told the *Louisville Courier-Journal*, "We're not going to teach one theory and not teach another theory" and that the textbook's recall "had nothing to do with censorship or anything like that" (August 23, 1996, A1, p. 1). It seems doubtful that Shadowen was lobbying for equal time for the Steady State theory or Inflationary Cosmology. Perhaps Shadowen found his solution by consulting librarian Ray Martin's "Reviewing and Correcting Encyclopedias," a guide for Christians on how to doctor books:

> Encyclopedias are a vital part of many school libraries. . . . [They] represent the philosophies of present day humanists. This is obvious by the bold display of pictures that are used to illustrate painting, art, and sculpture. . . . One of the areas that needs correction is immodesty due to nakedness and posture. This can be corrected by drawing clothes on the figures or blotting out entire pictures with a magic marker. This needs to be done with care or the magic marker can be erased from the glossy paper used in printing encyclopedias. You can overcome this by taking a razor blade

and lightly scraping the surface until it loses it glaze. . . . [Regarding evolution] cutting out the sections is practical if the portions removed are not thick enough to cause damage to the spine of the book as it is opened and closed in normal use. When the sections needing correction are too thick, paste the pages together being careful not to smear portions of the book not intended for correction. (*Christian School Builder*, April 1983, pp. 205–207)

Fortunately, creationists have failed in their top-down strategy of passing antievolution, pro-creationism laws (Ohio, Tennessee, and Georgia recently rejected creationist legislation), but their bottom-up grassroots campaign bent on injecting Genesis into the public school curriculum has met with success. In March 1996, for example, Governor Fob James used a discretionary fund of taxpayers' money to purchase and send a copy of Phillip Johnson's anti-evolution book, *Darwin on Trial*, to every high school biology teacher in Alabama. Their success should not be surprising. Politically, the United States has taken a sharp turn to the right, and the political strength of the religious right has grown. What can we do? We can counter with our own literature. For example, the National Center for Science Education, Eugenie Scott's Berkeley-based group specializing in tracking creationist activities, countered Governor James's mailing with a mailing that included a critical review of Johnson's book. We can also try to understand the issue thoroughly so that we are prepared to counter procreationist arguments wherever we meet them.

The following is a list of arguments put forth by creationists and answers put forth by evolutionists. The arguments are primarily attacks on evolutionary theory and secondarily (in a minor way) positive statements of creationists' own beliefs. The arguments and answers are simplified due to space constraints; nonetheless, they provide an overview of the principal points of the debate. This list is not meant to substitute for critical reading, however. While these answers might be adequate for casual conversation, they would not be adequate for a formal debate with a well-prepared creationist. Numerous books offer fuller discussions (e.g., Berra 1990; Bowler 1989; Eve and Harrold 1991; Futuyma 1983; Gilkey 1985; Godfrey 1983; Gould 1983a, 1991; Lindberg and Numbers 1986; Numbers 1992; Ruse 1982; and, especially, Strahler 1987).

What Is Evolution?

Before reviewing creationists' arguments against evolution, a brief summary of the theory itself might be useful. Darwin's theory, outlined in his 1859 *On the Origin of Species by Means of Natural Selection*, can be summarized as follows (Gould 1987a; Mayr 1982, 1988):

Evolution: Organisms change through time. Both the fossil record and nature today make this obvious.

Descent with modification: Evolution proceeds via branching through common descent. Offspring are similar to but not exact replicas of their parents. This produces the necessary variation to allow for adaptation to an ever-changing environment.

Gradualism: Change is slow, steady, stately. *Natura non facit saltum*—Nature does not make leaps. Given enough time, evolution accounts for species change.

Multiplication of speciation: Evolution does not just produce new species; it produces an increasing number of new species.

Natural selection: The mechanism of evolutionary change, co-discovered by Darwin and Alfred Russel Wallace, operates as follows:

A. Populations tend to increase indefinitely in a geometric ratio: 2, 4, 8, 16, 32, 64, 128, 256, 512, ...

B. In a natural environment, however, population numbers stabilize at a certain level.

C. Therefore, there must be a "struggle for existence" because not all of the organisms produced can survive.

D. There is variation in every species.

E. In the struggle for existence, those individuals with variations that are better adapted to the environment leave behind more offspring than individuals that are less well adapted. This is known in the jargon of the trade as *differential reproductive success*.

Point E is crucial. Natural selection, and thus evolutionary change, operate primarily at the local level. It is just a game of who can leave behind the most offspring, that is, who can most successfully propagate their genes into the next generation. Natural selection has nothing to say about evolutionary direction, species progress, or any of the other teleological goals, such as human inevitability or the necessary evolution of intelligence, which are commonly attributed to it. There is no ladder of evolutionary progress with humans at the top, only a richly branching bush with humans as one tiny twig among millions. There is nothing special about humans; we just happen to be extremely good at differential reproductive success—we leave behind lots of offspring and are good at getting them into adulthood—a trait that could eventually cause our demise.

Of the five points of Darwin's theory, the most controversial today are gradualism, with Niles Eldredge (1971, 1985; Eldredge and Gould 1972) and Stephen Jay Gould (1985, 1989, 1991) and their supporters pushing for a theory called *punctuated equilibrium,* which involves rapid change and stasis, to replace gradualism; and the exclusivity of natural selection, with Eldredge, Gould, and others arguing for change at the level of genes, groups, and populations in addition to individual natural selection (Somit and Peterson 1992). Ranged against Eldredge, Gould, and their supporters are Daniel Dennett (1995), Richard Dawkins (1995), and those who opt for a strict Darwinian model of gradualism and natural selection. The debate rages, while creationists sit on the sidelines hoping for a double knockout. They will not get it. These scientists are not arguing about *whether* evolution happened; they are debating the *rate* and *mechanism* of evolutionary change. When it all shakes down, the theory of evolution will be stronger than ever. It is sad that while science moves ahead in exciting new areas of research, fine-tuning our knowledge of how life originated and evolved, creationists remain mired in medieval debates about angels on the head of a pin and animals in the belly of an Ark.

Philosophically Based Arguments and Answers

1. Creation-science is scientific and therefore should be taught in public school science courses.

Creation-science is scientific in name only. It is a thinly disguised religious position rather than a theory to be tested using scientific methods, and therefore it is not appropriate for public school science courses, just as calling something Muslim-science or Buddha-science or Christian-science would not mean that it requires equal time. The following statement from the Institute for Creation Research, which must be adhered to by all faculty members and researchers, is a powerful illumination of creationist beliefs: "The scriptures, both Old and New Testaments, are inerrant in relation to any subject with which they deal, and are to be accepted in their natural and intended sense . . . all things in the universe were created and made by God in the six days of special creation described in Genesis. The creationist account is accepted as factual, historical and perspicuous and is thus fundamental in the understanding of every fact and phenomenon in the created universe" (in Rohr 1986, p. 176).

Science is subject to disproof and is ever-changing as new facts and theories reshape our views. Creationism prefers faith in the authority of the Bible no matter what contradictory empirical evidence might exist: "The main reason for insisting on the universal Flood as a fact of history and as the primary vehicle for geological interpretation is that God's Word plainly teaches it! No geological difficulties, real or imagined, can be allowed to take precedence over the clear statements and necessary inferences of Scripture" (in Rohr 1986, p. 190). Here is an analogy. Professors at Caltech declare Darwin's *Origin of Species* dogma, the authority of this book and its author absolute, and any further empirical evidence for or against evolution irrelevant.

2. Science only deals with the here-and-now and thus cannot answer historical questions about the creation of the universe and the origins of life and the human species.

Science does deal with past phenomena, particularly in historical sciences such as cosmology, geology, paleontology, paleoanthropology, and archeology. There are experimental sciences and historical sciences. They use different methodologies but are equally able to track causality. Evolutionary biology is a valid and legitimate historical science.

3. Education is a process of learning all sides of an issue, so it is appropriate for creationism and evolution to be taught side-by-side in public school science courses. Not to do so is a violation of the principles of education and of the civil liberties of creationists. We have a right to be heard, and, besides, what is the harm in hearing both sides?

Exposure to the many facets of issues is indeed a part of the general educational process, and it might be appropriate to discuss creationism in courses on religion, history, or even philosophy but most certainly not science; similarly, biology courses should not include lectures on American Indian creation myths. There is considerable harm in teaching creation-science as science because the consequent blurring of the line between religion and science means that students will not understand what the scientific paradigm is and how to apply it properly. Moreover, the assumptions behind creationism comprise a two-pronged attack on all the sciences, not just on evolutionary biology. One, if the universe and Earth are only about ten thousand years old, then the modern sciences of cosmology, astronomy, physics, chemistry, geology, paleontology, paleoanthropology, and early human history are all invalid. Two, as soon as the creation of even one species is attributed to supernatural intervention, natural laws and inferences about the workings of nature become void. In each case, all science becomes meaningless.

4. There is an amazing correlation between the facts of nature and the acts of the Bible. It is therefore appropriate to use creation-science books and the Bible as reference tools in public school science courses and to study the Bible as a book of science alongside the book of nature.

There is also an amazing correlation between acts in the Bible for which there are no facts in nature and between facts in nature for which there are no acts in the Bible. If a group of Shakespeare scholars believe that the universe is explained in the bard's plays, does that mean science courses should include readings of Shakespeare? Shakespeare's plays are literature, the Bible contains scriptures sacred to several religions, and neither has any pretensions to being a book of science or a scientific authority.

5. The theory of natural selection is tautological, or a form of circular reasoning. Those who survive are the best adapted. Who are the best adapted? Those who survive. Likewise, rocks are used to date fossils, and fossils are used to date rocks. Tautologies do not make a science.

Sometimes tautologies are the beginning of science, but they are never the end. Gravity can be tautological, but its inference is justified by the way this theory allows scientists to accurately predict physical effects and phenomena. Likewise, natural selection and the theory of evolution are testable and falsifiable by looking at their predictive power. For example, population genetics demonstrates quite clearly, and with mathematical prediction, when natural selection will and will not effect change on a population. Scientists can make predictions based on the theory of natural selection and then test them, as the geneticist does in the example just given or the paleontologist does in interpreting the fossil record. Finding hominid fossils in the same geological strata as trilobites, for instance, would be evidence against the theory. The dating of fossils with rocks, and vice versa, could only be done *after* the geological column was established. The geological column exists nowhere in its entirety because strata are disrupted, convoluted, and always incomplete for a variety of

reasons. But strata order is unmistakably *nonrandom*, and chronological order can be accurately pieced together using a variety of techniques, only one of which is fossils.

6. There are only two explanations for the origins of life and existence of humans, plants, and animals: either it was the work of a creator or it was not. Since evolution theory is unsupported by the evidence (i.e., it is wrong), creationism must be correct. Any evidence that does not support the theory of evolution is necessarily scientific evidence in support of creationism.

Beware of the either-or fallacy, or the fallacy of false alternatives. If A is false, B must be true. Oh? Why? Plus, shouldn't B stand on its own regardless of A? Of course. So even if evolutionary theory turns out to be completely wrong, that does not mean that, ergo, creationism is right. There may be alternatives C, D, and E we have yet to consider. There is, however, a true dichotomy in the case of natural versus supernatural explanations. Either life was created and changed by natural means, or it was created and changed by supernatural intervention and according to a supernatural design. Scientists assume natural causation, and evolutionists debate the various natural causal agents involved. They are not arguing about whether it happened by natural or supernatural means. And, again, once you assume supernatural intervention, science goes out the window—so there can be no scientific evidence in support of creationism because natural laws no longer hold and scientific methodology has no meaning in the world of creationists.

7. Evolutionary theory is the basis of Marxism, communism, atheism, immorality, and the general decline of the morals and culture of America, and therefore is bad for our children.

This partakes of the *reductio ad absurdum* fallacy. Neither the theory of evolution in particular nor science in general is no more the basis of these "isms" and Americans' so-called declining morals and culture than the printing press is responsible for Hitler's *Mein Kampf* or *Mein Kampf* is responsible for what people did with Hitler's ideology. The fact that the atomic bomb, the hydrogen bomb, and many even more destructive weapons have been invented does not mean we should abandon the study of the atom. Moreover, there may well be Marxist, communist, atheistic, and even immoral evolutionists, but there are probably just as many capitalist, theist, agnostic, and moral evolutionists. As for the theory itself, it can be used to support Marxist, communist, and atheistic ideologies, and it has; but so has it been used (especially in America) to lend credence to laissez-faire capitalism. The point is that linking scientific theories to political ideologies is tricky business, and we must be cautious of making connections that do not necessarily follow or that serve particular agendas (e.g., one person's cultural and moral decline is another person's cultural and moral progress).

8. Evolutionary theory, along with its bedfellow, secular humanism, is really a religion, so it is not appropriate to teach it in public schools.

To call the science of evolutionary biology a religion is to so broaden the definition of religion as to make it totally meaningless. In other words, religion becomes any lens that we look through to interpret the world. But that is not what religion is. Religion has something to do with the service and worship of God or the supernatural, whereas science has to do with physical phenomena. Religion has to do with faith and the unseen, science focuses on empirical evidence and testable knowledge. Science is a set of methods designed to describe and interpret observed or inferred phenomena, past or present, and aimed at building a testable body of knowledge open to rejection or confirmation. Religion—whatever it is—is certainly neither testable nor open to rejection or confirmation. In their methodologies, science and religion are 180 degrees out of phase with each other.

9. Many leading evolutionists are skeptical of the theory and find it problematic. For example, Eldredge and Gould's theory of punctuated equilibrium proves Darwin wrong. If the world's leading evolutionists cannot agree on the theory, the whole thing must be a wash.

It is particularly ironic that the creationists would quote a leading spokesman against creationism—Gould—in their attempts to marshal the forces of science on their side. Creationists have misunderstood, either naively or intentionally, the healthy scientific debate among evolutionists about the causal agents of organic change. They apparently take this normal exchange of ideas and the self-correcting nature of science as evidence that the field is coming apart at the seams and about to implode. Of the many things evolutionists argue and debate within the field, one thing they are certain of and all agree upon is that evolution has occurred. Exactly how it happened, and what the relative strengths of the various causal mechanisms are, continue to be discussed. Eldredge and Gould's theory of punctuated equilibrium is a refinement of and improvement upon Darwin's theory of evolution. It no more proves Darwin wrong than Einsteinian relativity proves Newton wrong.

10. "The Bible is the written Word of God . . . all of its assertions are historically and scientifically true. The great Flood described in Genesis was an historical event, worldwide in its extent and effect. We are an organization of Christian men of science, who accept Jesus Christ as our Lord and Savior. The account of the special creation of Adam and Eve as one man and one woman, and their subsequent Fall into sin, is the basis for our belief in the necessity of a Savior for all mankind" (in Eve and Harrold 1991, p. 55).

Such a statement of belief is clearly religious. This does not make it wrong, but it does mean that creation-science is really creation-religion and to this extent breaches the wall separating church and state. In private schools funded or controlled by creationists, they are free to teach whatever they like to their children. But one cannot make the events in any text historically and scientifically true by fiat, only by testing the evidence, and to ask the state to direct teachers to teach a particular religious doctrine as science is unreasonable and onerous.

11. All causes have effects. The cause of "X" must be "X-like." The cause of intelligence must be intelligent—God. Regress all causes in time and you must come to the first cause—God. Because all things are in motion, there must have been a prime mover, a mover who needs no other mover to be moved—God. All things in the universe have a purpose, therefore there must be a purposeful designer—God.

If this were true, should not nature then have a natural cause, not a supernatural cause? But causes of "X" do not have to be "X-like." The "cause" of green paint is blue paint mixed with yellow paint, neither one of which is green-like. Animal manure causes fruit trees to grow better. Fruit is delicious to eat and is, therefore, very unmanure-like! The first-cause and prime-mover argument, brilliantly proffered by St. Thomas Aquinas in the fourteenth century (and more brilliantly refuted by David Hume in the eighteenth century), is easily turned aside with just one more question: Who or what caused and moved God? Finally, as Hume demonstrated, purposefulness of design is often illusory and subjective. "The early bird gets the worm" is a clever design if you are the bird, not so good if you are the worm. Two eyes may seem like the ideal number, but, as psychologist Richard Hardison notes cheerfully, "Wouldn't it be desirable to have an additional eye in the back of one's head, and certainly an eye attached to our forefinger would be helpful when we're working behind the instrument panels of automobiles" (1988, p. 123). Purpose is, in part, what we are accustomed to perceiving. Finally, not everything is so purposeful and beautifully designed. In addition to problems like evil, disease, deformities, and human stupidity which creationists conveniently overlook, nature is filled with the bizarre and seemingly unpurposeful. Male nipples and the panda's thumb are just two examples flaunted by Gould as purposeless and poorly designed structures. If God designed life to fit neatly together like a jigsaw puzzle, then what do you do with such oddities and problems?

12. Something cannot be created out of nothing, say scientists. Therefore, from where did the material for the Big Bang come? From where did the first life forms that provided the raw material for evolution originate? Stanley Miller's creation of amino acids out of an inorganic "soup" and other biogenic molecules is not the creation of life.

Science may not be equipped to answer certain "ultimate"-type questions, such as what there was before the beginning of the universe or what time it was before time began or where the matter for the Big Bang came from. So far these have been philosophical or religious questions, not scientific ones, and therefore have not been a part of science. (Recently, Stephen Hawking and other cosmologists have made some attempts at scientific speculations on these questions.) Evolutionary theory attempts to understand the causality of change after time and matter were "created" (whatever that means). As for the origin of life, biochemists do have a very rational and scientific explanation for the evolution from inorganic to organic compounds, the creation of amino acids and the construction of protein chains, the first crude cells, the creation of photosynthesis, the invention of sexual reproduction, and so on. Stanley Miller never claimed to have created life, just some of its building blocks. While these theories are by no means robust and are still subject to lively scientific debate, there is a reasonable explanation for how you get from the Big Bang to the Big Brain in the known universe using the known laws of nature.

Scientifically Based Arguments and Answers

13. Population statistics demonstrate that if we extrapolate backward from the present population using the current rate of population growth, there were only two people living approximately 6,300 years before the present (4300 B.C.E.). This proves that humans and civilization are quite young. If the Earth were old—say, one million years—over the course of 25,000 generations at a 0.5 percent rate of population growth and an average of 2.5 children per family, the present population would be 10 to the power of 2,100 people, which is impossible since there are only 10 to the power of 130 electrons in the known universe.

If you want to play the numbers game, how about this? Applying their model, we find that in 2600 B.C.E. the total population on Earth would have been around 600 people. We know with a high degree of certainty that in 2600 B.C.E. there were flourishing civilizations in Egypt, Mesopotamia, the Indus River Valley, and China. If we give Egypt an extremely generous one-sixth of the world's population, then 100 people built the pyramids, not to mention all the other architectural monuments—they most certainly needed a miracle or two . . . or perhaps the assistance of ancient astronauts!

The fact is that populations do not grow in a steady manner. There are booms and busts, and the history of the human population before the Industrial Revolution is one of prosperity and growth, followed by famine and decline, and punctuated by disaster. In Europe, for instance, about half of the population was killed by a plague during the sixth century, and in the fourteenth century the bubonic plague wiped out about one-third of the population in three years. As humans struggled for millennia to fend off extinction, the population curve was one of peaks and valleys as it climbed uncertainly but steadily upward. It is only since the nineteenth century that the rate of increase has been steadily accelerating.

14. Natural selection can never account for anything other than minor changes within species—microevolution. Mutations used by evolutionists to explain macroevolution are always harmful, rare, and random, and cannot be the driving force of evolutionary change.

I shall never forget the four words pounded into the brains of the students of evolutionary biologist Bayard Brattstrom at California State University, Fullerton: "Mutants are not monsters." His point was that the public perception of mutants—two-headed cows and the like at the county fair—is not the sort of mutants evolutionists are discussing. Most mutations are small genetic or chromosomal aberrations that have small effects—slightly keener hearing, a new shade of fur. Some of these small effects may provide benefits to an organism in an ever-changing environment.

Moreover, Ernst Mayr's (1970) theory of *allopatric speciation* seems to demonstrate precisely how natural selection, in conjunction with other forces and contingencies of nature, can and does produce new species. Whether they agree or disagree with the theory of allopatric speciation and punctuated equilibrium, scientists all agree that natural selection can produce significant change. The debate is over how much change, how rapid a change, and what other forces of nature act in conjunction with or contrary to natural selection. No one, and I mean no one, working in the field is debating whether natural selection is the driving force behind evolution, much less whether evolution happened or not.

15. There are no transitional forms in the fossil record, anywhere, including and especially humans. The whole fossil record is an embarrassment to evolutionists. Neanderthal specimens, for example, are diseased skeletons distorted by arthritis, rickets, and other diseases that create the bowed legs, brow ridge, and larger skeletal structure. *Homo erectus* and *Australopithecus* are just apes.

Creationists always quote Darwin's famous passage in the *Origin of Species* in which he asks, "Why then is not every geological formation and every stratum full of such intermediate links? Geology assuredly does not reveal any such finely graduated organic chain; and this, perhaps, is the gravest objection which can be urged against my theory" (1859, p. 310). Creationists end the quote there and ignore the rest of Darwin's chapter, in which he addresses the problem.

One answer is that plenty of examples of transitional forms have been discovered since Darwin's time. Just look in any paleontology text. The fossil *Archeopteryx*—part reptile, part bird—is a classic example of a transitional form. In my debate with Duane Gish, I presented a slide of the newly discovered *Ambulocetus natans*—a beautiful example of a transitional form from land mammal to whale (see *Science*, January 14, 1994, p. 180). And the charges about the Neanderthals and *Homo erectus* are simply absurd. We now have a treasure trove of human transitional forms.

A second answer is a rhetorical one. Creationists demand just one transitional fossil. When you give it to them, they then claim there is a gap between these two fossils and ask you to present a transitional form between these two. If you do, there are now two more gaps in the fossil record, and so on ad infinitum. Simply pointing this out refutes the argument. You can do it with cups on a table, showing how each time the gap is filled with a cup it creates

two gaps, which when each is filled with a cup creates four gaps, and so on. The absurdity of the argument is visually striking.

A third answer was provided in 1972 by Eldredge and Gould, when they argued that gaps in the fossil record do not indicate missing data of slow and stately change; rather, "missing" fossils are evidence of rapid and episodic change (punctuated equilibrium). Using Mayr's allopatric speciation, where small and unstable "founder" populations are isolated at the periphery of the larger population's range, Eldredge and Gould showed that the relatively rapid change in this smaller gene pool creates new species but leaves behind few, if any, fossils. The process of fossilization is rare and infrequent anyway, but it is almost nonexistent during these times of rapid speciation because the number of individuals is small and the change is swift. A lack of fossils may be evidence for rapid change, not missing evidence for gradual evolution.

16. The Second Law of Thermodynamics proves that evolution cannot be true since evolutionists state that the universe and life move from chaos to order and simple to complex, the exact opposite of the entropy predicted by the Second Law.

First of all, on any scale other than the grandest of all—the 600-million-year history of life on Earth—species do not evolve from simple to complex, and nature does not simply move from chaos to order. The history of life is checkered with false starts, failed experiments, local and mass extinctions, and chaotic restarts. It is anything but a neat Time/Life-book foldout from single cells to humans. Even in the big picture, the Second Law allows for such change because the Earth is in a system that has a constant input of energy from the Sun. As long as the Sun is burning, life may continue thriving and evolving, automobiles may be prevented from rusting, burgers can be heated in ovens, and all manner of other things in apparent violation of the Second Law may continue. But as soon as the Sun burns out, entropy will take over and life will cease and chaos come again. The Second Law of Thermodynamics applies to closed, isolated systems. Since the Earth receives a constant input of energy from the Sun, entropy may decrease and order increase (although the Sun itself is running down in the process). Thus, because the Earth is not strictly a closed system, life may evolve without violating natural laws. In addition, recent research in chaos theory suggests that order can and does spontaneously generate out of apparent chaos, all without violating the Second Law of Thermodynamics (see Kauffman 1993). Evolution no more breaks the Second Law of Thermodynamics than one breaks the law of gravity by jumping up.

17. Even the simplest of life forms are too complex to have come together by random chance. Take a simple organism consisting of merely 100 parts. Mathematically there are 10 to the power of 158 possible ways for the parts to link up. There are not enough molecules in the universe, or time since the beginning, to allow for these possible ways to come together in even this simple life form, let alone to produce human beings. The human eye alone defies explanation by the randomness of evolution. It is the equivalent of the monkey typing *Hamlet*, or even "To be or not to be." It will not happen by random chance.

Natural selection is not random, nor does it operate by chance. Natural selection preserves the gains and eradicates the mistakes. The eye evolved from a single, light-sensitive cell into the complex eye of today through hundreds if not thousands of intermediate steps, many of which still exist in nature (see Dawkins 1986). In order for the monkey to type the thirteen letters opening Hamlet's soliloquy by chance, it would take 26 to the power of 13 trials for success. This is sixteen times as great as the total number of seconds that have elapsed in the lifetime of our solar system. But if each correct letter is preserved and each incorrect letter eradicated, the process operates much faster. How much faster? Richard Hardison (1988) wrote a computer program in which letters were "selected" for or against, and it took an average of only 335.2 trials to produce the sequence of letters TOBEORNOTTOBE. It takes the computer less than ninety seconds. The entire play can be done in about 4.5 days.

18. Hydrodynamic sorting during the Flood explains the apparent progression of fossils in geological strata. The simple, ignorant organisms died in the sea and are on the bottom layers, while more complex, smarter, and faster organisms died higher up.

Not one trilobite floated upward to a higher stratum? Not one dumb horse was on the beach and drowned in a lower stratum? Not one flying pterodactyl made it above the Cretaceous layer? Not one moronic human did not come in out of the rain? And what about the evidence provided by other dating techniques such as radiometry?

19. The dating techniques of evolutionists are inconsistent, unreliable, and wrong. They give false impressions of an old Earth, when in fact it is no **older than ten thousand years, as proven by Dr. Thomas Barnes from the University of Texas at El Paso when he demonstrated that the half-life of the Earth's magnetic field is 1,400 years.**

First of all, Barnes's magnetic field argument assumes that the decay of the magnetic field is linear when geophysics has demonstrated that it fluctuates through time. He is working from a false premise. Second, not only are the various dating techniques quite reliable on their own but there is considerable independent corroboration between them. For example, radiometric dates for different elements from the same rock will all converge on the same date. Finally, how can creationists dismiss all dating techniques with a sweep of the hand except those that purportedly support their position?

20. Classification of organisms above the species level is arbitrary and man-made. Taxonomy proves nothing, especially because so many of the links between species are missing.

The science of classification is indeed man-made, like all sciences, and of course it cannot prove anything about the evolution of organisms absolutely. But its grouping of organisms is anything but arbitrary, even though there is an element of subjectivity to it. An interesting crosscultural test of taxonomy is the fact that Western-trained biologists and native peoples from New Guinea identify the same types of birds as separate species (see Mayr 1988). Such groupings really do exist in nature. Moreover, the goal of modern cladistics—the science of classification through nested hierarchies of similarities—is to make taxonomy less subjective, and it successfully uses inferred evolutionary relationships to arrange taxa in a branching hierarchy such that all members of a given taxon have the same ancestors.

21. If evolution is gradual, there should be no gaps between species.

Evolution is not always gradual. It is often quite sporadic. And evolutionists never said there should not be gaps. Finally, gaps do not prove creation any more than blank spots in human history prove that all civilizations were spontaneously created.

22. "Living fossils" like the coelacanth and horseshoe crab prove that all life was created at once.

The existence of living fossils (organisms that have not changed for millions of years) simply means that they evolved a structure adequate for their relatively static and unchanging environment, so they stopped once they could maintain their ecological niche. Sharks and many other sea creatures are relatively unchanged over millions of years, while other sea creatures, such as marine mammals, have obviously changed rapidly and dramatically. Evolutionary change or lack of change, as the case may be, all depends on how and when a species' immediate environment changes.

23. The incipient structure problem refutes natural selection. A new structure that evolves slowly over time would not provide an advantage to the organism in its beginning or intermediate stages, only when it is completely developed, which can only happen by special creation. What good is 5 percent of a wing, or 55 percent? You need all or nothing.

A poorly developed wing may have been a well-developed something else, like a thermoregulator for ectothermic reptiles (who depend on external sources of heat). And it is not true that incipient stages are completely useless. As Richard Dawkins argues in *The Blind Watchmaker* (1986) and *Climbing Mount Improbable* (1996), 5 percent vision is significantly better than none and being able to get airborne for any length of time can provide an adaptive advantage.

24. Homologous structures (the wing of a bat, the flipper of a whale, the arm of a human) are proof of intelligent design.

By invoking miracles and special providence, the creationist can pick and choose anything in nature as proof of God's work and then ignore the rest. Homologous structures actually make no sense in a special creation paradigm. Why should a whale have the same bones in its flipper as a human has in its arm and a bat has in its wing? God has a limited imagination? God was testing out the possibilities of His designs? God just wanted to do things that way? Surely an omnipotent intelligent designer could have done better. Homologous structures are indicative of descent with modification, not divine creation.

25. The whole history of evolutionary theory in particular and science in general is the history of mistaken theories and overthrown ideas. Nebraska Man, Piltdown Man, Calaveras Man, and *Hesperopithecus* are just a few of the blunders scientists have made. Clearly science cannot be trusted and modern theories are no better than past ones.

Again, it is paradoxical for creationists to simultaneously draw on the authority of science and attack the basic workings of science. Furthermore, this argument reveals a gross misunderstanding of the nature of science. Science does not just change. It constantly builds upon the ideas of the past, and it is cumulative toward the future. Scientists do make mistakes aplenty and, in fact, this is how science progresses. The self-correcting feature of the scientific method is one of its most beautiful features. Hoaxes like Piltdown Man and honest mistakes like *Hesperopithecus* are, in time, exposed. Science picks itself up, shakes itself off, and moves on.

Debates and Truth

These twenty-five answers only scratch the surface of the science and philosophy supporting evolutionary theory. If confronted by a creationist, we would be wise to heed the words of Stephen Jay Gould, who has encountered creationists on many an occasion:

> Debate is an art form. It is about the winning of arguments. It is not about the discovery of truth. There are certain rules and procedures to debate that really have nothing to do with establishing fact—which they are very good at. Some of those rules are: never say anything positive about your own position because it can be attacked, but chip away at what appear to be the weaknesses in your opponent's position. They are good at that. I don't think I could beat the creationists at debate. I can tie them. But in courtrooms they are terrible, because in courtrooms you cannot give speeches. In a courtroom you have to answer direct questions about the positive status of your belief. We destroyed them in Arkansas. On the second day of the two-week trial, we had our victory party! (Caltech lecture, 1985)

"CONFRONTING CREATIONISTS"

Michael Shermer

1) What are the three models that Shermer suggests are representative of the range of beliefs that people have regarding the relationship between science and religion?

2) What tactics have creationists used to protect their beliefs from the impact of science?

3) Does Shermer consider refuting creationist ideas to be an attack on religion? Do you believe this? Why or why not?

4) Discuss in broad outline evolutionary theory using Shermer's summary.

5) Select one or two arguments employed by creationists and using Feder's "Epistomology . . ." article ask the following questions about the arguments:

a) Does the argument follow the four operating principles of science that Feder defines?

b) What are the scientific, social, legal, and religious issues involved?

c) Does this creationist argument (and thus creationism) fit the definition of a *theory* as employed in science?

EMPIRE OF UNIFORMITY

Jared Diamond

Immigration, affirmative action, multilingualism, ethnic diversity—my state of California pioneered these controversial policies, and it is now pioneering a backlash against them. A glance into the classrooms of the Los Angeles public schools, where my sons are being educated, fleshes out the abstract debates with the faces of children. Those pupils speak more than 80 languages in their homes; English-speaking whites are in the minority. Every single one of my sons' playmates has at least one parent or grandparent who was born outside the United States. That's true of my sons also—three of their four grandparents were immigrants to this country. But the diversity that results from such immigration isn't new to America. In fact, immigration is simply restoring the diversity that existed here for thousands of years and that diminished only recently; the area that now makes up the mainland United States, once home to hundreds of Native American tribes and languages, did not come under the control of a single government until the late nineteenth century.

In these respects, ours is a thoroughly "normal" country. Like the United States, all but one of the world's six most populous nations are melting pots that achieved political unification recently and that still support hundreds of languages and ethnic groups. Russia, for example, once a small Slavic state centered on Moscow, did not even begin its expansion beyond the Ural Mountains until 1582. From then until the late nineteenth century, Russia swallowed up dozens of non-Slavic peoples, many of whom, like the people of Chechnya today, retain their original language and cultural identity. India, Indonesia, and Brazil are also recent political creations (or re-creations, in the case of India) and are home to about 850, 703, and 209 languages, respectively.

The great exception to this rule of the recent melting pot is the world's most populous nation, China. Today China appears politically, culturally, and linguistically monolithic. (For the purposes of this article, I exclude the linguistically and culturally distinct Tibet, which was also politically separate until recently.) China was already unified politically in 221 B.C. and has remained so for most of the centuries since then. From the beginnings of literacy in China over 3,000 years ago, it has had only a single writing system, unlike the dozens in use in modern Europe. Of China's billion-plus people, over 700 million speak Mandarin, the language with by far the largest number of native speakers in the world. Some 250 million other Chinese speak seven languages as similar to Mandarin and to each other as Spanish is to Italian. Thus, while modern American history is the story of how our continent's expanse became American, and Russia's history is the story of how Russia became Russian, China's history appears to be entirely different. It seems absurd to ask how China became Chinese. China has *been* Chinese almost from the beginning of its recorded history.

We take this unity of China so much for granted that we forget how astonishing it is. Certainly we should not have expected such unity on the basis of genetics. While a coarse racial classification of world peoples lumps all Chinese people together as Mongoloids, that category conceals much more variation than is found among such (equally ill-termed) Caucasian peoples as Swedes, Italians, and Irish. Northern and southern Chinese, in particular, are genetically and physically rather different from each other: northerners are most similar to Tibetans and Nepali, southerners to Vietnamese and Filipinos. My northern and southern Chinese friends can often distinguish each other at a glance: northerners tend to be taller, heavier, paler, with more pointed noses and smaller eyes.

The existence of such differences is hardly surprising: northern and southern China differ in environment and climate, with the north drier and colder. That such genetic differences arose between the peoples of these two regions simply implies a long history of their moderate isolation from each other. But if such isolation existed, then how did these peoples end up with such similar languages and cultures?

China's linguistic near-unity is also puzzling in comparison with the linguistic *dis*unity of other parts of the world. For instance, New Guinea, although it was first settled by humans only about 40,000 years ago, evolved roughly 1,000 languages. Western Europe has by now about 40 native languages acquired just in the past 6,000 to 8,000 years, including languages as different as English, Finnish, and Russian. Yet New

Guinea's peoples are spread over an area less than one-tenth that of China's. And fossils attest to human presence in China for hundreds of thousands of years. By rights, tens of thousands of distinct languages should have arisen in China's large area over that long time span; what has happened to them? China too must once have been a melting pot of diversity, as all other populous nations still are. It differs from them only in having been unified much earlier: in that huge pot, the melting happened long ago.

A glance at a linguistic map is an eye-opener to all of us accustomed to thinking of China as monolithic. In addition to its eight "big" languages—Mandarin and its seven close relatives (often referred to collectively as Chinese), with between 11 million and 700 million speakers each—China also has some 160 smaller languages, many of them with just a few thousand speakers. All these languages fall into four families, which differ greatly in their distributions.

At one extreme, Mandarin and its relatives, which constitute the Chinese subfamily of the Sino-Tibetan language family, are distributed continuously from the top of the country to the bottom. One distinctive feature of all Sino-Tibetan languages is that most words consist of a single syllable, like English *it* or *book*; long, polysyllabic words are unthinkable. One could walk through China, from Manchuria in the north to the Gulf of Tonkin in the south, without ever stepping off land occupied by native speakers of Chinese.

The other three families have broken distributions, being spoken by islands of people surrounded by a sea of speakers of Chinese and other languages. The 6 million speakers of the Miao-Yao family are divided among five languages, bearing colorful names derived from the characteristic colors of the speakers' clothing: Red Miao, White Miao (alias Striped Miao), Black Miao, Green Miao (alias Blue Miao), and Yao. Miao-Yao speakers live in dozens of small enclaves scattered over half a million square miles from southern China to Thailand.

The 60 million speakers of languages in the Austroasiatic family, such as Vietnamese and Cambodian, are also scattered across the map, from Vietnam in the east to the Malay Peninsula in the south to northeastern India in the west. Austroasiatic languages are characterized by an enormous proliferation of vowels, which can be nasal or nonnasal, long or extra short, creaky, breathy, or normal, produced with the tongue high, medium high, medium low, or low, and with the front, center, or back of the tongue. All these choices combine to yield up to 41 distinctive vowel sounds per language, in contrast to the mere dozen or so of English.

The 50 million speakers of China's fourth language family, Tai-Kadai, are scattered from southern China south ward into peninsular Thailand and west to Myanmar (Burma). In Tai-Kadai languages, as in most Sino-Tibetan languages, a single word may have different meanings depending on its tone, or pitch. For example, in Thai itself the syllable *maa* means "horse" when pronounced at a high pitch, "come" at a medium pitch, and "dog" at a rising pitch.

Seen on a map, the current fragmented distribution of these language groups suggests a series of ancient helicopter flights that dropped speakers here and there over the Asian landscape. But of course nothing like that could have happened, and the actual process was subtractive rather than additive. Speakers of the now dominant language expanded their territory and displaced original residents or induced them to abandon their native tongues. The ancestors of modern speakers of Thai and Laotian, and possibly Cambodian and Burmese as well, all moved south from southern China and adjacent areas to their present locations within historical times, successively inundating the settled descendants of previous migrations. Chinese speakers were especially vigorous in replacing and linguistically converting other ethnic groups, whom they looked down on as primitive and inferior. The recorded history of China's Chou Dynasty, from 1111 B.C. to 256 B.C., describes the conquest and absorption of most of China's non-Chinese-speaking population by Chinese-speaking states.

Before those relatively recent migrations, who spoke what where? To reconstruct the linguistic map of the East Asia of several thousand years ago, we can reverse the historically known linguistic expansions of recent millennia. We can also look for large, continuous areas currently occupied by a single language or related language group; these areas testify to a geographic expansion of that group so recent that there has not been enough time for it to differentiate into many languages. Finally, we can reason conversely that modern areas with a high diversity of languages within a given language family lie closer to the early center of distribution of that language family. Using those three types of reasoning to turn back the linguistic clock, we conclude that speakers of Chinese and other Sino-Tibetan languages originally occupied northern China. The southern parts of the country were variously inhabited by speakers of Miao-Yao, Austroasiatic, and Tai-Kadai languages—until they were largely replaced by their Sino-Tibetan-speaking neighbors.

An even more drastic linguistic upheaval appears to have swept over tropical Southeast Asia to the south of China, in Thailand, Myanmar, Laos, Cambodia, Vietnam, and peninsular Malaysia. It's likely that whatever languages were originally spoken there have now become extinct—most of the modern languages of those countries appear to be recent invaders, mainly from southern China. We might also guess that if Miao-Yao languages could be so nearly overwhelmed, there must have been still other language families in southern China that left no modern descendants whatsoever. As we shall see, the Austronesian family (to which all Philippine and Polynesian languages belong) was probably once spoken on the Chinese mainland. We know about it only because it spread to Pacific islands and survived there.

The language replacements in East Asia are reminiscent of the way European languages, especially English and Spanish, spread into the New World. English, of course, came to replace the hundreds of Native American languages not because it sounded musical to indigenous ears but because English-speaking invaders killed most Native Americans by war, murder, and disease and then pressured the survivors into adopting the new majority language. The immediate cause of the Europeans' success was their relative technological superiority. That superiority, however, was ultimately the result of a geographic accident that allowed agriculture and herding to develop in Eurasia 10,000 years earlier. The consequent explosion in population allowed the Europeans to develop complex technologies and social organization, giving their descendants great political and technological advantages over the people they conquered. Essentially the same processes account for why English replaced aboriginal Australian languages and why Bantu languages replaced subequatorial Africa's original Pygmy and Khoisan languages.

East Asia's linguistic upheavals thus hint that some Asians enjoyed similar advantages over other Asians. But to flesh out the details of that story, we must turn from linguistics to archeology.

As everywhere else in the world, the eastern Asian archeological record for most of human history reveals only the debris of hunter-gatherers using unpolished stone tools. The first eastern Asian evidence for something different comes from China, where crop remains, bones of domestic animals, pottery, and polished stone tools appear by around 7500 B.C. That's no more than a thousand years after the beginnings of agriculture in the Fertile Crescent, the area with the oldest established food production in the world.

In China plant and animal domestication may even have started independently in two or more places. Besides differences in climate between north and south, there are also ecological differences between the interior uplands (which are characterized by mountains like our Appalachians) and the coastal lowlands (which are flat and threaded with rivers, like the Carolinas). Incipient farmers in each area would have had different wild plants and animals to draw on. In fact, the earliest identified crops were two drought-resistant species of millet in northern China, but rice in the south.

The same sites that provided us with the earliest evidence of crops also contained bones of domestic pigs, dogs, and chickens—a livestock trinity that later spread as far as Polynesia. These animals and crops were gradually joined by China's many other domesticates. Among the animals were water buffalo (the most important, since they were used for pulling plows), as well as silkworms, ducks, and geese. Familiar later Chinese crops include soybeans, hemp, tea, apricots, pears, peaches, and citrus fruits. Many of these domesticated animals and crops spread westward in ancient times from China to the Fertile Crescent and Europe; at the same time, Fertile Crescent domesticates spread eastward to China. Especially significant western contributions to ancient China's economy were wheat and barley, cows and horses, and to a lesser extent, sheep and goats.

As elsewhere in the world, food production in China gradually led to the other hallmarks of "civilization." A superb Chinese tradition of bronze metallurgy arose around 3000 B.C., allowing China to develop by far the earliest cast iron production in the world by 500 B.C. The following 1,500 years saw the outpouring of a long list of Chinese inventions: canal lock gates, deep drilling, efficient animal harnesses, gunpowder, kites, magnetic compasses, paper, porcelain, printing, stern-post rudders, and wheelbarrows, to name just a few.

China's size and ecological diversity initially spawned many separate local cultures. In the fourth millennium B.C. those local cultures expanded geographically and began to interact, compete with each other, and coalesce. Fortified towns appeared in China in the third millennium B.C., with cemeteries containing luxuriously decorated graves juxtaposed with simpler ones—a clear sign of emerging class differences. China became home to stratified societies with rulers who could mobilize a large labor force of commoners, as we can infer from the remains of huge urban defensive walls, palaces, and the Grand Canal—the longest canal in the world—linking northern and southern China. Writing unmistakably ancestral to that of modern China is preserved from the second millennium B.C., though it probably arose earlier. The first of China's dynasties, the Hsia Dynasty, arose around 2000 B.C. Thereafter, our archeological knowledge of China's emerging cities and states becomes supplemented by written accounts.

Along with rice cultivation and writing, a distinctively Chinese method for reading the future also begins to appear persistently in the archeological record, and it too attests to China's cultural coalescence. In place of crystal balls and Delphic oracles, China turned to scapulimancy— burning the scapula (shoulder bone) or other large bone of an animal, such as a cow, then prophesying from the pattern of cracks in the burned bone. From the earliest known appearance of oracle bones in northern China, archeologists have traced scapulimancy's spread throughout China's cultural sphere.

Just as exchanges of domesticates between ecologically diverse regions enriched Chinese food production, exchanges between culturally diverse regions enriched Chinese culture and technology, and fierce competition between warring chiefdoms drove the formation of ever larger and more centralized states. China's long west–east rivers (the Yellow River in the north, the Yangtze in the south) allowed crops and technology to spread quickly between inland and coast, while their diffusion north and south was made easy by the broad, relatively gentle terrain north of the Yangtze, which eventually permitted the two river systems to be joined by canals. All those geographic factors contributed to the early cultural and political unification of China. In contrast, western Europe, with an area comparable to China's but fragmented by mountains such as the Alps, and with a highly indented coastline and no such rivers, has never been unified politically.

Some developments spread from south to north in China, especially iron smelting and rice cultivation. But the predominant direction of spread seems to have been the other way. From northern China came bronze technology, Sino-Tibetan languages, and state formation. The country's first three dynasties (the Hsia, Shang, and Chou) all arose in the north in the second millennium B.C. The northern dominance is clearest, however, for writing. Unlike western Eurasia, with its plethora of early methods for recording language, including Sumerian cuneiform, Egyptian hieroglyphics, Hittite, Minoan, and the Semitic alphabet, China developed just one writing system. It arose in the north, preempted or replaced any other nascent system, and evolved into the writing used today.

Preserved documents show that already in the first millennium B.C. ethnic Chinese tended to feel culturally superior to non-Chinese "barbarians," and northern Chinese considered even southern Chinese barbarians. For example, a late Chou Dynasty writer described China's other peoples as follows: "The people of those five regions—the Middle states and the Jung, Yi, and other wild tribes around them— had all their several natures, which they could not be made to alter. The tribes on the east were called Yi. They had their hair unbound, and tattooed their bodies. Some of them ate their food without its being cooked by fire." The author went on to describe wild tribes to the south, west, and north indulging in equally barbaric practices, such as turning their feet inward, tattooing their foreheads, wearing skins, living in caves, not eating cereals, and, again, eating their food raw.

States modeled on the Chou Dynasty were organized in southern China during the first millennium B.C., culminating in China's political unification under the Chin Dynasty in 221 B.C. China's cultural unification accelerated during that same period, as literate "civilized" Chinese states absorbed or were copied by the preliterate "barbarians." Some of that cultural unification was ferocious: for instance, the first Chin emperor condemned all previously written historical books as worthless and ordered them burned, much to the detriment of our understanding of early Chinese history. That and other draconian measures must have helped spread northern China's Sino-Tibetan languages over most of China.

Chinese innovations contributed heavily to developments in neighboring regions as well. For instance, until roughly 4000 B.C. most of tropical Southeast Asia was still occupied by hunter-gatherers making pebble and flake stone tools. Thereafter, Chinese-derived crops, polished stone tools, village living, and pottery spread into the area, probably accompanied by southern Chinese language families. The southward expansions from southern China of Laotians, Thai, and Vietnamese, and probably Burmese and Cambodians also, completed the "Sinification" of tropical Southeast Asia. All those modern peoples appear to be recent offshoots of their southern Chinese cousins.

So overwhelming was this Chinese steamroller that the former peoples of the region have left behind few traces in the modern populations. Just three relict groups of hunter-gatherers—the Semang Negritos of the Malay Peninsula, the Andaman Islanders, and the Veddoid Negritos of Sri Lanka—remain to give us any clue as to what those peoples were like. They suggest that tropical Southeast Asia's former inhabitants may have had dark skin and curly hair, like modern New Guineans and unlike southern Chinese and modern tropical Southeast Asians. Those people may also be the last survivors of the source population from which New Guinea and aboriginal Australia were colonized. As to their speech, only on the remote Andaman Islands do languages unrelated to the southern Chinese language families persist—perhaps the last linguistic survivors of what may have been hundreds of now extinct aboriginal Southeast Asian languages.

While one prong of the Chinese expansion thus headed southwest into Indochina and Myanmar, another headed southeast into the Pacific Ocean. Part of the evidence suggesting this scenario comes from genetics and linguistics: the modern inhabitants of Indonesia and the Philippines are fairly homogeneous in their genes and appearance and resemble southern Chinese Their languages are also homogeneous, almost all belonging to a closely knit family called Austronesian, possibly related to Tai-Kadai.

But just as in tropical Southeast Asia, the archeological record in the Pacific shows more direct evidence of the Chinese steamroller. Until 6,000 years ago, Indonesia and the Philippines were sparsely occupied by hunter-gatherers. Beginning in the fourth or fifth millennium B.C., pottery and stone tools of unmistakably southern Chinese origins appear on the island of Taiwan, which is in the straits between the southern Chinese coast and the Philippines. Around 3000 B.C.. that same combination of technological advances spread as a wave to the Philippines, then throughout the islands of Indonesia, accompanied by gardening and by China's livestock trinity (pigs, chickens, and dogs). Around 1600 B.C. the wave reached the islands north of New Guinea, then spread eastward through the previously uninhabited islands of Polynesia. By 500 A.D. the Polynesians, an *Austronesian* speaking people of ultimately Chinese origin, had reached Easter Island, 10,000 miles from the Chinese coast. With Polynesian settlement of Hawaii and New Zealand around the same time or soon thereafter, ancient China's occupation of the Pacific was complete.

Throughout most of Indonesia and the Philippines, the Austronesian expansion obliterated the region's former inhabitants. Scattered bands of hunter-gatherers were no match for the tools, weapons, numbers, subsistence methods, and probably also germs carried by the invading Austronesian farmers. Only the Negrito Pygmies in the mountains of Luzon and some other Philippine islands appear to represent survivors of those former hunter-gatherers, but they too lost their original tongues and adopted Austronesian languages from their new neighbors. However, on New Guinea and adjacent islands, indigenous people had already developed agriculture and built up numbers sufficient to keep out the Austronesian invaders. Their languages, genes, and faces live on in modern New Guineans and Melanesians.

Even Korea and Japan were heavily influenced by China, although their geographic isolation from the mainland saved them from losing their languages or physical and genetic distinctness. Korea and Japan adopted rice from China in the second millennium B.C.., bronze metallurgy in the first millennium B.C., and writing in the first or early second millennium A.D.

Not all cultural advances in East Asia stemmed from China, of course, nor were Koreans, Japanese, and tropical Southeast Asians noninventive "barbarians" who contributed nothing. The ancient Japanese developed pottery at least as early as the Chinese did, and they settled in villages subsisting on Japan's rich seafood resources long before the arrival of agriculture. Some crops were probably domesticated initially or independently in Japan, Korea, and tropical Southeast Asia. But China's role was still disproportionately large. Indeed, the influence of Chinese culture is still so great that Japan has no thought of discarding its Chinese-derived writing system despite its disadvantages for representing Japanese speech, while Korea is only now replacing its clumsy Chinese-derived writing with its wonderful indigenous Hangul alphabet. The persistence of Chinese writing in Japan and Korea is a vivid twentieth-century legacy of plant and animal domestication that began in China 10,000 years ago. From those achievements of East Asia's first farmers, China became Chinese, and peoples from Thailand to Easter Island became their cousins.

"EMPIRE OF UNIFORMITY"

Jared Diamond

1) In what ways—culturally, politically, linguistically—does China differ from other state-level societies in the modern world?

2) Why does Diamond state that China's uniformity is remarkable when compared to other cultures?

3) What advantage did Mandarin/Chinese speakers have over speakers of other languages that originally held sway over large parts of prehistoric China?

4) What influences has Chinese culture exerted over other Asian cultures in terms of language, writing systems, technology, and other cultural traits?

THE PRICE OF PROGRESS

John Bodley

Until recently, government planners have always considered economic development and progress beneficial goals that all societies should want to strive toward. The social advantages of progress—as defined in terms of increased incomes, higher standards of living, greater security, and better health—are thought to be positive, *universal* goods, to be obtained at any price. Although one may argue that tribal peoples must sacrifice their traditional cultures to obtain these benefits, government planners generally feel that this is a small price to pay for such obvious advantages.

In earlier chapters, evidence was presented to demonstrate that autonomous tribal peoples have not *chosen* progress to enjoy its advantages, but that governments have *pushed* progress upon them to obtain tribal resources, not primarily to share with the tribal peoples the benefits of progress. It has also been shown that the price of forcing progress on unwilling recipients has involved the deaths of millions of tribal people, as well as their loss of land, political sovereignty, and the right to follow their own life style. This chapter does not attempt to further summarize that aspect of the cost of progress, but instead analyzes the specific effects of the participation of tribal peoples in the world-market economy. In direct opposition to the usual interpretation, it is argued here that the benefits of progress are often both illusory and detrimental to tribal peoples when they have not been allowed to control their own resources and define their relationship to the market economy.

Progress and the Quality of Life

One of the primary difficulties in assessing the benefits of progress and economic development for any culture is that of establishing a meaningful measure of both benefit and detriment. It is widely recognized that *standard of living*, which is the most frequently used measure of progress, is an intrinsically ethnocentric concept relying heavily upon indicators that lack universal cultural relevance. Such factors as GNP, per capita income, capital formation, employment rates, literacy, formal education, consumption of manufactured goods, number of doctors and hospital beds per thousand persons, and the amount of money spent on government welfare and health programs may be irrelevant measures of actual *quality* of life for autonomous or even semiautonomous tribal cultures. In its 1954 report, the Trust Territory government indicated that since the Micronesian population was still largely satisfying its own needs within a cashless subsistence economy, "Money income is not a significant measure of living standards, production, or well-being in this area" (TTR, 1953:44). Unfortunately, within a short time the government began to rely on an enumeration of certain imported goods as indicators of a higher standard of living in the islands, even though many tradition-oriented islanders felt that these new goods symbolized a lowering of the quality of life.

A more useful measure of the benefits of progress might be based on a formula for evaluating cultures devised by Goldschmidt (1952:135). According to these less ethnocentric criteria, the important question to ask is: Does progress or economic development increase or decrease a given culture's ability to satisfy the physical and psychological needs of its population, or its stability? This question is a far more direct measure of quality of life than are the standard economic correlates of development, and it is universally relevant. Specific indication of this *standard* of living could be found for any society in the nutritional status and general physical and mental health of its population, the incidence of crime and delinquency, the demographic structure, family stability, and the society's relationship to its natural resource base. A society with high rates of malnutrition and crime, and one degrading, its natural environment to the extent of threatening its continued existence, might be described as at a lower standard of living than is another society where these problems did not exist.

Careful examination of the data, which compare, on these specific points, the former condition of self sufficient tribal peoples with their condition following their incorporation into the world-market economy, leads to the conclusion that their standard of living is *lowered*, not raised, by economic progress—and often to a dramatic degree. This is perhaps the most outstanding and inescapable fact to emerge from the years of research that anthropologists have devoted to the study of culture change and modernization. Despite the best intentions of those who have promoted change and improvement, all too often the results have been poverty, longer working hours, and much greater physical exertion, poor health, social disorder, discontent, discrimination, overpopulation, and environmental deterioration—combined with the destruction of the traditional culture.

Diseases of Development

Perhaps it would be useful for public health specialists to start talking about a new category of diseases . . . Such diseases could be called the "diseases of development" and would consist of those pathological conditions which are based on the usually unanticipated consequences of the implementation of development schemes [Hughes & Hunter, 1972:93].

Economic development increases the disease rate of affected peoples in at least three ways. First, to the extent that development is successful, it makes developed populations suddenly become vulnerable to all of the diseases suffered almost exclusively by "advanced" peoples. Among these are diabetes, obesity, hypertension, and a variety of circulatory problems. Second, development disturbs traditional environmental balances and may dramatically increase certain bacterial and parasite diseases. Finally, when development goals prove unattainable, an assortment of poverty diseases may appear in association with the crowded conditions of urban slums and the general breakdown in traditional socioeconomic systems.

Outstanding examples of the first situation can be seen in the Pacific, where some of the most successfully developed native peoples are found. In Micronesia, where development has progressed more rapidly than perhaps anywhere else, between 1958 and 1972 the population doubled, but the number of patients treated for heart disease in the local hospitals nearly tripled, mental disorder increased eightfold, and by 1972 hypertension and nutritional deficiencies began to make significant appearances for the first time (TTR, 1959,1973, statistical tables).

Although some critics argue that the Micronesian figures simply represent better health monitoring due to economic progress, rigorously controlled data from Polynesia show a similar trend. The progressive acquisition of modern degenerative diseases was documented by an eight-member team of New Zealand medical specialists, anthropologists, and nutritionists, whose research was funded by the Medical Research Council of New Zealand and the World Health Organization. These researchers investigated the health status of a genetically related population at various points along a continuum of increasing cash income, modernizing diet, and urbanization. The extremes on this acculturation continuum were represented by the relatively traditional Pukapukans of the Cook Islands and the essentially Europeanized New Zealand Maori, while the busily developing Rarotongans, also of the Cook Islands, occupied the intermediate position. In 1971, after eight years of work, the team's preliminary findings were summarized by Dr. Ian Prior, cardiologist and leader of the research, as follows:

We are beginning to observe that the more an islander takes on the ways of the West, the more prone he is to succumb to our degenerative diseases. In fact, it does not seem too much to say our evidence now shows that the farther the Pacific natives move from the quiet, care-free life of their ancestors, the closer they come to gout, diabetes, atherosclerosis, obesity, and hypertension [Prior, 1971:2].

In Pukapuka, where progress was limited by the island's small size and its isolated location some 480 kilometers from the nearest port, the annual per capita income was only about thirty-six dollars and the economy remained essentially at a subsistence level. Resources were limited and the area was visited by trading ships only three or four times a year; thus, there was little opportunity for intensive economic development. Predictably, the population of Pukapuka was characterized by relatively low levels of imported sugar and salt intake, and a presumably related low level of heart disease, high blood pressure, and diabetes. In Rarotonga, where economic success was introducing town life, imported food, and motorcycles, sugar and salt intakes nearly tripled, high blood pressure increased approximately ninefold, diabetes two to threefold, and heart disease doubled for men and more than quadrupled for women, while the number of grossly obese women increased more than tenfold. Among the New Zealand Maori, sugar intake was nearly eight times that of the Pukapukans, gout in men was nearly double its rate on Pukapuka, and diabetes in men was more than fivefold higher, while heart disease in women had increased more than sixfold. The Maori were, in fact, dying of "European" diseases at a greater rate than was the average New Zealand European.

Government development policies designed to bring about changes in local hydrology, vegetation, and settlement patterns and to increase population mobility, and even programs aimed at reducing certain diseases, have frequently led to dramatic increases in disease rates because of the unforeseen effects of disturbing the preexisting order. Hughes and

Hunter (1972) published an excellent survey of cases in which development led directly to increased disease rates in Africa. They concluded that hasty development intervention in relatively balanced local cultures and environments resulted in "a drastic deterioration in the social and economic conditions of life."

Traditional populations in general have presumably learned to live with the endemic pathogens of their environments, and in some cases they have evolved genetic adaptations to specific diseases, such as the sickle-cell trait, which provided an immunity to malaria. Unfortunately, however, outside intervention has entirely changed this picture. In the late 1960s, sleeping sickness suddenly increased in many areas of Africa and even spread to areas where it did not for merly occur, due to the building of new roads and migratory labor, both of which caused increased population movement. Large-scale relocation schemes, such as the Zande Scheme, had disastrous results when natives were moved from their traditional disease-free refuges into infected areas. Dams and irrigation developments inadvertently created ideal conditions for the rapid proliferation of snails carrying schistosomiasis (a liver fluke disease), and major epidemics suddenly occurred in areas where this disease had never before been a problem. DDT spraying programs have been temporarily successful in controlling malaria, but there is often a rebound effect that increases the problem when spraying is discontinued, and the malarial mosquitoes are continually evolving resistant strains.

Urbanization is one of the prime measures of development, but it is a mixed blessing for most former tribal peoples. Urban health standards are abysmally poor and generally worse than in rural areas for the detribalized individuals who have crowded into the towns and cities throughout Africa, Asia, and Latin America seeking wage employment out of new economic necessity. Infectious diseases related to crowding and poor sanitation are rampant in urban centers, while greatly increased stress and poor nutrition aggravate a variety of other health problems. Malnutrition and other diet-related conditions are, in fact, one of the characteristic hazards of progress faced by tribal peoples and are discussed in the following sections.

The Hazards of Dietary Change

The traditional diets of tribal peoples are admirably adapted to their nutritional needs and available food resources. Even though these diets may seem bizarre, absurd, and unpalatable to outsiders, they are un-

likely to be improved by drastic modifications. Given the delicate balances and complexities involved in any subsistence system, change always involves risks, but for tribal people the effects of dietary change have been catastrophic.

Under normal conditions, food habits are remarkably resistant to change, and indeed people are unlikely to abandon their traditional diets voluntarily in favor of dependence on difficult-to-obtain exotic imports. In some cases it is true that imported foods may be identified with powerful outsiders and are therefore sought as symbols of greater prestige. This may lead to such absurdities as Amazonian Indians choosing to consume imported canned tunafish when abundant high-quality fish is available in their own rivers. An other example of this situation occurs in tribes where mothers prefer to feed their infants expensive and nutritionally inadequate canned milk from unsanitary, but *high status*, baby bottles. The high status of these items is often promoted by clever traders and clever advertising campaigns.

Aside from these apparently voluntary changes, it appears that more often dietary changes are forced upon unwilling tribal peoples by circumstances beyond their control. In some areas, new food crops have been introduced by government decree, or as a consequence of forced relocation or other policies designed to end hunting, pastoralism, or shifting cultivation. Food habits have also been modified by massive disruption of the natural environment by outsiders—as when sheepherders transformed—the Australian Aborigine's foraging territory or when European invaders destroyed the bison herds that were the primary element in the Plains Indians' subsistence patterns. Perhaps the most frequent cause of diet change occurs when formerly self-sufficient peoples find that wage labor, cash cropping, and other economic development activities that feed tribal resources into the world market economy must inevitably divert time and energy away from the production of subsistence foods. Many developing peoples suddenly discover that, like it or not, they are unable to secure traditional foods and must spend their newly acquired cash on costly, and often nutritionally inferior, manufactured foods.

Overall, the available data seem to indicate that the dietary changes that are linked to involvement in the world-market economy have tended to *lower* rather than raise the nutritional levels of the affected tribal peoples. Specifically, the vitamin, mineral, and protein components of their diets are often drastically reduced and replaced by enormous increases in starch and carbohydrates, often in the form of white flour and refined sugar.

Any deterioration in the quality of a given population's diet is almost certain to be reflected in an increase in deficiency diseases and a general decline in health status. Indeed, as tribal peoples have shifted to a diet based on imported manufactured or processed foods, there has been a dramatic rise in malnutrition, a massive increase in dental problems, and a variety of other nutrition-related disorders. Nutritional physiology is so complex that even well-meaning dietary changes have had tragic consequences. In many areas of Southeast Asia, government-sponsored protein supplementation programs supplying milk to protein deficient populations caused unexpected health problems and increased mortality. Officials failed to anticipate that in cultures where adults do not normally drink milk, the enzymes needed to digest it are no longer produced and milk *intolerance* results (Davis & Bolin, 1972). In Brazil, a similar milk distribution program caused an epidemic of permanent blindness by aggravating a preexisting vitamin A deficiency (Bunce, 1972).

Teeth and Progress

There is nothing new in the observation that savages, or peoples living under primitive conditions, have, in general excellent teeth . . . Nor is it news that most civilized populations possess wretched teeth which begin to decay almost before they have erupted completely, and that dental caries is likely to be accompanied by periodontal disease with further reaching complications [Hooton, 1945:xviii].

Anthropologists have long recognized that undisturbed tribal peoples are often in excellent physical condition. And it has often been noted specifically that dental caries and the other dental abnormalities that plague industrialized societies are absent or rare among tribal peoples who have retained their traditional diets. The fact that tribal food habits may contribute to the development of sound teeth, whereas modernized diets may do just the opposite, was illustrated as long ago as 1894 in an article in the *Journal of the Royal Anthropological Institute* that described the results of a comparison between the teeth of ten Sioux Indians and a comparable group of Londoners (Smith, 1894:109–116). The Indians were examined when they came to London as members of Buffalo Bill's Wild West Show and were found to be completely free of caries and in possession of all their teeth, even though half of the group were over thirty-nine years of age. Londoners' teeth were conspicuous for both their caries and their steady reduction in number with advancing age. The difference was

attributed primarily to the wear and polishing caused by the traditional Indian diet of coarse food and the fact that they chewed their food longer, encouraged by the absence of tableware.

One of the most remarkable studies of the dental conditions of tribal peoples and the impact of dietary change was conducted in the 1930s by Weston Price (1945), an American dentist who was interested in determining what caused normal, healthy teeth. Between 1931 and 1936, Price systematically explored tribal areas throughout the world to locate and examine the most isolated peoples who were still living on traditional foods. His fieldwork covered Alaska, the Canadian Yukon, Hudson Bay, Vancouver Island, Florida, the Andes, the Amazon, Samoa, Tahiti, New Zealand, Australia, New Caledonia, Fiji, the Torres Strait, East Africa, and the Nile. The study demonstrated both the superior quality of aboriginal dentition and the devastation that occurs as modern diets are adopted. In nearly every area where traditional foods were still being eaten, Price found perfect teeth with normal dental arches and virtually no decay, whereas caries and abnormalities increased steadily as new diets were adopted. In many cases the change was sudden and striking. Among Eskimo groups subsisting entirely on traditional food he found caries totally absent, whereas in groups eating a considerable quantity of store-bought food approximately 20 percent of their teeth were decayed. The figure rose to more than 30 percent with Eskimo groups subsisting almost exclusively on purchased or government-supplied food, and reached an incredible 48 percent among the Vancouver Island Indians. Unfortunately for many of these people, modern dental treatment did not accompany the new food, and their suffering was appalling. The loss of teeth was, of course, bad enough in itself, and it certainly undermined the population's resistance to many new diseases, including tuberculosis. But new foods were also accompanied by crowded, misplaced teeth, gum diseases, distortion of the face, and pinching of the nasal cavity. Abnormalities in the dental arch appeared in the new generation following the change in diet, while caries appeared almost immediately even in adults.

Price reported that in many areas the affected peoples were conscious of their own physical deterioration. At a mission school in Africa, the principal asked him to explain to the native school children why they were not physically as strong as children who had had no contact with schools. On an island in the Torres Strait the natives knew exactly what was causing their problems and resisted—almost to the point of bloodshed—government efforts to establish a store that would make imported food available. The government prevailed, however, and Price was able to establish a relationship between the length of time the government store had been established and the increasing incidences of caries among a population that showed an almost 100 percent immunity to them before the store had been opened.

In New Zealand, the Maori, who in their aboriginal state are often considered to have been among the healthiest, most perfectly developed of peoples, were found to have "advanced" the furthest. According to Price:

> Their modernization was demonstrated not only by the high incidence of dental caries but also by the fact 90 percent of the adults and 100 percent of the children had abnormalities of the dental arches [Price, 1945:206].

Malnutrition

Malnutrition, particularly in the form of protein deficiency, has become a critical problem for tribal peoples who must adopt new economic patterns. Population pressures, cash cropping, and government programs all have tended to encourage the replacement of traditional crops and other food sources that were rich in protein with substitutes high in calories but low in protein. In Africa, for example, protein-rich staples such as millet and sorghum are being replaced systematically by high-yielding manioc and plantains, which have in significant amounts of protein. The problem is in creased for cash croppers and wage laborers whose earnings are too low and unpredictable to allow purchase of adequate amounts of protein. In some rural areas, agricultural laborers have been forced systematically to deprive nonproductive members (principally children) of their households of their minimal nutritional requirements to satisfy the need of the productive members. This process has been documented in northeastern Brazil following the introduction of large-scale sisal plantations (Gross & Underwood, 1971). In urban centers the difficulties of obtaining nutritionally adequate diets are even more serious for tribal immigrants, because costs are higher and poor quality foods are more tempting.

One of the most tragic, and largely overlooked, aspects of chronic malnutrition is that it can lead to abnormally undersized brain development and apparently irreversible brain damage; it has been associated with various forms of mental impairment or retardation. Malnutrition has been linked clinically with mental retardation in both Africa and Latin America (see, for example, Mönckeberg, 1968), and this appears to be a worldwide phenomenon with serious implications (Montagu, 1972).

Optimistic supporters of progress will surely say that all of these new health problems are being overstressed and that the introduction of hospitals, clinics, and the other modern health institutions will over come or at least compensate for all of these difficulties. However, it appears that uncontrolled population growth and economic impoverishment probably will keep most of these benefits out of reach for many tribal peoples, and the intervention of modern medicine has at least partly contributed to the problem in the first place.

The generalization that civilization frequently has a broad negative impact on tribal health has found broad empirical support (see especially Kroeger & Barbira-Freedman [1982] on Amazonia; Reinhard [1976] on the Arctic; and Wirsing [1985] globally), but these conclusions have not gone unchallenged. Some critics argue that tribal health was often poor before modernization, and they point specifically to tribals' low life expectancy and high infant mortality rates. Demographic statistics on tribal populations are often problematic because precise data are scarce, but they do show a less favorable profile than that enjoyed by many industrial societies. However, it should be remembered that our present life expectancy is a recent phenomenon that has been very costly in terms of medical research and technological advances. Furthermore, the benefits of our health system are not enjoyed equally by all members of our society. High infant mortality could be viewed as a relatively inexpensive and egalitarian tribal public health program that offered the reasonable expectation of a healthy and productive life for those surviving to age fifteen.

Some critics also suggest that certain tribal populations, such as the New Guinea highlanders, were "stunted" by nutritional deficiencies created by tribal culture and are "improved" by "acculturation" and cash cropping (Dennett & Connell, 1988). Although this argument does suggest that the health question requires careful evaluation, it does not invalidate the empirical generalizations already established. Nutritional deficiencies undoubtedly occurred in densely populated zones in the central New Guinea highlands. However, the specific case cited above may not be widely representative of other tribal groups even in New Guinea, and it does not address the facts of outside intrusion or the inequities inherent in the contemporary development process.

Ecocide

"How is it," asked a herdsman . . . "how is it that these hills can no longer give pasture to my cattle? In my father's day they were green and cattle thrived there; today there is no grass and my cattle starve." As one looked one saw that what had once been a green hill had become a raw red rock [Jones, 1931].

Progress not only brings new threats to the health of tribal peoples, but it also imposes new strains on the ecosystems upon which they must depend for their ultimate survival. The introduction of new technology, increased consumption, lowered mortality, and the eradication of all traditional controls have combined to replace what for most tribal peoples was a relatively stable balance between population and natural re sources, with a new system that is imbalanced. Economic development is forcing *ecocide* on peoples who were once careful stewards of their resources. There is already a trend toward widespread environmental deterioration in tribal areas, involving resource depletion, erosion, plant and animal extinction, and a disturbing series of other previously unforeseen changes.

After the initial depopulation suffered by most tribal peoples during their engulfment by frontiers of national expansion, most tribal populations began to experience rapid growth. Authorities generally at tribute this growth to the introduction of modern medicine and new health measures and the termination of intertribal warfare, which lowered mortality rates, as well as to new technology, which increased food production. Certainly all of these factors played a part, but merely lowering mortality rates would not have produced the rapid population growth that most tribal areas have experienced if traditional birth-spacing mechanisms had not been eliminated at the same time. Regardless of which factors were most important, it is clear that all of the natural and cultural checks on population growth have suddenly been pushed aside by culture change, while tribal lands have been steadily reduced and consumption levels have risen. In many tribal areas, environmental deterioration due to overuse of resources has set in, and in other areas such deterioration is imminent as resources continue to dwindle relative to the expanding population and in creased use. Of course, population expansion by tribal peoples may have positive political consequences, be cause where tribals can retain or regain their status as local majorities they may be in a more favorable position to defend their resources against intruders.

Swidden systems and pastoralism, both highly successful economic systems under traditional conditions, have proven particularly vulnerable to increased population pressures and outside efforts to raise productivity beyond its natural limits. Research in Amazonia demonstrates that population pressures and related resource depletion can be created indirectly by official policies that restrict swidden peoples to smaller territories. Resource depletion itself can then become a powerful means of forcing tribal people into participating in the world-market economy—thus leading to further resource depletion. For example, Bodley and Benson (1979) showed how the Shipibo Indians in Peru were forced to further deplete their forest resources by cash cropping in the forest area to replace the resources that had been destroyed earlier by the intensive cash cropping necessitated by the narrow confines of their reserve. In this case, a certain species of palm trees that had provided critical housing materials were destroyed by forest clearing and had to be replaced by costly purchased materials. Research by Gross (1979) and others showed similar processes at work among four tribal groups in central Brazil and demonstrated that the degree of market involvement increases directly with increases in resource depletion.

The settling of nomadic herders and the removal of prior controls on herd size have often led to serious overgrazing and erosion problems where these had not previously occurred. There are indications that the desertification problem in the Sahel region of Africa was aggravated by programs designed to settle nomads. The first sign of imbalance in a swidden system appears when the planting cycles are shortened to the point that garden plots are re-used before sufficient forest regrowth can occur. If reclearing and planting continue in the same area, the natural pattern of forest succession may be disturbed irreversibly and the soil can be impaired permanently. An extensive tract of tropical rainforest in the lower Amazon of Brazil was reduced to a semi-arid desert in just fifty years through such a process (Ackermann, 1964). The soils in the Azande area are also now seriously threatened with laterization and other problems as a result of the government-promoted cotton development scheme (McNeil, 1972).

The dangers of overdevelopment and the vulnerability of local resource systems have long been recognized by both anthropologists and tribal peoples themselves, but the pressures for change have been overwhelming. In 1948 the Maya villagers of Chan Kom complained to Redfield (1962) about the shortening of their swidden cycles, which they correctly attributed to increasing population pressures. Redfield told them, however, that they had no choice but to go "forward with technology" (Redfield, 1962:178). In Assam, swidden cycles were shortened from an average of twelve years to only two or three within just twenty years, and anthropologists warned that the limits of swiddening would soon be reached (Burling, 1963:311–312). In the Pacific, anthropologists warned of population pressures on limited resources as early as the 1930s (Keesing, 1941:64–65). These warnings seemed fully justified, considering the fact that the crowded Tikopians were prompted by population pressures on their tiny island to suggest that infanticide be legalized. The warnings have been dramatically reinforced since then by the doubling of Micronesia's population in just the fourteen years between 1958 and 1972, from 70,600 to 114,615, while consumption levels have soared. By 1985 Micronesia's population had reached 162,321.

The environmental hazards of economic development and rapid population growth have become generally recognized only since worldwide concerns over environmental issues began in the early 1970s. Unfortunately, there is as yet little indication that the leaders of the now developing nations are sufficiently concerned with environmental limitations. On the contrary governments are forcing tribal peoples into a self reinforcing spiral of population growth and intensified resource exploitation, which may be stopped only by environmental disaster or the total impoverishment of the tribals.

The reality of ecocide certainly focuses attention on the fundamental contrasts between tribal and industrial systems in their use of natural resources. In many respects the entire "victims of progress" issue hinges on natural resources, who controls them, and how they are managed. Tribal peoples are victimized because they control resources that outsiders demand. The resources exist because tribals managed them conservatively. However, as with the issue of the health consequences of detribalization, some anthropologists minimize the adaptive achievements of tribal groups and seem unwilling to concede that ecocide might be a consequence of cultural change. Critics attack an exaggerated "noble savage" image of tribals living in perfect harmony with nature and having no visible impact on their surroundings. They then show that tribals do in fact modify the environment, and they conclude that there is no significant difference between how tribals and industrial societies treat their environments. For example, Charles Wagley declared that Brazilian Indians such as the Tapirape

are not "natural men." They have human vices just as we do. . . . They do not live "in tune" with nature any more than I do; in fact, they can often be as destructive of their environment, within their limitations, as some civilized men. The Tapirape are not innocent or childlike in any way [Wagley, 1977:302].

Anthropologist Terry Rambo demonstrated that the Semang of the Malaysian rain forests have measurable impact on their environment. In his monograph *Primitive Polluters,* Rambo (1985) reported that the Semang live in smoke-filled houses. They sneeze and spread germs, breathe, and thus emit carbon dioxide. They clear small gardens, contributing "particulate matter" to the air and disturbing the local climate because cleared areas proved measurably warmer and drier than the shady forest. Rambo concluded that his research "demonstrated the essential functional similarity of the environmental interactions of primitive and civilized societies" (1985:78) in contrast to a "noble savage" view (Bodley, 1983) which, according to Rambo (1985:2), mistakenly "claims that traditional peoples almost always live in essential harmony with their environment."

This is surely a false issue. To stress, as I do, that tribals tend to manage their resources for sustained yield within relatively self-sufficient subsistence economies is not to make them either innocent children or natural men. Nor is it to deny that tribals "disrupt" their environment and may never be in absolute "balance" with nature.

The ecocide issue is perhaps most dramatically illustrated by two sets of satellite photos taken over the Brazilian rain forests of Rôndonia (Allard & McIntyre, 1988:780–781). Photos taken in 1973, when Rôndonia was still a tribal domain, show virtually unbroken rain forest. The 1987 satellite photos, taken after just fifteen years of highway construction and "development" by outsiders, show more than 20 percent of the forest destroyed. The surviving Indians were being concentrated by FUNAI (Brazil's national Indian foundation) into what would soon become mere islands of forest in a ravaged landscape. It is irrelevant to quibble about whether tribals are noble, childlike, or innocent, or about the precise meaning of balance with nature, carrying capacity, or adaptation, to recognize that for the past 200 years rapid environmental deterioration on an unprecedented global scale has followed the wresting of control of vast areas of the world from tribal groups by resource-hungry industrial societies.

Deprivation and Discrimination

Contact with European culture has given them a knowledge of great wealth, opportunity and privilege, but only very limited avenues by which to acquire these things [Crocombe,1968].

Unwittingly, tribal peoples have had the burden of perpetual relative deprivation thrust upon them by acceptance either by themselves or by the governments administering them—of the standards of socioeconomic progress set for them by industrial civilizations. By comparison with the material wealth of industrial societies, tribal societies become, by definition, impoverished. They are then forced to transform their cultures and work to achieve what many economists now acknowledge to be unattainable goals. Even though in many cases the modest GNP goals set by development planners for the developing nations during the "development decade" of the 1960s were often met, the results were hardly noticeable for most of the tribal people involved population growth, environmental limitations, inequitable distribution of wealth, and the continued rapid growth of the industrialized nations have all meant that both the absolute and the relative gap between the rich and poor in the world is steadily widening. The prospect that tribal peoples will actually be able to attain the levels of resource consumption to which they are being encouraged to aspire is remote indeed except for those few groups who have retained effective control over strategic mineral resources.

Tribal peoples feel deprivation not only when the economic goals they have been encouraged to seek fail to materialize, but also when they discover that they are powerless, second-class citizens who are discriminated against and exploited by the dominant society. At the same time, they are denied the satisfactions of their traditional cultures, because these have been sacrificed in the process of modernization. Under the impact of major economic change family life is disrupted, traditional social controls are often lost, and many indicators of social anomie such as alcoholism, crime, delinquency, suicide, emotional disorders, and despair may increase. The inevitable frustration resulting from this continual deprivation finds expression in the cargo cults, revitalization movements, and a variety of other political and religious movements that have been widespread among tribal people following their disruption by industrial civilization.

References

Ackermann, F. L. 1964. *Geologia e Fisiografia da Região Bragantina, Estado do Pará*. Manaus, Brazil: Conselho Nacional de Pesquisas, Instituto Nacional de Pesquisas da Amazônia.

Allard, William Albert, and Loren McIntyre. 1988. Rôndonia's settlers invade Brazil's imperiled rain forest. *National Geographic* 174(6):772–799.

Bodley, John H. 1983. The World Bank tribal policy: Criticisms and recommendations. *Congressional Record,* serial no. 98–37, pp. 515–521. (Reprinted in Bodley, 1988.)

Bodley, John H., and Foley C. Benson. 1979. Cultural ecology of Amazonian palms. *Reports of Investigations,* no. 56. Pullman: Laboratory of Anthropology, Washington State University.

Bunce, George E. 1972. Aggravation of vitamin A deficiency following distribution of non-fortified skim milk: An example of nutrient interaction. In *The Careless Technology: Ecology and International Development*, ed. M. T. Farvar and John P. Milton, pp. 53–60. Garden City, N.Y.: Natural History Press.

Burling, Robbins. 1963. *Rengsanggri: Family and Kinship in a Garo Village*. Philadelphia: University of Pennsylvania Press.

Crocombe, Ron. 1968. Bougainville!: Copper, R. R. A. and secessionism. *New Guinea* 3(3):39–49.

Davis, A. E., and T. D. Bolin. 1972. Lactose intolerance in Southeast Asia. In *The Careless Technology: Ecology and International Development*, ed. M. T. Farvar and John P. Milton, pp.61 –68. Garden City, N.Y.: Natural History Press.

Dennett, Glenn, and John Connell. 1988. Acculturation and health in the highlands of Papua New Guinea. *Current Anthropology* 29(2):273–299.

Goldschmidt, Walter R. 1952. The interrelations between cultural factors and acquisition of new technical skills. In *The Progress of Underdeveloped Areas*, ed. Bert F. Hoselitz, pp. 135–151. Chicago: University of Chicago Press.

Gross, Daniel R., and Barbara A. Underwood. 1971. Technological change and caloric costs: Sisal agriculture. *American Anthropologist* 73(3):725–740.

Gross, Daniel R., et al. 1979. Ecology and acculturation among native peoples of Central Brazil. *Science* 206(4422):1043–1050.

Hooton, Earnest A. 1945. Introduction. In *Nutrition and Physical Degeneration: A Comparison of Primitive and Modern Diets and Their Effects* by Weston A. Price. Redlands, Calif.: The author.

Hughes, Charles C., and John M. Hunter. 1972. The role of technological development in promoting disease in Africa. In *The Careless Technology: Ecology and International Development*, ed. M. T. Farvar and John P. Milton, pp. 69–101. Garden City, N.Y.: Natural History Press.

Jones, J. D. Rheinallt. 1934. Economic condition of the urban native. In *Western Civilization and the Natives of South Africa,* ed. I. Schapera, pp. 159–192. London: George Routledge and Sons.

Keesing, Felix M. 1941. *The South Seas in the Modern World.* Institute of Pacific Relations International Research Series. New York: John Day.

Kroeger, Axel, and Françoise Barbira-Freedman. 1982. *Culture Change and Health: The Case of South American Rainforest Indians/* Frankfurt am Main: Verlag Peter Lang. (Reprinted in Bodley, 1988:221–236).

Maunier, René. 1949. *The Sociology of Colonies.* Vol. 2. London: Routledge and Kegan Paul.

McNeil, Mary. 1972. Lateritic soils in distinct tropical environments: Southern Sudan and Brazil. In *The Careless Technology: Ecology and International Development,* ed. M. T. Farvar and John P. Milton, pp. 591–608. Garden City, N.Y.: Natural History Press.

Mönckeberg, F. 1968. Mental retardation from malnutrition. *Journal of the American Medical Association* 206: 30–31.

Montagu, Ashley. 1972. Sociogenic brain damage. *American Anthropologist* 74(5):1045–1061.

Price, Weston Andrew. 1945. *Nutrition and Physical Degeneration: A Comparison of Primitive and Modern Diets and Their Effects.* Redlands, Calif.: The author.

Prior, Ian A. M.1971. The price of civilization. *Nutrition Today* 6(4):2–11.

Rambo, A. Terry. 1985. *Primitive Polluters: Semang Impact on the Malaysian Tropical Rain Forest Ecosystem.* Anthropological Papers no. 76, Museum of Anthropology, University of Michigan.

Redfield, Robert. 1962. *A Village That Chose Progress: Chan Kom Revisited.* Chicago: University of Chicago Press, Phoenix Books.

Reinhard, K. R. 1976. Resource exploitation and the health of western arctic man. In *Circumpolar Health: Proceedings of the Third International Symposium, Yellowknife, Northwest Territories,* ed. Roy J. Shephard and S. Itoh, pp. 617–627. Toronto: University of Toronto Press. (Reprinted in Bodley, 1988.)

Smith, Wilberforce. 1894. The teeth of ten Sioux Indians. *Journal of the Royal Anthropological Institute* 24:109–116.

TTR: *See under* United States.

United States, Department of State. 1955. *Seventh Annual Report to the United Nations on the Administration of the Trust Territory of the Pacific Islands* (July 1, 1953, to June 30, 1954).

_____. 1959. *Eleventh Annual Report to the United Nations on the Administration of the Trust Territory of the Pacific Islands* (July 1, 1957, to June 30, 1958).

_____. 1973. *Twenty-Fifth Annual Report to the United Nations on the Administration of the Trust Territory of the Pacific Islands* (July 1, 1971, to June 30, 1972).

Wagley, C. 1977. *Welcome of Tears: The Tapirape Indians of Central Brazil.* New York: Oxford University Press.

Wirsing, R. 1985. The health of traditional societies and the effects of acculturation. *Current Anthropology* 26:303–322.

"THE PRICE OF PROGRESS"

John Bodley

1) How do western cultures define the term *progress*?

2) How do western and traditional cultures compare in terms of quality of life, and how do you define this quality?

3) What diseases has Bodley defined as "diseases of development" and how have they impacted traditional societies?

4) Has a change in diet from traditional foods to western foods had a beneficial or deleterious effect on the health and well-being of traditional peoples?

5) According to Bodley, what have been the ecological impacts of development and westernization?

6) What other social ills has impact with western society brought to traditional peoples?